The Tradition

A New History of Welsh Art
1400 – 1990

PETER LORD

The Tradition

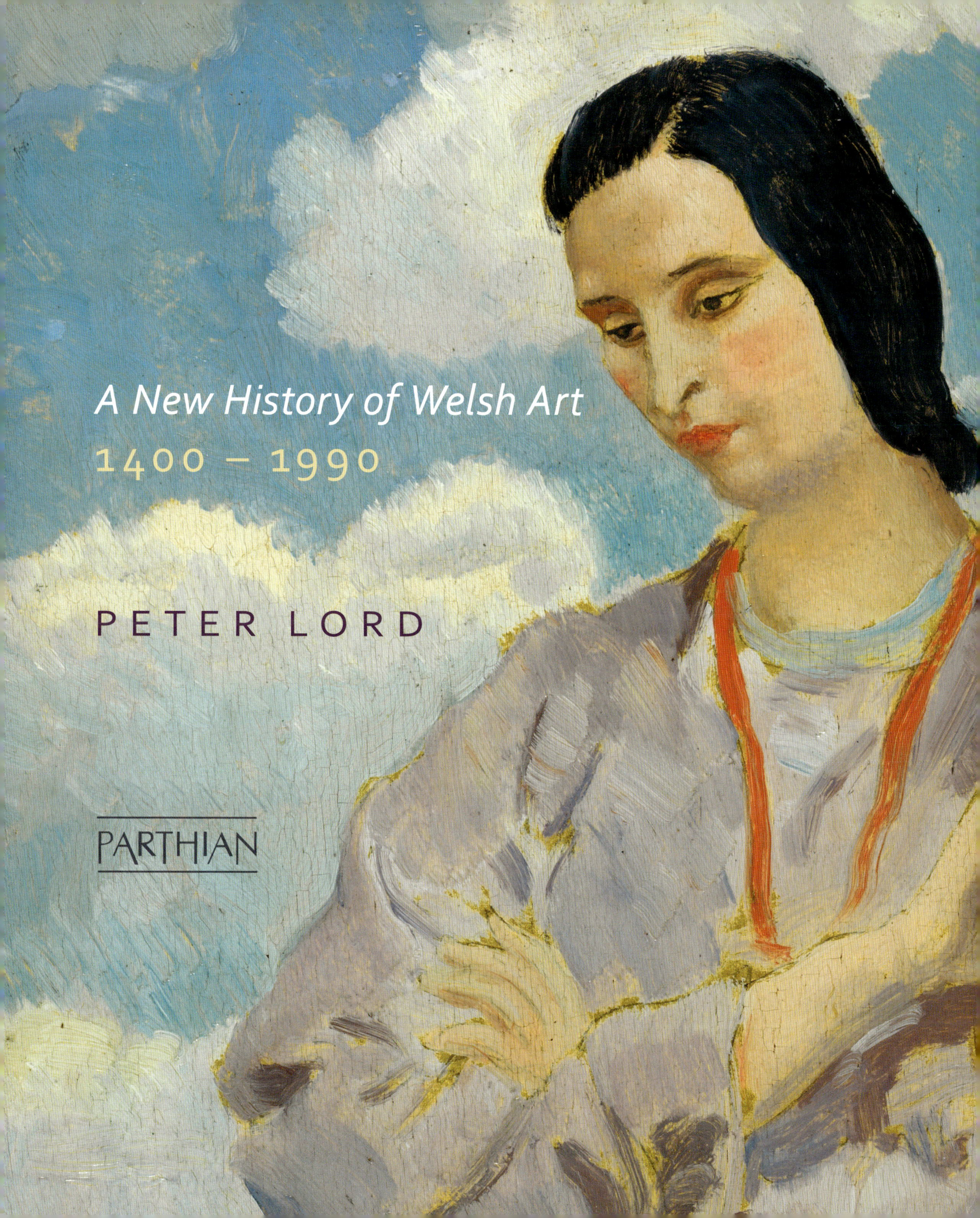

A New History of Welsh Art

1400 – 1990

PETER LORD

PARTHIAN

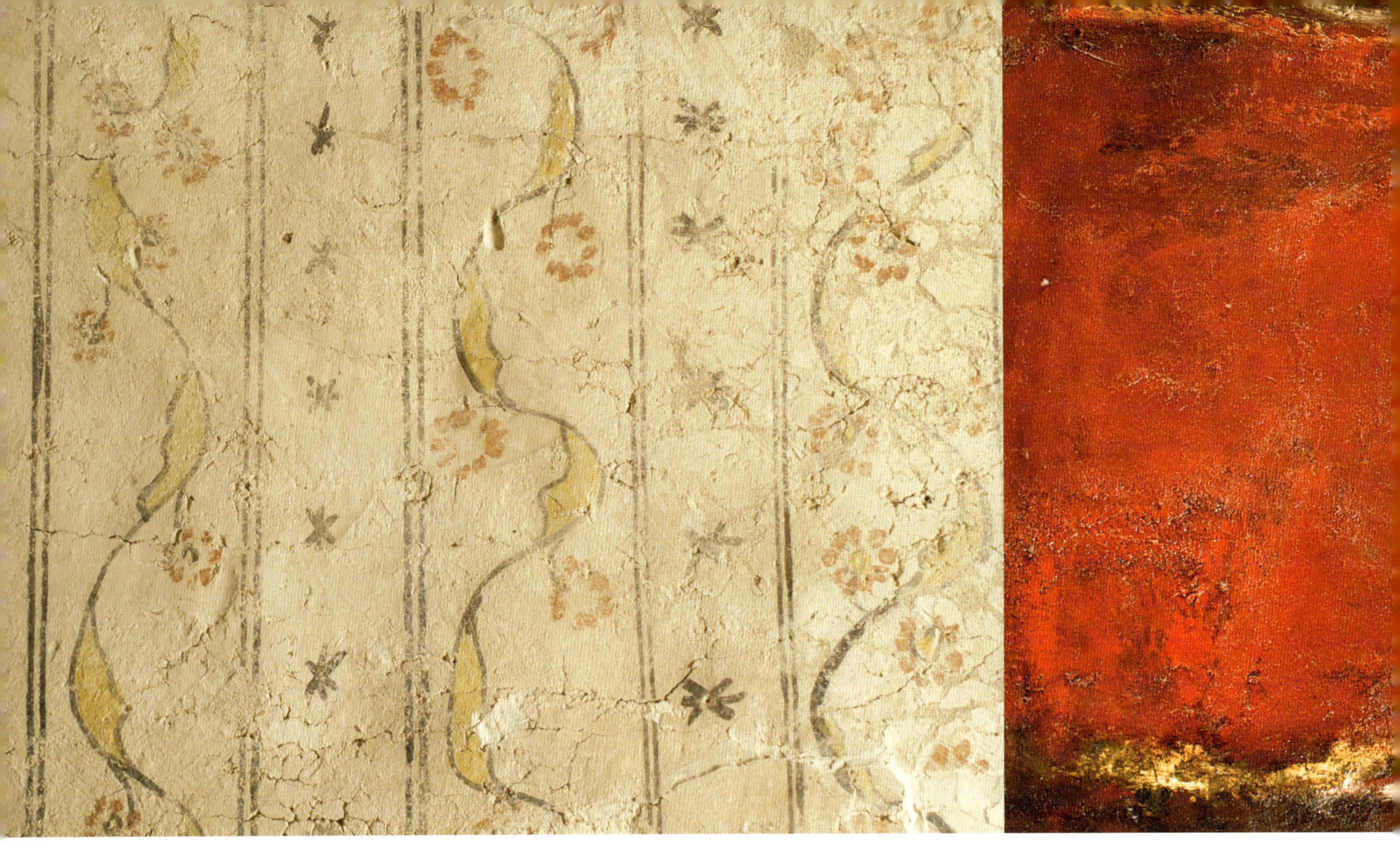

PARTHIAN

Parthian
The Old Surgery
Napier Street
Cardigan
SA43 1ED

www.parthianbooks.com

First published in 2016
Reprinted in 2017

ISBN 978-1-910409-62-6

Editor: Ceridwen Lloyd-Morgan

Designed by Olwen Fowler

Printed and bound by Gomer Press
Llandysul SA44 4JL

Published with the financial support
of the Welsh Books Council.

British Library Cataloguing in Publication Data

A cataloguing record for this book
is available from the British Library.

CYNGOR LLYFRAU CYMRU
WELSH BOOKS COUNCIL

PAUL MELLON CENTRE
for Studies in British Art

MARC FITCH FUND

national museum wales
amgueddfa cymru

LLGC
NLW

CREW

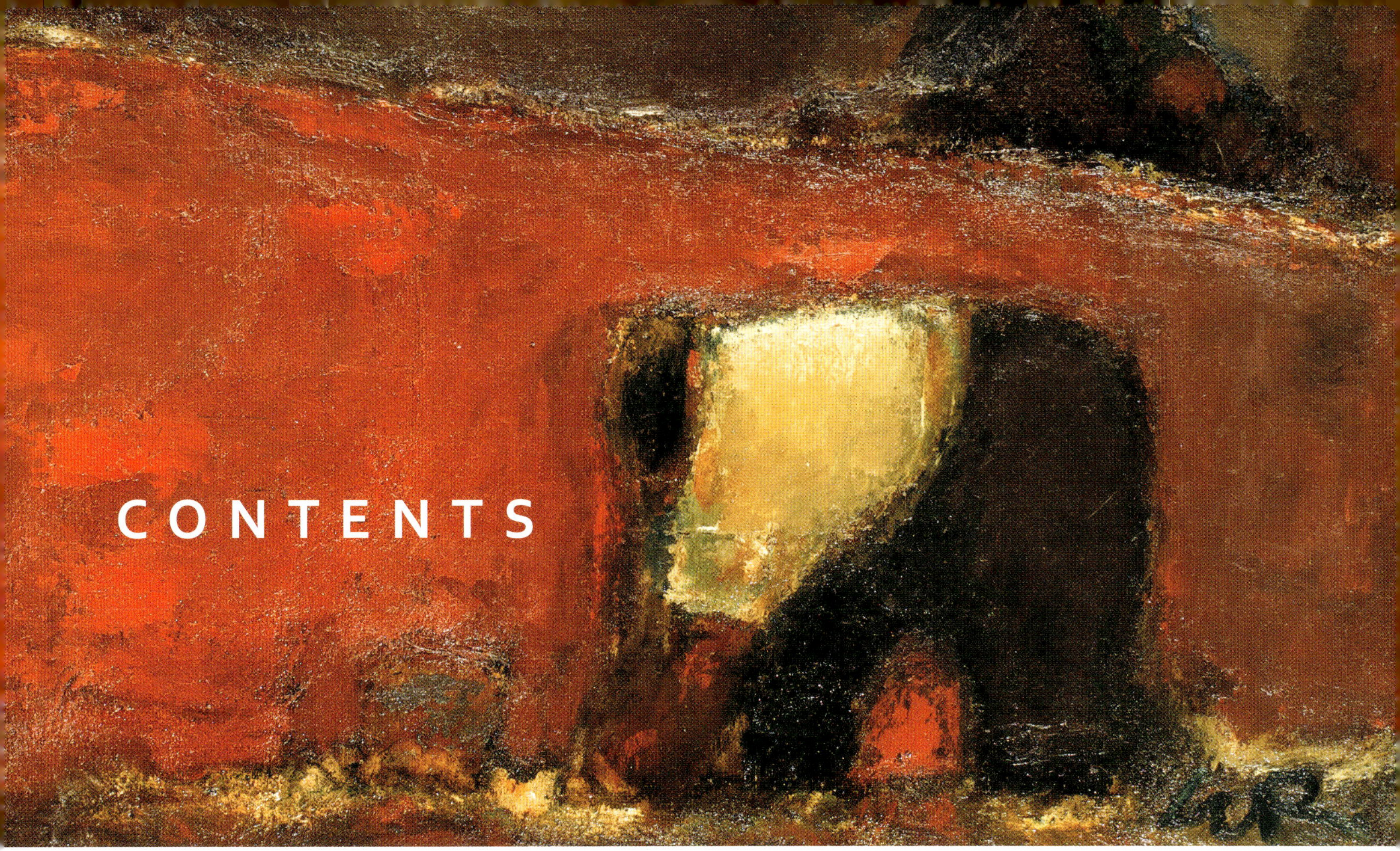

CONTENTS

FOREWORD

This landmark volume is the summation of Peter Lord's distinguished career as the premier social historian of Wales's visual culture. It is a distillation of the dozen and more books he has published over some three decades that have opened our eyes to a valuable native tradition of image-making.

A 1490 alabaster effigy in Tenby commemorates not only the deceased (John White) but also the occasion of a notable service performed by him for the future Henry VII that made possible the financing of such a grand sepulchral statement. History is written as much in visual images and artefacts as in words and deed, but we too often lack the skill to read it. Peter Lord shows us how.

This authoritative study is brimful of intriguing examples. The rise of personal portraits was triggered by the Puritan prohibition on religious images; landscape art evolved out of the display culture of an aristocracy keen to have its lavish holdings in land advertised in the panoramic rural backgrounds of grand family portraits; shifts in social taste facilitated the elevation of humble artisan to the dignity of artist.

As for Wales itself, visual art provides us with a riveting record of its serial transformations of identity. Instructed in his native country's prestigious antiquity by the scholars, intellectuals and antiquarians of the Cymmrodorion society, Richard Wilson was moved to represent Castell Dinas Brân as the 'Celtic equivalent of Mount Olympus.' In the later eighteenth century the 'opening up' of Wales by picturesque travellers paralleled the 'voyages of discovery' of explorers such as Captain Cook, whose botanist, Joseph Banks, found this seemingly familiar land to be 'terra incognita' almost as much as Australia. And awed artists struggling to master a new graphic vocabulary were among the first to register Wales's dramatic metamorphosis into the fiery furnace of industrial revolution.

The rise of 'the nonconformist nation' brought with it the golden age of the artisan painter, whose neglected body of work Peter Lord was the first to uncover, champion and celebrate; and as a national cultural renaissance gathered momentum from the mid-nineteenth-century onwards the new patriotism was imaged in monumental sculpture, public buildings and of course paint.

Different regions of Wales figure large in the story from time to time. Between the two world wars, the Swansea area produced a remarkable crop of talent in the context of which Dylan Thomas's work might be profitably re-viewed. Immediately following the second world war it was the turn of Cardiff and its feeder valleys to become the cradle of talent, shortly before an increasingly institutionalised and state-sponsored 'art scene' turned its face away from representational images and towards the 'international style' of abstract expression.

In its affirmation of the tolerant plurality of Welsh artistic practice over the last twenty and more years this timely study reveals itself to be the product of its (post-devolution) era. And in its mode of procedure it is clearly indebted to that revolutionary turn in art history towards the material, social and cultural that we associate with such important figures of the seventies as T. J. Clarke and John Berger.

In his seminal volume, *Ways of Seeing*, Berger welcomed the decay of the 'holy authority of art,' and the arrival in its place of a new literacy – an ability to read 'the [social] language of images.' 'What matters now,' he added, 'is who uses that language for what purpose.' This, he emphasised, was a political issue that could influence the fate of a whole society, because a 'people...which is cut off from its own past is far less free to choose and to act as a people...than one that has been able to situate itself in history.'

Peter Lord's invaluable *New History of Welsh Art* should therefore be regarded as his gift to the Welsh people. In teaching us how to read 'the language of images' he has enabled us to situate ourselves much more securely in our own distinctive history as a nation.

M. Wynn Thomas
CREW (Centre for Research into the
English Literature and Language of Wales),
Swansea University,
July, 2015

INTRODUCTION

With colleagues at the Centre for Advanced Welsh and Celtic studies, twenty years ago I began the work that led to the publication of the three volume history entitled *The Visual Culture of Wales*. In those volumes I sought to do two things. Firstly, to make available a large selection of the visual images that emerged in Welsh cultures over a period of 1500 years, from the collapse of Roman authority to the mid-twentieth century. Secondly, in the texts, I sought to relate those images to the broader political, economic and social evolution of the Welsh nation.

The three volumes of *The Visual Culture of Wales* have been out of print for some years. Once again (and perhaps uniquely in Europe), Wales finds itself a nation without a readily accessible book that describes its visual culture to its own people and to the world. This new work seeks to reoccupy that space. I have tried to write in a straightforward way, not just for specialists in the field, but for everyone with an interest in Wales and in art. I have been assisted, since the publication of the third volume of the earlier series in 2003, by the appearance of many studies of individual artists and aspects of Welsh visual culture. I would like to thank all the authors of those studies for their contribution to the deepening of my own understanding and I hope, therefore, to the richness of this text. New images and previously unknown makers of images have emerged during the last decade, and there have been developments both in our understanding of relationships between artists and the wider context within which they worked. Nevertheless, there are many images in this book that are retained from the previous three volumes. Their cultural significance, or simply their visual impact, make it vital that they are presented again, especially for a new generation of readers perhaps unfamiliar with them.

opposite
John Cyrlas Williams,
The Life Studio, Newlyn,
c.1920-1 (detail)

However, since the publication of *The Visual Culture of Wales*, there has been a huge inflation in the charges, on occasion to prohibitive levels, made by some institutions and holders of copyrights for the right to reproduce paintings. I am particularly grateful, therefore, to the private owners of many works reproduced here who have, without

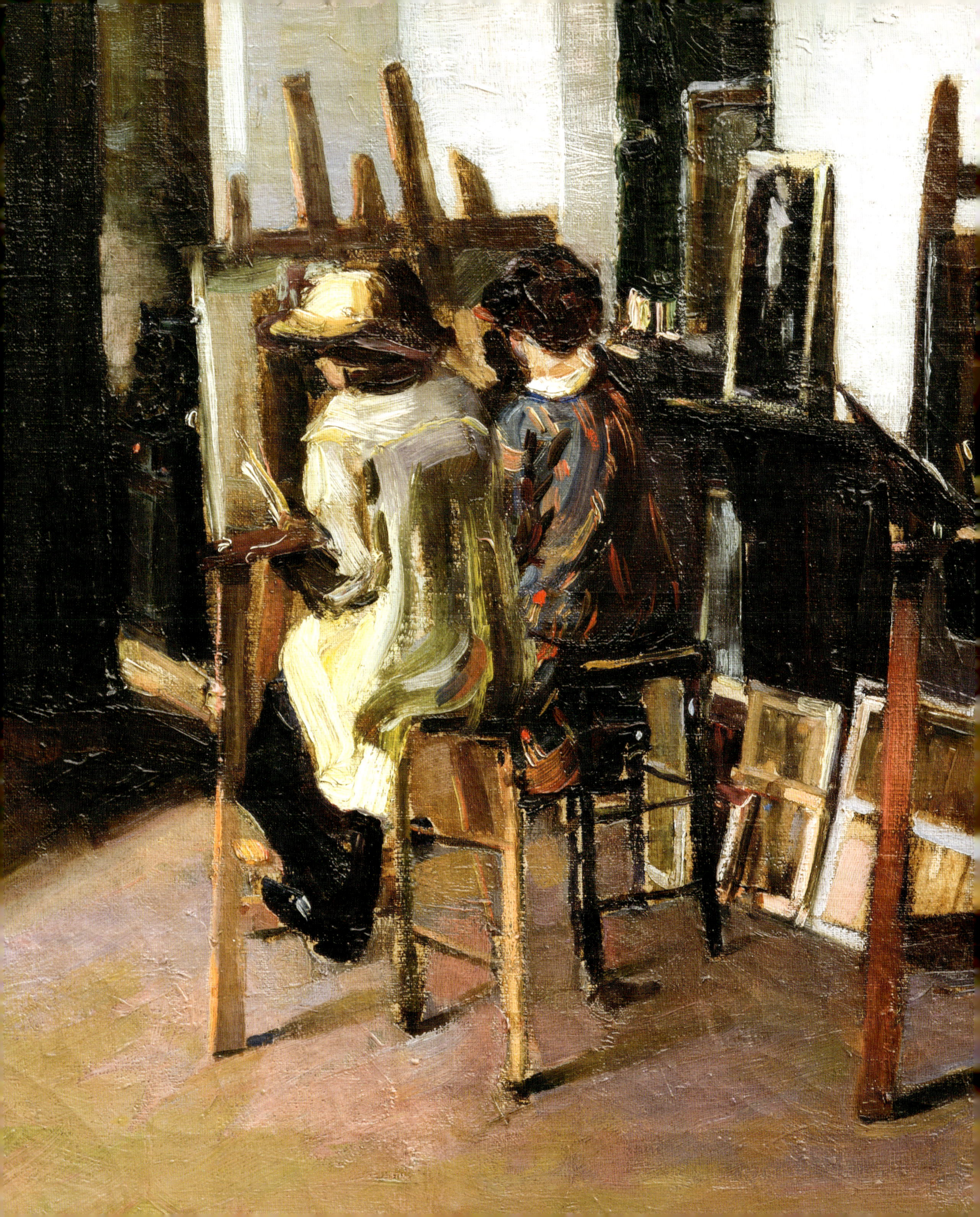

exception, been generous in freely granting permissions. Similarly, images from the two major Welsh collections, at the National Museum and the National Library, have been given without charge. Without the help of these two institutions this book would not have been possible. In particular I wish to acknowledge the enthusiasm and support expressed for this project at the outset by David Anderson, Director General of National Museum Wales, and by Oliver Fairclough, who was, until 2015, Keeper of Art at the National Museum. Oliver also read the text and offered much useful advice, as did other friends and colleagues. Shelagh Hourahane, Jill Piercy, Miles Wynn Cato and Thomas Lloyd all offered advice in fields in which they have specialist knowledge. I am grateful to the former National Librarian, Aled Jones, for his support of this publication, and to members of his staff who assisted with picture acquisition.

I was able to complete much of the text of this book as a research fellow at the Centre for Research into the English Literature and Language of Wales at Swansea University, and I extend my thanks to the university for its support, and to my colleagues at CREW, Professors Neil Reeve and M. Wynn Thomas. Publication has been assisted further by grant aid from the Paul Mellon Centre for Studies in British Art, the Marc Fitch Fund, and the Welsh Books Council, where I am indebted to Elwyn Jones. My thanks go to my publisher, Parthian Books, and to Richard Davies and Gillian Griffiths for their continuing enthusiasm for an ambitious project. Claire Houguez worked with commitment on the huge and sometimes frustrating task of securing the 400 images in the book. The text was edited by Ceridwen Lloyd-Morgan, whose expertise extends beyond the technical aspects of editing into a detailed knowledge of visual culture and Welsh history, and I thank her for her invaluable contribution. The book has been designed with equal commitment and finesse by Olwen Fowler.

The constraints of a single volume led to a decision at the outset to confine the story of Welsh visual culture to the modern period. Nevertheless, I have taken the opportunity to correct what I realise now was a misapprehension, built into the earlier publications, of the depth of the roots of that modern period. It has become clear that Renaissance attitudes to visual imagery emerged at a much earlier date among Welsh patrons than I had presumed, when writing twenty years ago. Any starting point for a history is arbitrary to a degree, but it seems to me that the period of reconstruction following the Glyndŵr Revolt at the beginning of the fifteenth century exemplified much that would divide attitudes and belief systems in the middle ages from those prevalent subsequently, at least into the early-twentieth century. I have also taken the opportunity to bring the closing point of this study forward to the beginning of the 1990s. The reasons for this choice are expressed in the text, but the inclusion of the last twenty years of the time span did present particular challenges to me as author, because I myself became directly involved in the Welsh art world during that period. Inevitably, my initial perceptions of the period were influenced by my proximity to particular people, institutions and events, perhaps at the expense of a wider view. With the assistance of colleagues, and in particular the work of Huw David Jones, I hope I have succeeded in broadening my understanding, though without any claim to objectivity – a false notion in history, in my opinion. Histories have always been written to meet the needs of their own present, and to reflect the aspirations of the writers for the future, and this text is no exception.

Peter Lord
October 2015

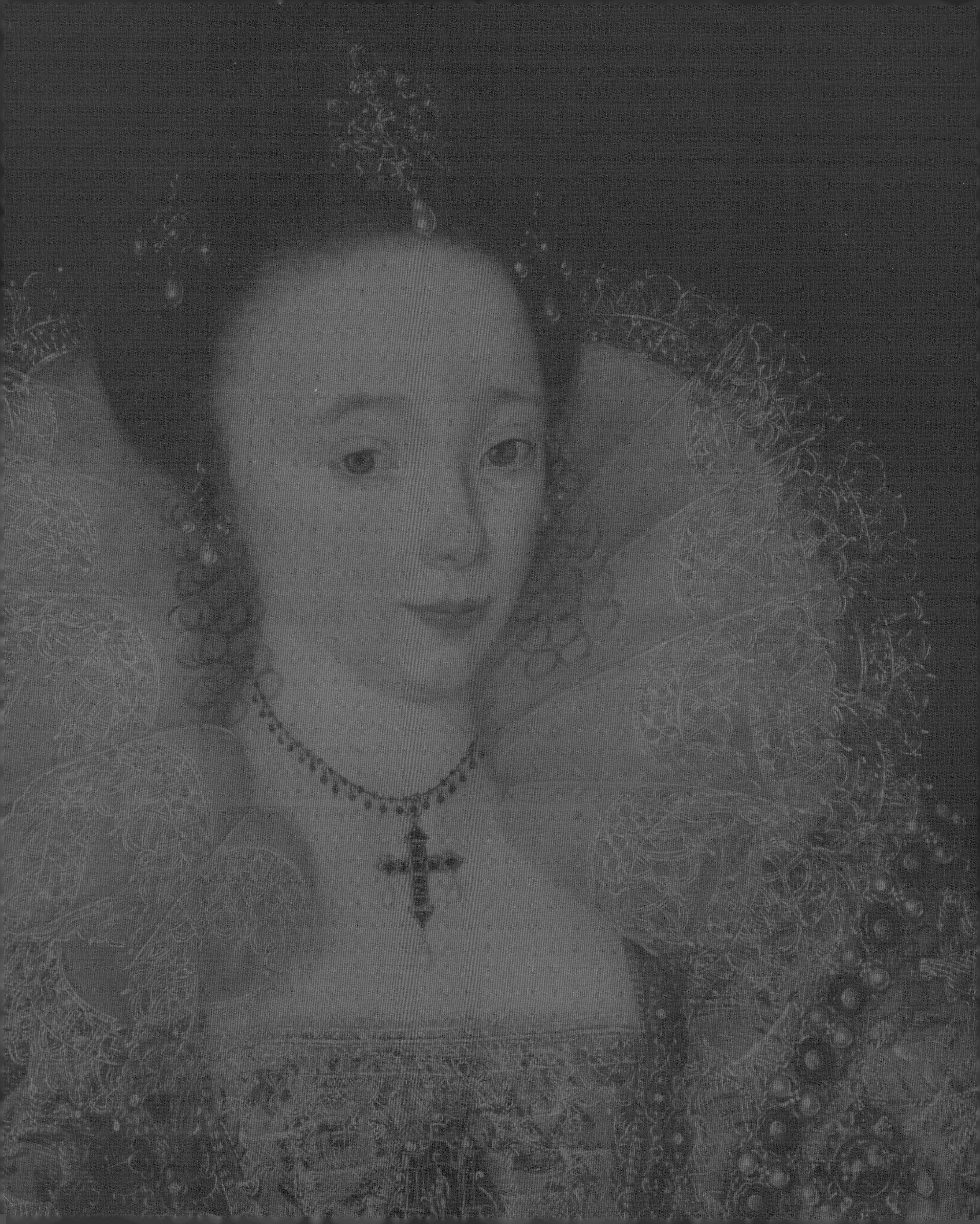

CHAPTER 1

1400–1660

CHAPTER 1 1400–1660

An age of uncertainty

In 1401, reacting to the defeat by Owain Glyndŵr of a loyalist force at the Battle of Hyddgen, the English King Henry IV despoiled the Cistercian abbey of Strata Florida in Ceredigion. The following year, the forces of Owain himself ruined the Cathedral Church of St Asaph, where Bishop John Trefor remained – for the moment – a supporter of the king. All 'was brent [burnt] and utterly destroyed, and in likewys the Byshop's Palays and all his other three Mannoirs no Styk left …'[1] It was the third year of a revolt against the English crown that would last for a further twelve years. Both sides contributed to the damage or destruction of religious paintings, carvings, manuscripts, glass and textiles, along with the buildings that contained them.[2] Over the ensuing hundred years the country would recover, and some fine architecture and artefacts would be produced. The poet Guto'r Glyn reported that Abbot Rhys installed 'rows of glass windows, flowery ornament of a court, the chancel of Strata Florida', dating reconstruction there as early as the 1430s.[3] However, the recovery did not take place against a background of political and social stability. On the contrary, Welsh people became deeply embroiled in the Wars of the Roses – towns were again burnt and the fortunes of prominent families waxed and waned as dynastic power shifted in England. The struggle for the English throne lasted until the defeat in 1485 of Richard III by Henry Tudor at the Battle of Bosworth Field.

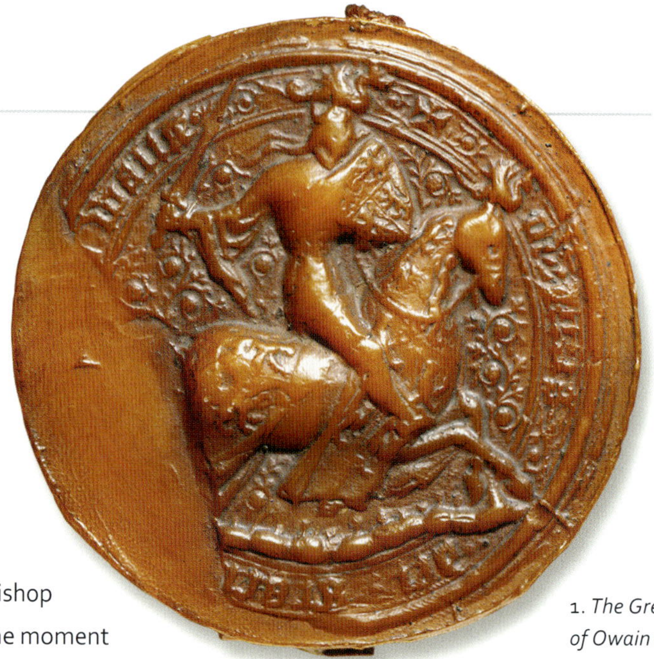

1. *The Great Seal of Owain Glyndŵr*, 1404–5, wax

1 … the Chirch Cathedrall of Saint Asaph, with the Steple, Bells, Quere, Porch, and Vestiary, with all other Contentis, Bokes, Chaliz, Vestimentis, and other Ornaments, as the Bokes, Stalles, Deskes, Altres, and all the aparaill longying to the same Church, was brent …' Browne Willis, *Willis' Survey of St Asaph* (2nd ed., 2 vols., Wrexham, 1801), II, p. 116, Appendix no. LI. Henry VI to his chancellor, the Bishop of Bath, 3 August 1442. The early medieval St Asaph Gospel Book was probably lost in the fire, for which see Peter Lord, *The Visual Culture of Wales: Medieval Vision* (Cardiff, 2003), p. 24.

2 For instance, John Leland reported 'Montgomerike deflorichid by Owen Glindour' and 'Radenor partely destroied by Owen Glindour', Lucy Toulmin Smith, ed., *The Itinerary of John Leland in or about the years 1535-1543*, part VI, p. 41.

3 For the poem and the translation by Dafydd Johnston, see <gutorglyn.net>, poem 8, lines 57–8. Similarly, Guto'r Glyn praised Abbot Dafydd ap Ieuan of Valle Crucis abbey who 'gilded and constructed the images and the choir,/ and the chalices and the books …', ibid., poem 113, lines 13-14, translated by Ann Parry Owen.

The victory of this descendant of an Anglesey family, who had invaded England through Wales, had profound psychological and practical implications for the Welsh gentry and intellectuals. Henry's accession to the English throne came to be understood as the fulfilment of the prophecy, by now deeply rooted in Welsh tradition, that the island of Britain, divided by the Anglo-Saxon creation of England in the early Middle Ages, would ultimately be reunited under a native king – a Welsh king, the spiritual descendant of King Arthur. In the climate created by this powerful myth, the Welsh gentry that were loyal to the Tudors would profit mightily in wealth and offices at home, and in status at court.

The marriage of the Lancastrian Henry to Elizabeth of York, the heir to the claims of the enemy, settled the English succession by uniting the rival camps. Nevertheless, Henry Tudor's descendants did not reign in peace and security. In the 1530s, his son, Henry VIII, having broken with the Church of Rome by denying the authority of the Pope, dissolved the monasteries, confiscated all their property and turned much of the intrinsic value of their contents into cash. The consequence was, once again, massive material damage, but also an unprecedented redistribution of wealth, as the monastic lands passed into secular ownership. Church dogma and ritual were revised along Protestant lines. The religious upheaval of this Reformation divided the people of Wales deeply. All in all, it was a profoundly disturbed period.

Two complementary tendencies drove the response of the rich and the powerful to the uncertainty of the age, as expressed in their commissions to painters and other craftspeople. The first was the reaffirmation of traditional values through new religious pictures, sculptures, manuscripts and textiles. By the 1530s, many Welsh churches, large and small, had been restored to their earlier condition as galleries of highly coloured painting, sculpture and glass, which provided the backdrop to the dramatic celebration of the sacraments and the many saints' days. The second response was to advertise visually changes in the balance of power. By encrusting them with heraldry and portraiture, patrons clearly identified themselves on many of the new buildings and artefacts of the period. The second half of the fifteenth and the sixteenth centuries would be an age of ostentatious patronage by successive new orders, sometimes short-lived, as if such dynastic displays would, in themselves, affirm their legitimacy and ensure their survival.

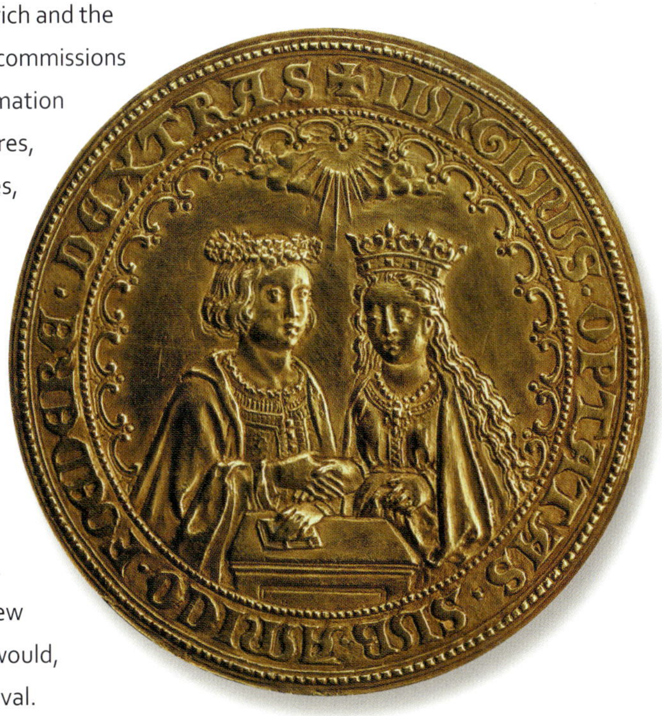

2. *Portrait Medallion of Henry VII and Elizabeth of York*, 1485, copper alloy, d. 6

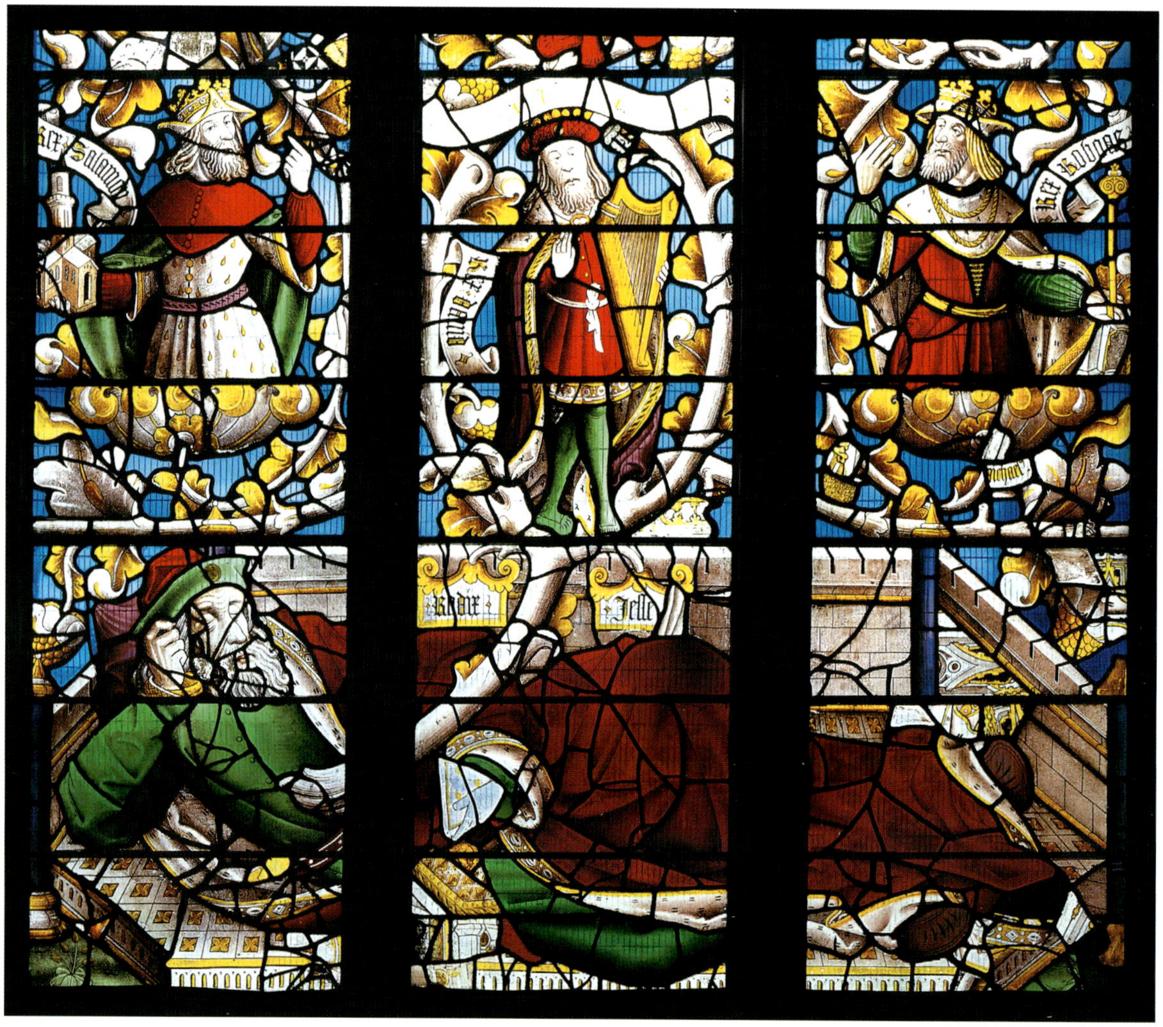

3. *Jesse Window, Church of St Dyfnog, Llanrhaeadr-yng-Nghinmeirch*, 1533, painted glass, detail of lower section

Restoration

Among the finest expressions of the spirit of restoration that drove the commissioning of religious pictures in the century following the Glyndŵr Revolt was the magnificent Jesse window at the Church of St Dyfnog at Llanrhaeadr-yng-Nghinmeirch, Dyffryn Clwyd. Images of Jesse were found all over Europe, and Welsh examples survive from as early as the first half of the thirteenth century. They serve to demonstrate that, far from being an isolated outpost, after the decline of the Celtic Church in the eleventh century, Wales stood in the mainstream of a biblical iconography that extended from the east of the continent to the very west, disseminated by religious institutions under the ultimate authority of the papacy in Rome. The idea of the Tree of Jesse had originated as a visualisation of a

4 Isaiah 11:1.

5 Much of the lower part of the window at the Church of St Bridget in Diserth, including the figure of Jesse himself, is lost.

6 At the Church of St Illtud, Llantwit Major, for instance, an early thirteenth-century example, where the tree frames a niche that probably once contained a statue or painting of the Virgin and Child. See Lord, *Medieval Vision*, p. 207.

sentence in the Book of Isaiah: 'And there shall come forth a rod out of the stem of Jesse, and a Branch shall grow out of his roots'.[4] Following the established convention, the Llanrhaeadr window depicted the tree with its roots in the stomach of Jesse, the branches carrying portraits of Jewish prophets who were visualised as the antecedents of Jesus. King David, son of Jesse, holding his symbol of a harp, was set at the centre but below the Virgin Mary, carrying the infant Jesus.

The Jesse window at Llanrhaeadr, and another example at Diserth, were made in about 1533, but by different masters.[5] Their styles of drawing were distinct. The Llanrhaeadr master followed what was a common workshop practice in re-using the patterns designed for the drawing of faces. Some of the prophets share the same features, but reversed. It also seems clear that this master had seen a drawing of Jesse reproduced as a woodcut, published in Paris in 1498 and widely distributed. The century of restoration in Wales was also the first century of printing in Europe. The widespread dissemination of pictures printed on paper began even before the adoption of moveable type in about 1439, with its radical implications for the spread of literacy.

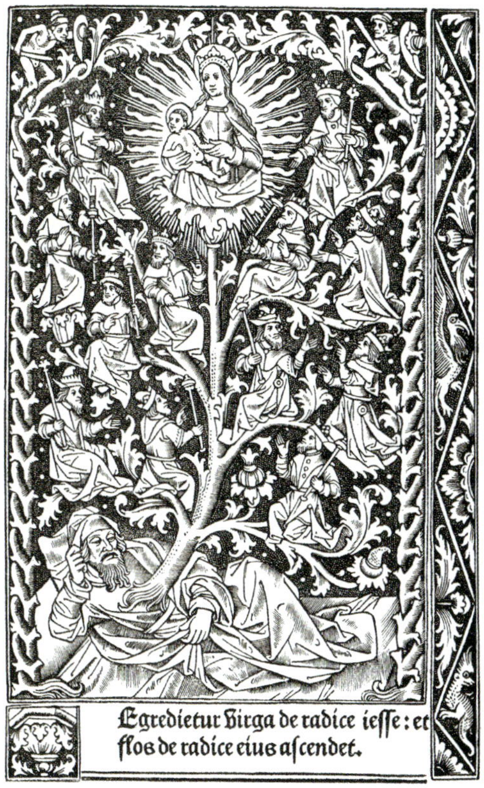

4. *Figure of Jesse*, 1498, woodcut, printed in Paris by Jean Pigouchet

Jesse was a popular subject. His carved figure, made in wood on a monumental scale, survives at the Priory Church of St Mary, Abergavenny. Like most of the earlier depictions of the king, it differed from the Llanrhaeadr image by showing him asleep.[6] Now stripped of its original painted and gilt surface, the Abergavenny figure once lay at the base of what must have been an enormous and dramatic structure, presumably supported against a wall.

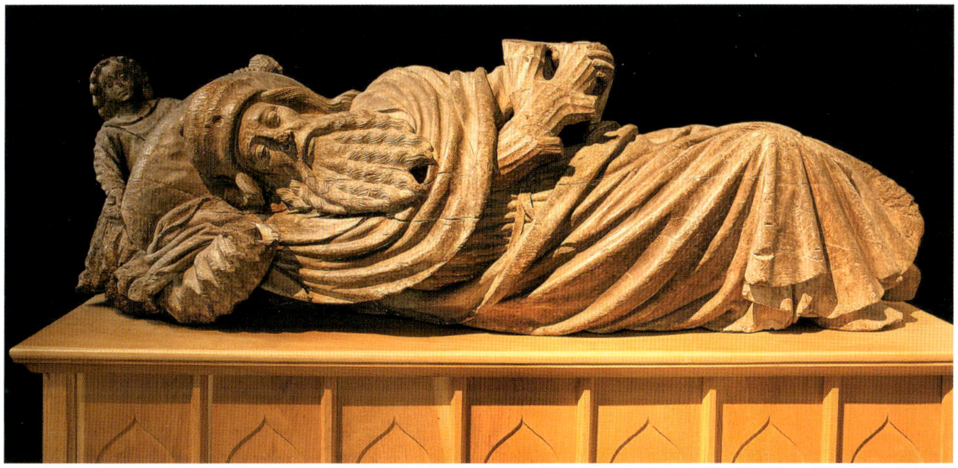

5. *Sleeping Jesse, Priory Church of St Mary, Abergavenny*, early 15th century, wood, l. 129.4

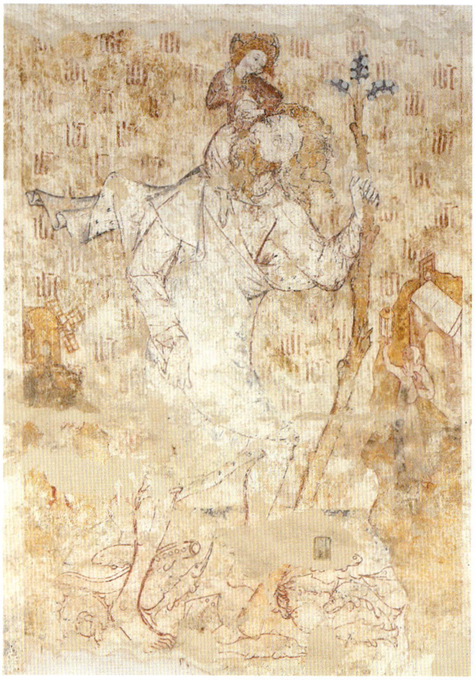

6. *St Christopher, Church of St Saeran, Llanynys*, 15th century, wall painting

The style of its carving links it to a large wall-painting of St Christopher in the Church of St Saeran, Llanynys, in Denbighshire, and both works may be the product of the same workshop.[7] Originally there were probably many more paintings on the wall at Llanynys, which are now lost, but some sense of the extent of the painting in churches of the period can be gained from murals that survive at Llancarfan in Glamorgan. The paintings include depictions of the Seven Deadly Sins, Death and the Gallant, and a large and dramatically painted St George and the Dragon. Although of eastern origin, by the late medieval period the legend of St George was known throughout Europe and, no doubt, there were once other paintings of the subject in Wales. Similarly, paintings of the ultimate Christian theme of the Last Judgement were widespread, though only a single example survives. As at the Church of St Giles in Wrexham, the Doom was conventionally painted above the chancel arch, the most effective location for the intimidation of the congregation who stood at services in the medieval period, confined to

7. *St George and the Dragon, Llancarfan, Glamorgan*, late 15th century, wall painting

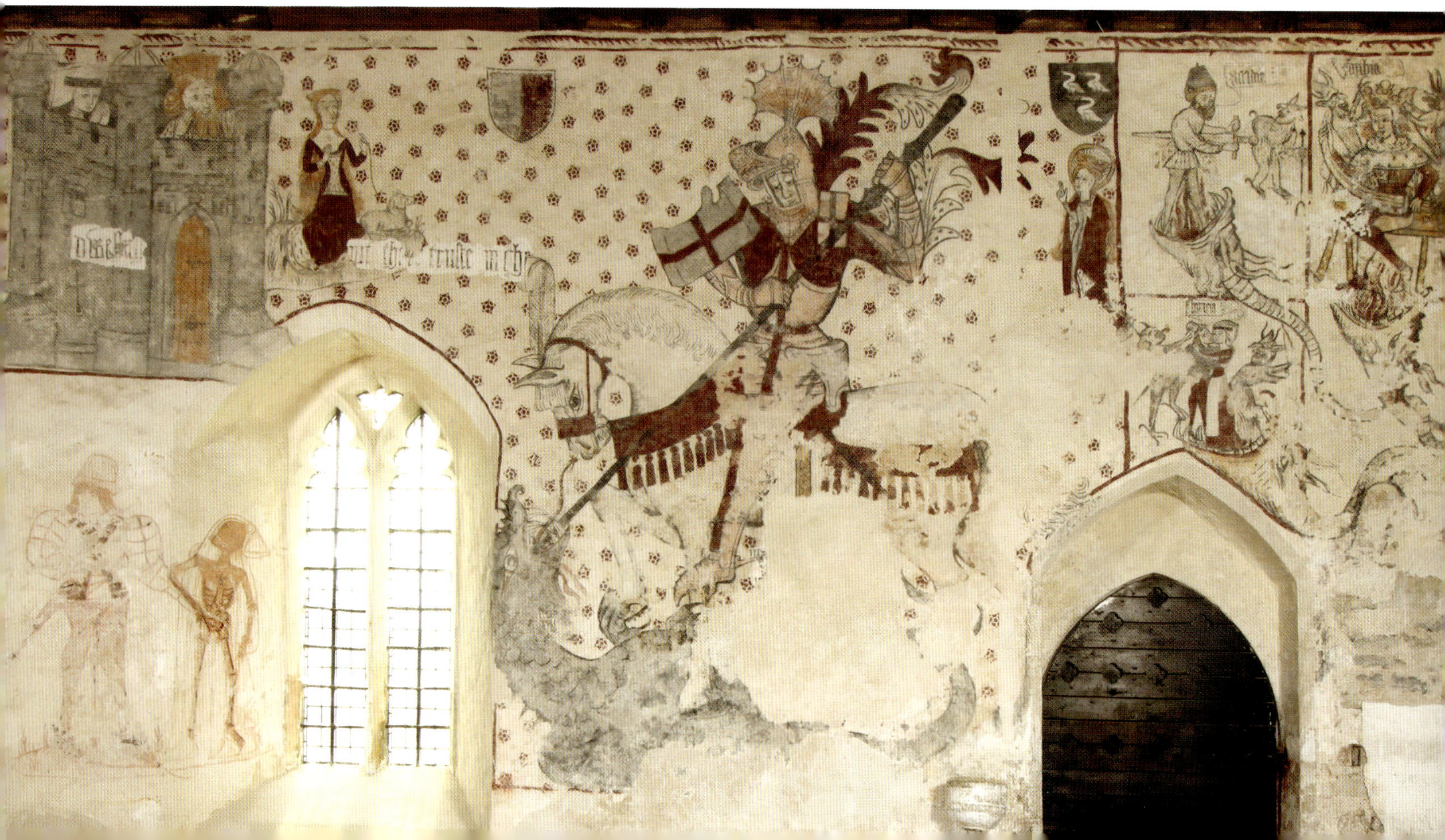

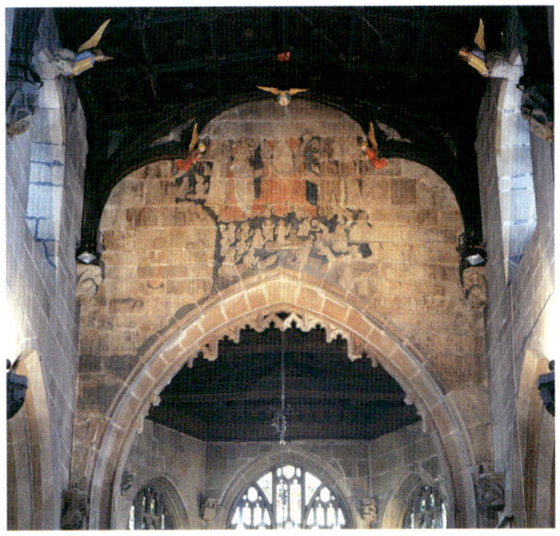

the nave. Above them they saw the virtuous, grouped to the right hand of God, admitted to heaven. The sinful, to God's left, were damned and dispatched to burn in hell.[8]

During the turbulent years of the Glyndŵr Revolt and the Wars of the Roses, woodwork was particularly prone to destruction. Yet, almost as if in defiance of its vulnerability, the use of wood both architecturally and for carving had reached a high degree of sophistication in Wales at the end of the fifteenth century. By 1500, elegant cruck-built hall houses, initially commissioned on a substantial scale for the wealthiest individuals, were also being constructed in smaller versions for tenant farmers.[9] In churches, the wooden rood screens that

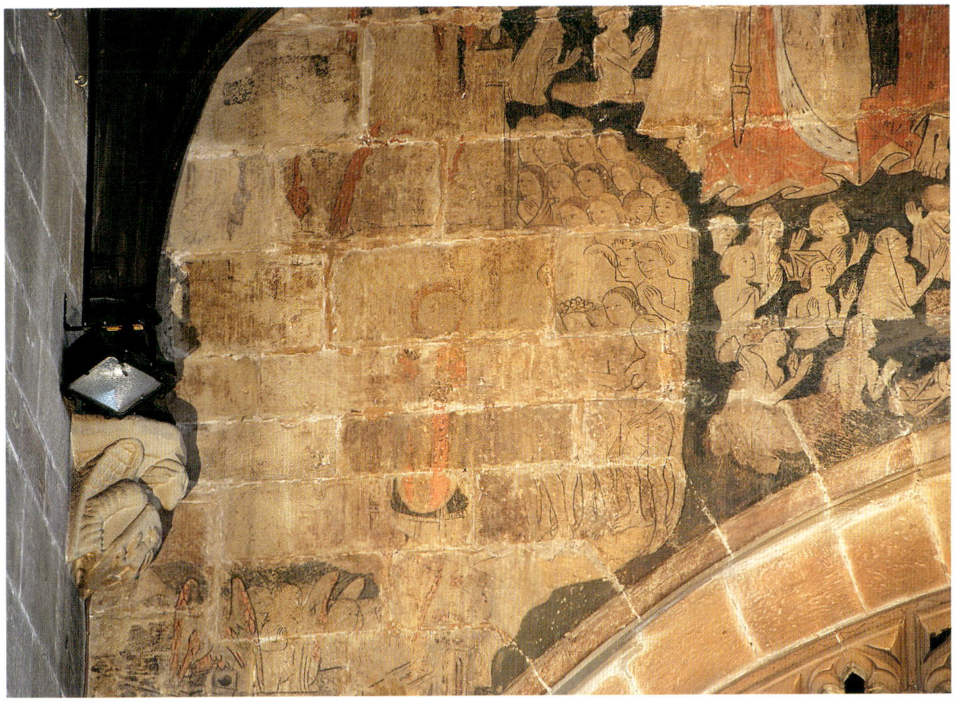

8. *The Doom, Church of St Giles, Wrexham,* 15th century, wall painting

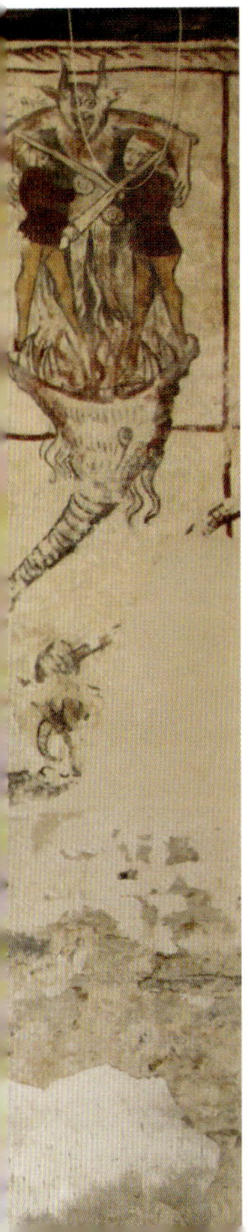

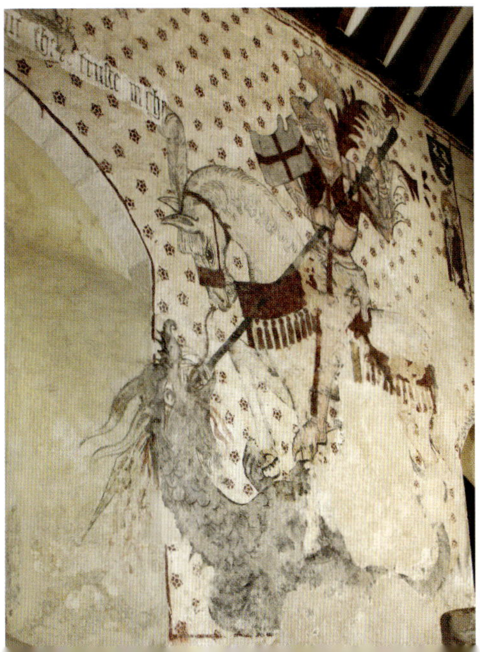

7 The association of these two images is made through a stone statue of St Christopher carrying the infant Jesus at Norton Priory in Cheshire, which seems likely to be the work of the same carver as the Abergavenny Jesse. See Lord, *Medieval Vision*, pp. 214–5.

8 It was suggested by Eve Baker, who conserved the picture, that the Wrexham Doom was painted by the master also responsible for the Llanynys St Christopher. See Lord, *Medieval Vision*, p. 215, note 175.

9 See Richard Suggett, 'Creating the Architecture of Happiness', in Dylan Foster Evans, Barry J. Lewis and Ann Parry Owen (eds.), *Gwalch Cywyddau Gwŷr: Essays on Guto'r Glyn and Fifteenth-Century Wales*, (Aberystwyth, 2013), pp. 393–427.

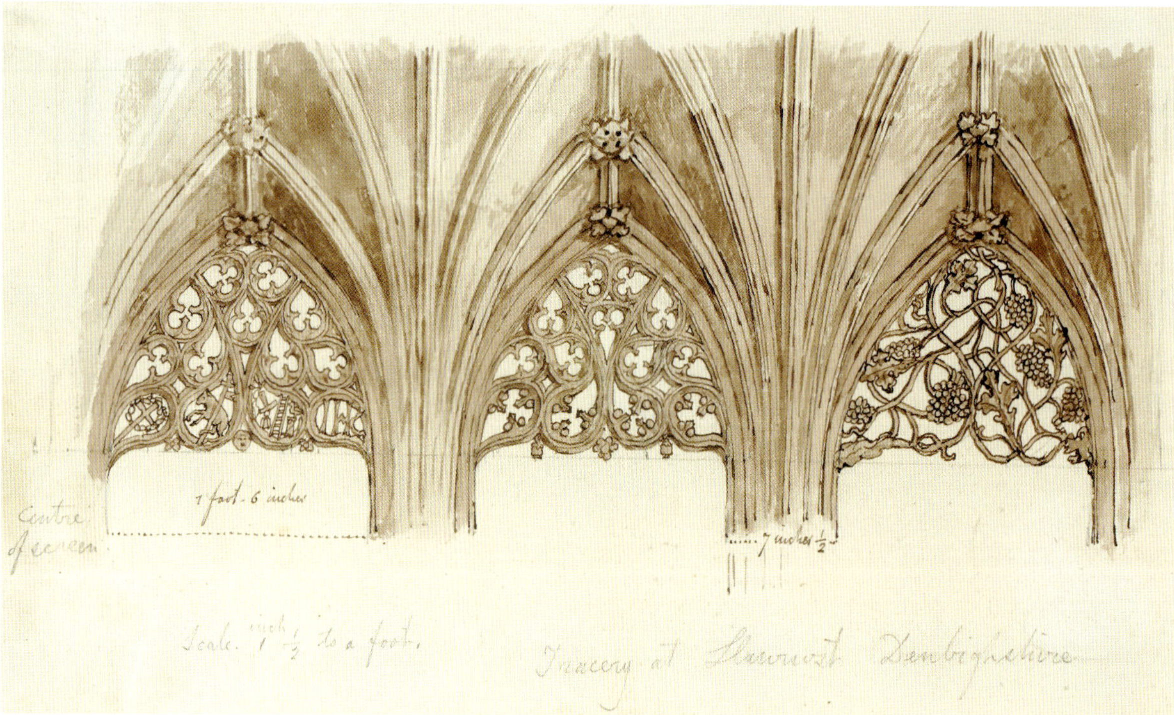

9. Revd John Parker, *Late 15th century screen, Church of St Crwst, Llanrwst*, c.1830, pen and wash

divided nave from chancel in the Middle Ages, provided opportunities for carvers – probably, in many cases, the same individuals responsible for the joinery of the new houses – to create both decorative and narrative schemes of considerable complexity. In 1468, the 1st Earl of Pembroke, William Herbert of Raglan Castle, burned Llanrwst in the Yorkist cause. The woodwork in the church was surely among the casualties, but by the end of the century one of the finest new screens in Wales had been installed. The style of such screens reflected the development of regional workshops as well as of individual artisans, and their imagery sometimes combined the Europe-wide iconography of the faith with devotion to local saints.[10]

As well as dividing the nave from the chancel (and so the laity from the clergy), the screen supported the rood – the image of Jesus on the cross, that was the focus for the contemplation of the faithful. It was often the most elaborate artefact in a church. The celebrity of particularly splendid examples was recorded by contemporary poets:

> [Behold] yonder the rood of Brecon and the implements of the Crucifixion, the gilded feet and side of Christ['s image] all pierced through: [such] a treasure [it is which hangs] above the Choir! The icon is a worthy one; I shall go there, to the lands of the free-flowing Hodni [river]. On the Cross which [grew] from Moses' staff, [Christ] was of old hung between Dismas and [Gestas]; his two arms outstretched: his very body the means of his sacrifice.[11]

10 At Pennant Melangell, for instance, the myth of the local saint, Melangell, was illustrated in cartoon-strip fashion along the upper beam of the screen. For a thorough discussion of many aspects of woodwork in the period, see Richard Bebb, *Welsh Furniture 1250-1950* (Kidwelly, 2007), I.

11 For the text of this late fifteenth-century poem, see Henry Lewis, Thomas Roberts and Ifor Williams, (eds.), *Cywyddau Iolo Goch ac Eraill* (1st edn., Bangor, 1925), pp. 230–2.

It was the image of the crucifixion that most attracted the indignation of radical Christians during the Reformation of the Church, begun by Henry VIII and pursued by his son, Edward VI. Roods were taken down, the flanking carvings of the Virgin and St John with them, and destroyed. No fifteenth-century rood figures of Jesus remain, but other images of the Crucifixion, carved, painted and embroidered, have survived.[12] They demonstrate an intensification of focus by believers on the bodily suffering of Jesus that is characteristic of the late medieval period. Broadly speaking, early depictions of the Crucifixion tended to present Jesus on the cross as if at peace, his arms outstretched horizontally, suggesting his godliness in overcoming pain. Although there are many exceptions, by the fifteenth and early sixteenth centuries, crucifixion iconography generally presented a tortured and contorted body on the cross, an image that presented Jesus as a suffering human being. The five wounds made by the nails and the spear that pierced his side, with the blood collected in cups carried by angels, exercised a particular fascination for the pious. The painted glass at the Church of St Ust and St Dyfrig, Llanwrin, Montgomeryshire, is remarkable in this respect. A sixth angel is present, a servant of Satan called Apollyon, who is described in the biblical Book of Revelation and depicted in the glass with a black halo.[13] At the Church of St Cadwaladr, Llangadwaladr in Anglesey, the shadowy image of the skeleton of Jesus is visible beneath the flesh, illustrating the fulfilment of the prophecy, quoted in the Gospel of St John, that at the crucifixion 'A bone of him shall not be broken'.[14] Clearly, the patrons or the painters of these windows had sophisticated understandings of Christian theology.

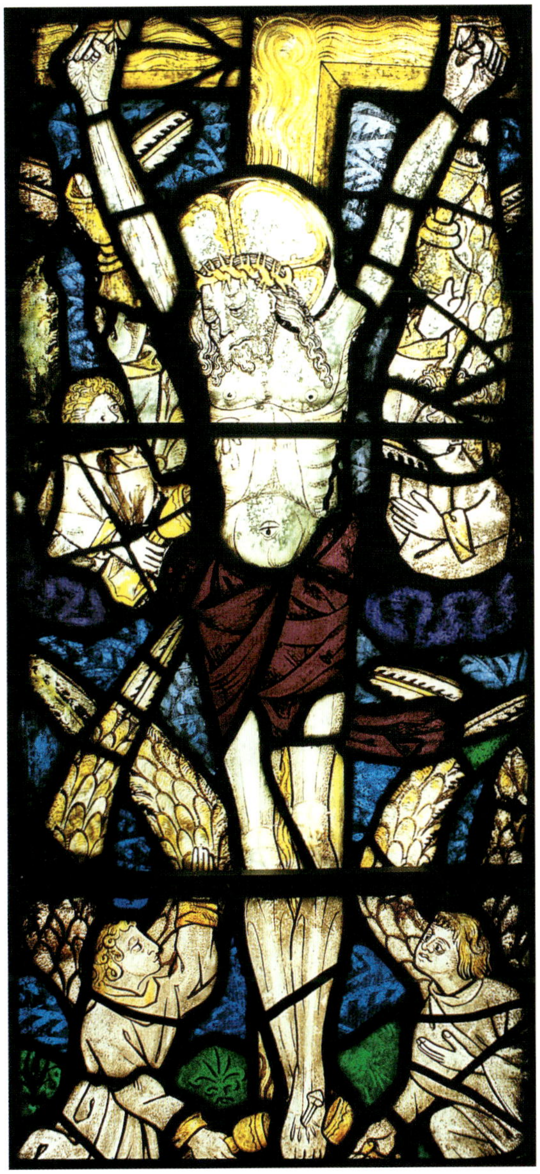

10. *The Crucifixion*, Church of St Cadwaladr, Llangadwaladr, *c.*1500, painted glass

12 The screen at Llanrwst can only briefly have carried its rood – either newly carved or preserved from the flames of 1468 and restored to its position. However, the figure of Jesus on the cross survived both the Reformation and the civil wars of the mid-seventeenth century, hidden from the public gaze, and was seen by Thomas Dineley in 1684: 'Over the Timber Arch of the Chancell neer the Rood Loft, lieth hid the ancient figure of the Crucifixion as bigg as the life. This I suppose is shewn to none but the curious, and rarely to them.' Thomas Dineley, *The Account of the Official Progress of His Grace Henry the First Duke of Beaufort through Wales in 1684* (London, 1888), p. 147. The two medieval rood figures of Jesus that have survived in Wales predate the disturbed fifteenth century. Originally located at the churches of Kemeys Inferior, Monmouthshire, and Mochdre, Montgomeryshire, both are now held at the National Museum of Wales.

13 Revelation 9:11. See also Matthew 25:41.

14 John 19:36, reflecting Exodus 12:46.

11. *The Angel of the Abyss*, Church of St Ust and St Dyfrig, Llanwrin, *c.*1461–83, painted glass

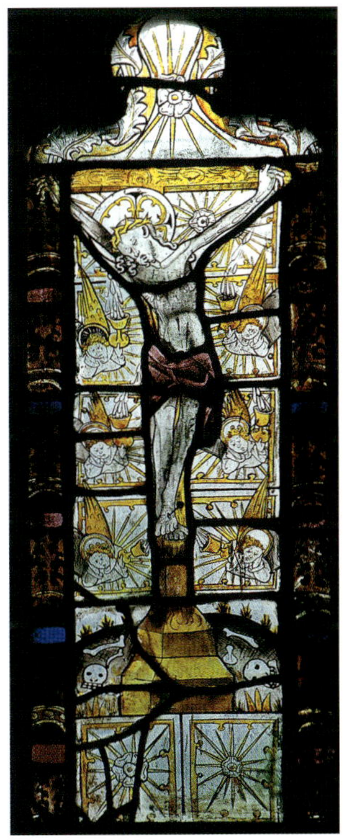

The intensification of religious feeling that is suggested by the concentration on the suffering of Jesus in large-scale public images of the Crucifixion was reflected in small, personal artefacts. The most pious among the gentry and the wealthy mercantile class might make space in their houses for an altar on which a depiction of the Virgin or the Crucifixion could stand, along with a devotional book, such as a Book of Hours. An early surviving example is the Llanbeblig Hours, probably made in the late fourteenth century. It appears to have belonged to Isabella Godynogh, whose husband's family held lands in Conwy, though the book's calendar of saints' days included St Deiniol of Bangor and St Peblig of Caernarfon. The main part of the manuscript is English work, but is preceded by four leaves of miniatures, probably added in Wales. These include an image of the Virgin and Child and a sophisticated portrayal of the Annunciation, in which a premonition of the Crucifixion was inserted between the Archangel Gabriel and the Virgin. The cross on which Jesus would die was transformed into a lily, the symbol of purity overcoming human sin. The local associations of the text and other evidence in the Llanbeblig Hours suggest that the miniatures may have been painted by an employee at the Caernarfon treasury.[15]

15 Daniel Huws, *Medieval Welsh Manuscripts* (Cardiff and Aberystwyth, 2000), p. 19. The manuscript is NLW MS 17520A.

In the Llanwrin crucifixion window, at the foot of the cross the painter depicted skulls and other bones. These were among the symbols that featured not only in representations of the Crucifixion itself, but of the other events in the sequence leading up to it, and following it, known collectively as the Passion. The skull and bones were those of Adam and Eve, whose burial place was believed to be Golgotha, the site of the crucifixion of Jesus, and so they represented the completion of the cycle from the fall of mankind to the redemption through his death and resurrection. For the pious, such symbols stimulated the recreation of the events of the Passion in the imagination, and the contemplation of their meaning. The imagery transcended the many different media in which the Passion was

12. *The Annunciation to the Virgin Mary*, from the *Llanbeblig Book of Hours*, late 14th–early 15th century, 17.5x12.0

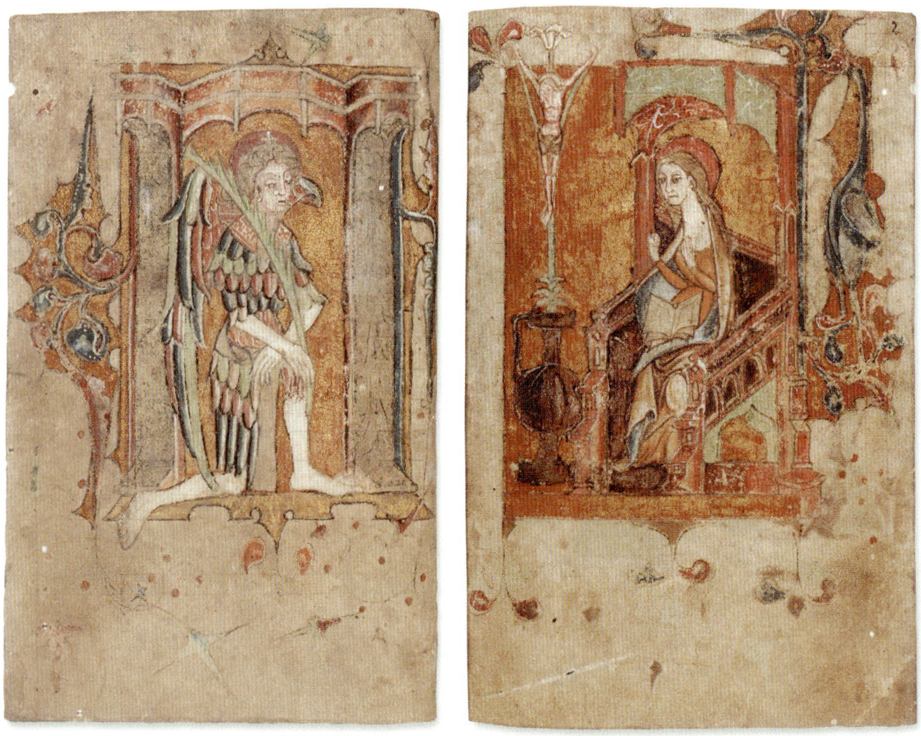

represented. Like the glass at Llanwrin, a crucifixion scene, finely embroidered on a chasuble that survives at the Church of Our Lady and St Michael at Abergavenny, depicted both the skull of Adam and angels collecting the blood from the wounds on the hands of Jesus. The chasuble, worn by the priest at mass, was part of a set of elaborate vestments probably given to Elizabeth Herbert of Raglan Castle by the queen, Elizabeth of York, who was her cousin. The queen visited the castle in 1502. Similarly, a life-size carved figure of Jesus, associated with the Mostyn family of Flintshire and perhaps originally located at Maenan Abbey, Llanrwst, also included the skull of Adam. Jesus was depicted seated and bound, prior to the Crucifixion. Though it is not described in the bible, this

13. *Chasuble*, Church of Our Lady and St Michael, Abergavenny, early 16th century, embroidery

14. *The Mostyn Christ*, Bangor Cathedral, 15th century, wood, ht. 157.5

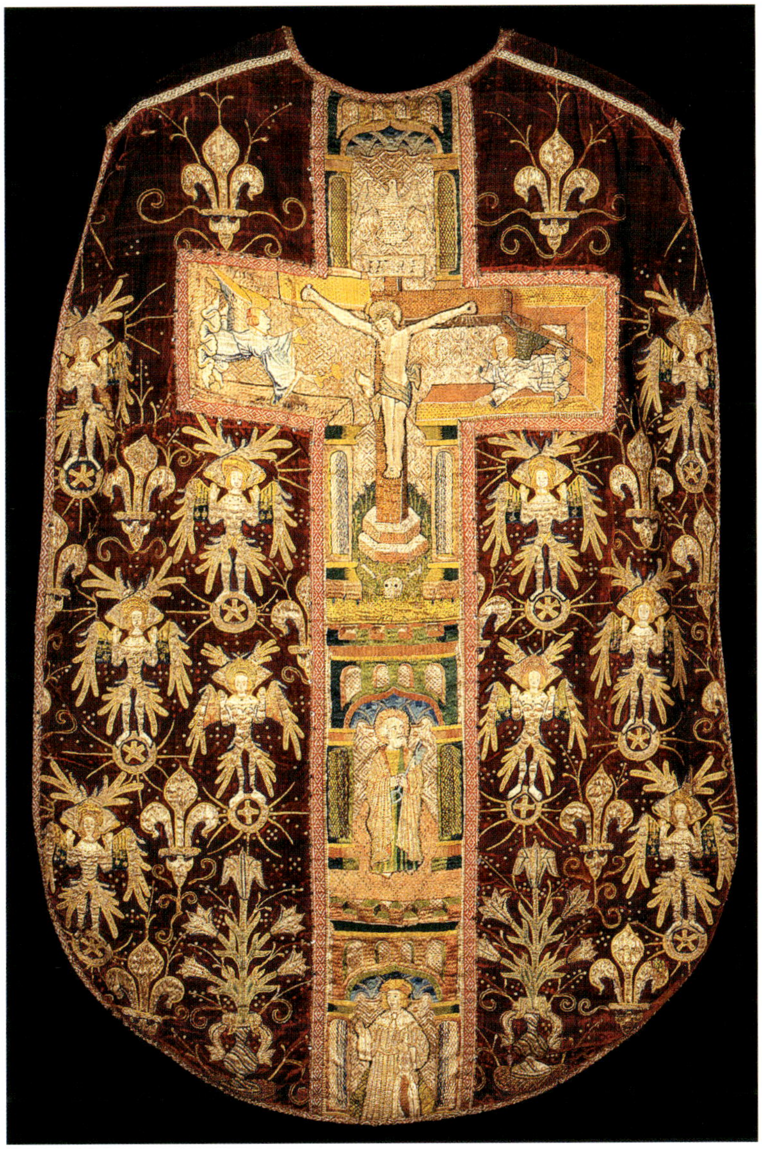

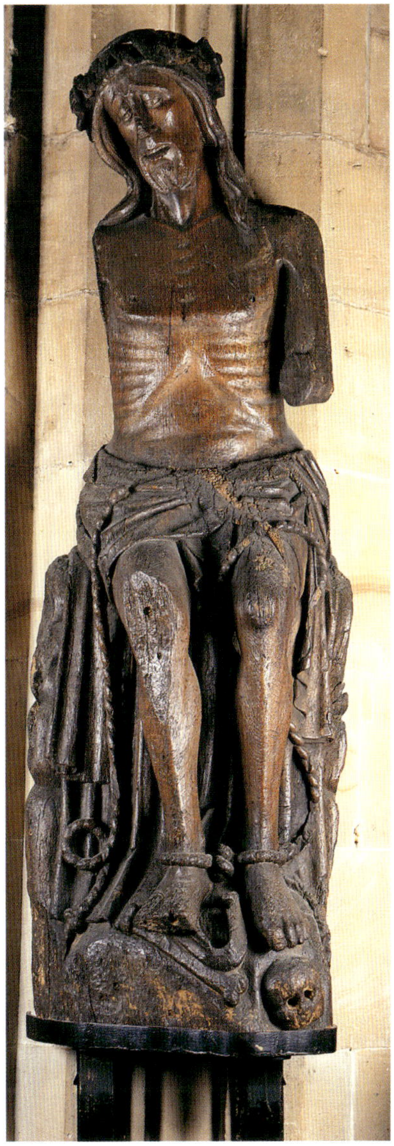

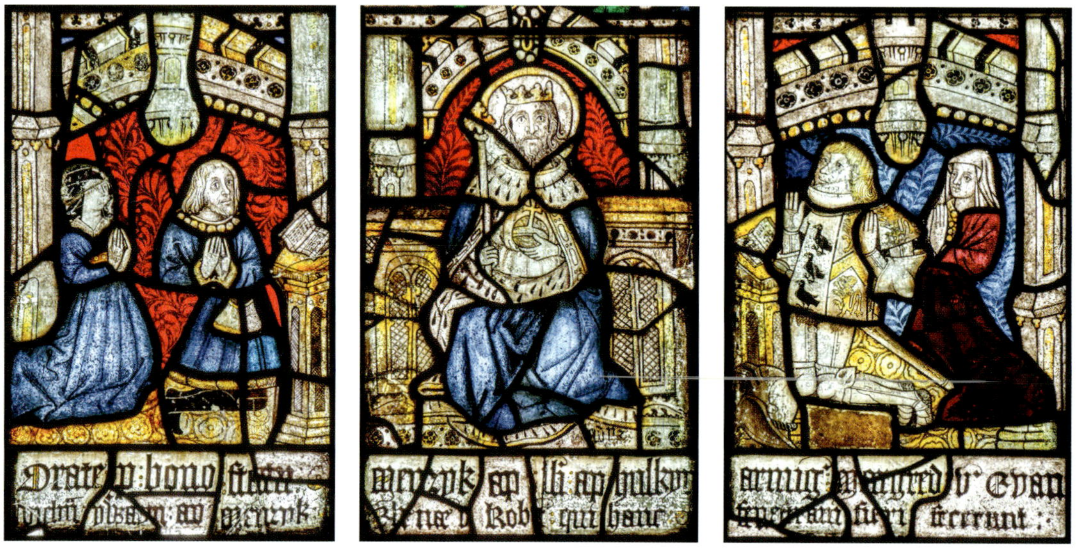

15. *Donor portraits with King Cadwaladr*, Church of St Cadwaladr, Llangadwaladr, Anglesey, painted glass fragments *c.*1490, reassembled *c.*1850

portrayal of Jesus as 'the Man of Sorrows' was a favourite subject. It appears again among the extensive group of wall paintings that survive from the Church of St Teilo at Llandeilo Tal-y-bont, in Glamorgan, where the painter added the symbolic representations of the Crucifixion itself, known as the Instruments of the Passion – the nails driven through the hands and feet of Jesus, the lance that pierced his side, the ladder used to take down his body from the cross, and the pincers used to withdraw the nails.[16]

Works on the scale of the Mostyn Christ, the Wrexham and Llancarfan murals, and the Jesse windows at Llanrhaeadr and Diserth, were expensive to commission. In general, the most dramatic surviving examples are clustered in what were the richest parts of late-medieval Wales, that is, the north-east counties of Flint and Denbighshire, and Glamorgan. Commissions were usually the benefactions of individual patrons – royalty, in the case of the Raglan embroideries, but more often the gentry and wealthy clergy. The patrons of the murals at Llancarfan, for instance, are likely to have been the local Bawdrip family, since their arms survive among the paintings.[17] The Diserth Jesse window was the gift of Archdeacon Peter Conwey, who left money for the project in his will. The desire of patrons to advertise their public spirited generosity alongside their piety was not an innovation of the period, but the increasing number of examples through the fifteenth century, recorded in the form of heraldry, inscriptions or portraits, demonstrated a growing tendency among both laity and clergy to assert individual identity and social status through their commissions. At Llangadwaladr, in Anglesey, two generations of the same family were portrayed kneeling under the images of St John and the Virgin at the Crucifixion. Between them was the enthroned seventh-century King Cadwaladr, a figure of pious association.

16 The reconstructed church from Llandeilo Talybont is at the National History Museum, St Fagans.

17 The family was very well connected. Margaret Bawdrip was, by her previous marriage to Richard Herbert of Ewyas, the mother of William Herbert, 1st Earl of Pembroke.

16. *Man of Sorrows*, Church of St Teilo, formerly at Llandeilo Tal-y-bont, wall painting, 15th century

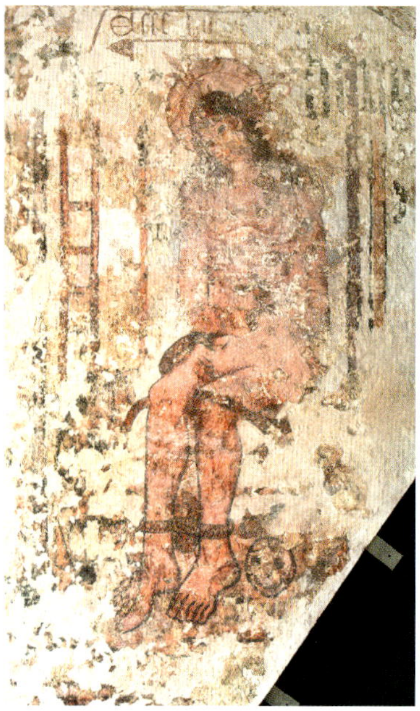

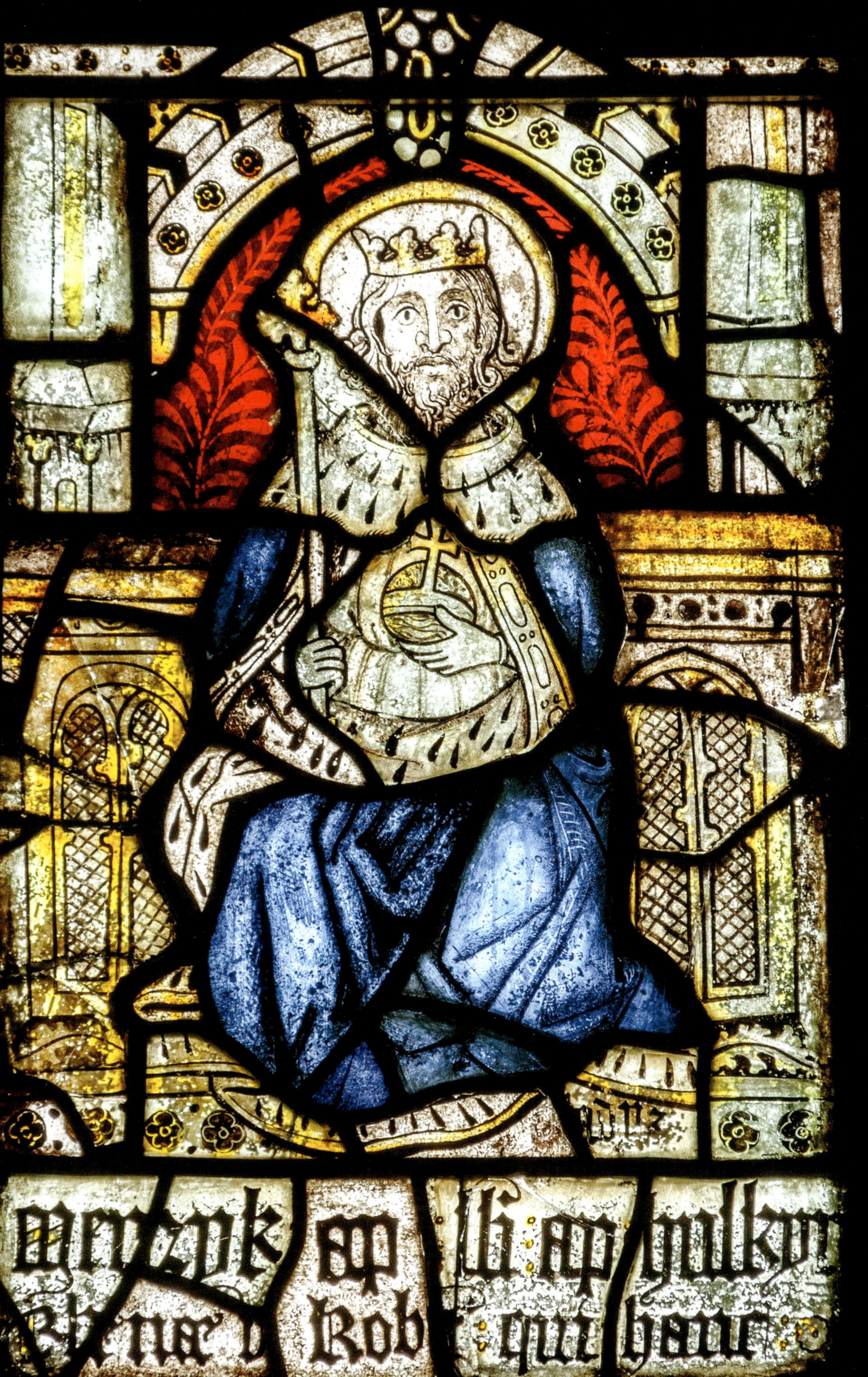

18 A roof boss at Holywell, showing the heads of a couple in close proximity, has been regarded traditionally as a portrait of Sir William and Elizabeth, though this is not confirmed by heraldry.

19 See also a cupboard of continental origin, believed to have been at Chirk and of the late fifteenth century, Bebb, *Welsh Furniture*, I, p. 199.

The king had died on pilgrimage at Rome, but his depiction in the window also signified the patrons' secular association with ancient Welsh lineage and their allegiance to the Tudor dynasty. Henry VII claimed direct descent in Anglesey from Cadwaladr. To their contemporary audience, what appear today to be pious representations of patrons in devotion before a favoured saint might also indicate a network of entwined secular and religious associations that legitimised the status of the family.

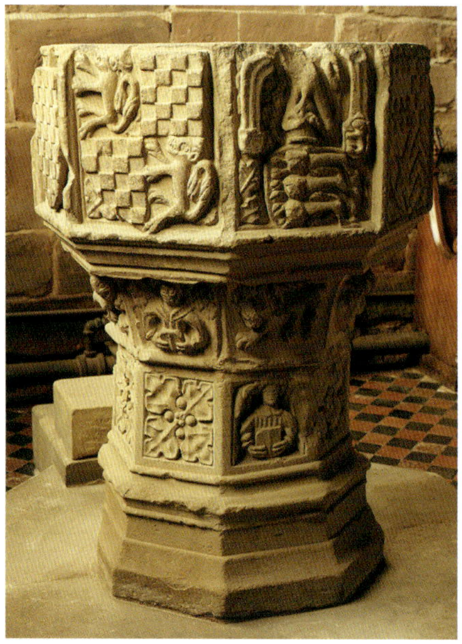

17. *Font*, Church of St Chad, Holt, *c.*1493

In the north-east of the country, the Stanley family became involved in church patronage on a lavish scale, though with a strong emphasis on dynastic celebration, alongside devotion. Sir William, his wife Elizabeth Hopton, and his brother, Sir Thomas, all identified themselves in heraldic devices at a group of Flintshire churches and at the shrine of St Winifred at Holywell, with which all three together may have been involved.[18] The font at the Church of St Chad at Holt is encrusted with heraldic emblems of Sir William and his association with the Lordship of Bromfield to the exclusion of any Christian imagery. Unfortunately, Sir William did not retain his Lordship for long, since he was executed in 1495 by Henry VII, the king whom he had helped bring to power.

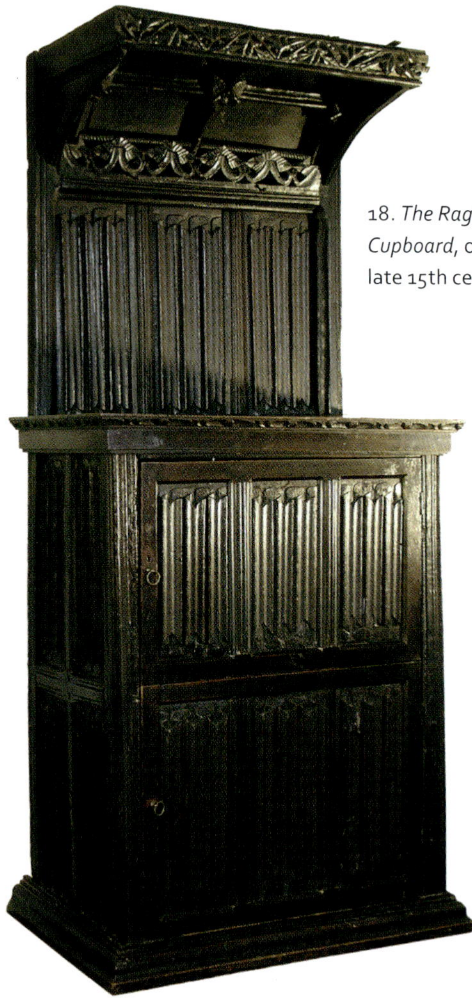

18. *The Raglan Cupboard*, oak, late 15th century

Domestic patronage

Among Sir William Stanley's briefly held gains under Henry VII was Chirk Castle, which he restored, apparently to a high quality and under the influence of continental fashions.[19] A few years later, when it was in the hands of a subsequent constable, the poet Tudur Aled noted its French form and the quality of its woodwork.[20] Fewer examples of wood carving and painting survive from a domestic context than from churches prior to the mid-sixteenth century, but it is clear that styles and techniques of manufacture spanned the two. A fine screen at the church of St Jerome, Llangwm Uchaf, Monmouthshire, included the carved pattern known as 'linenfold' (since it was derived from the imitation of the folds of draped fabrics), as did the remarkable 'Raglan Cupboard', made in the same period and, at that time, a new form of artefact. Raglan is just a few miles from Llangwm, and the similarity in the style and quality of the carving from the church screen and the domestic furniture strongly suggest at least the influence of the one upon the other, if not a common origin in a local workshop. Similar parallels existed in many parts of the country. In the north, it is clear that the plentiful supplies of good timber, along with wealthy patrons, made the Conwy Valley a particular focus for the production of high quality furniture and fittings for both ecclesiastical and domestic use.[21]

Among the most elaborately carved domestic artefacts of the period are the front panels of another cupboard, though its origins are more obscure than the Raglan example. It includes a depiction of the expulsion of Adam and Eve from the Garden of Eden, the symbolic representation of the Crucifixion in the form of the Instruments of the Passion, musicians

20 'Dal sylw ar dy lys, Wiliam,/Dull Ffrainc yw dyall ei ffrâm ...' Tudur Aled, 'I Wiliam ap Siôn Edwart, Cwnstabl y Waun'. See Thomas Parry (ed.), *The Oxford Book of Welsh Verse* (Oxford, 1962), p. 177.

21 The Gwydir Cupboard, which is similar in form to the Raglan piece but of a slightly later date, reflects contemporary carving in Llanrwst Church.

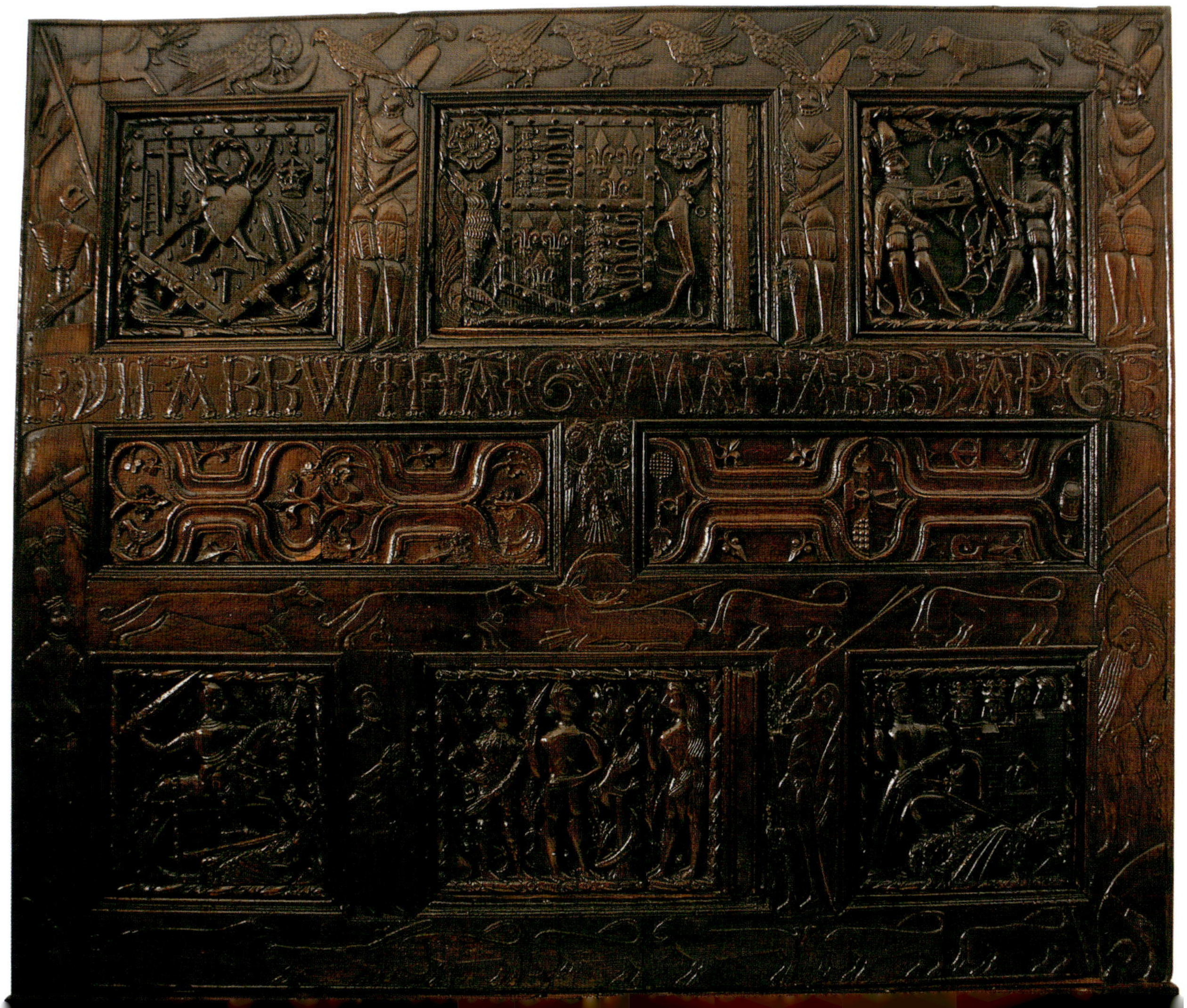

19. *The Newcourt Cupboard Front* (also known as the 'Cotehele Tester'), *c.*1515–30, oak

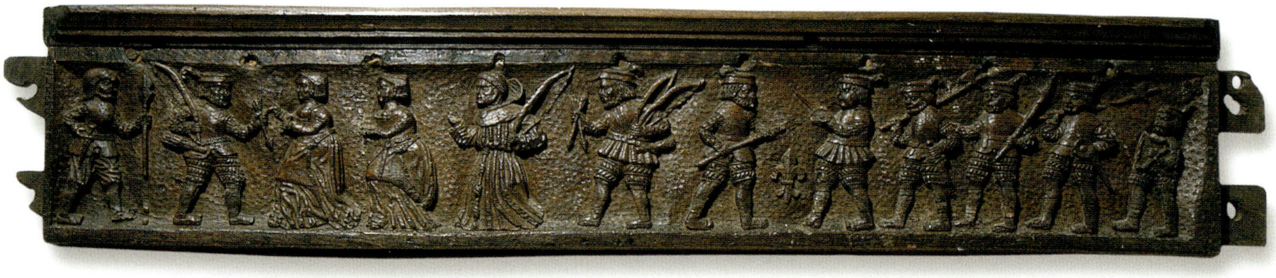

20. *Bedstead of Sir Rhys ap Thomas*, c.1507, oak

playing the harp and the *crwth*, and Tudor heraldry. The panels are held in a frame elaborated with hunting scenes and an inscription that includes, in abbreviated form, the name 'Harri ap Gruffudd'. The inscription may identify the maker or perhaps a patron from the Golden Valley in Monmouthshire, where the style of the work is reflected in elaborate church screens and other figurative carving.[22] Harri ap Gruffudd's cupboard panel subsequently came into the possession of descendants of the family of Sir Rhys ap Thomas of Carew in Pembrokeshire, causing confusion as to its origins, since Sir Rhys was also a patron of skilled local woodworkers. Carved chairs and an extraordinary bedstead made for Sir Rhys both survive as testimony to the elaboration of his court, from which he dominated the administration of south-west Wales in the early sixteenth century. The bedstead decoration took the form of a frieze populated by knights on horseback, pikemen, longbowmen and crossbowmen, who commemorated a tournament organised by Sir Rhys at Carew in 1506. It was an elaborate affair, expressing the growing fascination manifested by the gentry of the period for an imagined past age of chivalry and deeds of arms. It attracted participants and observers from all parts of Wales, and from England. Painters were among those who benefitted by commissions associated with the tournament – 'images, scutcheons, and coat armours' being prominently displayed along with a 'table' (that is, a painting on board) that celebrated the coming together of two nations under the Tudor monarchy:

> ... Sir Rice having reserved a great companie of the better sort for his guests, he leads them to the castle, with drummes, trumpetts, and other warlike musicke. Over the gate, at the entrance, was hung up a goodlie faire table, wherein was represented the species and pourtraiture of St George and St David embracing one another with this mottoe, *Nodo plus quam Gordiano*.[23]

Sir Rhys's bed, and his painted panel of St George and St David, represented a world far removed from that of the common people, in an age when the poor were very poor. Little is known of their visual culture, and it may be that the only pictures with which they were familiar were those they saw in church. Nor were they often depicted in the works

22 The case for Harri ap Gruffudd as patron is argued by Bebb, *Welsh Furniture*, I, pp. 161-8.

23 'Knot stronger than the Gordian'. See Ralph A. Griffiths, *Sir Rhys ap Thomas and his Family: A Study in the Wars of the Roses and Early Tudor Politics* (Cardiff, 1993), p. 252.

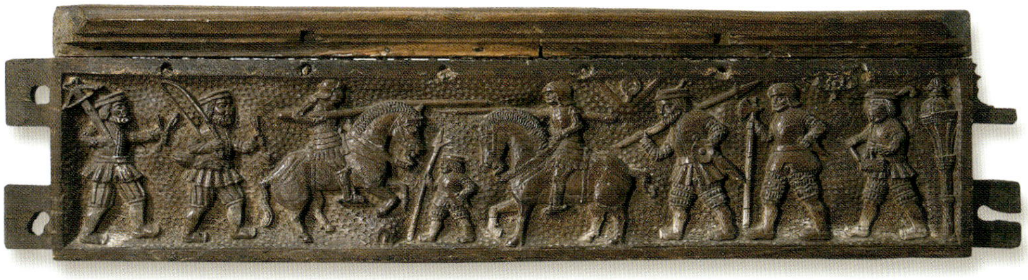

commissioned by their social superiors. Above the level of these poor, though below the ranks of the gentry, existed a class of yeoman and, in the towns especially, of merchants, professionals and craftspeople. It was from their ranks that the artisans who produced the carving in wood and stone and the painted decoration that adorned the court of Sir Rhys were drawn though, like the poor, they seldom imaged themselves before the mid-fifteenth century. Glass commissioned for the Church of St Tyrnog, Llandyrnog in Denbighshire, may present one of the few glimpses of the lives of this small but important class of people. The subject of the window was the seven sacraments of the faith. Fragments of five remain recognisable, of which Holy Matrimony is the most complete. The painter of the glass succeeded in creating a convincing depiction of his cheerful subjects, whose faces give the impression of living individuals rather than drawings made from recycled patterns.

The relative material prosperity of this nascent middle class – among whom were individuals wealthier than some who could call themselves gentry – enabled them to adorn their houses and occasionally urban public buildings, such as market and guild halls. At a merchant's house in Tenby, one of the few examples of interior painted decoration survives. Both freehand and stencilled painting on plaster was practiced in the period as a cheaper alternative to textile hangings. The flowing pattern of leaves within vertical bands in the Merchant's House was light and delicate. Most unusually, Tenby also retains portraits of two individuals of the kind who would have

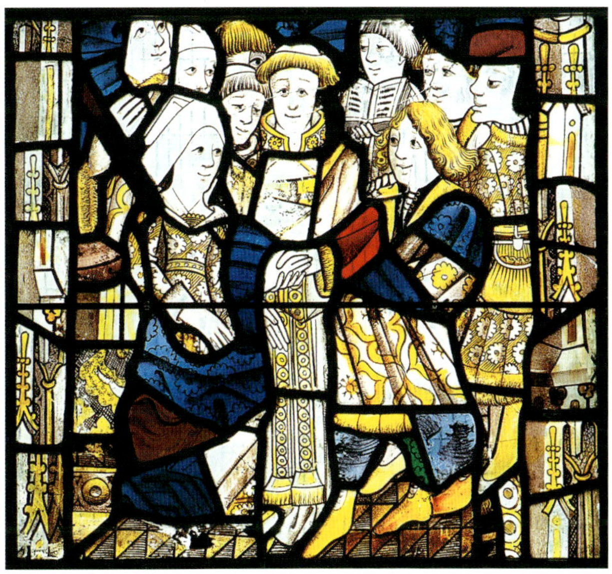

21. *Holy Matrimony*, Church of St Tyrnog, Llandyrnog, late 15th century, painted glass

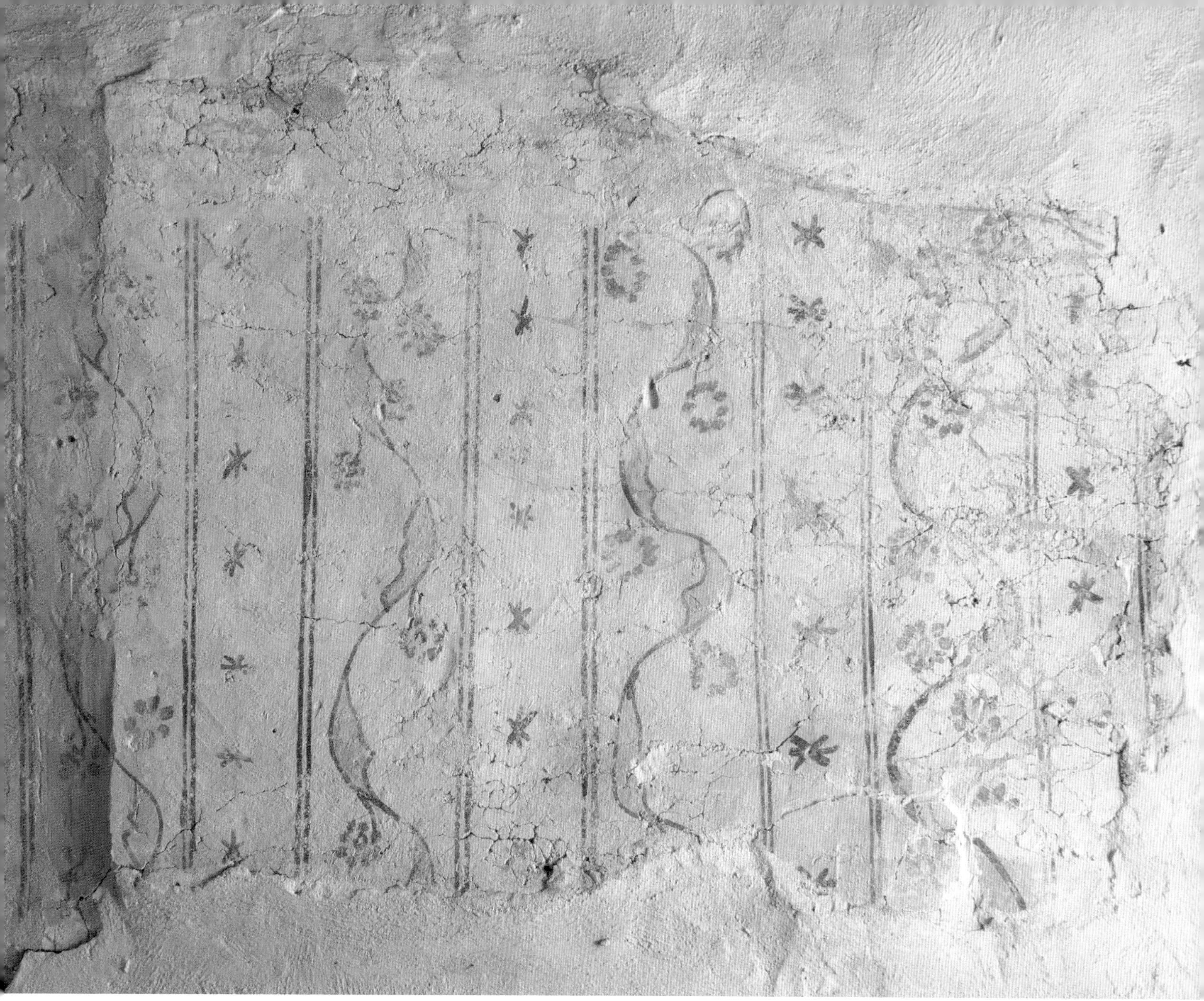

22. Unknown painter, *Decoration at the Merchant's House*, Tenby, wall painting, c.1500

occupied such a residence. Thomas and John White were portrayed in the form of tomb effigies. However, the exceptional status which accorded their elaborate memorials a prominent place in the parish church lay not simply in commercial success. John White was the beneficiary of his father's loyalty to the Lancastrian cause in the Wars of the Roses. Following the battle of Tewkesbury in 1471, he had provided the boat in which the young Henry Tudor escaped with his uncle Jasper, Earl of Pembroke, to Brittany. As king, a decade and a half later, Henry Tudor did not forget this service, and rewarded the family handsomely. John White probably commissioned the alabaster effigies of himself and his deceased father, with other family members in adoration before their favoured saints, in about 1490.

The tournament organised by Sir Rhys ap Thomas at Carew in 1506 reflected the influence of the court of Burgundy on that of the new Tudor monarchy. Along with other supporters of the Lancastrian cause, Sir Rhys had experienced directly the splendours of the cities of the Low Countries when he was a political exile, with his father, during the second half of the 1460s. Such personal experience of continental life was not unusual among the Welsh gentry and clergy. Bishop John Trefor of St Asaph, whose house and cathedral had been burnt by Owain Glyndŵr before he prudently changed sides in the revolt, had spent time in Rome. However, rather than the culture of the city states of Italy, it was the northern renaissance of the Burgundian empire, enriched by world-wide trade, that exercised the greatest influence on Welsh patrons. The Burgundian heartland of the Low Countries

23. *The Tomb and Effigy of Thomas White*, Church of St Mary, Tenby, late 15th century, alabaster

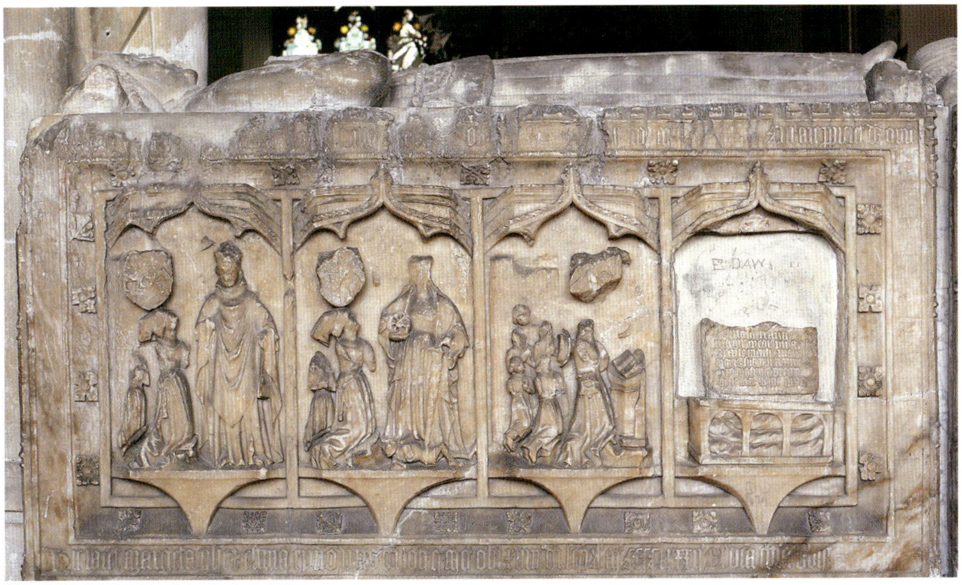

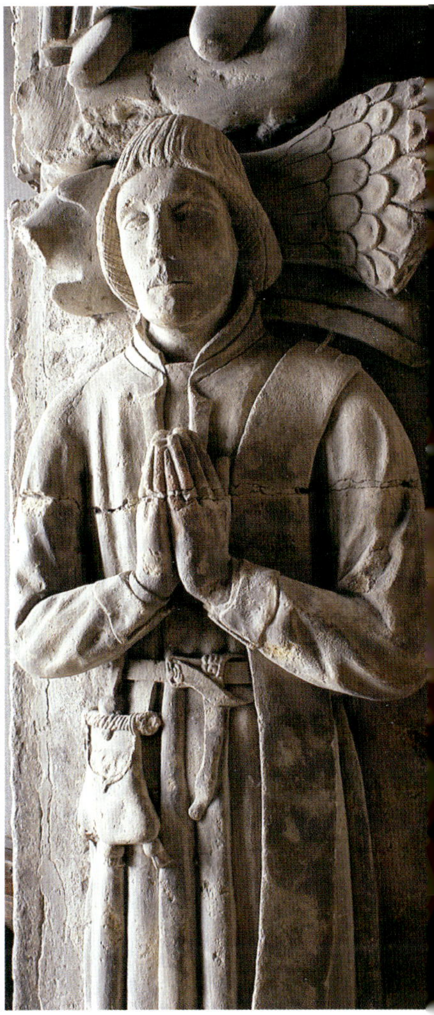

became the medium of transmission from Italy for humanist ideas, and in the early sixteenth century, the Protestant Reformation would reinforce a sense of the north as the home of radical thinking. The Welsh elite became increasingly aligned with Burgundy in culture.

Sir John Dwnn of Cydweli was among the earliest Welsh gentlemen to acquire a taste for the artistic products of Burgundy. He had profited both in wealth and courtly status by his support for King Edward IV, who himself had spent a brief period of exile in the Hague and Bruges. In the 1470s Dwnn acted as a diplomat on the king's behalf at the Burgundian and French courts, and became an enthusiast for elaborately decorated books. In the age of printing, courtly fashion for illuminated manuscripts had turned a medieval necessity into a desirable modern luxury. Dwnn's first known acquisition came as the gift of Margaret, Duchess of Burgundy, the sister of Edward IV. His sumptuously illustrated history of the exploits of Alexander the Great testified both to the elevated company that he kept and to the northern renaissance taste for the classical world.[24] Nevertheless, the humanist scholars who were refreshing interest in the authors of ancient Greece and Rome did not do so

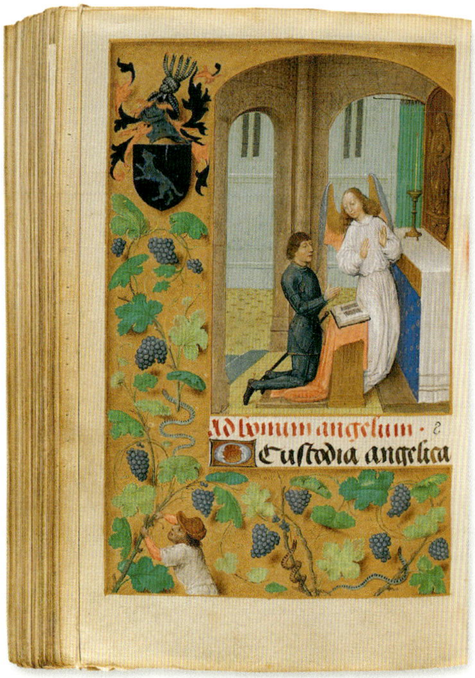

24. *Sir John Dwnn and a Guardian Angel*, illumination from the *Louthe Hours*, before 1483

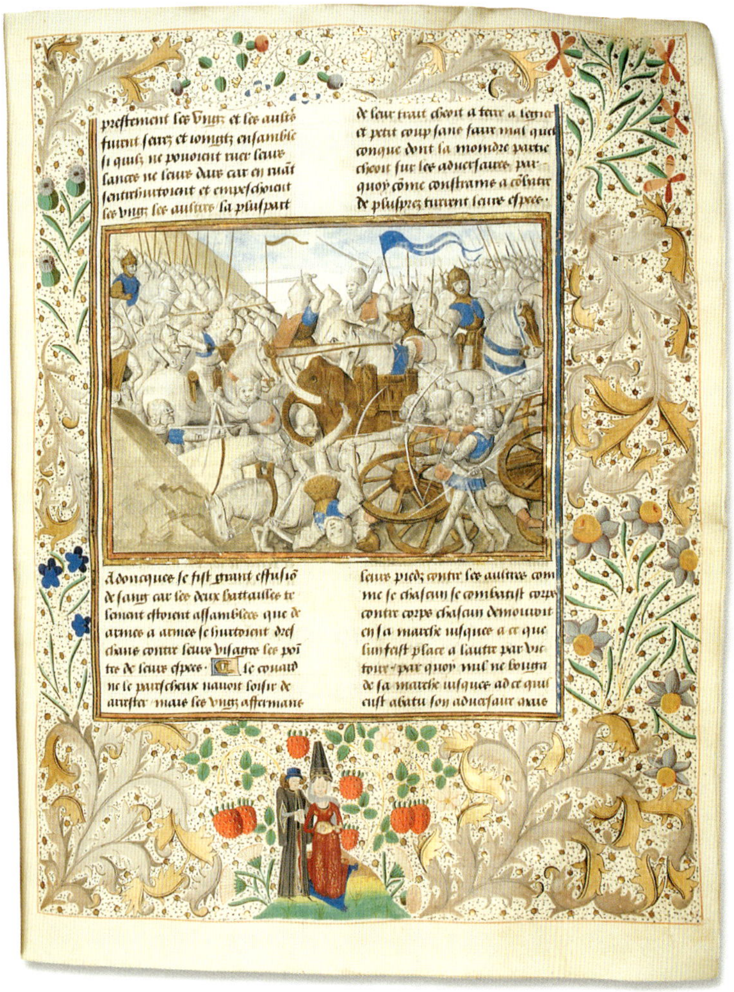

25. *The Battle of Issus*, illumination from *Quinte Curse Ruffe des faix du grant Alexandre*, 1467–77, 43.2x33.1

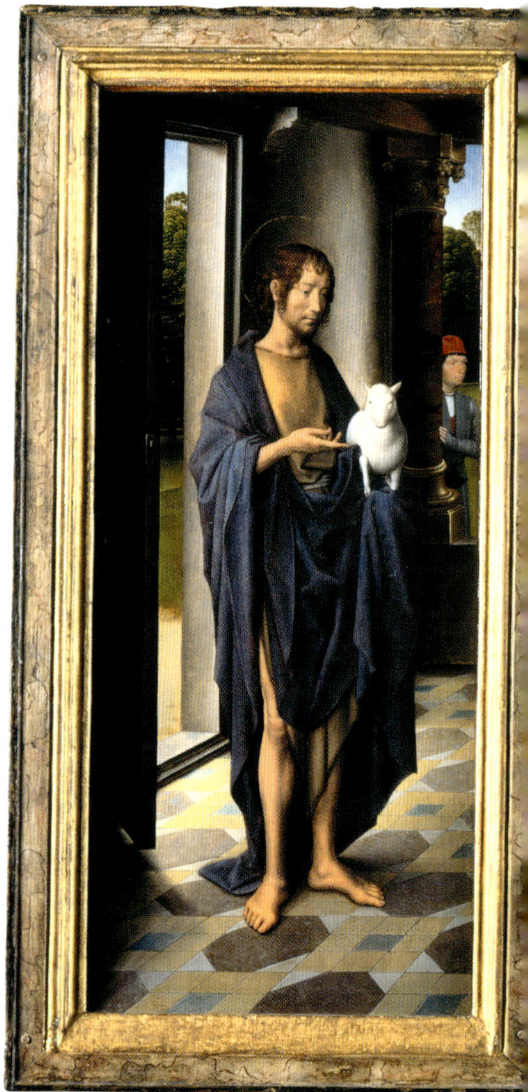

26. Hans Memling, *The Virgin and Child with Saints and Donors*, c.1479, oil on panel, centre 71.0x70.3, wings 71.0x30.5

in a way that opposed 'pagan' classical culture to Christianity. Also among the four Flemish illuminated manuscripts that Dwnn would acquire was a book of hours, now known as the Louthe Hours, which is among the finest devotional works of its period.[25] Dwnn himself was portrayed in two of its illuminations – kneeling at a prayer desk, and as a devotee of the Virgin Mary, observing the Annunciation. The physical appearance of the donor was confirmed by his portrait, opposite that of his wife, Elizabeth, and his daughter, in another major act of artistic patronage. In about 1479, Dwnn commissioned one of the most prominent painters of the period, Hans Memling, to make him an altarpiece in the form of a triptych, depicting the Virgin and Child with St Catherine and St Barbara. St John the Baptist and St John the Evangelist were portrayed in the side panels.[26]

24 British Library, MS Royal D 15.IV.

25 Louvain-la-Neuve, Archives de l'Université, MS A2. See Janet Backhouse, 'Sir John Donne's Flemish Manuscripts' in Peter Rolfe Monks and D.D.R. Owen (eds.), *Medieval Codicology, Iconography, Literature, and Translation: Studies for Keith Val Sinclair* (London, New York and Köln), 1994, pp. 48–53. Some texts refer to Dwnn using the Anglicised form 'Donne'.

26 On the closed doors of the triptych Memling painted *trompe l'oeil* statues of St Christopher carrying the infant Jesus, and of St Antony.

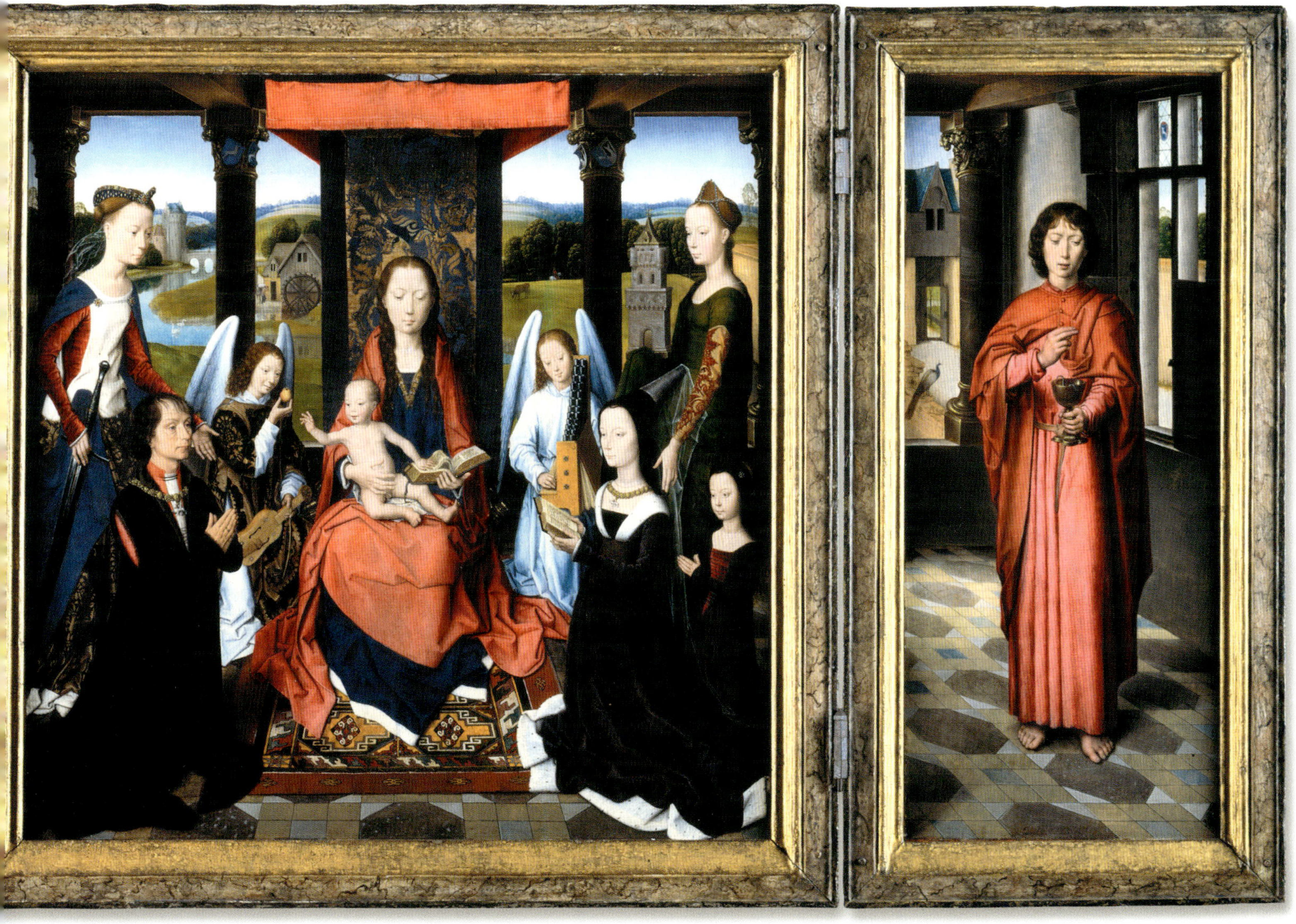

In 1461, Dwnn had fought alongside William Herbert of Raglan at the Battle of Mortimer's Cross, which installed Edward IV on the English throne. Herbert was similarly rewarded for his services and invested heavily in the development of his home. Among his continental acquisitions may have been two large Arras tapestries, described later at Raglan as 'full of lively figures and ancient British stories.' The subject matter suggests that they would have been specially designed, and were an early manifestation of the search for an insular foundation myth that equated with the stories of ancient Rome.[27] Herbert certainly commissioned an illuminated copy of John Lydgate's Troy Book, an English reworking of a medieval version of a Classical tale. In the manuscript Herbert was portrayed with his wife, Ann Devereux, presenting it to the king – though whether this was Edward IV or his predecessor, Henry VI, is a matter of debate.[28] For himself, Herbert commissioned a lavishly illustrated combined Book of Hours and Psalter. The Pembroke Hours is the only such book known to have been produced in the fifteenth century in Flanders.[29] A team of at least six illuminators appear to have worked on the magnificent manuscript, which included 10 full page illustrations and 174 smaller ones within the text. Sadly, the manuscript was incomplete at the time of Herbert's death. When the tide of war turned briefly in favour of the Lancastrians in 1469, he was captured at the Battle of Banbury, following which he was summarily executed.[30]

27 The precise date of the tapestries is uncertain. They are noted in John Rowland Phillips, *Memoirs of the Civil War in Wales and the Marches* (London, 1844–7), II, p. 27. Other references to tapestries in gentry houses of the period are given in Suggett, 'Creating the Architecture of Happiness', pp. 415–6.

28 See Dylan Foster Evans, 'William Herbert of Raglan (d.1469): Family History and Personal Identity' in *Gwalch Cywyddau Gwŷr*, pp. 98–100.

29 Philadelphia Museum of Art.

30 In its unfinished condition, the manuscript was probably claimed for the family from the Flemish workshop by William's daughter, Maud. See Lord, *Medieval Vision*, pp. 262–3. Maud married Henry Percy, into whose family the manuscript then passed, between 1473 and 1476. It is unclear whether or not the Pembroke Hours had reached Raglan prior to her marriage.

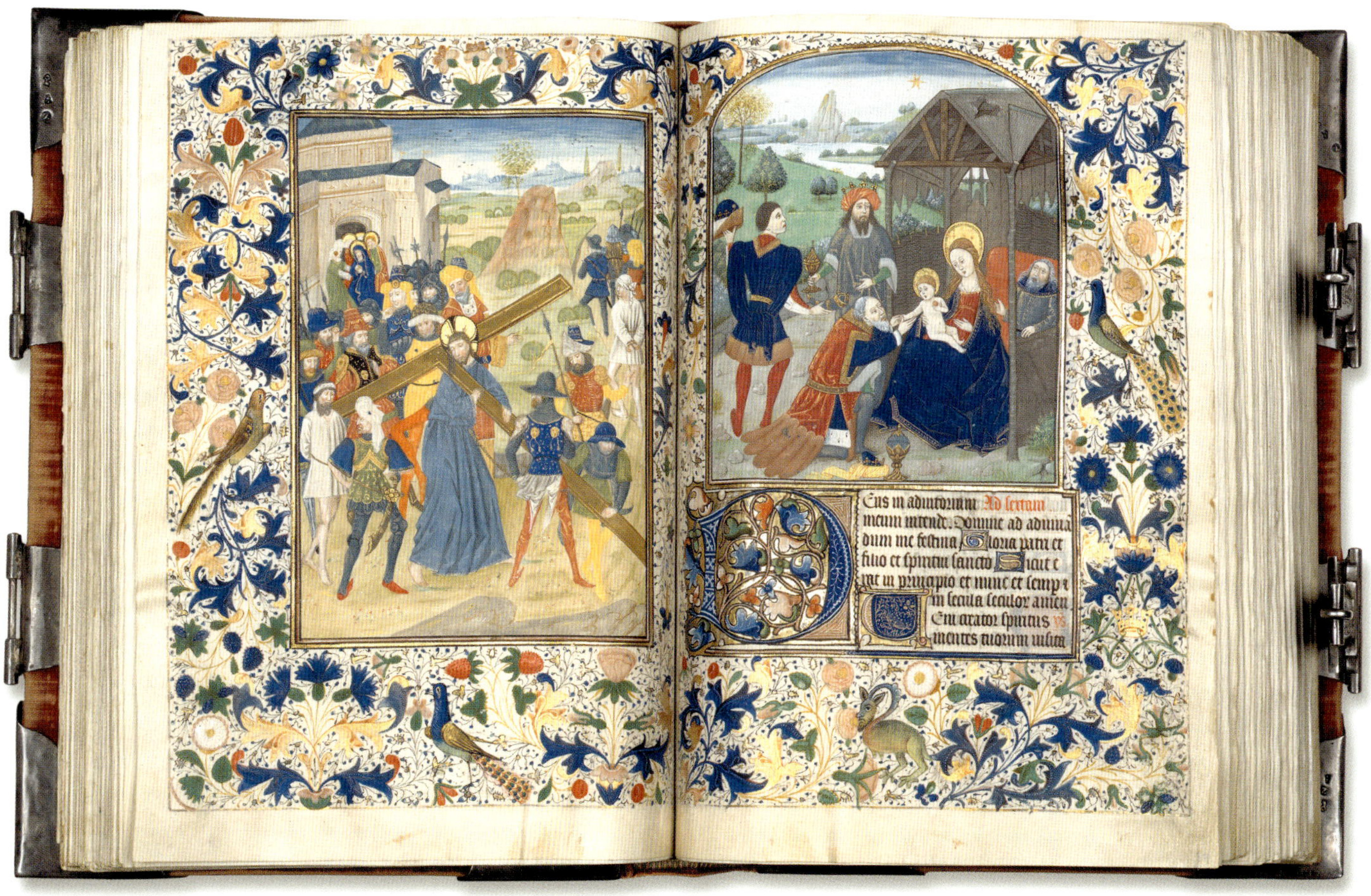

27. The Master of Anthony of Burgundy, and others, *Jesus Carrying the Cross and the Nativity*, illuminations from the *Pembroke Hours*, before 1469, 290x210

right
28. *Sir William Herbert and his wife Ann Devereux before King Edward IV*, illumination from the *Troy Book*, c.1462, 39.5x27.9

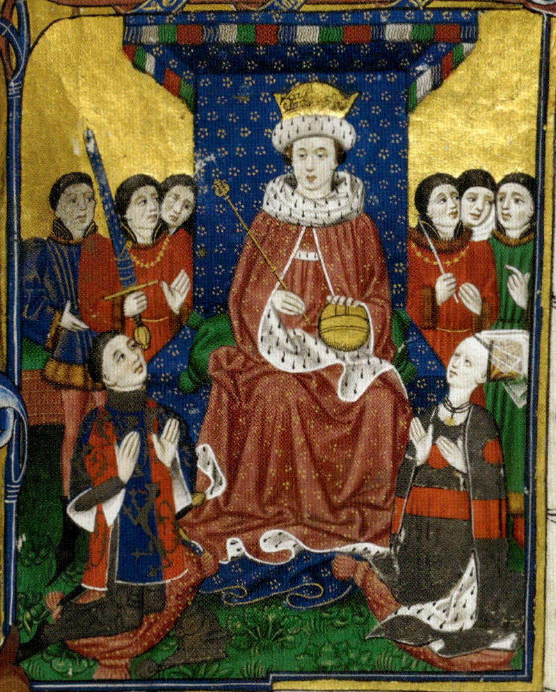

O myghty Mars · that with
thy sterne lyght ·
In armes hast · the powere
and the myght ·
And namyde art · frome
Est tyle the Occydent ·
The myghty lorde · the
god Armypotent ·
That with the shynynge · of thy stremes rede ·
By influence · dost the brydele lede ·
Of chyvalry · as sovereyne and patrone ·
Ful hote and dry · of complexione ·
Irouse and wode · and malyncolyk ·
And of nature · brent and Coleryk ·
Of coloure shewynge · lyke the fyrye glede ·
Whose fers lokys · bene as ful of drede ·
As the levene · that alyghtith lowe ·
Downe by the skye · frome Iubiters bowe ·
Thy sterne bene · so passynge dispitone ·
To loke [illegible] fresyoun ·
And causes [illegible] with thy fyre bemes ·
Of corn and [illegible] in many sundry reames ·
Whos [illegible] in [illegible] ·
But [illegible] thy powere [illegible] ·
And [illegible] of [illegible] of strif ·
[illegible] of [illegible] ·
With [illegible] at myschef take ·
[illegible] only for here sake ·

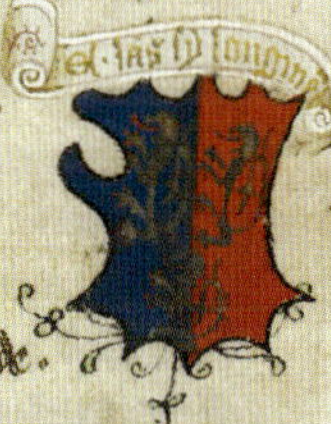

And for the love · of thy Bellona ·
That with the dwellyth · byyonde Cyrea ·
In lybie londe · upon the sondes rede ·
So be myne help · in this grete nede ·
To do socoure · my style to direct ·
And of my penne · the traces to correct ·
Which bareyne is · of Aureate licoure ·
But in thi grace I fynde some socoure ·
For to converte it · with thyne Influence ·
That stumbleth ay · for fawte of eloquence ·
For to reherce · or writene ony worde ·
Now help O Mars · that art of knyghthode lorde ·
And hast of manhode · the magnyficence ·
And Othea · the goddes of prudence ·
This werke tenplente · that ye not refuse ·
But maketh Clio · for to be my muse ·
With here sustres · that on parnasa dwells ·
In Cirea · by Elycon the wells ·
Rennynge full clere · with stremes Cristallyne ·
And callyd is · the welle Cabalyne ·
That sprange by touche · of the Pegase ·
And help also · O thowe Caliope ·
That wer modere · unto Orpheus ·
Whos dytees wern · so melodeus ·
That the werbylles · of his resownynge harp ·
Apeced dyd · the bitter wordys sharp ·
Both of Parchas · and ffuryes infernalle ·
And Cerberus · so cruel founde at alle ·
He Cesed also · of bestes fowlles and trees ·
Now of thy grace · be helpynge unto me ·
And of thy golde dewyth · let the streme enter ·
My dulled brest · that with thyne hony swete ·
Sugerest tonges · of Rethoryciens ·
And maystresse art · to musyciens ·
Now be myne help · enluminyne of this wer ·
Which am byset · with cloudys dymme and derk ·
Of ignorance · in makynge to procede ·
To be lusty to hem that it shall rede ·
Also in hert · I am so full of drede ·
When prudent lesters herto shall take hede ·
That in makynge · more stel ben than I ·
To whome I pray · full lowlyly ·
Of here goodenesse · to have compassyon ·
Where as I erre · in my translacyon ·
For god I take highly to wetnysse ·
That I this worke · of hertly lowe humblesse ·
Toke upon me · of full entencyon ·
Devoyde of pryde · and presumpcyon ·
For to obeye · withoute variaunce ·

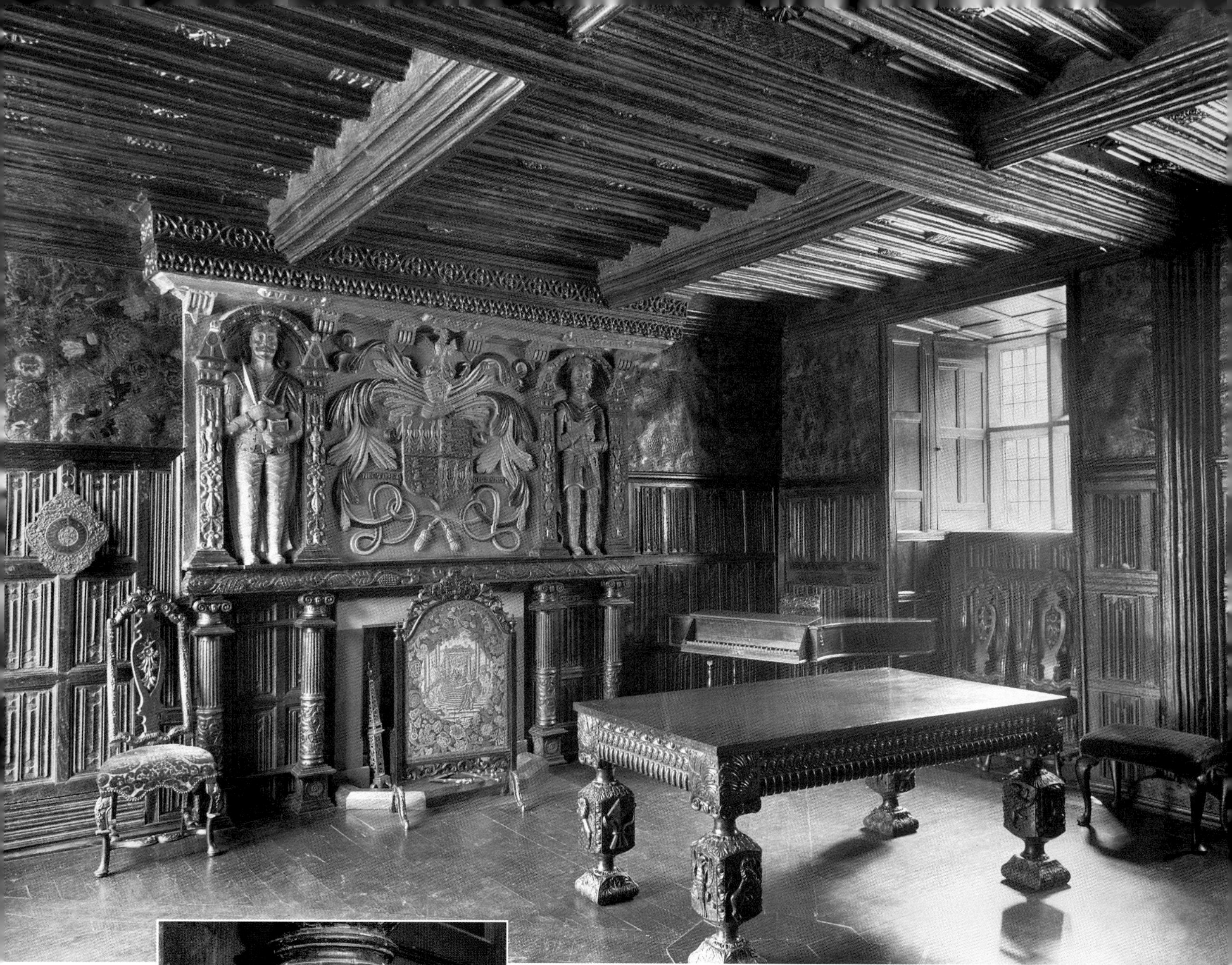

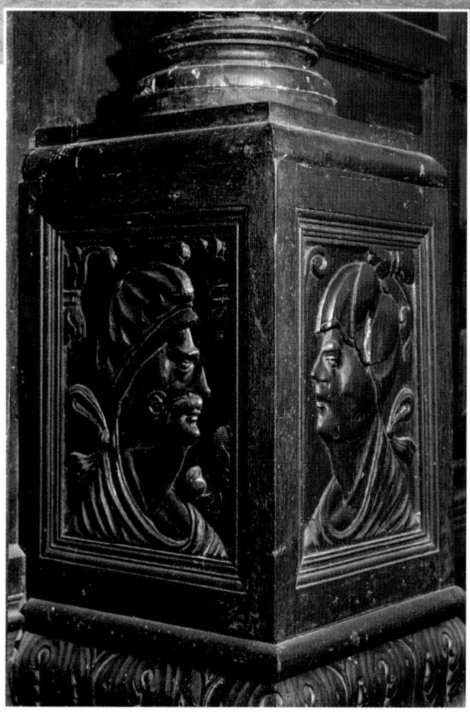

The fashion for things continental resulted both in the import of particular artefacts, and in the adoption of styles and motifs in locally made furniture and fittings.[31] Prominent among imported motifs were profile heads, designed in imitation of classical medallions, which demonstrate that humanist enquiry extended beyond written texts to include the visual culture of the ancient world. In the early sixteenth century, such heads animated the surfaces of woodwork in the town houses of the Welsh gentry in Cardiff and in the country seats of the north alike.[32] They transcended the religious upheaval of the period that otherwise radically curtailed the range of the visual culture. Although Henry

VIII's Church of England initially represented a political rather than a religious reformation, within its shelter the influence of Puritan churchmen, for whom the elaborate ceremony and rich visual images of the old Roman Church were anathema, rapidly increased. During the brief reign of Edward VI, the destruction of religious images, appropriated by his father from the monasteries for the fiscal benefit of the crown, extended to the parish churches for reasons of Protestant dogma. The attempt to turn back the clock made by the Roman Catholic Mary, when she ascended the throne on the death of Edward in 1553, was short

opposite
29. *Chimneypiece* formerly at Gwydir, Llanrwst, 1597, oak

opposite, bottom
30. *Romaine Heads*, Gwydir, Llanrwst, ht. 40, oak

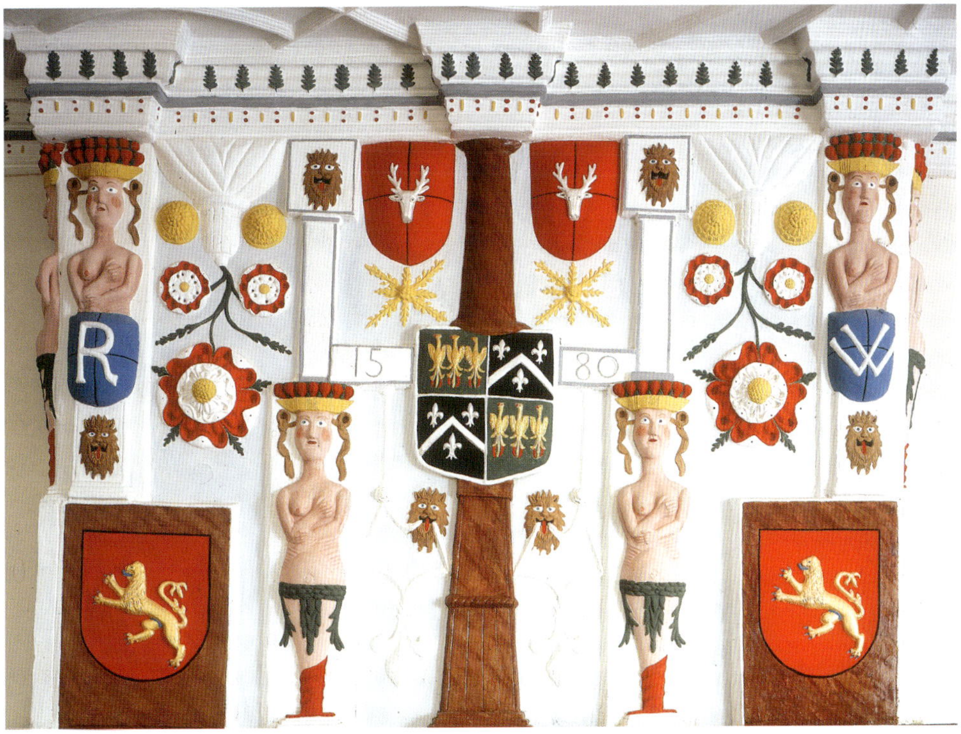

31. *Overmantel*, Plas Mawr, Conwy, 1580, painted plaster, 180x257

lived.[33] Biblical imagery all but disappeared, to be replaced by the visual vocabulary of the classical world. In 1597, Sir John Wynn of Gwydir, a man deeply engaged with antiquarian studies after the humanist fashion, commissioned a chimneypiece for a new library above his gatehouse. Flanking his arms stood full-length figures of Julius and Augustus Caesar.

The dramatic impact of the colour that originally enlivened Sir John Wynn's carved chimneypiece can be estimated by comparison with the restored plaster work that adorns the fireplaces and ceilings of Plas Mawr at Conwy, the slightly earlier town house built for his uncle, Robert Wynn. Like so many of his predecessors and his sixteenth-century contemporaries, Robert Wynn had travelled extensively on the continent. He had been in the service of the English courtier, Sir Philip Hoby, whom he accompanied to Spain and

31 Elaborate chandeliers in the neighbouring parish churches of Llanarmon-yn-Iâl and Llandegla in Denbighshire exemplify the range of the imports. They were made in Flanders in the late fifteenth or early sixteenth century. See Lord, *Medieval Vision*, pp. 228–9.

32 For the Cardiff carvings, now at the Church of St John, Cardiff, see Lord, *Medieval Vision*, p. 271.

33 Images of Jesus and the Virgin Mary that had been torn down were briefly reinstated. For instance, at the Church of St Laurence in Ludlow, on the Welsh border, painted cloths were commissioned to cover the gap left by the rood screen that had been removed. See Thomas Wright (ed.), *Churchwarden's accounts for the town of Ludlow, Shropshire, from 1540 to the end of the reign of Queen Elizabeth* (London, 1869).

Portugal on diplomatic missions. Hoby was a notable patron of the arts, and of painters in particular. The planning of Wynn's new house, begun in 1576, reflected his experience of the continent in fashion-conscious company, though it was combined with many local traditions of construction. It represents now a rare survivor, but its avant-garde continental style was not unique in Wales in the period. By the time Wynn began work, to the east in Denbighshire and Flintshire, Richard Clough had already constructed Plas Clough, with its Dutch stepped gables, and Bachegraig, which was an even more radical conception.

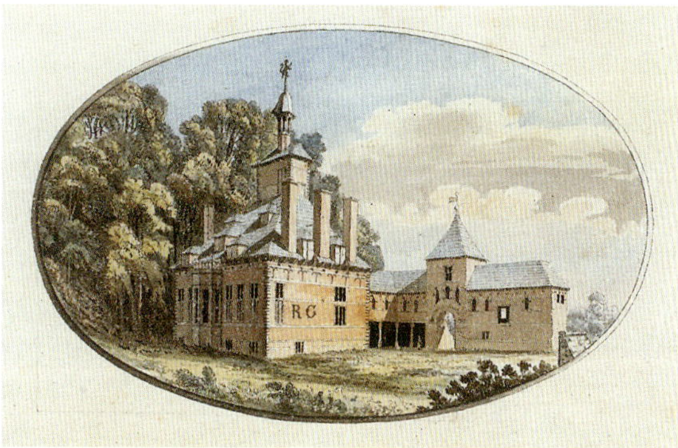

32. Moses Griffith, *Bachegraig*, c.1781, watercolour on paper, 7.7x12.5

Though Clough enjoyed less elevated origins, like Robert Wynn he made money in trade and progressed socially by association with an English courtier. Clough spent most of his working life at Antwerp, the centre of the European financial world, where he was employed by Sir Thomas Gresham, who was among the richest Englishman of his period. Clough's Bachegraig was built in the continental manner with bricks imported from the Low Countries. It was remarkable enough still to impress the antiquarian Thomas Pennant, when he visited in the late 1770s:

> It consists of a mansion, and three sides, inclosing a square court. The first consists of a vast hall, and parlour: the rest of it rises into six wonderful stories, including the cupola and forms from the second floor the figure of a pyramid ... In the windows of the parlour are several pieces of painted glass, of the arms of the knight of the *holy sepulchre*; as his own with a heart at the bottom.[34]

As Pennant noted, Clough's knighthood had not been bestowed by an English monarch. It was a title assumed as a result of a pilgrimage to Jerusalem made in his youth, a journey indicating Roman Catholic leanings which, wisely, he did not choose to express on his visits to London. Nevertheless, the appalled tone of his account of Protestant iconoclasm that he witnessed in Antwerp in 1566 indicates his sympathies, and underlines the fragility of social stability not only in the Low Countries but at home in this period. Clough observed that after the disturbances in Antwerp, the Church of Our Lady 'lookyd lyke a hell: where were above 1000 tourches brynnyng, and syche a noise! as yf heven and erth had gone togeder, with fallyng of Images and betyng down of costyly works; in syche sort, that the spoil was so grett that a man could not well pass through the church.'[35] Prudently retreating to Wales, in the following year Clough married Katheryn of Berain in Denbighshire and began to build Bachegraig. Following the taste expressed in that house, they marked their return to Antwerp in 1568 with a commission for a portrait of Katheryn.[36] Clough's choice of painter presented a further hint of his religious tendencies – he was probably Adriaen van Cronenburgh, a Roman Catholic himself, much favoured by clients from Catholic families.

34 Thomas Pennant, *Tours in Wales* (3 vols., Caernarfon, 1883), II, p. 135.

35 John William Burgon, *Life and Times of Sir Thomas Gresham, Knt.*, (London, 1839), vol II, p. 139.

36 Gresham patronised the Flemish portrait painter Antonis Mor.

37 Holbein's first visit to London was for two years. He then worked in Basel, returning to London in 1532, and by 1536 was on the king's payroll.

During the time that Robert Wynn remained in the service of his master, Philip Hoby, the diplomat was despatched by Henry VIII to Brussels and then to France with Hans Holbein, the German-born painter. His responsibility was to draw or paint the portraits of likely marriage candidates for the king's inspection. Holbein had arrived in London, via Antwerp, in 1526, and influenced both the style of portraits and the intellectual context in which they were produced, especially after he became an official painter at the king's court in the mid-1530s.[37] As the manuscripts of Sir John Dwnn and William Herbert, and the painted glass depictions of patrons at Llangadwaladr demonstrate, wealthy individuals had begun to have their appearance recorded by painters considerably earlier. However, in the fifteenth century, the context was always devotional, as at Llandaf Cathedral, where a portrait of Bishop John Marshall was commissioned in 1485 to adorn his throne. The bishop chose to be identified in particular with the Virgin, who was portrayed at her assumption into heaven. After the 1530s, Protestant suspicion of religious subjects resulted in their disappearance from the repertoire of acceptable images. The visual vacuum was filled by the portrait pure and simple, divested of pious justification by Christian iconography. Painted on canvas or panel and framed to hang on a wall, portraits would be the foundation on which gentry patronage of painting in Wales was built for the subsequent three hundred years.

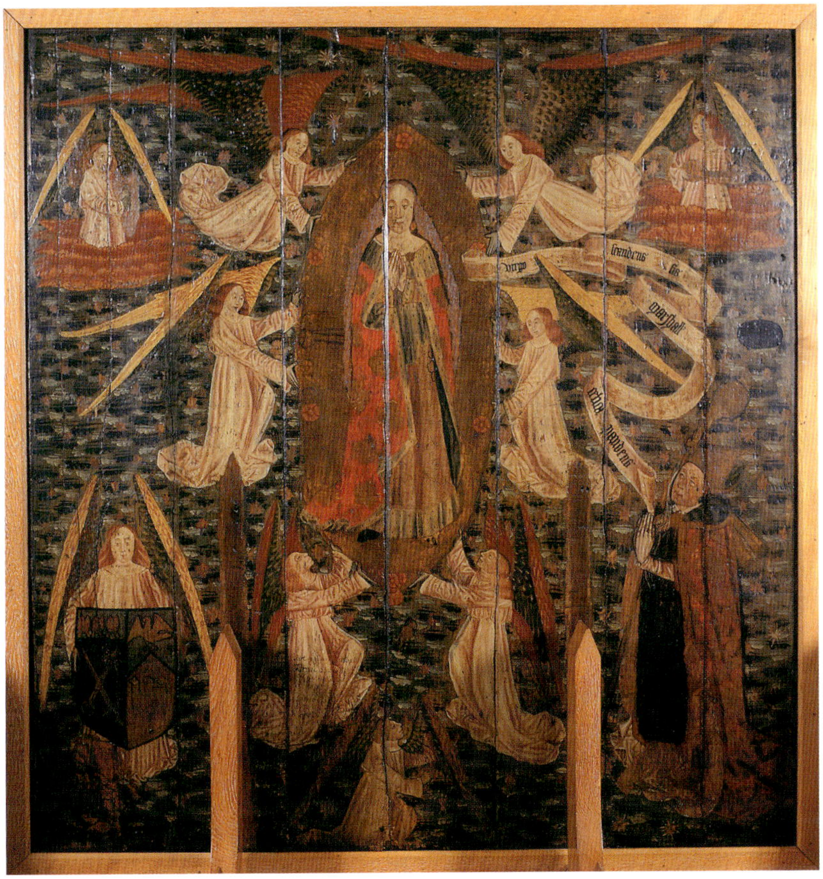

33. *The Assumption of the Virgin*, from the throne of Bishop John Marshall, Llandaf Cathedral, panel painting, late 15th century, 150x144

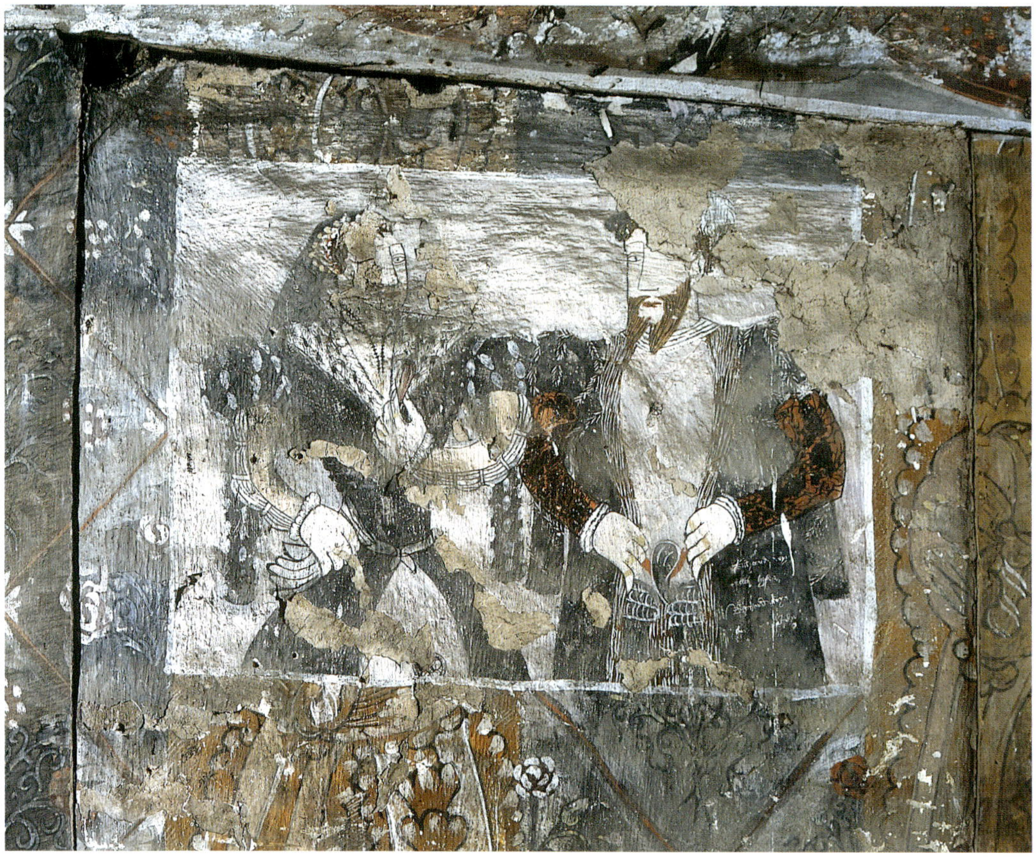

34. Unknown painter, *Elis ap Richard and Jane Hanmer*, Althrey Hall, c.1545–58, wall painting

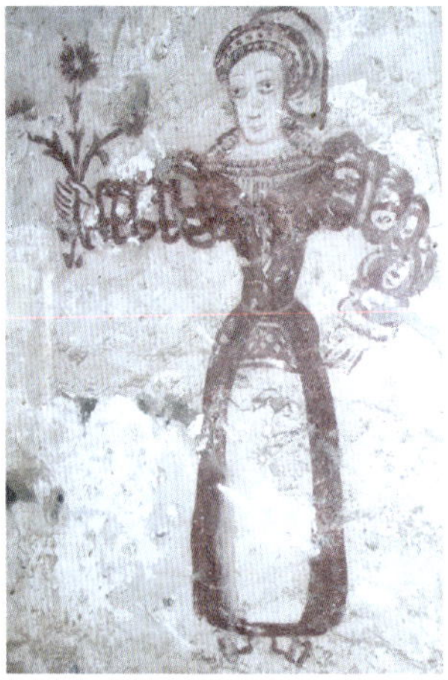

35. Unknown painter, *Jane Andrew*, Coal Farm, Barry, late 16th century, wall painting

At Althrey Hall in Flintshire, a remarkable double portrait survives that can be seen as representing the transition from one form of picture to another. Following the medieval tradition, the double portrait was painted in about 1550 directly on a plastered wall, at the head of what was probably a private chamber. It formed a part of a larger decoration designed to simulate the tapestry hangings of the very wealthy.[38] However, it was separated from the overall scheme by a painted frame, as if in imitation of the new discrete portrait painted on panel or canvas. Furthermore, it was an entirely secular image – quite different in conception to the earlier family portrait of Sir John and Elizabeth Dwnn. It represented Elis ap Richard and Jane Hanmer, one of whose male ancestors had appeared, painted in the older tradition in windows installed in 1500 by Margaret Hanmer at the Church of St Chad, Holt. As a continuing alternative to the new framed pictures, wall painted portraits would penetrate some way down the social scale. At Coal Farm, a yeoman house at Barry in Glamorgan, a simple mural painting probably represented Jane Andrew.[39] She appears to hold in her hand a posy of gillyflowers, a symbol particularly associated with representations of Queen Elizabeth, both in visual art and poetry.

36. Unknown painter, *Sir John Wynn of Gwydir*, 1619, oil, 91.4x72.3

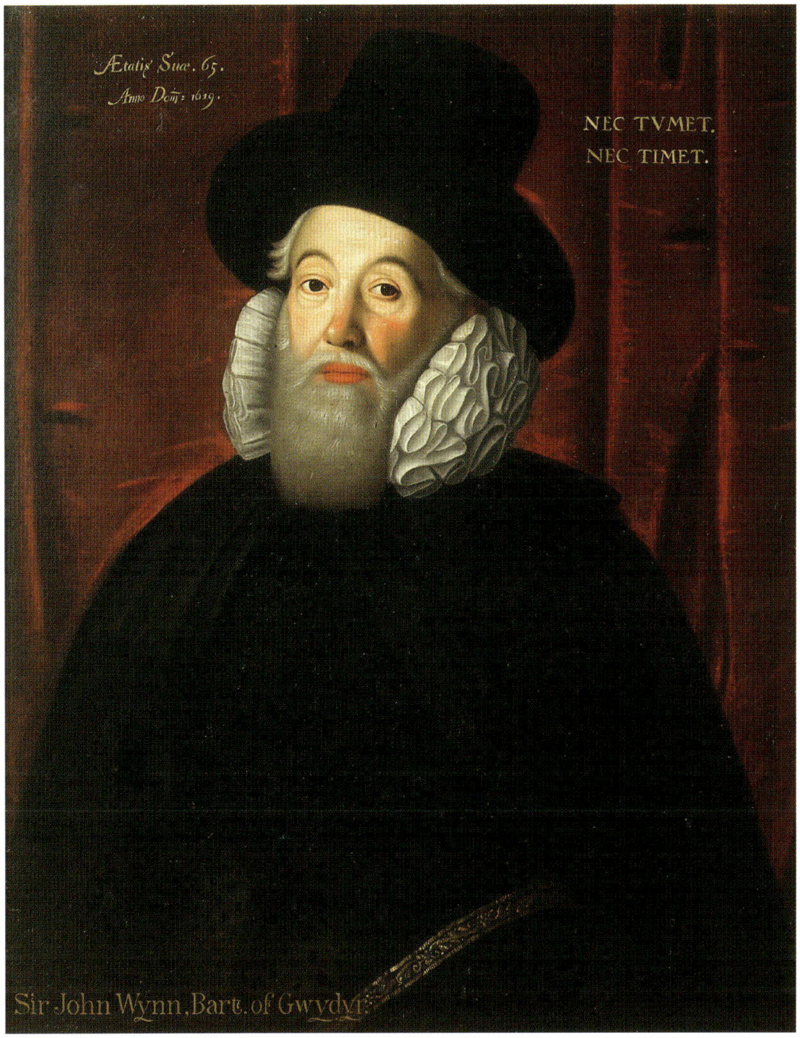

The emergence of the portable painted portrait was stimulated both by philosophical development and change in the domestic arrangements of wealthy families. More sophisticated houses, exemplified by Gwydir, built by the Wynn family in about 1500, contained new kinds of room and a degree of comfort that encouraged not only the embellishment of fixtures, such as fireplaces, but also the elaboration of portable furniture and the hanging of framed pictures. Nevertheless, it is the correspondence between the increasing popularity of the portrait and deep changes in the world of ideas, including religious ideas, that is most striking. The influence of humanist thought, particularly in the context of the Reformation, brought about a change in the self-perception of the upper classes, and in the very definition of a gentleman. A move away from the emphasis on military prowess and towards learning, opened up for individuals such as Sir John Wynn the world of classical Greece and Rome. From reading the classical writers, among the virtues that became apparent to the likes of Sir John was the ability to appreciate sculpture and painting. Furthermore, the uncertainty of the times for the upper gentry, both in terms of changes in family fortune flowing from dynastic upheaval and, especially in the mid-sixteenth century, the removal of medieval certainties concerning the most profound issues of death and salvation, certainly contributed to the need for personal reassurance in the form of symbols of permanence and transcendence. For nouveaux riches families, whose fortunes were made as a consequence of the acquisition of the monastic lands disposed of by Henry VIII, affirmations of legitimacy in the form of portraiture and heraldry were especially important.

38 The practice of painting in imitation of tapestry was probably widespread. A further example survives at Ciliau in Radnorshire. Suggett, 'Creating the Architecture of Happiness', pp. 416–7.

39 See Kathryn Davies, *Artisan Art. Vernacular wall paintings in the Welsh Marches 1550-1650* (Almeley, 2008), p. 199.

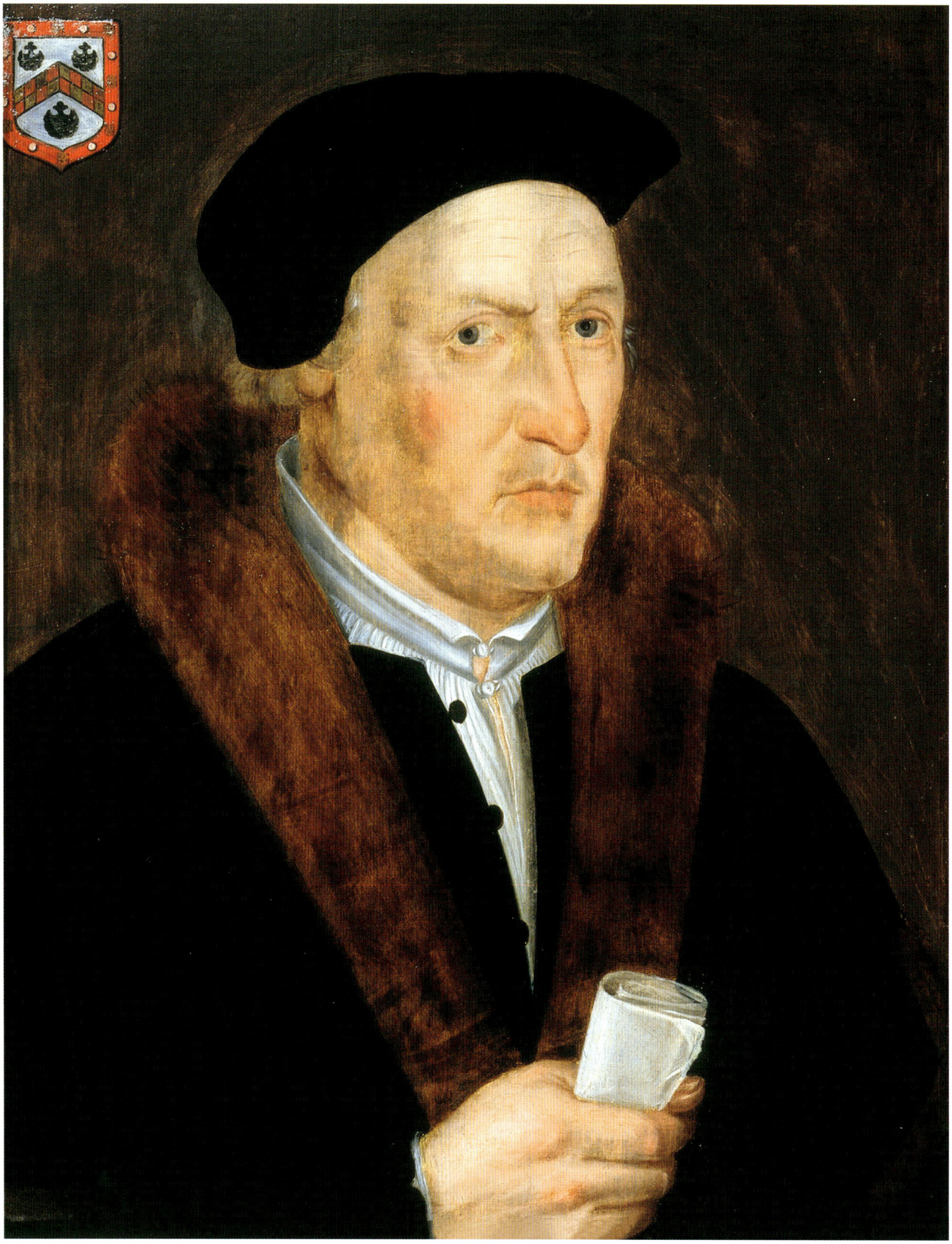

Also consequent on the deep structural changes wrought in society during the Tudor period was the emergence of civic authorities of various kinds. The celebration of offices held as a result of the incorporation of new boroughs, for instance, further widened the market for portraits. As if to signify these deep social changes, the earliest surviving example of a modern framed portrait, commissioned by a Welsh patron, represents not a gentleman but a wealthy member of the urban middle class. In 1517 Thomas Exmewe of Ruthin became Lord Mayor of London, though the Holbein-like style of his portrait suggests that it was painted some ten years later.[40] Where it was made is unclear, but eventually it hung at Exmewe House, the patron's home in Ruthin, and it remained there when the house became the property of the Goodman family. It seems certain that the example it set lay behind the portrait commissions given subsequently by three generations of the prosperous Goodmans themselves. That the portraits were highly valued tokens of their family identity was confirmed by Gawen Goodman in his will, which specified not only who should inherit the Exmewe portrait (along with his own and that of his father), but that the pictures should remain *in situ* in Exmewe House:

opposite
37. Unknown painter, *Sir Thomas Exmewe*, c.1526–9, oil, 54x43.2

38. Unknown painter, *Gawen Goodman*, 1582, oil, 49.5x43.2

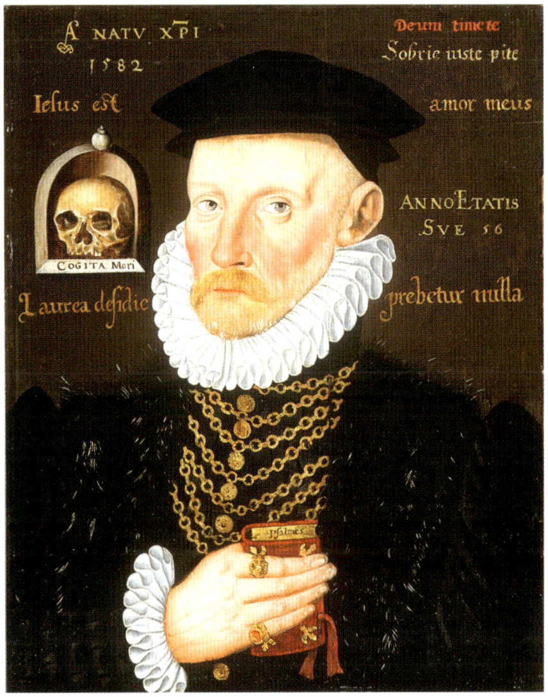

> I give and bequeath to my Sonne Edward Goodman all those three Pictures viz the Picture of Sir Thomas Exmewe the Picture of my father Edward Goodman and my owne Picture being now in the Parlour of the hose wherein I now dwell. And my will is that the said pictures should remaine in the said parlour ...[41]

Gawen Goodman's own portrait was the most complex of the group. Notwithstanding a contemporary poem that suggests he fell somewhat short of being a paragon of Christian virtue, Gawen surrounded himself with pious Latin inscriptions, and held in his hand a book of psalms.[42] With an eye on the uncertainties of the future, the portrait's most prominent feature was a *momento mori* in the form of a skull, the symbol most frequently employed to suggest the awareness of the sitter of the transitory nature of human life.[43]

Nowhere was the correspondence between the Protestant prohibition on religious images and the rise of the personal portrait more evident than in the brazen iconisation of Queen Elizabeth I during the 45 years of her reign. It was court poets and painters who played the central role in the creation of the image of the queen as a surrogate Virgin Mary, undefiled mother of the nation, but in an age in which the Welsh gentry were prominent figures in London as well as at home, some of their work had a direct bearing on the development

40 One of Exmewe's close friends, Thomas Kytsonne, was painted by Holbein.

41 The will of Gawen Goodman, The National Archives. The house is Exmewe House, not Nantclwyd House. Gawen's second son, Godfrey Goodman, also commissioned a portrait.

42 For the poem, see Peter Lord, *The Visual Culture of Wales: Imaging the Nation* (Cardiff, 2000), p. 27, note 4.

43 The rejection by Protestants of the doctrine of purgatory contributed to this state of uncertainty.

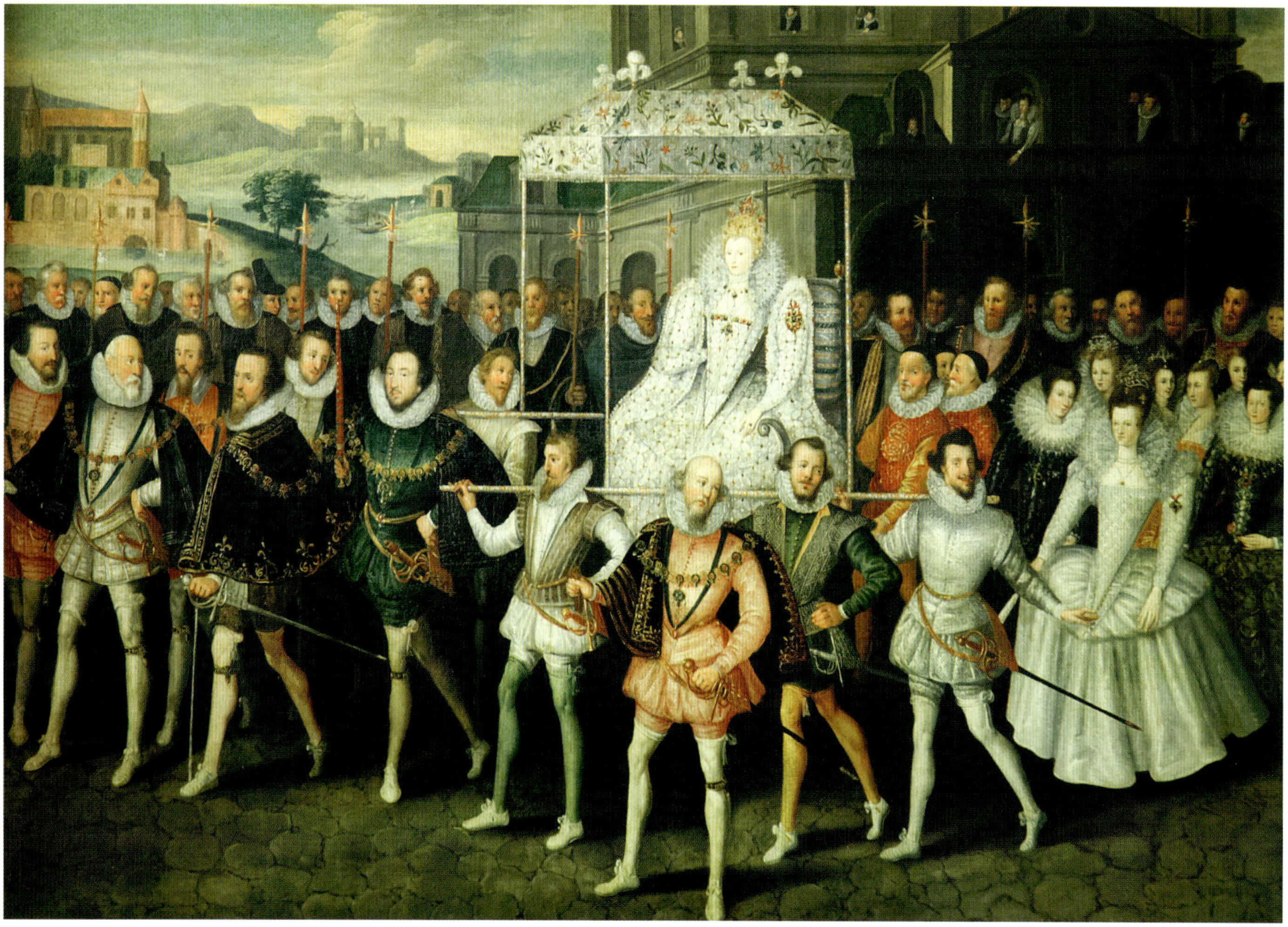

39. Robert Peake, *Queen Elizabeth going in Procession*, c.1600, oil, 132x190.5

of Welsh patronage at this socially elevated level. After the queen, the most prominent individual represented in a remarkable group portrait, made near the end of the queen's reign and known as *Queen Elizabeth going in Procession*, was Edward Somerset, 4th Earl of Worcester. Somerset posed in the foreground, directly below the queen herself, conveyed on a carriage below a canopy carried by other leading courtiers. As the queen's last Master of the Horse, the earl was closely involved in the creation of such ceremonials. The picture was probably painted by Robert Peake, and Somerset may well have been the patron. It has been argued that the two fantasy castles seen in the background of the picture symbolise Chepstow, which he owned, and his primary home at Raglan, where he had grown up during the lavish development undertaken by his father.[44]

Not long after Edward Somerset was painted at the heart of the procession picture, the earl's distant cousin, Edward Herbert, 1st Baron Herbert of Chirbury, also availed himself of the services of Robert Peake. He recorded his sitting with the painter in London and the

44 The picture is analysed in Roy Strong, *The Cult of Elizabeth* (London, 1977), pp. 17–55.

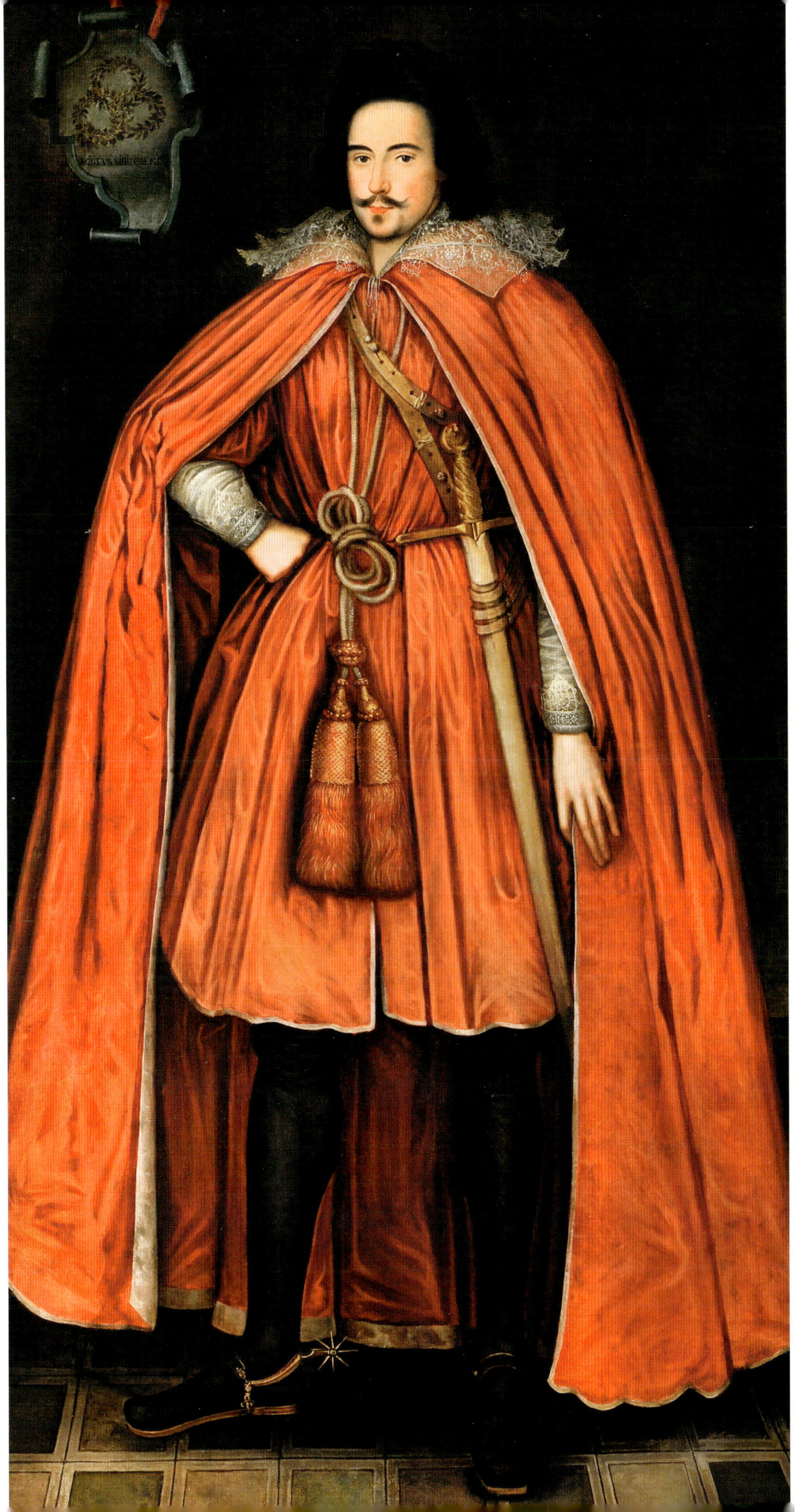

40. Robert Peake, *Edward Herbert, First Baron Herbert of Chirbury*, 1604, oil, 218.4x114.3

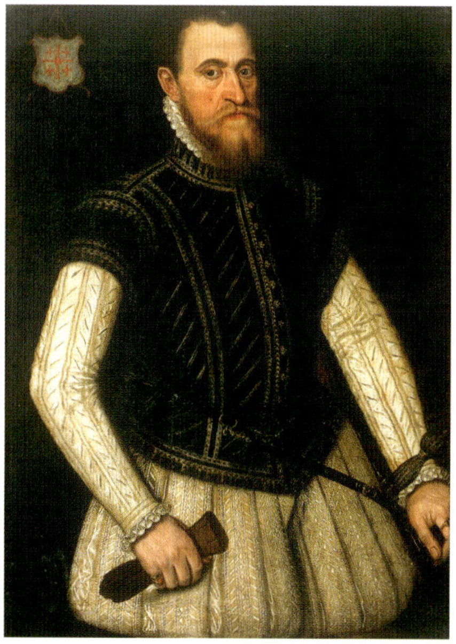

41. Unknown painter,
Richard Clough, *c.*1550,
oil, 93.9x68.5

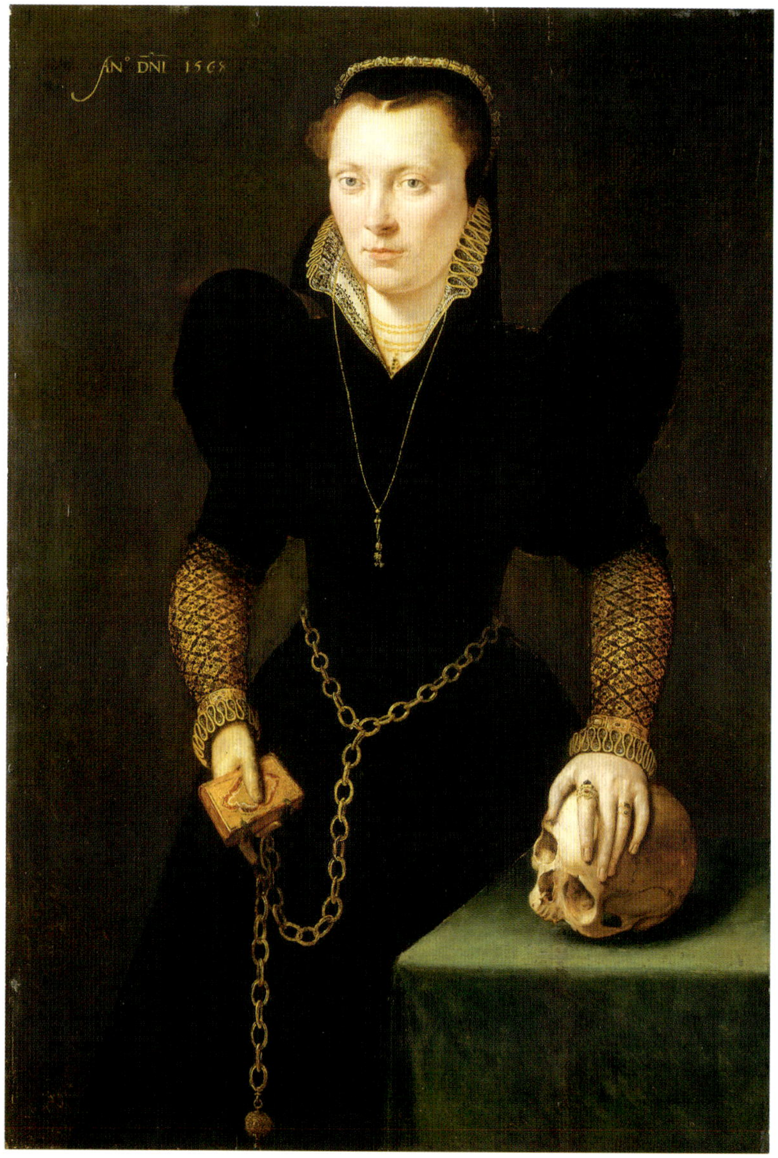

42. Adriaen van Cronenburgh,
Katheryn of Berain, 1568,
oil, 97.2x68.6

fashionable atmosphere of medieval fantasy that surrounded it. Clearly, the need to obscure vanity behind a veil of piety in portraiture had entirely disappeared by the early 1600s:

> The second day to wear Robes of crimson Taffita (in which I am painted in my Study) and so to ride from St James's to Whitehall with our Esquires before us, and the third day to wear a Gown of Purple Satin, upon the left sleeve whereof is fastned certain Strings weaved of white Silk and Gold tied in a knot, and tassells to it of the same, which all the Knights are obliged to wear untill they have done something famous in Arms, or 'till some Lady of Honour takes it off, and fasten it on her Sleeve, saying I will answer he shall prove a good Knight.[45]

45 Edward Herbert, *The Life of Edward Lord Herbert of Chirbury* (London, 1770), pp. 54–5. Edward Herbert seems to have had an exceptional fondness for his own image. He would go on to commission several other painted portraits, and a bust from the French sculptor Hubert le Sueur.

46 Llwyd thought Clough 'a verie honest man.' See F.J. North, *Humphrey Lhuyd's Maps of England and Wales* (Cardiff, 1937), p. 9.

In both his procession picture and his portrait of Edward Herbert, Robert Peake placed his sitters in a three-dimensional space – that is, by means of perspective he conveyed a sense of foreground and background. Throughout the first century of portrait painting, realism of this kind competed with a residual taste for a more symbolic approach, in which sitters were painted against a plain dark backdrop and sometimes, as in the case of Gawen Goodman's portrait, were surrounded by a personal narrative of texts and heraldry. In about 1550, Richard Clough sat for a portrait of this kind, which was probably painted in Wales or in England. Nearly twenty years later, the difference in the approach of the artist from the Low Countries who painted Clough's wife, Katheryn of Berain, was immediately apparent. Katheryn was set in a realistic space, defined by a projecting table that displayed a *momento mori* in the form of a skull on which she laid her hand, while in her other hand she held a devotional book.

Among Richard Clough's Denbighshire friends was the scholar Humphrey Llwyd. Clough put Llwyd in touch with the Antwerp map maker, Abraham Ortelius, and the result of their 'love and acquaintance' was the first map of Wales as a distinct entity, published in 1573.[46] Like the portraits of Clough and Katheryn, Humphrey Llwyd's painted portrait and the carved memorial made after his death, though separated only by some seven years, illustrated the contrast between visual conventions in the period. The portrait of 1561 was a severely heraldic affair, whereas the memorial was distinctly modern in conception. Certainly, Llwyd knelt in medieval fashion at a prayer desk, but he did so within a fully three-dimensional space created by pillars and arches cut in perspective. This central image was framed within a setting of Corinthian columns linked by a frieze. Christian angels competed for attention with pagan masks.

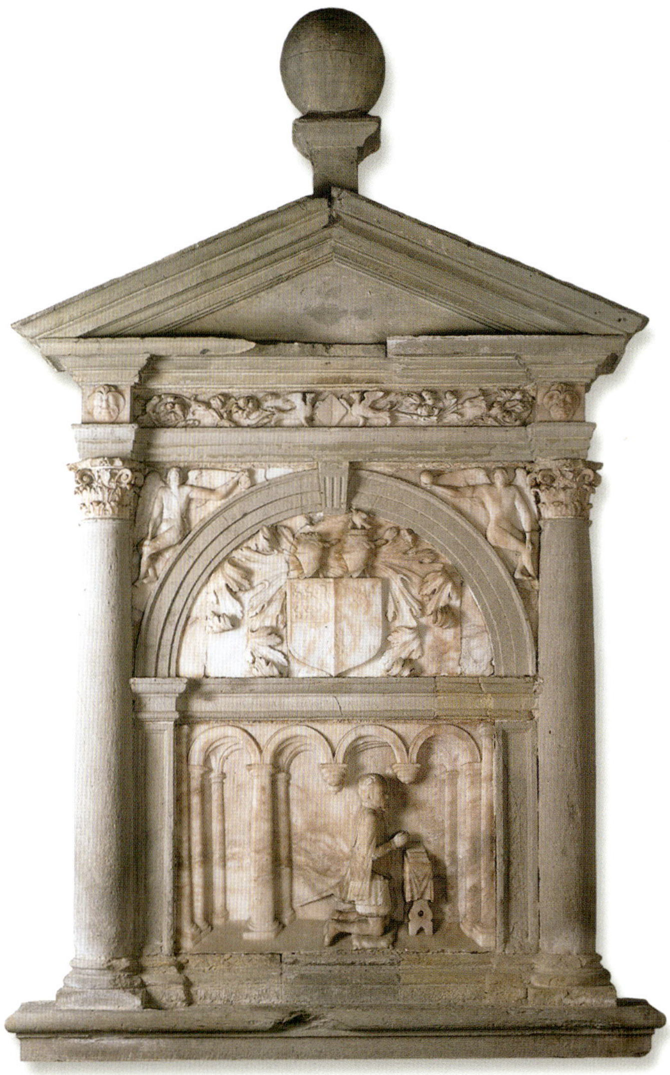

43. *Memorial to Humphrey Llwyd*, Church of St Marcella, Llanfarchell, 1568, stone

At about the same time, William Herbert, 1st Earl of Pembroke, also chose the modern manner for a painted portrait. As in Llwyd's memorial, Pembroke was presented standing in a realistic pillared interior, a classical reference to his cultured outlook which was reinforced by his leaning on a fragment of ancient fluted column. Around his neck on a ribbon he wore the insignia of a Knight of the Garter – St George slaying the dragon. The image had been adopted by Henry VII and so, to this patriotic and Welsh-speaking Welshman, by no means did it represent the uncomplicated Englishness of which it would become the token in succeeding centuries.[47] Pembroke's portrait retained an element of the heraldic tradition in the dominant display of arms, but again, these were presented as if carved in three dimensions. Such old and new conventions co-existed for at least a generation, though no doubt portraits reflected not simply differences in the taste of patrons, but also the ability to locate or afford appropriate painters. In a portrait of one of Pembroke's grandsons, William Herbert, 1st Baron Powis, an unknown painter made a token gesture towards creating an illusion of three-dimensional space (in the form of a table), but

opposite
44. Attributed to Steven van Herwijck, *Sir William Herbert, First Earl of Pembroke*, c.1560, oil, 115x85.8

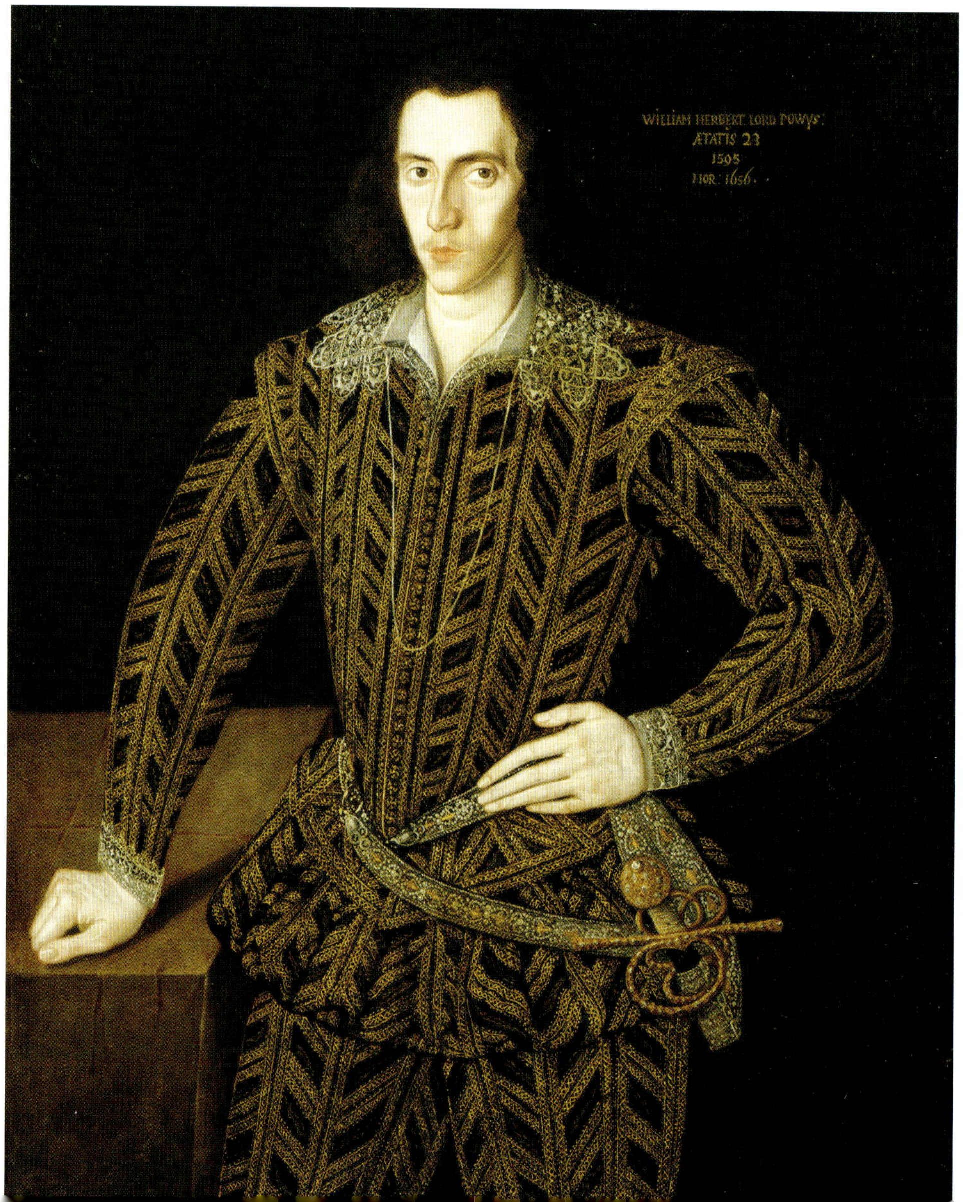

45. Unknown painter, *William Herbert, First Baron Powis*, 1595, oil, 106x84

47 See for instance the panel painting *The Family of Henry VII with St George and the Dragon*, illustrated in Lord, *Medieval Vision*, p. 278.

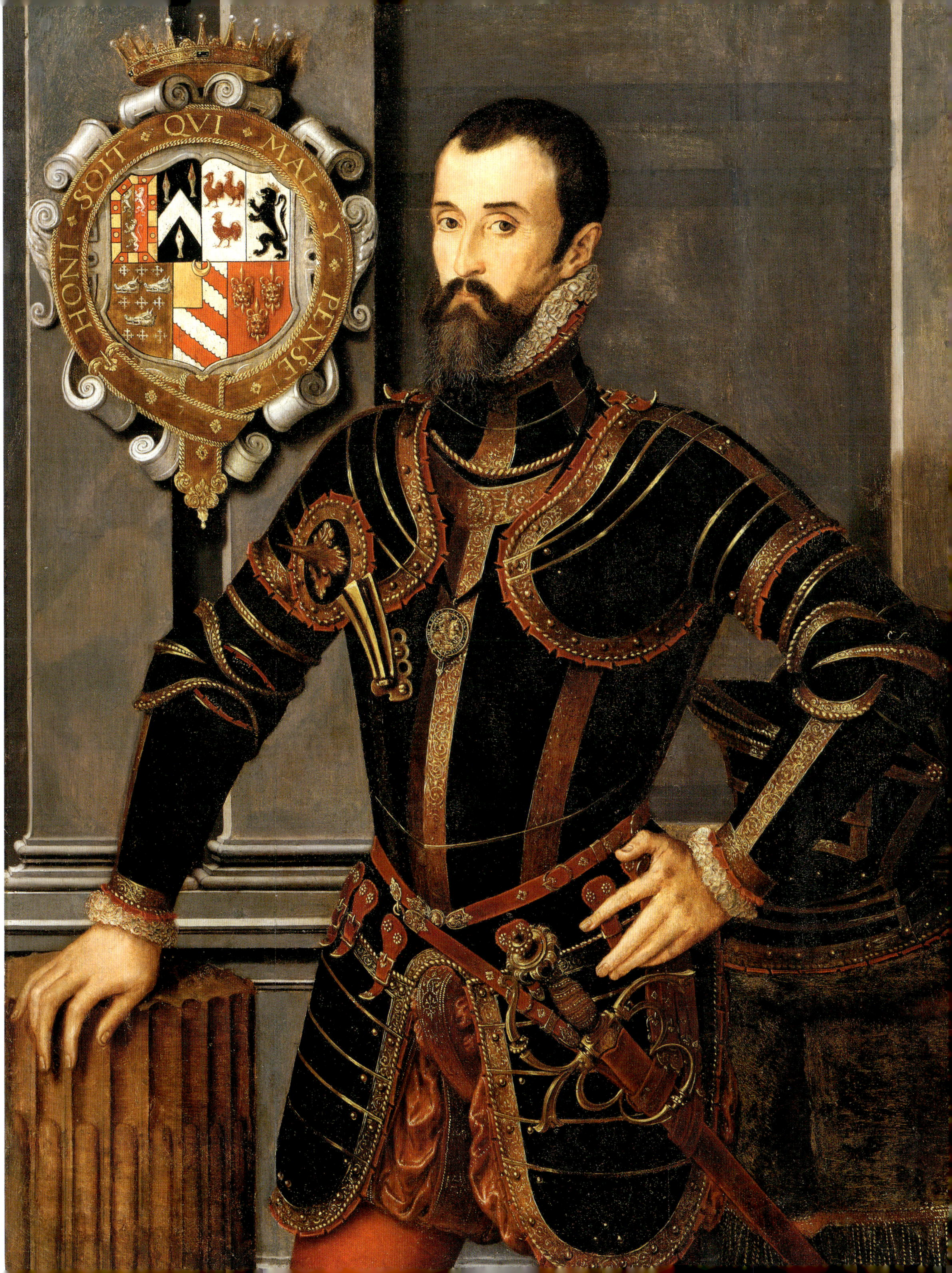
HONI SOIT QVI MAL Y PENSE

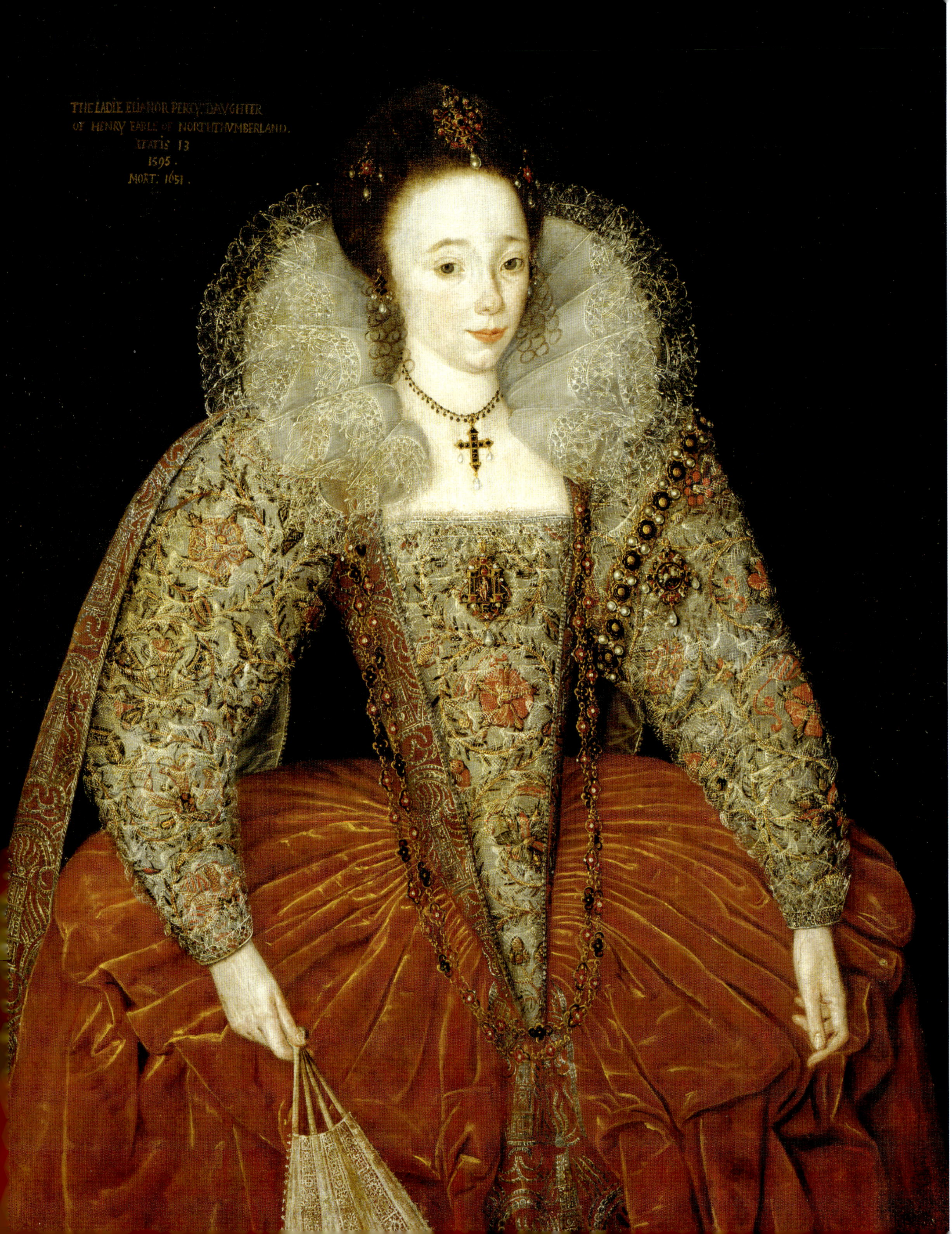
THE LADIE ELIANOR PERCY. DAUGHTER
OF HENRY EARLE OF NORTHTHUMBERLAND.
ÆTATIS 13
1595.
MORT: 1651.

left
46. Unknown painter, *Lady Eleanor Percy*, 1595, oil, 106x84

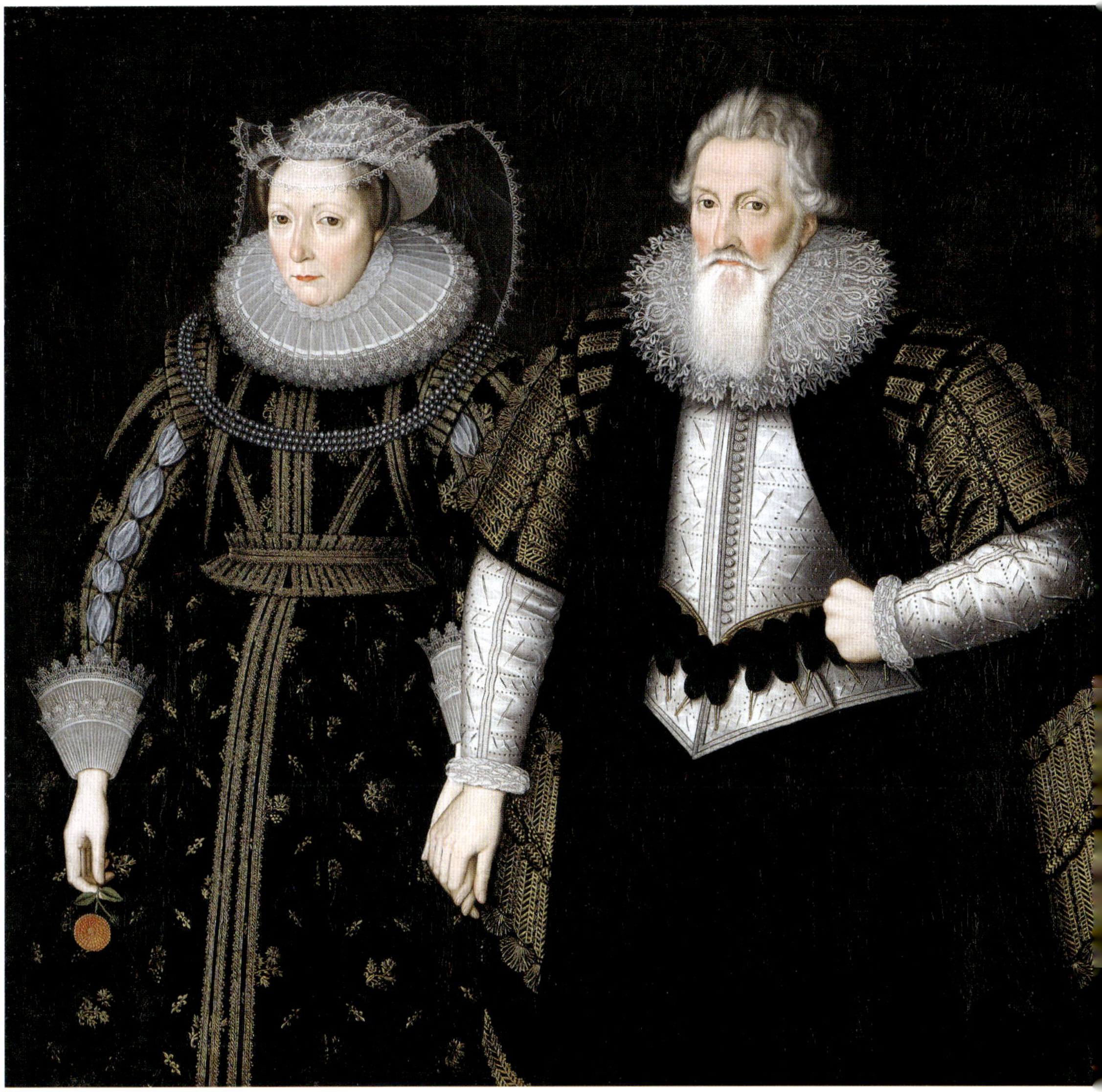

47. Unknown painter, *Sir Thomas and Jane Mansel*, c.1625, oil, 118x126

below
48. Maximilian Colt, *Thomas and Jane Mansel*, Church of Margam Abbey, 1639, alabaster

in the portrait of Herbert's wife, Eleanor Percy, no attempt at all was made to present the sitter in the modern manner. The pictures were both painted in 1595 and presumably related to the couple's marriage in that year, when Eleanor was just thirteen. The flat, heraldic style was still considered appropriate by a few patrons even thirty years later again. Posing for the minutely detailed double portrait of Sir Thomas and Jane Mansel of Glamorgan, Jane held a marigold, probably an allusion to her grief at the death of her first husband. The picture makes a remarkable contrast

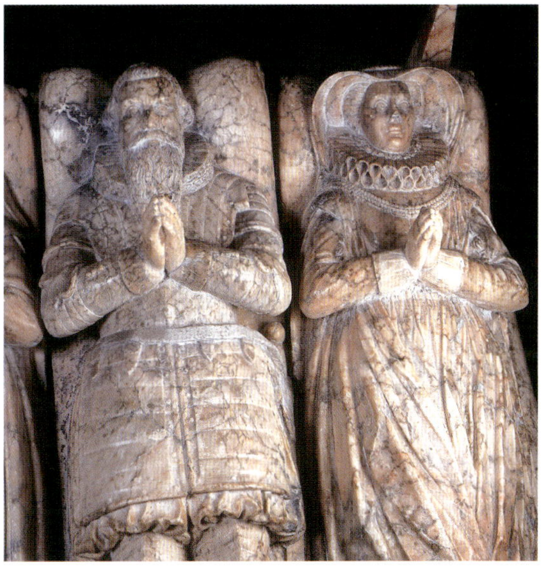

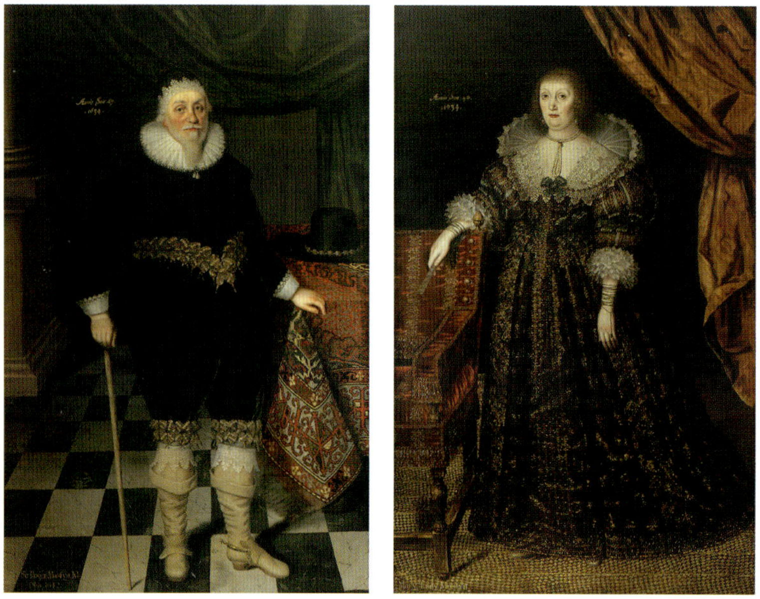

49. Possibly Daneil Mytens, *Sir Roger and Lady Mary Mostyn*, 1634, oil, 210.8x134.6

with near-contemporary portraits of Sir Roger and his wife Mary Mostyn, eldest daughter of Sir John Wynn of Gwydir. Here, the taste for spacial realism and modern painting had reached its full expression. The Mostyn portraits were not signed, but they strongly suggest the work of the Dutch painter Daniel Mytens.[48]

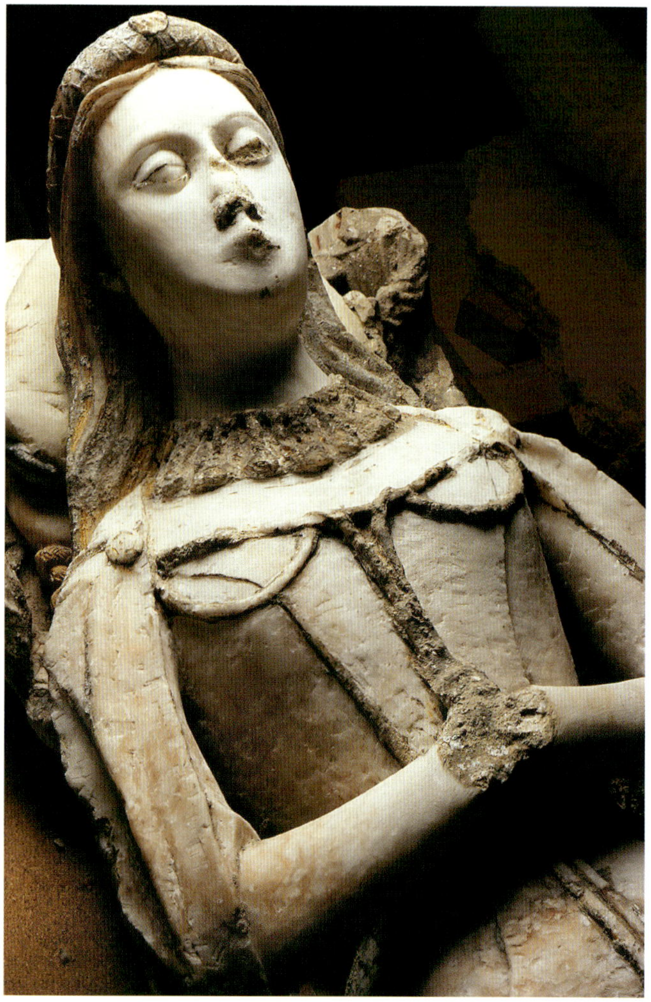

right
50. *Margaret Wogan*, formerly at the Church of St John, Slebech, before 1483, alabaster

The fashion for portable portraits painted on panel or canvas emerged in parallel with the evolution of an older form, also devoted to the affirmation of personal and dynastic identity – the tomb effigy. Only the very wealthy could afford a carved effigy and were in a position to demand its insertion in the body of a parish church, or to commission the building of a family chapel, though alongside the old gentry these did include a few who had prospered in trade, such as the Whites of Tenby.[49] In Glamorgan, the Mansel family, though long established, had substantially increased their wealth and status by acquiring Margam Abbey at the Dissolution and the memorial commissioned for Lady Jane and Sir Thomas Mansel, also flanked by Mary, his first wife, represented patronage at the very top of the market. The memorial was carved in alabaster by Maximilian Colt, among the most celebrated sculptors of the early seventeenth century, who earlier in his career had carved the memorial to Queen Elizabeth, commissioned for Westminster Abbey by James I. Colt was a Huguenot who, like many other sculptors and painters, had fled to London to escape Catholic oppression of Protestants on the continent.

In the age of the painted portrait, the stylised representation of individuals that characterised most medieval memorial effigies was no longer acceptable. As early as the 1480s, the facial deformity reproduced on the effigy of a Pembrokeshire woman, Margaret Wogan, makes it clear that likeness was considered important. Margaret may have been drawn in life for the sculptor to copy, since it was not uncommon for effigies to be commissioned before death. Drawing a cadaver must also have been practiced, though the earliest record of it in Wales is considerably later.[50] A third option was to copy from an existing image, and it would seem that the Mansel effigies were derived from the painted double portrait. A drawing may have been taken from it in Wales by or on behalf of the sculptor, or the painting itself may have been carried to London for Colt to copy. It was in London workshops or in the quarries of Nottingham and Derby that alabaster effigies were carved. The delicate image of Margaret Wogan retains its original restrained colouring, confined to her hair, head band and collar. Carved a century and a half after the Wogan memorial, the Margam effigies of Sir Thomas, Mary and Jane Mansel would have been more elaborately painted, though they were subsequently stripped of their colour. Among the many early seventeenth-century memorials that retain their original polychrome appearance, that of Richard and Magdalen Herbert at the Church of St Nicholas in Montgomery is perhaps the most elaborate.

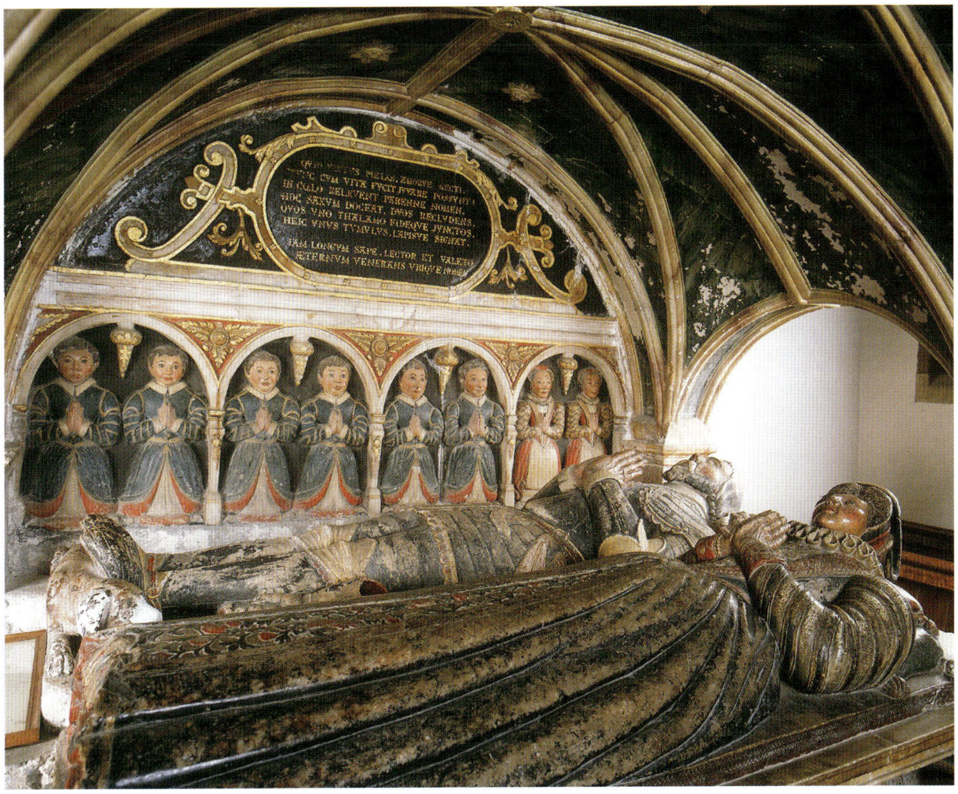

51. Possibly Walter Hancock, *Memorial to Richard and Magdalen Herbert*, Church of St Nicholas, Montgomery, 1600, alabaster

48 If the Mostyn pictures are the work of Mytens, they would be among the last that he painted before returning to the Hague, where he lived most of the remainder of his life. Another Flintshire family, Davies of Gwysaney, may also have patronised Mytens. See John Steegman, *A Survey of Portraits in Welsh Houses, Volume I, Houses in North Wales* (Cardiff, 1957), p. 162 and plate 27A.

49 A second example at the Church of St Mary, Tenby, is the memorial to Margaret Mercer, commissioned by her husband in 1610. The memorial is illustrated in Lord, *Imaging the Nation*, p. 39.

50 See Lord, *Imaging the Nation*, p. 42.

Presumably the effigy of Richard was based on a painted portrait, since the memorial was commissioned by Magdalen a few years after the death of her husband.[51] On the other hand, Magdalen's eight children, who included the celebrated poet George Herbert, were tokenistic, lined up with no differentiation of feature or even of size, behind her husband. Such an arrangement, more often with the children portrayed in profile at prayer, had become conventional by the early seventeenth century, but the inclusion in the Herbert memorial not only of Richard's effigy as in life but also as a cadaver was unusual. The *momento mori* theme was maintained in the painted decoration of the elaborate canopy with the allegorical figures of Vanity and Time.

Surmounting the Herbert tomb at Montgomery is the family arms. Creating an authoritative record of the origins of important dynasties was a central function of Elizabethan and Jacobean gentry imagery. Public displays of heraldic devices were accompanied in private by the confirmation of ancient ancestry in the form of family trees, recorded by specialist herald painters. Their work was presented in the form of inscribed rolls, some of enormous length and elaboration, illustrated by heraldic devices and occasionally also by miniature portraits. Heralds were responsible both for researching and making the rolls, and also for the banners and escutcheons displayed at the elaborate funerals and other ceremonials which they devised for their gentry clients. The main centre of activity for painters serving the northern Welsh gentry was Chester. Detailed civic records survive in the city, and through them it is possible to trace the evolution of painting workshops from the late sixteenth to the early eighteenth century.[52] The central figures were four generations of the Holme family, all named Randle, though the first Randle Holme took over the existing business of his own master, Thomas Chaloner, by marrying his widow in about 1598. The surviving notebooks of this first Randle Holme show that he worked as far away from his base as Anglesey, where he copied carved and painted armorial devices in Beaumaris church.[53] These were his sources for the research and production of heraldry for his clients. However, Randle Holme also painted other types of picture, and it is clear that many early sixteenth-century portraits – especially those produced beyond court circles – were the work of such heralds. The painters remain largely unidentified, since the medieval workshop tradition from which Randle Holme and his contemporaries emerged did not consider it appropriate for individual makers to name themselves on their work. They were simply tradesmen, and it would have been regarded as impertinent for them to place their signatures beside the images of their employers, implying equality of status. In 1584 William Somerset, 3rd Earl of Worcester, wrote from Raglan to his friend John Scudamore in Shropshire, asking to borrow a painting that he wished to have copied. His tone clearly implies the status of the unidentified painter in his employ:

51 No portrait of Richard is known. A portrait of Magdalen survives, but as a younger woman than the depiction in the effigy. It is unlikely to be the work of Federico Zuccaro, to whom it is often attributed.

52 For an analysis of the records, see Robert Tittler, *Portraits, Painters, and Publics in Provincial England, 1540–1640* (Oxford, 2012). Among other heralds who can be identified with surviving rolls, Rhys Cain worked at Oswestry from the last quarter of the sixteenth century. Rhys Cain also painted religious images, for which he was criticised in a contemporary verse. See Lord, *Imaging the Nation*, p. 45.

53 The notebooks and much other material relating to the Randle Holme family are among the Harleian Manuscripts in the British Library. See Robert Tittler and Shaun Evans, 'Randle Holme the elder and the development of portraiture in north Wales c.1600-1630', *British Art Journal*, XVI, no. 2 (2015), pp. 24-9.

54 William Somerset, 3rd Earl of Worcester at Raglan to John Scudamore, Holme Lacy, Shropshire, 6 November 1584, The National Archives MS C115/100/7373. A further letter, C115/101, also refers to the loan of an unidentified picture. A portrait of John Scudamore survives at Holme Lacy, painted at about this time by an unidentified painter.

> Whereas you doe offer that your mann shoulde doe the picture for mee I yelde your thanks. But I am of opinion that I have a very sufficient workeman here with me. Wherefore if yo wilbe soe good as to sende mee the picture rowled upp by this bearer I will cause my mann to Draw ytt, and it shalbe slfye returned againe unto you with thankes. … yf yor comyng … my Paynter shall drae you allso.[54]

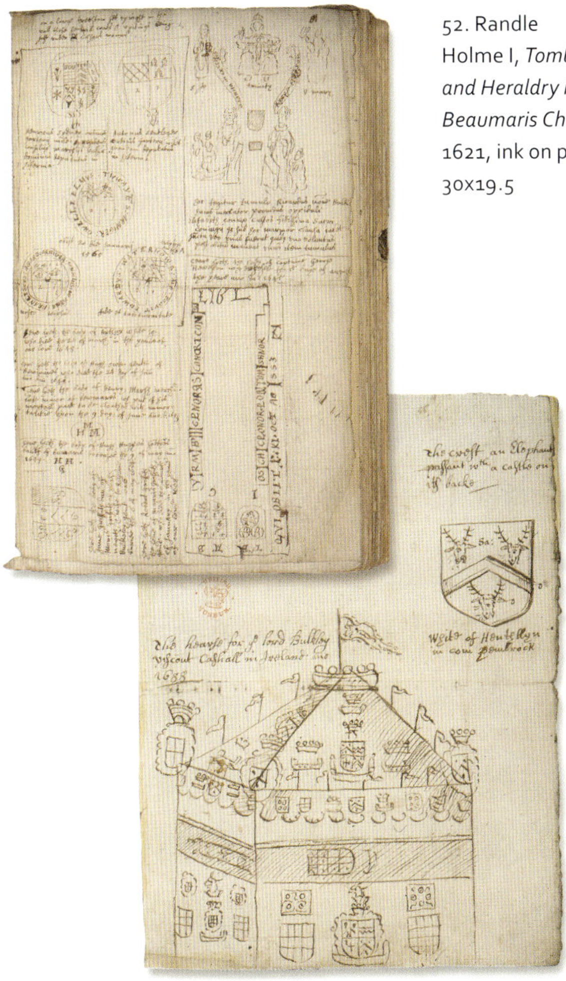

52. Randle Holme I, *Tombs and Heraldry in Beaumaris Church*, 1621, ink on paper, 30x19.5

Given the extent of the 3rd Earl's enrichment of Raglan, it is possible that his 'workeman' was an artisan employed there over a long period, painting everything from wainscot to portraits. However, by this time, under the influence of continental courtly fashion, the idea of some painters as specialists, and of the portrait in particular as a form of 'polite art' as distinct from a craft product, was beginning to take hold among elite patrons. A fashion for collecting paintings not on the basis of who or what they represented, but for their quality as artefacts, began to develop, and along with it a hierarchy of painters. In England, Holbein emerged among the earliest of these collectable names. Responding to this trend,

53. Rhys Cain, *The Pedigree Roll of Edward Almer*, 1602, gouache, 57.5x215.9

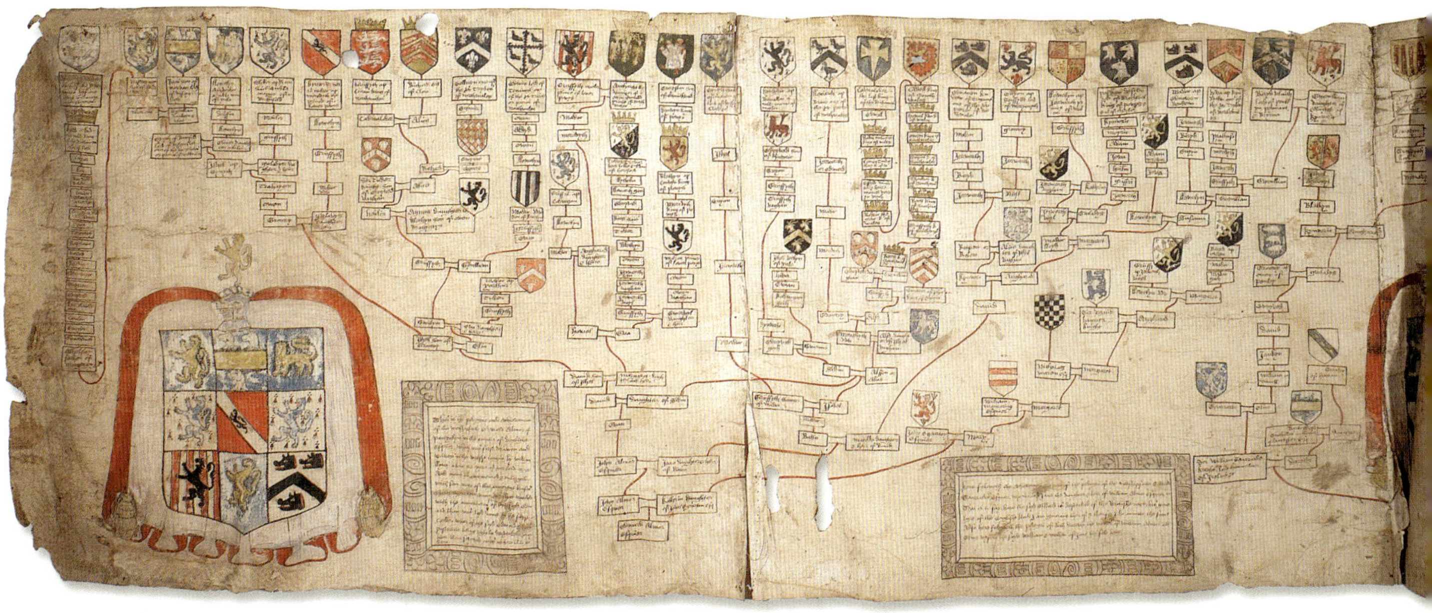

practitioners such as the Elizabethan miniaturist Nicholas Hilliard began to conceive of themselves, and to present themselves both socially and in theoretical writing, as a breed apart from the artisan. A conceptual gap opened between the products of the fashionable polite painters – the emerging 'artists' of the modern world – and the more conservative artisans. By the early seventeenth century, filtering down from courtly practice, the concept of the artist as an individual practitioner was made apparent by the fact that signatures became more common even in the products of some trained in the workshop tradition. A portrait of Thomas ap Ieuan ap David, painted in 1610, was signed with a monogram, though the painter has yet to be identified. However, alongside this emblem of change, the portrait retained the conventions of heraldic painting in the form of an inscription – 'Resurgam' (May I rise again) – and a robin, whose red breast symbolised the blood of Christ, drawn by the crown of thorns. The painters John Souch, first apprenticed in Chester in 1607, and Thomas Leigh, who worked for Souch from 1618, after he had achieved independent status, also both signed portraits painted for the north Wales gentry. Indeed, albeit in muted colour, Thomas Leigh's signature on his portrait of Robert Davies of Gwysaney was inscribed adjacent to his patron's face, in large flowing script.

Unfortunately, like many of his well-placed predecessors, Robert Davies would not have long to enjoy his portrait. Two years after it was painted, he was taken from his home and imprisoned for Royalist sympathies, as order broke down and the civil wars began.

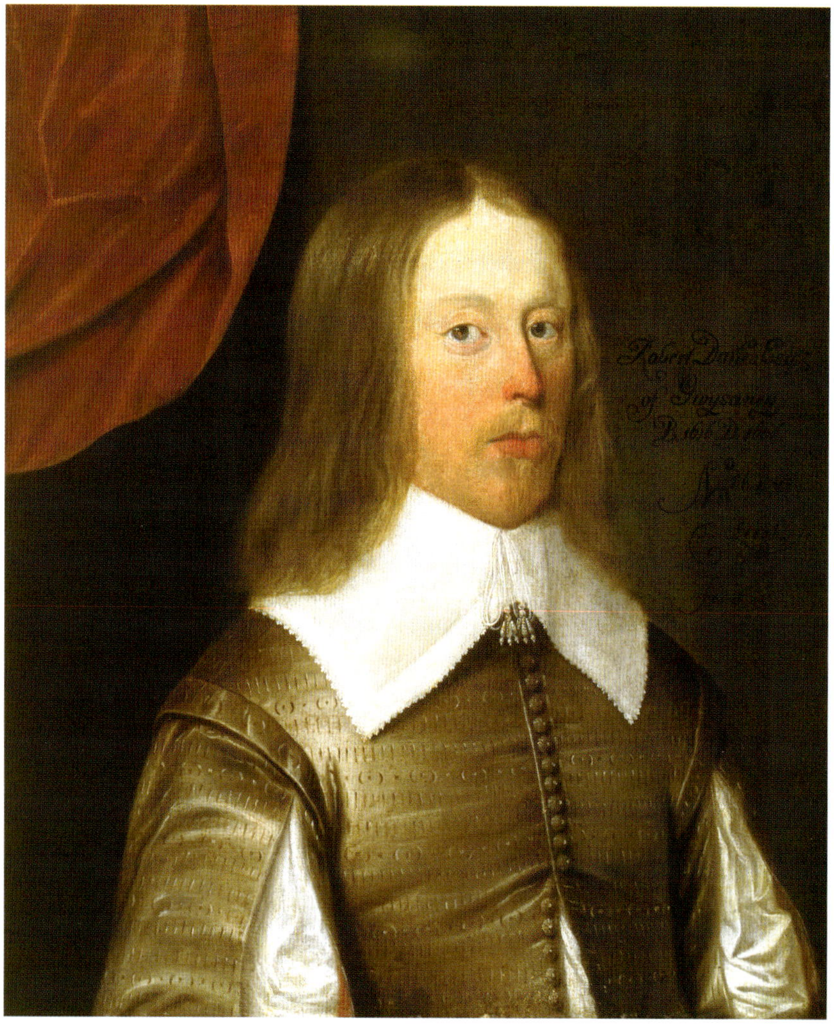

54. Thomas Leigh,
Robert Davies of Gwysaney,
1643, oil, 69.9x58.4

55. Unidentified painter,
Thomas ap Ieuan ap David of Arddynwent, 1610,
oil, 67.5x54.3

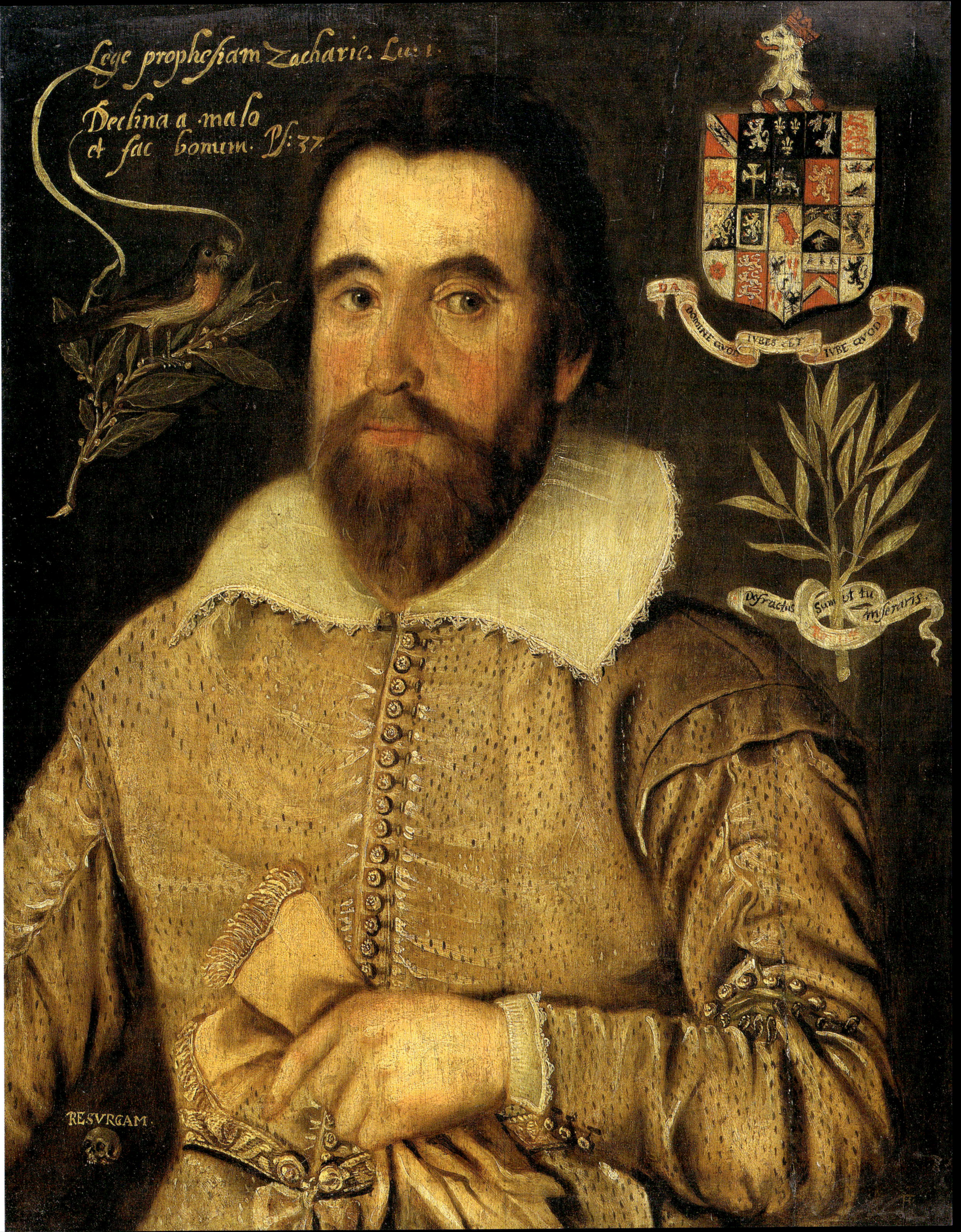
Lege prophesiam Zacharie. Lu: 1.
Declina a malo
et fac bonum. Ps: 37
DA DOMINE QVOD IVBES ET IVBE QVOD VIS.
Defractus Sum ut tu miseraris.
RESVRGAM

Things fall apart – the English Civil Wars

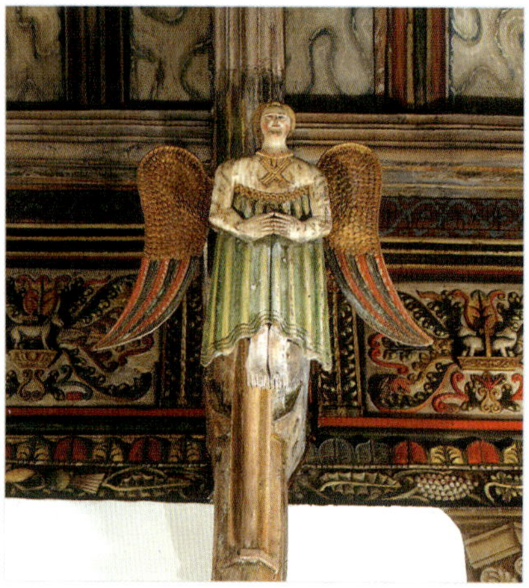

During her long reign, that came to an end in 1601, Queen Elizabeth had succeeded for the most part in keeping a grip on public order. Nevertheless, the religious tensions that had disturbed the world of her predecessors continued to smoulder into the early period of the Scottish Stuart dynasty, which succeeded the Tudors. In this context, the decision by William Salusbury of Rhug, near Corwen, to build a private chapel is particularly interesting. By the mid-1630s, when Salusbury commissioned the building, Charles I had considerably relaxed the attitude of the state towards ritual and dogma. Puritans suspected the edge of a slippery slope leading down to Popery, and Salusbury was certainly among those nostalgic for the old church. The atmosphere of the Rhug chapel, elaborately carved and brilliantly coloured, recalled the visual riches of the medieval Roman tradition of Welsh churches down to the 1530s, and yet the theology of its imagery was diplomatically cautious. Below the angels flying in the roof, in the body of the chapel the patron placed a characteristic Reformation emphasis on texts written in the Welsh language of the people. A tableau, designed around words taken from a fifteenth-century poem, presented a remarkable collection of the *momento mori* usually found in isolation on portraits and memorials – a skull, a cadaver, an hourglass and a sundial, with two burning candles specifically reinforcing the words of the poet: 'as the flame gradually consumes the tallow of the lighted candle so life under the firmament perishes daily.'[55]

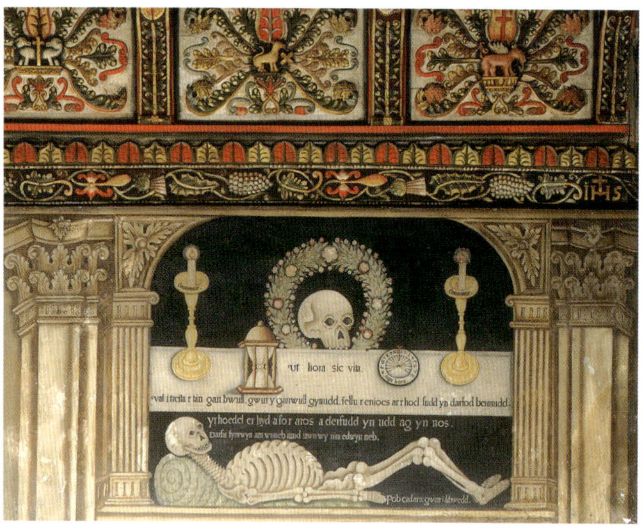

top
56. *Angel*, Rug Chapel, *c.*1637, oak

bottom
57. *Image of Death*, Rug Chapel, *c.*1637, wall painting

The simplicity and vigour of the carving and painting at Rhug suggest that it was carried out by local craftspeople. Its character well illustrates the parting of the ways between the conservative tradition of the artisan and the sophistication of the court painter – the artist – that crystallised once and for all during the reign of Charles I.[56] Remarkably, the work at Rhug was contemporary with the sophisticated religious painting of Rubens and the portraits of Van Dyck, both of whom were patronised lavishly in London. Even among the court painters themselves, the conceptual evolution that took place in the forty years of the first two Stuart monarchs was startling, and left almost all Welsh gentry patrons in its wake. Van Dyck flamboyantly eclipsed other fashionable Dutch portrait painters of the preceding generations – Gheerhaerts, Mytens and Janssens – and their English contemporaries, including Peake and Gilbert Jackson, who painted for Welsh clients. Although in later years loyal gentry houses would become well stocked with studio versions and copies of Van Dyck's portraits of Charles I and Henrietta Maria, it appears that no Welsh patron sat to him. Of the older generation of painters, Jackson in particular availed himself of Welsh commissions, the key to which was his portrait of Eubule Thelwall of Bathafarn Park in Flintshire, in his role

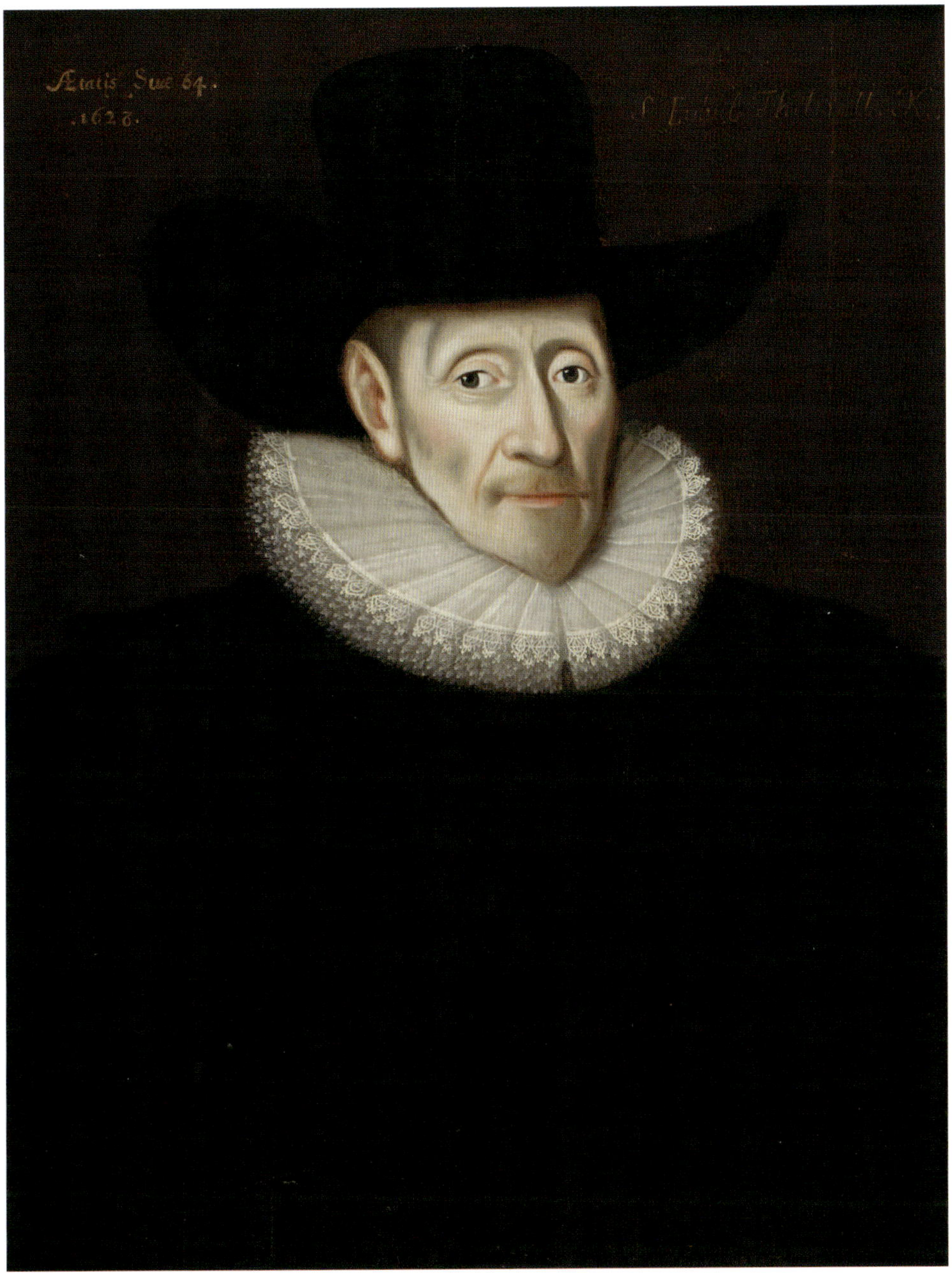

58. Gilbert Jackson, *Eubule Thelwall*, 1628, oil, 77×59

55 'val i treila r tan gan bwull, gwur y ganwull gynudd. fellu r enioes ar r hod sudd yn darfod beunudd', from Ieuan ap Rhydderch, 'Englynion y Misoedd', quoted in D.B. Hague, 'Rug Chapel, Corwen', *Journal of the Merioneth Historical and Record Society*, III, part II (1958), p. 176.

56 The effects of the patronage and collecting of Charles I were far reaching both in terms of setting court taste firmly in an international mainstream, and – as a consequence of his untimely demise in 1649 and the sale of his collection – for creating a London art market.

as Principal of Jesus College Oxford, painted in 1628.[57] In 1631, Cornelius Johnson (the anglicised form of Janssens, by which name he became best known) painted Sir Thomas Hanmer, whose family tradition of portraits went back 150 years by this time, and Elizabeth, his first wife. Sir Thomas, then only 19 years of age, would distinguish himself in the pacific role of horticulturalist.[58] With a significant difference of iconography, four years after the Hanmer portraits, Johnson painted Richard Herbert, 2nd Baron Herbert of Chirbury.

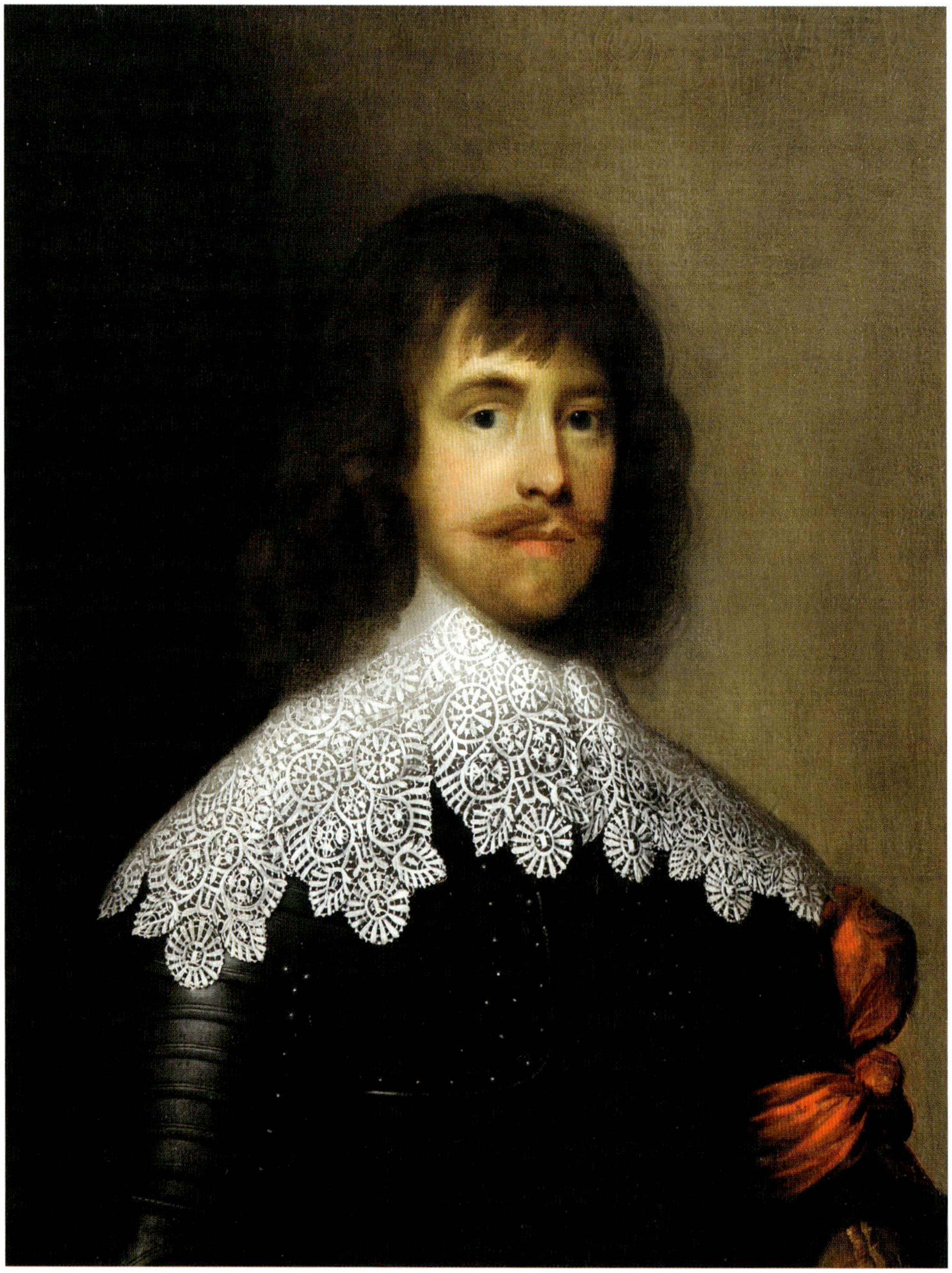

59. Cornelius Johnson, *Richard Herbert, Second Baron Herbert of Chirbury*, 1635, oil, 75x62

opposite
60. Cornelius Johnson, *Sir Thomas Hanmer*, 1631, oil, 77.5x62.2

57 Thelwall was the fifth of ten brothers, several of whom subsequently commissioned portraits from Jackson, along with members of neighbouring families in the north-east. The subsequent Thelwall portraits were painted to a common format, but at least two of the surviving pictures appear to be the work of a less sophisticated painter. A painting purporting to represent Eubule Thelwell as a child with his mother, also at Jesus College, is far too late to represent these sitters.

58 A portrait of his second wife, Susan, shows her studying *Gerard's Herbal*. See Steegman, *North Wales*, p. 139 and plate 22B, present whereabouts unknown.

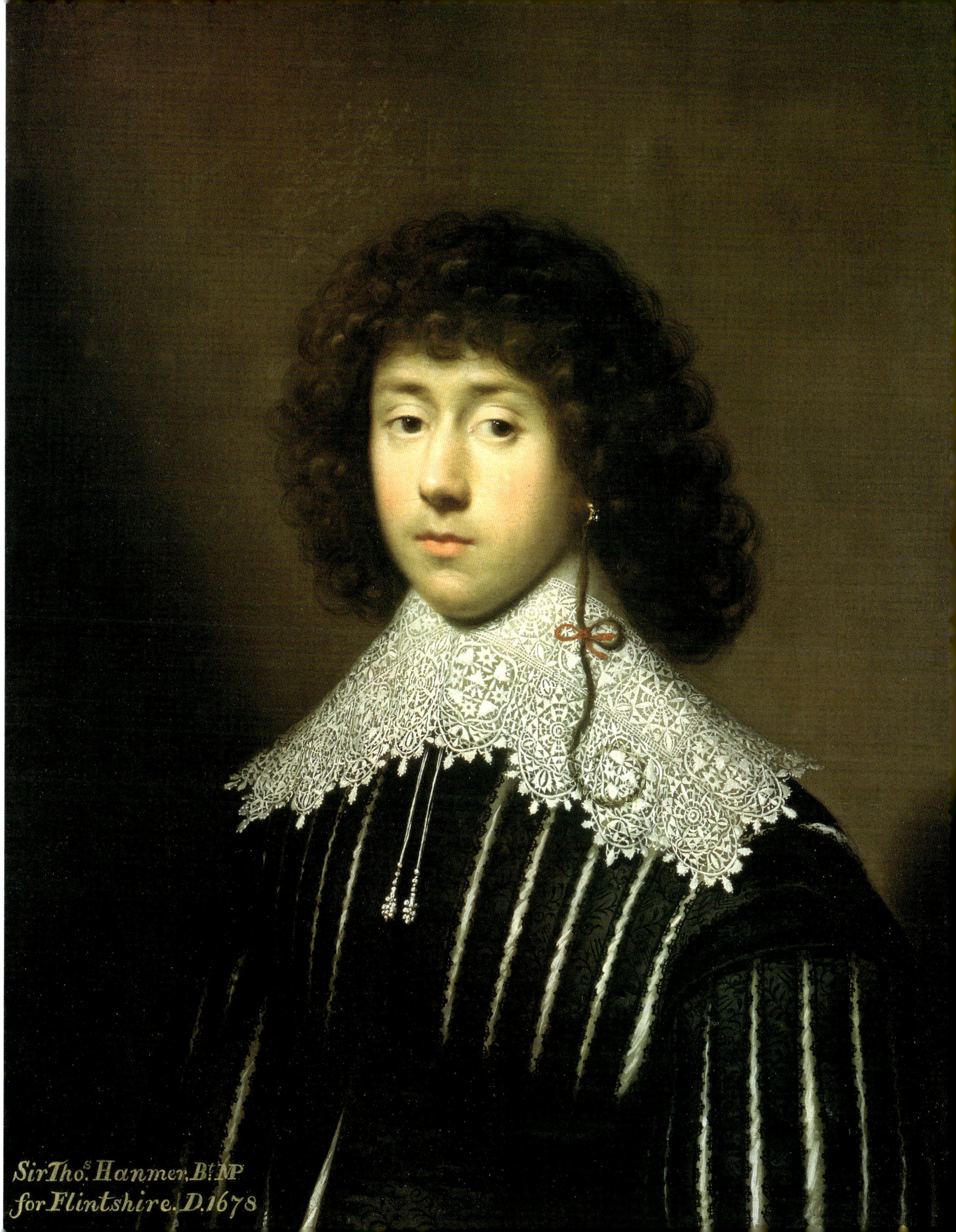
Sir Thos. Hanmer, Bt. MP
for Flintshire. D.1678

Herbert posed in his armour. Forty-one years after the death of Queen Elizabeth, things fell apart once again, in a contest for secular authority between the king and parliament that would result in civil war and the execution of Charles I in 1649. In addition to huge loss of life, the entanglement of religious belief in the struggle for power resulted in a further orgy of destruction aimed at the few surviving material relics of the religious culture of the middle ages, and at the property and monuments of those who, in the eyes of the parliamentary radicals, represented the old order:

> About 9 Nov., 1643, Sir W. Brereton and his forces came to Faringdon and Holt, and entered through the same, and went to Wrexham, Flint and Holywell, and did pull down the organs, defaced the windows in all the churches, and the monuments of divers, and pulled down the arms and hatchments.[59]

A contemptuous eye-witness account of destruction nearby, at Hawarden, calls to mind the scene witnessed by Richard Clough in Antwerp, some seventy years earlier:

> I myself coming into the church of Hawarden the morning after they were there, found the Common Prayer-Book scattered up and down the chancel, and some well read man, without doubt, conceiving that the Common Prayers had been in the beginning of a poor innocent old church bible, tore out almost all Genesis for failing. It stood so dangerously it was suspected to be malignant. Its windows where there was oriental glass they broke in pieces only the faces; to be as frugal as they could, they left sometimes the whole bodies of painted bishops, though in their rochets. But if there was anything in the language of the beast, though it was but an *hoc fecit*, or at worst, *orate* &c. (and I but guess, for I could not read it when it was gone), which had stood many years, and might many more, without idolatry, that was dashed out.[60]

Sir Richard Herbert, like the majority of the Welsh gentry, was a Royalist, but the powerful Sir Thomas Myddelton of Chirk Castle fought on the parliamentarian side. The labyrinthine Myddelton family was strongly associated with trading activities in London, and inclined to Puritan beliefs. Sir Thomas melted the organ pipes at Wrexham that had been pulled down by Brereton's forces, and made bullets of them. He was appointed Sergeant Major General of North Wales by parliament and among his military successes was the expulsion of Richard Herbert from Montgomery Castle in 1644. Later, with the restoration of the monarchy in sight, he jumped the Cromwellian ship prematurely, resulting in considerable depredations to Chirk Castle in 1659, but he managed to retain his property. The surviving Chirk castle portraits include those of prominent supporters of the Commonwealth, including Sir Henry Vane, and Sir Thomas's own military image, perhaps painted by Robert Walker, Oliver Cromwell's favourite painter.

59 British Library, Harleian MS 2125, f. 135.

60 J. Rowland Phillips, *Memoirs of the Civil War in Wales and the Marches 1642-1649* (2 vols., London, 1874), II, p. 114.

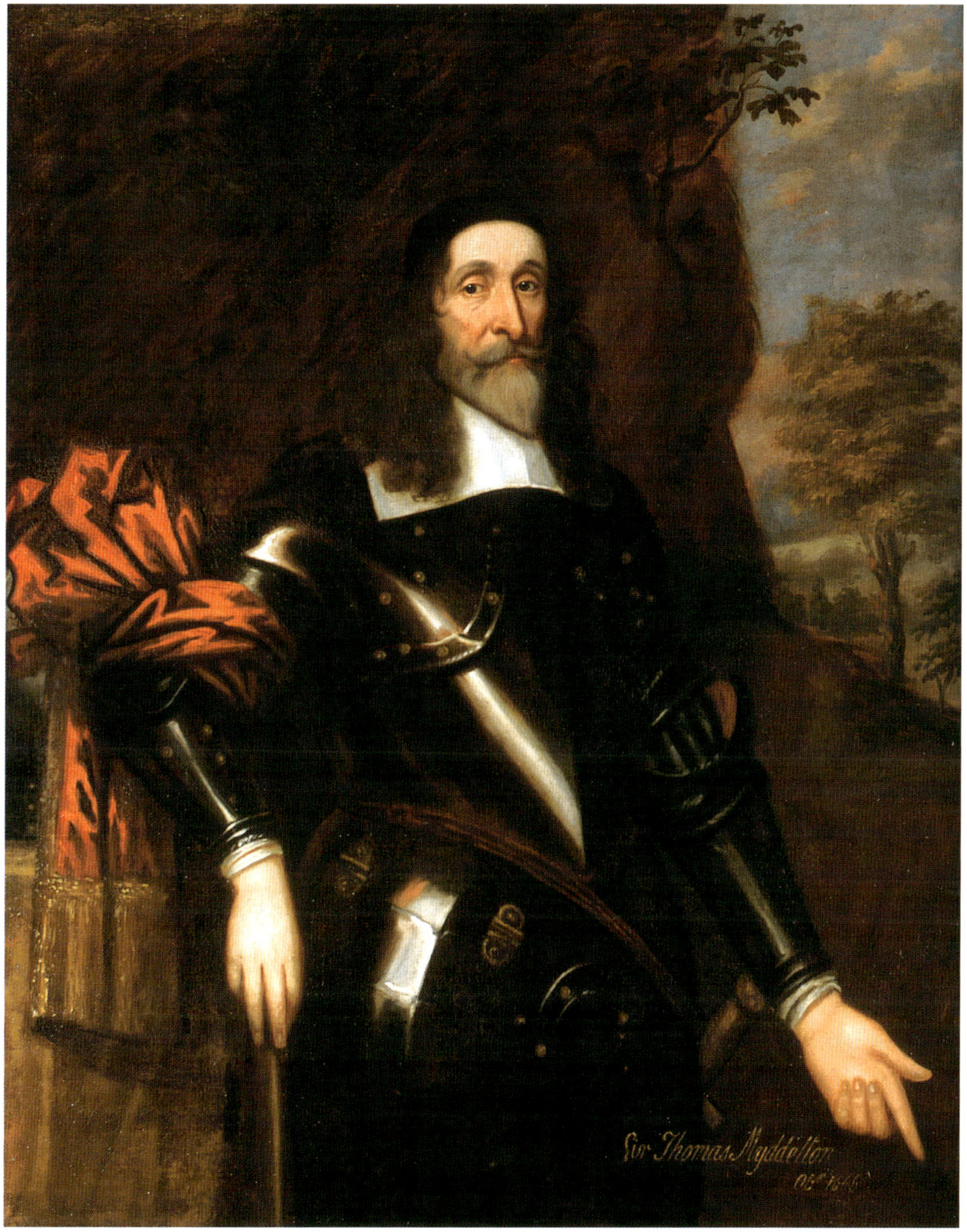

61. Probably Robert Walker, *Sir Thomas Myddelton*, c.1650-60, oil, 123x101

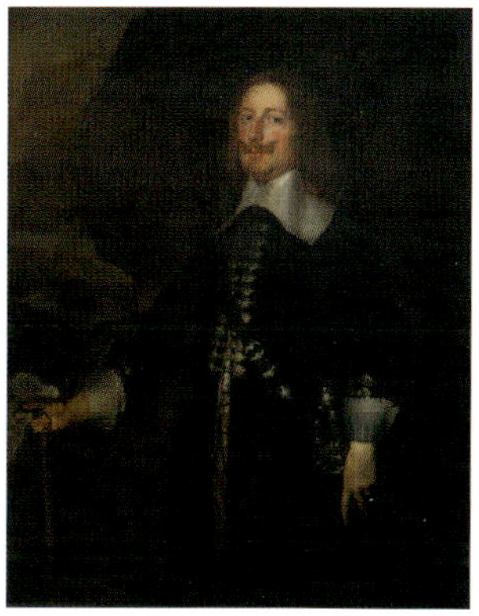

62. Unknown painter, *Colonel Philip Jones of Fonmon*, c.1655, 127x102

In the south, the most important parliamentarian was Colonel Phillip Jones of Fonmon, who was a close associate of Cromwell. The colonel's own portrait, similar in style to that of Sir Thomas Myddelton, hung in the house, along with that of Cromwell himself and Henry Ireton, the general largely responsible for the brutal suppression of Ireland.

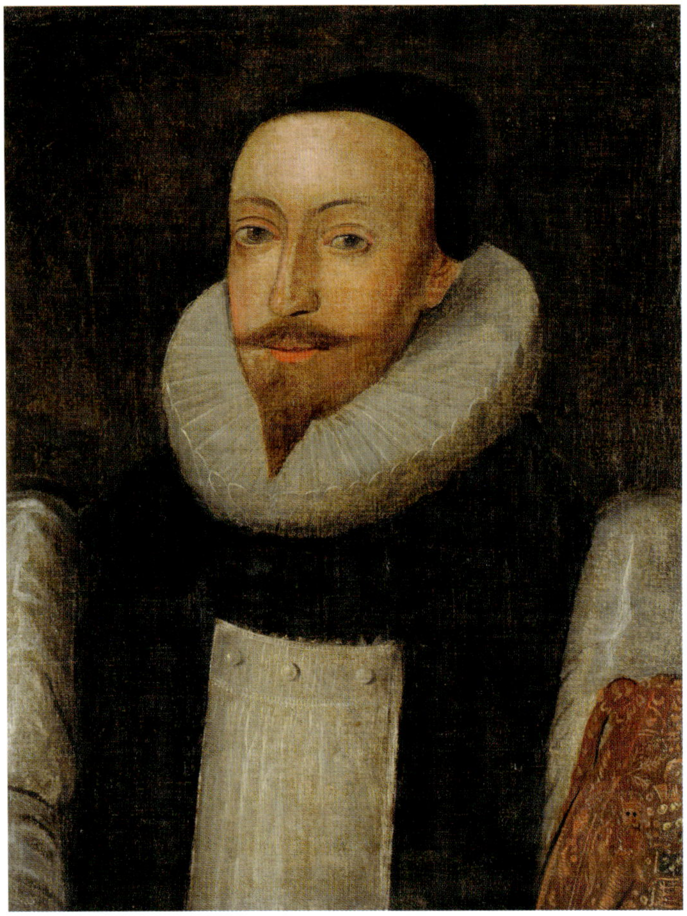

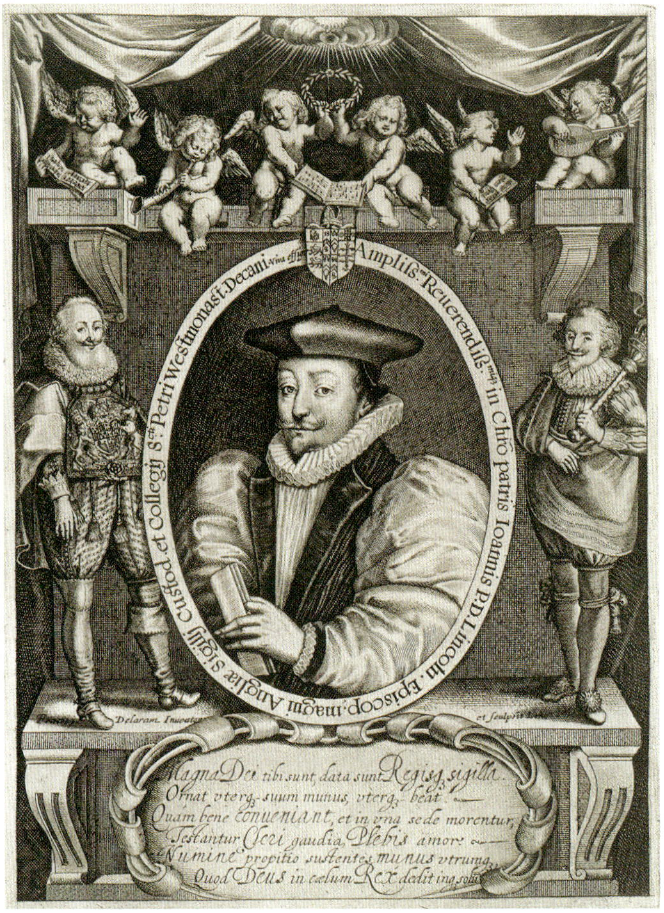

63. Unknown painter,
John Williams, subsequently Archbishop of York, c.1620, oil, 127x56

64. Francis Delaram,
John Williams, as Bishop of Lincoln, c.1621, engraving

However, by far the most frequently portrayed Welsh person embroiled in the Civil Wars was Archbishop John Williams. A product of Gabriel Goodman's grammar school at Ruthin, Williams rose rapidly in the church under James I, becoming the king's chaplain while still in his mid-30s. By 1621 he was both Bishop of Lincoln and Lord Keeper of the Great Seal, and in this elevated position he was depicted in an engraving based on a portrait at Trinity College, Cambridge. Through the medium of the engraving his image found its way home, translated into painted glass that probably formed part of a window at Bachegraig.[61] Williams was painted full length by Gilbert Jackson in 1627 for his Oxford college, St John's, a portrait that was copied and developed both in further oil paintings[62] and in many engravings. However, after the accession of Charles I in 1625, life did not proceed so smoothly for the bishop. He became embroiled in the religious and political disputes leading up to the war, and spent three years in the Tower of London. A brief period of liberty was followed by a

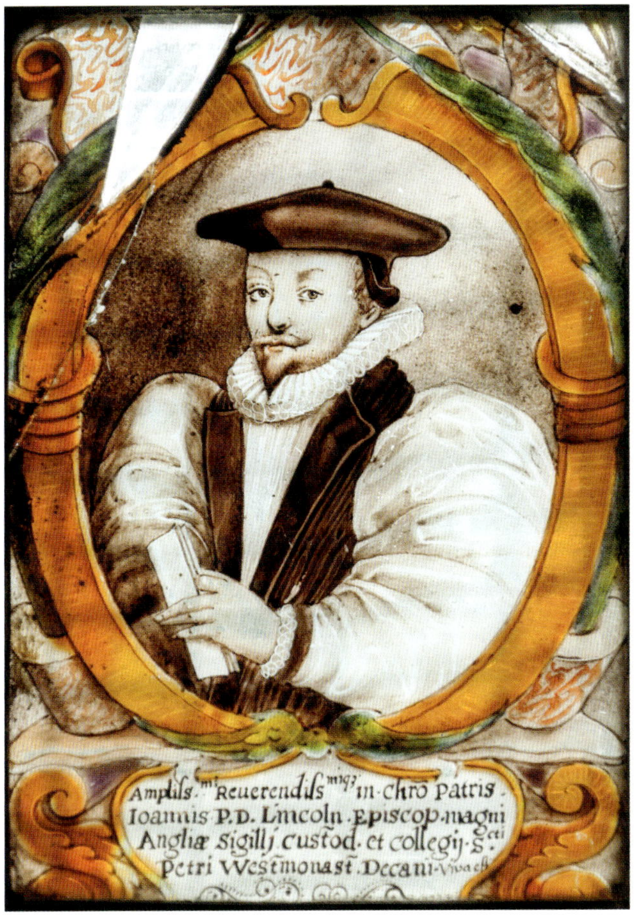

65. Unknown painter, *John Williams, as Bishop of Lincoln*, Church of Corpus Christi, Tremeirchion, *c*.1621-41, painted glass

66. Wenceslas Hollar, *Archbishop John Williams*, 1642, engraving, 23.0x16.9

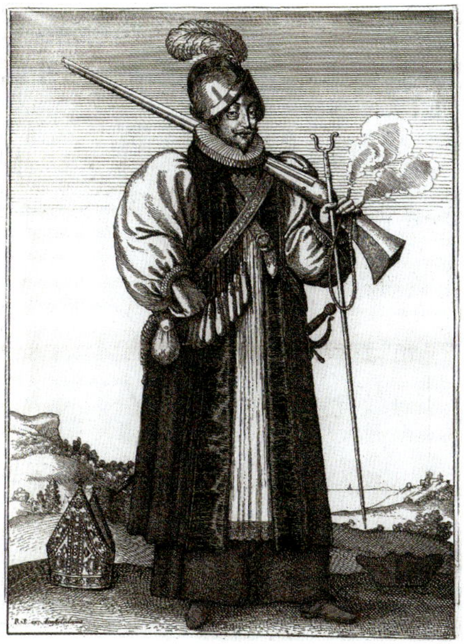

further six months' incarceration. On his release in 1642 he joined the king at York where he was enthroned as archbishop. The vicissitudes of his career resulted in his being satirised by the London popular press, complete with Wenglification of his speech. He was the first of many subsequent Welsh persons to be accorded this doubtful honour.

During the war, the complicated career of Williams stimulated the production of further engravings, including a remarkable image made by Wenceslas Hollar, based on his appearance in the Jackson portrait. Hollar set Williams at Conwy, before the castle that he occupied initially for the king (and subsequently for Parliament), clad both in Archbishop's robes and military crossbelts. His mitre lies on the ground, replaced with a soldier's helmet – an appropriate symbol not only of the condition of society in 1642, but of the divisions and conflicts that had formed the background to the visual culture for much of the previous two and a half centuries.

61 Mostyn Lewis, *Stained Glass in North Wales up to 1850* (Altrincham, 1970), p. 94. Clough's house had been bought by the Salusbury family. John Salusbury inherited in 1623 and became a Member of Parliament in 1626, the likely period of the glass portrait. It is now inserted in a window at the Church of Corpus Christi, Tremeirchion, along with portraits of James I and Charles I. However, the Charles I portrait is not in the same format as that of Williams and James, which were probably made between 1621 and 1625. Charles would have been added after his succession in 1625 and almost certainly before 1642. All are based on engravings.

62 There are variants at Lincoln College, Oxford and formerly at Penrhyn Castle, presently untraced, for which see Steegman, *North Wales*, p. 58 and pl. 10B.

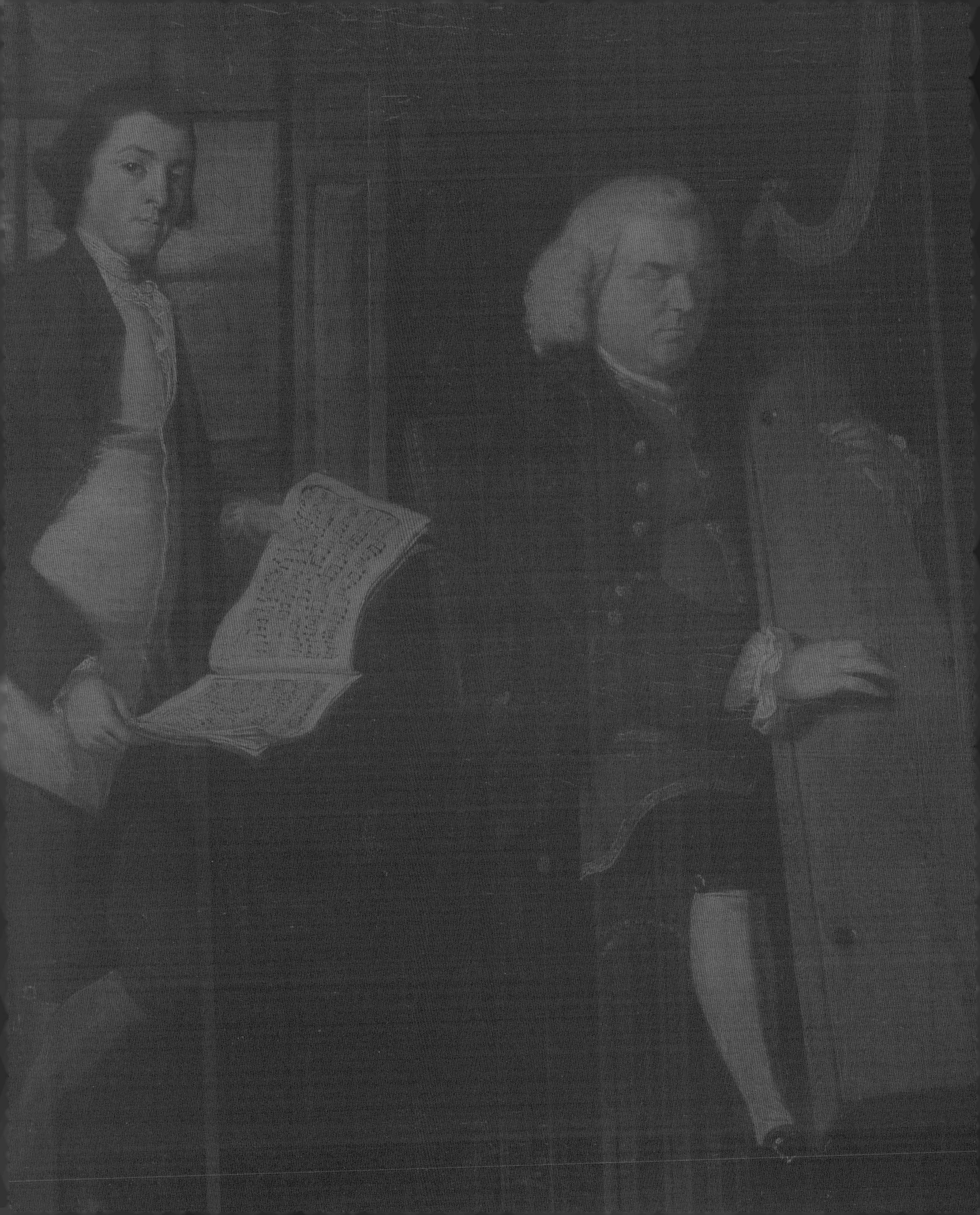

CHAPTER 2

1660–1820

CHAPTER 2 1660–1820

Retrenchment

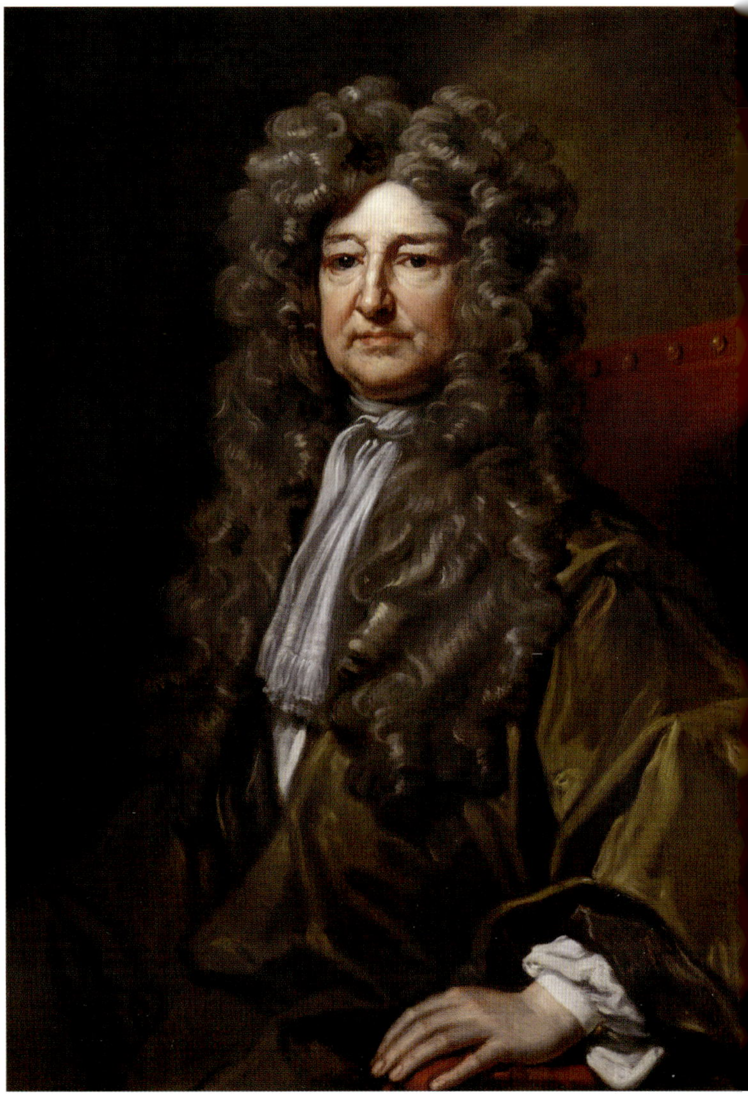

67. Godfrey Kneller, *Sir John Vaughan, 3rd earl of Carbery*, c.1700, oil, 90.8x71.1

The settlement that restored the Stuart monarchy in 1660 in the person of Charles II sought to chart a safe course through the minefield of entwined religious and political contention that had scarred the previous two and a half centuries. It marked the beginning of a long though by no means smooth process of transfer of power away from the monarchy and towards parliament. The Catholic and despotic instincts of Charles's brother, James II, together would result in his removal from the throne in 1688. He was replaced jointly by his daughter Mary and her husband (and cousin) William of Orange, who were firmly Protestant. Though not entirely bloodless, it was perhaps more of a *coup d'état* than a 'Glorious Revolution', and what emerged was not a parliamentary system that empowered the common people. The gentry remained the dominant force in Welsh society, and those people who sought power in

1 Despite attempts to link him to the Morgan family of Tredegar House, Harri Morgan was probably of lowly origin. The earliest contemporary document refers to him is as a labourer of Abergavenny.

2 In the illustration of children's literature, for instance, and on bottles of 'Captain Morgan' rum!

3 *The Diary of Samuel Pepys*, ed. Robert Latham and William Matthews (London, 1970), vol. VIII (1667), pp. 532–3 (entry for 16 November).

London or through government appointments elsewhere, continued to be drawn largely from their ranks. They celebrated their success in portraits, and the images of the most famous among them became known to a wider public through engravings.

The restoration of 1660 was the occasion for a general retrenchment of the Welsh gentry, but especially for those who, like Sir Richard Vaughan of Golden Grove in Carmarthenshire, the 2nd Earl of Carbery, had found themselves at best under a cloud or at worst deprived of their estates during the Commonwealth. Sir Richard's political indiscretions had obliged him to retire from public affairs and live quietly at home. He took as his chaplain the English clergyman Jeremy Taylor, also out of political favour, who wrote in Wales one of the most successful devotional books of the age. He entitled it *Golden Grove*, after his patron's house. Sir Richard's son John, the 3rd Earl of Carbery, became sufficiently secure and prosperous to sit to the most celebrated and prolific portrait painter of the Restoration age in London. Godfrey Kneller continued the tradition of dominance of court painting by continental artists that extended back through Van Dyck to Holbein. From a Welsh point of view, Sir John's celebrity rested on his role as Governor of Jamaica, where he became embroiled in a dispute with his compatriot and deputy, Sir Harri Morgan, whose Welsh origins were considerably more obscure.[1] Morgan rose in the West Indies through his profitable engagement in piracy, but his violent exploits against the Spanish and French threatened to disrupt the peace that Vaughan had been appointed to preserve. They would become the stuff of folklore, and resulted in the creation of a popular iconography that continues to evolve to this day.[2] Most of the images of Morgan derive from a seventeenth-century engraving by Frederick Hendrik van Hove, though no painted portrait source for the engraver's work has been identified. Morgan died in the West Indies in 1688, by which time Vaughan had returned to London, where he became a prominent and fashionable figure. Before his departure for the West Indies, the diarist Samuel Pepys was informed that he was 'one of the lewdest fellows of the age', but on his return he would become President of the Royal Society.[3]

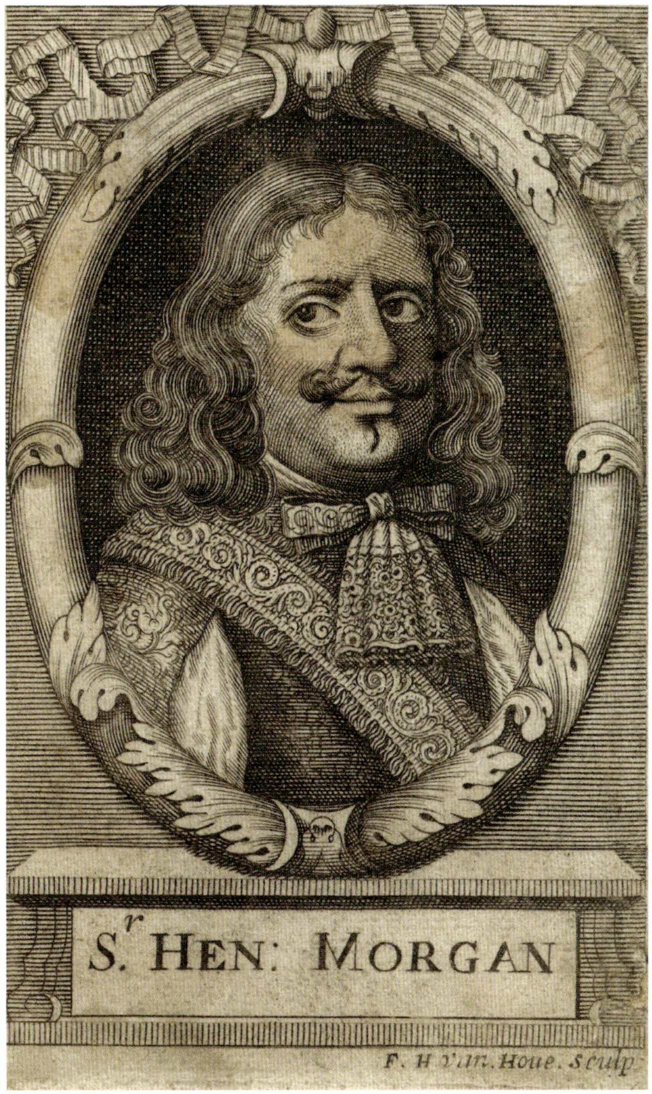

68. Frederick Hendrik van Hove, *Sr.Hen: Morgan* (Harri Morgan), late 17th century, engraving, 12.5x8.2

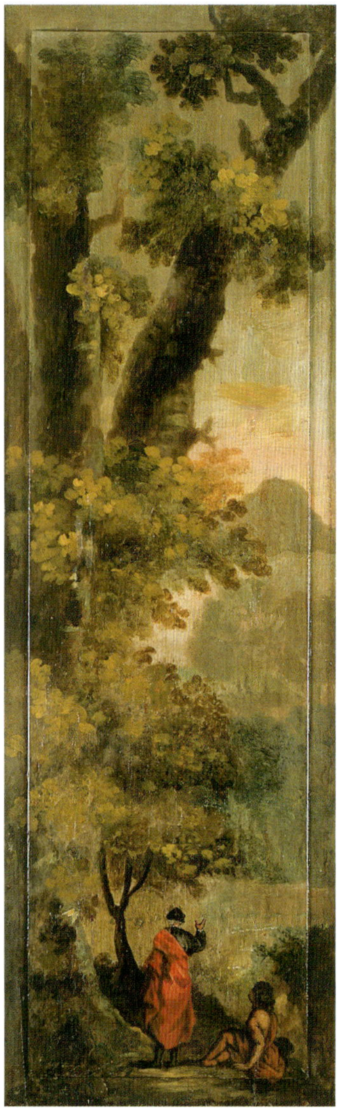

69. Unknown painter, *Landscape in the Gilt Room at Tredegar House, Newport*, oil, 160x52

The Vaughan family's Elizabethan Golden Grove would not be replaced until the mid-eighteenth century, but other Welsh gentry families reasserted dynastic authority with substantial rebuilding or completely new houses. The most notable from an architectural and artistic point of view was certainly Tredegar House, near Newport. Following in the long established tradition of those Welsh patrons who had experienced personally the cultures of the continent, Sir William Morgan had his builder[4] create a house which both in its general approach and in its detail reflected his awareness of international trends. Internally, the ground floor consisted of a series of richly carved and painted rooms, one opening into another. The most elaborate of them, the Gilt Room, was adorned with a copy of a ceiling at a palace in Rome, while paintings of the Virtues copied from sculptures in Amsterdam were set in the wall panels, and there was also a copy of a picture by Rubens. Nevertheless, a group of original landscape decorations seem to have been inspired locally. They strongly suggest views of the Brecon Beacons, albeit enlivened with classical figures in the foreground. Few records dating from the long period of the construction and decoration of the new house survive, and no individuals have been identified as responsible for these pictures. However, the Dutch painter Hendrick Danckerts was certainly working in the south of Wales in the period. Danckerts painted Troy House for Henry Somerset, 3rd Marquess of Worcester, in about 1672, in a modern style compatible with the Tredegar House landscapes.

In contrast to Tredegar House, detailed documentation of the contemporary enhancement of Chirk Castle in Denbighshire has survived, and it provides a remarkable insight into practice in the period. As the pictures at Tredegar House suggest, the interest of some of the gentry in painting was widening beyond the acquisition of dynastic portraits to include works esteemed for their quality as art. An emerging taste for landscape painting reflected this development, though the predominance of local subject matter before the 1730s suggests that affirmation of family status remained a powerful element in the motivation of patrons. Blanche Morgan, for instance, owned estates in Breconshire which the landscapes at Tredegar House were doubtless intended to call to mind. Nevertheless, that landscape paintings remained something of a novelty until the turn of the century is confirmed by the inventory made in 1699 of the property of Elizabeth Hoby, owner of the Neath Abbey estate. Her many 'great pictures' may safely be assumed to be portraits, since her two 'landskips', one in a gilt frame, the other in black, were specifically differentiated from the rest.[5]

The fashion for landscape, often with an overlaid mythological narrative, had taken hold much earlier in continental Europe and was held back in Wales partly by a legal ban on the import of paintings, imposed to protect indigenous practitioners in England and their guild monopolies. Although frequently circumvented, it remained in place until the 1690s, and

4 Perhaps Roger Hurlbutt of Warwickshire. See Howard Colvin, *A Biographical Dictionary of British Architects 1600-1840* (3rd ed., New Haven and London, 1995), pp. 521–2.

5 NLW Dynevor Papers, parcel 11, item 74. The yellow chamber contained 18 pictures, 'fram'd guilt and not guilt [sic]...' I am grateful to Gerald Morgan for this reference.

6 Edward Pugh, *Cambria Depicta* (London, 1816), p. 247.

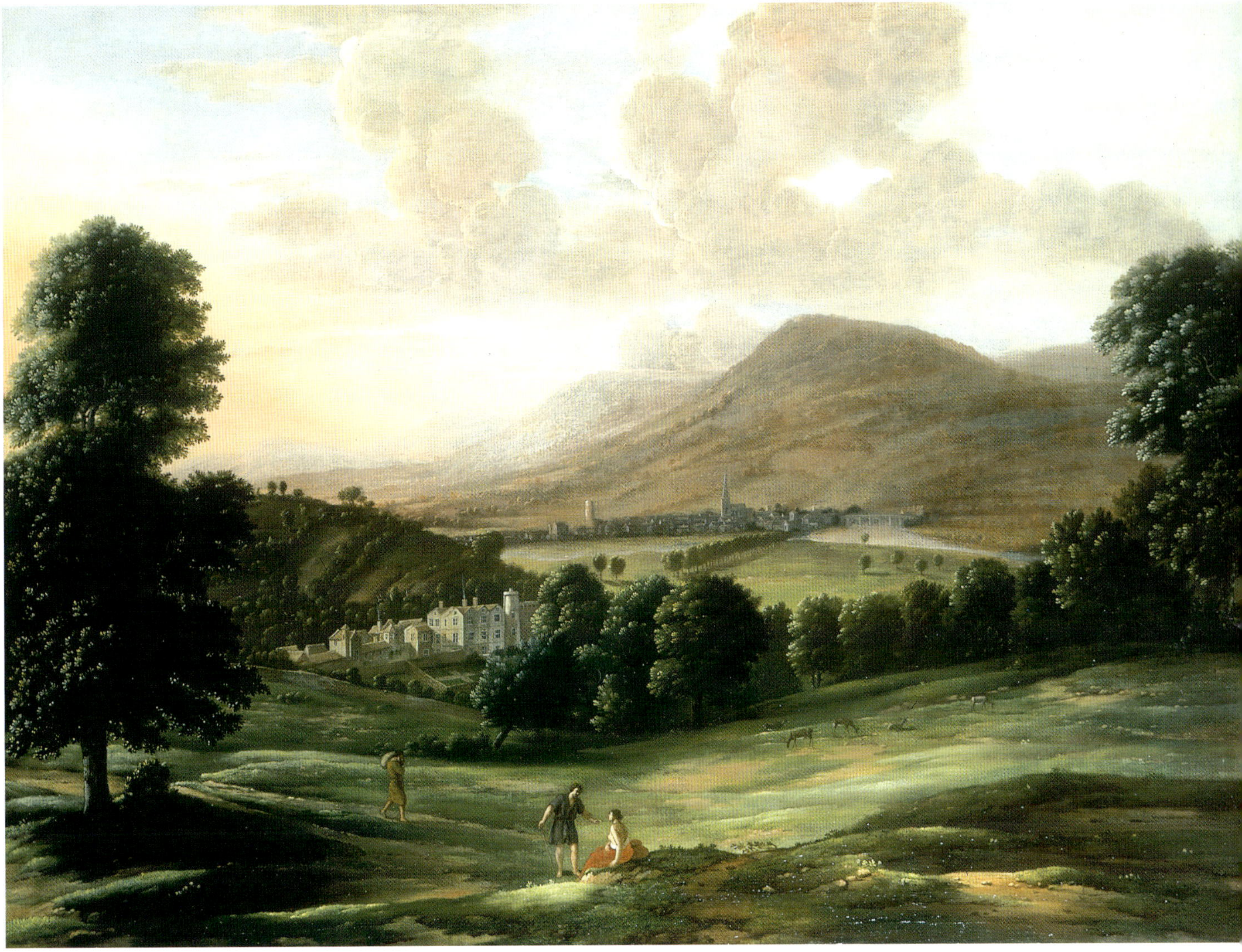

70. Hendrik Danckerts, *A Panorama of Monmouth with Troy House*, c.1672, oil, 126.5x181.8

among its unintended consequences was the added incentive it gave to foreign painters to come in person to supply directly the needs of patrons. The continuing influx exaggerated the widening conceptual gap between generalist artisans and those who presented themselves as artists. There was a rapid decline in the areas of overlap between the artisan who painted walls, coloured carvings, and carried out heraldic and decorative painting for installation in the complicated interior schemes of the richest patrons, and the artist, who painted free-hanging portraits, history pictures and landscapes. The redevelopment of Chirk Castle shows clearly how, although decorative schemes involving artisan work remained in fashion, the artist was taking the cream of the commissions. Artisans did not disappear, but their work became less highly esteemed. Indeed, at the end of the eighteenth century, the painter Edward Pugh would disparagingly group them under the heading 'sign painters', who followed 'the meanest, and lowest parts of the arts.' He regarded it as 'a question, indeed, whether they belong to them at all ...'[6]

The accounts of payments made to employees at Chirk provide detailed evidence of the differentiated roles of the artisan and the artist. In 1672, Sir Thomas Myddelton sent to Montgomery for Thomas Ffrancis, 'the herald painter', whose commissions were recorded by the castle accountant some four months later. He had been employed to carry out painting that ranged from the most basic decorative level up to sign painting:

> Paid Thomas ffrancis, the Herald Painter, for paintinge 119
> yards of wainscot in the draweinge room, at xviij^{d} p yard, 8 18 6
> Paid him for payntinge of 89 yards in the chambers in the newe
> Tower at xviij^{d} p yard, 6 13 6
> Paid him for Makeinge 3 landskips for 3 chimney peeces, one at the
> Draweinge roome, one at the red, and another at the blacke Chamber,
> in the newe Tower xij^{li} xs, & for the Bwll signe x^{s,} 8 0 0[7]

71. Thomas Ffrancis, *Orpheus Charming the Animals*, *Chirk Castle*, c.1672 oil, 111x165

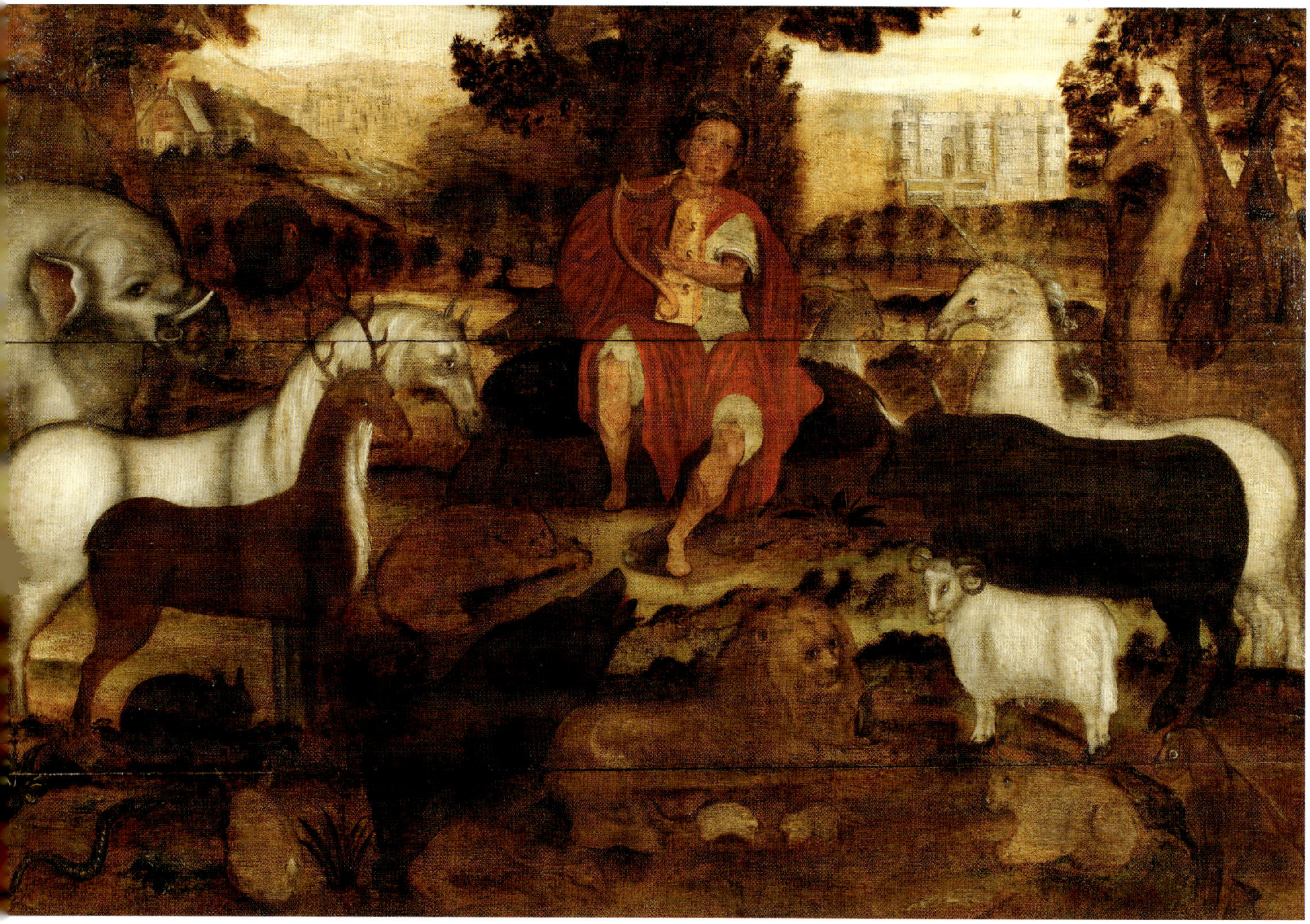

The 'landskips' painted by Thomas Ffrancis were not framed pictures to be hung wherever the patron chose, but permanently incorporated in the decorative scheme in the panelling above the fireplaces. A surviving painting of *Orpheus Charming the Animals*, set in woodland with the castle in the background, is likely to have been one of them.[8] In 1660, for a different type of client at the Drapers' Hall in Shrewsbury, Ffrancis had been employed to exercise a wider range of skills by painting a portrait of Edward IV with heraldry and inscriptions. A hundred years earlier, one of his herald predecessors might have been required also to paint the portrait of a living gentleman or lady, but times had changed. As Ffrancis worked at Shrewsbury, his employer at Chirk, Sir Thomas Myddelton, 2nd Baronet, repaired to London to have his portrait painted first by Peter Lely, the official painter at the Restoration court, and then by John Michael Wright, who was among the most celebrated of Lely's competitors – though Samuel Pepys did not have a high opinion of him. Curiously, at about the time that

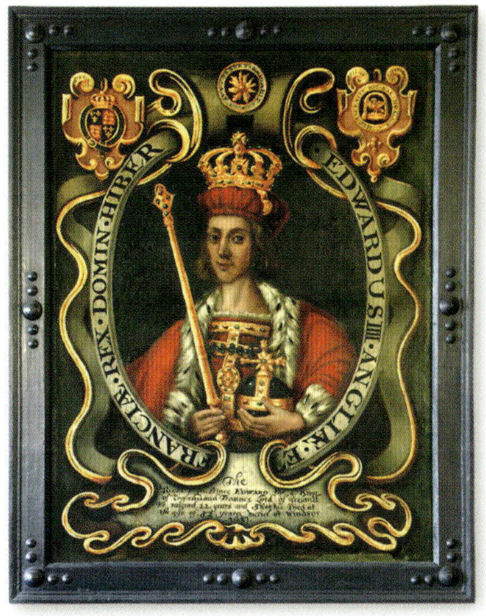

72. Thomas Ffrancis, *Portrait of Edward IV*, Drapers' Hall, Shrewsbury, 1660, oil, 130x99

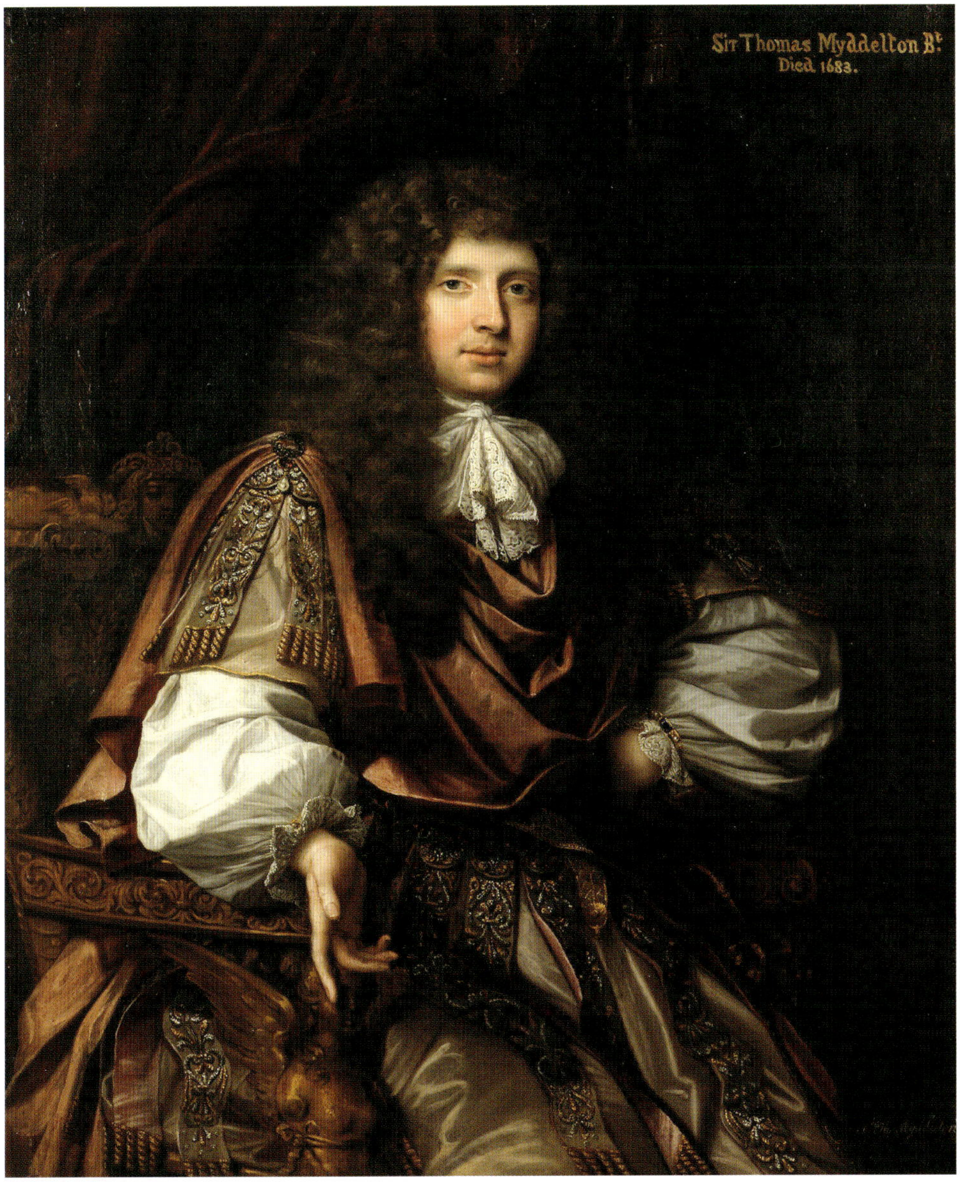

73. John Michael Wright, *Sir Thomas Myddelton, 2nd Baronet*, c.1670, oil, 126.5x109.5

7 *Chirk Castle Accounts (Continued) A.D. 1666–1735*, compiled by W.M. Myddelton (Horncastle, 1931), p. 95.

8 A second panel painting depicting *The Muse of Architecture* is also likely to be the work of Ffrancis, for which see Peter Lord, *The Visual Culture of Wales: Imaging the Nation* (Cardiff, 2000) p. 60.

74. Peter Tillemans, *Llangollen and the Dee Bridge*, 1720–30, oil, 96x172.5

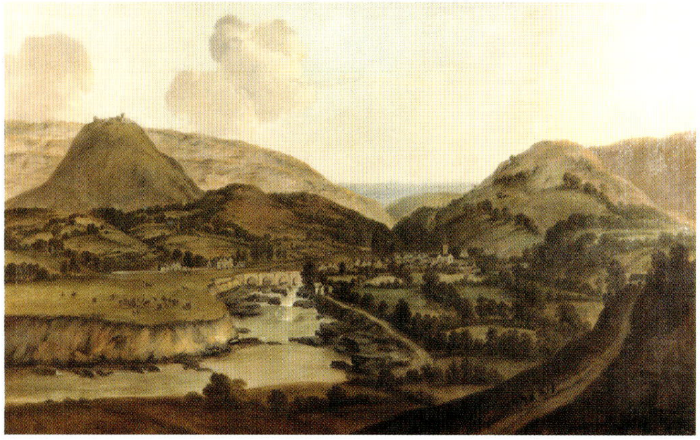

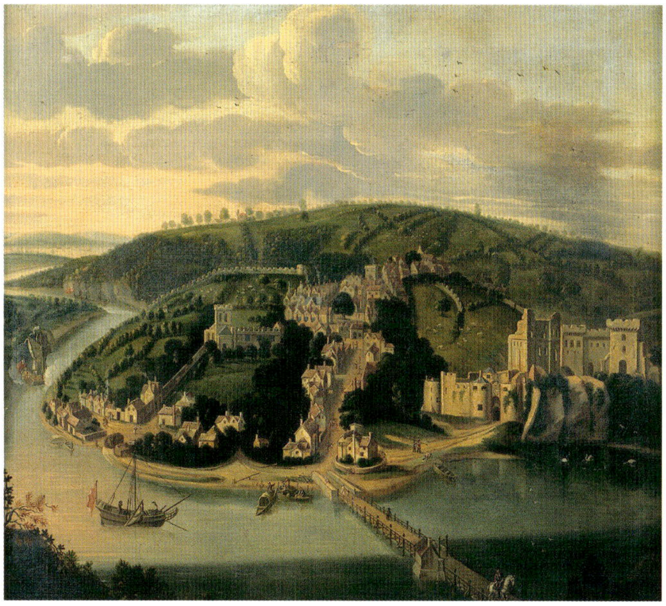

75. Thomas Smith, *Chepstow*, c.1680–90, oil, 61x71.1

Myddelton was sitting for the first portrait, one day in June 1662 Pepys called to view pictures in Lely's studio, of which he approved, then walked across London to inspect Wright's latest performances: 'Lord, the difference that is between their two works', he observed.[9] Perhaps Pepys did no more than repeat conventional snobbery by favouring the works of the more exotic foreigner. It was a powerful prejudice and the preference for continental painters continued into the early eighteenth century. In the 1720s, an Antwerp painter, Peter Tillemans, would be chosen to carry out both portrait and landscape commissions for Robert Myddelton, Sir Thomas's collateral descendent at Chirk. They included Castell Dinas Brân, which he owned.

Most of the landscape paintings commissioned by the Welsh gentry in the half century following the Restoration were notable for the conceptual contrast they made with portraits painted by Kneller, Lely and their metropolitan competitors. Hendrick Danckerts' landscape of Troy House was unusual in representing a continental modernity equivalent to that of the fashionable London portrait painters. The Dutch artist's patron, Henry Somerset, 3rd Marquess of Worcester, also commissioned a series of landscapes of his Welsh properties from the English painter Thomas Smith, and these were painted in a quite different manner. Somerset, lately become the 1st Duke of Beaufort, now viewed his properties from the perspective of his English house at Badminton, to which those treasures salvaged from the Civil War destruction of Raglan had been taken. A view of the ruined castle was among the pictures painted for him by Smith. Like the wider group of late seventeenth-century landscapes to which they belong, Smith's views depicted the world from an unnatural high angle, so that they might include all the details of buildings and everyday activities going on below – in the streets of Chepstow, for instance. Further west, the unknown painter of two views of Margam had employed the same map-like convention, revealing the full extent of the house and gardens, as well as much of the surrounding farm land, by taking north and south facing views. Both the Margam pictures included Sir Edward Mansel's summer banqueting house, newly 'built after ye Italian where regular simetrie Excellent sculpture delicate graving & an infinity

9 *The Diary of Samuel Pepys*, vol. III, pp. 112–13 (entry for 18 June 1662).

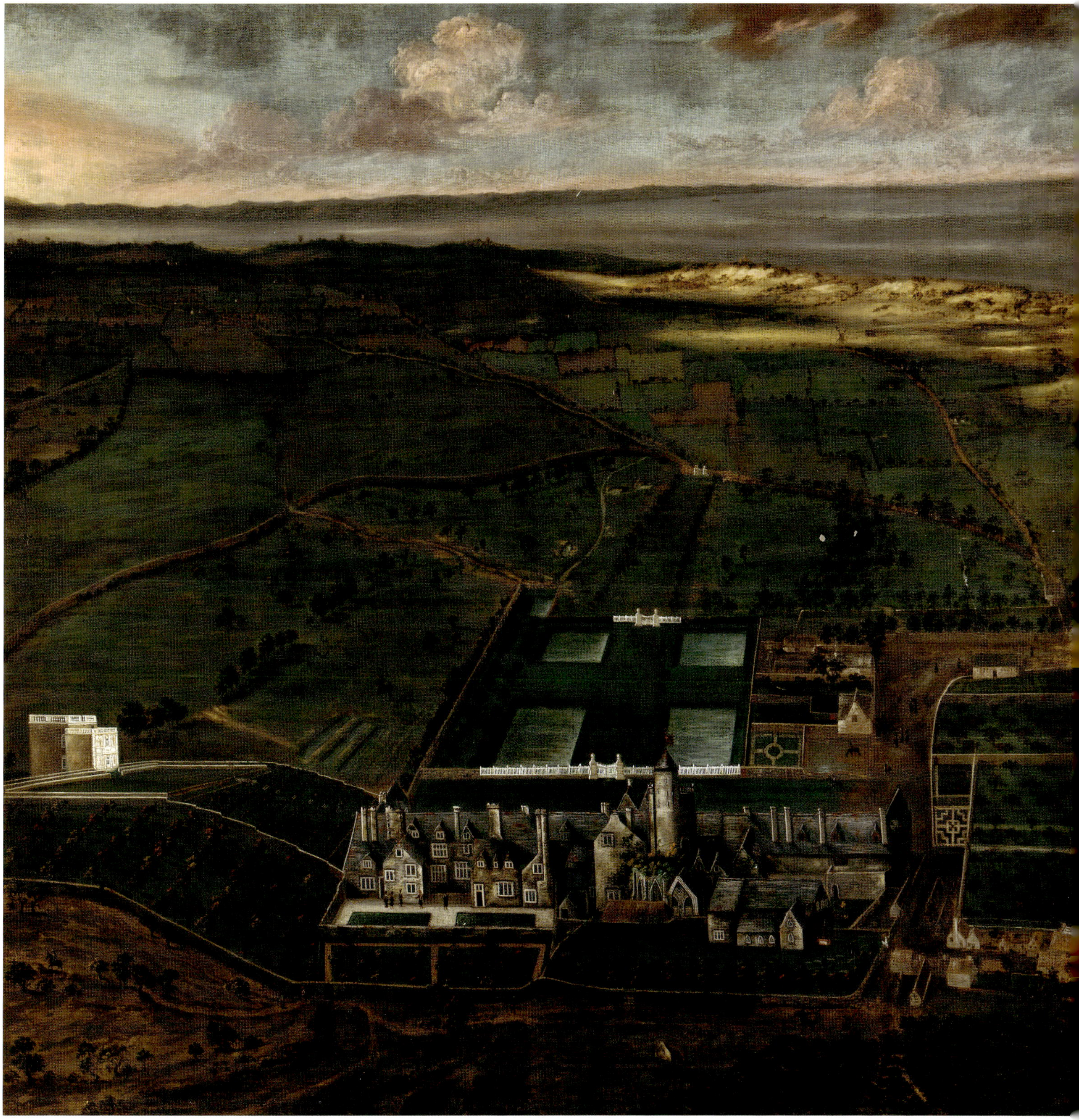

76. Unknown painter, *Margam House, Glamorgan, looking South*, c.1700, oil, 146x145

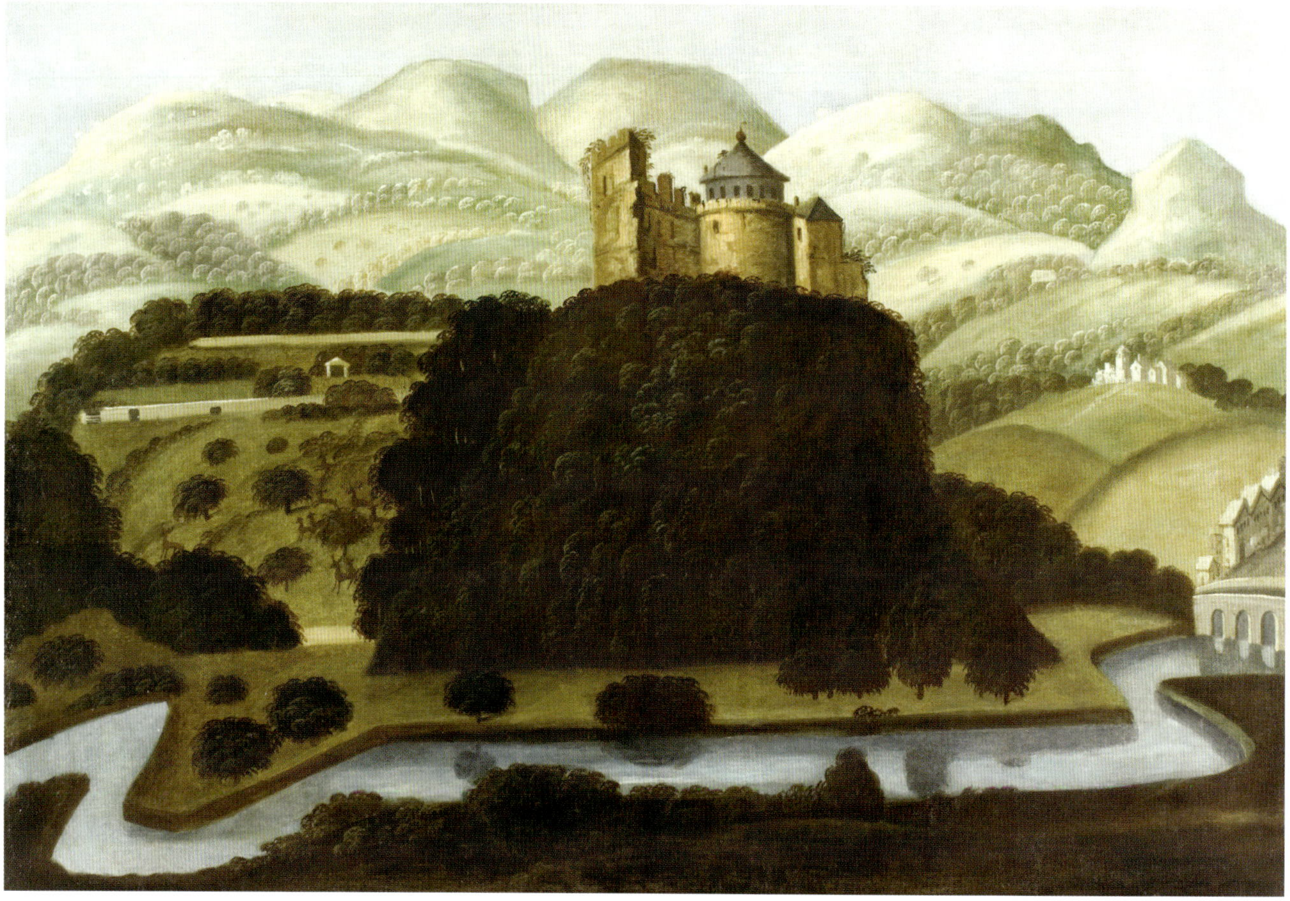

77. Unknown painter, *Dinefwr Castle from the South-West*, c.1700, oil, 83.8x124.5

of good Dutch and other paintings make a lustre not to be imagined'.[10] The Baroque symmetry of the summer house and its modern art collection contrasted strongly with the rambling Elizabethan building that had been home to the 1620s portrait of Sir Thomas and Jane Mansel.

The Margam landscapes, along with contemporary views of Llannerch in Denbighshire and Newton in Carmarthenshire, were essentially concerned with pride of possession, with wealth and prosperity. As its name indicates, Newton was a completely new house, though its builder, Edward Rice, who was portrayed strolling in the gardens in one of the pictures, also commissioned two views of his ancient castle of Dinefwr. In these, the castle stands out before rising ground in a landscape of a kind that would, in years to come, attract painters for its own sake, but in the late seventeenth century the naked hills were not the focus. As with the Duke of Beaufort's view of Raglan, dynasty was the subject matter of the Dinefwr pictures. Edward Rice was the direct descendent of Lord Rhys who, from the castle, had led Welsh resistance to the Norman invasion, five hundred years earlier.

10 Thomas Dineley, *The Account of the Official Progress of His Grace Henry the First Duke of Beaufort through Wales in 1684* (London, 1888), p. 313.

11 'Comsumlock' was Cwmsymlog, a few miles inland from Aberystwyth.

Restored dynasties, such as that of Dinefwr, which was still recovering from losses suffered as long ago as the reign of Henry VIII, were anxious to confirm their historical claim to power, but sterile mountain lands held little attraction for them. It was not to celebrate the beauty of the uplands of Ceredigion that an unidentified artist travelled to the far west in about 1670, but to illustrate the economic benefit of lead mining. Only by default did the artist produce the first views of what would later become celebrated as 'Wild Wales'. Alongside the tiny figures populating the urban landscapes of Thomas Smith, these depictions of *The Roman Works* and *Comsumlock Hill* also provided some of the earliest surviving representations of the common people of the country.[11]

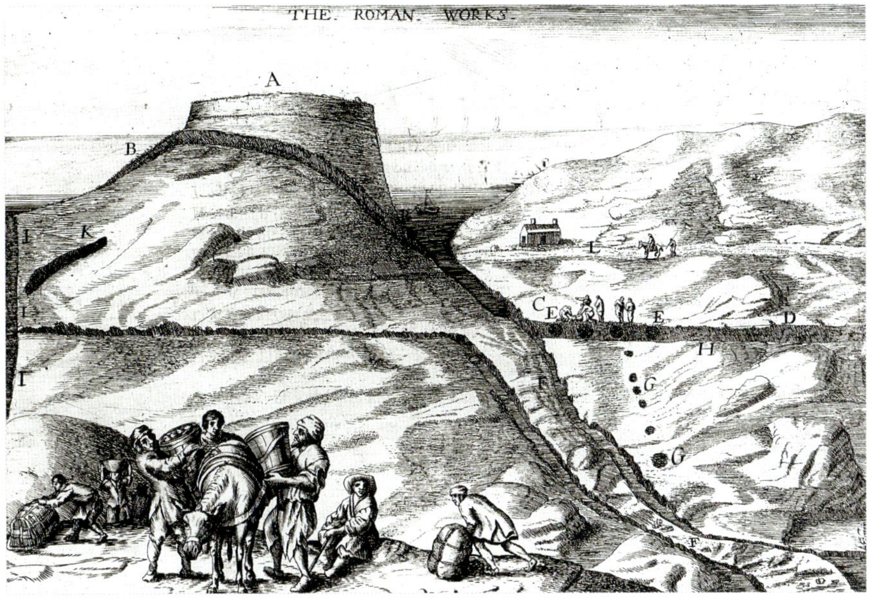

78. Unknown artist, *The Roman Works*, engraving, 17.3x26.3, from John Pettus, *Fodinae Regales*, 1670

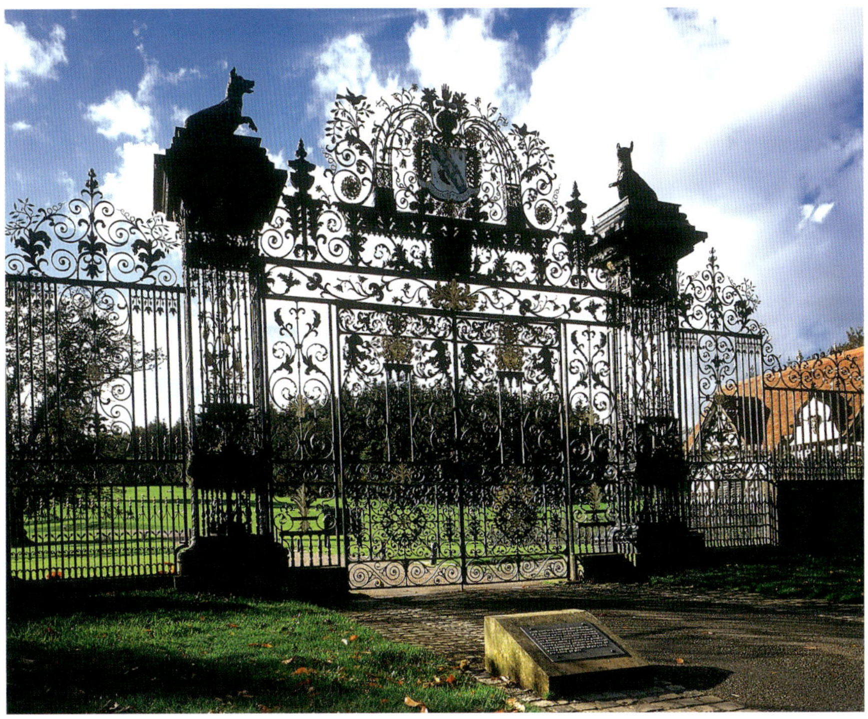

79. Robert and John Davies, *Gates at Chirk Castle*, 1712–19, wrought and cast iron

Among the jobs carried out by Thomas Ffrancis at Chirk was the colouring (for a shilling each) of 'Turke and blackeymore figures' on the staircase carved by Nicholas Needham. Facilitated by the patronage of the Myddelton family, such interactions continued into the early eighteenth century. Other improvements to the castle included the gates set up to enclose a courtyard before the entrance towers. When Peter Tillemans painted a prospect of the building in 1720 they were newly installed, though the finishing touch – a pair of statues depicting Hercules and Mars – would not arrive until the following year. The statues were made in London, but the impressive gates were the work

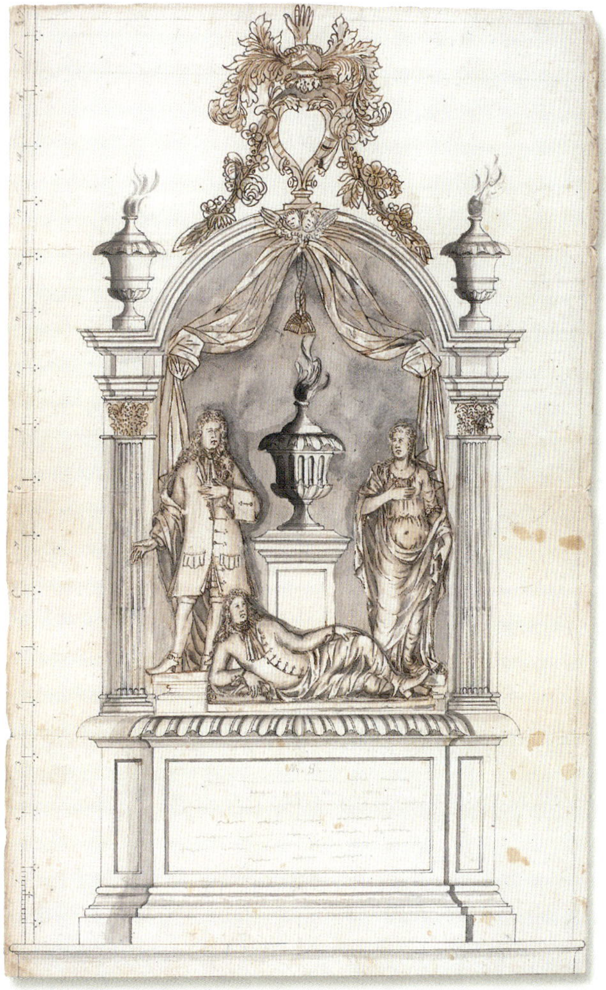

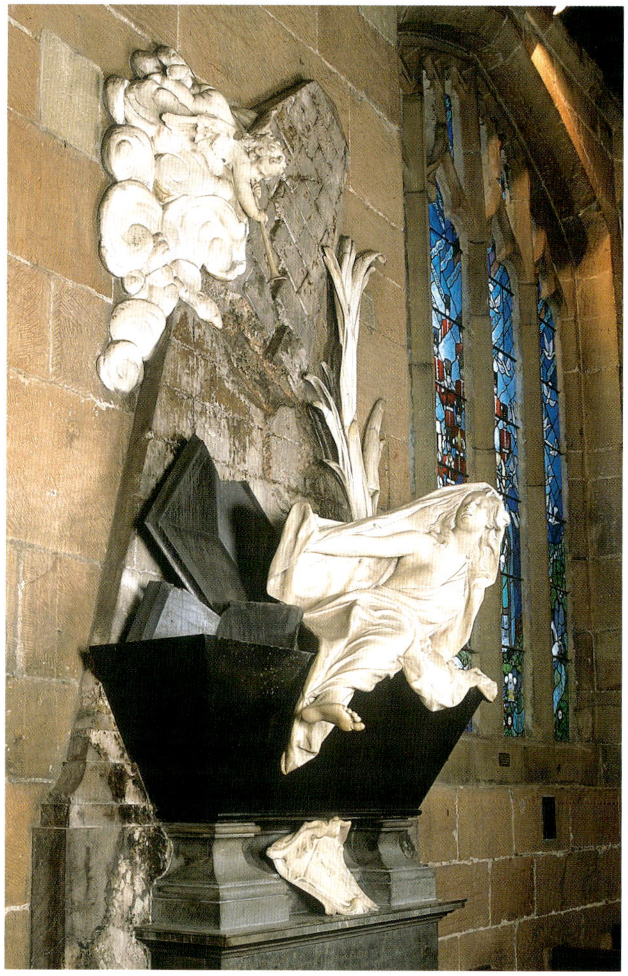

80. Robert Wynne, *Memorial to Richard Myddelton, 3rd Baronet*, Church of St Mary, Chirk, 1719, pen and wash, 46x28.5

above right
81. Louis-François Roubiliac, *Memorial to Mary Myddelton*, Church of St Giles, Wrexham, 1751–2, marble

of the Davies family business, that had been established at Croes Foel, near the Bersham ironworks, since the 1670s.[12] Helped by the Chirk commission, the brothers Robert and John Davies, sons of the founder of the business, would proceed to make equally imposing gates at Leeswood in Flintshire and at Eaton Hall, over the border in Cheshire. These were high status artefacts in this period, and it appears that the reputation of the Davies brothers may have gained them commissions as far south as Aldenham Park, beyond the centre of the English iron industry at Coalbrookdale. In addition to the use of wrought iron, their gates included cast elements, such as cherubs and small animals. In 1713, in the early stages of his influential commission at Chirk, Robert Davies had been supplied with a carved or modelled pattern for a casting of a bird by the sculptor Robert Wynne, whose workshop, 'the Elaboratory', was at Ruthin. Like the Davies family, Wynne would also soon become the beneficiary of Myddelton patronage. In 1719, he was commissioned by Mary

Myddelton to make a memorial to her father Richard, the 3rd Baronet (who commissioned the gates), her mother and her recently deceased brother William. The drawing survives, with a note in Wynne's hand:

> This is a draft picked upon by Agreement with the Honourable
> Madam Myddelton the 5th of May 1719 to be made & Erected
> in ye Church of Churk by me Robert Wynne.
> 17 foot high & 6 inches
> 8 Foot Broad
> All of Italian Marble.[13]

Robert Wynne was born in Dyffryn Clwyd in about 1655. He trained in London but seems to have returned to Wales by the early years of the new century.[14] The Myddelton memorial is one of three large scale commissions that he undertook, in addition to jobbing work such as carving fire surrounds and the pattern that he made for Robert Davies. Perhaps because of old age, his business failed in 1730 and he was incarcerated in a debtors' prison where he died the following year. Clearly, his Welsh work drew on his early metropolitan experience, reflecting the Baroque fashion of his youth for classical symmetry that presented to the world an image of protestant piety, of stability and substance. However, by the time of the death in mid-century of his patron, Mary Myddelton, fashions had changed. Her own memorial at Wrexham was commissioned from the French sculptor Louis-François Roubiliac, one of the leading London exponents of the more dynamic and florid Rococo style, which superseded the Baroque.

Gentry patronage in the first half of the eighteenth century reflected not only stylistic but also dynastic changes that would have important implications for visual culture in Wales. Anglicisation of various branches of the Herbert dynasty coincided with the steady rise at home of the Wynns of Wynnstay, at Ruabon. Through his mother (the great grand-daughter of Sir John Wynn of Gwydir) Watkin Williams, the 3rd Baronet, inherited estates that extended those of his father, a piece of good fortune that he celebrated by adding 'Wynn' to his name. He further enriched himself by marriage. Finding himself probably the wealthiest man in Wales, Sir Watkin challenged the Myddeltons for political domination of the north east. The machinations that ensued would attract the attention of the London satirists on several occasions. They based their caricatures of the Baronet on a series of increasingly impressive portraits that bore witness simultaneously to the expanding influence of the great man and to his expanding waistline. With the benefit of some fifty years' hindsight, Thomas Pennant, the antiquary from Downing in Flintshire, thought that 'His full wig and dress give a very disadvantageous idea of him ...', in the

12 The gates were later removed to a new site some distance from the castle, where they remain. For the Davies family, see Ifor Edwards, *The Davies Brothers Gatesmiths: 18th Century Wrought Ironwork in Wales* (Cardiff, 1977).

13 NLW Plas Power Papers, Box 12. Robert Wynne was paid £400 for the memorial.

14 He signed a tablet memorial to Sir Thomas Powell at Llanbadarn Fawr Church, near Aberystwyth, in 1707.

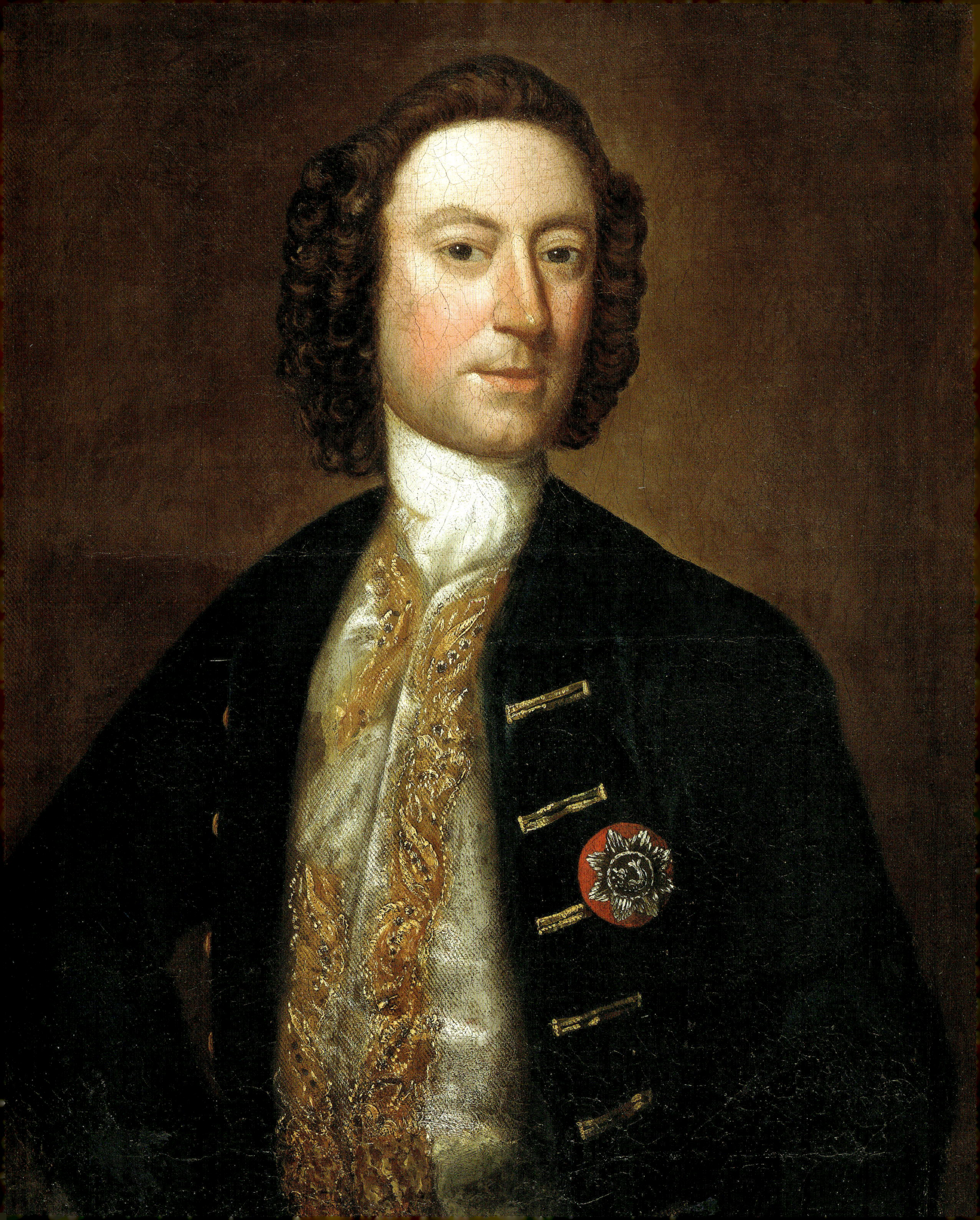

earliest picture. 'The fashion is equally the misfortune of the artist and his employer', he observed dryly.[15] Pennant, who had known Wynn, favoured a double portrait in the company of the Duke of Beaufort, inspecting a horse called Legacy, painted by John Wootton. An animal of this kind would be responsible for Sir Watkin's premature demise. In 1749, he fell while hunting, but before that unfortunate event, he had also been painted by Michael Dahl, by Allan Ramsay and by Thomas Hudson, an impressive list of contemporary top-drawer painters.

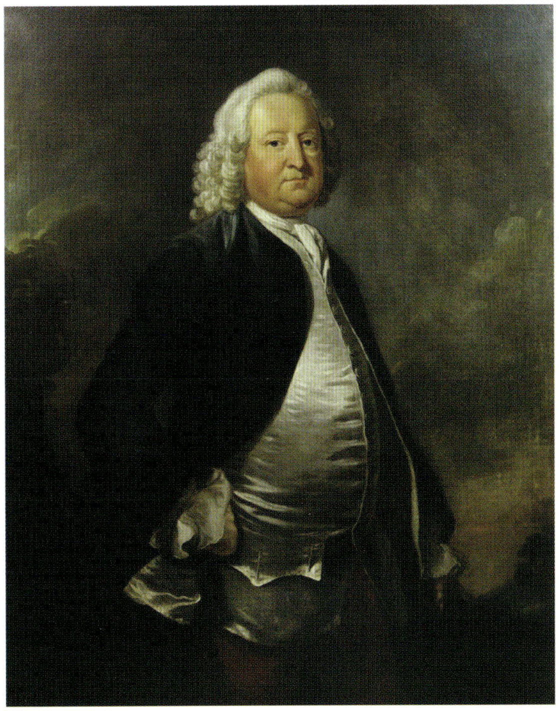

83. Thomas Hudson, *Sir Watkin Williams-Wynn*, c.1740, oil, 127x101.5

left
82. Robert Taylor, *Mansel Langdon, Sea Serjeant*, oil, 75.4x63

The rivalry between the Tory Wynns and the Whig Myddeltons expressed divisions rooted in the Civil Wars. Sir Watkin favoured the return of the Stuart monarchy to the English throne in the person of Charles Edward Stuart, 'the Young Pretender', and as the leading Welsh Jacobite, his portrait carried significance deeper than merely the image of a rich and powerful landowner. The Hudson picture exists in a number of versions that were in the possession of friends of a similar political persuasion. Sir Watkin was President of the 'Cycle of the White Rose', a Jacobite society that supported, at least in principal, the Scottish rising of 1745, though to what extent he would have afforded practical assistance had matters come to a head in Wales is debatable.[16] The use of visual imagery by Welsh Jacobites was most overtly expressed by a second society, known as the Sea Serjeants, whose insignia appears on a variety of artefacts, but most conspicuously to identify members in a series of 30 portraits commissioned in 1747 by Richard Gwynne of Taliaris, near Llandeilo in Carmarthenshire. The painter – presumably a fellow traveller, since his self-portrait was included in the series – was Robert Taylor. The series must have dominated the walls of Gwynne's fashionable Palladian-style house, and remained prized family heirlooms. Many years later, as an old woman, his daughter Elizabeth, who had inherited the title of President, was described 'sitting at the head of her table, in a fine old hall which was entirely surrounded with the portraits ...[17]

15 Thomas Pennant, *Tours in Wales*, ed. John Rhys (Caernarfon, 1883), vol. I, p. 373. Pennant thought this portrait, like another that he saw at Wynnstay, to be the work of Michael Dahl, but this is unlikely.

16 Hudson was a close friend of Louis-François Roubiliac, the sculptor chosen by the Myddeltons for the memorial to Mary Myddelton at Wrexham. He might have been the obvious choice to memorialise Sir Watkin also, and it may be that the decision to commission John Michael Rysbrack was governed by the rivalry between the families. Sir Watkin's memorial in the church at Ruabon is a considerably more sober affair than that at Wrexham.

17 By this time the family had moved from Taliaris to Tregib. Mary Morgan, *A Tour to Milford Haven in the year 1791* (London, 1795), pp. 373–5.

The emergence of Welsh art practice

Among the many pictures at Taliaris was a second portrait of Richard Gwynne, along with companion portraits of his wife and three of their children, including Elizabeth, inheritor of the presidency of the Sea Serjeants.[18] The pictures were painted in about 1736–7 by John Lewis, who at about the same time painted also for Sir John Pryce of Newtown a small celebration of his marriage to Mary Morris, and larger portraits of Sir John's daughters by his first wife.[19] He would return to Newtown 15 years later to paint one of them, Diana, for a second time, on this occasion in the guise of Diana the Huntress. Between these commissions, he painted portraits for the Vaughan family of Golden Grove and Derwydd in Carmarthenshire, and many others. It is unclear where Lewis was born, though his patrons and his name clearly suggest at least strong Welsh connections.

84. John Lewis, *Elizabeth Gwynne of Taliaris*, c.1736–7, oil, 102x65

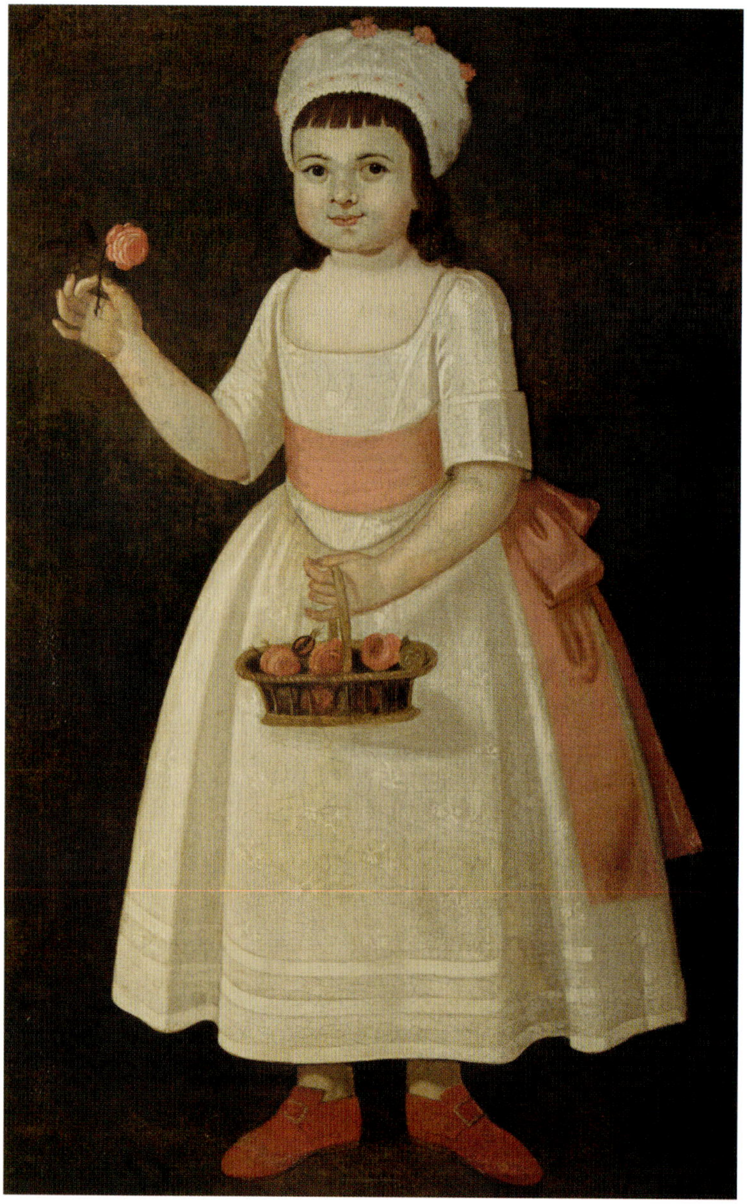

In the late 1740s and early 1750s he worked periodically also in Ireland, but it was in Wales that Lewis's career was of most significance, as the earliest sustained portrait practice of which we have detailed knowledge.[20] Along with the slightly earlier career of the sculptor Robert Wynne, it signifies the emergence of an expectation that it might be possible for an artist (rather than an artisan) to make a career on the basis of gentry patronage inside Wales. Furthermore, the development of his Welsh practice in the 1730s coincided with the emergence of three portrait painters who were certainly Welsh-born, though they all trained in London. John Dyer went to the metropolis in 1720, Edward Owen went in 1725, and Richard Wilson in 1729. Dyer and Owen came from minor gentry families in Carmarthenshire and Anglesey, and Wilson, who was born at Penegoes in Montgomeryshire, had gentry connections in the north-east of Wales through both his mother and father.

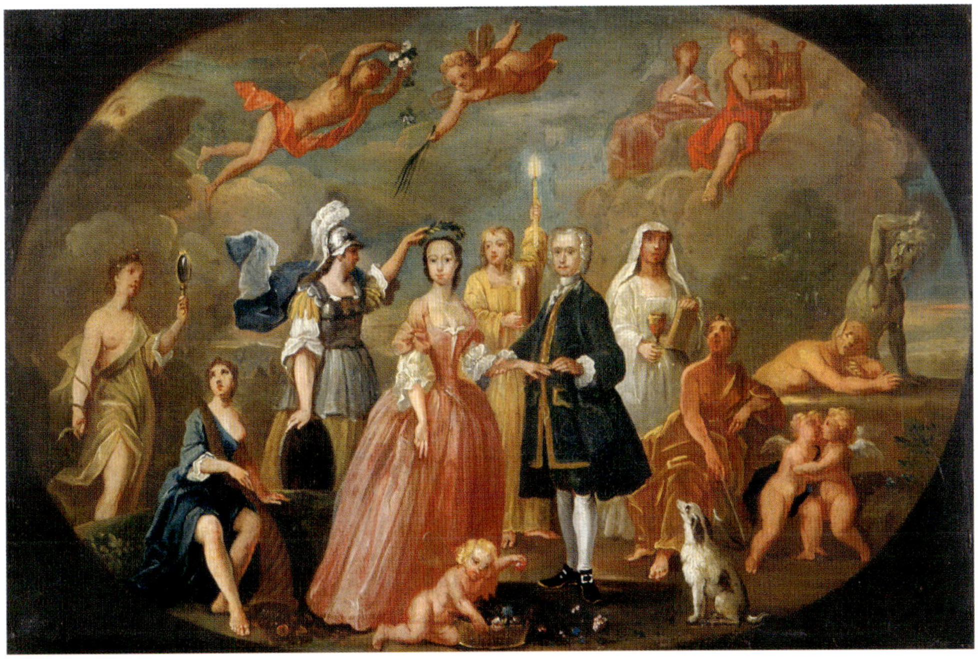

85. John Lewis, *The Marriage of Sir John Pryce of Newtown*, 1737, oil, 40.6x62.2

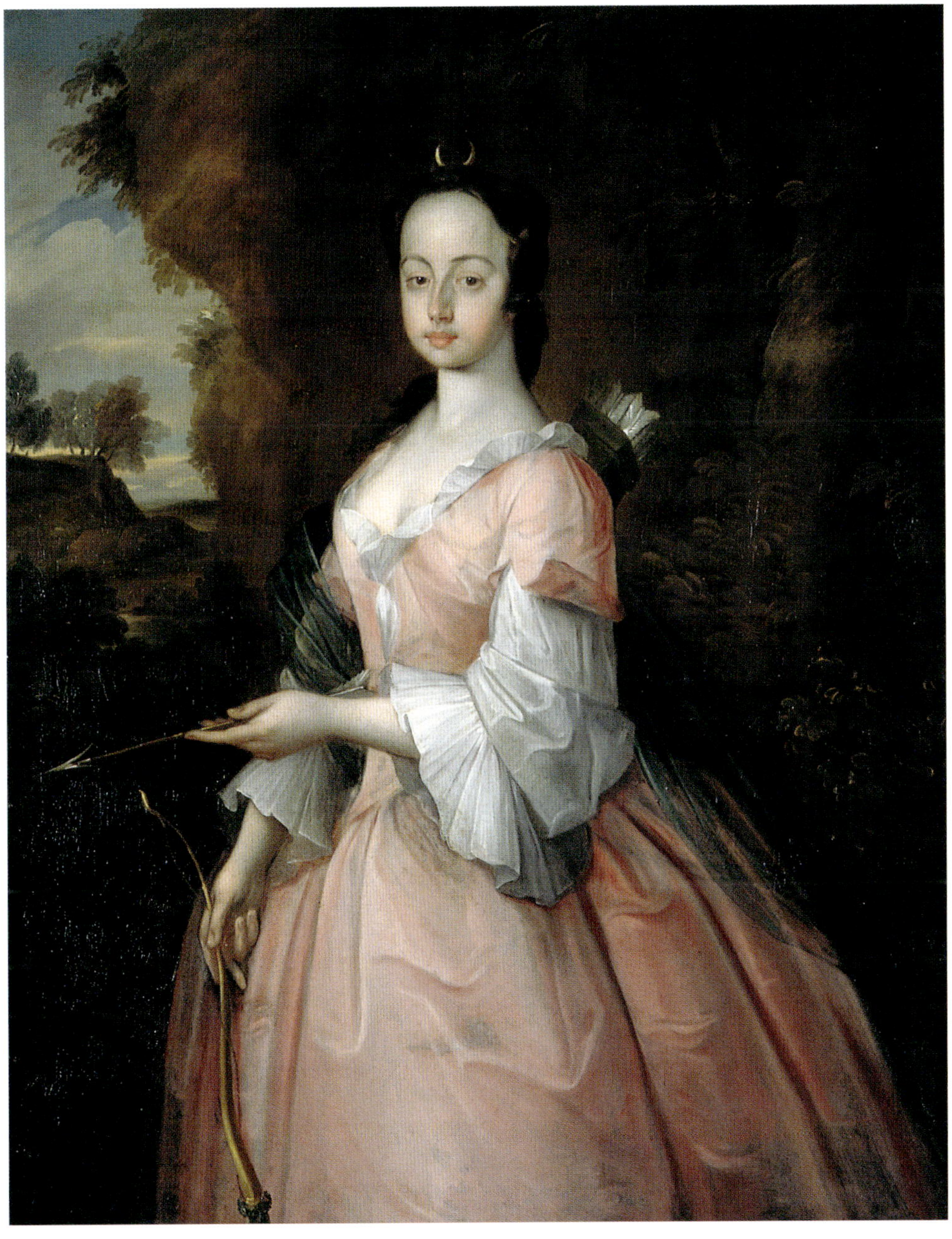

86. John Lewis, *Diana Pryce with the attributes of the Goddess Diana*, 1752, oil, 127.3x101.2

18 Noted by Joseph Gulston in 1785 and quoted in Francis Jones, 'Portraits and Pictures in Old Carmarthenshire Houses', *The Carmarthenshire Historian*, vol. V (1968), pp. 43–66.

19 Anna Elizabeth and Diana. The portrait of Anna Elizabeth was posthumous, though it may have been begun while she was alive. Her father was a curious individual, for whom see Peter Lord, *The Meaning of Pictures: Images of Personal, Social and Political Identity* (Cardiff, 2009), pp. 17–18.

20 Ibid., pp. 10–51.

The 1720s marked something of a turning point in professional practice in England also, as the increasing number of English names among the most prominent painters of the day in London suggests. A reaction against continental domination of the art market had begun, one of the leaders of which was John Dyer's master. In 1719, Jonathan Richardson had published *An Essay on the Whole Art of Criticism as it relates to Painting*, a text that would have a considerable influence both on ideas about the meaning of pictures and the status of the artists who painted them. In a letter dated 1727, Dyer's contemporary, Edward Owen expressed his frustration with his own master, Thomas Gibson, and made it clear that Richardson's portraits now represented the benchmark of quality.[21] Although Owen's career as a painter in his own right would be very brief, he left two important legacies. The first was the earliest known self-portrait painted by a Welsh artist – and it is, perhaps, significant that Richardson, whom he so much admired, was a prolific self-portraitist.[22] Owen's second legacy was a large body of letters written to members of his family that describe his training as a painter between 1725 and 1732 in Covent Garden, the hub of the metropolitan art world. Among the many aspects of the life of an apprentice upon which the letters throw light is the gentrification of the profession in the period. In sending him to London from Penrhos, near Holyhead, Owen's mother had been of the old-fashioned opinion that her son Ned would acquire 'a Good Honest Trade'. However, he soon discovered that it was necessary to cut a fashionable figure by, for instance, wearing ruffles on his shirts, like everybody 'that was anything genteel, and not one face painter Prentice but what did, especially my Master being one of the greatest I should go [a] litle tydy and clean'. The financial implications for a family of relatively limited means were worrying:

> There died about 4 months ago a famous History Painter whose paintings and drawings were last week sold by Auction and my master bought me some of his academy figures which were reckned the best that ever were drawn, which I now draw after. Mrs Lloyd's Landlord married this painters maid who proved a good fortune to him left her by her master which was about 1500 pound and as people say for standing naked to him to paint after, and for other favours. I find my business vastly expensive to what I thought it would be when I was first bound, theres not a week passes but it costs me above eighteen pence only in pens pencils chalks blew brown and white paper, besides what it costs me in things to coppy after as drawings prints and plaster figures. My Master tells me it will yearly cost me 10 pound in my business, it is not meerly coppying makes a painter but seeing and buying great masters performances, and minding where in one excell'd, here in another. Tho' master is the best Drawer in England, as allow'd by every one, yet he lays out above 40 or 50 pound a year in drawings.[23]

87. Edward Owen, *Self-portrait*, 1732, oil, 72.5x61

21 Along with those of John Vanderbank who, notwithstanding his name, was born in London and made his career there. Peter Lord, *Relationships with Pictures: an Oblique Autobiography* (Cardigan, 2013), pp. 249–50.

22 Richardson's pupil John Dyer also painted a self portrait in the 1730s, though unlike Owen he did not identify himself as a painter by including in the picture the tools of his trade. The whereabouts of a Wilson self-portrait of c.1735 is currently unknown.

23 Archives and Welsh Library, Bangor University, Penrhos Papers, I, item 997, quoted with other extracts from the letters of Edward Owen in Lord, *Relationships with Pictures*, pp. 241–58. The 'history painter' was perhaps Godfrey Kneller, better known now as a portraitist, who in fact had died in 1723.

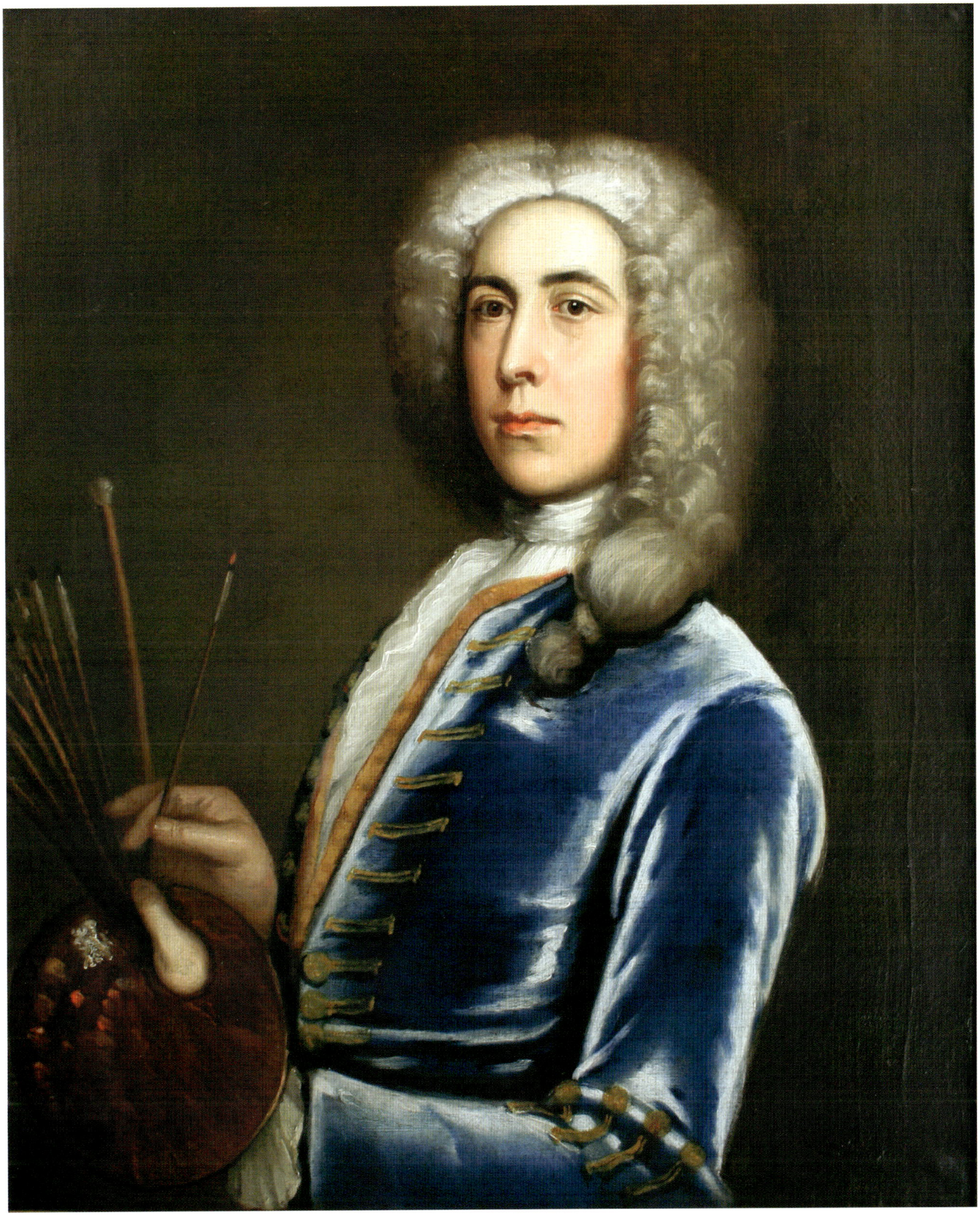

88. Richard Wilson, *John Jones of Pentre Mawr, Abergele*, 1738, oil, 74.5x62.5

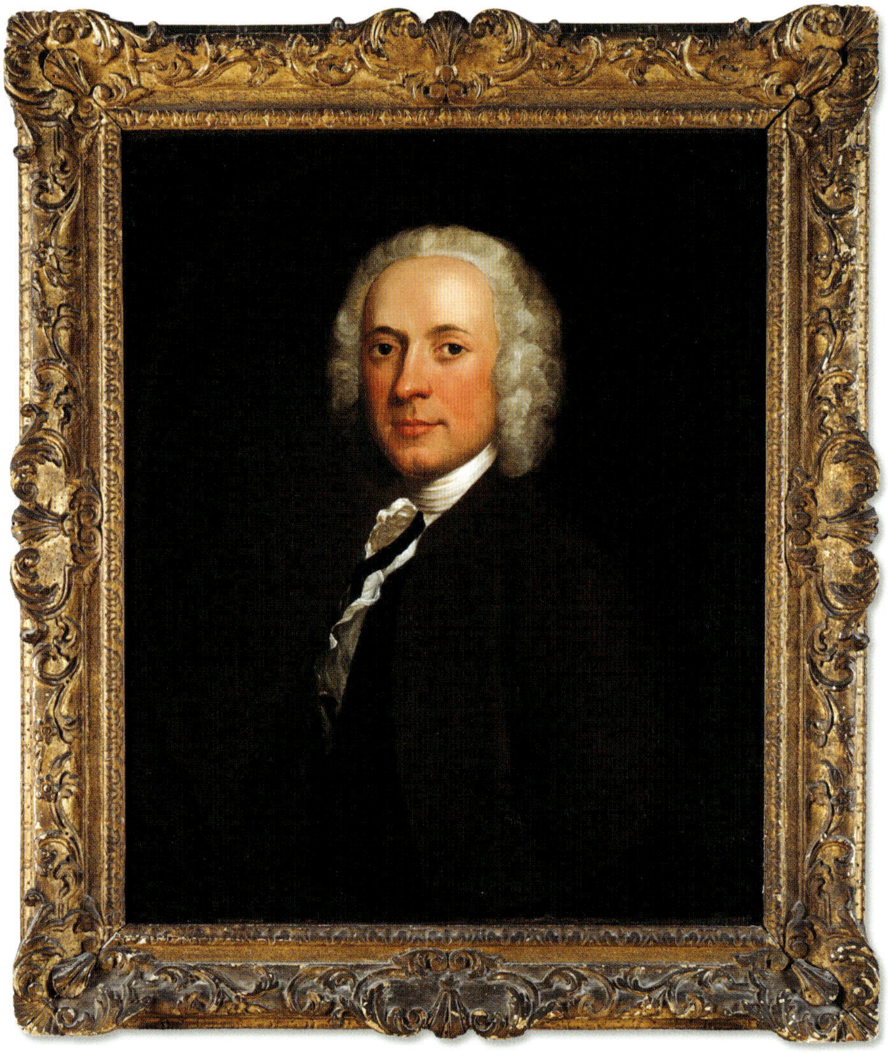

Sadly, in his letters, Ned Owen made no mention of the arrival of his fellow countryman Richard Wilson in Covent Garden in 1729. Wilson went to the studio of Thomas Wright, a less celebrated figure than Gibson or Richardson, but there is no reason to suppose that his experiences as an apprentice there differed greatly from those of Ned Owen. However, nothing is heard of him again until 1734, when he was in Wales taking the portrait of Hugh Jones of Pentre Mawr, Abergele. The Jones family were almost certainly family friends, and four years later, Wilson painted Hugh's younger brother, John – but, significantly, also in 1738 he painted the more elevated personage of John Myddelton at Chirk Castle.[24] By the mid-1740s Wilson had gained the patronage of the Lyttelton family of Worcestershire, and through them access to the fringes of the court. He was commissioned to paint Dr Francis Ayscough (who had married a Lyttelton) in the company of the princes Edward Augustus and George (the future George III) to whom he was tutor. Perhaps also through the Lytteltons he gained access to Flora MacDonald, incarcerated in the Tower of London for the assistance she had given the Young Pretender to escape following the Battle of Culloden in 1746. Wilson's portrait of her, dressed in tartan, would become an icon of Scottish identity but, given the strong Whig associations of his family, it is unlikely that this image indicated Jacobite leanings on the part of the painter. In London, far removed from the failed Scottish rising, MacDonald was probably presented in tartan to the fashionable world as a curiosity. Nevertheless, a second portrait, the background of which shows the boat in which Charles Stuart, disguised as a woman, fled to the Isle of Skye against the setting sun of the Jacobite claims, clearly evokes romantic Stuart fantasies.[25]

24 See Peter Lord, *Richard Wilson: Life and Legacy* (Conwy, 2009), p. 11. W.G. Constable, *Richard Wilson* (London, 1953), p. 20, incorrectly states that this portrait was of Robert Myddelton, which cannot be, as Robert died in 1733.

25 Wilson would later benefit from the patronage of the Jacobite Wynns of Wynnstay. The face of MacDonald in the second picture (National Portrait Gallery, London) is apparently based on the tartan portrait. MacDonald was also painted by Hudson at this time.

89. Richard Wilson, *Flora MacDonald*, 1747, oil, 117x93.3

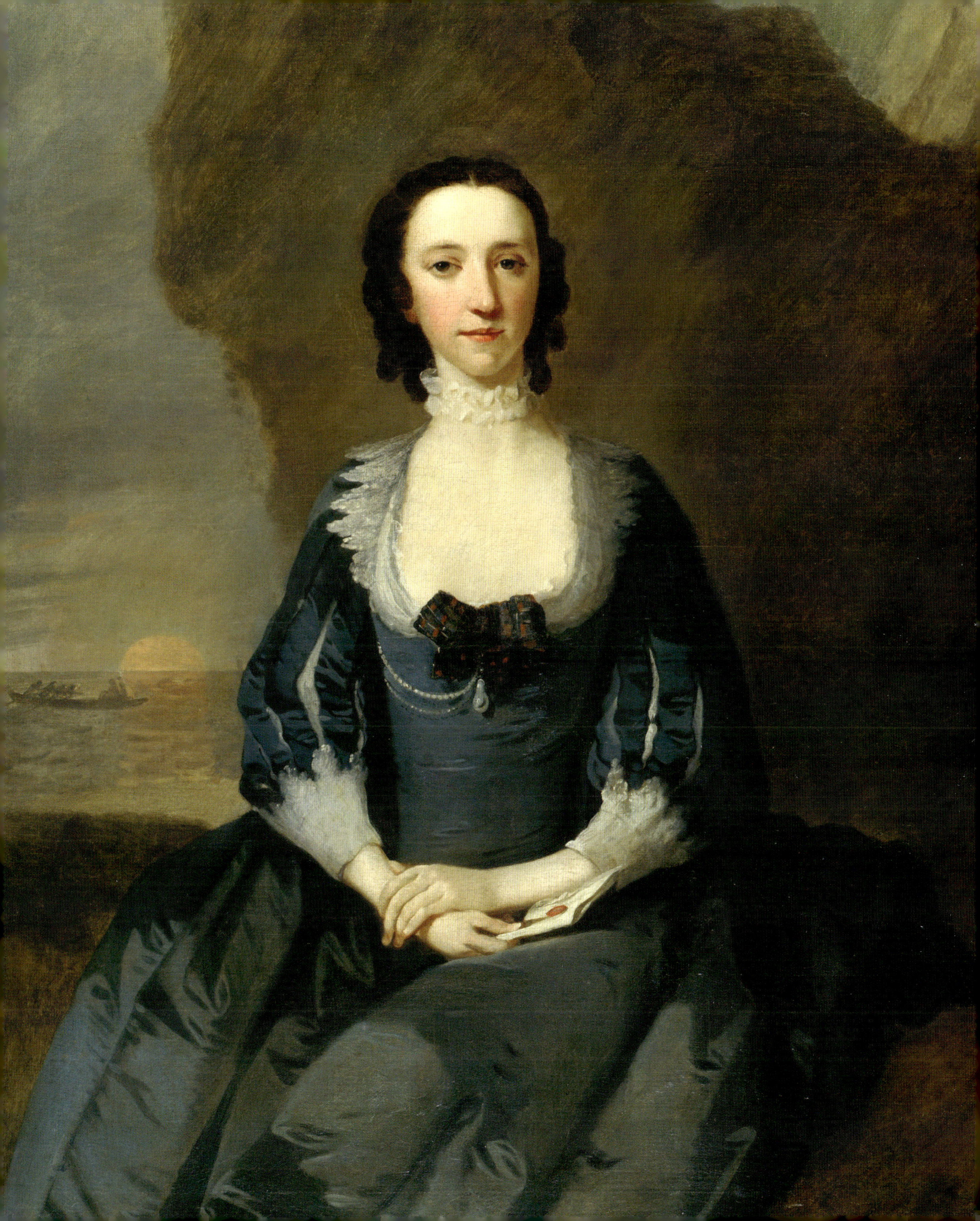

26 If the story is based in fact, the horse must have belonged to Robert Vaughan, the 1st Baronet (1723–1792), rather than to his son, Robert Williams Vaughan. It is reported in *Bye-Gones relating to Wales and the Border Counties*, new series, XIII, p. 18 (26 February 1913). I am grateful to Thomas Lloyd for this reference.

27 The oral tradition was recorded in 1888, in a pamphlet written by Robert Isaac Jones (Alltud Eifion) that included an engraving. The essay describes how John was well treated, married a local woman and had seven children. No doubt the positive gloss placed on the unsavoury incident of the kidnapping of the child was influenced by abolitionist guilt. Several instances are recorded in which the faces of African servants were painted out of portraits of white gentry sitters following the abolition of slavery.

28 Blackburn had earlier painted Thomas and Elizabeth Hughes, prominent townspeople in Cheltenham, but Thomas's father and grandfather had both been agents to the Morgan family, so presumably this commission was related to the Hugh Jones portrait.

29 Nearby, at Gwaenynog, another unidentified artisan painted a group portrait of servants below stairs celebrating the coming of age of Richard Myddelton in 1785. The painter explained the cause of the toasting both with an inscribed illustration of the Chirk Castle gatehouse, pinned to the wall, and by means of a short verse in *englyn* form in praise of the young man, inscribed in the archaic manner of the seventeenth century. A second coming of age picture, painted two years later in celebration of Myddelton's neighbour, Robert Williams Wynn, was painted by the same artisan, and also included an *englyn*.

A curious story, noted in the early twentieth century, concerns Wilson painting a portrait of the favourite horse of Sir Robert Williames Vaughan of Nannau.[26] The story may be apocryphal, but not necessarily so, since a tradition of equestrian portraits was emerging that would, later in the eighteenth century (as gentry interest in agricultural improvement deepened), extend to the commission of paintings of prize farm stock. Such work was usually given not to established portrait painters of high status, but less celebrated individuals who developed careers of a more generalist nature that included this sort of picture. Sir Robert Williames Vaughan is supposed to have presented the equine portrait to his butler, Hugh Jones, and indeed some gentry patrons were also inclined to commission portraits of particularly trusted or interesting servants. For instance, imperial expansion in the seventeenth and eighteenth centuries gave rise to a fashion for acquiring African servants. In the mid-1740s, presumably in west Africa, a member of the Wynne family of Ystumllyn kidnapped a young boy and brought him home. Known simply as John or Jack, he settled in Eifionydd, initially in the family's service at Ystumllyn, and became sufficiently celebrated to be painted in 1754.[27]

In 1777, Sir Charles Morgan, of Tredegar House and Ruperra, commissioned a portrait of Hugh Jones, for fifty years the family agent. Jones sat for his portrait at a desk on which estate account books identified his employer and the nature of the sitter's work. The painter, Joseph Blackburn, had developed his career in the United States, where he was a figure of some influence in colonial period portraiture.[28] At about the same time, at Chirk, an unidentified but clearly artisan-trained painter portrayed the castle scullion, John Wilkes, who was an individual of sufficient repute to become the subject of at least one other portrait.[29] Beneath the surface of well-documented high art patronage, gentry houses had continued to provide jobbing work for artisan painters. The Chirk pictures signal the occasional re-emergence of such artisans

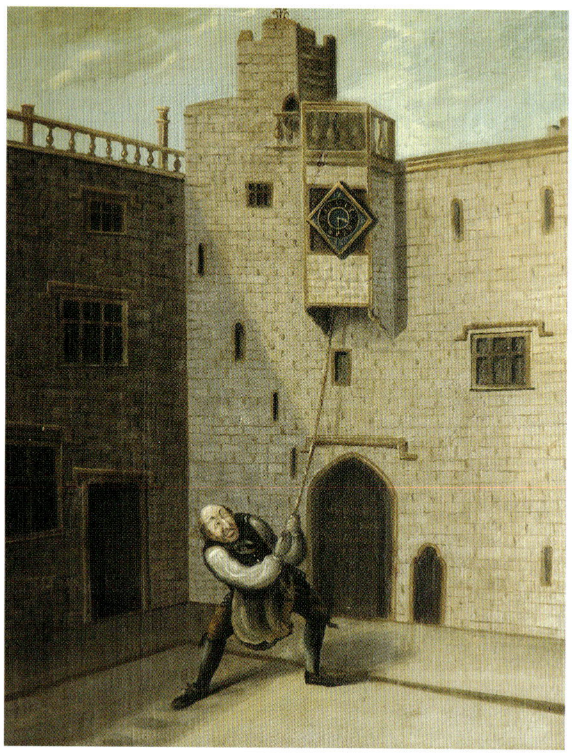

90. Unknown painter, *Welch Wilkes, the Chirk Castle Scullion*, c.1730-50, oil, 56x47

opposite
91. Joseph Blackburn, *Hugh Jones, Morgan Family Agent*, 1777, oil, 128.3x102.2

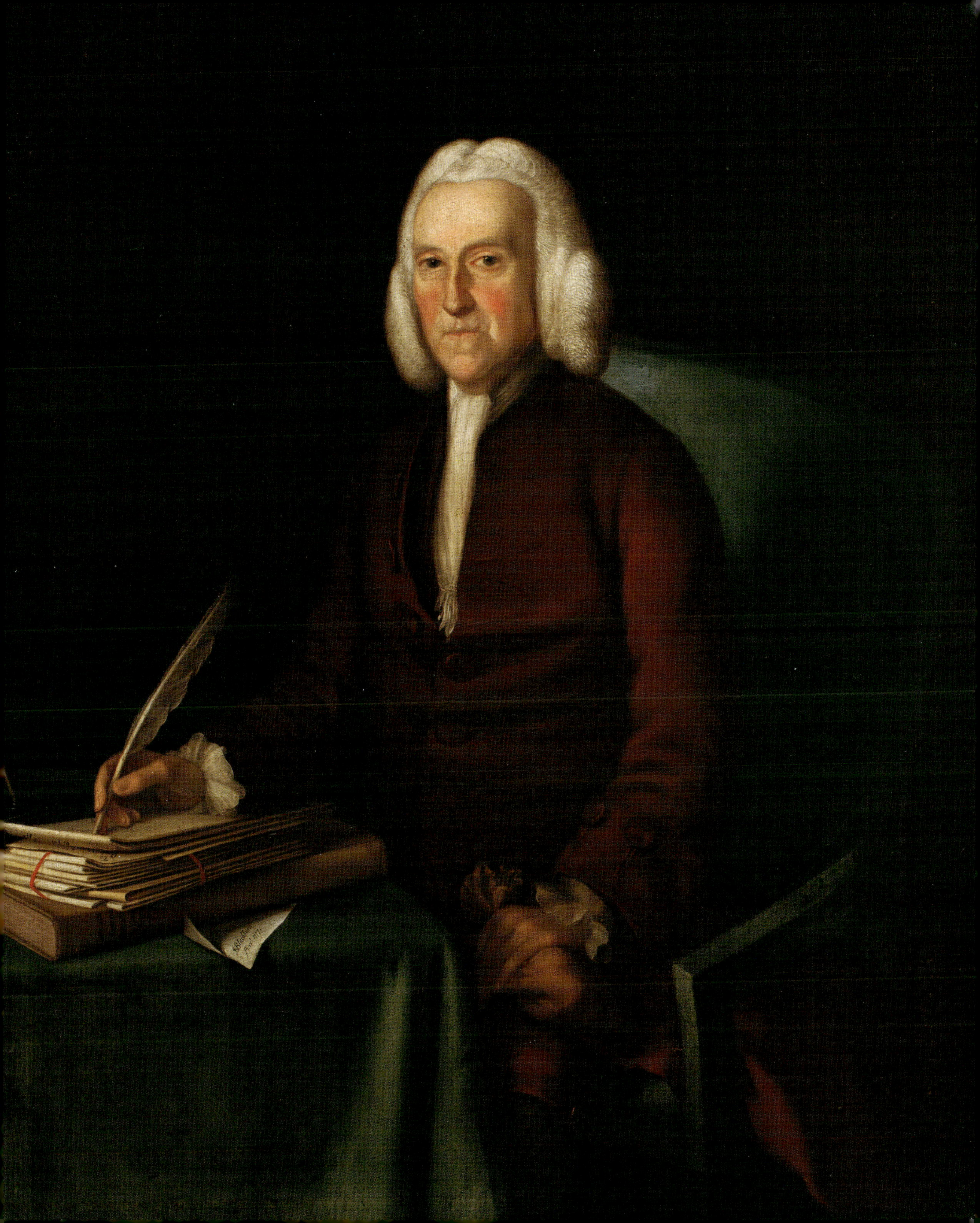

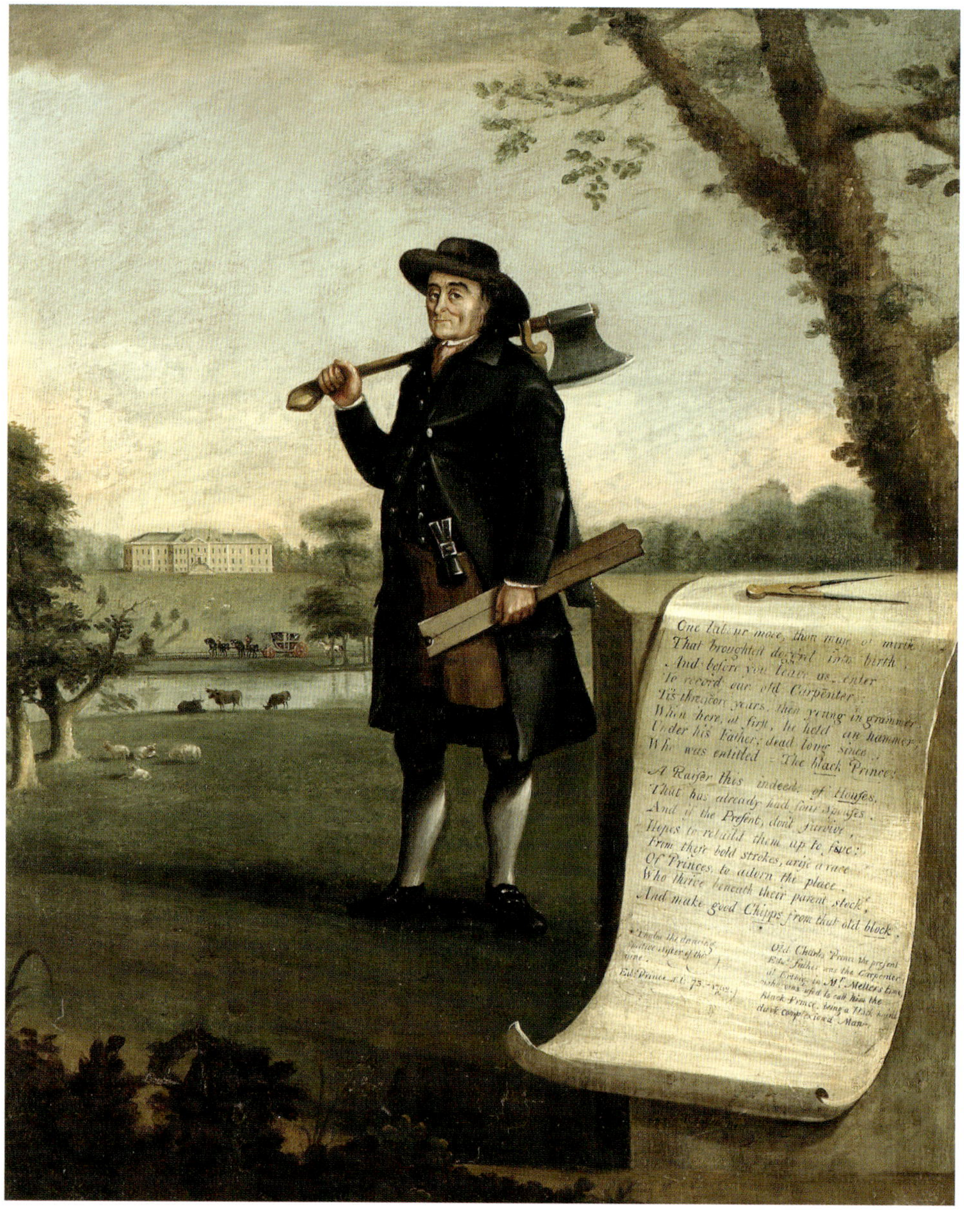

92. John Walters, *Edward Prince, Carpenter at Erddig, Aged 73*, 1792, oil, 113.5x93.5

in portraiture. The most ambitious eighteenth-century series of this type was painted by John Walters of Denbigh, and depicted six servants and tradespeople associated with the Erddig estate of Philip Yorke. They were painted for Yorke between 1791 and 1796, and all included verses describing the sitters, written by this gentleman patron – who, for his own portrait, travelled to London to sit to Thomas Gainsborough. Like his seventeenth-century artisan predecessor, Thomas Ffrancis, recorded in the Chirk Castle accounts, John Walters found work with gentry patrons over a wide area. In 1780, he was reported at Peniarth, near Dolgellau.[30]

30. The informant was Elizabeth Baker, for whom see Ben Bowen Thomas, *The Old Order, based on the Diary of Elizabeth Baker*, (Cardiff, 1945). For the divergence of 'polite' painting from the work of artisans, see James Ayres, *Art, Artisans and Apprentices* (Oxford, 2014).

Although Richard Wilson's reputation was established by the mid-eighteenth century as a portrait painter, he had also painted some landscapes. After 1750, he all but abandoned portrait painting in favour of landscape, a move that – although it was undertaken in Italy – would come to have profound implications for the perception of Wales both inside and outside the country.

In about 1538, near Whitland in Carmarthenshire, the English antiquarian John Leland had complained of 'meane hills and dales' slowing his journey to Pembroke. Further north, in Ceredigion, he observed that 'The ground all about Tyve, and a great mile toward Stratfler is horrible with the sighte of bare stones, as Cregeryri mountains be'.[31] Daniel Defoe, on a similar fact-finding tour nearly two centuries later, remained of much the same opinion, writing in the 1720s of disagreeable 'Rocks and Precipices', which caused him and his companions 'to repent our Curiosity' to cross the Black Mountain.[32] However, Defoe was in his sixties by this time, an old man by contemporary standards, and somewhat out of touch with a changing perception of landscapes 'unimproved' by the hand of man that was beginning to emerge. As early as 1709, the Earl of Shaftesbury considered the wilderness as having 'a Magnificence beyond the formal mockery of Princely Gardens'.[33] Through the subsequent writings of Joseph Addison and Edmund Burke, a positive perception of mountainous landscape, defined as 'sublime', replaced the negativity of the past, and with it a fascination with all awe-inspiring wonders of nature, such as great cataracts. The admirers of the 'sublime' distinguished the emotions it aroused in them from the gentler 'beautiful', which might be experienced, for instance, in contemplation of a pastoral scene.

As the product of a new generation, this change of perception may be understood in part as a rejection of the constraints, so apparent in the Baroque style in all the arts, that expressed a formality of manners and a utilitarian attitude to economic development in the age of expanding trade. The worldly pragmatism and political cynicism of the likes of Defoe bred a reactive fashion for meditation upon deeper things, manifested not only in attitudes to the natural world but also to the relics of human activity in ages past. Periods of rapid economic development tend to manifest a compensatory interest in the signs of the world left behind, in the minds of those at leisure to consider such matters. Entangled in the turn to untamed nature was a growing antiquarianism, which had both strong metaphysical connotations and a contemporary political dimension that made it doubly attractive to the ruling class. In a profoundly materialist age, the motif of the ruined castle, set in a landscape devoid of more recent human interventions, replaced the *momento mori*,

31 Lucy Toulmin Smith, *The Itinerary on Wales of John Leland*, Part VI, pp. 115, 121. 'Stratfler' is Strata Florida and 'Cregeryri' (Craig Eryri) is Snowdonia, which he had earlier experienced.

32 Daniel Defoe, *A Tour thro' the Whole Island of Great Britain* (London, 1725), p. 81.

33 Anthony Ashley Cooper, 3rd Earl of Shaftsbury, 'The Moralists, a Philosophical Rhapsody', in idem *Characteristicks of Men, Manners, Opinions, Times* (3 vols., 5th ed., London, 1732), II, pp. 393–4.

so commonly deployed in sixteenth- and seventeenth-century portraiture as a reminder of human transience.[34] At the same time, mercantile and political pragmatists found in the ruins of medieval castles an equivalent history to that called to mind by the ruins of the classical world, with which the eighteenth-century social elite was closely familiar. Imperial England would take up the fallen mantle of Rome. Wales manifested an abundance of appropriate motifs in support of this aspiration – of ancient ruins and unsullied nature in noble conjunction. Though they retained in their style something of the stiff formality of the Baroque, the widely distributed engravings made by the brothers Samuel and Nathaniel Buck did much to popularise the contemporary mood all over Britain – but the combination of image and text in their *East View of Dolwyddelan Castle*, published in 1742, hinted at the particular importance of the Welsh context:

> DOLWYDDELAN signifies the Castle of the Valley of Helen's Wood, and from hence there is an Ancient Road ... called Sarn Helen, or Helen's Way, which is supposed to have been made by Helena, mother of Constantine the Great; Dolwyddelan was therefore probably a Strong hold before the time of that Emperor ...[35]

John Dyer's long poem *The Ruins of Rome*, published just two years before *Dolwyddelan Castle*, presented a mirror image of this relationship between Wales and the classical world. For Dyer, the pine trees which he had seen growing among the ruins of the baths of Caracalla in Rome called to mind 'Britannia's oaks/On Merlin's mount, or Snowden's rugged sides'. Dyer was among the earliest of a succession of Welsh intellectuals, painters and patrons, through the eighteenth century, who would play an influential part in drawing to the country artists and intellectuals from outside who sensed in Wales, as a relic of Ancient Britain, a vague but appropriate back-story – a misty foundation myth – for the emerging imperial England.

Dyer travelled to Italy in 1724, by which time he had written his poem 'Grongar Hill', in which he described with the precision of intimate acquaintance the beauty of the landscape in which he had grown up. He revised the poem while abroad and published it in 1726, on his return. Alongside the Scottish poet James Thomson's long poem 'The Seasons', published four years later, it stood as an influential signpost towards the interest in ideas about landscape that would loom large in artistic discourse for the remainder of the century. Back in Wales, Dyer toured to every corner of the country, making notes and taking drawings. In 1728 he had 'a surprising escape on horseback, on a very narrow wooden bridge in North Wales, about fifty feet above rocks and a great torrent of water, which frightened the horse, who could not turn for the narrowness of the bridge, and

34 Shaftesbury had equated a 'wasted mountain' with a 'noble ruin' in *The Moralists* (1769), part III, Sec 1, pp. 390–1.

35 The tradition that Helena, mother of the Emperor Constantine, was a Briton, seems to originate in the 12th century in the work of Geoffrey of Monmouth, who conflated her with the Elen of Welsh tradition. Helena was widely regarded as the discoverer of the True Cross and revered as a saint.

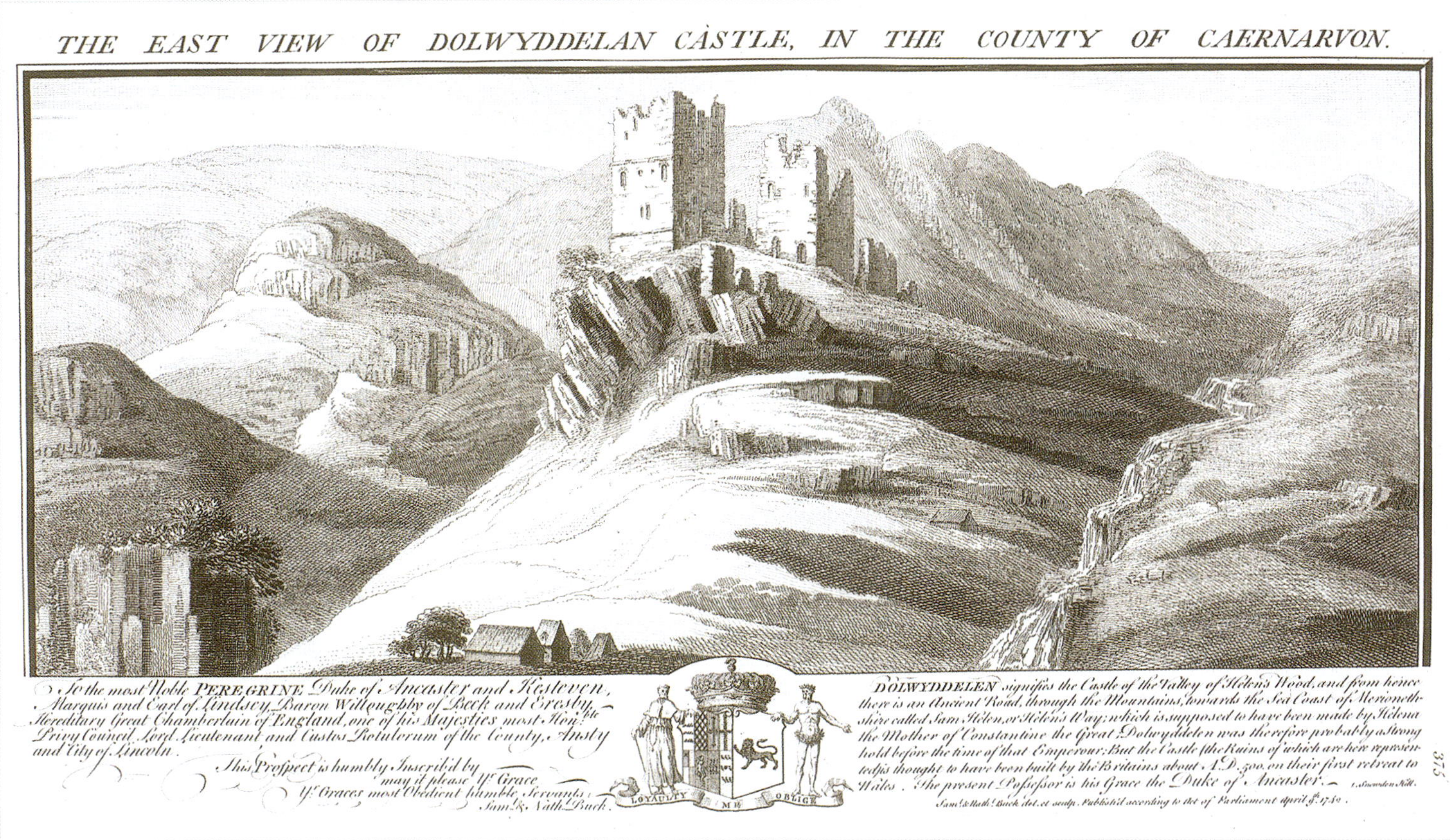

93. Samuel and Nathanial Buck, *The East View of Dolwyddelan Castle in the County of Caernarvon*, 1742, engraving, 19.3x37.5

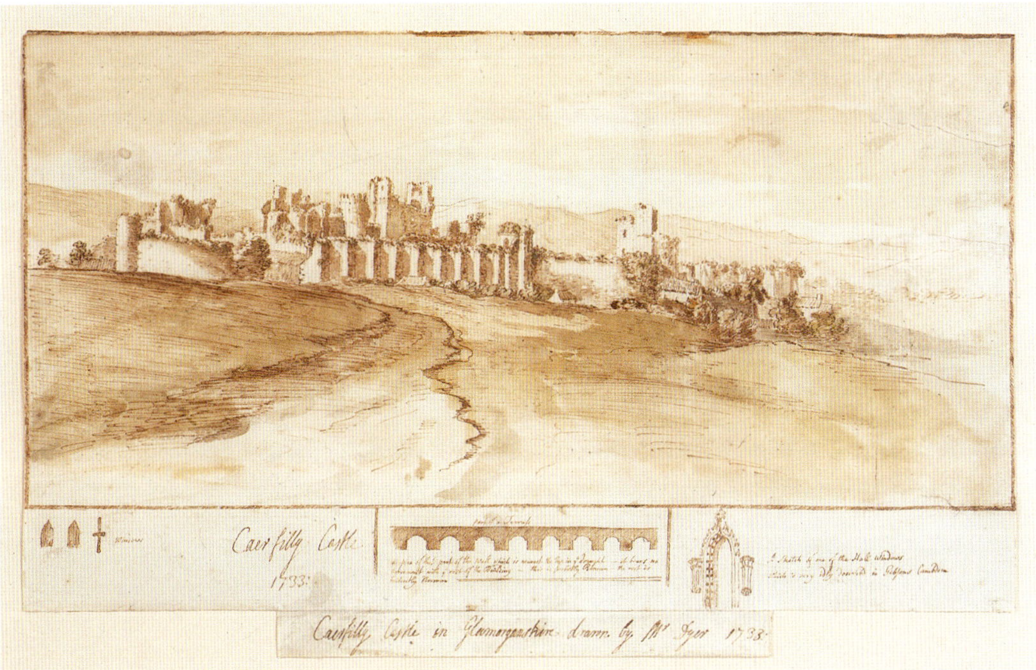

94. John Dyer, *Caerfilly Castle*, 1733, pen, ink and wash, 26.3x46.6

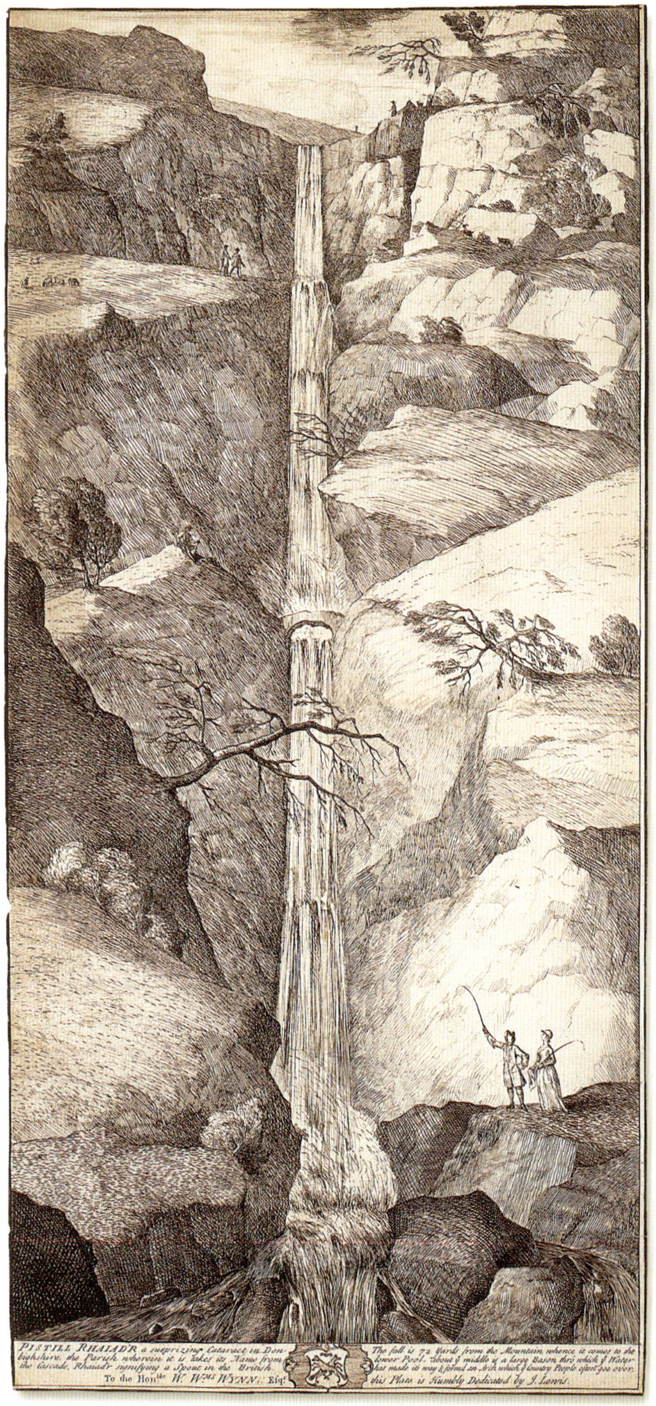

95. John Lewis,
Pistill Rhaiadr,
c.1736, engraving,
61.8x30.7

entangled his feet in the side rails.'[36] Dyer's travels were pioneering, though none of his Welsh pictures was engraved so as to contribute visually to the landscape fashion. However, the evolution from the residual formality of most of the Buck engravings, with their accompanying texts, to a more informal alignment of drawing style and the natural world can be traced through a group of engravings made in 1737 by John Lewis – almost certainly the same John Lewis who was painting portraits in Montgomeryshire and Carmarthenshire at that date.[37] On 30 June 1736, William Bulkeley of Anglesey noted in his diary that he had 'subscribed to a Proposal from one Mr Lewis a painter from Shrewsbury for 12 of the most Beautiful prospects in North Wales.'[38] Lewis's engravings retained the archaic tradition of heraldic dedication and explanation, but the drawing of the *View of Dyserth*, for instance, displayed a significant relaxation of the formality of earlier works. The concentration of *Pistill Rhaiadr* on a single 'wonder of nature' established a pattern that would still be marketable in the last decade of the century.[39]

Lewis's early engravings do not seem to have been produced in a large edition. The widespread dissemination of Welsh landscape prints would be pioneered by John Boydell, initially as designer and engraver as well as publisher, but eventually as the most powerful entrepreneur in England of the market for engravings of all categories. Boydell was born in Shropshire but spent the later part of his childhood at Hawarden in Flintshire. He identified with Wales and, as an entrepreneur of the metropolitan art world, he was claimed as a Welshman by his contemporaries.[40] His story became something of a legend, which described his rise from the status of 'a poor and ignorant lad in the obscure village of Hawarden', via an apprenticeship with the engraver William Henry Toms, to become an Alderman of the City of London.[41] His own drawing, *Rhaidder Fawr*, published in 1750 when he was about 30 years old, reveals the straightforward eye of a self-taught artist, but his later career saw him marketing

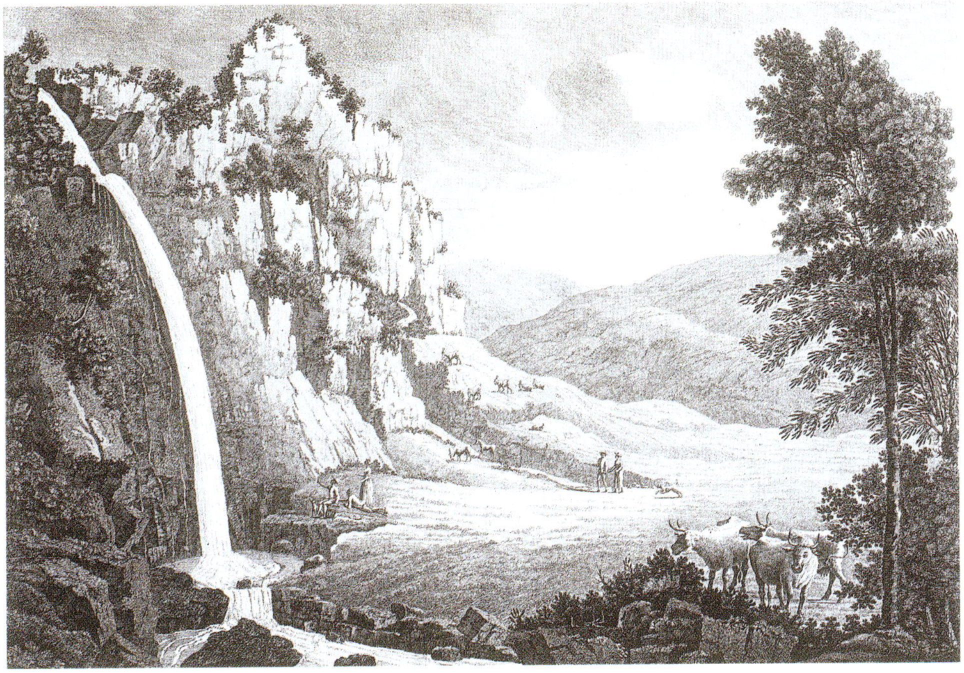

96. John Boydell, *Rhaidder Fawr, A great Cataract three Miles from Penmaen Mawr*, 1750, engraving, 31.5x46.8

36 J.P. Hylton Dyer Longstaffe, 'John Dyer as a Painter', *Montgomeryshire Collections*, XI (1878), pp. 396–402.

37 For the identification of John Lewis as both portrait and landscape painter, see Lord, *Meaning of Pictures*, pp. 10–51.

38 Archives and Welsh Library, Bangor University, William Bulkeley Diaries.

39 See J. Green after John Evans, *Pistyll Rhaiadr*, published in 1794, for instance, illustrated in Lord, *Imaging the Nation*, p. 131.

40 The Boydell family were established at several places in north-east Wales.

41 For the legend, see Lord, *Imaging the Nation*, p. 103 and note 12.

sophisticated engravings copied from the works of the most celebrated European painters. Among them would be Richard Wilson, and indeed, the legend has it that the engraving that he commissioned in 1761 from William Woollett, after Wilson's picture of *The Destruction of the Children of Niobe*, would earn him the huge sum of £2,000 – a measure both of his own entrepreneurial skills and the size of the market for art engravings in the mid-eighteenth century.

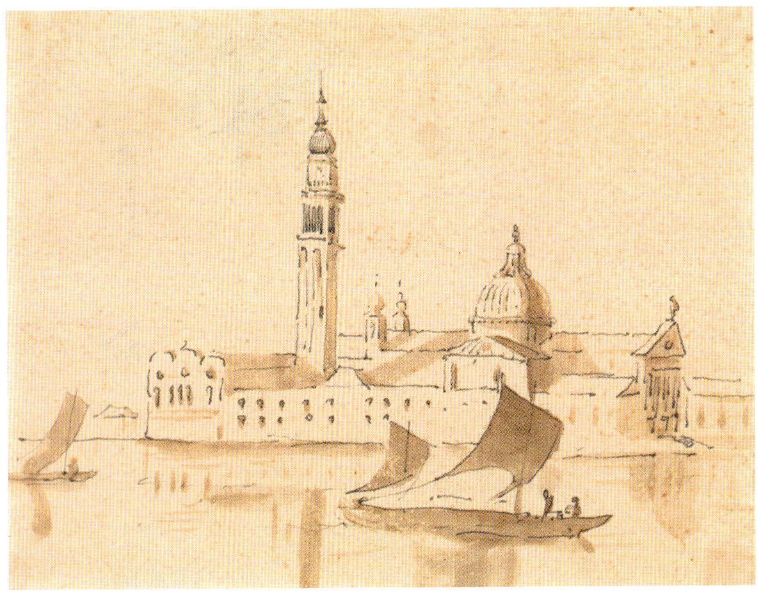

97. Richard Wilson, *The Church of San Giorgio, Venice*, c.1751, pen and wash, 12.8x22.8

It was in 1750 that Richard Wilson followed the path of artistic aspiration that led to Italy though, unusually for artists making the journey, he landed at Venice, where he stayed for about a year, before travelling south to Rome. Whether following his own artistic inclinations or because he sensed, through his contact with other painters, that it offered better economic prospects, by this time Wilson

42 The Grand Tour was largely a male affair in this period, though increasing numbers of women travelled in the late eighteenth and early nineteenth centuries. Among them was Charlotte Clive, whose portrait by Charles Grignion, painted in Rome in 1787, is at Powis Castle. She was depicted carrying a portfolio of drawings. A daughter of Clive of India, Charlotte was the sister of the 1st Earl of Powis of the 3rd creation. See Brian Dolan, *Ladies of the Grand Tour: British Women in Pursuit of Enlightenment and Adventure in Eighteenth-Century Europe* (London, 2001).

43 Dughet had been born in Rome, but was considered a part of the French school, since he was taught by Poussin and married his sister.

had decisively changed his career path from portraiture to landscape. He established a studio and frequented the Caffè degli Inglesi, where he courted the patronage of the many wealthy young men who arrived in the city at the high point of their European Grand Tour. The tour was designed to round off their qualification as educated gentlemen, though most of them were still in their late teens or early twenties.[42] The English predominated, but the city attracted the gentry and aristocracy of all Europe, and the artistic community that thrived on providing them with momentos in the form of portraits, subject pictures and landscapes was equally multi-national. It was a well established tradition, in which the names of the French painters Nicolas Poussin, Gaspard Dughet and Claude Lorrain loomed large.[43] Wilson would have been familiar with the landscape works of these painters before he went to Italy mainly through engravings, but now he had the opportunity to study many originals, and he took much from their style. At the same time, he drew on the experience of his contemporaries. Another French painter, Claude-Joseph Vernet, seems to have exercised a personal influence upon his decision to concentrate on landscape, and he came to know the German portrait painter Anton Raphael Mengs well enough to sit to him, in exchange for one of his own pictures. Wilson's relationship with Mengs is noteworthy of Wilson's status in Rome, since that painter's reputation was also rising rapidly. By the time the picture was painted in 1752, Mengs was regarded as a rival in Roman portraiture to the Italian Pompeo Batoni, though Batoni would eventually prove by far the more popular with British tourists. Among his Welsh patrons, George Herbert, 2nd Earl of Powis, would sit to him at the age of 20 on his Grand Tour in 1776.

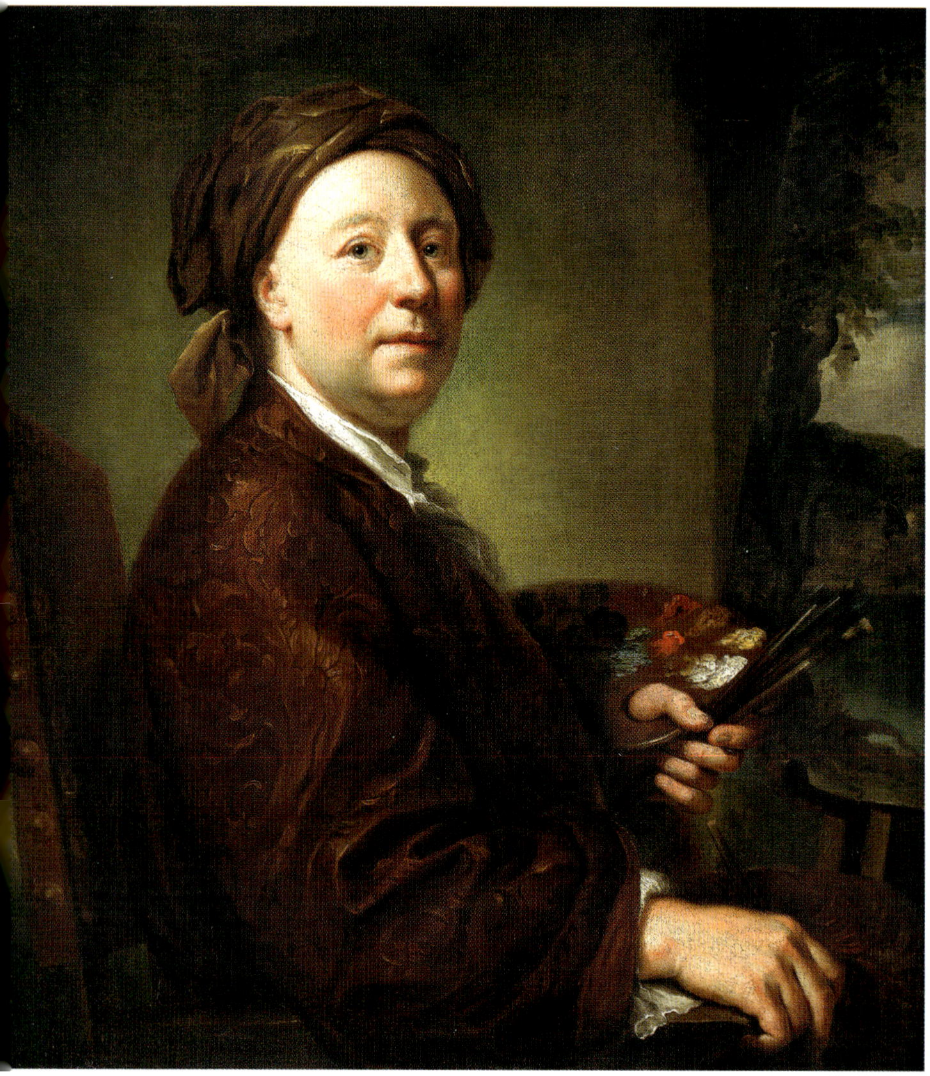

98. Anton Raphael Mengs, *Richard Wilson*, 1752, oil, 84.6x75.2

right
99. Pompeo Batoni, *George Herbert, 2nd Earl of Powis*, 1776, oil, 134.5x96.5

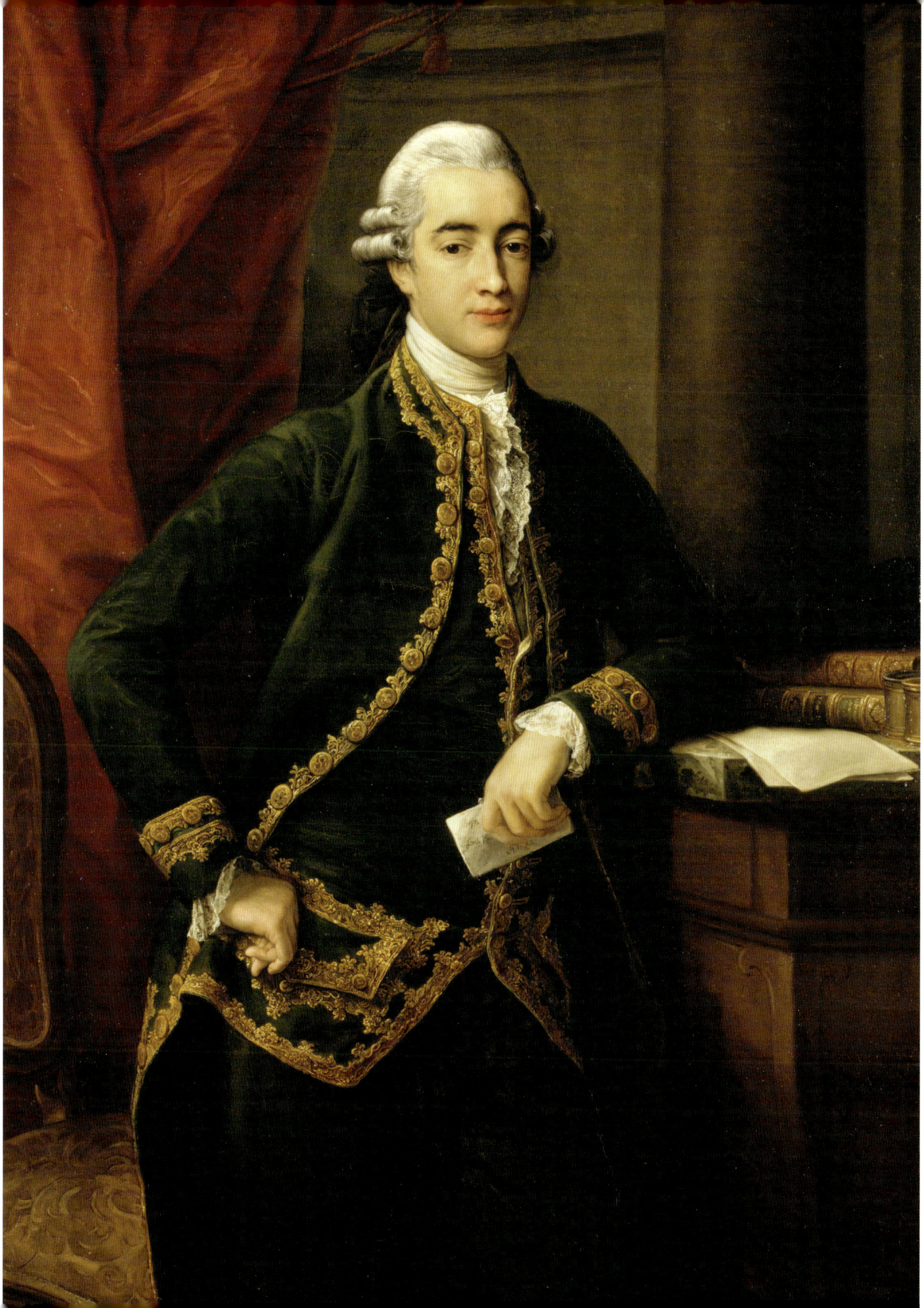

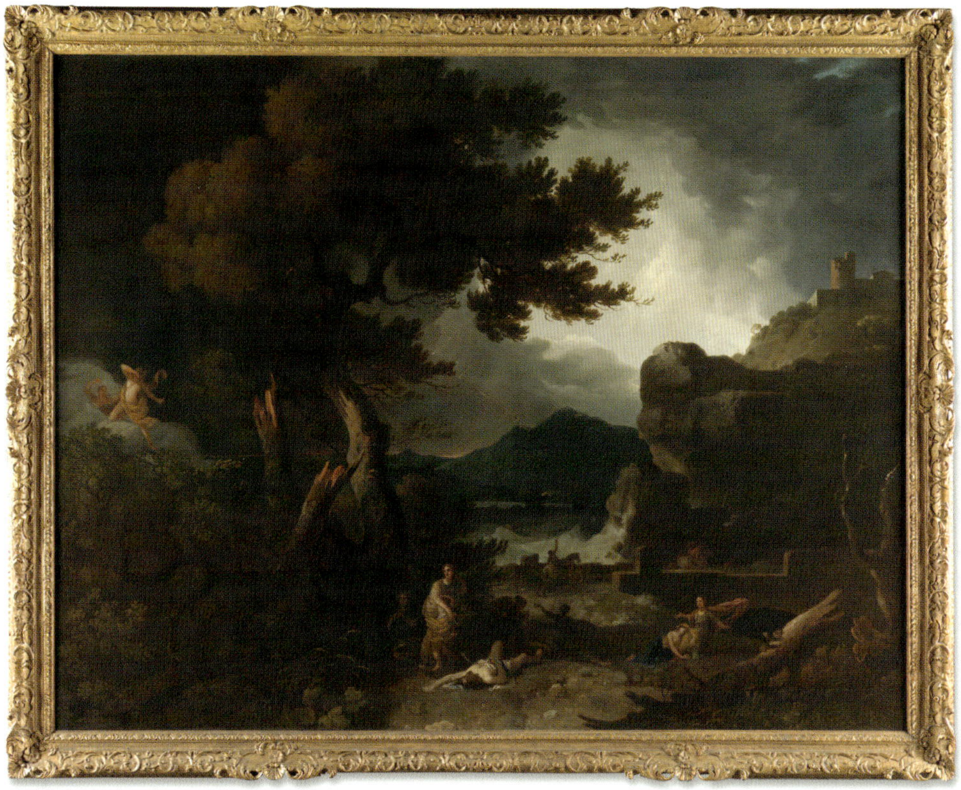

100. Richard Wilson, *The Destruction of the Children of Niobe*, 1760, oil, 147.3x188

Wilson's reputation as a landscape painter was established on the basis of the patronage that he found in Rome, among the Grand Tourists. Probably in 1753, he accompanied William Legge, 2nd Earl of Dartmouth, on a number of expeditions beyond the city, which resulted in the young man buying two large oil paintings and a series of over sixty drawings. In 1754, Wilson was observed near Tivoli in the company of the Earl of Pembroke and a group of equally elevated friends. Henry Herbert, the 10th Earl, was the direct descendent of the Welsh 1st Earl of Pembroke, William Herbert, and though the family was now domiciled in Wiltshire no doubt the Welsh connection assisted Wilson in his successful bid to gain the young man's patronage. By the time that Wilson returned to London in 1757, his name was, therefore, already familiar to connoisseurs, and through the following decade he would consolidate his position as the leading London landscape painter. Continuing to solicit the patronage of the returned Grand Tourists, Wilson produced many images based on his Italian experience, the most notable and influential of which was *The Destruction of the Children of Niobe*, so successfully published by Boydell. The painting had been presented to the public at the first annual exhibition of the Society of Artists.[44] Regular exhibitions of pictures were a new phenomenon, and the closeness of Wilson's involvement with the evolution of art marketing and professional practice in the period was confirmed in 1768 when he became one of the 34 founding members of the Royal Academy. These

44 Wilson painted the subject first in Rome in 1754–5, and repeated it on his return, though the sequence of painting these works, and a third version, now destroyed, has been a matter of debate. See Martin Postle and Robin Simon eds., *Richard Wilson and the Transformation of European Landscape Painting* (Newhaven and Cardiff, 2014), pp. 274–5, and the Richard Wilson Online Catalogue Raisonné.

45 'Memoirs of Thomas Jones of Penkerrig Radnorshire 1803' in *The Thirty-Second Volume of the Walpole Society 1946-1948* (London, 1951), p. 9.

46 loc.cit.

were the years of his greatest success. With the assistance of his apprentices and students, his studio produced large numbers of pictures, including many variants of successful themes. Among his paying students was Thomas Jones from Radnorshire, second son of the squire of Pencerrig. Along with his colleague Joseph Farington, Jones would be the source of some of the few authentic anecdotes that reveal a little of the character of Wilson, whose career is poorly documented, considering his high status in the 1760s:

> Wilson being an unmarried man, kept no house – but had commodious Appartments in the Piazza Covent Garden, which consisted of a *Study*, or painting room for himself – A large Exhibition or Show-room, a Study for his Pupils, Bed Chamber, Garrets &c. – The two Apprentices ..., not having advanced any Premium, were expected to make up that deficiency by their assistance in dead Colouring and forwarding the Pictures, in proportion to their Abilities, and were accordingly prescribed to certain stated hours daily attendance – As to the Other two Pupils, there being no claim on their time, They were left to their own Discretion – It would have been better indeed, if there had been more Restraint upon us all, too much of the time that ought to have been dedicated to Study, being squandered away in idle Mirth & frolick ...[45]

Jones went on to describe Wilson painting in his studio, but in 1765 Farington made a drawing of his teacher working directly from nature in the open air. Wilson was clearly not drawing but painting, which remained an unusual practice in England. It perhaps gave rise to a tension in his work that was criticised by contemporaries, between the classicism of style that conventional wisdom demanded should extend to smooth and polished paint surfaces, and what even Thomas Jones initially perceived as a 'course unfinished' quality that he felt marred his work. Jones would change his mind about the matter in due course, reinterpreting roughness as freshness, and one of the 'characteristick Beauties of this great Master'.[46] Painting before the subject, it is clear that Wilson – both in Italy and at home – was concerned to record not only with topographical accuracy but also to respond to light and atmosphere at a particular moment, much as his contemporary, John Dyer, did in his poetry.

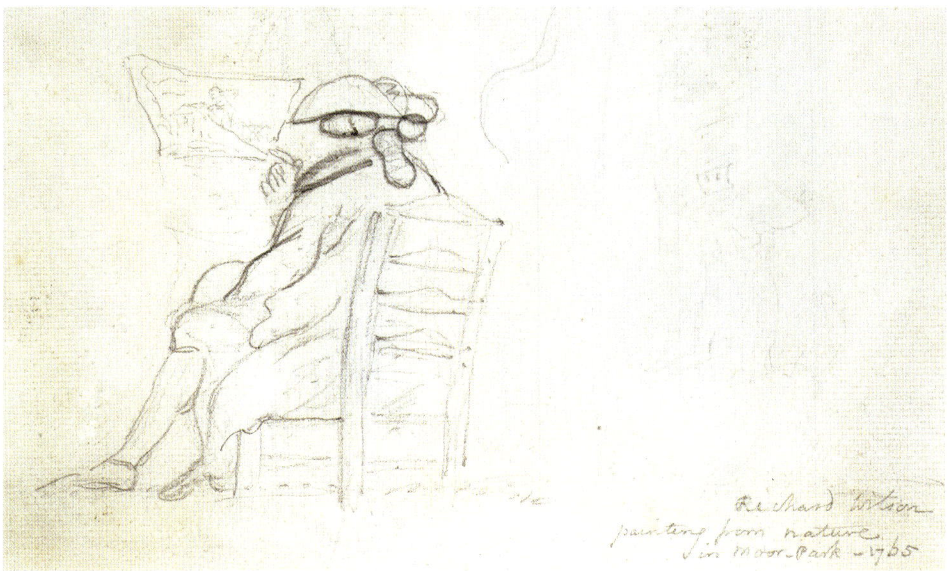

101. Joseph Farington, *Richard Wilson Painting from Nature*, 1765, pencil, 21x16.5

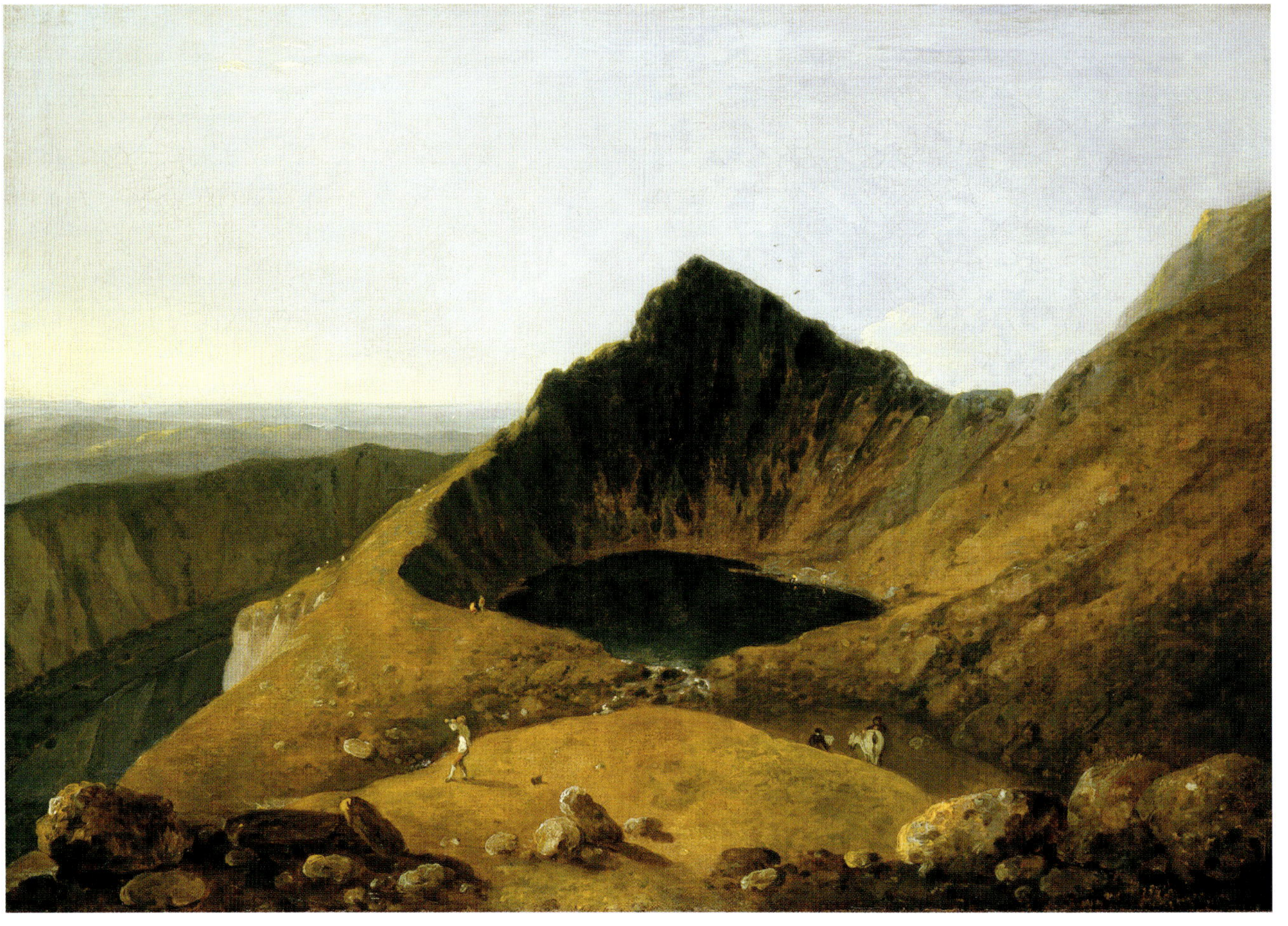

102. Richard Wilson,
Cader Idris, Llyn-y-Cau,
1774–6, oil, 51.1x73

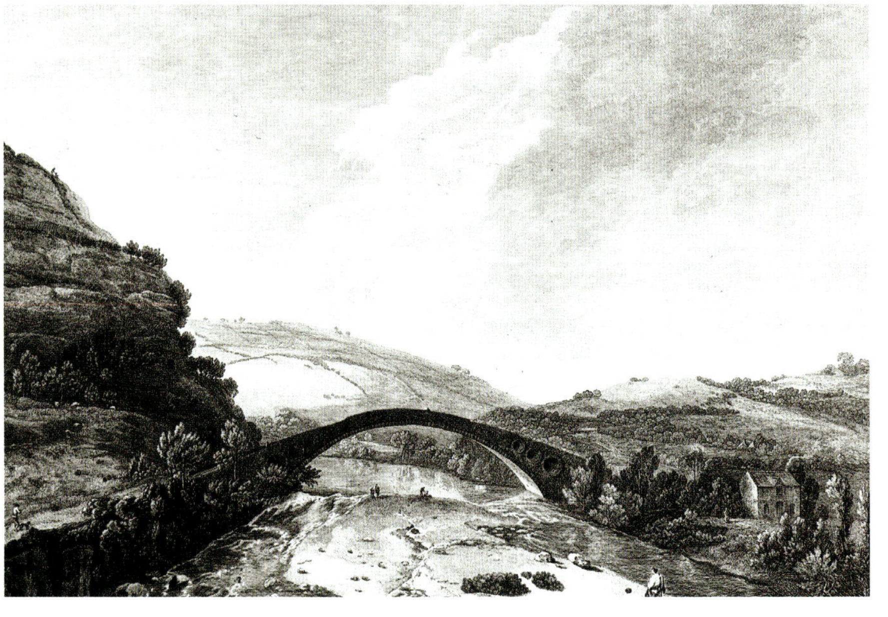

103. Peter Charles Canot
after Richard Wilson,
The Great Bridge over the Taaffe,
1775, engraving, 35.3x51.4

On his return from Italy, Wilson journeyed extensively to draw and to meet patrons, and his travels took him back to Wales. Six Welsh paintings were engraved as a group, and the first was certainly in circulation by 1766, so it appears that Wilson toured in both the north and south of the country in 1764 or 1765.[47] Naturally, his Welsh subjects particularly interested Welsh patrons. William Vaughan of Corsygedol bought views of Snowdon from Llyn Nantlle and of Pembroke and Cilgerran castles. Sir Roger Mostyn bought *Summer Evening, Caernarvon Castle*, and probably a version of *Cader Idris, Llyn-y-cau,* which with the help of the engraving would become one of Wilson's most celebrated works. That the engravings contributed substantially to the growing interest in Welsh landscape outside the country is clear from the fact that the images established themselves firmly in the minds of connoisseurs.[48]

Wilson's landscapes taken in the south of the country are especially intriguing, since he is not known to have had any particular contacts there. Taking his views of Cilgerran and Pembroke, he followed earlier travellers, but he broke new ground at Pontypridd. Nevertheless, although the grand bridge – advertised as the largest single-span in Europe – had been completed only in 1756, Wilson presented it so thoroughly embedded in the tranquil landscape that it might have been an ancient Roman monument.[49] His image gave no hint of the prosaic purpose for which the bridge had been constructed, which was to facilitate the transport eastwards of coal from the estates of Lord Windsor. It was an early manifestation of the industrialisation that would eventually transform not only the environs of the bridge but much of south Wales. Ironically, given the nature of his imagery, it could be argued that Wilson himself was an early beneficiary of this incipient process. His first cousin on his mother's side, Sir George Wynne of Leeswood, who seems to have looked after the adolescent Wilson's interests when his father died, had been made wealthy by the exploitation of lead ore on his land. The engraving after Wilson's view of Pontypridd may have been known to John Lewis. In 1767 and 1768 Lewis exhibited in London several landscapes painted in Glamorgan, and his own view of Pontypridd, taken from a point close to that from which Wilson had worked, almost certainly dates from these years.

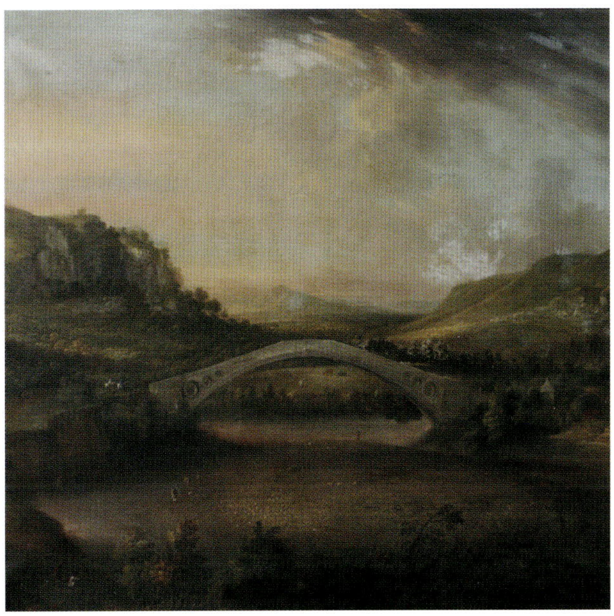

104. John Lewis, *Pontypridd*, *c.*1767, oil, 122x122

47 Considerable confusion exists about the issue dates of these engravings, which are best known in the complete edition of six published by Boydell in 1775.

48 A decade or so after Wilson, Thomas Pennant would feel that there was no need to describe Llyn-y-cau since it was 'so excellently expressed by the admirable pencil of my countryman, Mr Wilson'. *Tours*, p. 232. The celebrity of this view, which might well have been regarded as the epitome of barren ugliness a hundred years before, persisted into the early nineteenth century. An English tourist, John Skinner, echoed Pennant's sentiments, though he was less scrupulous on the matter of Wilson's nationality: 'Mr Wilson, the English Claude, has conferred celebrity on this spot by his pencil', he opined (Cardiff Central Library MS 1.503). It is unclear which of several extant versions was the view exhibited by Wilson in 1774.

49 Wilson may have been alerted to the bridge by an article and a technical drawing that appeared in the *Gentleman's Magazine* in 1764.

50 Though Constable, *Richard Wilson*, pp. 89–90, was of this opinion. See also Wilson's *Holt Bridge on the River Dee*, in which he evoked Claude Lorrain's *Rome and the Ponte Molle*, painted over a century earlier. Postle and Simon, *Richard Wilson*, pp. 260–2.

Among the Welsh landscapes of the mid-1760s, Wilson's views of *Llyn Peris and Dolbadarn Castle* most clearly demonstrate the complexity of his work. Though often concerned with the particularity of place and time, only the castle itself (and Snowdon beyond in other versions) are immediately recognisable, since Wilson reorganised the landscape to such an extent that it bore little relationship to topographical reality. However, it did follow closely the pattern of an *Ideal Landscape* painted in Italy some twenty years earlier by Gaspard Dughet – one of those fashionable painters who set the norms of taste for the Grand Tourists. Furthermore, probably shortly after painting his Welsh view, Wilson redeployed the entire composition as the Lake of Nemi, near Ariccia, otherwise known as 'Diana's Mirror', since the site was the centre of her cult. Notwithstanding the large scale production of pictures in his studio, it seems unlikely that a painter of Wilson's erudition, working for a public equally capable of learned interpretation of every element of a scene, would transpose Welsh and Italian images in this way simply as a matter of expediency.[50]

105. Richard Wilson, *Llyn Peris and Dolbadarn Castle*, 1760–5, oil, 92.4x126.2

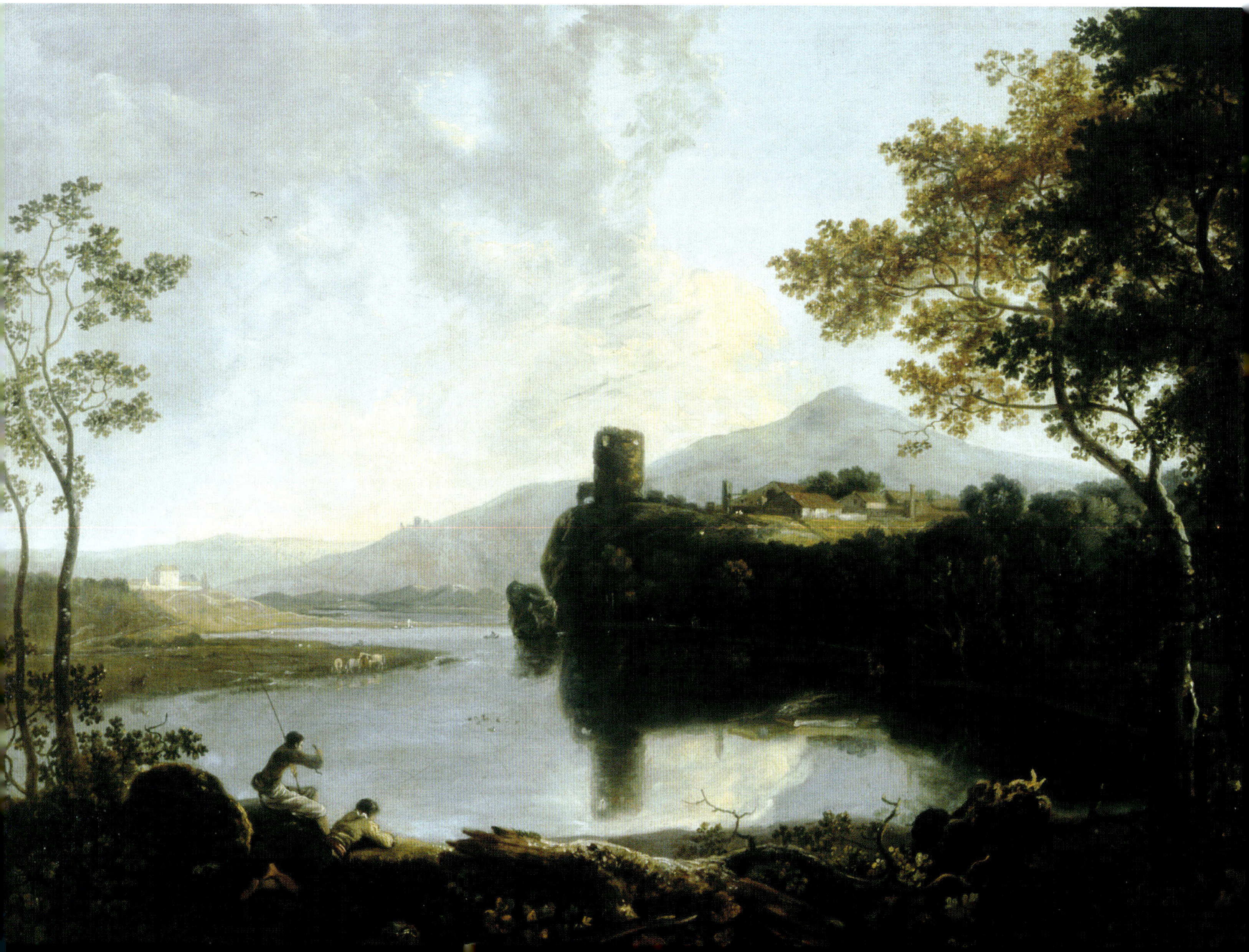

Wilson's Welsh tour of 1764 or 1765 reflected the fact that aesthetic and antiquarian interest in the country had grown in England through the 1750s, while he was in Italy. His early patron George Lyttelton had toured north Wales in 1755. He enthused about most of what he saw in letters that apparently circulated in manuscript among the small group of intellectuals who set artistic trends, and his descriptions appear to have impressed them.[51] A few years earlier, in 1751, the Cymmrodorion Society had been established in London, largely as a result of the efforts of the Morris brothers of Anglesey. Lewis Morris conceived of the Cymmrodorion as a Welsh equivalent of the Royal Society, and under the presidency of William Vaughan of Corsygedol it succeeded in attracting to its ranks some of the more thoughtful and energetic among the gentry and the literati. Wilson himself did not become a member, but Vaughan's patronage of the painter in the 1760s indicates that he was in touch with the activities of the society. In fact, it is clear even from the few scraps of direct evidence about Wilson which have survived that he was fully aware of the antiquarian aspect of what was now developing into a national revival. Before he left for Italy, he had been among the subscribers to Revd John Owen's *A Compleat and Impartial History of the Ancient Britons*, published in 1743. Wilson inscribed the name of the early British king Vortigern, whose unfortunate story was told in that volume, on two drawings.[52] Vortigern ('Gwrtheyrn' in Welsh) was believed to have invited the Saxons to Britain to assist him in resisting the attacks of the Picts. 'But human Foresight, which is exceedingly short and limited, oftentimes in thinking to prevent an Evil, procures it ...', the author had blandly observed.[53] Just as Wilson arrived home, in 1757, Thomas Gray published his celebrated poem 'The Bard', which refreshed the theme of foreign oppression of the Britons, and in the process did much to popularise the idea of Welsh poetic tradition among the intelligentsia in London. The contemporary poet Evan Evans ('Ieuan Fardd'), who had pointed Gray towards the source material for his work, was busy translating Welsh literature into English and manuscripts of his writings were in circulation even before the publication in 1764 of his book *Some Specimens of the Poetry of the Antient Welsh Bards*. It would be difficult to believe that Wilson was not caught up in the intellectual excitement surrounding the idea of Wales that was growing in the period. He was surely familiar with the most celebrated account of Welsh bardic and druidic

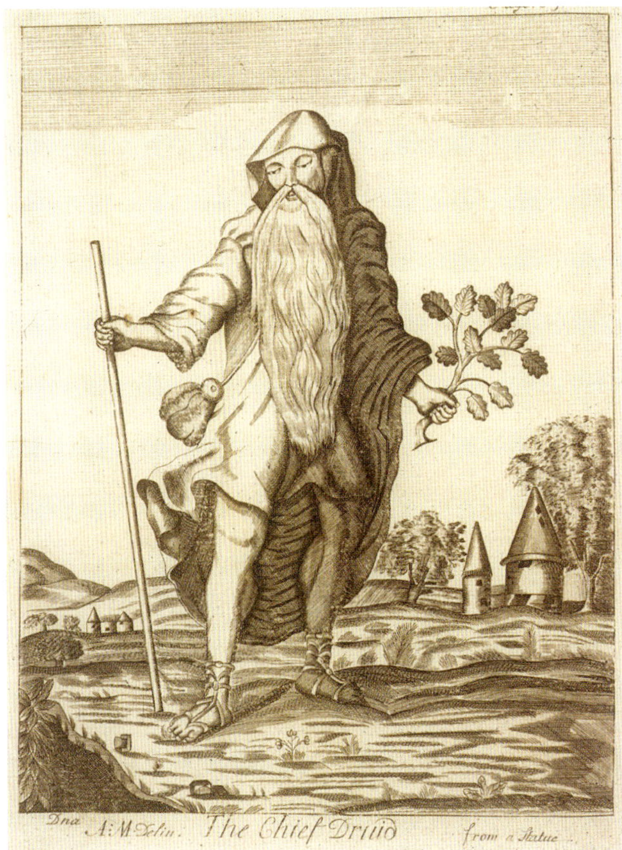

106. A.M., *The Chief Druid*, from Henry Rowlands, *Mona Antiqua Restaurata*, 1723, engraving, 19.2x150

51 The letters were not printed for some time, see George Lyttelton, *The works of George Lyttelton ...* (Dublin, 1774) and Henry Wyndham, *Tour through Monmouthshire and Wales* (Salisbury, 1781). Lyttelton was somewhat conservative in his views, not being an unequivocal enthusiast for the sublime. He was a close friend of James Thomson, author of *The Seasons*, and on the whole he preferred fertile lands to 'desart', though he did acknowledge 'savage beauty'.

52 BM 1867.12.14.775 and Victoria & Albert Museum, Dyce Collection, 661.

53 John Owen, *A Compleat and Impartial History of the Ancient Britons* ... (London, 1743), p. 121.

tradition, which was to be found in Henry Rowlands's volume *Mona Antiqua Restaurata*, published in 1723. There Rowlands had illustrated *The Chief Druid* with an image based on a seventeenth-century engraving, which would be taken up by the Cymmrodorion for their banner. In a picture shown in 1762 under the title *Landskip with hermits*, the eponymous hooded figures may reference the same source. Certainly, the Ancient Britain association with druids and bards was made when the picture, retitled *Solitude*, was published as an engraving in 1778.[54] It was captioned with lines quoted from 'Summer', in Thomson's 'The Seasons', though it is not clear whether this was done at Wilson's suggestion, or represented an interpretation of the picture made by the publisher:

107. Richard Wilson, *Solitude*, c.1762, oil, 100.3x125.1

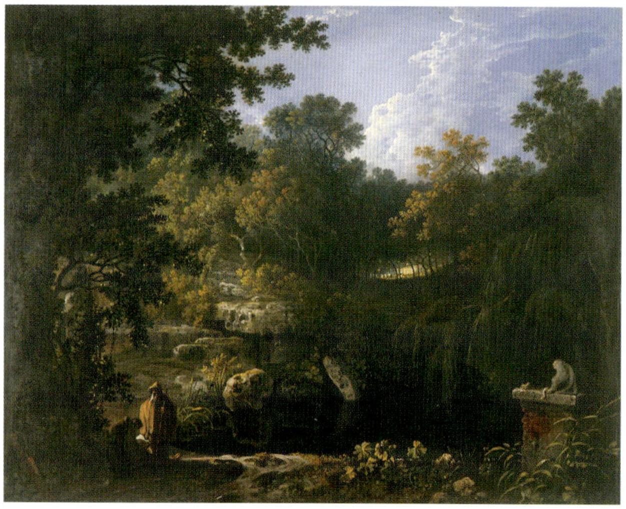

> THESE are the Haunts of Meditation, These
> The Scenes where antient Bards th'inspiring Breath,
> Extatic felt; and, from this World retir'd ...

The setting is a grove of oak trees, and in the background the sun filters through the otherwise shady scene to illuminate Christian devotion. The scene reflects both an earlier Italian picture, *Ariccia*, and Rowlands's description of Anglesey – 'a Country by Nature remov'd from the Noise and Tumults of the World ... full of delicious Groves, pleasant Shades, bubling Springs' – an Elysium, where walked and meditated 'a Company of divinely Inspir'd Souls, abounding with instructive Documents of Virtue, and profound Discoveries of Nature.'[55] It may well be that, just as he would soon transfer the image of Dolbadarn Castle to Lake Nemi, near Ariccia, Wilson was playing a game of association between Wales and Italy in the interests of deep philosophical concerns. The painter suggested the continuity of the spiritual druidic tradition amid the remains of the vanished Roman imperium, represented by the fractured sculpture of a lion – a lesson in the concept of virtuous living, consisting in the contemplation of god in nature. The idea of virtue achieved through contemplation was current. In one of the few contemporary observations of Wilson that reveal something of his intellect, Thomas Hollis, the buyer of the *Ariccia* picture, noted a breakfast conversation with the painter: 'Much discourse concerning his own situation and views; and about virtu.'[56]

The opportunity for Wilson to pursue on a large scale the equation between Wales and the classical civilizations came in 1770. The young Sir Watkin Williams-Wynn, son of the long-deceased equestrian, had returned from his Grand Tour. In Italy he had spent lavishly on artefacts and paintings, commissioning the obligatory portrait from Batoni, and a large picture of *Perseus and Andromache* from Mengs. Now he commissioned

54 An earlier edition of the engraving, published in 1770, does not carry the lines from Thomson.

55 Henry Rowlands, *Mona Antiqua Restaurata* (Dublin, 1723), p. 73. David H. Solkin, *Richard Wilson. The Landscape of Reaction* (London, 1982), p. 213, interpreted the symbolism of the picture in a different way. Subsequently, it emerged from x-ray examination that *Solitude* had started life as a different subject picture. Wilson painted over a group of young ladies, bathing in the foreground, and probably added the druid and the enactment of the mysteries in the sunlit grove. The subject of the picture in its earlier form may have been Diana and Actaeon. The x-ray photograph was published in *British Art Journal*, Spring 2001, p. 68.

56 Houghton Library, Cambridge, Mass., MS Eng 1191, 2, 26 October, 1761, 35, quoted in Postle and Simon eds., *Richard Wilson*, p. 86. Wilson had painted a portrait of Hollis in 1752.

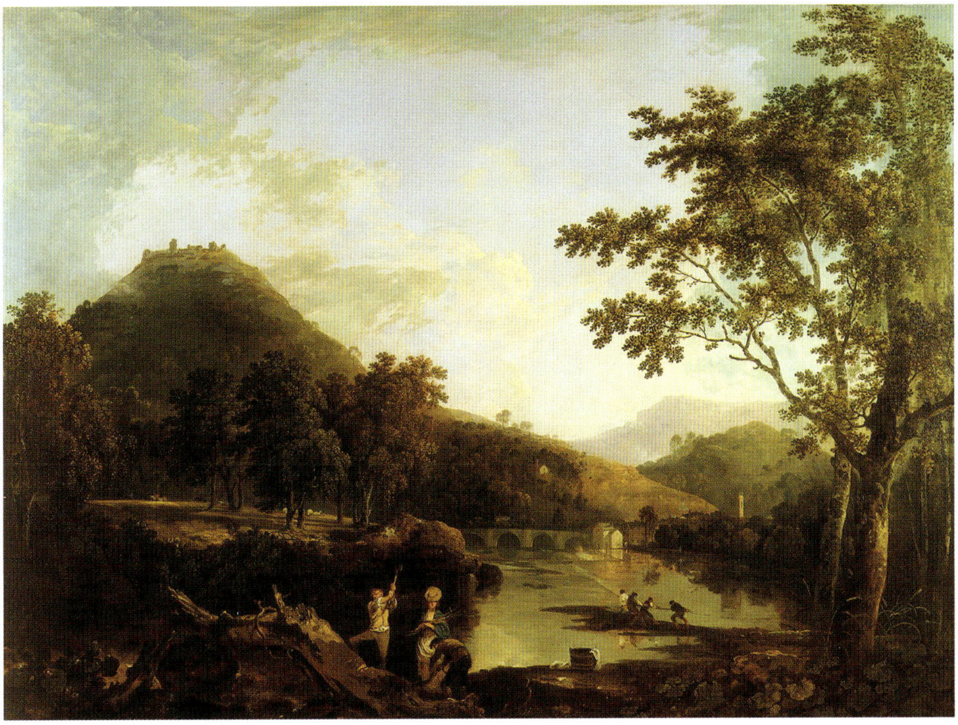

108. Richard Wilson, *Castell Dinas Bran from Llangollen*, 1770–1, oil on canvas, 180.3x244.8

two landscapes from Wilson. How the subject was decided upon is unknown, but the central feature of both paintings was highly significant. Castell Dinas Brân was laden with Welsh mythological and historical associations. In 1772, a year after Wilson exhibited his paintings, the patriotic contemporary mood surrounding the choice of subject would be exemplified by Ieuan Fardd, now also under the wing of Sir Watkin's patronage:

> Nor did this genius shine in Greece alone,
> In other nations equally it shone,
> Witness the Bards that grac'd the Celtic clime,
> Whose images were bold and thoughts sublime ...
>
> Old Llywarch and Aneurin still proclaim,
> How Britons fought for glory and for fame;
> Whole troops of Saxons in the field they mow'd,
> And stain'd their lances red with hostile blood ...[57]

In the closer of the two views Wilson emphasised the significance of Dinas Brân both by choosing the only viewpoint from which the summit appears to stand clear of its surrounding hills, and by enfolding the ruins of the summit castle in a halo of light, created by a circular opening in the cloud.[58] What Ieuan Fardd would describe as 'the spacious palace of Brân',[59] the giant god-king of Britain, was presented by Wilson as a Celtic equivalent of Mount

57 Ieuan Fardd, *For the Love of Our Country*, dedicated to Sir Watkin. See D. Silvan Evans (ed.), *Gwaith y Parchedig Evan Evans (Ieuan Brydydd Hir)* (Caernarfon, 1876), pp. 135–6.

58 Benjamin Booth, the early collector of Wilson's work, reported that the painter worked in the open air, sheltered from the weather by a tent erected for him at Sir Watkin's expense, Booth MS (Brinsley Ford Collection, London), document 4, p. 2. Whether Wilson worked on the large finished canvases in the open air, as Booth seems to suggest, or on the smaller oil of the view from Llangollen (NLW), is unclear.

59 Evans, *Gwaith y Parchedig Evan Evans*, p. 15.

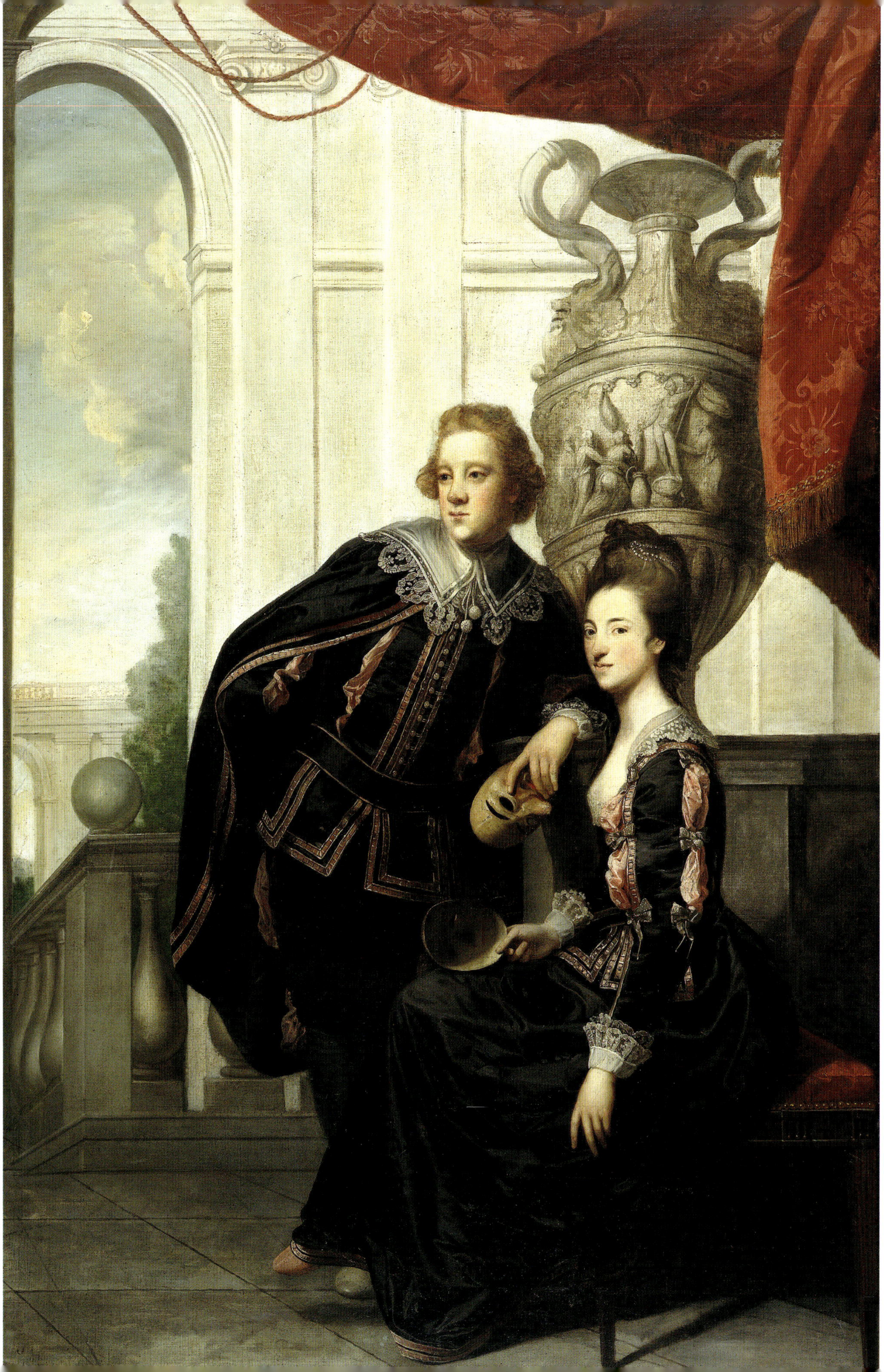

Olympus, home of the Greek pantheon. The evidence for understanding the picture in terms of national pride is even stronger when considered from the patron's point of view. Sir Watkin did not own Castell Dinas Brân – indeed, the site was the property of the family's old political rivals, the Myddeltons. Sir Watkin commissioned the picture not because he owned the place it depicted, but to demonstrate his understanding of its aesthetic and mythological significance. Furthermore, it was the work of a Welsh painter. Sir Watkin would eventually hang the pictures not at Wynnstay, in Wales, but in London where they could be admired by the English cognoscenti visiting his new house in St James' Square, commissioned from the architect Robert Adam.

60 Gray's observations on Parry are quoted in Sam Smiles, *The Image of Antiquity* (New Haven, 1994), p. 49.

61 A quarter of a century earlier, John Lewis had worked closely with Sheridan's father, Thomas, in Dublin, where he managed the Smock Alley Theatre. Lewis painted the manager's portrait and the scenery for his productions. See Lord, *Meaning of Pictures*, pp. 22–7.

Wales revealed to the English public – the 1770s

Wilson's commission to paint the Castell Dinas Brân landscapes was just one aspect of a remarkable burst of creative patronage involving architecture, music and theatre, as well as the visual arts, in which Sir Watkin indulged on his return from Italy in 1769. In April, he married Lady Henrietta Somerset, daughter of the 4th Duke of Beaufort, the close friend of his father who had stood with him admiring the racehorse 'Legacy' in Wootton's picture, a quarter of a century earlier. The young couple commissioned a double portrait from Reynolds, but its celebratory intent turned rapidly to memorial when the young lady died only three months after the wedding. Both sitters were shown wearing black, but in truth Sir Watkin seems to have been little disturbed by this turn of events, and continued to pursue his patronage of the arts with enthusiasm. He promoted further the career of his already celebrated harper, John Parry, whose music Thomas Gray famously reported had stimulated him to complete the composition of *The Bard*.[60] Parry lived long enough to perform at Sir Watkin's new London house. For the music room there, he paid Reynolds 150 guineas to paint a picture of St Cecilia, the patron saint of music, personified by the celebrated singer Elizabeth Ann Linley, wife of the playwright Richard Brinsley Sheridan.[61] Theatre featured strongly among Sir Watkin's enthusiasms, and one of his first ventures on his return home was to organise at Wynnstay a series of summer theatrical seasons that he maintained until his death in 1789. They attracted many of the London fashionable set, including David Garrick, the most celebrated actor-manager of the age.

Theatre remained the one field in which art painters could legitimately venture beyond portraits, subject pictures and landscapes, without being regarded as working beneath their dignity. It may well be that the backdrops for the first performances at Wynnstay

opposite
109. Joshua Reynolds, *Sir Watkin Williams-Wynn and Lady Henrietta Williams-Wynn*, 1769, oil, 253.5x167.4

110. Henry William Bunbury and John Evans, *The Wynnstay Theatre*, c.1786, engravings, 81x117

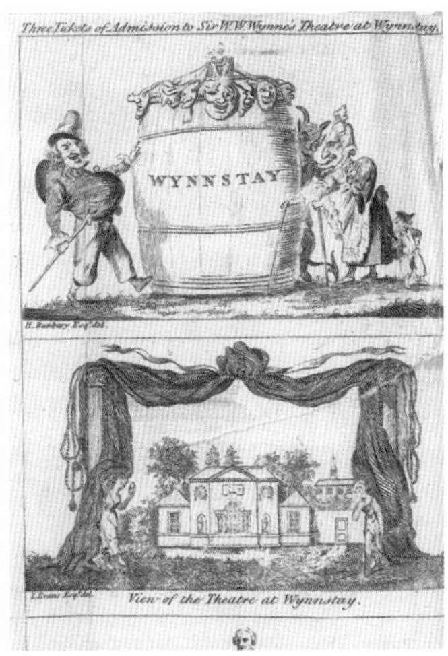

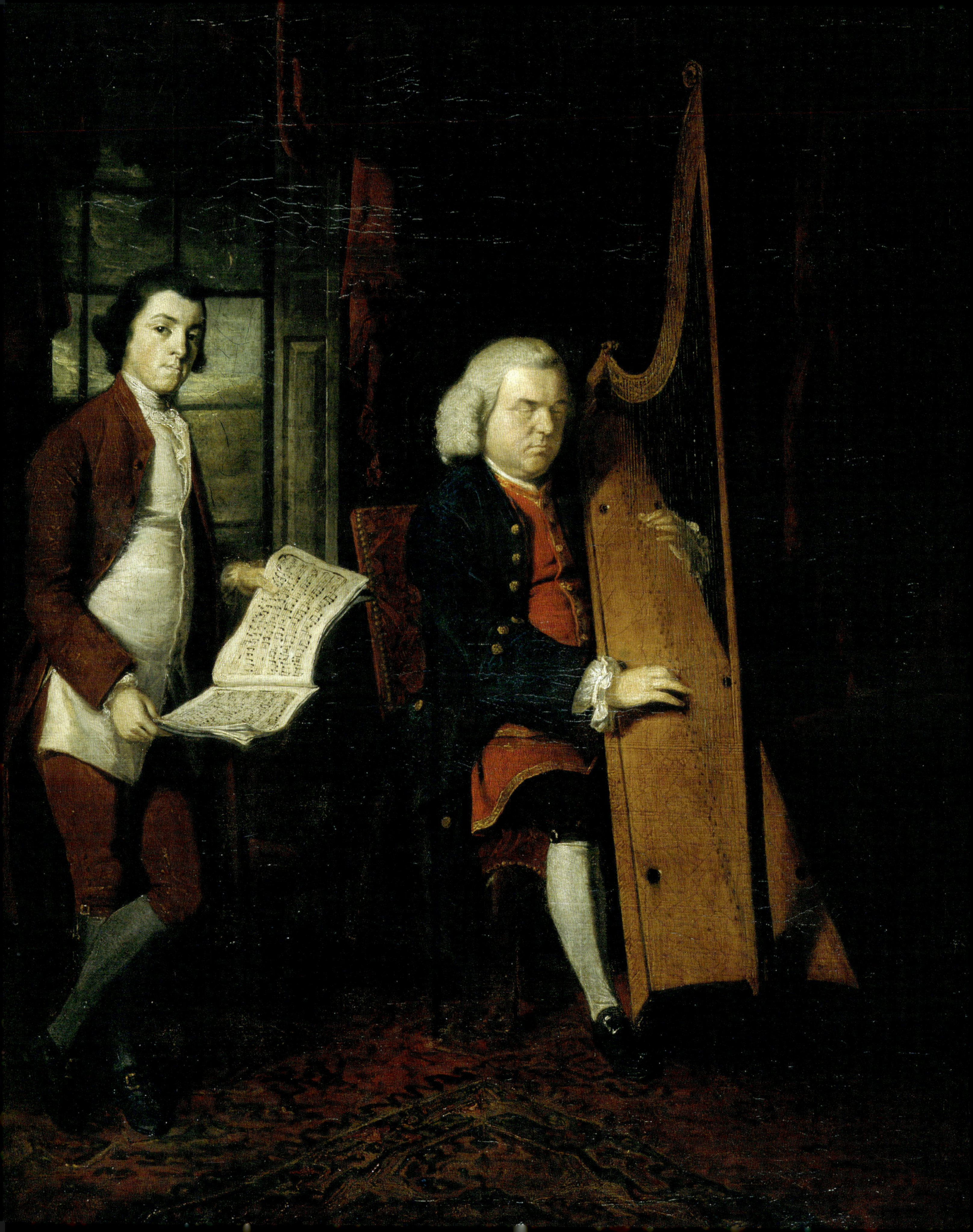

were painted by William Parry, son of Sir Watkin's harper. The Wynn family had begun its patronage of the younger Parry as early as 1759 when, with their support, he had entered the academy of William Shipley in London. Subsequently they paid for him to study at the St Martin's Lane Academy and finally in the studio of Reynolds.[62] After a decade of training Parry returned to Wynnstay, and it was probably at this time that he painted the first of several portraits of his famous father. John Parry sat for the picture with his other son, David, who was also a musician. In his hand David held a copy of Handel's anthem *Zadok the Priest* – a detail certainly aimed at their collective patron, Sir Watkin, who would become a great promoter of the work of his favourite composer.[63] Parry was also able to take advantage of his patron's friends in the Cycle of the White Rose. The Jacobite society, of which the elder Sir Watkin had been the leading light in the days of its political significance, was now largely a forum for Tory socialising, but it provided commissions for Parry in the form of two groups of pastel portraits, one monochrome and the other coloured, as well as portraits in oil of some members and their children. His portrait of Frances Puleston demonstrates the easy sophistication which the London-trained painter could deploy by this time.

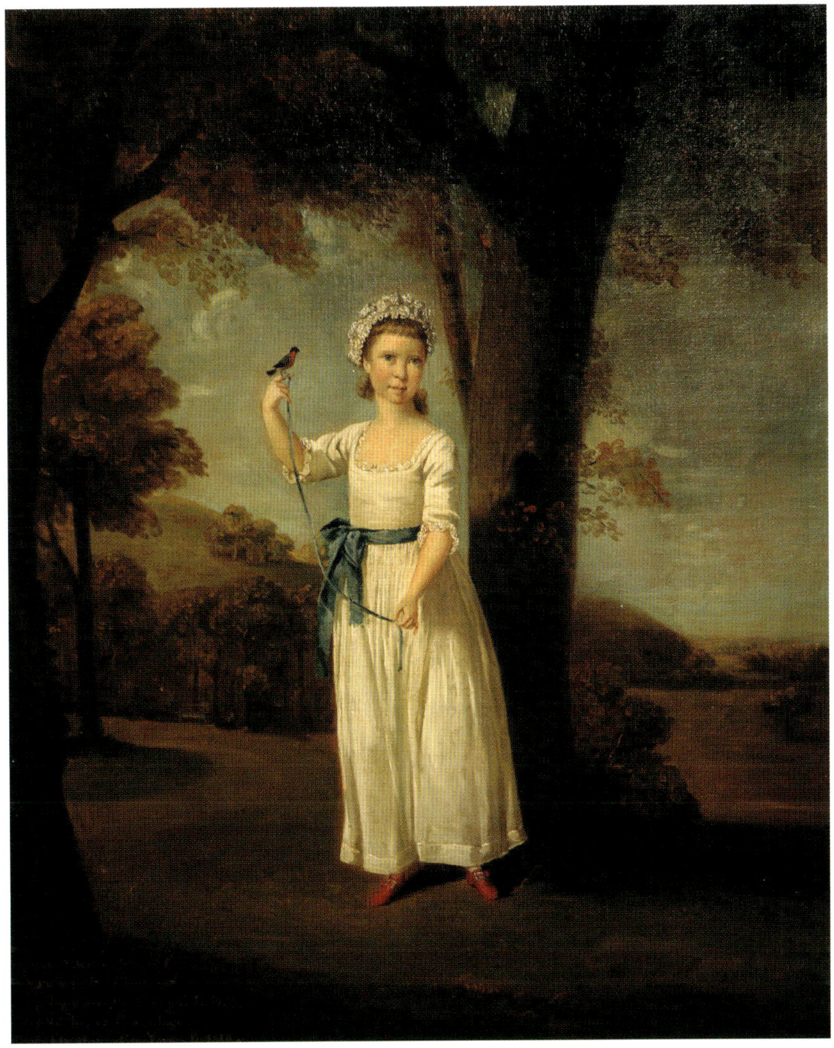

112. William Parry, *Frances Puleston*, 1770, oil, 75x62.4

In parallel with his intensive patronage, Sir Watkin himself was being taught to paint by the English artist Paul Sandby. In 1770, he paid Sandby for 46 lessons, and a drawing of the painter at work, made by Parry, survives. However, the interactions that clearly occurred between the artists working under Sir Watkin's patronage were not confined to Wynnstay. Interactivity in Wales

left
111. William Parry, *John Parry, the Blind Harper, with his son David*, oil, 87x71.2

62 For the career of Parry, and in particular his relationship with Sir Watkin, see Miles Wynn Cato, *Parry. The Life and Works of William Parry A.R.A. (1743–1791)* (London, 2008).

63 Sir Watkin's promotion of Handel reached its high point in the Handel Commemoration Concert at Westminster Abbey in 1784.

reflected relationships established in London, where William Parry, pupil of Reynolds, was acquainted with Thomas Jones, pupil of Wilson, along with the Welsh satirist Evan Lloyd[64] and the celebrated Garrick. Jones reported several instances of such interactions in his *Memoirs*:

> On the 16th [of July 1769] Evan Lloyd the Poet, Charles Hemmings an old fellow collegian, Parry, late a pupil of Reynolds, and my self, hired a Coach for the day, dined at the Toy at Hampton, and after dinner Lloyd introduced us to Mr Garrick at his elegant Villa there, who very politely shewed the house, attended us round the walks and Shrubberies, and as a particular Compliment, conducted us to his study, a detached Building in the Garden, which being, as he told us, dedicated to his Retirement, had only one Chair in it – A bottle of Wine was ordered, and standing round his writing desk, The glass was circulated and enlivened with the flippant Conversation of these two Wits, untill a Coach driving up, announced My Lord Somebody – upon which we took our leave and returning to the Toy to the other Bottle – concluded the Evening together at the Crown and Anchor tavern in the Strand.[65]

The other Wilson pupil, Joseph Farington, was also drawn into the circle. In 1770 he co-operated with Parry on a painting illustrating Shakespeare's *King Lear.* Two decades later, the picture was masquerading as a much more valuable Wilson, of whose works Thomas Jones – and perhaps Farington also – had produced 'a few *innocent* Impostures' to supplement the income they gained as young men from their own original productions.[66] Yet another Welsh-born painter, John Downman, must also have been known to Parry and Jones at this time. Indeed, Downman had been born in 1750 at Ruabon, by the gates of Wynnstay, though strangely he appears never to have received the patronage of Sir Watkin.[67] Downman was training in London under Benjamin West while Parry was with Reynolds, and in 1769 he was among the first students to enrol at the Royal Academy Schools.

In 1770, as Parry worked on his elegant portraits in Wales and Wilson on his learned landscapes, the epic circumnavigation of the globe undertaken by Captain James Cook was underway. At the time, on board HMS Endeavour, Cook was charting the east coast of Australia. It might seem fanciful to mention, in the same breath, that the year 1770 also saw Thomas Gray boating down the River Wye, and an English cleric, the Revd William Gilpin, composing a learned discourse on the aesthetics of his own experience of that leisurely journey, but in fact both the circumnavigation and the gentle descents of the Wye expressed a common desire to discover and disclose to the sedentary public unfamiliar places, peoples and phenomena. It was a time of revelation of things remote, whether located thousands of miles away or – for the likes of Sir Watkin – in their unexplored back yard, since the spirit infused Welsh and English intellectuals alike. Indeed, as Cook mapped the coast of Australia, Thomas Pennant was engaged in a 'discovery' of Scotland, which

64 For Evan Lloyd and his circle see Peter Lord, *Words with Pictures: Images of Wales and Welsh Images in the Popular Press, 1640–1860* (Aberystwyth, 1995).

65 Jones, *Memoirs*, p. 21.

66 For the relationship between Farington and Parry see Cato, *Parry*, p. 37, and for Jones's 'impostures', see *Memoirs*, p. 141.

67 Though the next Sir Watkin, the 5th Baronet, would purchase an allegorical painting made towards the end of the artist's career. *A late Princess personifying Peace crowning the Glory of England reflected on Europe* was exhibited at the Royal Academy in 1819. Downman lived the last years of his life at Wrexham. See Jane Munro, *John Downman 1750–1824* (Cambridge, 1996).

68 See H.P. Carter, *Sir Joseph Banks, 1743–1820* (London, 1988). The draughtsman on Cook's second voyage was William Hodges, fellow pupil with Thomas Jones in Wilson's studio.

69 The origins of the Wye Tour are described in Malcolm Andrews, *The Search for the Picturesque* (Aldershot, 1989), pp. 84–107.

70 Gilpin's first publication on the subject was *An Essay on Prints ...* (London, 1768).

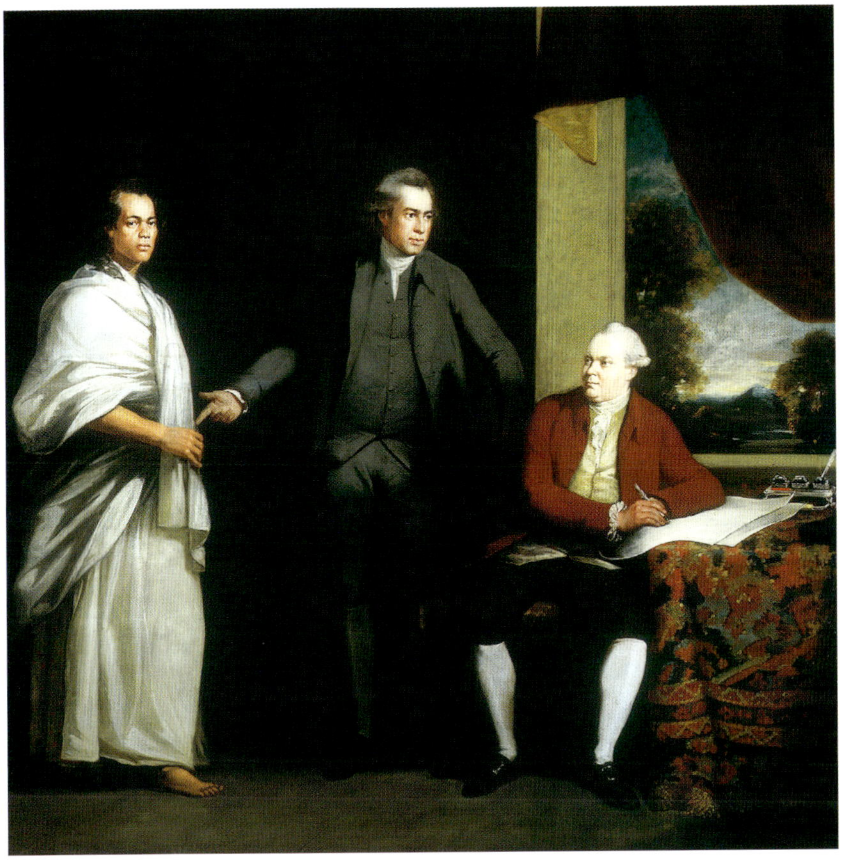

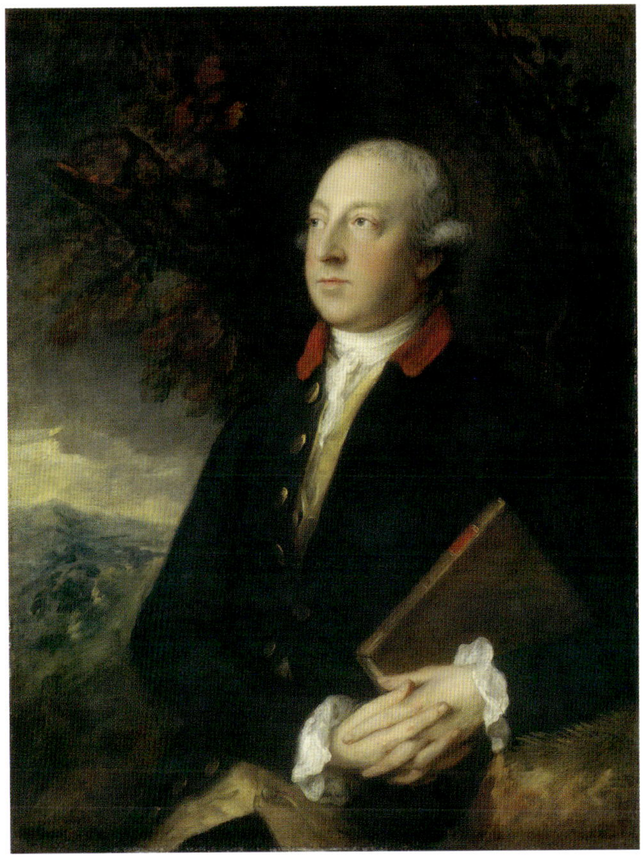

114. Thomas Gainsborough, *Thomas Pennant with his 'Tour in Scotland'*, 1776, oil, 95x74

above left
113. William Parry, *Omai, Joseph Banks and Dr Daniel Solander*, *c.*1775–6, oil, 150x150

he would reveal to the English public in his illustrated *Tour in Scotland and Voyage to the Hebrides* in 1774. In the context of these varied contemporary explorations, it is worthy of note that among Pennant's circle of acquaintances was the botanist Joseph Banks, who had visited him at Downing during a stay in Wales in 1767. The Banks family was related by marriage to the Williams family of Edwinsford in Carmarthenshire, where Joseph had based himself after he 'determin'd to visit the land of Cymri before any foreign soil'. Shortly afterwards, he embarked on the *Endeavour* with Cook. Some years later, back in London, he would be painted by William Parry in the company of Omai, a native chief who Cook had taken to England after his second expedition to the South Seas. The next exploratory tour undertaken by Banks would be to south Wales.[68]

The excursion down the River Wye was already known to landscape enthusiasts by the time the Revd William Gilpin arrived at Ross-on-Wye in the summer of 1770.[69] Gilpin, the headmaster of Cheam School, was well-connected among the metropolitan cognoscenti, counting Gray and Horace Walpole among his associates. He had grown up in an artistic family but his particular delight was aesthetic theory.[70] He recorded in detail, both in words

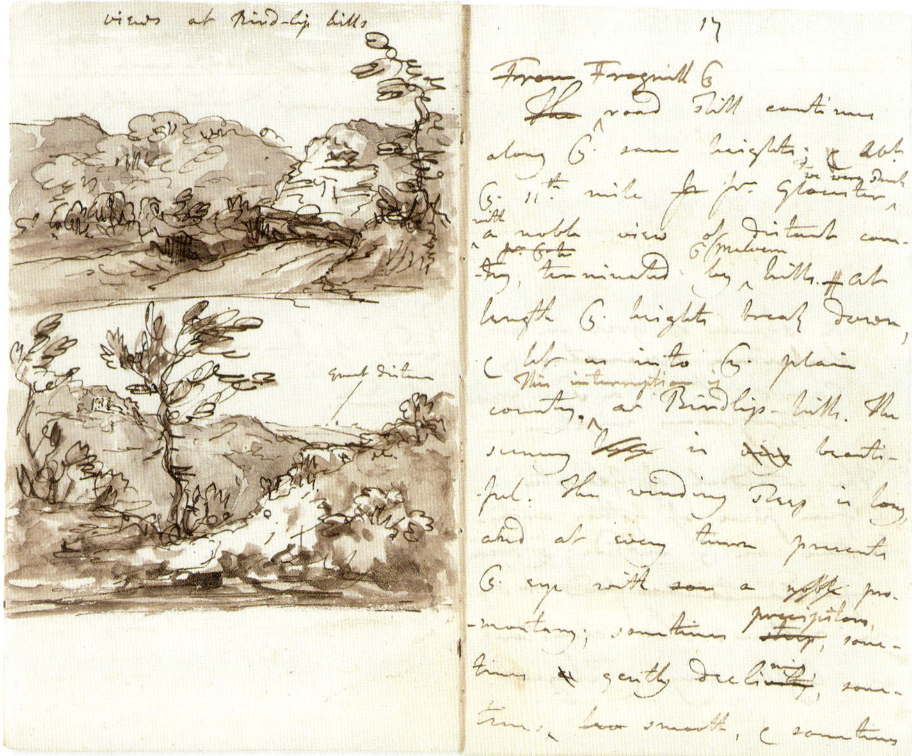

115. William Gilpin, *Views at Bird-Lip Hills*, pages from *The Wye Tour Sketchbook*, 1770, pen, ink and wash, 19.7x24.5

and pictures, his observations on the scenery of the Wye valley, which were directed towards the development of his concept of the picturesque landscape – of how trees, hills, rocks and water might be composed to create 'that kind of beauty which is agreeable in a picture'. Gilpin sought out for praise those viewpoints from which various natural and man-made elements were juxtaposed so as to conform to the rules of what he conceived the ideal pictorial composition. He criticised those places that did not conform – including Tintern Abbey, the stone surfaces of which he found insufficiently animated, such that they 'hurt the eye with their regularity; and disgust it by the regularity of their shape. A mallet judiciously used (but who durst use it?) might be of service in fracturing some of them', he observed in a passage that would become celebrated for its extreme devotion to his esoteric vision.[71] For John Dyer as for Richard Wilson – artists of the same generation – landscape poetry and painting had been both a contemplation of particular place and time, and vehicles to carry the philosophical and social concepts that arose from their observations.[72] Notwithstanding the fact that he was a clergyman, Gilpin's enjoyment of landscape was closer in kind to that experienced by a bureaucrat in the enforcement of regulations. Nevertheless, it is one of the more remarkable consequences of the intellectual activity of the 1770s that – albeit divested of its pedantry and infected with alternative perceptions – Gilpin's picturesque would become the default position for the appreciation of landscape that remains fundamental to mass tourism.

As Gilpin was absorbing the lessons of his Wye tour, Sir Watkin Williams-Wynn ventured into Snowdonia. It was a journey that, illustrated by his painting teacher, Paul Sandby, would also have an important impact on perceptions of landscape. Sir Watkin's relationship with Sandby had flourished during 1770, and so in August 1771, following in the footsteps

71 William Gilpin, *Observations on the River Wye* (London, 1782), p. 33.

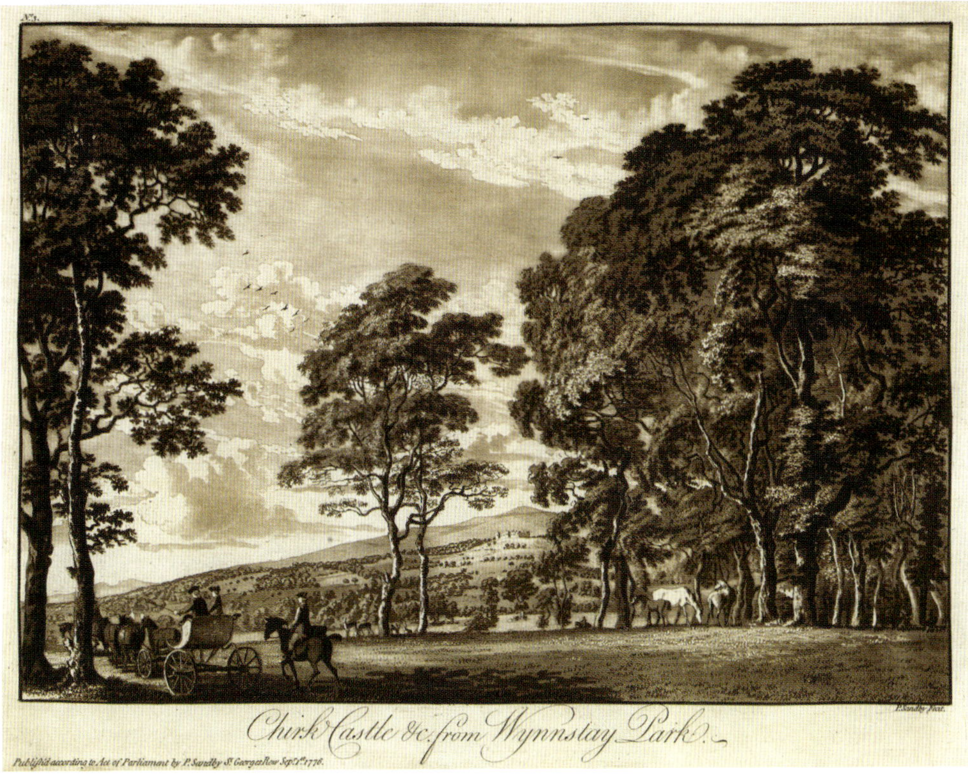

116. Paul Sandby, *Chirk Castle, &c. from Wynnstay Park*, from *XII Views in North Wales*, 1776, aquatint, 23.8x31.4

of George Lyttelton and a growing band of gentry connoisseurs, he set out with his teacher on tour. Sir Watkin took care to travel adequately supplied. Along with Sandby and his Grand Tour friend Thomas Apperly, the gentleman was accompanied by nine servants, fifteen horses and a large cart for his belongings. The travellers drew and painted from Llangollen to Snowdon. Two years later, Sandby would join forces with Joseph Banks on his similar exploration of the south of the country. It was the results of this latter journey that first become known to the public, when in 1775 Sandby published *XII Views in South Wales*. In 1776 they were followed by *XII Views in North Wales*, based on his earlier journey with Sir Watkin. The volumes were remarkable not because of the sites they portrayed, many of which were familiar to a public informed by the earlier work of Wilson and others, but for the means that Sandby employed to illustrate them. The engravings were made using the new print process of aquatint, which enabled the artist to reproduce subtle changes of tone and effects of light previously to be achieved only in painted originals.[73] With little topographical reorganisation, Sandby allowed the natural world to display itself with drama. His rise coincided with a serious decline in the fortunes of Wilson in the mid-1770s, perhaps partly as the result of changes of taste represented by the work of Sandby and others of his generation.[74]

72 In the course of the exposition of his theories, Gilpin reflected on the work of John Dyer. His comments on the poem 'Grongar Hill' confirm the importance of Dyer as an early influence on the landscape movement, and reveal the evolution in ideas that Gilpin's own concepts represented. Ibid., pp. 59–60.

73 For Sandby's involvement in the development of aquatint, and also that of another Welsh tourist, the Hon. Charles Greville, see Ann V. Gunn, 'Sandby, Greville and Burdett, and the "Secret" of Aquatint', *Print Quarterly*, XXIX, no. 2 (2012), pp. 178–80.

74 Wilson left London and returned to Wales to live with a cousin near Mold in 1781, where he died the following year.

75 Wright was also indirectly involved in the development of aquatint. His friend Peter Perez Burdett (who modelled in some of his pictures) had introduced Greville and Sandby to the technique.

76 Anon [Henry Penruddocke Wyndham], *A Gentleman's Tour through Monmouthshire and Wales* (London, 1775), 1781 edition, p. iii. On the other hand, he found the turnpikes 'excellent' and the mountain roads 'as good as the nature of the country will admit of', and 'the people universally civil and obliging'. Wyndham came again in 1777 with the Swiss painter Samuel Hieronymous Grimm, enabling him to enhance the 1781 and 1797 editions of his *Gentleman's Tour.*

77 'I speak now of my native country' is the opening sentence of Pennant's *Tours*.

78 Pennant, *Tours*, p. 261.

79 In a printed advertisement of 1784 Griffith 'Takes the Liberty of offering his Services to the Public, at his leisure Hours'. See Lord, *Imaging the Nation*, p. 134. The reason for Pennant's adoption of Griffith, who was born to poor parents, is unclear from the account given in his *Literary Life* (London, 1793), p. 10. Pennant also gives an incorrect birth date for the painter. Griffith was born in 1747 and died in 1819.

Sandby was notable as a barometer of changing times in one further respect. Travelling with Sir Watkin near Dolgellau, the party paused at an iron forge. Sandby's sketch of the site (or one very similar to it) was straightforward, and included a figure – presumably Sir Watkin – drawing under a sunshade held by a servant. However, in his subsequent aquatint Sandby employed a low viewpoint and intense lights and darks to convey with dramatic effect the beginnings of a new world of science and technology – the counterpoint between the power of nature and its employment by man in industrial processes. Between Sandby's initial drawing and his aquatint, a precedent had been established by the painter Joseph Wright, whose intensely-lit images of blacksmiths and farriers at work, made between 1771 and 1773, had become well known through exhibition and distribution as engravings.[75] Sandby himself showed a consistent interest in early industrial sites, depicted in juxtaposition to their natural landscape setting, and had painted both coal mines and copper works in the Vale of Neath before the end of the 1770s.

On tour in Wales in 1774, Henry Penruddocke Wyndham, an English gentleman, complained of the 'little intelligence' available about the country to facilitate his progress.[76] This difficulty would not begin to be alleviated by the availability of a guide-book until 1778. Having completed his expeditions to Scotland, Thomas Pennant turned his attention to his 'native country' in the early 1770s, though his explorations were facilitated by bed and breakfast

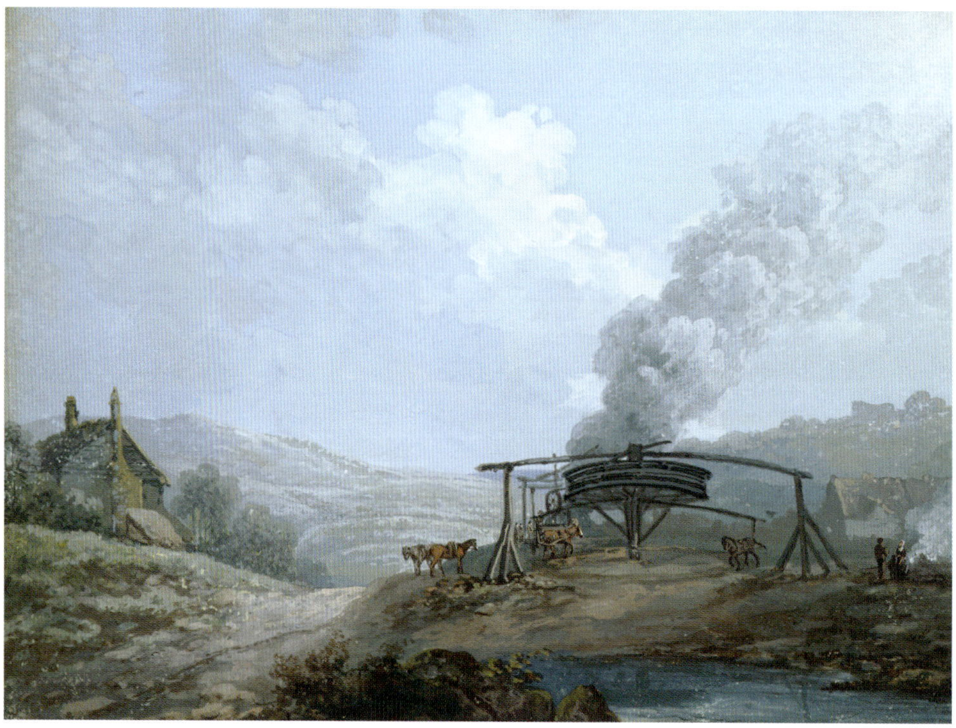

117. Paul Sandby, *Landscape with a Mine*, c.1775, gouache, 25x34.3

(and supper) at a succession of gentry houses, largely insulating him from the common people.[77] At Corsygedol, for instance, where he must have inspected Wilson's *Snowdon from Llyn Nantlle*, he was entertained by William Vaughan for several days 'in the style of an antient baron'.[78] Pennant was accompanied on his tour by Moses Griffith, a young painter born at Bryncroes in the Llŷn peninsula. Griffith was required to paint a wide range of subjects, from heraldry to architecture and scientific specimens, and also to copy portraits. The *Tour in Wales*, to which was added in 1781 *A Journey to Snowdon*, was illustrated by engravings after his work, but Pennant also had printed on large paper twelve extra copies, which his painter illustrated with a profusion of original watercolours. Some were made for distribution to friends, Sir Watkin among them, and these copies also included paintings made by John Ingleby of Halkin, whom Pennant occasionally employed. Ingleby was commissioned by Pennant on a conventional basis to carry out specific tasks, but Griffith had been taken into his household on a master-servant basis. As a result, although he became known within Pennant's own social and intellectual circle, his career as a painter would be constrained. He produced a great number of pictures, but it would be many years before he was able to practice with a degree of independence. Not until he was in his late thirties was he able to offer his services as a portrait painter, and even then only 'By permission from his master'.[79]

118. Moses Griffith, *Thomas Mostyn with 'Bay Bess'*, 1792, watercolour 24.8x36.8

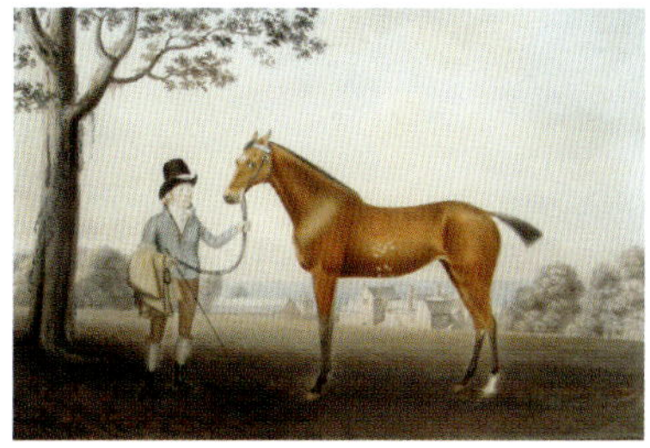

119. Moses Griffith, pages from an extra-illustrated copy of Thomas Pennant, *A Tour in Wales*, *c.*1778, watercolour, 29x44.5

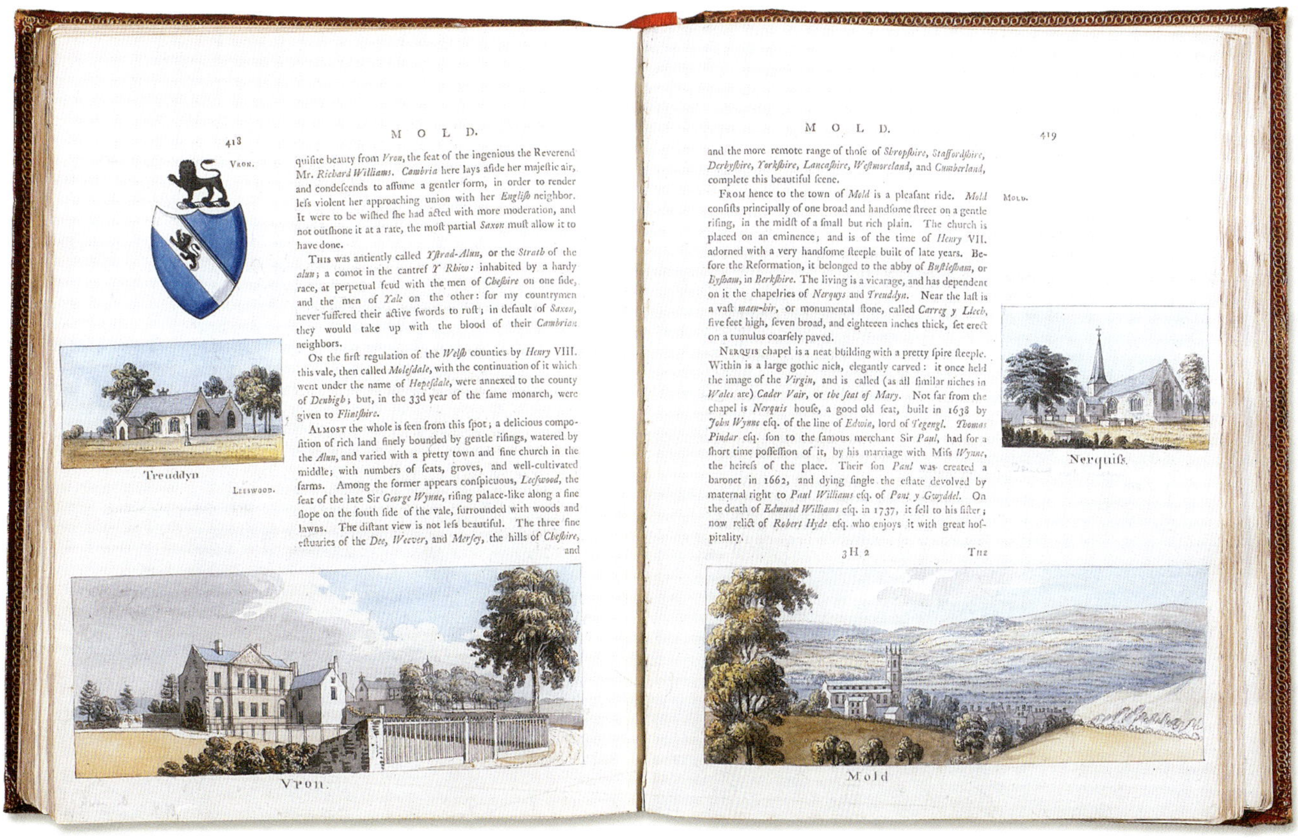

418 M O L D.

VRON.

quiſite beauty from *Vron*, the ſeat of the ingenious the Reverend Mr. *Richard Williams*. *Cambria* here lays aſide her majeſtic air, and condeſcends to aſſume a gentler form, in order to render leſs violent her approaching union with her *Engliſh* neighbor. It were to be wiſhed ſhe had acted with more moderation, and not outſhone it at a rate, the moſt partial *Saxon* muſt allow it to have done.

THIS was antiently called *Yſtrad-Alun*, or the *Strath* of the *alun*; a comot in the cantref *Y Rhiw:* inhabited by a hardy race, at perpetual feud with the men of *Cheſhire* on one ſide, and the men of *Yale* on the other: for my countrymen never ſuffered their active ſwords to ruſt; in default of *Saxon*, they would take up with the blood of their *Cambrian* neighbors.

ON the firſt regulation of the *Welſh* counties by *Henry* VIII. this vale, then called *Moleſdale*, with the continuation of it which went under the name of *Hopeſdale*, were annexed to the county of *Denbigh*; but, in the 33d year of the ſame monarch, were given to *Flintſhire*.

ALMOST the whole is ſeen from this ſpot; a delicious compoſition of rich land finely bounded by gentle riſings, watered by the *Alun*, and varied with a pretty town and fine church in the middle; with numbers of ſeats, groves, and well-cultivated farms. Among the former appears conſpicuous, *Leeſwood*, the ſeat of the late Sir *George Wynne*, riſing palace-like along a fine ſlope on the ſouth ſide of the vale, ſurrounded with woods and lawns. The diſtant view is not leſs beautiful. The three fine eſtuaries of the *Dee*, *Weever*, and *Merſey*, the hills of *Cheſhire*, and

Treuddyn

LEESWOOD.

Vron.

M O L D. 419

and the more remote range of thoſe of *Shropſhire*, *Staffordſhire*, *Derbyſhire*, *Yorkſhire*, *Lancaſhire*, *Weſtmoreland*, and *Cumberland*, complete this beautiful ſcene.

MOLD.

FROM hence to the town of *Mold* is a pleaſant ride. *Mold* conſiſts principally of one broad and handſome ſtreet on a gentle riſing, in the midſt of a ſmall but rich plain. The church is placed on an eminence; and is of the time of *Henry* VII. adorned with a very handſome ſteeple built of late years. Before the Reformation, it belonged to the abby of *Buſtleſham*, or *Byſham*, in *Berkſhire*. The living is a vicarage, and has dependent on it the chapelries of *Nerquys* and *Treuddyn*. Near the laſt is a vaſt *maen-hir*, or monumental ſtone, called *Carreg y Llech*, five feet high, ſeven broad, and eighteeen inches thick, ſet erect on a tumulus coarſely paved.

NERQUIS chapel is a neat building with a pretty ſpire ſteeple. Within is a large gothic nich, elegantly carved: it once held the image of the *Virgin*, and is called (as all ſimilar niches in *Wales* are) *Cader Vair*, or *the ſeat of Mary*. Not far from the chapel is *Nerquis* houſe, a good old ſeat, built in 1638 by *John Wynne* eſq. of the line of *Edwin*, lord of *Tegengl*. *Thomas Pindar* eſq. ſon to the famous merchant Sir *Paul*, had for a ſhort time poſſeſſion of it, by his marriage with Miſs *Wynne*, the heireſs of the place. Their ſon *Paul* was created a baronet in 1662, and dying ſingle the eſtate devolved by maternal right to *Paul Williams* eſq. of *Pont y Gwyddel*. On the death of *Edmund Williams* eſq. in 1737, it fell to his ſiſter; now relict of *Robert Hyde* eſq. who enjoys it with great hoſpitality.

Nerquiſs.

3H 2 THE

Mold

The next generation – Parry, Lewis, Downman and Jones in Italy

At the end of 1770, William Parry left Wynnstay for Italy, with the promise of a stipend paid by Sir Watkin in return for which he was to present his patron with original pictures and copies of old masters. He would complete four large-scale copies, including the Raphael *Transfiguration*, which would be hung in a prominent place on the staircase at Sir Watkin's new London house.[80] Parry's letters to his parents from Italy give a sense of the life led by expatriate connoisseurs and the artists with whom they surrounded themselves, which clearly had changed little since Wilson's day:

> I have made acquaintance with several english Gentlemen here ... I was last night at the Duke of Dorsett's Concert. His Grace plays on the violin very well, he very obligingly invited me to come whenever I pleased and offer'd to lend me any of the Pictures that he has collected here, that I chose to study from ...[81]

Parry fell in with a young Welsh architect, James Lewis. They spent much time together, looking at pictures, inspecting ancient and Renaissance architecture, visiting the theatre and socialising at the Caffè degli Inglesi.[82] Three years later, Parry was followed to Italy by more of his artist acquaintances, in the persons of Joseph Wright and John Downman. Unlike Parry, who spent five days in Paris on his overland route, they travelled by sea, via Spain and Nice, where Downman made drawings on the seashore and in the town which displayed for the period remarkable and prescient informality. The new generation of young painters were accompanied by a continuing flow of equally young gentlemen to Rome.

In 1772, Thomas Bulkeley of Baron Hill in Anglesey, the 7th Viscount Bulkeley to be, began his Grand Tour. It seems unlikely that he remained long unaware of the presence of his artist compatriots in town, but he favoured neither Downman nor Parry with commissions – nor, indeed, did he employ the established favourites Mengs or Batoni. The painter of Bulkeley's Grand Tour portrait has yet to be identified. Curiously, the English painter George Romney was also in Rome at this time, and Bulkeley, on his return home, would soon acquire a fine picture by this painter, though only as a result of his marriage. His future wife had recently sat to Romney, who painted her as Hebe, cup bearer to the gods, with a ewer at her feet and an eagle, symbol of her father, Zeus, looming rather ominously above her.[83]

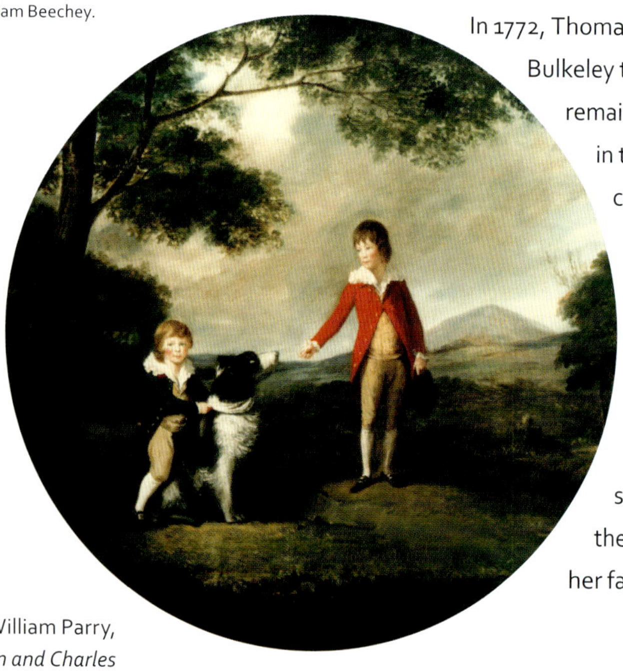

120. William Parry, *Watkin and Charles Watkin Williams-Wynn*, 1783–4, oil, d.132

80 Presumably working from the same tracing, later Parry would produce a second copy for Sir Roger Newdigate, the only one of his old master copies which is known to survive. See Cato, *Parry*, pp. 113–9.

81 NMW Archives A 11469.

82 The relationship is revealed in the diary of the English architect Richard Norris, BL Add MS 52497A-D. Lewis, who was born at Brecon, travelled to Italy with Norris, while Parry lodged with Dederick Dusign, an English portrait painter whom he had met in Reynolds's studio. Norris, Lewis, Parry and Dusign were frequently together until the architects departed for Venice in June 1772. Their circle included the resident agents James Byres and Thomas Jenkins, and also Dr Johnson, in Rome at that time. I am grateful to Miles Wynn Cato for the reference to the diary of Richard Norris.

83 Elizabeth Harriet Warren was the heiress of Sir George Warren of Poynton in Cheshire. Several of Romney's preparatory drawings for the portrait, made in 1776, survive. Elizabeth was painted later by Richard Cosway, again in strongly classical mode, with a cornucopia, though the marriage had no issue. The image was engraved by Bartolozzi in 1785. Husband and wife were also painted by William Beechey.

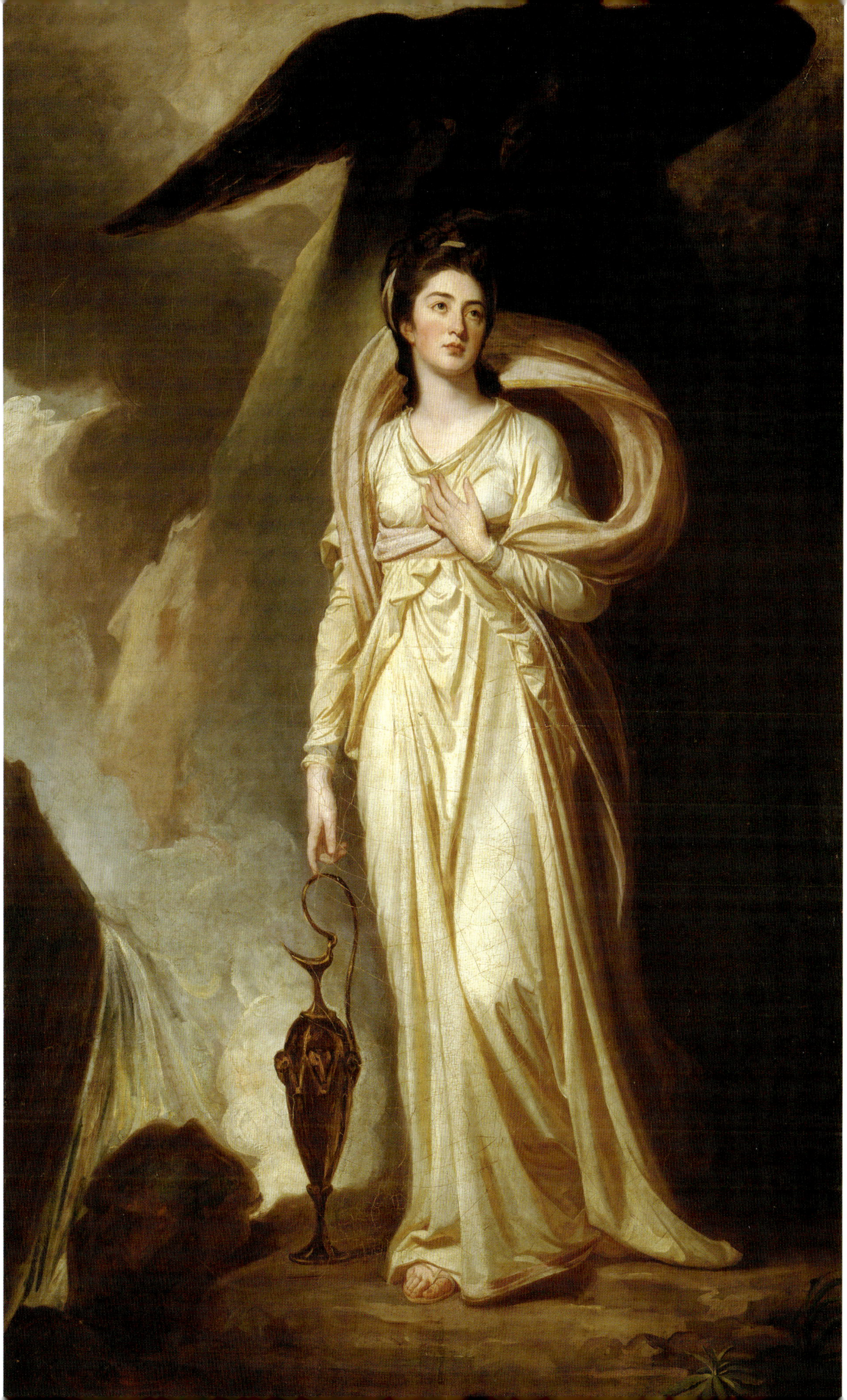

121. George Romney, *Elizabeth Warren, Viscountess Bulkeley, as Hebe*, 1775–6, oil on canvas, 238.5x148

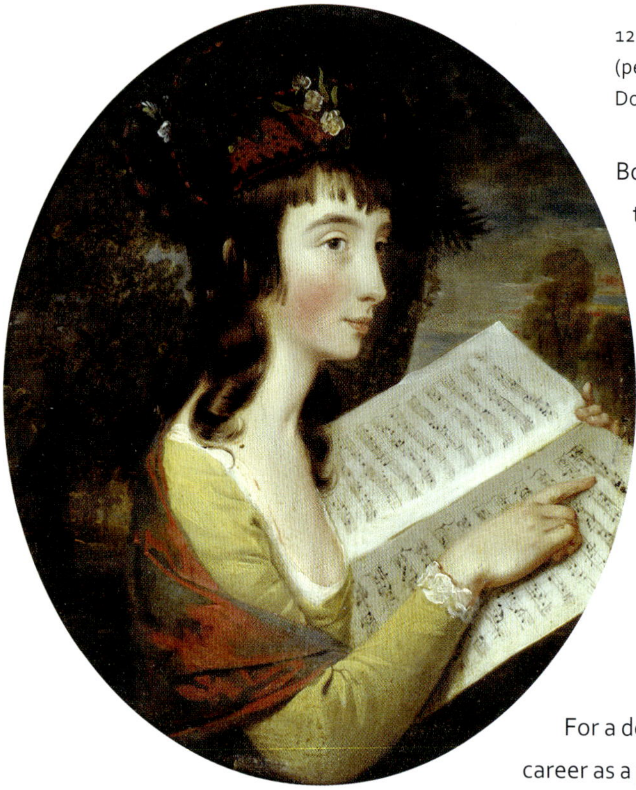

122. John Downman, *Miss Jackson* (perhaps subsequently Mrs John Downman), 1778, oil, 22.9x19

Both Welsh painters – Downman and Parry – had returned home by 1775 to resume their portrait careers. Parry would re-establish relationships with Welsh patrons, but Downman found sitters for his pastels and miniatures mainly among English people. On 7 October the following year, Thomas Jones noted a fortunate meeting in his diary:

> I had been for some time looking out for a Ship in which I meant to take my Passage, and had already found One, when meeting Parry, formerly a pupil of Sr Joshua Reynolds, who had just arrived from Italy accidentally in the Street, he told me that I now had a very lucky Opportunity of going by land as Mr Norton of Rome was in town and setting off on his return – He accordingly introduced me to this Gentleman and I was received with great form and Ceremony.[84]

For a decade after leaving Wilson's studio in 1765, Jones had developed his career as a painter of landscape and mythological subjects. His style reflected that of his master in various ways. He made both classical subject pictures, such as the *Death of Orpheus*, painted in about 1770 in co-operation with John Hamilton Mortimer, who was responsible for the figures, and fresher contemporary landscapes such as the *River Landscape with Figures beside a Weir* of 1775, probably inspired by the River Wye.[85] However, in the middle of this sequence, he painted a picture which was exceptional in his career because of its theme. Jones's *Memoirs* do not suggest that the history and mythology of his own country loomed large in his consciousness. Gray's poem 'The Bard' had early inspired a painting by Paul Sandby, that achieved considerable celebrity, but the *Memoirs* do not reveal why, fourteen years later, Jones also interested himself in the subject. The picture was painted during a long stay at the country house of his patron and pupil Oldfield Bowles, and perhaps it was he who suggested it. Some years earlier, Jones had visited Stonehenge, which he relocated in his picture in a fanciful Snowdonia, where he had never been.[86] Nevertheless, years later he would look back on the picture as 'one of the best I ever painted'. It attracted some attention when it was exhibited, but the engraving published in 1775 made so little impression that Jones believed it had been suppressed 'by that great Leviathan, Mr Alderman Boydel'.[87] The next year, following in the footsteps of Dyer, Wilson, Lewis, Parry and Downman, Jones set off for Italy.

Jones spent three years in and around Rome. Such was his familiarity with the work of Wilson that 'Every scene seemed anticipated in some dream – It appeared a Magick Land.'[88] He mixed with other artists in residence, several of whom he had known in London, including

84 Jones, *Memoirs*, p. 38. Norton was several times noted in the Italian diary of Richard Norris.

85 Mortimer worked on at least four Jones paintings, and in a further instance of interconnectedness among artists and patrons, also painted Joseph Banks with Cook (and others) on their return from the South Seas in 1771. The picture is in the collection of the National Library of Australia.

86 Curiously, when viewing the 'Stupendous Monument of remote Antiquity', Jones had felt that its 'grandeur and Magnificence' owed much to its location in the 'void' of the surrounding plain: '...were this Mass situated amidst high rocks, lofty mountains, and hanging Woods – however it might contribute to the richness of the scene in general – [it] would lose much of its own grandeur as a Single Object – The Experiment is easily tried upon Canvass.' Jones, *Memoirs*, p. 21.

87 Ibid., p. 33. Although the picture was painted in the period in which the figures for several of Jones's subject paintings were executed by Mortimer, he made no mention of co-operation in this case.

88 Ibid., p. 55.

the sculptor Thomas Banks, with whom he drank coffee at the Caffè degli Inglesi on the day of his arrival, and to whom he would sit for a bust in exchange for a painting. He would also associate with the painter John 'Warwick' Smith:

> Went with *Smith* the Landscape Painter & *Hardwick* to see a picture of *Perseus & Andromache* which the Caval're Mengs had just finished for Sr Watkin William Wynne & which was now exhibiting to the Public at his Palace near St Peter's ... In the room where this famous piece was placed for public Admiration, decorated with a Superb frame & green silk curtain, the Senior Pupils attended in form, ready to explain the Subject, point out the different beauties of the Performance, & expatiate on the transcendent excellencies of their great Master ...[89]

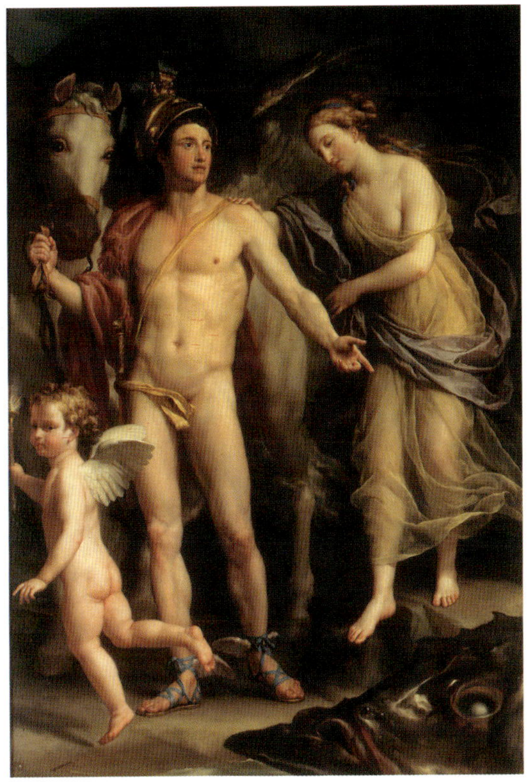

89 Ibid., pp. 68–9. Sir Watkin never saw his commission, which was taken by a French privateer on its way home, and eventually found its way to Russia, where it remains. Among other experiences shared with John Warwick Smith, Jones celebrated St David's day in 1780 on board a barque trading in Spanish wine, Jones, *Memoirs*, p. 93.

123. Anton Raphael Mengs, *Perseus and Andromache*, 1774–7, oil, 227x153.5

124. Thomas Jones, *The Bard*, 1774, oil, 114.5x168

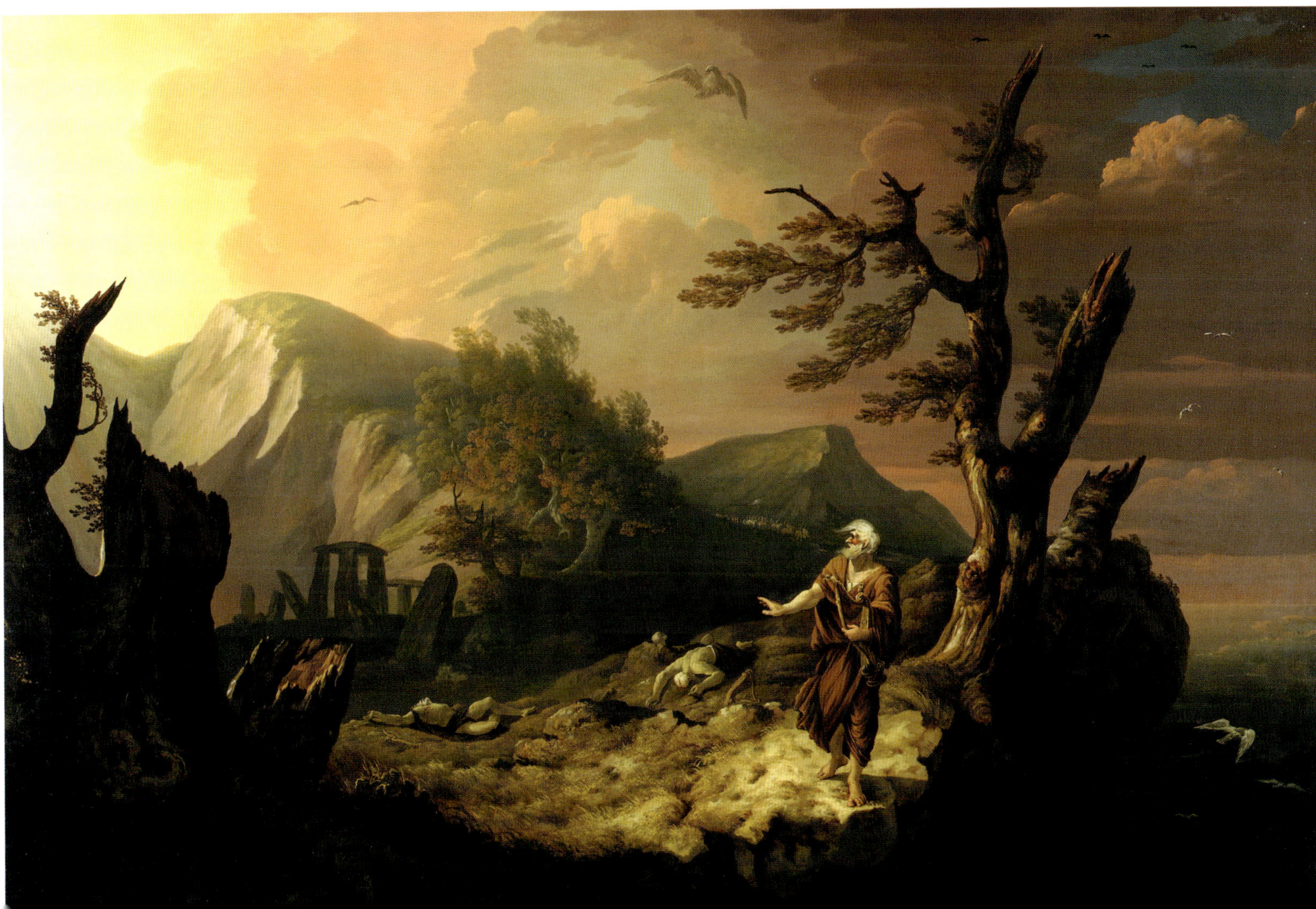

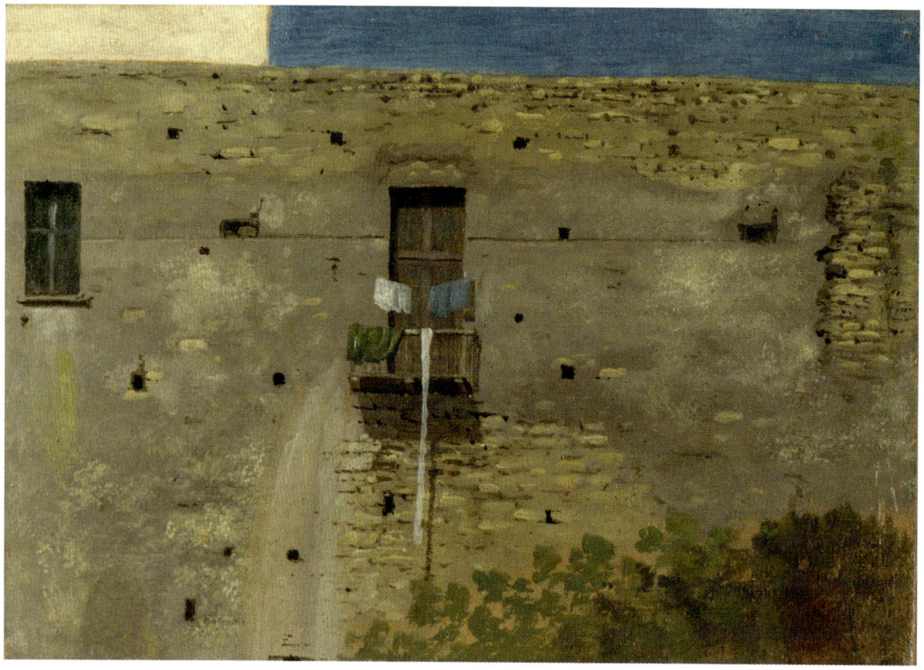

125. Thomas Jones, *A Wall in Naples*, c.1782, oil, 11.2x15.8

However, Jones took the view that the large picture was more 'The result of German flegmatic Industry' than of inspiration, a manifestation of sour grapes that perhaps reflected his own lack of success in attracting patrons. Despite treading the minefield of dealing with both Thomas Jenkins and James Byres, the rival artists' agents in Rome, by 1780 his commissions had dwindled to such an extent that he decided to move to Naples. He hoped that the British ambassador there, Sir William Hamilton, might be of more assistance to him. Hamilton's wife, Catherine, was Welsh – a Barlow of Lawrenny in Pembrokeshire. In Naples, Jones's life-style changed. He lived there with the woman that he would later marry, Maria Moncke, whom he had employed initially as a servant, and she quickly bore him two daughters. The financial implications of Jones's changed status obliged him to live simply, with the consequence that he seems to have become more closely involved with the Italian community than he had been in Rome. This change of life-style may have a bearing on one group of paintings that he produced in Naples. Jones painted small but finished pictures in oil of buildings around his apartments. He observed his urban environment apparently without attempting to select views on the basis of conventional aesthetic ideas or to manipulate the scene as it presented itself. It is from these paintings that the reputation he would acquire a century and a half after his death initially sprang, though they were of little use to him professionally in his lifetime. Nevertheless, as a harbinger of a change in taste that would eventually break down the formality of academic landscape painting, Jones was not an entirely isolated phenomenon, and indeed perhaps he had sensed a change of mood among some other young painters. Downman's French and Italian sketchbook showed similar inclinations to his own, and even before leaving home, Jones was certainly familiar with the work of Vernet, Wilson's friend in Italy, who had made informal oil sketches. Neither had Jones's own paintings of the countryside around Pencerrig, made shortly before his departure, conformed to academic norms. The urban studies that he would make in Naples seem less startling when considered in the context of these earlier, informal rural landscapes.

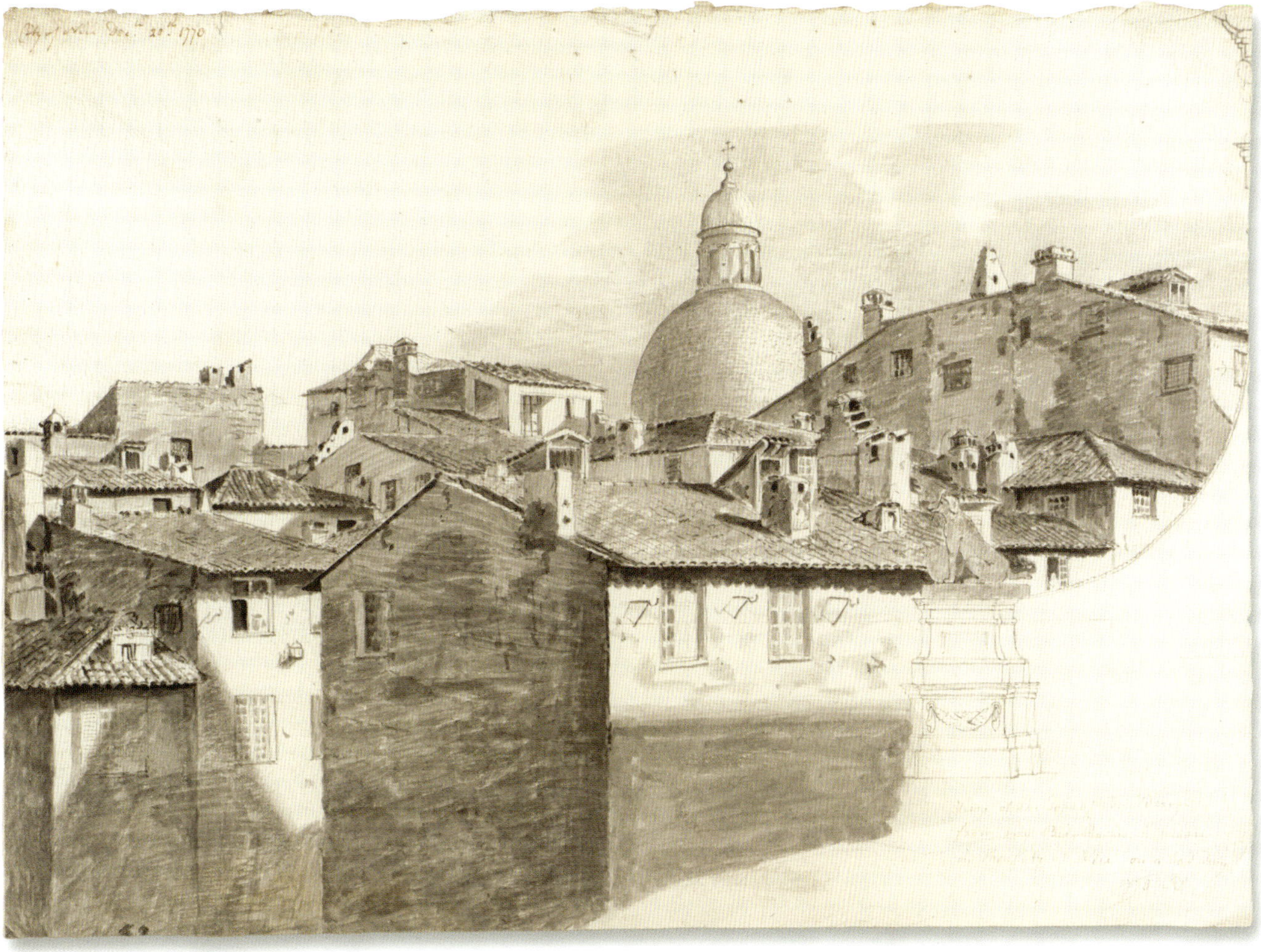

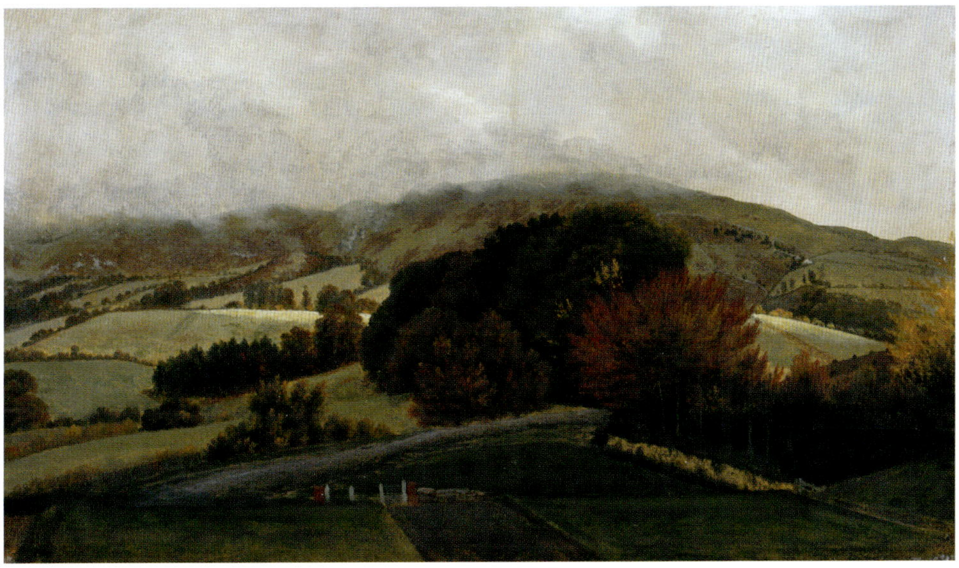

126. John Downman, *View of Roof Tops in Nice*, 1773, pencil and watercolour, 26.5x36.7

127. Thomas Jones, *Carneddau Mountains from Pencerrig*, c.1775, oil, 29.5x51

90 Gilpin to William Mason, 1787, quoted in Carl Paul Barbier, *William Gilpin. His Drawings, Teaching and Theory of the Picturesque* (Oxford, 1963), p. 72.

91 See Richard Suggett, *John Nash: Architect in Wales* (Aberystwyth, 1995), and for a survey of early Welsh architects, see Thomas Lloyd, 'The emergence of the architectural profession in Wales', *Archaeologia Cambrensis* 157 (2008), pp. 1–8.

Jones left Italy in 1783, and attempted to re-establish himself in London, but he met with little critical success. Financially it mattered not, since in 1787 he unexpectedly inherited Pencerrig, and was able to continue as a gentleman painter, not reliant on selling his work. Among the few patrons and friends who did support him in the interim was Thomas Johnes, owner of the Hafod estate in Cardiganshire. At the time of Jones's first visit there, probably made in 1785, Johnes was beginning the development of Hafod into what would become one of the most celebrated managed landscapes in Britain. He was enthusiastic about the painting of his fellow gentleman, and bought pictures that Jones painted on the estate. However, they did not please the aesthetic authorities. In 1787, Johnes showed to the Revd William Gilpin 'a large port-folio full of paintings (on paper) of a variety of views around his house. They were done by Jones, a pupil of Wilson', he noted. 'On the whole, they were not amiss, considering he is one of your *religious copyists* ...'[90] Gilpin's patronising comments on the lack of theoretical rigour evident in Jones's views did not deter his patron, and it seems likely that they were the basis of the images painted on an elegant dessert service produced for Johnes at the Derby factory in the following year.

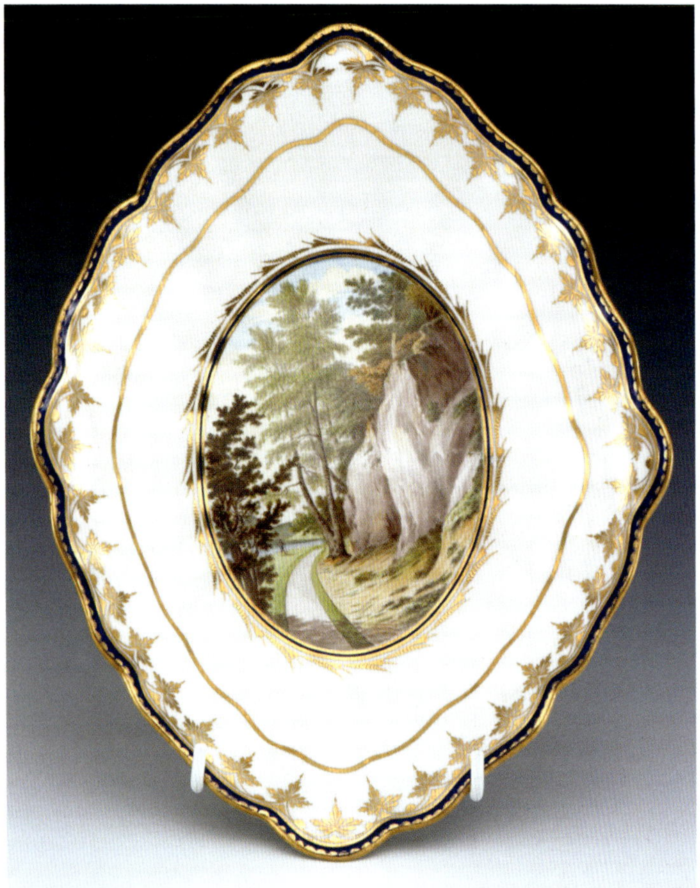

Like so many of his gentry contemporaries, Thomas Johnes had visited the continent as a young man, though he travelled more widely than most. In 1769 he returned to his mother's home county of Herefordshire, where he kept the company of local landowners Richard Payne Knight and Uvedale Price, enthusiastic contributors to the developing theory of landscape. All three would participate in the debates that interested the increasing flow of painters and connoisseurs visiting Wales during the closing decades of the eighteenth century. The publication in 1794 of Knight's poem, 'The Landscape' and Price's *Essay on the Picturesque, As Compared with the Sublime and the Beautiful* coincided with the high-point of Johnes's energetic enterprise in developing the

128. After Thomas Jones,
Ladies' Walk, Hafod, from the Hafod Dessert Service,
Derby Porcelain Factory, 1787, porcelain, 26.5x21

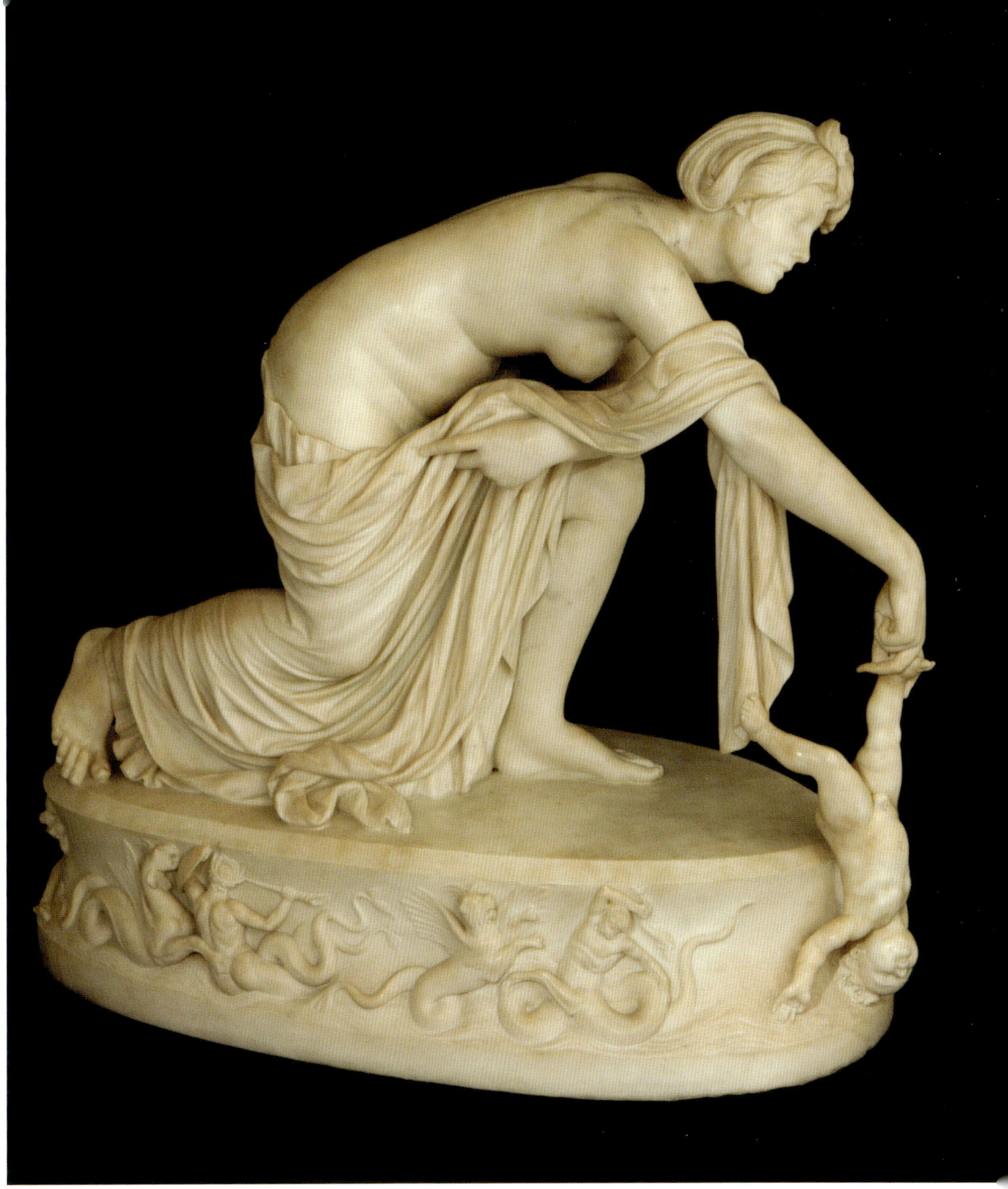

129. Thomas Banks, *Thetis dipping Achilles in the River Styx*, 1789–90, marble

Hafod landscape, and of his collecting activities. Johnes commissioned his new house on the estate from Thomas Baldwin of Bath in 1786, and in the early 1790s John Nash made additions that would help to develop his own subsequent career. Nash was of a London Welsh family, and had started work there, but following bankruptcy spent twelve years based in Carmarthen, from where he was occasionally able to design in a manner intended to complement the picturesque landscape aesthetic.[91] The most dramatic of Nash's additions to Hafod was the octagonal library which, with its 'vast collection of valuable and rare publications, methodically arranged and carefully preserved', would be enhanced with sculpture made by Thomas Banks.[92] It is possible that Johnes was encouraged to patronise Banks by Thomas Jones, and the relationship between them would result in the production of one of the sculptor's most celebrated works, *Thetis dipping Achilles in the River Styx*, completed to critical acclaim in 1790. As a classical subject piece, it was regarded as somewhat radical because of its use of Jane and Mariamne Johnes, the patron's wife and daughter, as models: 'The figure of the infant hero is in the highest degree exquisite', reported the London *Morning Post*, even before the completion of the work.[93]

92 R. Warner, *A Second Walk through Wales* (2nd edn., London, 1802), p. 148.

93 *Morning Post*, 13 June 1789. For an introduction to the wide range of Johnes's activities at Hafod, and his letters, see Richard J. Moore-Collyer, *A Land of Pure Delight. Selections from the letters of Thomas Johnes of Hafod, 1748–1816* (Llandysul, 1992). However, Moore-Collyer is mistaken in stating that Johnes had met Banks in Italy, p. 17. The sculptor did not arrive there until 1772.

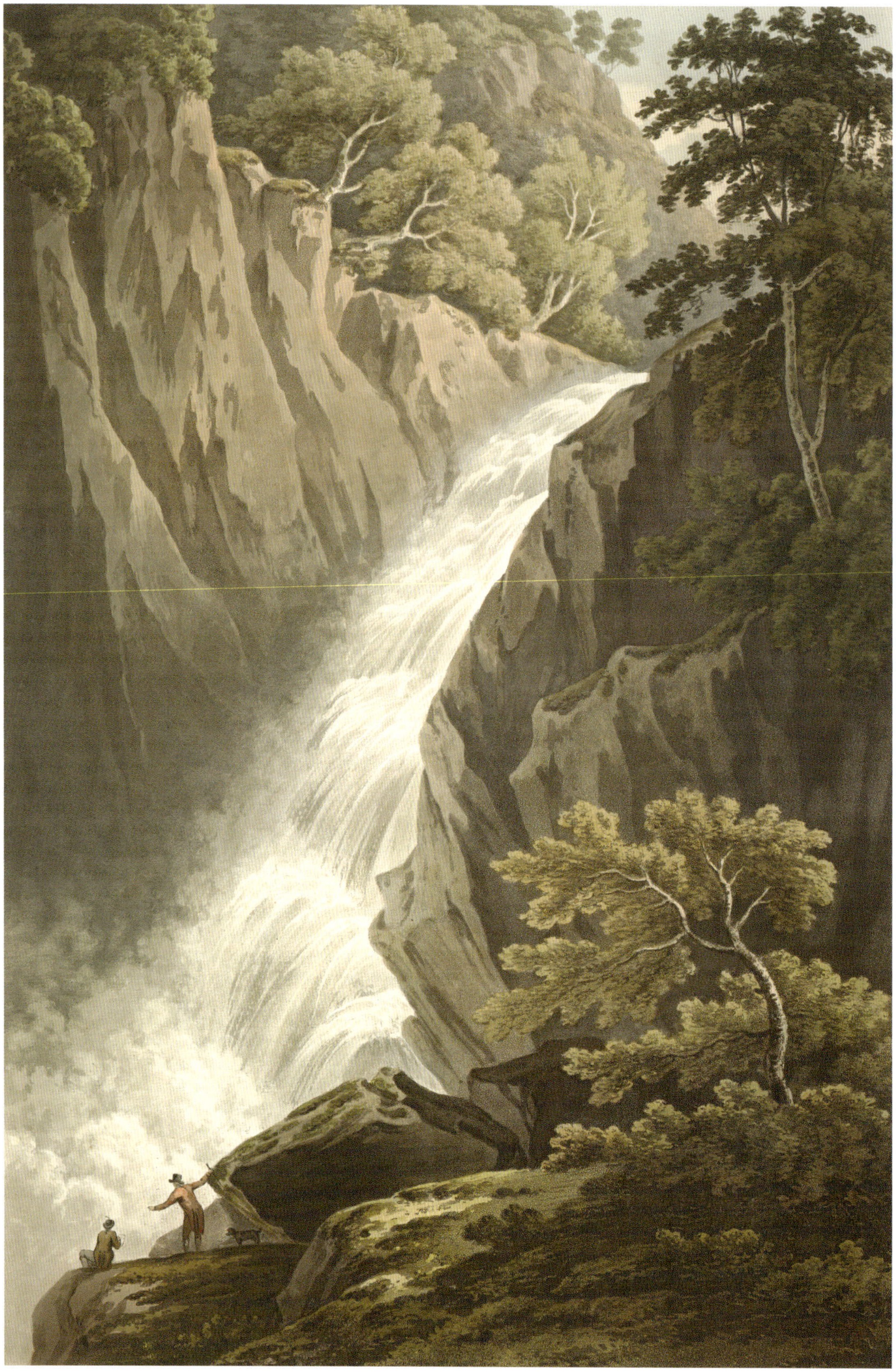

130. J.C.Stadler after John Warwick Smith, *Lower Part of the Great Fall of the Fynach*, from James Edward Smith, *Fifteen views illustrative of a tour to Havod in Cardiganshire*, 1810, aquatint, 51x34.5

Hafod was celebrated in several published tours in Wales, but in most detail in George Cumberland's *An Attempt to Describe Hafod*, published in 1796. Immediately afterwards, Johnes floated the idea of an illustrated guide, based on 'some beautiful drawings by Smith', that were in his possession, and others that he could borrow from Robert Fulke Greville. The 'Smith' in question was Thomas Jones's friend from Italy, the landscape painter John Warwick Smith. He had visited Hafod in 1792 in the company of Greville and a younger painter, Julius Caesar Ibbetson. The volume was eventually published in 1810 as *Fifteen views illustrative of a tour to Havod in Cardiganshire*, the views being engraved after Smith's paintings. They became the definitive images of the picturesque landscape of Hafod in its prime.[94]

John Warwick Smith was among the most enthusiastic of tourists in Wales, returning many times between 1784 and 1806. Aided by the publication of new descriptions of country that had been 'rarely visited' in the 1770s, when Henry Penruddocke Wyndham 'did not meet with a single party' during his six-week tour, the roads were now regularly frequented in the summer. Thomas Johnes felt able to encourage George Cumberland, whose *Attempt to Describe Hafod* was published twenty years after Wyndham's *Gentleman's Tour*, with the observation that 'a good sale might be made of your work at the Devil's Bridge where crowds still increasing come every year'. Johnes had provided them with a convenient hotel, twenty yards from the head of the waterfalls.[95] The menu of sights and the routes to them were now well defined, especially along the River Wye, where Tintern Abbey became a beggar-infested mecca, and in Snowdonia, where blind harpers proliferated. Indeed, Smith, Greville and Ibbetson were treated to a performance by John Smith of Conwy, a harper whom Wyndham had publicised two decades earlier. He was immortalised by Ibbetson in an image that emerged in 1802 in engraved form (relocated to Llanberis in a landscape drawn by Smith) as the frontispiece to the latest publication on the subject of traditional Welsh music, *The Bardic Museum*.[96]

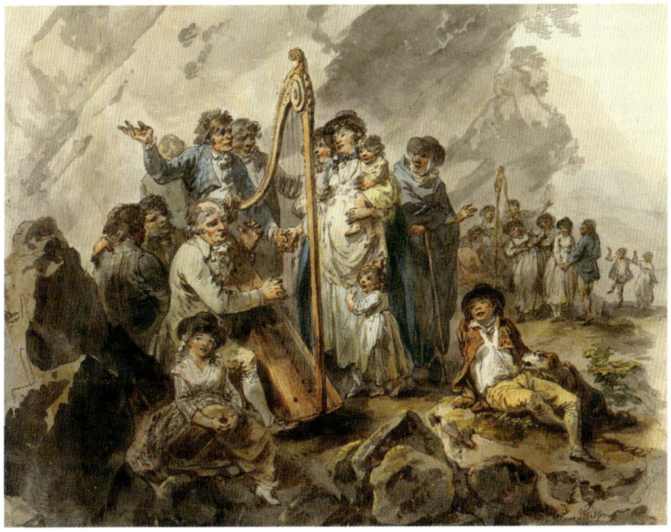

131. Julius Caesar Ibbetson, *Penillion Singing near Conway*, c.1792–3, watercolour, 21.5x29.2

94 The volume was proposed in a letter to James Edward Smith, dated 1 February 1796, Linnean Society of London (Smith), 16, f. 45, given in Moore-Collyer, ibid., p. 115. Smith, Chairman of the Linnean Society, was a close friend of Johnes, and would write the text to the illustrations by John Warwick Smith. Between conception and publication, in 1807 the house at Hafod was severely damaged by fire, along with much of its contents. It was rebuilt, again to designs by Baldwin. John Warwick Smith was offered employment as tutor and painter in residence at Hafod, but declined. The place was filled by Thomas Stothard.

95 BL Add. MS 36498, f. 100, given in Moore-Collyer, ibid., p.114.

96 Edward Jones, *The Bardic Museum* (London, 1802). At the time, Jones was harpist to the Prince of Wales, subsequently King George IV, and so became known as 'Bardd y Brenin'.

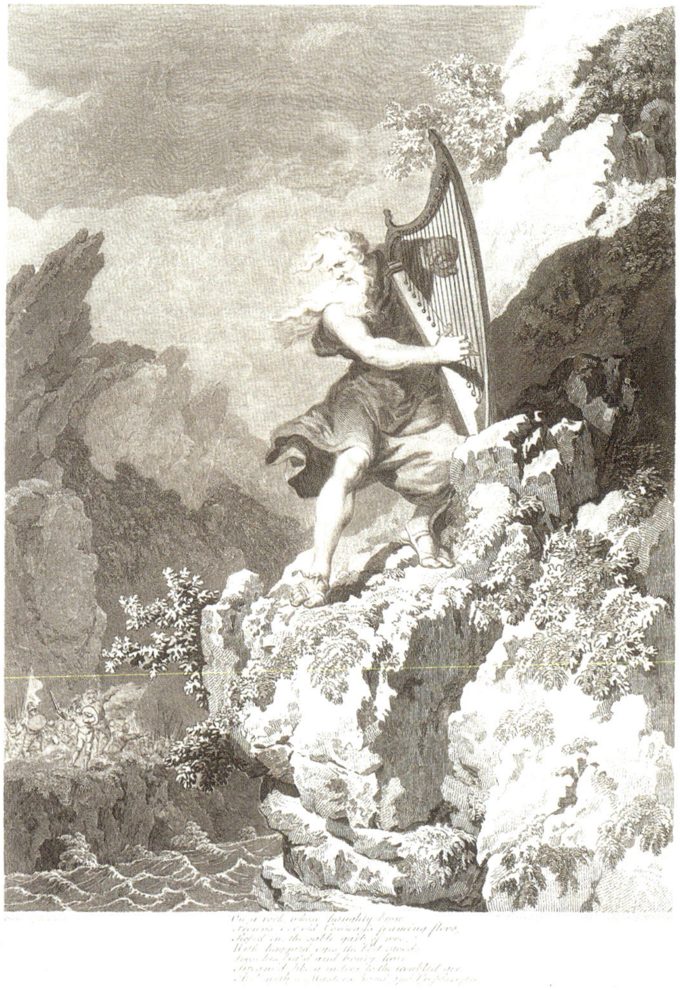

132. Hall and Middiman after Philippe de Loutherbourg, *The Last Bard*, frontispiece to Edward Jones, *Musical and Poetical Relicks of the Welsh Bards*, 1784, engraving 31x22.8

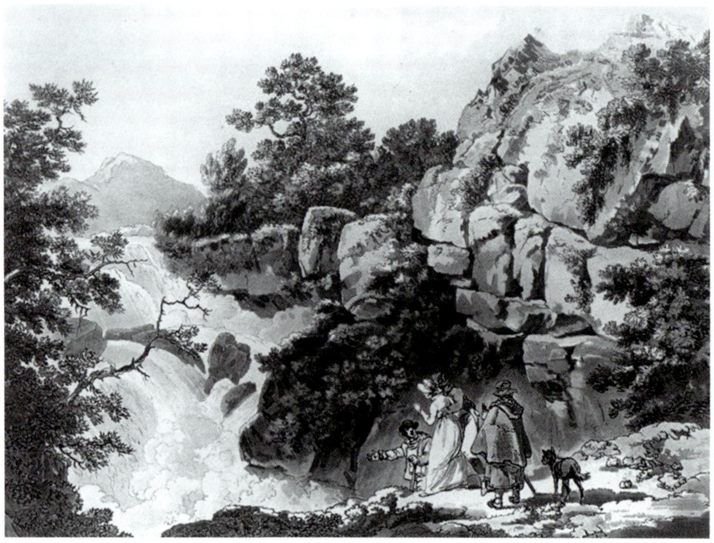

133. William Pickett after Philippe de Loutherbourg, *Cataract on the Llugwy*, from *The Romantic and Picturesque Scenery of England and Wales*, 1805, aquatint, 23.1x31.7

Inspired by such publications, almost all the painters prominent in the London exhibitions of the late eighteenth and early nineteenth centuries now took tours in north Wales. Indeed, some painted Welsh themes even before they had set foot in the country. Philip de Loutherbourg produced what would become one of the most familiar images of the Last Bard legend, engraved as the frontispiece to Edward Jones's *Musical and Poetical Relicks of the Welsh Bards* in 1784, two years before he and his wife visited Snowdonia. When they did so, their hunt for primitive ancient Britons lurking in sublime settings was duly rewarded at the Swallow Falls, near Betws-y-coed:

> After we had struck out of the high road, we came to a hovel, not unlike those of Oonalashka, as delineated in Cook's Voyages, where we found a man and his daughter, who conducted us to the spot. By this man we were informed, that it was the place to which the devil conveys the souls of bad stewards ...[97]

Some prominent London figures became acquainted with Wales over a longer period. George Beaumont, though more influential as an arbiter of taste than as a painter, was in residence at Benarth House, Conwy, every summer between 1799 and 1806. In 1801 the poet Samuel Rogers met him on the street in Conwy with Joseph Farington, Wilson's pupil of nearly forty years earlier. In a letter to William Gilpin, he reported that 'Their port-folios were full of rocks & cataracts & ruin'd Castles'.[98] Farington had visited Wales with Thomas Jones as early as 1769, and came again on several occasions at the turn of the century. Though his own preference was for the lakes of Cumbria, the catalogues of the newly formed Society of Painters in Water Colours demonstrated the dominance of Wales as a destination for artists in the early years of the nineteenth century. In 1805, the society's first exhibition displayed fifty-two Welsh views, compared with ten from Scotland and just one from the Lake District.

Back in London in September 1798, Joseph Farington noted in his diary that 'William Turner called on me. He has been in South and North Wales this summer – alone and on horseback – out 7 weeks.'[99] Although he was still only 23 years old, J.M.W. Turner had just returned from the fourth of five tours in Wales that he made before 1800. The range of pictures that he produced over the decade during which he interested himself in Welsh subject matter demonstrates how the country played an important role in the early evolution of his work, as he set out on the road from child prodigy (he had entered the Royal Academy Schools at the age of 14), to the grand old man of English art. His Welsh journeys were among the most thorough undertaken by any English painter. In 1792 – the same summer that Smith, Ibbetson and Greville were on the road – he proceeded well beyond the conventional Wye tour, following the river to its source on Pumlumon and on to Hafod. Many year later he recalled in a letter to a friend that 'The view from the Inn near the Devil's Bridge commands the falls of the Ridol – the Devil's Bridge torrent rushes down a steep chasam, under two bridges one over the other ... You are in the neighbourhood of Havord ... I dare say yet known by being the Seat of Esquire Johns a fine place well wooded ...'[100] In 1794 Turner was in Llangollen, and in 1795 he explored the south as far west as St David's. On the way he produced both rapid pencil sketches and more intensive coloured studies, which provided the source material that he refined in his London studio into large-scale watercolours and oils for exhibition at the Royal Academy. Although these attracted much attention, at this stage they did not set him decisively apart from the competition of painters such

97 Philippe de Loutherbourg, *Romantic and Picturesque Scenery in England and Wales* (London, 1805), no pagination.

98 Rogers to Gilpin, 12 January 1801, quoted in C.P.Barbier, *Samuel Rogers and William Gilpin. Their Friendship and Correspondence* (London, 1959), p. 57.

99 'Much rain but better effects – one clear day and Snowdon appeared green and unpicturesque to the top ...' Quoted in Andrew Wilton, *Turner in Wales* (Llandudno, 1984), p. 52.

100 John Gage, *Collected Correspondence of J.M.W. Turner* (1980), no. 307, Turner to Hawkesworth Fawkes, 27 December 1847. Turner came to Aberystwyth on his tour in 1798, but it is unclear if he visited Hafod for a second time on that occasion.

101 *True Briton*, 4 May 1799, quoted in Martin Butlin and Evelyn Joll, *The Paintings of J.M.W. Turner* (2 vols. New Haven, 1977), 1984 edition, text volume, pp. 7–8 . For Turner's attitude to the tradition of landscape painting, see *Turner and the Masters*, ed. David Solkin (London, 2009).

as de Loutherbourg and Ibbetson, who also worked up sketches taken on the spot into substantial exhibition paintings. In 1794 Turner showed *Tintern Abbey* at the Academy, and in the same exhibition Ibbetson showed *Conway Castle, Moonlight Effect*. An artist – Ibbetson himself, perhaps, or his colleague Smith – observed the ferrymen on a remarkably busy night-time crossing. Ibbetson combined a scene redolent of ages past with the silvery light effects beloved of the art market in the period. Turner seems to have taken note, and two years later showed his own moonlit scene of *Fishermen at Sea*.

134. J.M.W. Turner, *Interior of Tintern Abbey, Monmouthshire*, 1794, watercolour, 32.1x25.1

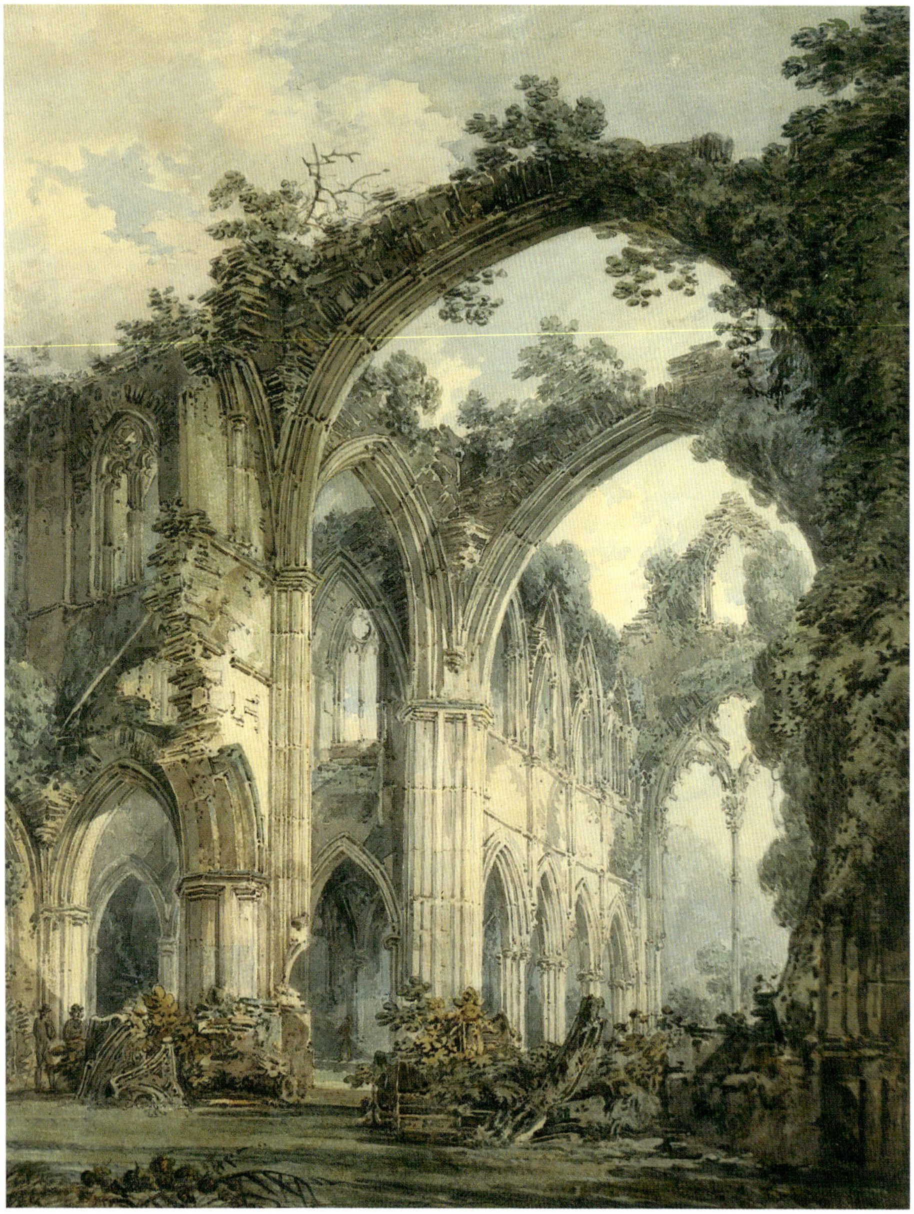

In 1798 Turner undertook his most extensive tour – that mentioned by Farington – in the course of which he accomplished almost a complete circuit of the country, beginning at Chepstow and finishing at Hereford. On his way, he visited Penegoes, the birthplace of Richard Wilson. His Academy picture of the following year, *Harlech Castle from Tygwyn Ferry*, illustrates the path that the young painter was attempting to walk between acknowledgement of earlier masters of landscape painting and the originality that was increasingly required to make a mark in the London art world. The picture met with the approval of one critic in precisely these terms: 'This Landscape, though it combines the style of CLAUDE and of our excellent WILSON, yet wears an aspect of originality that shows the painter looks at Nature with his own eyes.'[101]

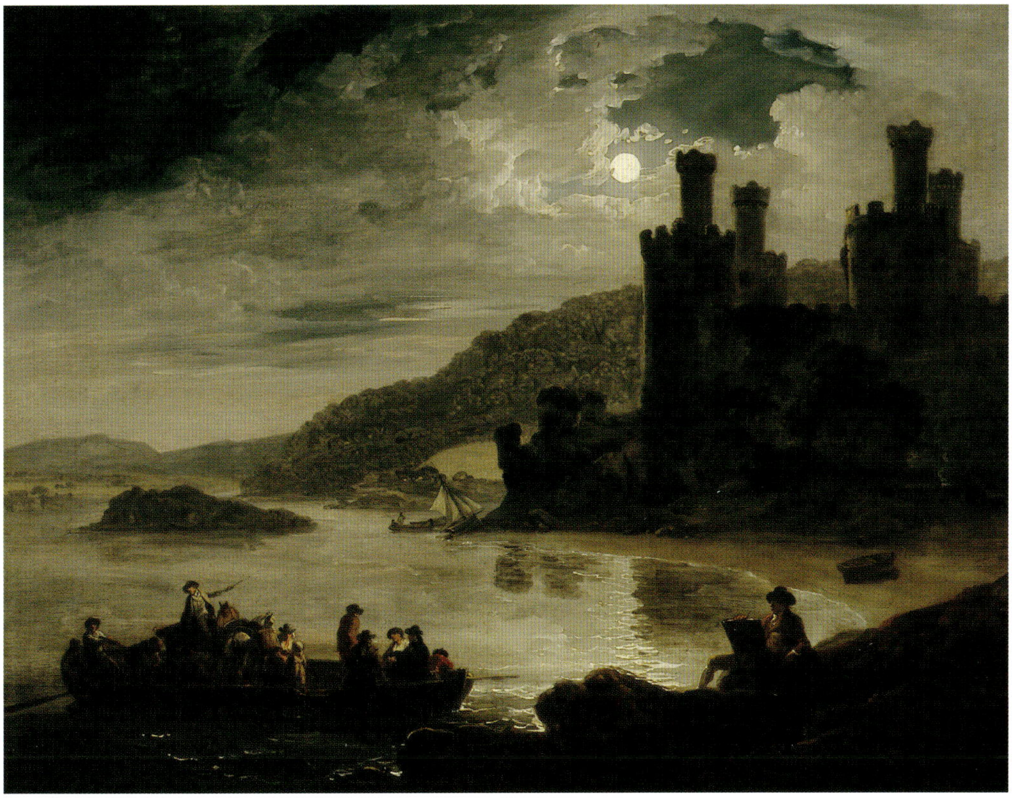

135. Julius Caesar Ibbetson, *Conway Castle, Moonlight Effect*, 1794, oil, 34.3x45.1

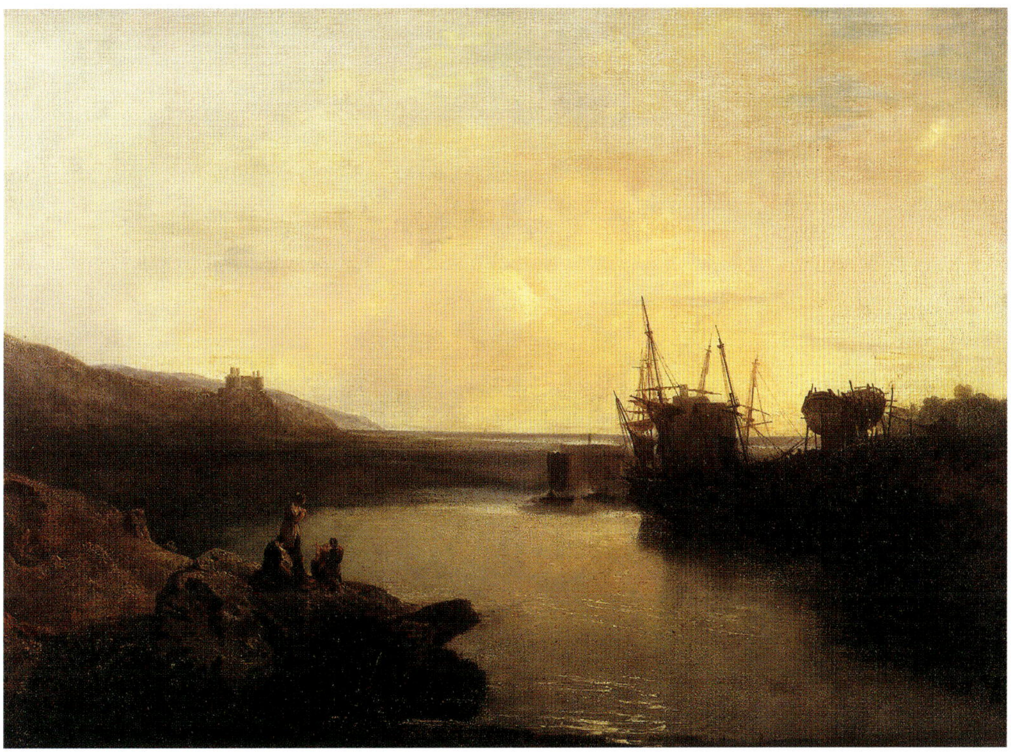

136. J.M.W. Turner, *Harlech Castle from Tygwyn Ferry, Summer's Evening Twilight*, 1799, oil, 87x119.4

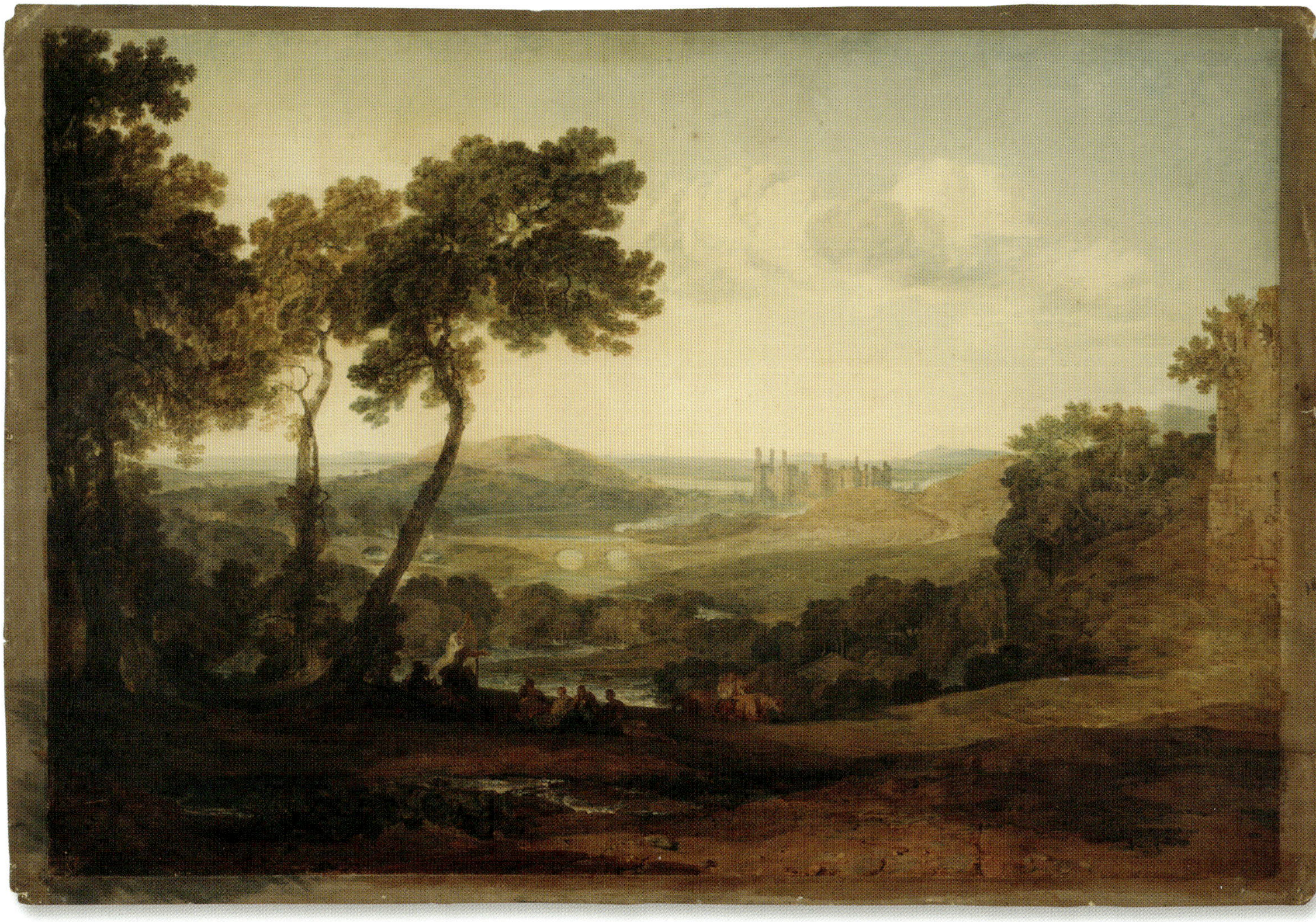

137. J.M.W. Turner, *Caernarvon Castle, North Wales*, 1799–1800, watercolour, 70.6x105.5

102 In 1799 Turner visited the Conwy Valley and Snowdonia, but with the exception of a brief excursion along the River Dee in 1808, he did not again return to Wales. His final exhibited Welsh pictures were largely confined to the first years of the nineteenth century, though in the mid-1820s he revisited material he had gathered as a young man. In his series *Picturesque Views in England and Wales*, he retrospectively applied his mature, luminous style to views of Penmaenmawr and Llanberis Lake.

Like Wilson before him, the young Turner aspired to paint landscape infused with mythic content and a high moral tone. A group of sketches and unfinished watercolours suggest that he intended to paint a picture inspired by the Last Bard legend. In the end, his large exhibited watercolour, *Caernarvon Castle, North Wales*, was a lament on the subject of the violent conquest by Edward I of Wales, 'Where jealous of the minstrel band,/The tyrant drench'd with blood the land.' The accompanying verses were probably of the painter's own composition. In his picture, Turner presented his audience with an aesthetic paradox by opposing a sublime subject – a bard singing of violence and bloodshed in the rugged mountains – to a composition and restrained use of colour that alluded unambiguously to the classical landscape tradition represented by Wilson. However, in two other historical pictures of the period, *Looking down a Deep Valley towards Snowdon, with an Army on the March* – the army of Edward I – and *Dolbadern Castle, North Wales*, content and painting

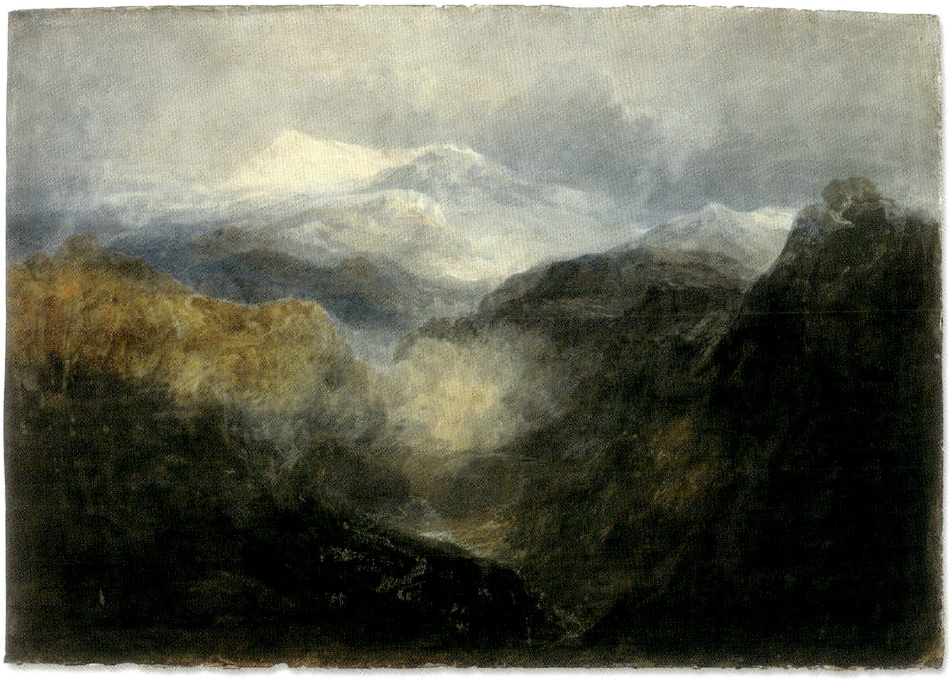

138. J.M.W. Turner, *Looking down a Deep Valley towards Snowdon, with an Army on the March*, 1799–1800, watercolour, 67.9x99.6

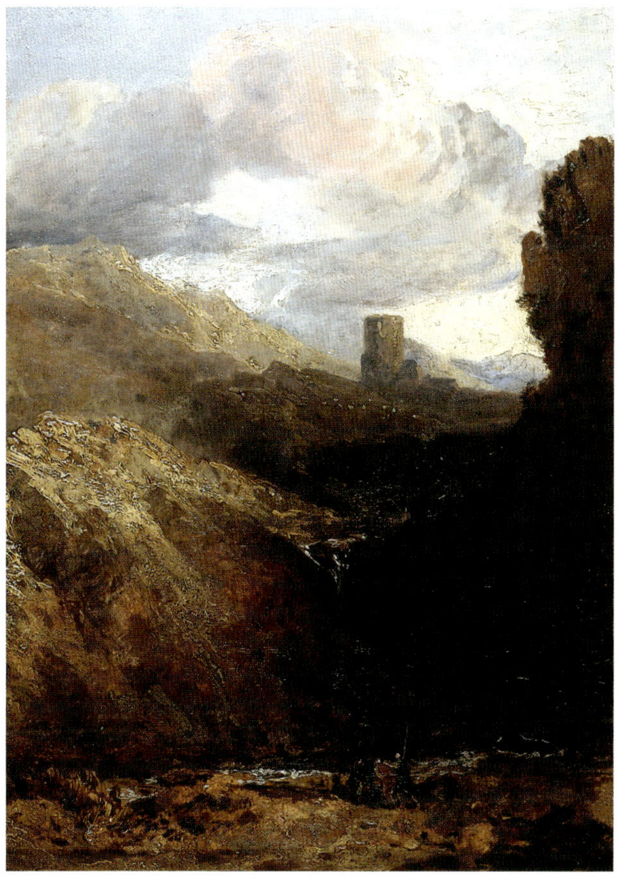

139. J.M.W. Turner, Sketch for *Dolbadern Castle, North Wales*, 1799–1800, oil, 46.5x34.0

style were not conflicted. In the first, the misty atmospherics for which Turner would later become celebrated were foreshadowed, and in the second he presented an undiluted Romanticism. Human vulnerability, exemplified by the tiny figure of Owain Goch, dragged to imprisonment on the orders of his brother, Llywelyn, was emphasised by the towering mountains and the dark fortress above. The importance of this picture to Turner was made apparent when he chose it as the diploma work to be presented to the Royal Academy on his being elected a member in 1802.[102]

New views

Beneath the surface of elevated sentiment presented to the public in London by artists at the end of the eighteenth century lay both the age-old hard reality of earning a living, and the challenge of dealing with a world in which environmental and social change was occurring at an unprecedented rate. In 1789, on his first visit to Wales, under the patronage of the Earl of Bute, Julius Caesar Ibbetson wrote in a sarcastic frame of mind to his friend William Anderson, a Scottish marine painter:

> I pray God that all Bakers, Butchers, Landlords ... may have (as in duty bound) the highest respect for Artists and their wives in general. We are Gentlemen and ought, for that matter, to be maintained at the publick expense [and] that in purple and fine linen and fare sumptuously every day – but we live in a damned lechrous age, when every maggot of a Duke or a Lord imagines Himself almost upon an equality with the professors of the Noblest of Arts – an Art which enables the Artist to starve in a superb manner and to wear ragged breeches when every body knows that in the days of Protogenes and Apelles the princes of the earth from the most remote regions surrounded their palaces and in the most submissive manner begged to have the honour of cleaning their shoes and wiping their backsides. And if the painter honoured them with a kick on the arse or a good lick on the jaws, the Prince or King or any other rascal went home perfectly satisfied and prouder of recounting that honour than any other title belonging to them – [103]

It is significant that such earthy and anti-elitist sentiments emanated from Ibbetson in particular, and also that they did so in the year of the French Revolution – to which the painter also made reference in his letter. It has often been observed by art historians that 1789 marked the beginning of a quarter century during which painters and patrons were no longer able to travel freely to the continent.[104] Certainly, a side effect of the French wars was a stimulus to internal tourism in the British Isles, but as the tone of Ibbetson's letter suggests, the more fundamental and important effect of the Europe-wide conflicts of the period was a liberation of mind. As the work of James Gillray and other metropolitan satirists confirms, deference was not a characteristic of late eighteenth-century intellectual life. Although the French wars engendered a degree of patriotic solidarity within the British Isles, nevertheless a democratising spirit was abroad, stimulated by a realisation that the prevailing order was not god-given and therefore fixed. Alongside industrialisation, this spirit would facilitate the transformation of Welsh society, and that of the rest of Britain, in the first half of the nineteenth century. Ibbetson himself came not from the metropolitan elite or the gentry, but from a Nonconformist background in trade in the English provinces. Of all the painters

103 'The women too, in those days – o Lord! o Lord!! I shall go mad! I think I see them now, the most beautiful princesses and damsels of the universe on their knees, supplicating the honour of laying [*sic*] for a night under the painter's bed, or on a mat at his chamber door. And if he designed once to command one of them to [*word scraped away*] him, she was a match directly for the Emperor of the World!!!' NLW MS 5484C. The offending word was apparently scraped away by a puritanical subsequent reader or owner of the letter. I have adjusted Ibbetson's indignant orthography and punctuation. Ibbetson had been introduced to the Earl of Bute by the Scottish dealer and connoisseur, Captain William Baillie.

104 A lull in the French wars in 1802 briefly enabled artists and patrons to travel again. Among the beneficiaries was Turner, who visited France and Switzerland.

105 His works exhibited at the Academy in the years following his 1792 tour with Smith and Greville, included nine views of the common people at work, mounted together in a single frame.

106 Ibbetson made three watercolour versions of his image of Smith (in addition to that which became the frontis to *The Bardic Museum*), as well as the Royal Aacademy oil painting.

140. Julius Caesar Ibbetson, *An Iron Forge at Merthyr Tydfil*, 1789, watercolour, 22x29

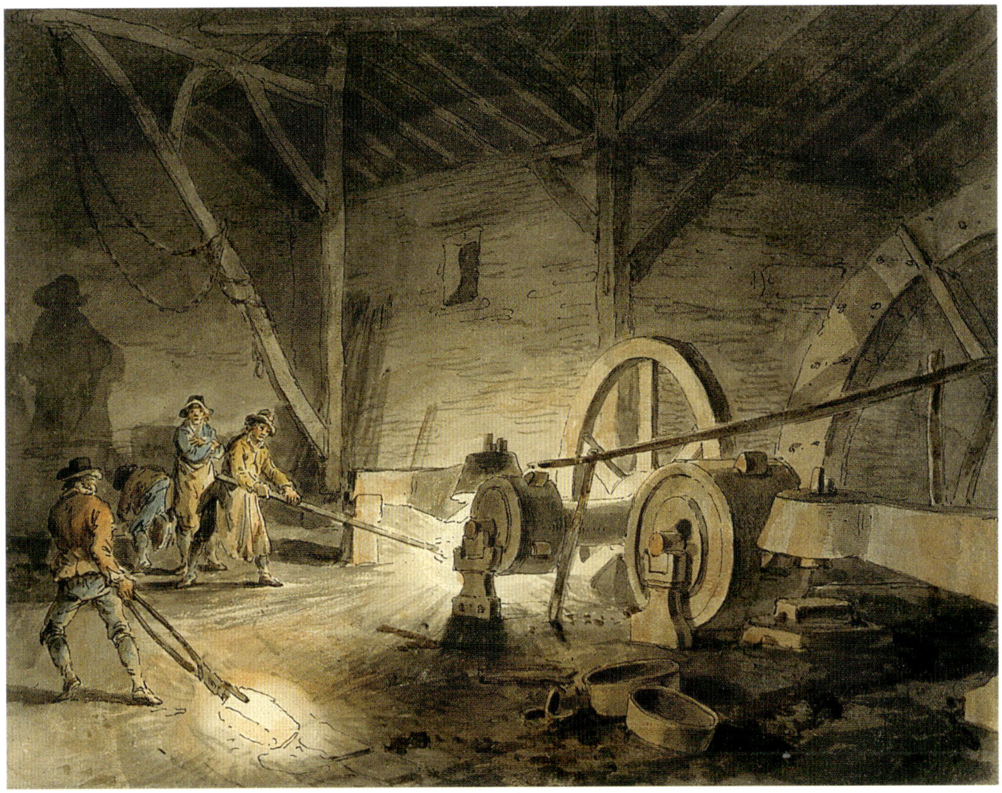

visiting Wales in the late eighteenth century, it was in his work that the common people came closest to emerging from the obscurity to which high art had for the most part condemned them. While he cannot be characterised as a social critic in his painting, Ibbetson was certainly a social observer both of rural communities and of life in emerging industrial Wales. In Glamorgan in 1789 he painted workers at the Cyfarthfa ironworks and, further west, women labourers at the coal staithes in Swansea, where the copper smelting industry was expanding rapidly.[105]

From Ibbetson's subsequent visit to Wales, three years later, the first fruit to appear in public was an oil painted version of his image of the Conwy harper, John Smith.[106] It was shown at the Royal Academy in the summer of 1793. In the same exhibition, the Welsh painter Edward Pugh made his London debut, showing a pair of miniature portraits, and it is likely that painting pictures of this kind had been his primary occupation for the previous ten years or so. However, much of Pugh's subsequent work would echo the change of atmosphere perceptible in the work of the older Ibbetson – a democratisation that reflected an increasingly complex interaction of forces in a society in transformation. Pugh was born in Ruthin and probably educated there, though nothing is known of his art training, if indeed he received any, or of his early career. In 1794 his work was reproduced for the first time in print, and it is in this form that his painting, alongside his writing, now seems most significant. His *Six Views in Denbighshire* was advertised in a newspaper in Chester, where he sought to establish himself as a miniaturist and silhouette painter.

None of the views depicted a major tourist site, but together they presented a more intimate and layered awareness of the atmosphere of north west Wales in the period than did the work of strangers to the area. Indeed, it has been persuasively argued that the view entitled *Llanfwrog, Ruthin and Llanbedr* incorporates a powerful social narrative in the implied relationship between a young couple in the foreground of the picture and a shadowy third figure, whom they observe. She may represent a war widow.[107]

In 1813, reflecting on the conception of his remarkable volume of images and texts, *Cambria Depicta*, Pugh recalled a discussion with John Boydell that had taken place in about 1802, in which the elderly publisher suggested that the deep acquaintance of a 'native artist' with Wales would invest the proposed work with particular authority. It was an idea to which Pugh himself would allude on several occasions in his text. The ten years' work of writing

141. William Ellis after Edward Pugh, *Llanfwrog, Ruthin and Llanbedr*, 1794, aquatint

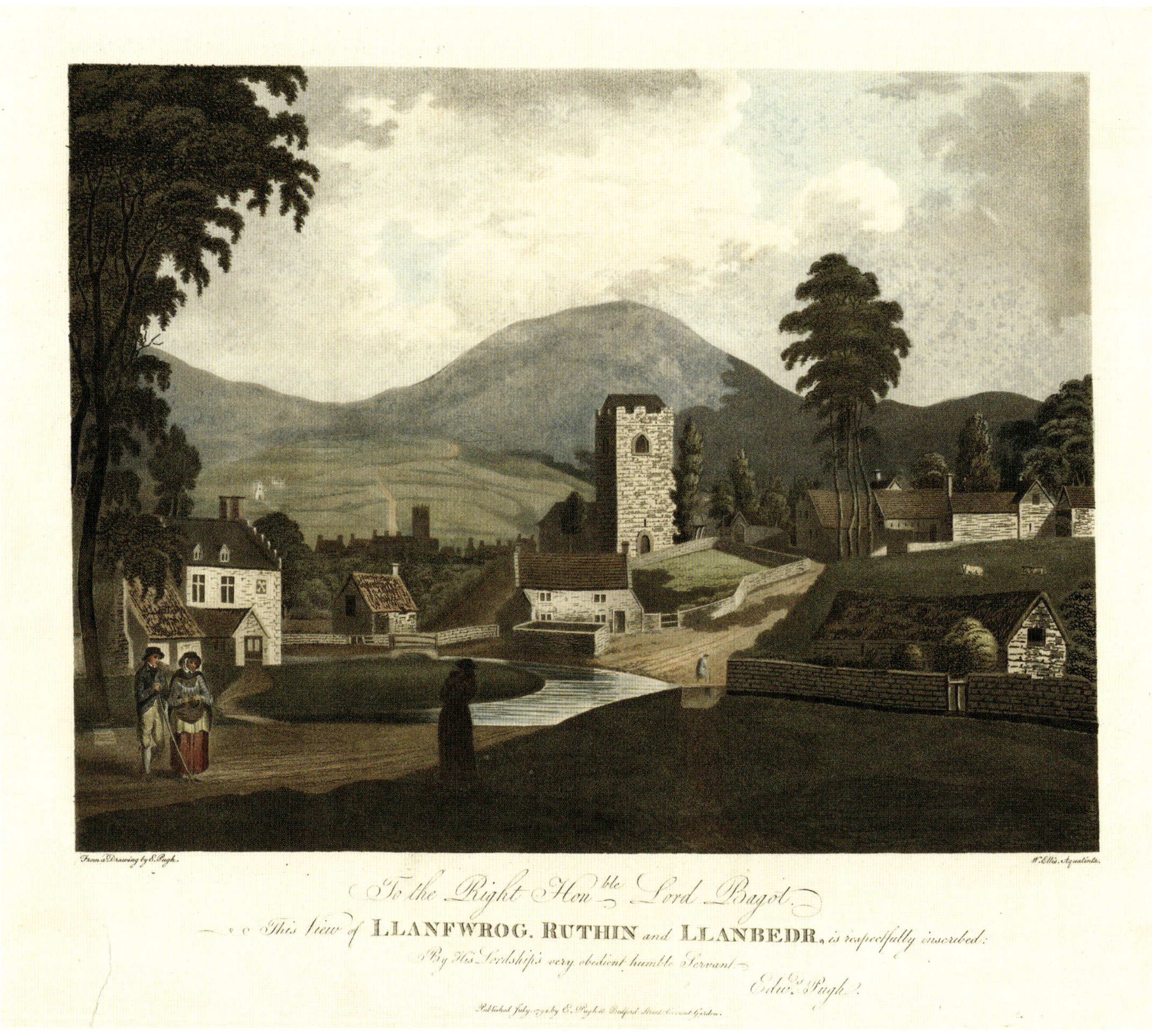

and illustrating the book, undertaken on the basis of tours made exclusively on foot, was initially interrupted by a commission to illustrate a volume which, superficially at least, represented a vivid contrast to *Cambria Depicta*. Pugh provided twenty of the images that would illustrate *Modern London; being the History of the Present State of the British Metropolis*. Pugh's illustrations teemed with people from all sections of society, and although the context of a guide book for artistic travellers in north Wales was radically different to the urban *Modern London*, in *Cambria Depicta* Pugh's interest in people would again be among the factors that distinguished his narrative.

Notwithstanding the general implications of his being a 'native artist', Pugh was not in any simple sense an insider. His mindset was modern, formed in a period of almost ceaseless war, social change and economic development. His was a new voice, that considered the people with gossipy familiarity which was leavened occasionally with the intellectual objectivity of one who had been away. His writing certainly manifested bursts of patriotism, but also criticism of his nation. Like Thomas Pennant before him, in ascending Cadair Idris Pugh recalled the work of Richard Wilson, whom he acclaimed enthusiastically when viewing his modest tomb in Mold churchyard – but, equally, he bemoaned what he perceived to be a lack of patronage for painters among an unsophisticated Welsh gentry.[108]

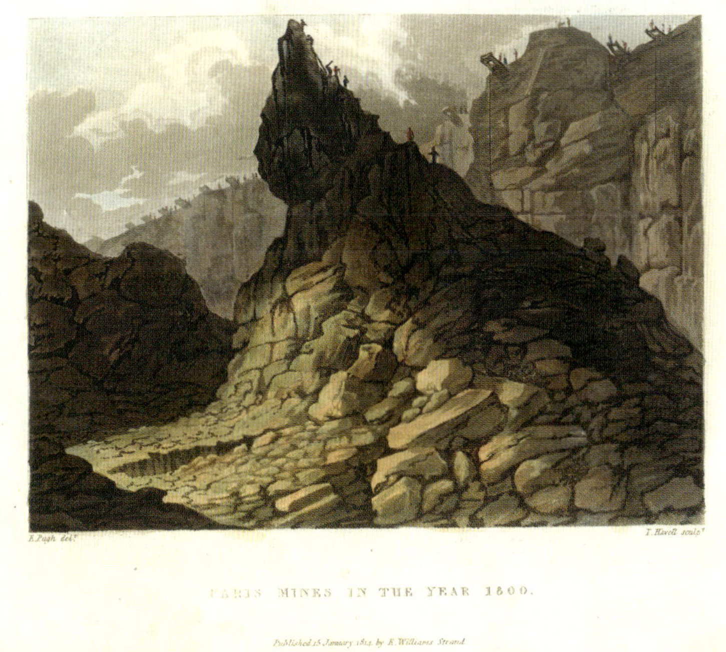

142. I. Havell after Edward Pugh, *Paris Mines in the Year 1800*, from *Cambria Depicta*, 1816, aquatint, 14x19

Pugh's observations in *Cambria Depicta* were confined to the north, though he was familiar with other parts of Wales, where industrial development did not escape his attention. In 1810 he seems to have visited Monmouthshire, where he drew for subsequent engraving the impressive 'Long Bridge' that carried the Sirhowy tramway on its way from the Tredegar ironworks to Newport.[109] In Anglesey, he had visited the copper mines at Mynydd Parys at least twice. Returning after an absence of five years, he noted with a characteristic combination of purple prose and levity that 'the internal part had much altered its appearance; the great and lofty pyramid of copper ore had been destroyed, and also the arch, which at that time was a grand object, has been since converted into pans, kettles, and penny-pieces.'[110]

107 See John Barrell, *Edward Pugh of Ruthin 1763-1813, 'A Native Artist'* (Cardiff, 2013), pp. 66–76.

108 Pugh, *Cambria Depicta*, pp. 344–5

109 The image may have been commissioned by the engineer John Hodgkinson. See Barrell, *Edward Pugh*, pp. 17–19.

110 See the watercolour of the arch by François Louis Francia, painted in 1799, illustrated in Peter Lord, *The Visual Culture of Wales: Industrial Society* (Cardiff, 1998), p. 26.

111 Pugh, *Cambria Depicta*, p. 47. For the cave, see depictions by John Warwick Smith, 1790, and William Havell, 1803–4, in Lord, *Industrial Society*, pp. 24–5.

112 The Buck brothers drew the copper works at Llangyfelach in about 1750, but did not publish the view. See ibid., p. 16.

> The great cave, so long as it may retain its present form, is a subject by itself; but the mine will afford the artist a variety, and if he be a man of taste, he will feel highly gratified with the sight. It is necessary for those who descend to take a guide with them, for, from the frequent blasting of the rocks, they will otherwise be in danger, from the situation which they may be in, the workmen not being able to see them ... Even ladies, with trifling assistance, may easily go down. Nothing can impress upon the mind a greater awe than this mine, and all produced by manual labour of thirty years.[111]

Artists on tour as early as the Buck brothers in the mid-eighteenth century and Sandby in the 1770s had sometimes paused on their way to draw mines, smelting works and foundries.[112] For most of them industrial sites provided only an incidental diversion, though Smith and Ibbetson worked more intensively at Mynydd Parys and Philippe de Loutherbourg seems to have spent a considerable amount of time in and around Swansea, producing both detailed and distant views of the Hafod and other works. In contrast to his exhibition pictures and his published engravings, the objectivity of these industrial drawings set them apart from the aesthetic posturing that characterised most of the landscape painting produced at the time.[113]

143. Philippe de Loutherbourg, *Iron Works near Swansea*, 1786 or 1800, pen, ink and pencil on paper, 8x11.9

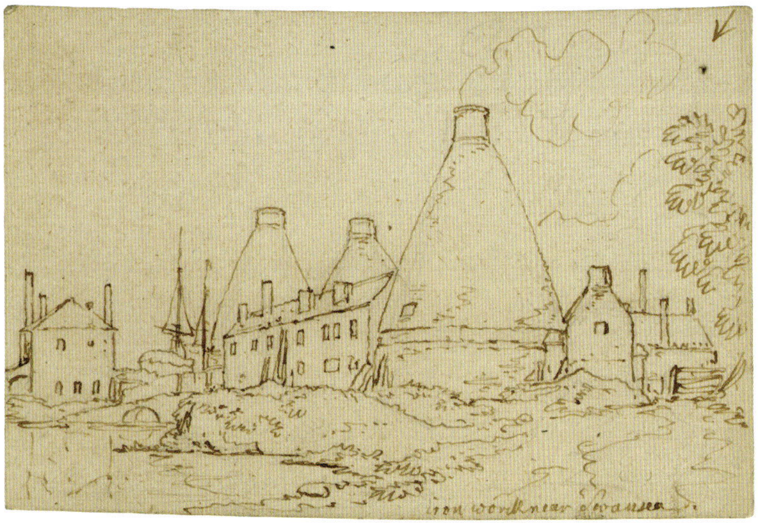

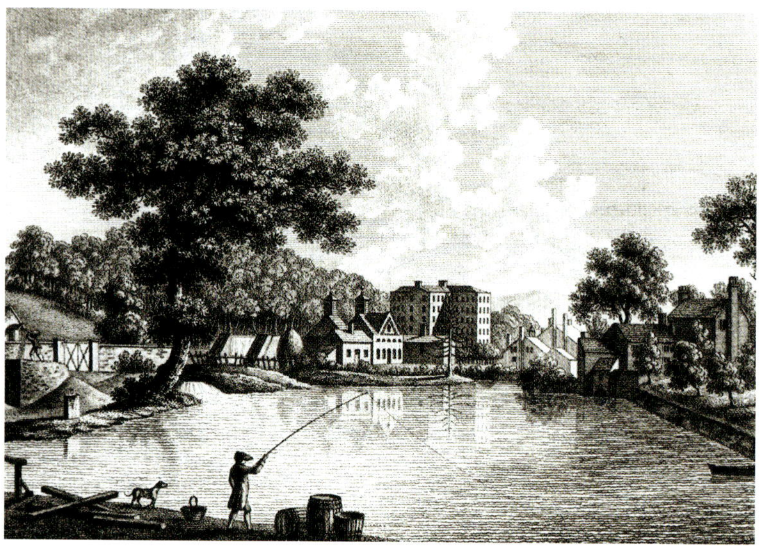

144. John Ingleby, *Cotton Works near Holywell, Flintshire*, from *Four Views on Holywell Stream*, 1792, engraving, 12.2x18

The last decade of the century saw not only a distinct increase in the imaging of the emerging industrial world but also the first attempts to profit by it through engravings. In 1792, Boydell published *Four Views on Holywell Stream* after drawings by John Ingleby, depicting copper works and cotton mills. The venture must surely also have involved Ingleby's patron, Thomas Pennant, engaged at the time in writing his *History of the Parishes of Whiteford and Holywell* (1796). Both Ingleby and Moses Griffith would illustrate in watercolour Pennant's personal large-paper copy of this volume, though the engravings chosen for the standard edition were all the work of Griffith. At about the same time in the south, Thomas Rothwell, a painter employed at the Cambrian Pottery in Swansea, diversified his work by producing a series of engravings that included views not only of his own workplace but also of the copper works at Morriston, and of Clasemont, the elevated seat of John Morris, the eponymous founder of the workers' settlement.[114]

The earliest industrial engravings issued in colour were produced by the painter and engraver John Hassell, who probably toured in 1797.[115] The first of his four views, published in the following year, depicted a coal mine at Neath. Like Thomas Pennant's painters, Hassell presented such sites as benign, located within a rural environment. However, at the same time as Hassell and in the same area, a Breton traveller, Count Maudet de

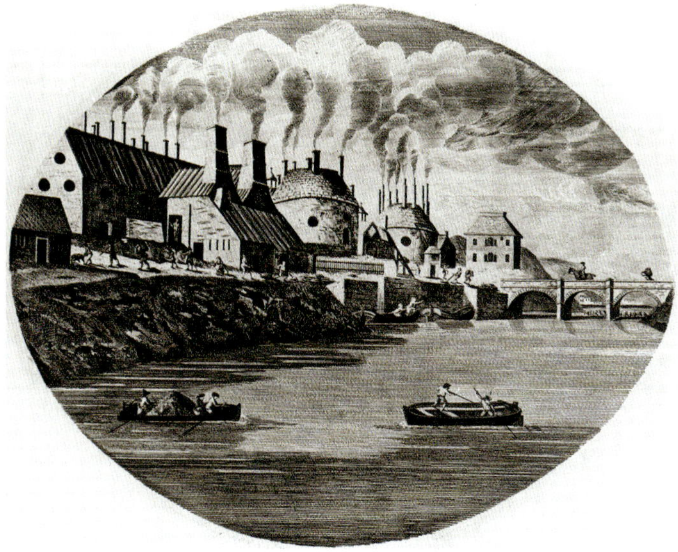

145. Thomas Rothwell, *The Forest Copper Works, Morriston*, 1791, engraving, 19.4x24.4

146. John Hassell, *Coal Works. A view near Neath in Glamorganshire*, 1798, aquatint, 21.8x33

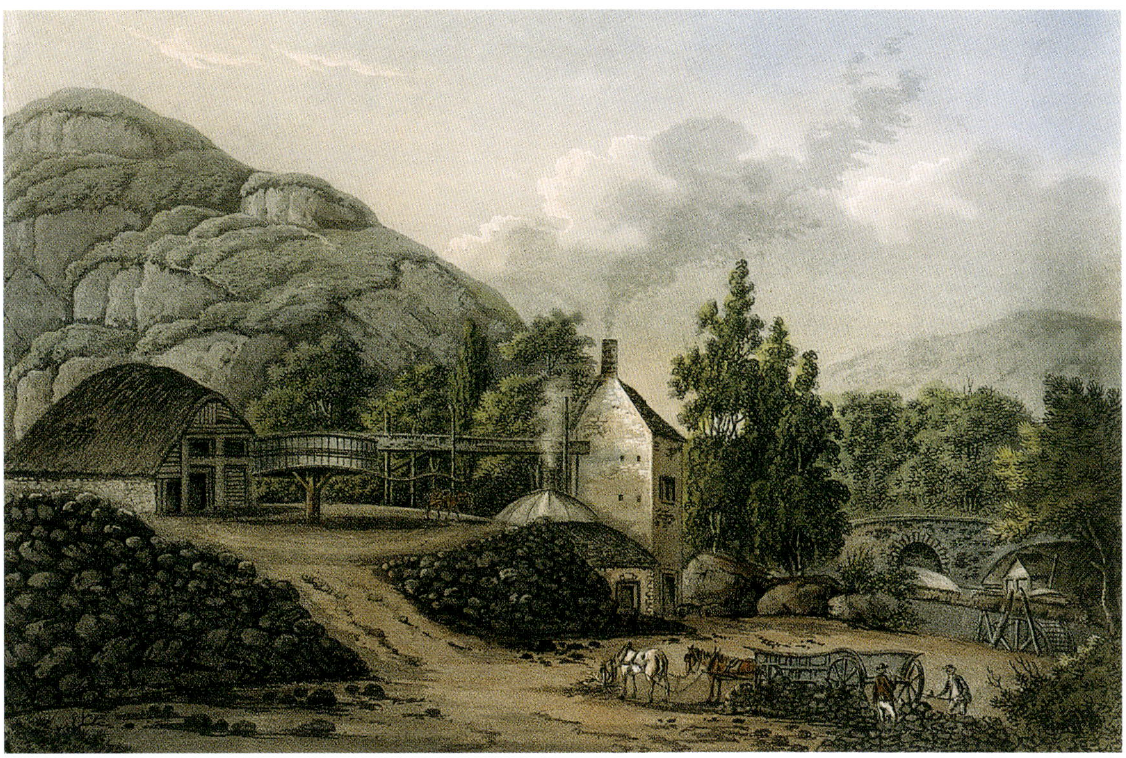

113 They contrasted strongly with a view of a copperworks at Swansea produced by John Sell Cotman, for instance. As a young man learning his trade on a tour in Wales, it seems that only on this one occasion did Cotman search for the misty light effects that his watercolour technique exploited so well in the man-made atmosphere of industrial pollution. Also while on the obligatory young English painter's tour of Wales, William Havell produced a dramatic but apparently isolated image of the mines at Parys Mountain.

114 Morris commissioned William Edwards, builder of Pontypridd, celebrated by Wilson and Lewis, to design the village of Morris Town in 1768, to house the copper workers.

115 Hassell would later be employed to engrave one of the views in Edward Pugh's *Cambria Depicta*.

Penhouet, took a less sanguine view of industrial exploitation. One of the favourite objects of peaceful contemplation by earlier travellers, Neath Abbey, was now adjoined by coal mines and a copper smelting works. Maudet de Penhouet described and drew the dismal situation of the common people who found shelter there with no trace of the picturesque but equally with little compassion:

> ... the cells of it serve as a retreat to an inumerable gang of mendicants, whose figures are hideous beyond all that can be imagined: the air which they respire in these subterranean caverns is, without doubt, the cause of that livid complexion and lean aspect which so particularizes them. As soon as I entered into one of the vaulted outer parts, several women came out of holes that communicated with it; they surrounded me, and the farther I advanced, the more the troop augmented: they carried almost all of them infants upon their backs, and the tone of voice in which they begged of us could be compared only to that of those women who headed the rebels at Paris ...[116]

The creators and beneficiaries of the industrial world viewed matters in a more pragmatic way, that had little in common with either the tirades of the indignant Maudet de Penhouet or the pastorals of Hassell. Like Morris of Morriston, those newly enriched either by the good fortune of finding natural resources beneath the surface of their lands or by the exercise of entrepreneurial skills, soon began to manifest the taste for self-imaging and for the patronage of artists and architects that would, in their eyes at least, set their descendants on the road to social equality with the old gentry. As a young man, Samuel Homfray, one of the founding fathers of the iron industry at Merthyr, commissioned a portrait that adapted the Gainsborough formula for the portrayal of the landed gentry by replacing the background view of the country seat with an image representing the pride of the sitter in the industrialisation which was the source of his wealth. Homfray was painted in sporting mode against a background of ironworks, probably by William Williams.[117] In fact, Homfray managed rapidly to achieve the gentry status to which his portrait suggested he aspired by marrying Jane, sister of Sir Charles Gould Morgan of Tredegar House. A little later, Richard Crawshay, who developed the Cyfarthfa works previously leased by Homfray, also commissioned a portrait, though he chose to project a more sober image than his younger contemporary. His painter was the intriguingly named but obscure artisan Richard Wilson of Birmingham, who travelled to Cyfarthfa to carry out the work. The ironmaster sat with a copy of Adam Smith's *The Wealth of Nations* on the table at his side. As the founder of a powerful industrial dynasty, Crawshay was not in a position to surround himself at home with pictures of illustrious ancestors, so he commissioned portraits of his entrepreneurial contemporaries. Presumably having given satisfaction, Wilson was

116 Comte Maudet de Penhouet, *Letters describing a Tour through part of South Wales* (London, 1797), p. 38. A more compassionate description of the situation of these unfortunate women was given in 1803 by an English tourist: 'The poor creatures were the wives of miners and women that worked in the manufactories, who burrowed and brought up their families in the cells of the ruin. Unceasing drudgery, however, was unable to obtain for them the necessaries of life, much less a taste of the comforts, to which the exertion of useful labour might seem to have just claim.' J.T. Barber, *A Tour through South Wales and Monmouthshire* (London, 1803).

117 In 1777 William Williams had painted at Ironbridge in Shropshire, where at least one of his works was bought by the ironmaster Abraham Darby III. The Welsh and Shropshire ironmasters were in close touch at the end of the eighteenth century.

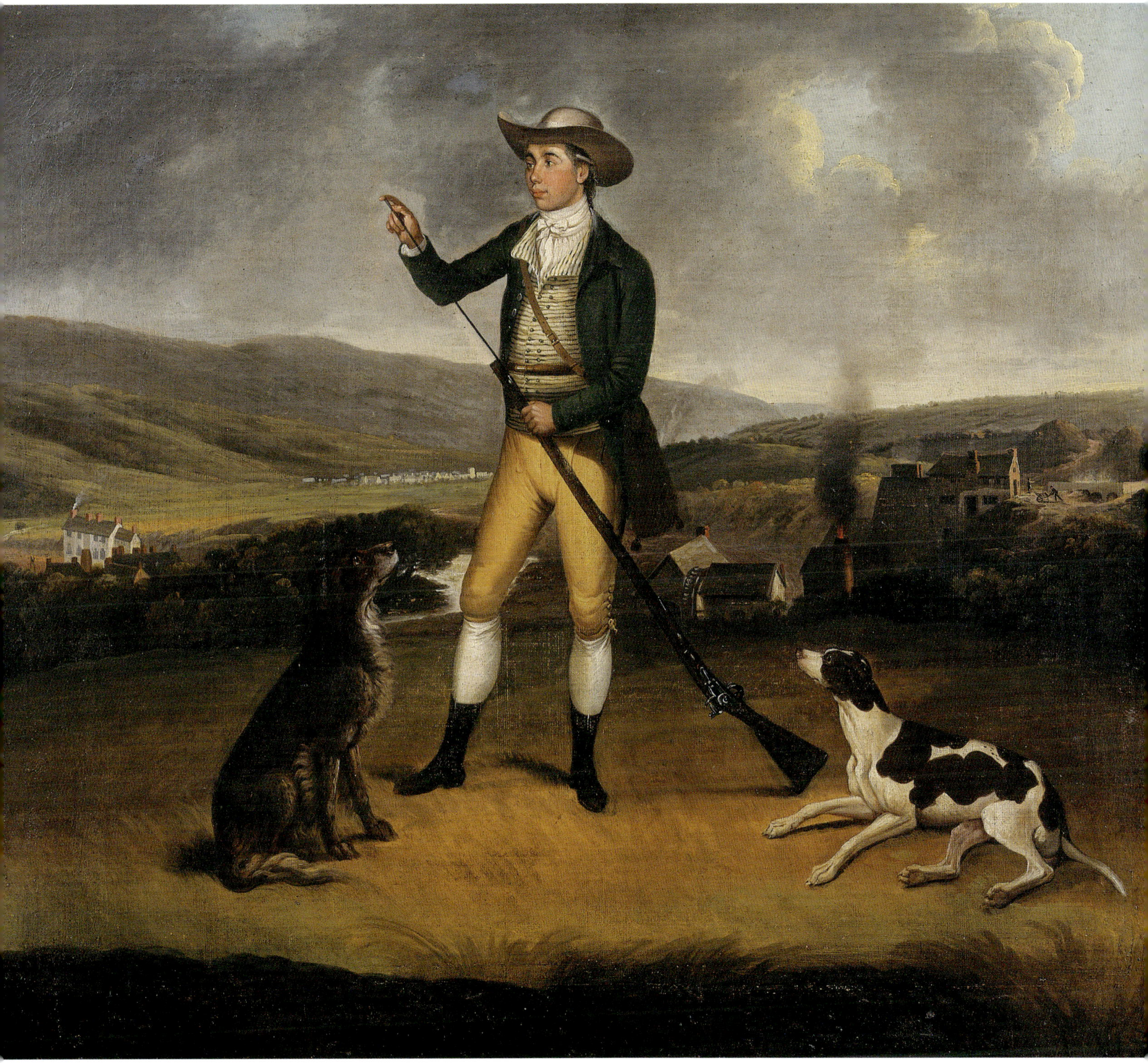

147. William Williams,
Samuel Homfray, *c*.1790,
oil on canvas, 100.8x88.1

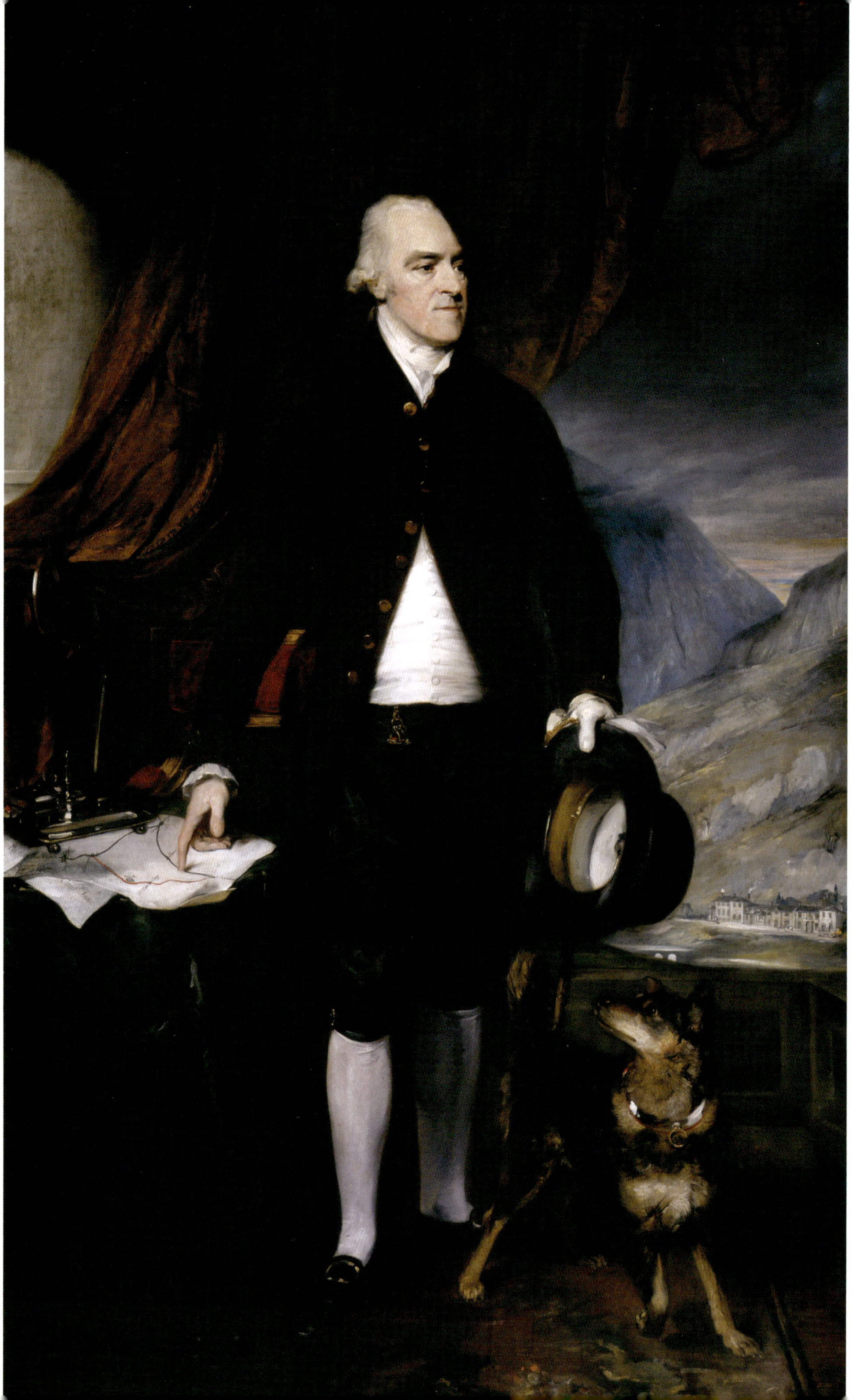

dispatched to Shropshire to paint the ironmasters William Reynolds and John Wilkinson, who were joined for the occasion by Crawshay's son William. By the following year, 1797, all the portraits had arrived at Cyfarthfa, where they were seen by Gilbert Gilpin of Abergavenny: 'In Crawshay's parlour I observed the following pictures, himself, son & daughter, your brother [John Wilkinson of Bersham] & Mr Reynolds. They are all striking likenesses.'[118]

In the north, Richard Pennant, developer of the Penrhyn slate quarries, also celebrated his enterpreneurial flair in a portrait, though his painter, Henry Thomson, was somewhat more illustrious than Crawshay's Richard Wilson. Pennant pointed to a map showing the location of his new Royal Hotel at Capel Curig, on the Shrewsbury road whose improvement he was financing. The new road avoided the inconvenience of the river crossing at Conwy, where the ferrymen had acquired a reputation for extorting excessive sums from inexperienced tourists.[119] In the background was the hotel itself, designed by Wyatt as a boon both to artistic travellers like Edward Pugh, who was much impressed with it, and to those on their way to Ireland on government or commercial business.[120]

left
148. Henry Thomson, *Richard Pennant, 1st Baron Penrhyn of Penrhyn and His Dog 'Crab'*, c.1800, oil, 236.5x143

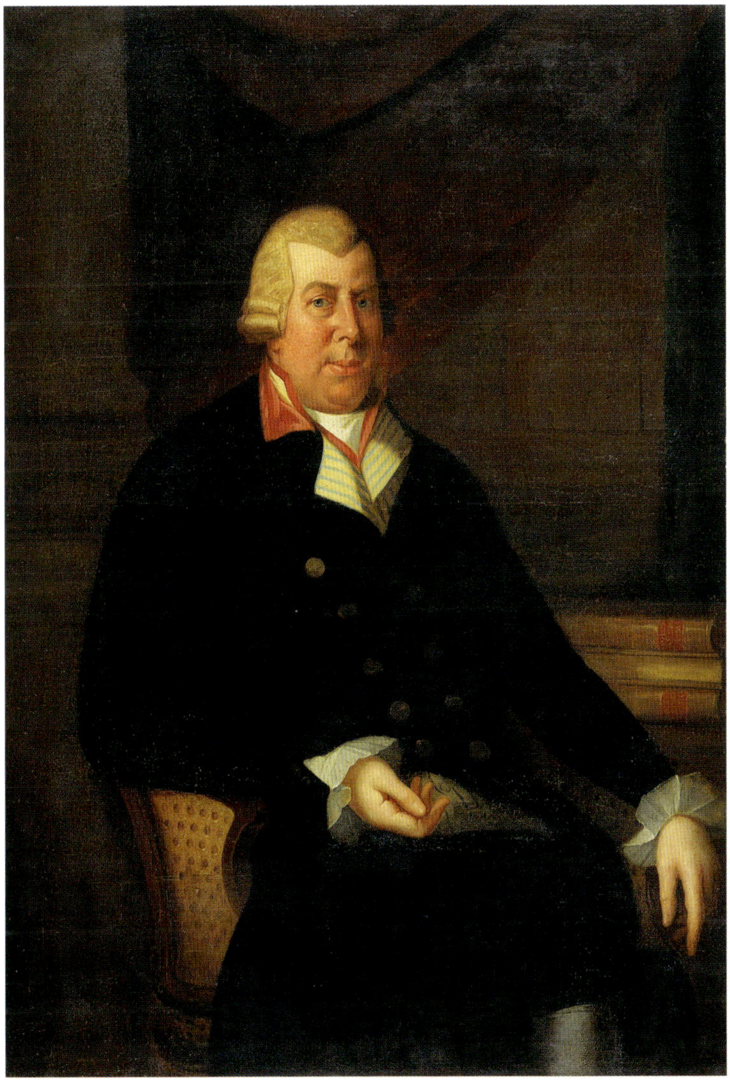

149. Richard Wilson of Birmingham, *William Crawshay I*, 1796, oil, 135x94.5

118 Shropshire Record Office 1781/6/25. I am grateful to Prof. Chris Evans of the University of South Wales for this reference. See Chris Evans, 'Gilbert Gilpin: A witness to the South Wales Iron Industry in its ascendancy', *Morgannwg*, 34 (1990), p. 36. The information concerning the sitting at Reynolds's house in Shropshire is contained in a letter from John Wilkinson to Matthew Boulton, 23 October 1796, Birmingham Reference Library, Matthew Boulton Collection. Richard Wilson of Birmingham is currently known by only one other portrait. However, he appears to have been the designer of tokens used to pay workers at the Anglesey copper mines, which display a druid's head (see the example of 1791 at the Fitzwilliam Museum, Cambridge, CM.BI.2219-R). John Wilkinson was involved with the extraction of copper ore in Anglesey, and was in frequent contact with Richard Crawshay. The other portraits commissioned by Crawshay are at present untraced.

119 Even for locals, the experience was irritating. The painter Hugh Hughes, on his way home to Meddiant, Glan Conwy, recorded in his diary 'Arrive at Conway and soon get over, but the well-known blackguard ferrymen would make me believe myself much obliged to them for getting out of Conway before to-morrow.' NLW MS Cwrt Mawr 130A, 8 June 1820.

120 Edward Pugh, *Cambria Depicta* (London, 1816), pp. 110–12.

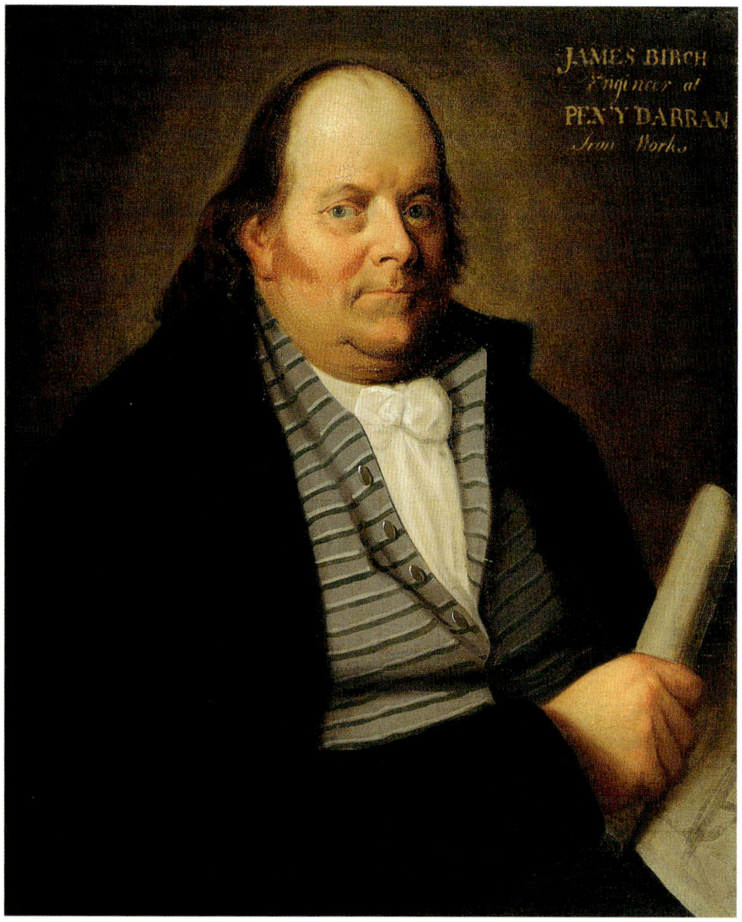

150. Unknown painter, *James Birch, Engineer, Penydarren Works*, *c*.1820, oil on canvas, 72x60

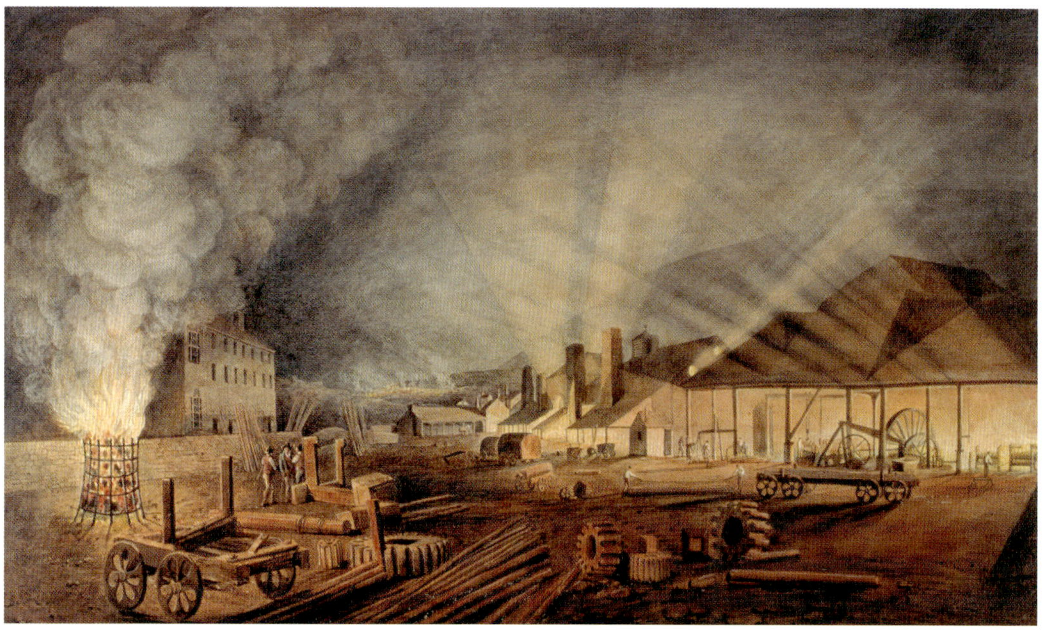

151. Thomas Hornor, *Rolling Mills, Penydarren Iron Works*, *c*.1817, watercolour, 27.9x47.6

Individuals such as Homfray, Crawshay and Pennant acted not simply as remote financiers but were engaged in a practical way in the management of businesses in which inventiveness and enterprise were valued. The engineers with whom they worked also enjoyed high status and celebrity. Both Richard Crawshay's chief engineer at Cyfarthfa, William Williams, and James Birch, of the rival Penydarren ironworks, sat for portraits in which they were identified with symbols of their vocation and achievements. The pictures may have been paid for by their employers, though it is equally possible that the engineers had prospered sufficiently by this time to commission them for themselves.[121] The identities of the painters have been lost, but Birch's place of employment at Penydarren was recorded in the same period by the remarkable Thomas Hornor, in a landscape that has come to symbolise the dynamism and drama that excited those who chose to observe the new industrial world from a positive standpoint – though their enthusiasm often simultaneously conjured medieval images of the fires of hell:

> ... the singular effect of the fire from the numerous iron works viewed by night, where the immense columns of flame, the incessant noise of hammers, and the continued buzz of voices, impresses the mind with a sensation perfectly new, and not easy to be defined ... add to all this, the strong reflexion of the fire upon the figures covered with the black dirt of the works, and it will not be surprising that such a scene should recall to the recollection the fabulous descriptions of the infernal regions and their inhabitants.[122]

For some five years, Hornor, who had trained in England as a surveyor, worked profitably at producing albums of painted views and written descriptions of the properties of wealthy Glamorgan landowners and industrialists, for at least one of which he charged 500 guineas.[123]

The engineer William Williams remained at Cyfarthfa for many years, eventually becoming celebrated not only for his technical ability but also for his physical bulk, as a result of which a special trolley was built to convey him about the works. In this condition, and surrounded by domestic paraphernalia that signified his arrival in the middle class, he was painted for a second time, on this occasion by the most celebrated of the artistic beneficiaries of Merthyr industrial patronage, Penry Williams. Echoing the rise of William Parry under the wing of Sir Watkin Williams-Wynn, the drawing skill of Penry Williams

121 A third engineer portrait of the period was reported in Charles Wilkins, *History of Merthyr Tydfil* (Merthyr, 1908), p. 250. The sitter was Rees Jones of Penydarren.

122 John George Wood, *The Principal Rivers of Wales Illustrated* (London, 1813), pp. 57–8. The location of Hornor's image, usually entitled simply *Rolling Mills*, is confirmed by comparison with the view of the site drawn by Wood.

123 Hornor's success in Wales seems to have provided the financial foundation for the extraordinary panorama of London which he subsequently executed and displayed to the public in the specially built Colosseum in Regents Park. Sadly, his ambition exceeded his resources, and bankruptcy ensued. Hornor was obliged to emigrate to New York, where he died in 1844. See Elis Jenkins, 'Thomas Hornor', *Glamorgan Historian*, 7 (Cowbridge, 1971), pp. 37–50.

152. Penry Williams, *William Williams, Cyfarthfa*, c.1825, watercolour, 18.5x15

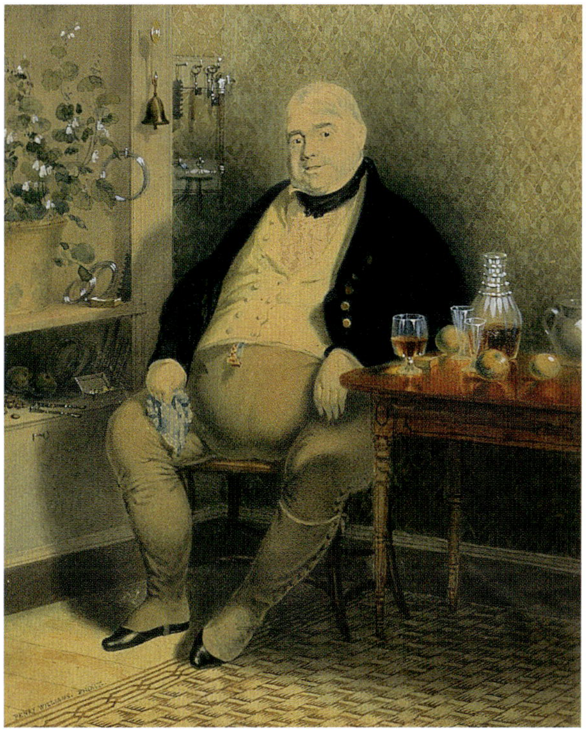

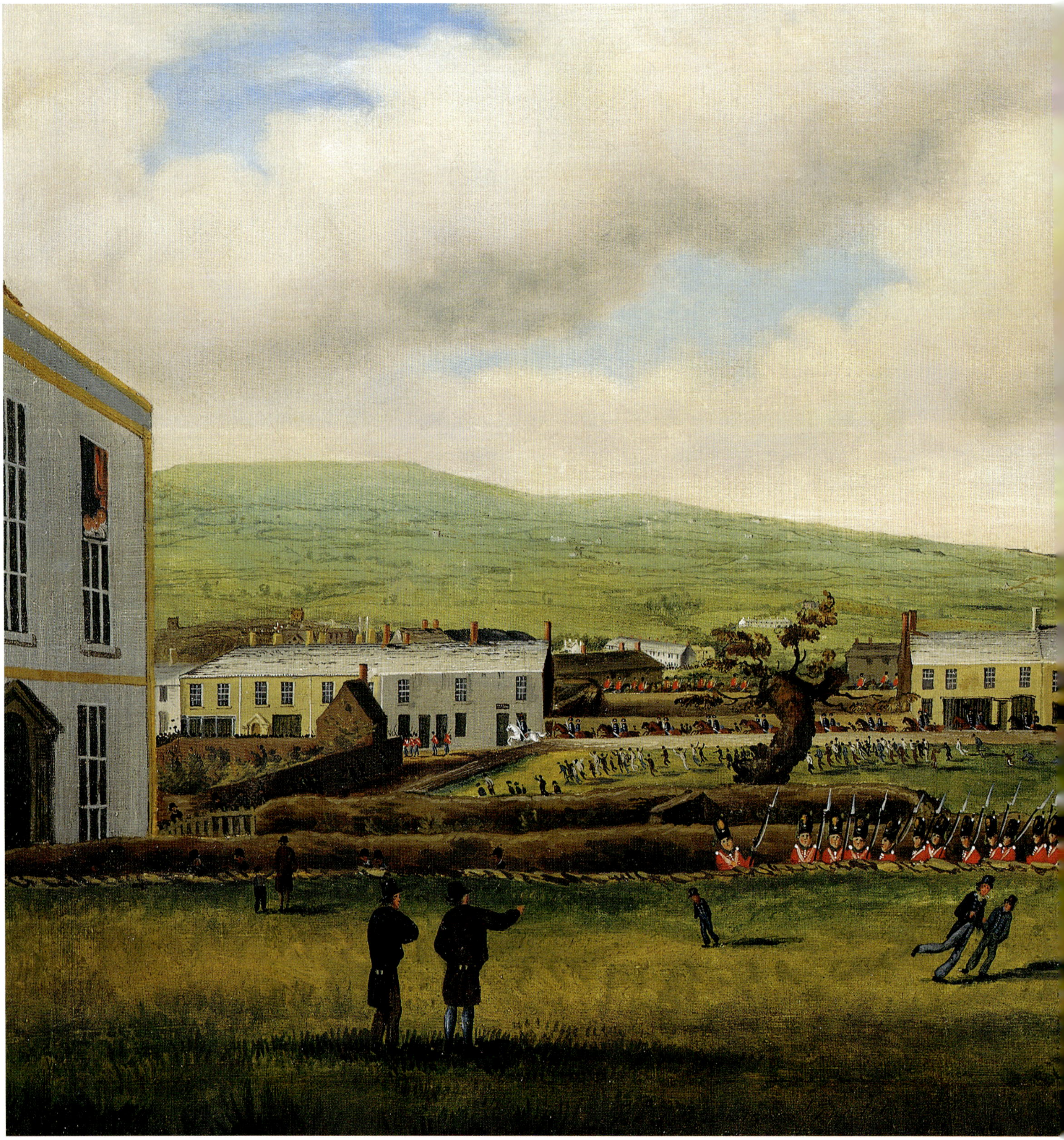

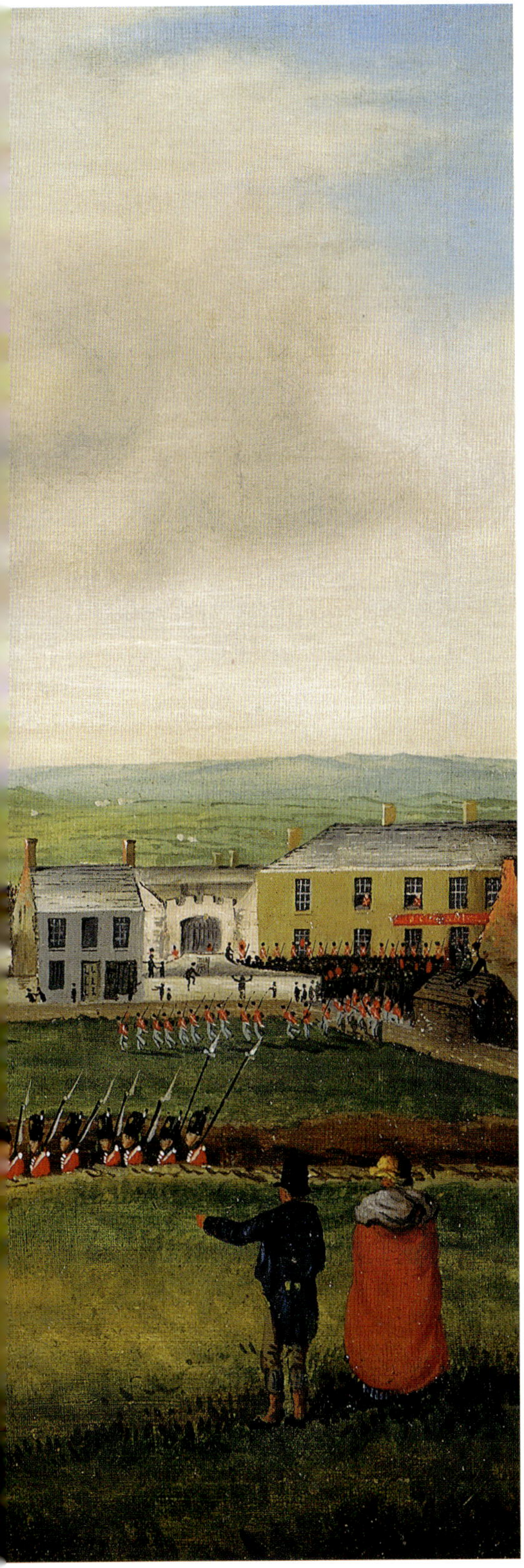

came to the attention of his social superiors, and their patronage enabled him to train in London. However, Williams appears to have attracted a wider range of early supporters than did Parry, and certainly more than Moses Griffith, tied for so many years to Thomas Pennant. Williams was the son of a house painter, and in 1816, at the age of 14, painted pictures of the quelling by the militia of disturbances that began with workers at the Tredegar ironworks protesting against wage cuts. There were attacks on the manager at Penydarren, and William Crawshay II, grandson of Richard and manager of the Cyfarthfa works, fled to the hills. However, once order was restored, Crawshay was prominent among a number of individuals who commissioned pictures from the young Williams.[124] He painted views of the ironworks for Crawshay, but also worked for less illustrious patrons, including Jenkin Price, landlord of the Lamb and Flag at Glyn Neath, who acquired a group of views of the natural beauties of the Vale of Neath. These were seen in the inn by the scientist Michael Faraday, on tour in the area, who through the good offices of his host at the Dowlais ironworks, Josiah John Guest, requested a similar set of 'eight or ten' at four shillings each.[125] All these individuals seem to have played a part in enabling Williams to train at the Royal Academy Schools, which he entered in 1822. Four years later he would depart for Italy, under the patronage of another ironmaster, Joseph Bailey, but not before completing a remarkable documentation of the Cyfarthfa works and surrounding area, in the form of twenty-one delicately painted watercolours.

153. Penry Williams, *Merthyr Riots*, 1816, oil, 38.5x54

124 Though Crawshay did not own either of the two versions of the picture of the disturbances. For a discussion of the early patronage of Williams, and his subsequent career, see Derrick Pritchard Webley, *Cast to the Winds. The Life and Work of Penry Williams (1802-1855)* (Aberystwyth, 1997).

125 Dafydd Tomos, *Michael Faraday in Wales* (Denbigh, 1972), p. 147.

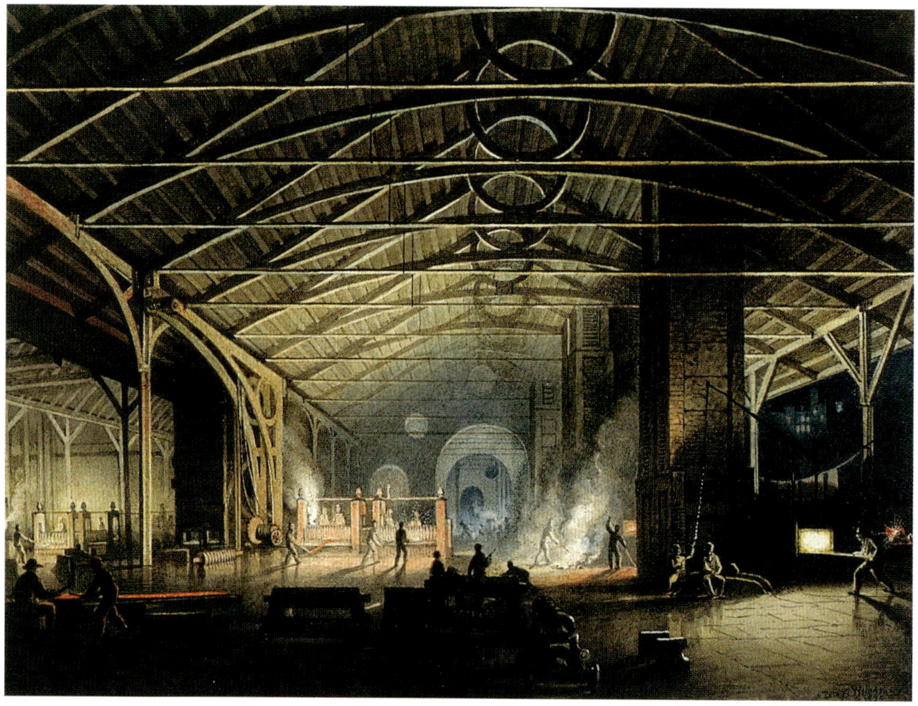

154. Penry Williams, *Cyfarthfa Ironworks Interior at Night*, 1825, watercolour, 15.7x21.0

In the most elaborate of the views, Williams depicted the interior of the works at night. Through the open side of the building, the lights of Cyfarthfa Castle, William Crawshay's grand statement of *arriviste* assertiveness, reminded his employees of their indebtedness to their master.[126]

Penry Williams probably received his early education at the school in Merthyr taught by Taliesin Williams, son of the celebrated antiquarian Iolo Morganwg. In 1821, both men were visited by the painter and engraver Hugh Hughes, who was on the last stage of a three-year series of tours in Wales. Born in Llandudno in 1790 but domiciled in London since 1814, Hughes was drawing for a collection of wood engravings called *The Beauties of Cambria* that, with the exception of its unusual print technique, stood firmly in the eighteenth century tradition of Sandby and Pennant.[127] Indeed, the text that accompanied the engraver's minutely detailed landscapes was heavily dependant on the writing of Pennant and other earlier antiquarians. Not so, however, the diary that Hughes kept on tour, in which he recorded primarily his perceptions of the condition of the people of Wales. Before meeting with Iolo Morganwg and Taliesin Williams, Hughes had rested at the Crown Inn at Merthyr:

> I will not forget the name of the place until it is impossible for me ever to come close to it again. The company was four or five men of a sort that my heart would not tolerate, my whole heart would do nothing but despise them; I sat in the same room

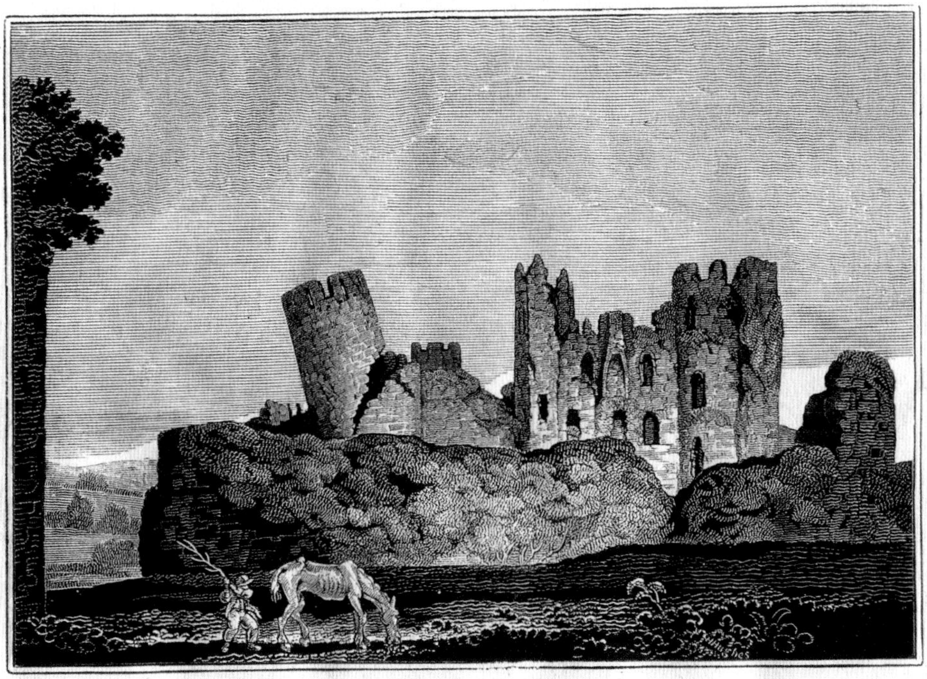

155. Hugh Hughes, *Caerphily Castle*, from *The Beauties of Cambria*, 1819-23, wood engraving, 85x126

as these for two or three hours without once opening my mouth. It was a blessing to me that nothing I loved was praised by them. To me, they were so vile that their disapproval excited me to love the objects of their abuse as if they necessarily deserved it, and to permanently detest whatever their kind found praiseworthy.[128]

Like Pugh's *Cambria Depicta*, the voice recorded in Hughes's diary was distinctly different from the voices of travellers that preceded it. Remarkably, he passed no comment on the visual quality of the industrial landscape of Merthyr, choosing to remark exclusively on the moral condition of those few people he met that worked there. In fact, his perceptions were as deeply rooted in eighteenth-century tradition as were his images, but it was a tradition belonging to people disregarded or despised by almost all of those who had commissioned, bought or produced paintings about Wales in the previous century. They were, however, the people of the future, and it fell to Hughes to produce the earliest substantial imaging of the communities from which a new intellectual leadership would emerge in the early years of the nineteenth century. As Hughes's observations of the workers at Merthyr suggest, it was a leadership that for many years would stand in uneasy relationship with Welsh industrial society. Drawn initially from the common people, but increasingly from a rapidly expanding middle class, it was largely, though not exclusively, Nonconformist in religion, but it was the social as well as the religious ideas emanating from that system of belief that would create the *Zeitgeist* of the nineteenth century.

126 William Crawshay commissioned the building from Robert Lugar in 1824, in the boom which followed the post-war slump that gave rise to the disturbances of 1816. His father, William Crawshay I opposed his son's social aspirations: 'A great house and expensive establishment will not fight our Battle in Trade', he observed. NLW Cyfarthfa Papers, 22 September 1820, letter from William Crawshay I to William Crawshay II.

127 Hughes was one of several young wood engravers who flourished during a revival of interest in the technique. Nearly all traced their professional credentials back to Thomas Bewick, the English engraver who had revitalised the medium. See Peter Lord, *Hugh Hughes, Arlunydd Gwlad 1790-1863* (Llandysul, 1995), pp. 43–7.

128 My translation from the Welsh, NLW MS Cwrt Mawr 130A, 31 October 1821. The English language sections of the diary of Hugh Hughes were published in full in *Wales*, ed. O.M. Edwards III (1896) and the Welsh sections in *Cymru*, ed. O.M. Edwards, VIII (1895). The diary is analysed, with extensive quotation, in Lord, *Hugh Hughes*.

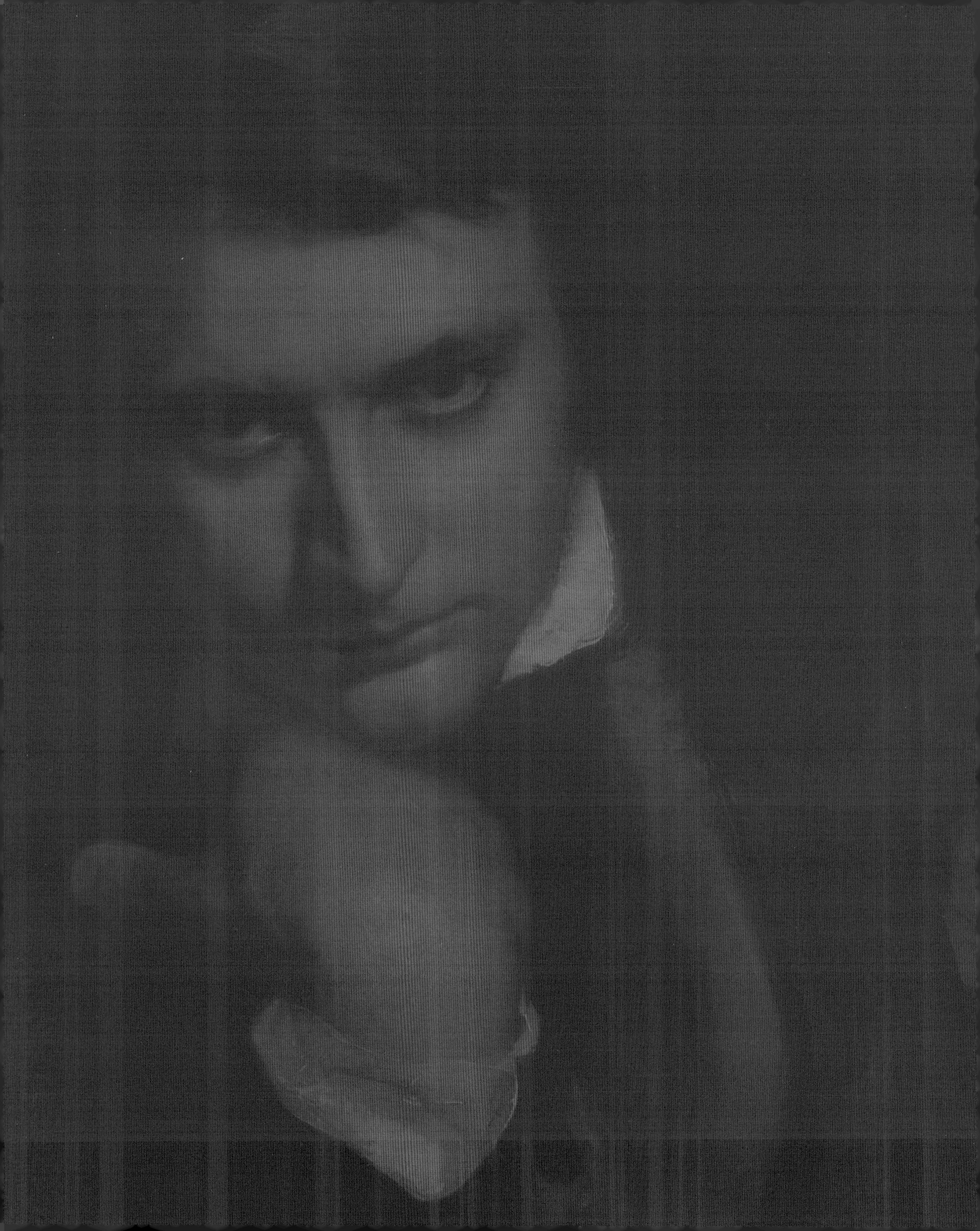

CHAPTER 3

1820–1914

CHAPTER 3 1820–1914

Origins

The Act of Uniformity that was passed in 1662 to settle religious issues arising from the restoration of the monarchy had the effect of legally marginalising a growing section of the population of the British Isles, with particularly important consequences in Wales. Those who dissented from the dogmas of the established Anglican church became defined as 'Nonconformists' and although not so severely constrained as the Roman Catholics, whose beliefs they despised, nevertheless they also found themselves deprived of civil rights – barred from public office and from university education, for instance. The impact of the creation of this new Nonconformist section of society, into which the common people and the middle classes were increasingly drawn, would be of fundamental importance in the evolution of Wales, and indeed the idea of Wales, in the subsequent two hundred years. Yet there is little pictorial record of the growth of Nonconformity or, indeed, of the rise of Calvinistic Methodism, from its emergence in the Great Revival in the late 1730s until the secession of the sect from the Church of England in 1811. At that point it too became officially Nonconformist. The remarkable paucity of evidence reflects the continuing dominance of patronage of visual culture by a gentry and an intellectual community largely dependant upon it, that was generally hostile to the movement. Comments by gentlemen like Thomas Pennant tended to be expressed as dismissive asides, though intellectuals were more forthright. Iolo Morganwg's opinion, expressed in 1799 to his patron Owain Jones, 'Owain Myfyr', that 'The north, by now, is as Methodistical as the south, and the south is as Methodistical as hell', has become one of the most celebrated observations of the eighteenth century.[1] Many among the new industrial elite also took a dim view of the 'fanatick Sectarys' as Richard Crawshay saw them, though there were exceptions. Among them were the Guests, Crawshay's rivals at Dowlais, where the works manager, Thomas Guest, was a Wesleyan lay preacher. Among the gentry, an important (if somewhat eccentric) exception was the wealthy Madam Sidney Griffith of the Thelwall family of Denbighshire. She funded the buildings at Trefeca, home of the Methodist community established by Howell Harris in the early 1750s.

1 Earlier anti-Methodist sentiments were expressed by members of the circle of Evan Lloyd, friend of William Parry and Thomas Jones in London. An example is given in 'Improvement: the visualisation of "y werin", the Welsh folk', in Lord, *The Meaning of Pictures: Images of Personal, Social and Political Identity* (Cardiff, 2009), p. 79. For Iolo, see *Rattleskull Genius: The Many Faces of Iolo Morganwg*, ed. Geraint H. Jenkins, (Cardiff, 2005).

2 'She sent Mr. Bowyer, the King's miniature painter, to draw his picture. He died the week following. William Williams [Pantycelyn] had just time to write his elegy before he William Williams died.' Cardiff Central Library MS 5.36, letter from William Pryce of Caerphilly to David Williams, 23 January 1791. Bowyer also painted Lady Huntingdon. A portrait of Revd Howel Davies, another prominent early Calvinistic Methodist, was posthumously engraved. Davies, who had been converted by the preaching of Howell Harris, had married into the gentry. Among the Welsh Baptists, Hugh Evans (1712-81), became head of the Bristol Baptist Academy, where he was painted by George Roth.

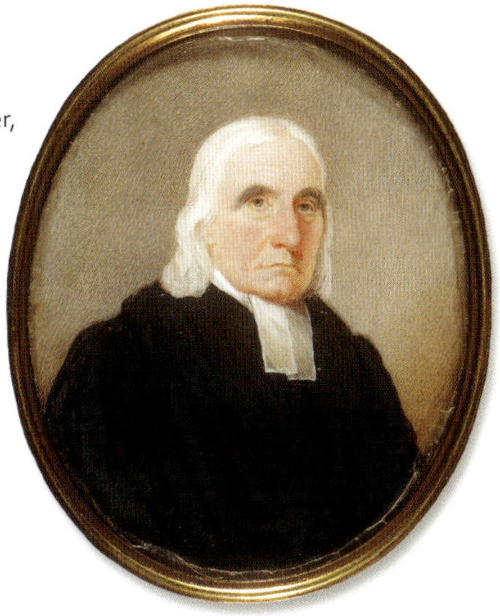

156. Robert Bowyer, *Daniel Rowland of Llangeitho*, 1790, watercolour, 85x67

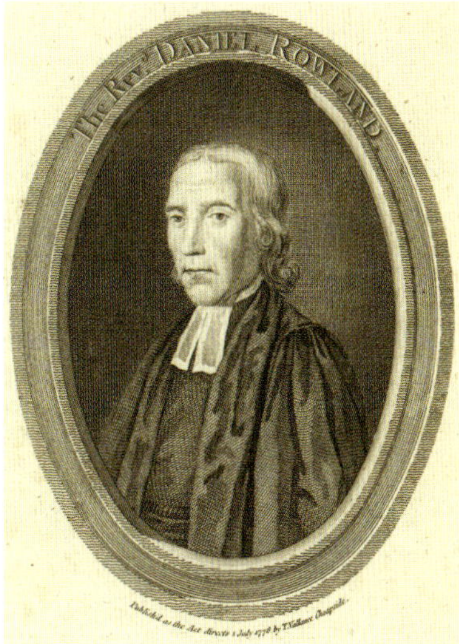

157. *The Rev.ᵈ Daniel Rowland*, from the *Gospel Magazine*, 1778, engraving

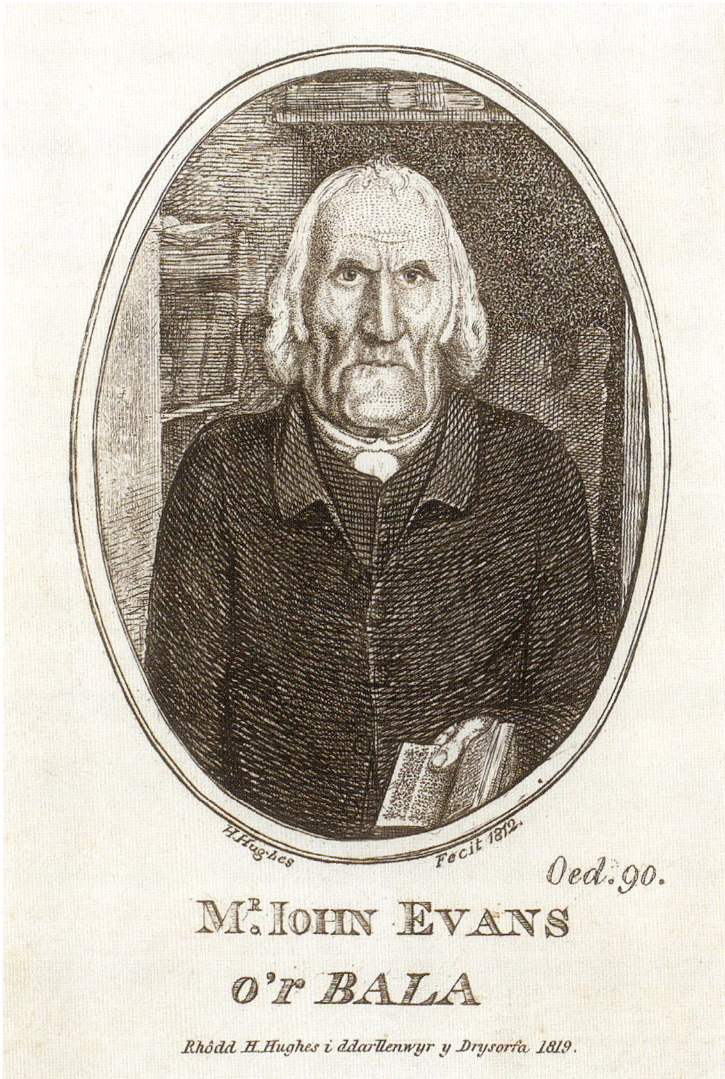

158. Hugh Hughes, *Mr John Evans o'r Bala*, 1812, from *Y Drysorfa*, 1819, engraving, 17.6x12.5

Their avant-garde Gothic style, probably the work of Harris himself, expressed the radicalism of the religious and social concepts that drove the establishment of the community. Some of the few portraits that recorded the early Methodist leadership were also the result of the patronage of gentry supporters. Daniel Rowland of Llangeitho was painted just a week before his death in 1790 by the distinguished miniaturist Robert Bowyer, at the request of Lady Huntingdon.[2]

However, the earliest known portrait of Daniel Rowland was published by the *Gospel Magazine* in 1778. The contrast between its earnest severity and the soapy complacency of the contemporary Gainsborough portrait of Thomas Pennant, who published his *Tour in Wales* in the same year, says much about the philosophical gulf opening between waxing and waning sections of Welsh society. The Rowland portrait offered the model that was adopted by Hugh Hughes when, in the wake of the secession of the Methodists, he painted a series of portraits of the leaders of the movement. The engraved interpretation by Hughes of his original oil painting of John Evans of Bala at ninety years of age exudes the same conviction as the Rowlands portrait of three decades earlier. Evans too was a Methodist of the first generation, though one who survived to play an important role in the ordination of ministers at the Bala *sasiwn* of 1811, which marked the secession. The painter was a second-generation Methodist, one of the thousands who attended the *sasiwn* to listen to the preaching, and one who would always draw inspiration from the example of the early leaders. John Evans in particular came to be regarded as 'an embodiment ... of the traditions of the Methodism of the north'.[3] His engraved portrait was distributed with the denominational magazine, *Y Drysorfa*, the first instance of a deep engagement with the Welsh-language press that Hugh Hughes would maintain, in both words and pictures, for most of his life.[4] During 1812 his other sitters included Thomas Hughes of Liverpool, Mr and Mrs John Roberts of Llangwm, John Elias of Anglesey, Mr and Mrs Thomas Jones of Denbigh and Thomas Charles of Bala. Many of these portraits were engraved, and that of Charles in particular – though not the earliest depiction of the figurehead of the secession – became the foundation for dozens of reinterpretations that would constitute perhaps the most extensive popular iconography of the nineteenth century. By crystallising a particular concept of Welsh national identity, the secession proved to be comparable in symbolic importance with the events of 1485. Through his images, Hughes was prominent among those who invested it with its meaning.

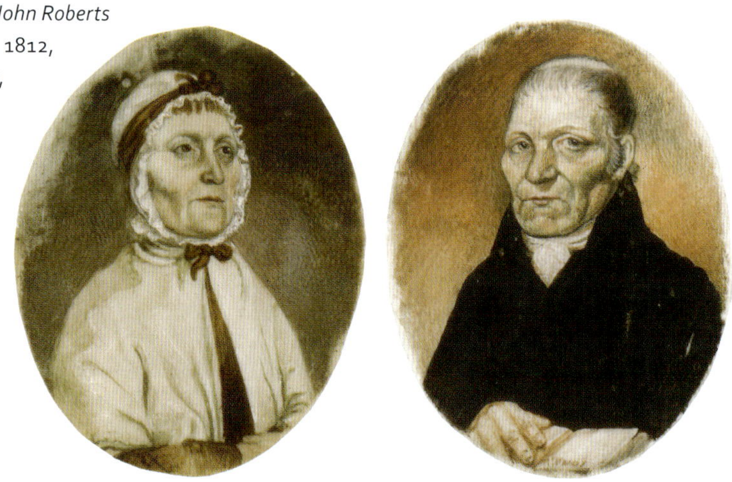

159. Hugh Hughes, *Mr and Mrs John Roberts of Llangwm*, 1812, watercolour, 8.2x6.9

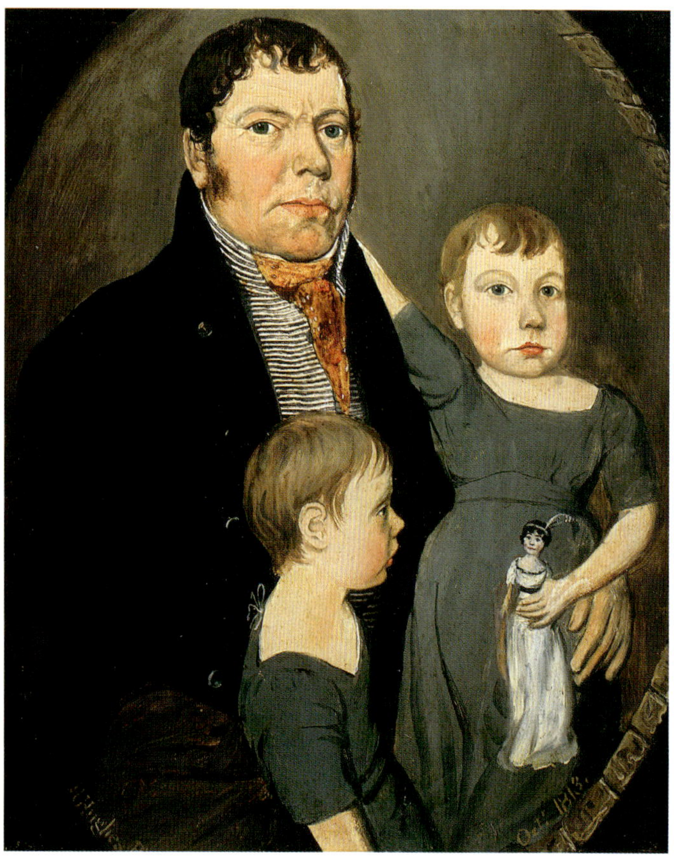

160. Hugh Hughes, *Huw Griffith of Bodwrdda, with his Children*, 1813, oil, 46x30.5

Most of Hughes's original portraits of the Methodist leaders were miniatures, whereas almost all of his contemporary portraits of lay people were small-scale oils. These pictures signified the beginning of a half-century during which the middle class rapidly overtook the gentry as the main source of patronage in Wales. By doing so they facilitated the re-emergence in portraits of the visual conventions of painters who were not academically trained. The manner in which Hughes painted the tenant farmer Huw Griffith of Bodwrdda, Caernarfonshire, with two of his children, placed the portrait firmly in the tradition of artisan work maintained in more marginal fields through the eighteenth century. Nevertheless, the art practice that developed in the first decades of the nineteenth century in Wales cannot be presented as a simple division between the products of academic and non-academic painters. As we have seen, by 1819 Hughes himself was engaged in a project firmly rooted in eighteenth-century high art tradition – travelling to draw the picturesque landscapes and historical monuments of the country, subsequently engraved and sold to a range of patrons that extended to the very top of society. *The Beauties of Cambria* was issued in six parts between 1819 and 1823, and dedicated to Sir Watkin Williams-Wynn, son of the patron of Richard Wilson. How Hughes initially gained Sir Watkin's favour is unclear, but at the regional eisteddfod held at Wrexham in 1820, which was attended by both men, he was praised by his patron in his role as president:

> ... meet Sir Watkin and Sir E[dward] Lloyd and various gentlemen who pay me the most kindly attention, and praise my work to the gentlemen around them far beyond my expectation. I am admitted into the company and get to know various famous and respectable men, among them the Revd Walter Davies, the most important poet and critic of the present time.[5]

The eisteddfod at Wrexham was the second in the series of regional eisteddfodau that had begun the previous year at Carmarthen. Central to their conception was the literary and antiquarian enthusiasm of a group of Anglican priests known as *yr hen bersoniaid llengar* ('the old literary parsons') of whom Walter Davies – 'Gwallter Mechain' – was one. The Carmarthen eisteddfod was also notable as the first to which were attached the ceremonies of the Gorsedd, devised by Iolo Morganwg. The eisteddfodau were the product of the old order, therefore, but were frequented by a mixed audience that included, certainly at Wrexham, the new generation of middle-class Nonconformist intellectuals, like Hughes and his friend William Williams, 'Caledfryn'. The Wrexham event may be visualised as a fulcrum – a symbolic point of balance following which the old intellectual culture rapidly gave way to the new. Even ardent proponents of the idea that the eighteenth-century Welsh revival was a golden age acknowledge that 'Nonconformity had produced by the eighteen-thirties and forties a higher culture more vigorous than that of the scholars and patriots of the Renaissance.'[6] That culture was visual as well as literary.[7]

3 J. Morgan Jones and W. Morgan, *Y Tadau Methodistaidd*, vol. ii (Swansea, 1895), p. 33.

4 The engraving carries the Welsh text 'The gift of H. Hughes to readers of the Drysorfa.'

5 NLW MS Cwrt Mawr 130A, 13 September 1820; my translation.

6 Prys Morgan, *The Eighteenth-Century Renaissance* (Llandybïe, 1981), pp. 147–8.

7 For the relationship between the eisteddfod movement and visual culture, see Peter Lord, *Y Chwaer-Dduwies. Celf, Crefft a'r Eisteddfod* (Llandysul, 1992).

A new cultural climate

In 1821, Hugh Hughes visited Carmarthen for the first time. Relationships that he established there provided a foundation for his elevation within the decade into a public figure not only as a portrait painter but as the earliest illustrator of Welsh language texts, and as a controversialist. He became a close friend of Revd David Charles, brother of Thomas Charles, and eventually married his daughter, Sarah. For her brother, David Charles the younger, he would illustrate the first children's magazine in Welsh, *Yr Addysgydd*. It was printed in Carmarthen by John Evans, who also became a friend and colleague. In the early 1820s, Evans was probably the most productive printer and publisher in Wales, and in addition to their co-operation on illustrated publications, like several other Carmarthen tradesmen John Evans employed Hugh Hughes in his capacity as a portrait painter.[8] *The Family of John Evans at Breakfast* was not only among the most ambitious portraits of the period, but also the most significant. It is the portrait of an idea. The Evans family represented for Hughes a model of the virtues of the progressive Nonconformist middle class, whose aspiration to spiritual and material improvement he championed in his painting, in his engraving, and in his writing: 'It is with people of the middling sort that all reform begins', he would observe in 1831.[9] Like its gentry precedents of the previous three centuries, the picture was a dynastic statement which, by the inclusion of a portrait silhouette of the deceased father, spanned three generations. At the exact centre Hughes placed the matriarch, and in puritan denial of the sin of pride, painted her hare lip distinctly. The room she dominated was plain but its accoutrements were good – blue china and silverware, acquired through the application of enterprise and knowledge.[10] Both were epitomised by the family publishing business, represented in the picture by the local newspaper, the *Carmarthen Journal*. The newspaper symbolised literacy which, to Hughes and many like him, was the key to the spread of progressive social attitudes in Wales and the world beyond.[11]

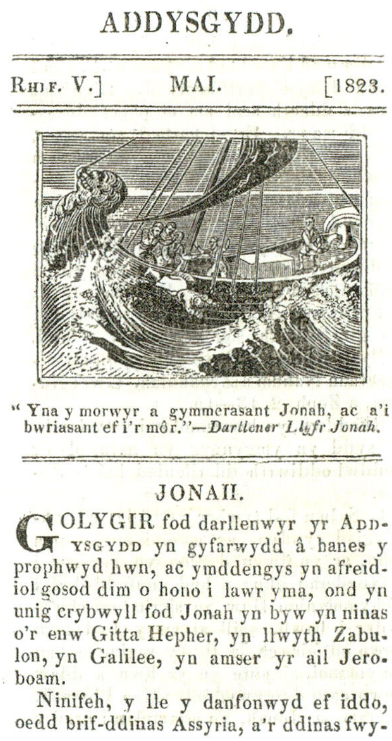

ADDYSGYDD.

RHIF. V.] MAI. [1823.

"Yna y morwyr a gymmerasant Jonah, ac a'i bwriasant ef i'r môr."—*Darllener Llyfr Jonah.*

JONAH.

GOLYGIR fod darllenwyr yr ADDYSGYDD yn gyfarwydd â hanes y prophwyd hwn, ac ymddengys yn afreidiol gosod dim o hono i lawr yma, ond yn unig crybwyll fod Jonah yn byw yn ninas o'r enw Gitta Hepher, yn llwyth Zabulon, yn Galilee, yn amser yr ail Jeroboam.

Ninifeh, y lle y danfonwyd ef iddo, oedd brif-ddinas Assyria, a'r ddinas fwy-

161. Hugh Hughes, *Jonah*, from *Yr Addysgydd*, 1823, wood engraving, 37x21

8 The others included David Charles, who in addition to being a Methodist minister was a rope and paper maker; David Morley, a flourishing cabinet maker; and Hannah White, a stationer.

9 'Gyda dynion canolig y dechreua pob diwygiad.' Hugh Hughes, 'Cyfoeth, Dysg a Synnwyr', in *Seren Gomer* (1831), p. 261.

10 The Evans family were members of an Independent chapel.

11 In Caernarfon, Hugh Hughes would found in 1836 the first weekly Welsh language newspaper, *Y Papyr Newydd Cymraeg*. See Peter Lord, *Hugh Hughes, Arlunydd Gwlad 1790–1863* (Llandysul, 1995), pp. 212–5. *The Family of John Evans at Breakfast* is discussed in detail in Lord, *The Meaning of Pictures*, pp. 65–67.

All over the country, middling sorts like the Evans family expressed their emerging confidence as a class by imaging themselves for the first time. They employed a new generation of Welsh painters, of whom Hugh Hughes was the pioneer, along with itinerant painters of miniatures and silhouettes venturing into Wales from England for the first time as the market for their work expanded. Often the itinerants found it easier to travel by sea than overland. Their movements can be traced by the handbills they had printed and the advertisements they placed in local newspapers as they voyaged from coastal town to coastal town – Swansea, Tenby, Haverfordwest, Cardigan, Aberystwyth – though their pictures are difficult now to identify, as they were frequently unsigned. Sometimes,

162. Hugh Hughes, *The Family of John Evans of Carmarthen at Breakfast*, c.1823, oil, 71x107

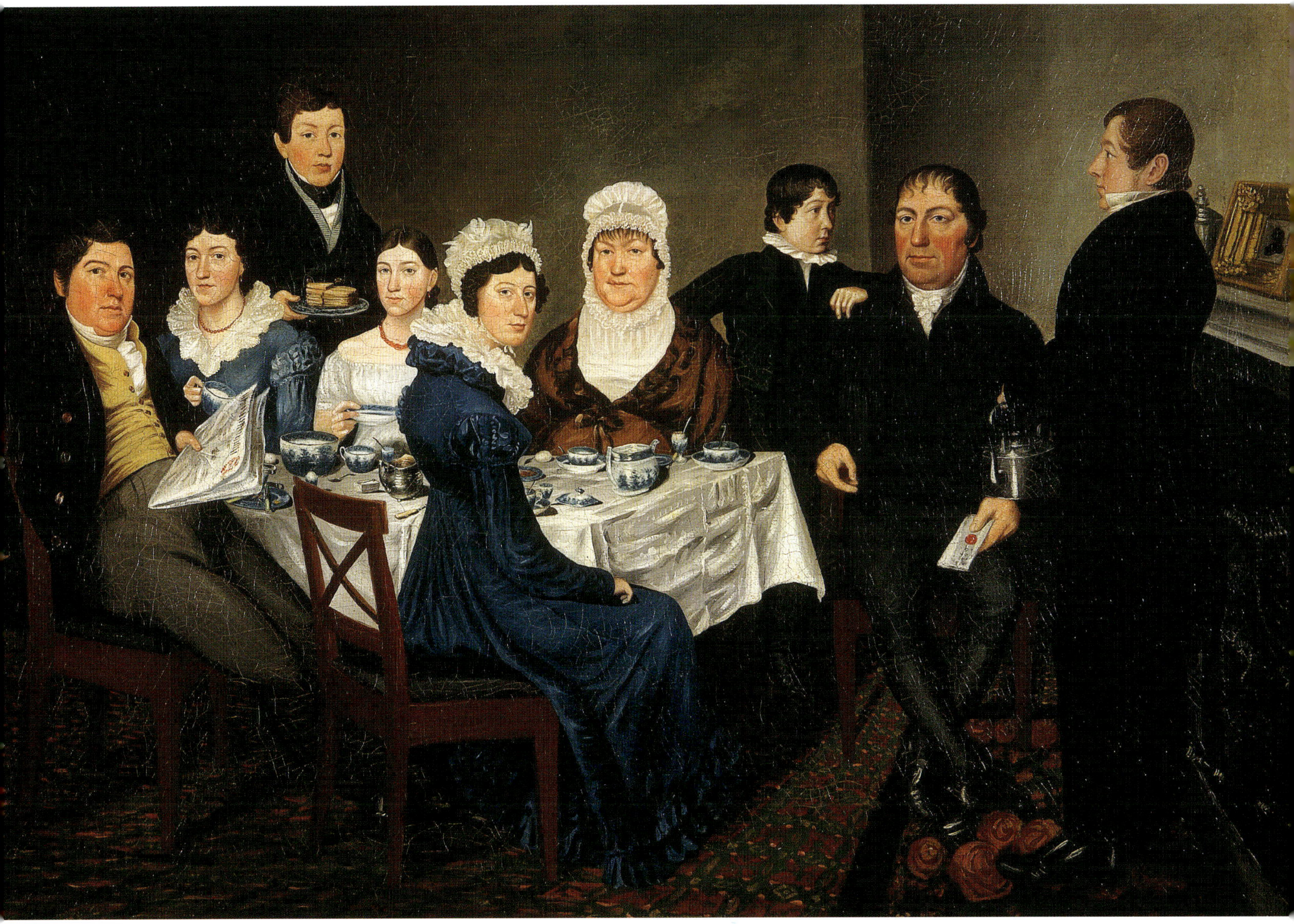

163. James Sparrow,
Captain Skinner's House,
Holyhead, 1828,

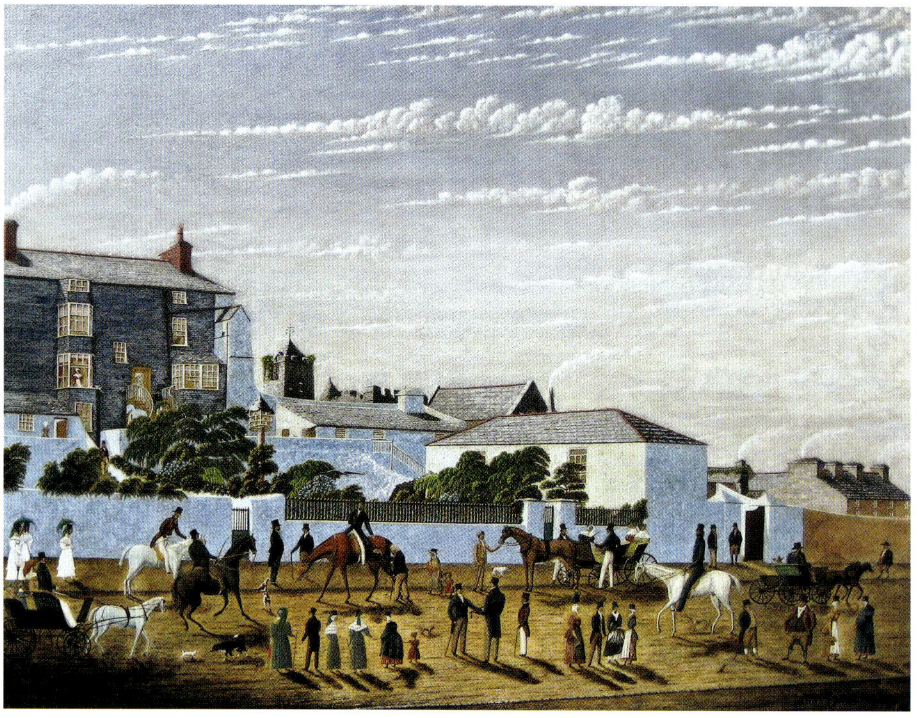

164. Unknown painter,
Margaret Rowlands with her daughter Ann and her son Robert Hugh, and *Hugh Rowlands with his son Owen*, c.1845, oil, 84x67.6

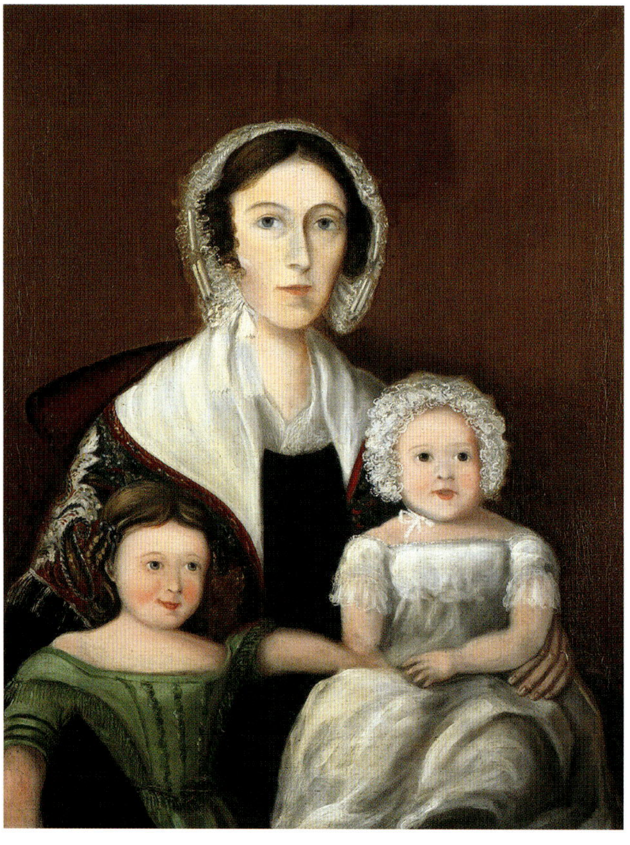

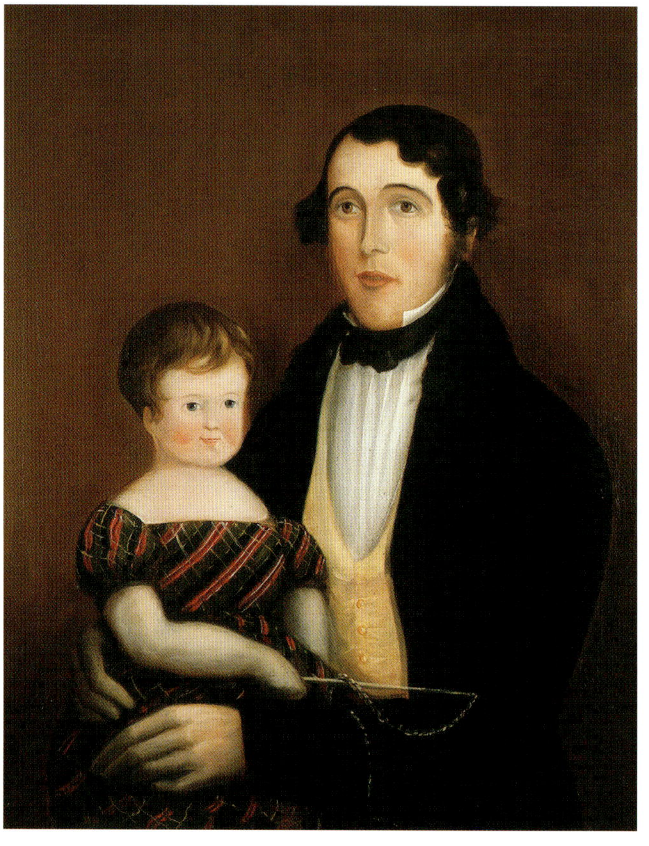

members of the rising middle class produced their own images, employing their amateur talents in the leisure time that their prosperity provided. In 1828, James Sparrow, a customs officer of Holyhead, painted a view of the house of his friend John Skinner, captain of the Dublin mail packet and a celebrated figure in the town. Sparrow peopled the street below with portraits of fellow townspeople, ranging from the minor gentry to the fishmonger, but dominated by those who, like himself, had risen with the maritime trade of the port.[12]

The towns of the Welsh seaboard, trading both coastally and world-wide, became a particularly rich source of patronage in the period. A decade or so after the Holyhead street scene, Hugh and Margaret Rowlands of the town would commission from an unidentified artisan a pair of portraits of themselves and their children. Hugh Rowlands was a purser on the Dublin steam packets that Captain Skinner had first commanded.[13] In mid-Wales, Captain John Evans of Aberaeron also commissioned an artisan to paint his portrait. He wore an earring, sign of the seaman, but chose to emphasise his Nonconformist piety rather than his profession by posing with his hand on his Bible. Other Welsh seamen commissioned their portraits while abroad, some as far away as China.[14] Both captains and owners also invested in pictures of their vessels, some of which were, again, painted while away from home. Particularly popular were pictures acquired in the Bay of Naples, where artisans flourished on the quays, working to a conventional pattern that enabled them to produce a work in the short time it took to discharge and reload cargo. On a calm sea and against a clear blue sky, vessels were depicted with Vesuvius smoking, apparently

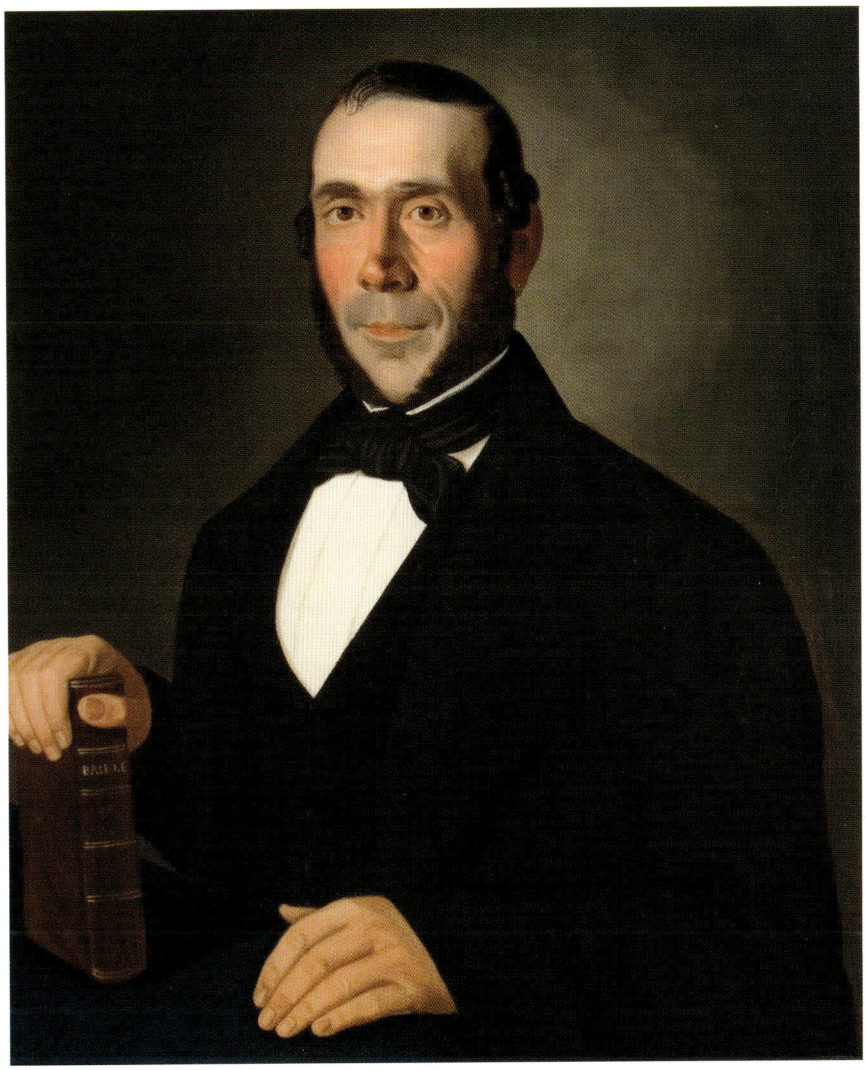

165. Unknown painter, *Captain John Evans, Milford House, Aberaeron*, c.1845, oil, 77x64

12 In a lithograph of the painting, all the individuals portrayed were identified. The gentry were represented by the Misses Stanley of Penrhos, descendants of the family of the painter Edward Owen.

13 The portraits are characteristic products of the artisan tradition. The 1841 census records the presence of William Hopson, a generalist painter, in the town.

14 Captain Evans of Swansea was painted by a Chinese artisan. Notable among earlier Welsh seafarers to be painted was Captain William Owen (1737-78) of Glansevern, Powys.

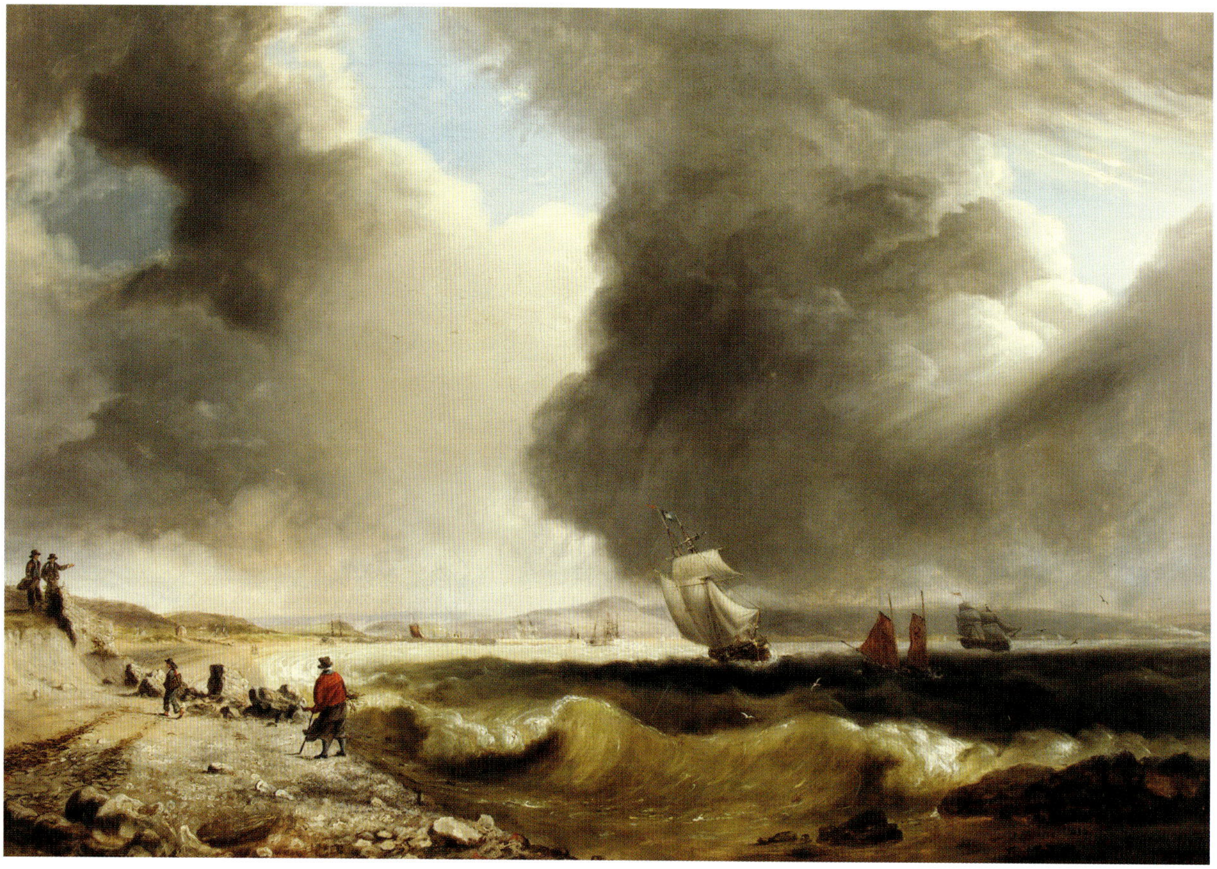

166. James Harris, *Swansea Bay in Stormy Weather*, 1834, oil, 60.3x88.9

benign, in the background. Ship pictures painted at home, in Welsh ports as in Bristol and other parts of England, were produced in a wide variety of styles. They ranged from simple, descriptive artisan products, usually painted in the smaller ports, to the sophisticated seascapes, sometimes of dramatic storm scenes, produced in Swansea by James Harris. His pictures were painted in a tradition that extended back to the work of Dutch artists of the seventeenth century, to which he may have gained access through training with George Chambers, who had also found customers among the industrialist families of Swansea for some years.[15] Harris may have trained with Chambers under the patronage of the wealthy Calvert Richard Jones, himself an amateur painter. Pictures of the kind painted by Chambers and Harris appealed to a wider range of clients than the artisan products painted specifically for an owner or captain. They satisfied a growing taste for seascape (and landscape) in the Victorian parlour.

Many of the artisan painters of ships remain unidentified, though John Roberts, who worked between Porthmadog and Pwllheli, was documented.[16] Roberts was a generalist artisan in the long tradition represented early on by Thomas Ffrancis. He undertook

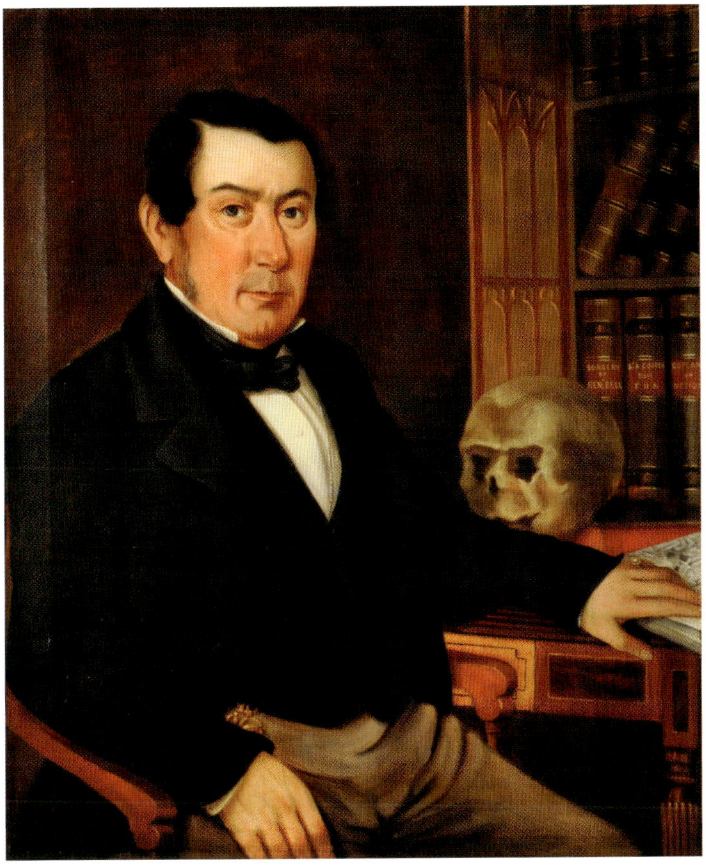

167. John Roberts, *Dr Hugh Hunter Hughes, Pwllheli*, *c*.1840-5, oil, 70x59

painting work of all sorts, including inscriptions, shop and pub signs, ship pictures and occasionally portraits. A painting of the doctor and coroner Hugh Hunter Hughes of Pwllheli, who sat sometime in the early 1840s, may well represent his work. Perhaps the picture hung over the mantelpiece in the parlour or dining room of the practitioner's town house, surrounded by fashionable furniture, like the cabinet before which he posed.[17] Such portraits became part of an ensemble of domestic display that informed the visitor and reassured the owner of his or her social status. A few patrons went further, employing artisans to paint decorative schemes directly on the walls of their houses. Examples of this kind of domestic elaboration were more common among the middle class in the small towns of the north-east of the United States than in Wales, but Hugh Hughes is known to have painted a mural scheme for Rowland Jones at Broom Hall, Pwllheli. This work is lost, but a complete scheme survives in Elwy Bank, a house at St Asaph, that may be in part the work of Albin Roberts Burt, a painter and engraver briefly associated with Hughes.[18] All four walls of the front room of the town house were painted with portraits of notable public figures, and with symbolic representations of Justice and Britannia. The portraits, that included Lord Nelson and the Duke and Duchess of Gloucester, were based on engravings, but one of those engravings

15 Chambers also knew Thomas Hornor, who may have encouraged him to seek patrons in Swansea, where he himself had been successful. See R.G. Howell, *Under Sail. Swansea Cutters, Tallships and Seascapes 1830-1880* (Swansea, 1987), p. 88.

16 John Roberts was the subject of one of the very few accounts of artisans written by a contemporary. Myrddin Fardd, 'John Roberts, Llanystumdwy', *Cymru*, VIII (1895), p. 63.

17 Hugh Hughes's portrait of *The Family of John Evans* was seen in just such a location in the 1820s by John Deffett Francis, NLW MS 6358B, unpaginated.

18 Both Hughes and the painter William Roos were in the north-east of Wales during the summer of 1820, including at St Asaph. Burt was engaged to engrave Hughes's portrait of Thomas Jones of Denbigh in the same year.

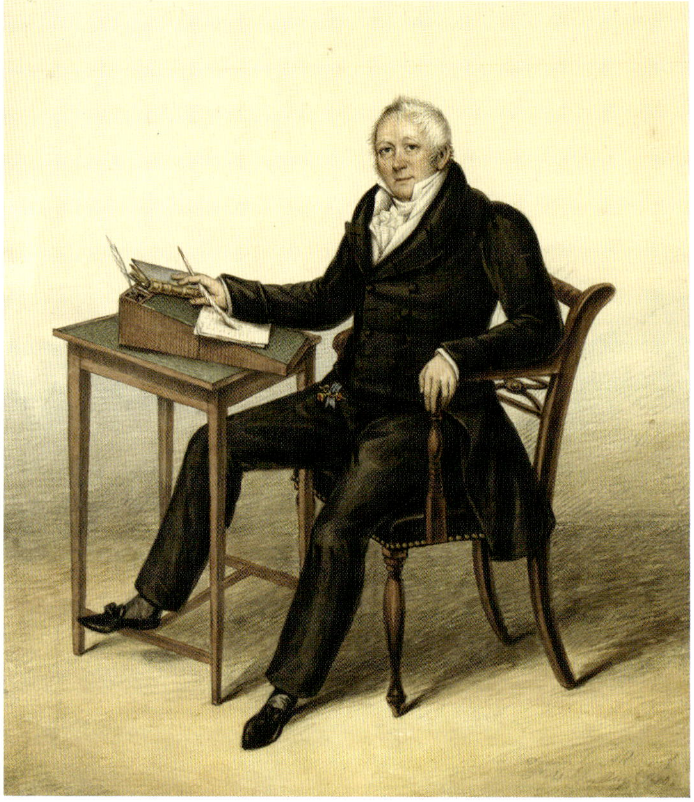

168. Albin Roberts Burt, *Lewis Hughes, St Asaph*, 1820, watercolour, 26x18

was Burt's own, after his cabinet miniature of William Shipley, the once controversial but now aged Dean of St Asaph Cathedral.[19] Another picture, probably representing the cathedral organist Henry Hayden (and not based on an engraving), is close in style to portraits known to have been painted by Burt at St Asaph in 1820.[20]

It is not clear if the St Asaph mural scheme was entirely domestic, or if the room was also used for meetings of a society of some kind. In the 1820s, antiquarian and literary societies proliferated, once again led mainly by members of the urban middle class. Some were modelled on the London Welsh societies of the second half of the eighteenth century, the Cymmrodorion, Gwyneddigion and Cymreigyddion, all of which occasionally commissioned portraits of members to adorn their meeting rooms. In 1824, the *Carmarthen Journal* advised its readers that

> On Tuesday night last, the members of the Carmarthen Cymreigyddion Society held their Quarterly meeting at the old Ivy Bush Inn, in this town, the Rev. Archdeacon Beynon in the chair. Previously to entering on the business of the evening, a full length portrait of the Rev. President was introduced into the room, which cost the Society twenty five guineas, made up by Private Subscriptions. This affords at once an evidence of the liberality and spirit of the members of the association, and the high estimation in which they hold their worthy President. The likeness was no less admired for its fidelity to the original than for its excellence as a painting, and reflects much credit on the Artist, Mr Hugh Hughes, author of *The Beauties of Cambria*.[21]

19 In the early 1780s, Shipley had attracted the enmity of Thomas Pennant, who had him satirised in political cartoons. The dispute and the images are described in Peter Lord, *Words with Pictures. Welsh Images and Images of Wales in the Popular Press, 1640–1860* (Aberystwyth, 1995), pp. 75–80.

20 Peter Lord, 'Murals and Mysteries at Elwy Bank, St Asaph', *Cambria*, 14, no. 1 (2014), pp. 42–5. Burt lived at Chester, from where he travelled to portray several notable Welsh people, ranging from Sir Watkin Williams-Wynn in 1820 to the eccentric Richard Robert Jones, known as 'Dic Aberdaron', in 1823.

21 *Carmarthen Journal*, 10 December 1824, p. 3.

22 Bangor University Archives MS Amlwch 4. The unidentified writer, a priest at Bala, rather overstated the case in his use of the word 'revolutionary', if he intended it in a political sense. Nevertheless, the magazine represented a radical departure in the wide range of its content, and its campaigning on issues of particular Welsh concern.

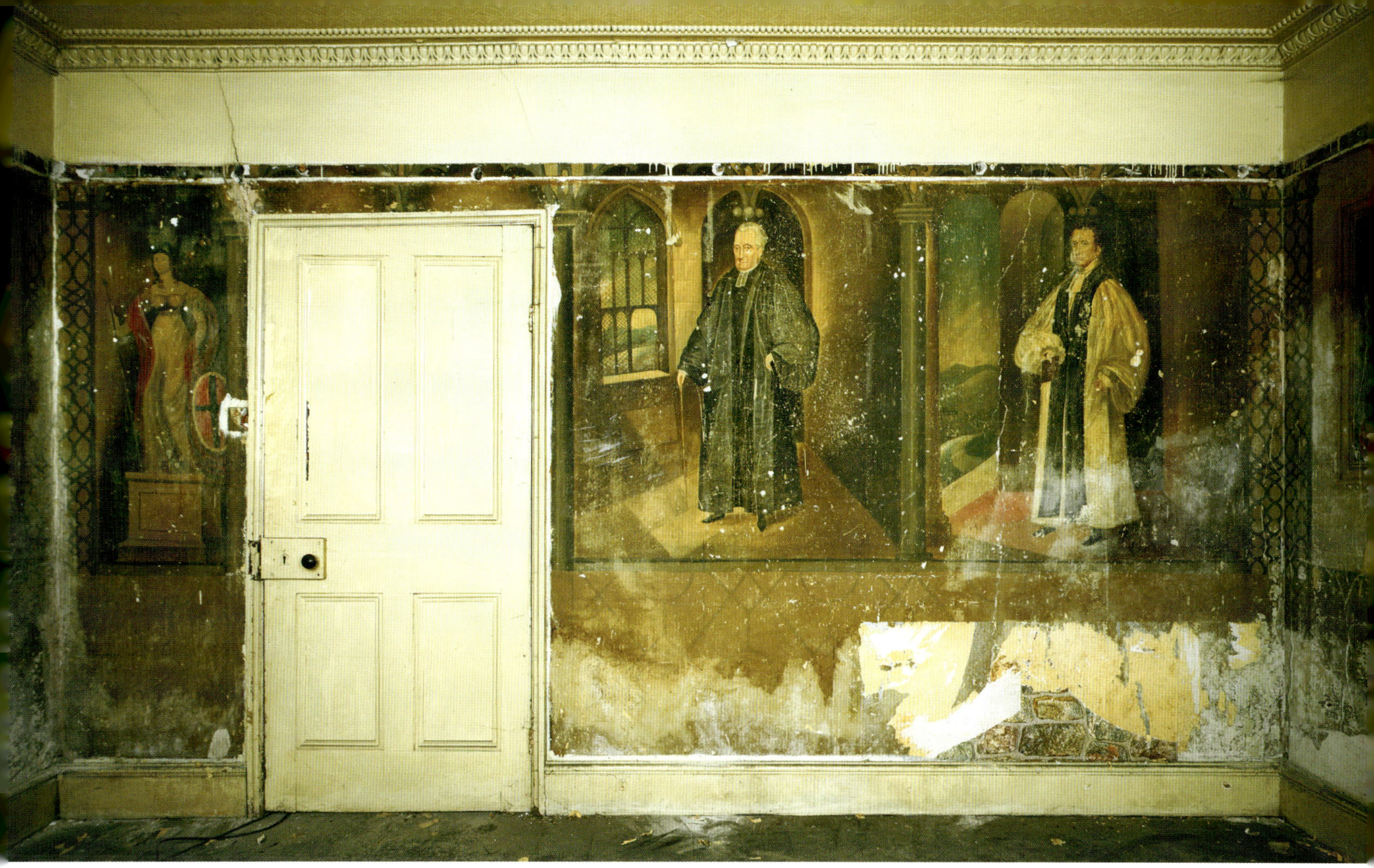

169. Probably Albin Roberts Burt, *Britannia, William Shipley (Dean of St Asaph), and Reginald Heber*, mural paintings at Elwy Bank, St Asaph, *c.*1823–6

Contact with the Society's president led Hughes socially upwards, in the direction of those he had encountered briefly at Wrexham in 1820. Over the next three years he was commissioned to paint not only the other members of the antiquarian and literary circle in which Beynon moved but also some gentry sitters. Since these patrons did not regard the artisan conventions of the painter's early portraits as appropriate, Hughes changed his style to imitate the work of academic artists. Briefly, his patronage base became hybrid, but following a bitter dispute within the Methodist church over the granting of civil rights to Roman Catholics, Hughes gained a reputation as an extreme radical, alienating both the increasingly conservative leadership of his church (from which he was expelled) and his newly-acquired gentry patrons. Still living in London, he became closely associated with the Welsh-speaking Cymreigyddion Society, writing and engraving for their 'revolutionary Welsh periodical', *Y Cymro*. Hughes designed the image through which the magazine presented its manifesto in 1830 – a new Welshman, aware of a deep history, but engaged with the contemporary world of politics, economics, science, and technology.[22]

170. Hugh Hughes, *Y Cymro*, 1830, wood engraving, 21.2x12.6

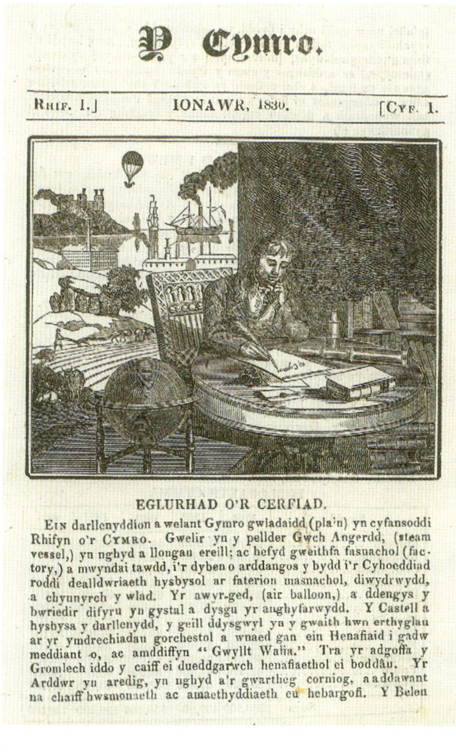

Y Cymro.

RHIF. 1.] IONAWR, 1830. [CYF. 1.

EGLURHAD O'R CERFIAD.

EIN darllenyddion a welant Gymro gwladaidd (plain) yn cyfansoddi Rhifyn o'r CYMRO. Gwelir yn y pellder Gwch Angerdd, (steam vessel,) yn nghyd a llongau ereill; ac hefyd gweithfa fasnachol (factory,) a mwyndai tawdd, i'r dyben o arddangos y bydd i'r Cyhoeddiad roddi dealldwriaeth hysbysol ar faterion masnachol, diwydrwydd, a chynnyrch y wlad. Yr awyr-ged, (air balloon,) a ddengys y bwriedir difyru yn gystal a dysgu yr anghyfarwydd. Y Castell a hysbysa y darllenydd, y geill ddysgwyl yn y gwaith hwn erthyglau ar yr ymdrechiadau gorchestol a wnaed gan ein Henafiaid i gadw meddiant o, ac amddiffyn "Gwyllt Walia." Tra yr adgoffa y Gromlech iddo y caiff ei dueddgarwch henafiaethol ei boddâu. Yr Arddwr yn aredig, yn nghyd a'r gwartheg corniog, a addawant na chaiff hwsmonaeth ac amaethyddiaeth eu hebargofi. Y Belen

Among Hughes's associates at this time was another painter, Thomas George, originally from Fishguard. Nothing is known of any training that George may have received, and his earliest known works were miniatures of Pembrokeshire sitters. However, he was in London by 1826 and soon mixing with the Welsh intellectual community. The diary of the antiquarian and lexicographer William Owen Pughe contains numerous references to portrait sittings with George, who sometimes arrived in the company of Hughes.[23]

171. Thomas George, *Gentleman by a Window, possibly B.S. Davies*, 1824–6, watercolour, 32x28

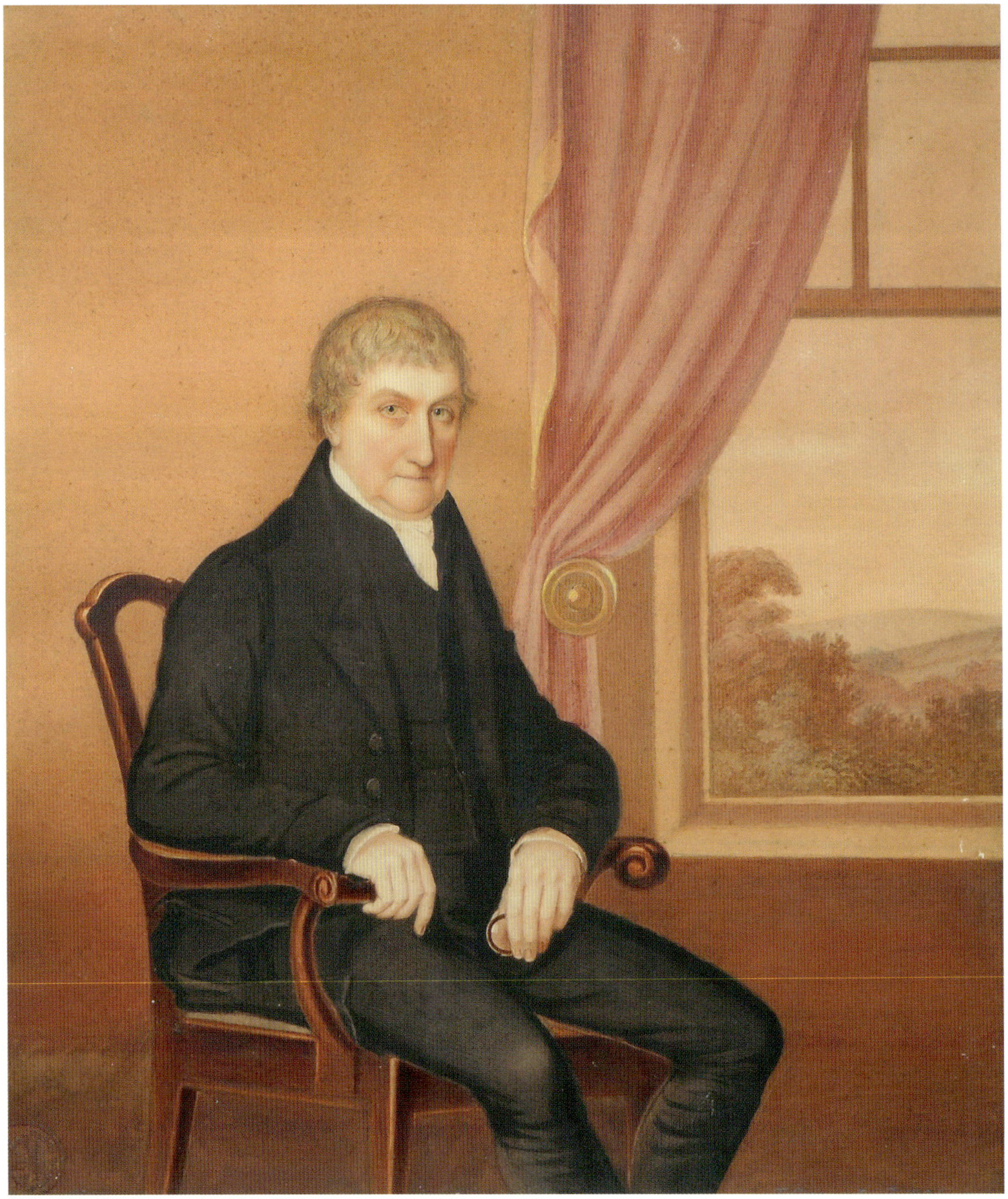

23 The diary, 1811–35, is now NLW MS 13248.

24 NLW MS Cwrt Mawr 74C, f. 38, my translation from the Welsh. John William Thomas, 'Arfonwyson', provides a classic example of the development of the Welsh middle class. He rose from humble origins at Pentir, Caernarfonshire, largely through his own efforts, publishing in the Welsh language on mathematics, engaging in public debate in *Seren Gomer*, and writing poetry. On moving to London he was noticed by the Astronomer Royal, G.B. Airy, who employed him at Greenwich. He died at the age of only 35, of tuberculosis.

Both men painted Pughe, and it would seem from the number of sittings that at least one of George's portraits was an oil. Unlike Hughes, however, in 1829 George succeeded in exhibiting at the Royal Academy, and would do so five times in all.

In 1832, Hugh Hughes left London. His return to Wales coincided with the beginning of two decades of unprecedented patronage of portrait painters at home and among the Welsh diaspora. The beneficiaries were both locally based general artisans and a number of portrait specialists, for whom there now existed sufficient work to earn a living exclusively within the Welsh community, providing they were prepared to follow a peripatetic lifestyle. Hughes pursued his career mainly in the north, and among the diaspora, especially in Liverpool. His main rival was William Roos, born at Amlwch in Anglesey in 1808. Although his public profile was lower, as a result of Hughes's continuing activity as a polemicist, Roos soon overtook the older painter in the number of commissions that he gained.

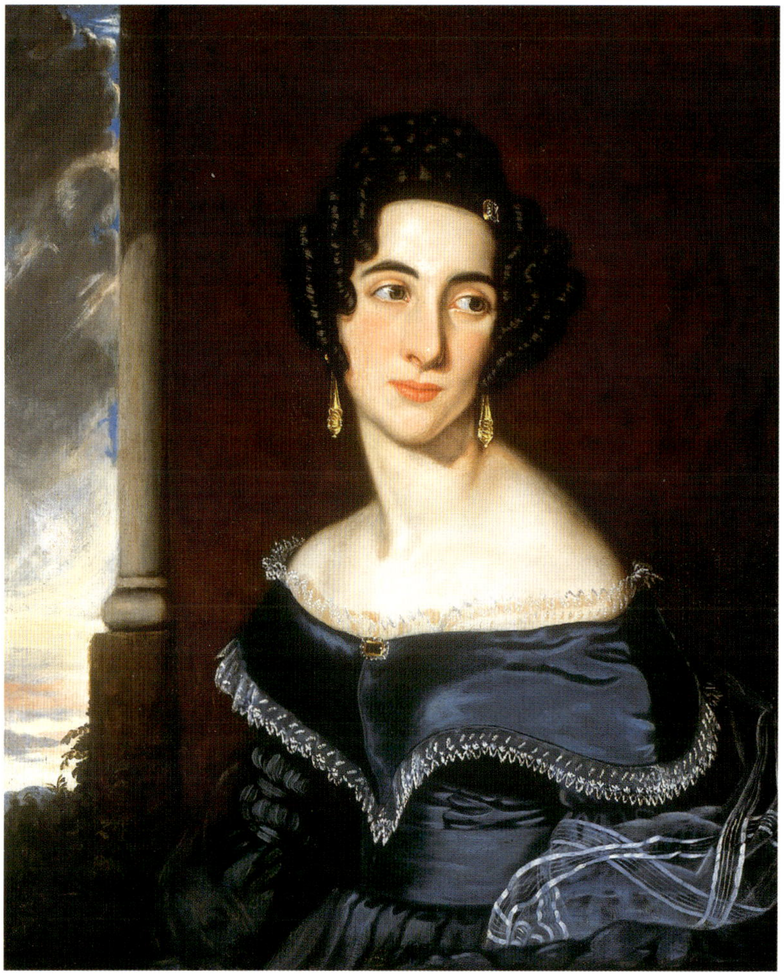

172. William Roos, *Woman in Blue*, 1839, oil, 76x63

Roos appears to have been self-taught and his earliest portraits did not imitate academic style. However, in 1836, he wrote to his friend, the poet Dewi Wyn o Eifion, describing the recent development of his career:

> Now I'll write a little about what I've been doing since I was in Pwllheli with you. I've wandered hundreds of miles. I was in London for three months, painting also in Woolwich and Dulwich; in Greenwich I stayed a week to paint J.W. Thomas, Arfon ... the famous Welshman, presently Astronomer to the King at the Royal Observatory. His picture has been hung in the meeting room of the Cymreigyddion in London ...[24]

Roos did not mention that while in London he had also been able to take a few lessons from an academically trained painter. The portrait known as *Woman in Blue*, that probably represents a London Welsh sitter, demonstrates the effect of exposure to academic style on a self-taught but talented painter. Roos learned quickly to produce pictures that reflected contemporary London fashion. The portrait bears a striking similarity to that painted in 1835 by William Etty of Louisa Vaughan, a member of the Rolls family of Hendre in Monmouthshire. The Etty portrait represents the ongoing patronage of sophisticated metropolitan painters by the upper echelons of Welsh society.[25] Nevertheless, notwithstanding his obvious ability, the patronage base for Roos widened only very occasionally to include the gentry. His middle-class clientele preferred a plainer style, on which he settled to paint a flood of distinctive portraits in the 1840s.

In his letter to Dewi Wyn, Roos mentioned that he was 'thinking about engraving two or three of the most famous Preachers.' An unusual characteristic of artisan painting in Wales was that the normal patronage base of the painters included important public figures of the day, especially Nonconformist religious leaders, and poets. As in the case of the depictions of prominent Methodists made by Hugh Hughes, engraved versions of Roos portraits played a role in the development of the reputation of these individuals – indeed, in some cases, of their iconisation. Finding himself lodged next door to Christmas Evans in Caernarfon, Roos had painted the celebrated Baptist minister in 1835, before the change of style brought about by his visit to London. In his letter of the following year to Dewi Wyn, he noted that he had just engraved the picture, and that it was his first experiment with mezzotint. The importance of this simple portrait, and that made by Hughes and engraved four years later, can be measured by the number of their derivatives. They range from other engravings to copies by amateur painters and sculptors, and include a Staffordshire ceramic figure, which must have been prepared exclusively for the Welsh market, since Evans was little known to English speakers.[26]

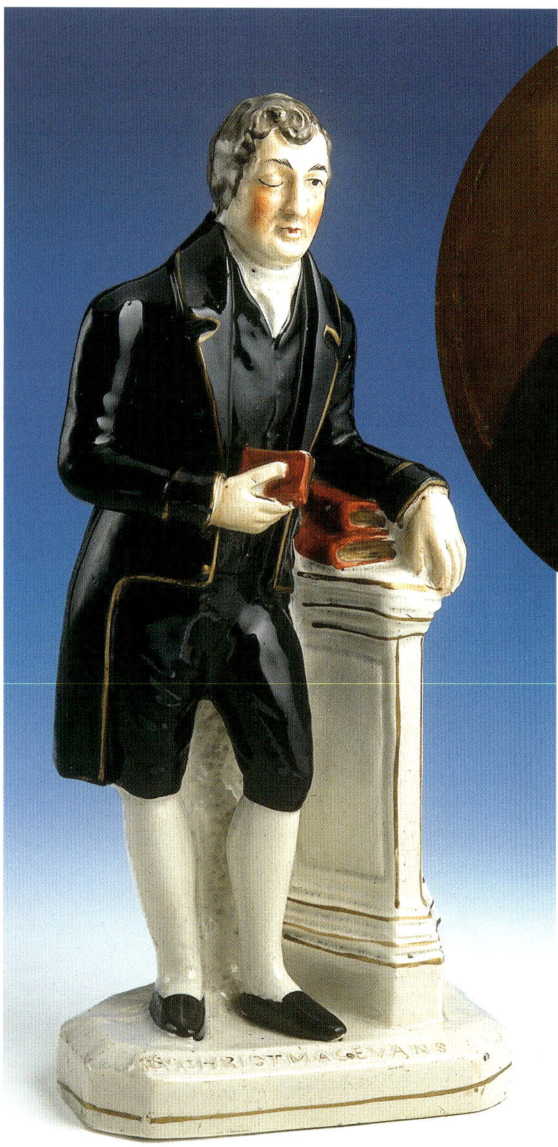

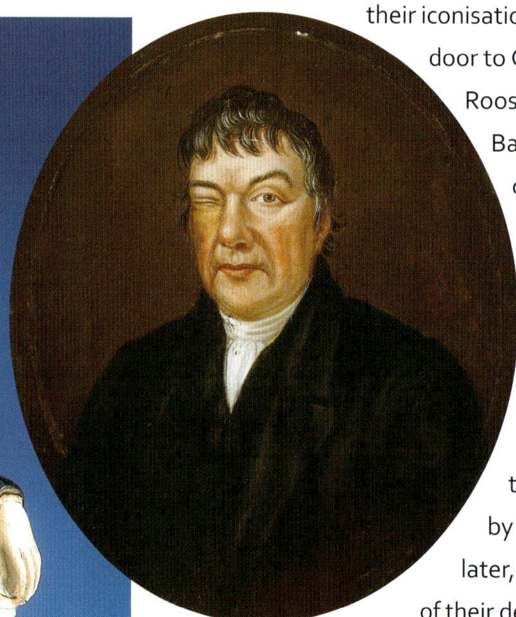

left
173. *Christmas Evans*, c.1850, Staffordshire pottery figure, h.36

above
174. William Roos, *Christmas Evans*, c.1835, oil, 39.4x33.2

175. William Etty, *Louisa Vaughan, née Rolls, of Hendre*, 1839, oil, 76.2x63.5

25 The sitter was painted with uncharacteristic restraint by Etty. Louisa had married into a pious Roman Catholic family, and became mother to four priests, four nuns and an Archbishop of Westminster! Etty painted also for the Williams-Wynns in the 1830s, in a more typically sumptuous manner. His double portrait of Charlotte and Mary, daughters of Charles, younger brother of Sir Watkin, is held by York Art Gallery.

26 Remarkably, Christmas Evans appears to have been one of only two individuals to have sat both to Hughes and to Roos. The other was the poet and literary patron, Ellis Owen of Cefn-y-Meusydd in Llŷn, who composed an epitaph for Roos: 'He painted life so well that Death/Envied his art; – withdrew his breath:/Although with mortals here he lies,/His Fame both Time and Death defies.' Ellis Owen, *Cell Meudwy* (Tremadog, 1877), p. 48.

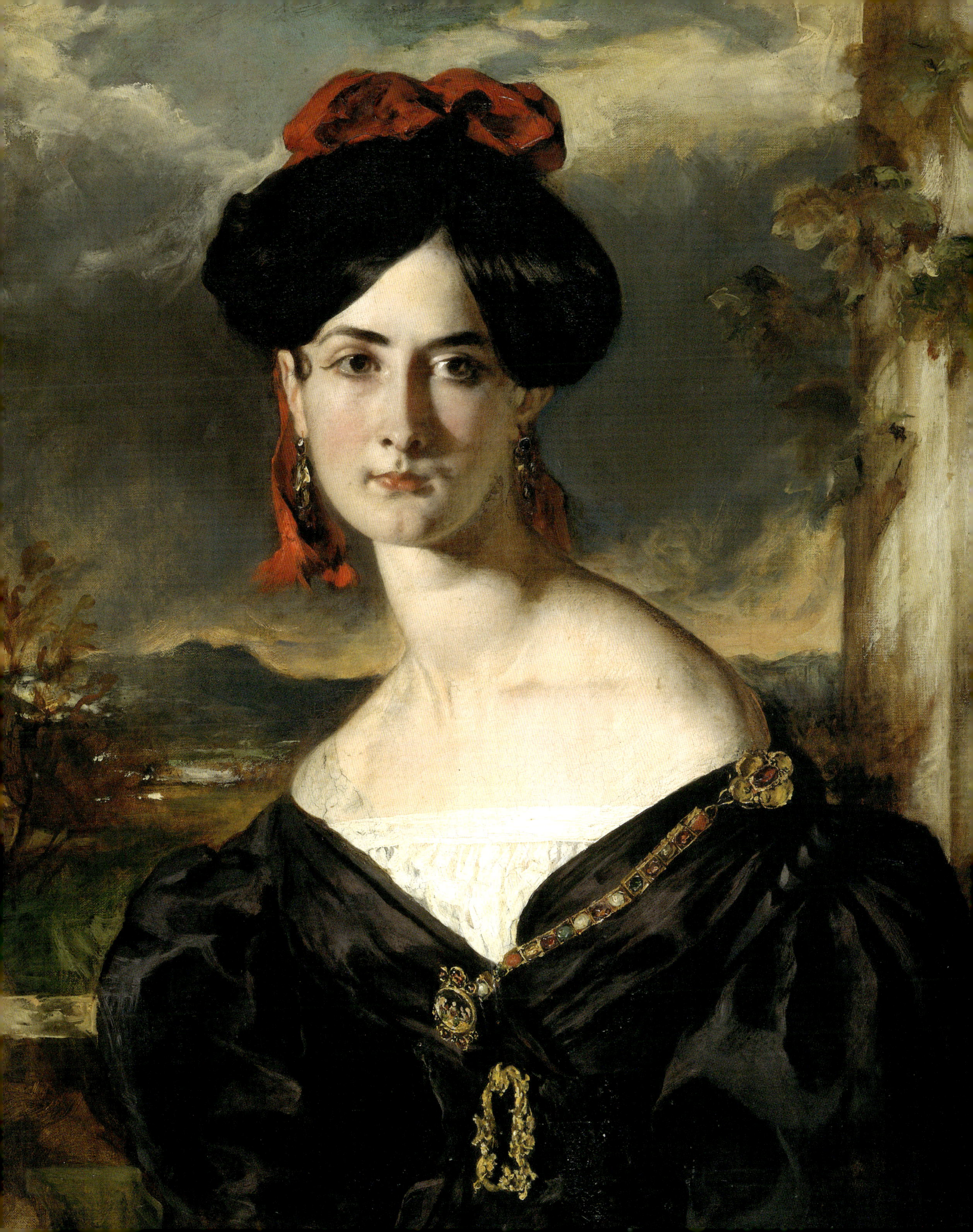

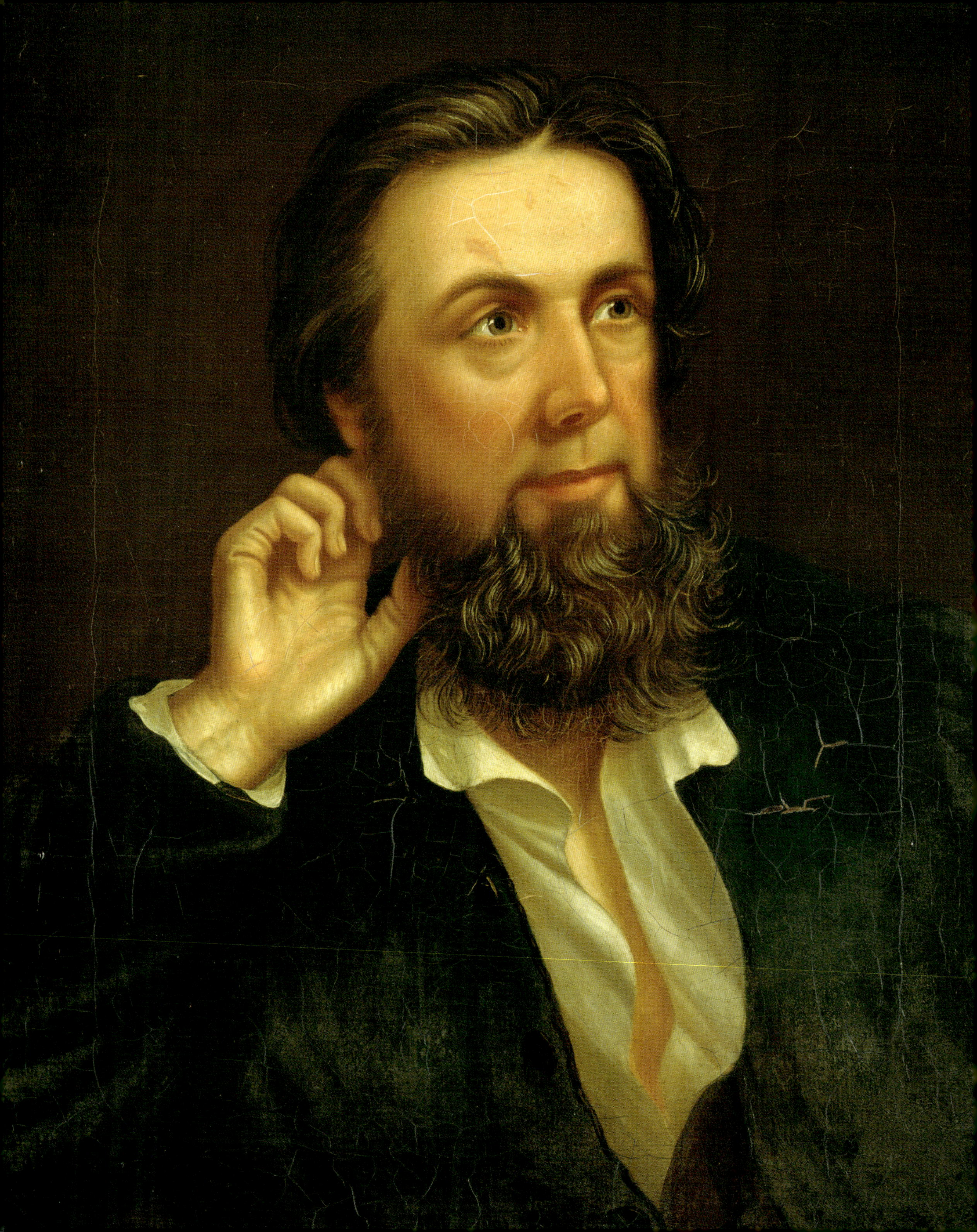

The literati figured prominently in the output of William Roos, whose versatility was demonstrated in the two portraits that he made of the poet John Jones, 'Talhaiarn', in successive years.[27] The commission for the first was probably associated with the eisteddfod held in 1850 at Rhuddlan. Talhaiarn was one of the promoters of the event, and the portrait was certainly displayed there. It is the most dramatic example of an inclination to Romanticism that occasionally emerged in the painter's work, and revealed his awareness of the tradition of high art bardic imagery. On the back of the painting Roos inscribed the words: 'The Bard in Meditation'. Talhaiarn was engaged with the eisteddfod both as a poet and in his other guise as a successful engineer. He designed the eisteddfod pavilion, though that commission paled into insignificance when compared with his work on the Crystal Palace, home of the Great Exhibition of 1851. Talhaiarn was an assistant to Joseph Paxton on the construction of that radical building and, in the same year as the opening, Roos painted the engineer again, this time in the sober guise of the successful London Welshman.[28]

A striking characteristic of the practice both of Roos and of Hugh Hughes, was that neither sought work in the increasingly wealthy south east of the country. Nevertheless, the middle-class patronage that sustained these two in other parts of Wales also provided employment in the industrialised areas for a range of painters who had not been academically trained. In 1830, William Jones Chapman, a peripatetic artisan who would travel throughout Wales over the ensuing forty years, made his earliest known painting. Although the society whose meeting it represented was known as the Cyfarthfa Hunt, the members were not those traditionally associated with hunting on horseback. The sitters were shopkeepers, professional people, musicians and engineers, including the celebrated William Williams.

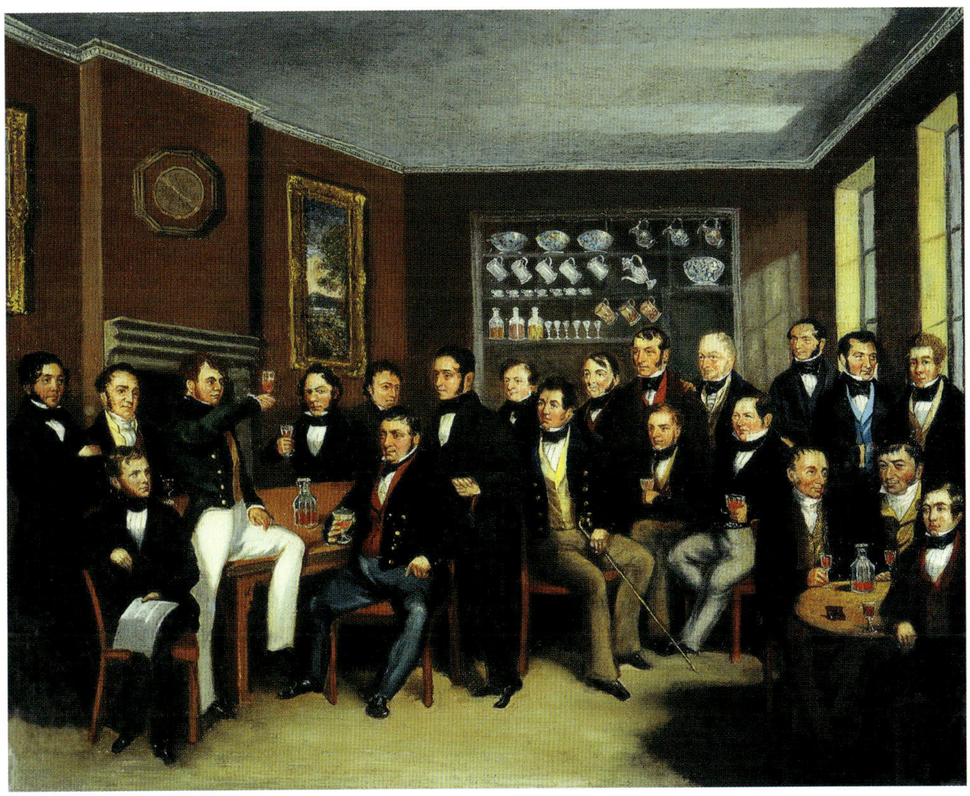

27 Roos painted two versions of the more formal portrait, one on a larger scale than the other.

28 Though sobriety was not a characteristic for which he was known in Wales. Talhaiarn appears to have suffered from an addiction to alcohol, for which he was satirised in the Welsh press. The ambiguity of his reputation was partly the result of the fact that he was an Anglican, and much of the comment upon him emanated from Nonconformists. Talhaiarn died by his own hand in 1869.

opposite
176. William Roos, *John Jones, Talhaiarn*, 1850, oil, 63.5x53

177. William Jones Chapman, *The Cyfarthfa Hunt*, 1830, oil, 71x90

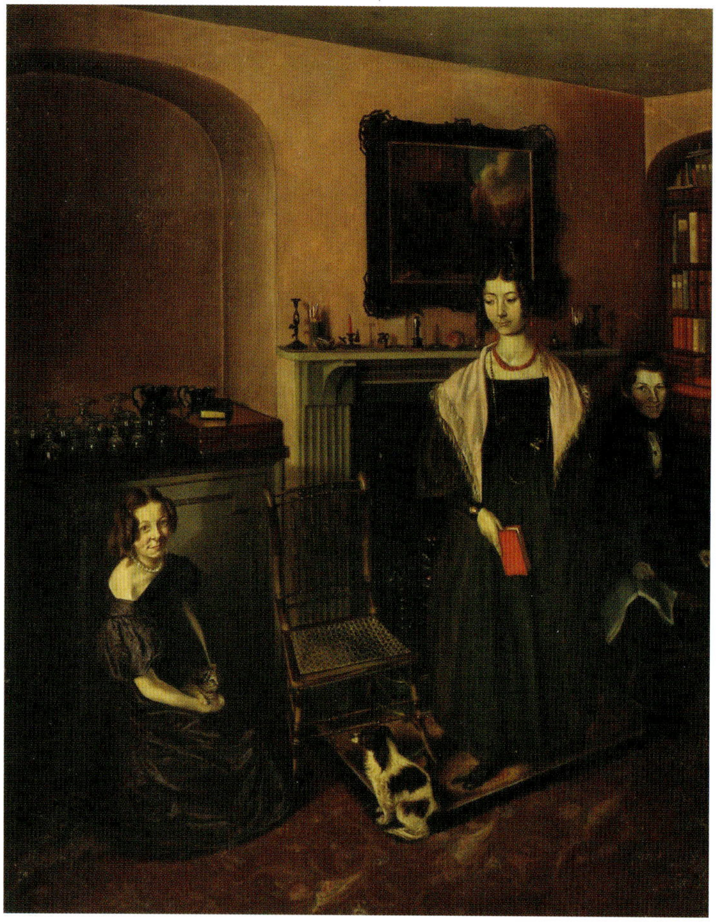

178. John Petherick, *Fireside in the Family Home*, c.1830–5, oil, 53.6x43.6

179. William Jones Chapman, *Thomas Euston, Lodge Keeper, Hirwaun*, from the Crawshay Worker Portraits series, oil, 35.5x26.5

A near-contemporary group portrait depicted a domestic scene. The family of John Petherick, manager of the Penydarren ironworks, was portrayed in mourning, grouped around an empty chair – presumably that of the recently deceased Petherick himself. A few years earlier this gentleman had been depicted in weighty maturity on a similar chair, in a watercolour painted by one of his sons, John Petherick junior. Family tradition ascribes the group portrait also to this son, but although finer in its representation of details, the faces of the family members resemble those painted by Chapman in the Cyfarthfa Hunt picture.[29] Whoever was responsible for painting them, the details of the interior of the Petherick house indicate both the prosperity of the family and their sophistication. On the wall hangs a late seventeenth-century Dutch subject painting. A commission received by Chapman in about 1835 presents a remarkable contrast with this comfortable world. It was given by Francis Crawshay, grandson of Richard, but an eccentric character, who found himself the unwilling manager of two family businesses at Hirwaun and Treforest. Francis Crawshay had Chapman paint a series of portraits of workers at the two sites. The seventeen small portraits depicted managers and agents in an informal manner, in their workaday clothes, and were particularly notable for the fact that they also presented some of the manual workers. Although such workers had appeared earlier in the pictures of Ibbetson and Penry Williams, they had not done so as named individuals. The Chapman portraits were remarkable for the interest they represented in individuals of no celebrity beyond their own community.[30]

29 Attribution is complicated by the fact that Chapman is known only to have completed *The Cyfarthfa Hunt*, which had been begun by another painter, A.W. Salter. However, the evidence of Chapman's subsequent work suggests strongly that he was responsible for painting the faces, which resemble those of the Petherick portrait. The only works known for certain to be by Petherick are landscape watercolours, dating from 1827 to the 1850s. However, documentary evidence also points to him as the painter of two remarkable industrial landscapes in oil, that depict the Bute Furnaces at Rhymney. See Peter Lord, *The Visual Culture of Wales: Industrial Society* (Cardiff, 1998), p. 57, note 8, and pp. 58-9.

30 One of the very few earlier portraits of a collier to name the sitter was made in 1819 by Albin Roberts Burt, but the subject, John Evans, was the celebrated survivor of a rock fall in his pit. He was a miner in the north-east Wales coalfield, and survived after twelve days underground. For this and the Chapman portraits, see Peter Lord, *The Francis Crawshay Worker Portraits* (Aberystwyth, 1996).

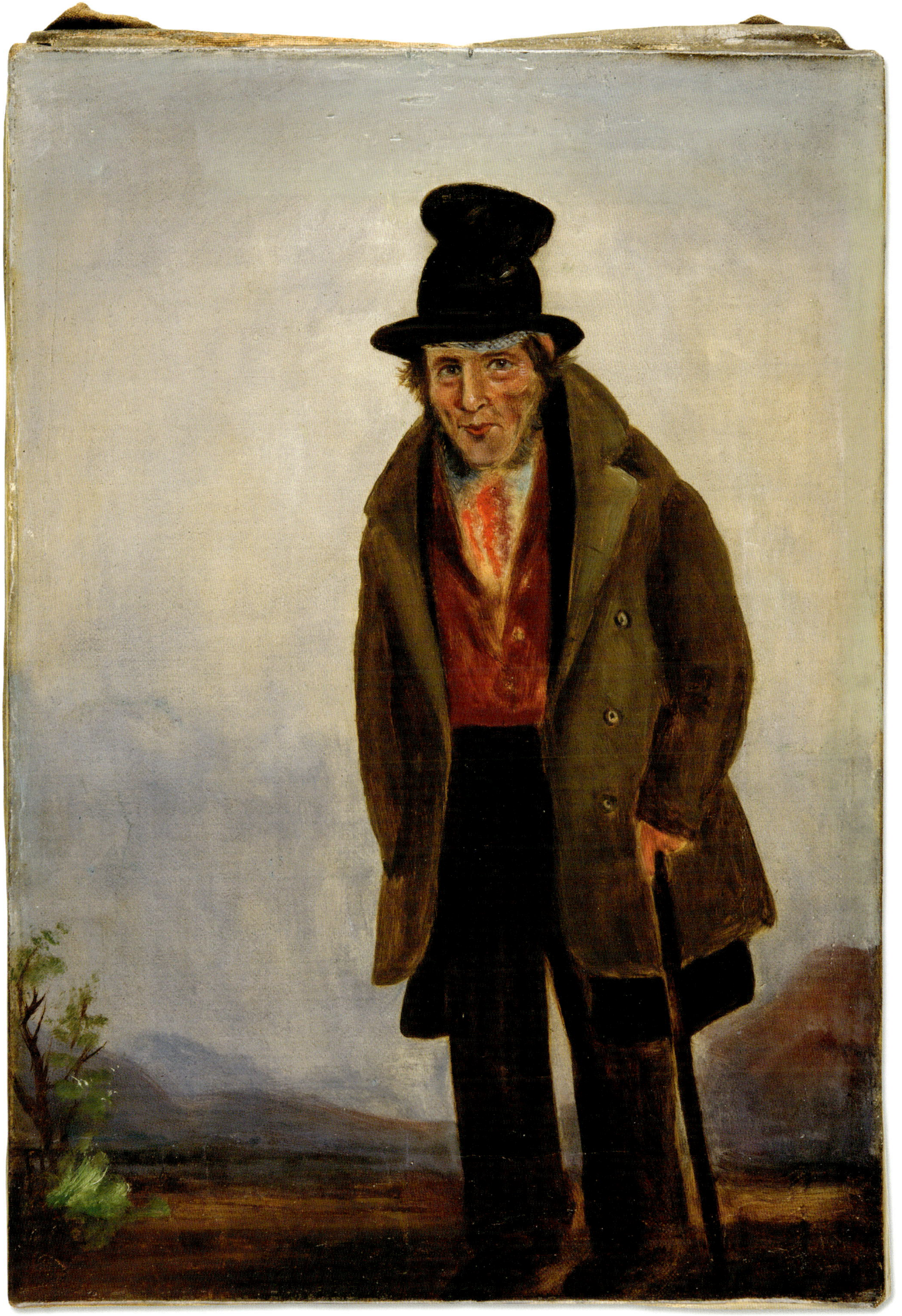

Like *The Cyfarthfa Hunt*, the worker portraits were not hidden inside a private house. They hung in an office where they would be seen by many members of the community that they depicted. Similarly, the remarkable *Homfray Coal Train*, painted in 1821 by an otherwise unknown artisan who signed himself 'In: Thomas', hung in the communal space of a public house in Newport. It depicted the arrival of a coal train at the Pillgwenlly terminus of the Sirhowy Tramway, drawn a decade earlier by Edward Pugh. The picture was dedicated to Samuel Homfray, 'The Independent Iron Master & Coal Merchant', whose entrepreneurial exertions had been to the public good, it was proclaimed, by reducing the price of coals in the area. The inscription did not note the fact that Homfray had profited doubly by his enterprise, as a result of his marriage into the Morgan family of Tredegar Park. For a short distance the tramway crossed Morgan land, a stretch that became known as 'the golden mile', since the family extracted a toll on every load that passed over it.

Curiously, the painting practice of the chief artistic beneficiary of the increasing wealth of Newport had little to say about the industrial source of the town's prosperity. James Flewitt Mullock was born in the town in 1818, and enjoyed an unusually long career there, that lasted into the 1880s. In the 1840s in particular, the agricultural and sporting interests of Sir Charles Morgan and his landed neighbours provided him with commissions to paint farm animals and equestrian portraits in the tradition that extended back into the eighteenth century.[31] In fact, Mullock and his family were also deeply involved in urban life, contributing to civic development in particular as instrumental figures in the creation of the Museum and Art Gallery, and the School of Science and Art. Mullock's earliest known work depicted the Chartist Rising at Newport in 1839, an event indicative of the pressure

opposite
181. James Flewitt Mullock, *Dr Fothergill Rowlands of Nantyglo on Tom Llewelyn Brewer's Horse 'Bold Davy'*, c.1845, oil, 61x74.5

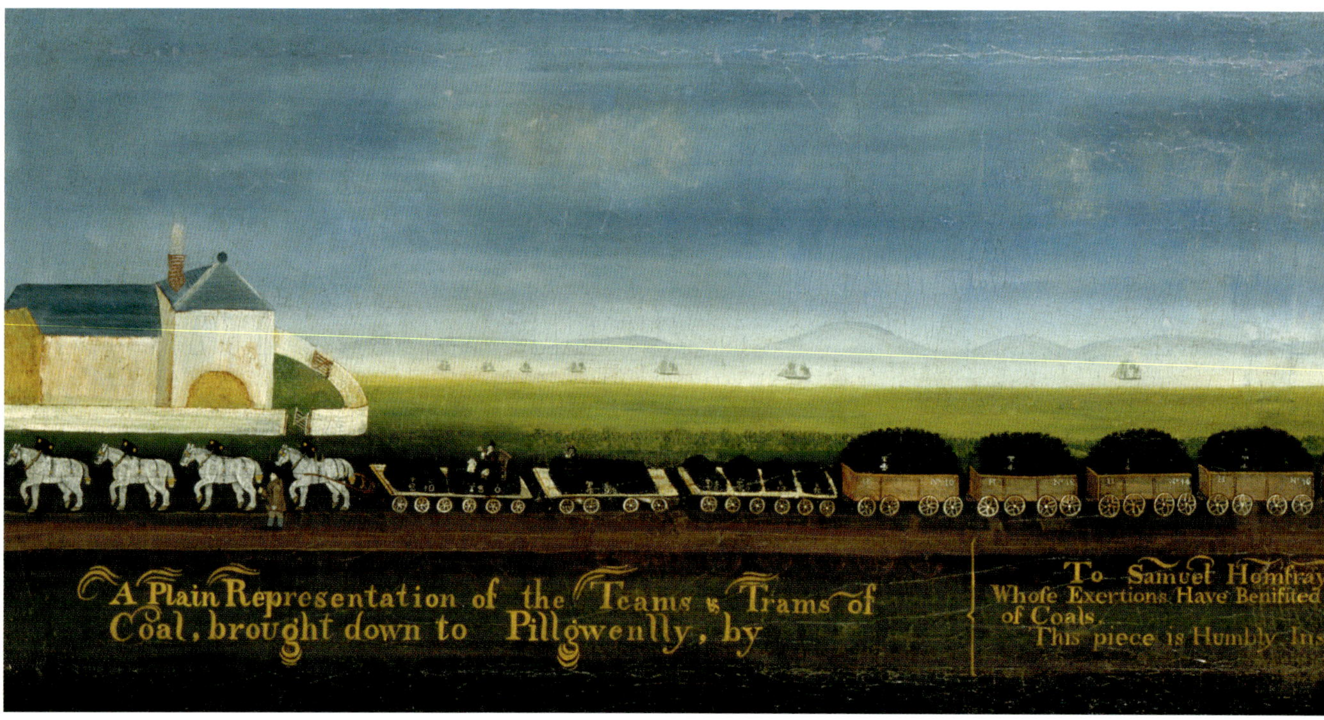

180. In: Thomas, *A Plain Representation of the Teams and Trams of Coal brought down to Pillgwenlly by Samuel Homfray Esq.*, 1821, oil, 86x376

31 W.J. Chapman was also able to benefit from this type of patronage in his later career. Only very occasionally did Hughes and Roos paint agricultural and sporting pictures.

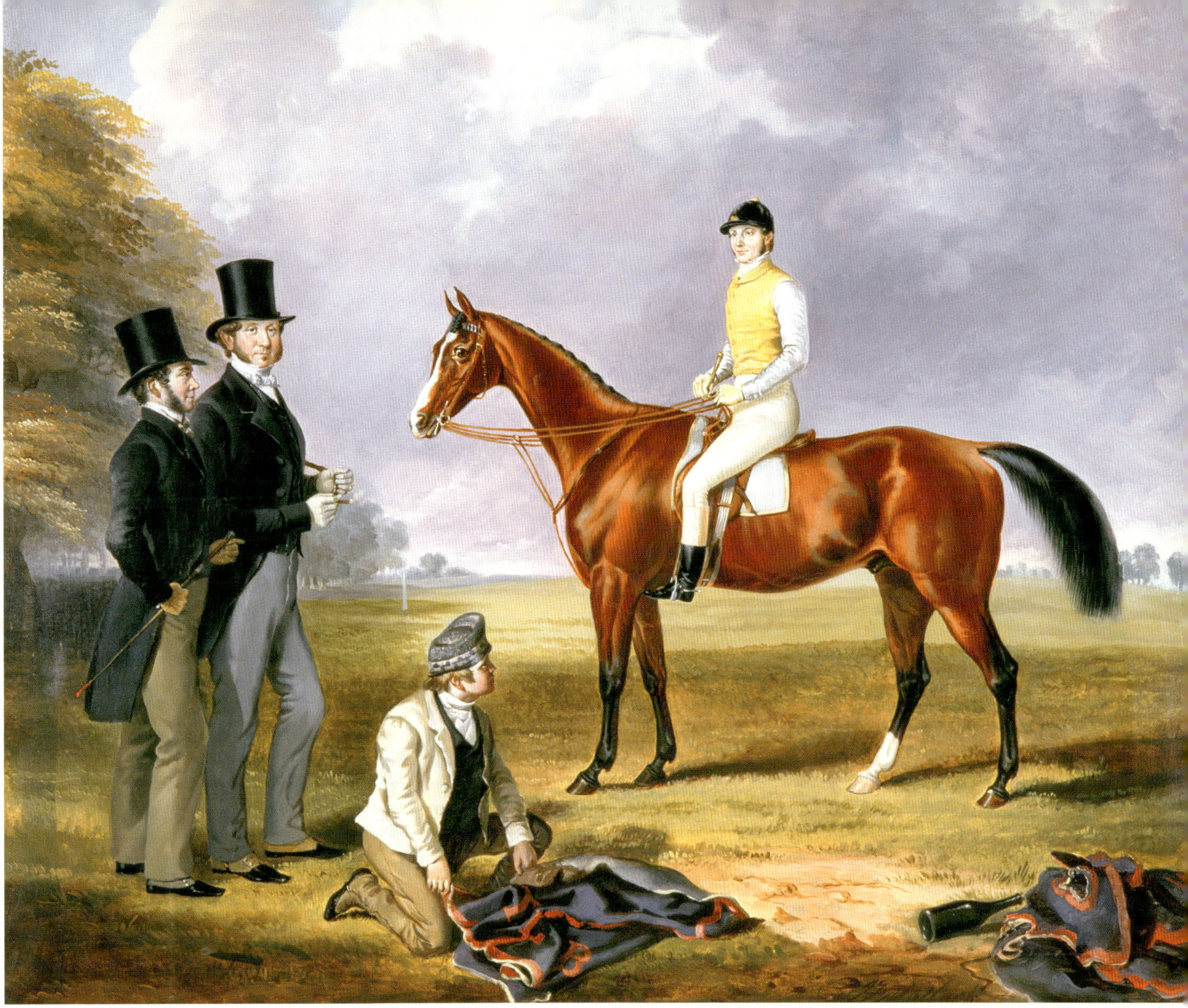

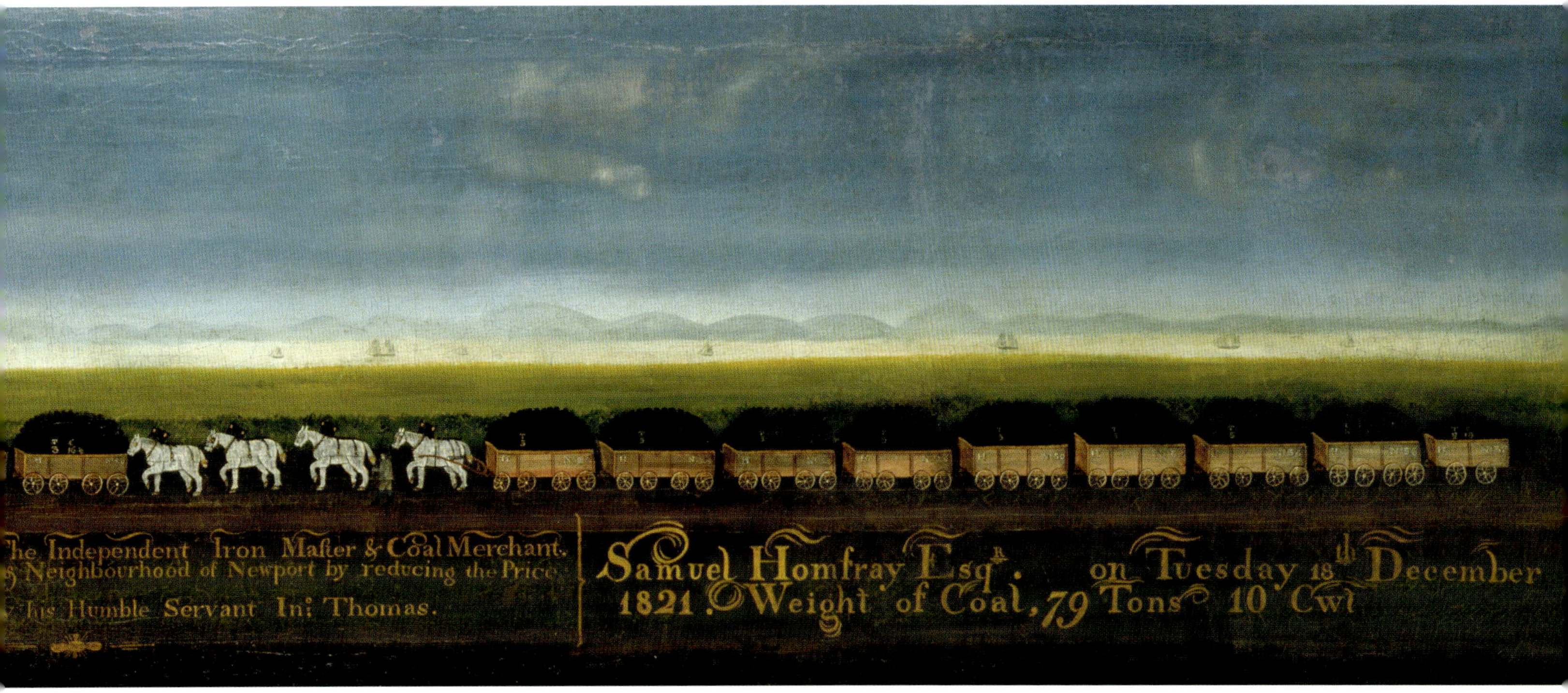
he Independent Iron Master & Coal Merchant.
Neighbourhood of Newport by reducing the Price
his Humble Servant Jn. Thomas.
Samuel Homfray Esqr. on Tuesday 18th December
1821. Weight of Coal, 79 Tons 10 Cwt

182. James Flewitt Mullock, *The Attack of the Chartists on the Westgate Hotel, Newport, November 4th, 1839*, c.1840, lithograph, 17.2x26

from below that would contribute to the stirring of the Victorian social conscience among the middle class, and result in such developments. Like the Penry Williams painting of the disturbances at Merthyr, Mullock's engraving was surely the result of eye witness observation, if not by the artist himself, then certainly by people with whom he would have spoken in preparing what became a celebrated and widely distributed image.[32]

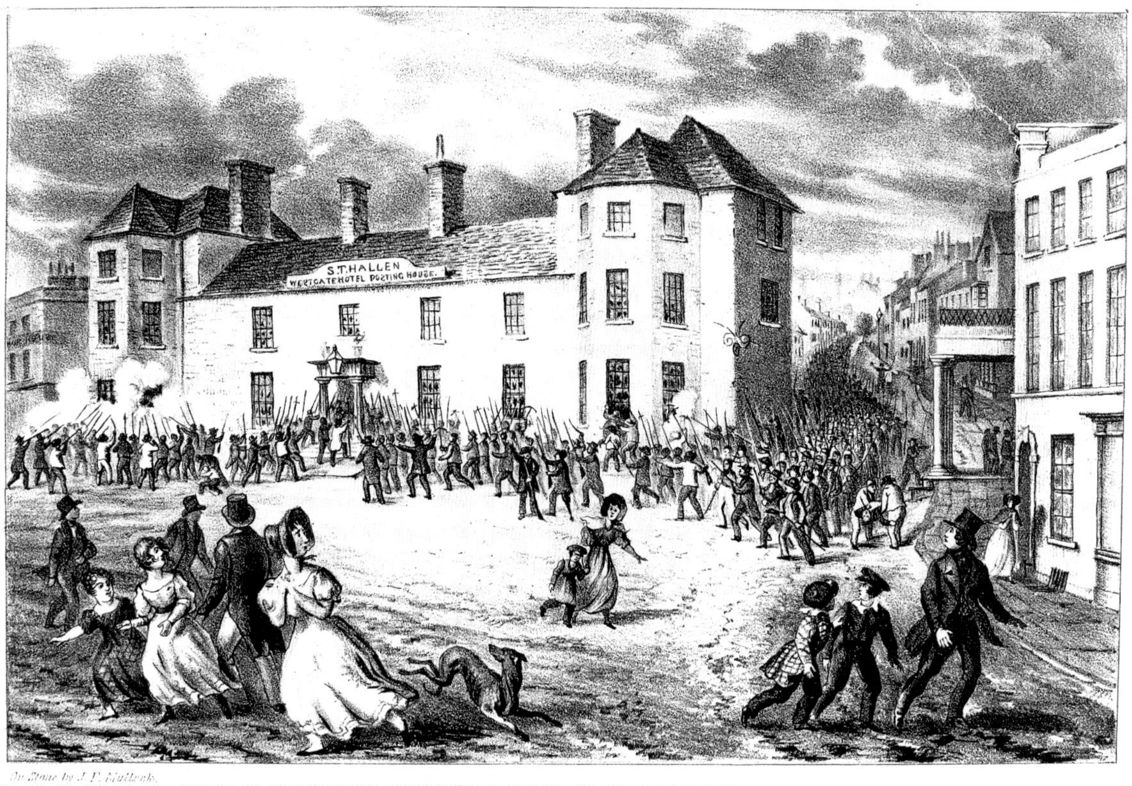

Pictures for the Common People

News of events such as the Chartist march on Newport and the disturbances in the rural south-west, known as the Rebecca Riots, was spread through the increasing number of newspapers in Wales. However, for many of the common people, and those who could not read, the itinerant composers and performers of ballads, sung at fairs and markets, remained an important source of information as well as entertainment. The ancient oral tradition had been reinforced in the eighteenth century by the sale of cheaply printed texts or broadsheets. By this time, in equivalent traditions in London and in continental towns, ballads and prose narratives of public events were illustrated by simple woodcut pictures.

32 For Mullock, see John Wilson, *Art and Society in Newport: James Flewitt Mullock and the Victorian Achievement* (Newport, 1993).

33 For early satires, and the subsequent imaging of Welsh people in popular prints, see Lord, *Words with Pictures*.

34 For Jones, see Gerald Morgan, *Y Dyn a Wnaeth Argraff* (Llanrwst, 1982).

The subjects ranged from politics and religion to scandals. Welsh subject matter, generally treated from a hostile London perspective, had arisen as early as the Civil War, when the Welsh mercenaries who were engaged on the Royalist side at the Battle of Edge Hill were visually and verbally mocked.[33] The generic Welsh gentleman, Shôn ap Morgan or 'Poor Taff', made his first appearance in a large-format woodcut in the middle of the eighteenth century, and his factual descendants, including assorted Wynns and Myddeltons, involved in London politics, attracted the attention of visual satirists later in the period. However, it was not until the 1830s that Welsh printers and publishers began to combine ballads and pictures. Although by this time Hugh Hughes had ceased to work as a wood engraver, he may well have been indirectly responsible for the development. In the preceding two decades Hughes had almost certainly worked for London ballad printers, and it is significant that among the Welsh publishers with whom he was involved in the earliest book illustrations in Wales was John Jones of Trefriw and Llanrwst.[34] Jones was the first of his trade to venture into the popular print market, and remained the most successful in the field. He established a relationship with the illustrator James Cope, and together they produced a substantial body of work. Cope was born in Caernarfonshire in 1805 or 1806, and by 1841 was established at Chapel Street in Caernarfon town. It is unclear if he was self-taught or had received a craft training, perhaps outside Wales.

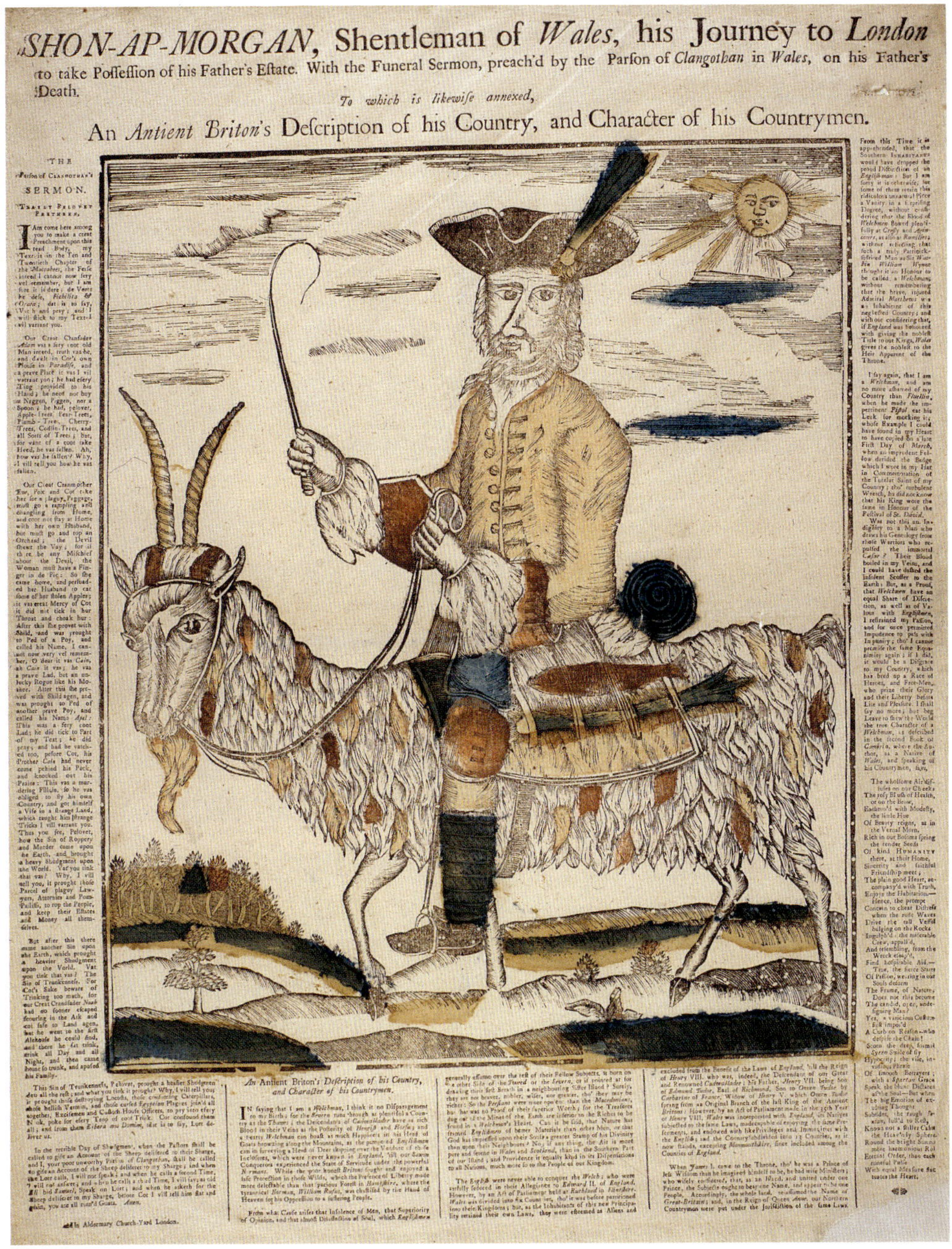

183. *Shon ap Morgan, Shentleman of Wales*, c.1747, published by William Dicey, London, woodcut, 45x35

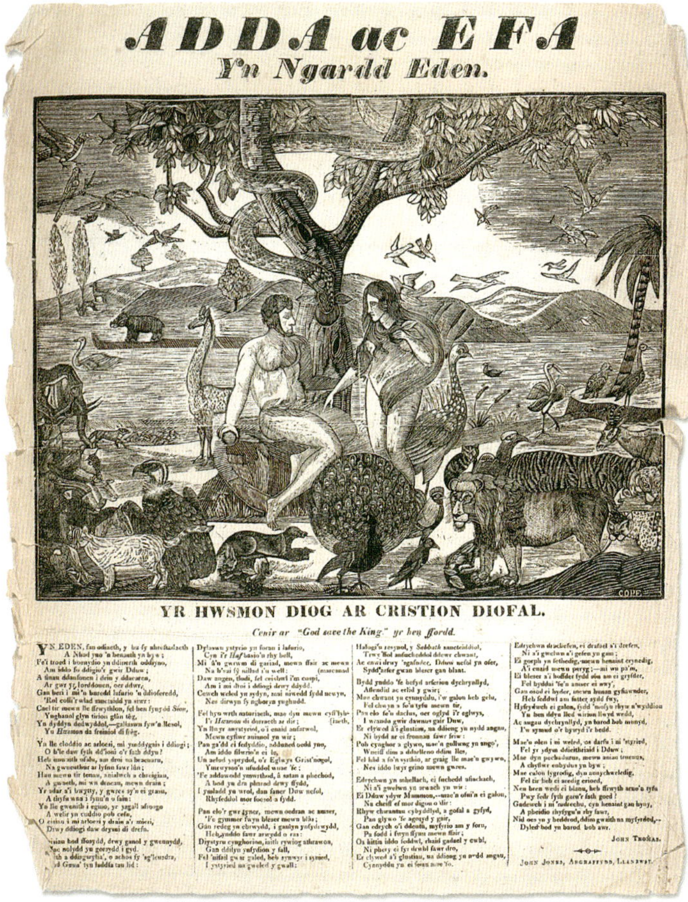

184. James Cope,
Adda ac Efa Yn Ngardd Eden,
*c.*1832–42, printed by John Jones, Llanrwst, woodcut, 42x33

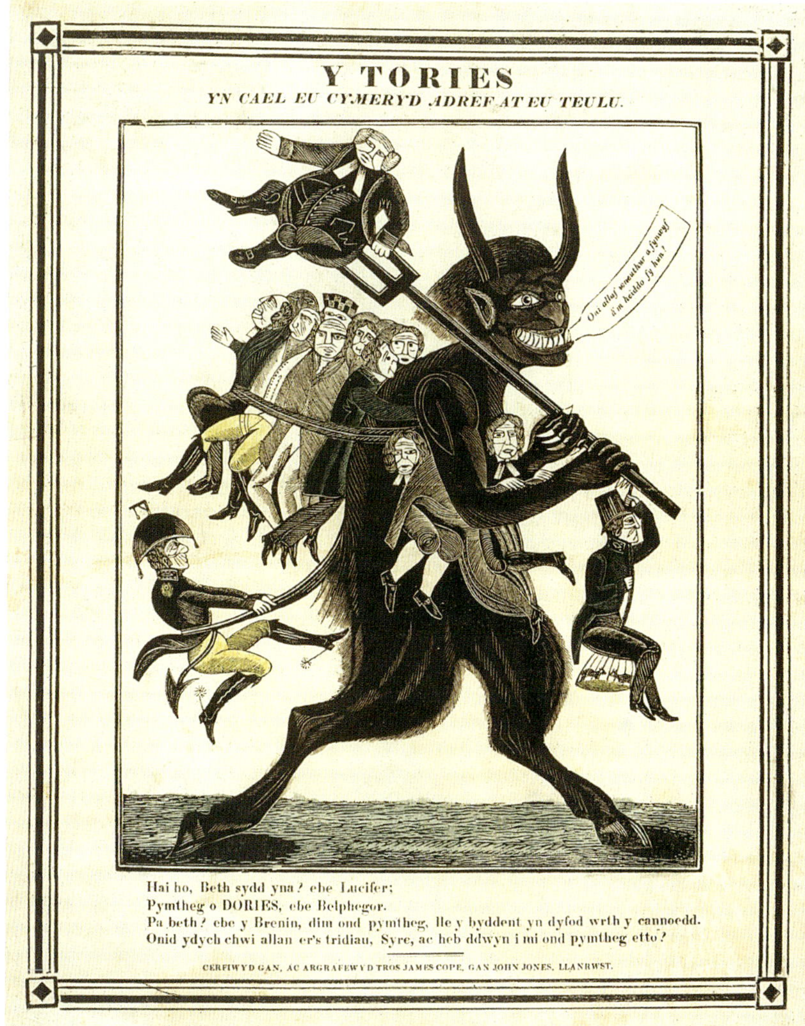

185. James Cope,
Y Tories yn cael eu cario adref tuag at eu teulu, *c.*1834–6,
printed by John Jones, Llanrwst, woodcut, 40x31.5

Prints designed by Cope were published mainly as large-format single sheets, sometimes in response to particular verses. Biblical subjects were popular, but particularly prone to recycling by the publisher to illustrate new ballads, sometimes resulting in strange combinations of picture and text. Of the controversial issues of the day, Cope illustrated two ballad sheets related to the debate between promoters of total abstinence from alcohol and those who favoured moderation, and a number of tirades directed against the English Church and the establishment in general, represented by the character of John Bull. However, Cope's images made no reference to the specific issues of Chartism or the Rebecca Riots. Whether this omission represented control of the medium by a broadly

35 Williams published one illustrated ballad on the subject, but the pictures were recycled and bizarrely inappropriate. For politics and the Welsh popular prints, see Lord, *Words with Pictures*, pp. 117–59.

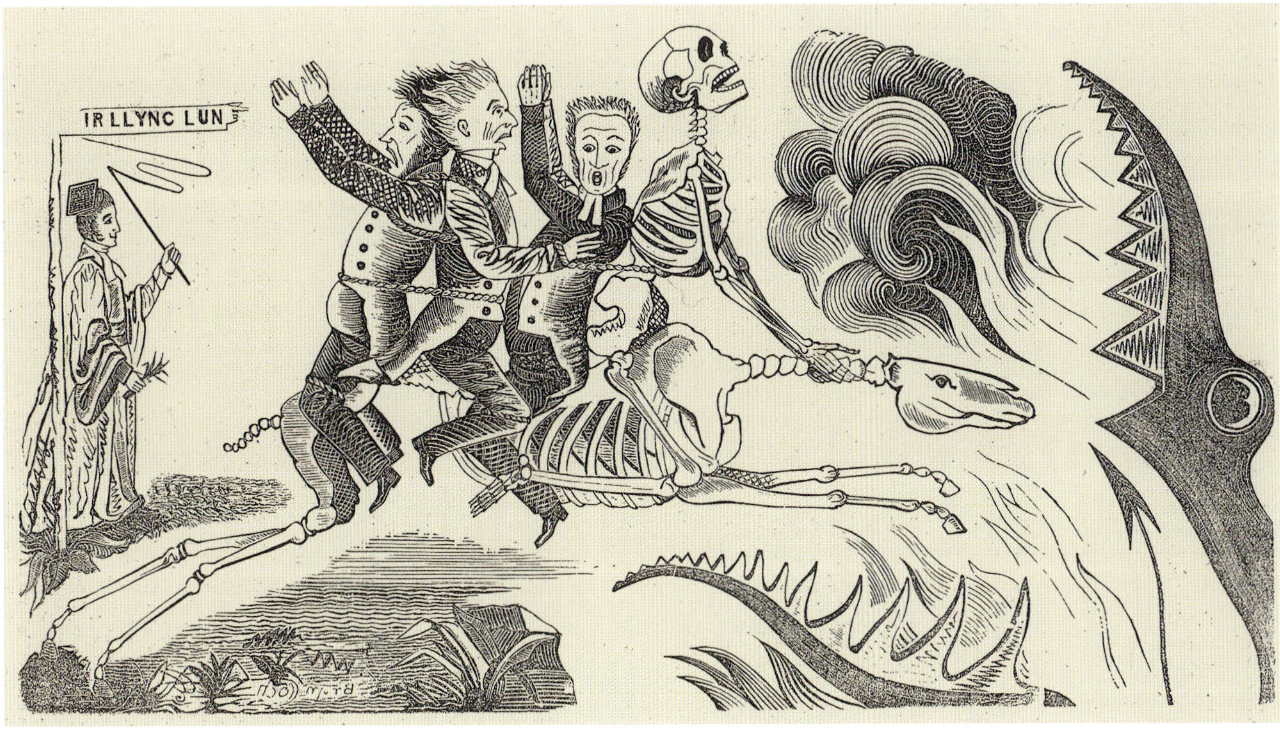

186. Ellis Owen Ellis, *Cyflawniad y Proffwydoliaethau*, from *Y Punch Cymraeg*, 1858, woodcut, 21x27.5

conservative publisher, or a perceived lack of interest in these subjects in the market place, is difficult to determine. It cannot be explained simply by the geographical remoteness of Cope and his publisher from the disturbances. The only other substantial producer of illustrated ballads was the printer and publisher Isaac Thomas at Cardigan, close to the centre of the Rebecca disturbances.[35] Prints produced by Thomas were more naively cut than those of Cope. They included at least one copy of Cope's work, and several based on London originals. Thomas also produced some material bilingually, in contrast with the monolingual Welsh publications of John Jones.

In the mid 1830s, Jones printed a small number of woodcuts made by Ellis Owen Ellis, a young painter and illustrator, born at Abererch in Llŷn, in 1813. Ellis seems to have received training in London, though the details are obscure, and he worked subsequently in Liverpool. However, his most important contribution to the visual culture was the substantial group of political and social satires that he engraved for *Y Punch Cymraeg* between the initial publication of the magazine in 1858, and 1861, when Ellis died. The illustrated ballad tradition was in terminal decline by this time, but Ellis reinvigorated it in the magazine, which at one penny per issue was within reach of a broad market. Developing increasingly grotesque and surreal imagery, Ellis satirised the pretensions of contemporary figures of note in the literary and religious establishment.

Improvement

The spirit of social improvement that infused in its various ways individuals as varied as Hugh Hughes and James Flewitt Mullock was expressed directly in the visual culture through intervention by wealthy patrons in the lives of young aspirants. Ellis Owen Ellis is believed to have been supported by Sir Robert Williames Vaughan of Nannau, just as Penry Williams had been assisted by the industrial aristocracy of Merthyr. The consequences of the 'elevation' of young artists from artisan backgrounds to academic practices were mixed. Penry Williams and his close friend, the sculptor John Gibson, both of whom spent most of their working lives in Rome, became highly successful. Indeed, these two would be presented by patriotic improvers at home in the second half of the nineteenth century as exemplars of what the Welsh people might achieve on the world stage. The case of Gibson was particularly telling, since he was born in poor circumstances within four months and a few miles of Hugh Hughes, at the lower end of the Conwy Valley. Economic depression and food shortages drove the Gibson family to emigrate to Liverpool in 1799, followed three years later by Hughes and his father. In that city, both attended the same Sunday school. However, their paths diverged dramatically soon afterwards as a result of the intervention of the leading light of Liverpool intellectual society, William Roscoe. Under Roscoe's patronage, Gibson was set on the path that would enable patriots, Welsh and English, to regard him in mid-life as the greatest sculptor in the world. In the meantime, Hugh Hughes made his way, unnoticed beyond the middle-class Welsh community. Only very occasionally did he benefit from the patronage of wealthy families like the Mostyns of Flintshire, perhaps condescending – sensitive to the spirit of the age – to promote 'native talent'.[36]

187. Hugh Hughes, *The Children of Sir Edward Mostyn Lloyd Mostyn and Lady Harriet Margaret Mostyn*, 1837, oil, 137x114

In Anglesey, the 7th Viscount Bulkeley and his wife Elizabeth, who twenty years earlier had sat to Romney, were employing the local artisan painter and decorator, Hugh Jones, to carry out a variety of improvements at their home, Baron Hill. Hugh Jones had two sons destined to work in the business, but in 1808, William, the elder of them, began training as an art painter at the Royal Academy schools. However successful the family business may have been, the sudden elevation of William Jones to the fringes of the London art world suggests at least the encouragement of artistically aware patrons – presumably the Bulkeleys. Unfortunately, once in London, Jones 'did not meet with the patronage promised him', though he was rendered a 'trifling service' by Edward Pugh.[37] Subsequently, his career hovered between loyalties derived from his upbringing and abilities that might have enabled him to rise in the art world, had he been possessed of a more competitive nature. Instead, he became a Wesleyan minister and at the behest of the denomination moved to Chester. Nevertheless, he gained the patronage of the local Grosvenor family, for whom he

36 See 'John Gibson and Hugh Hughes – British Attitudes and Welsh Art' in Peter Lord, *Gwenllian. Essays on Visual Culture* (Llandysul, 1994), pp. 8–35.

37 Pugh, *Cambria Depicta*, p. 91

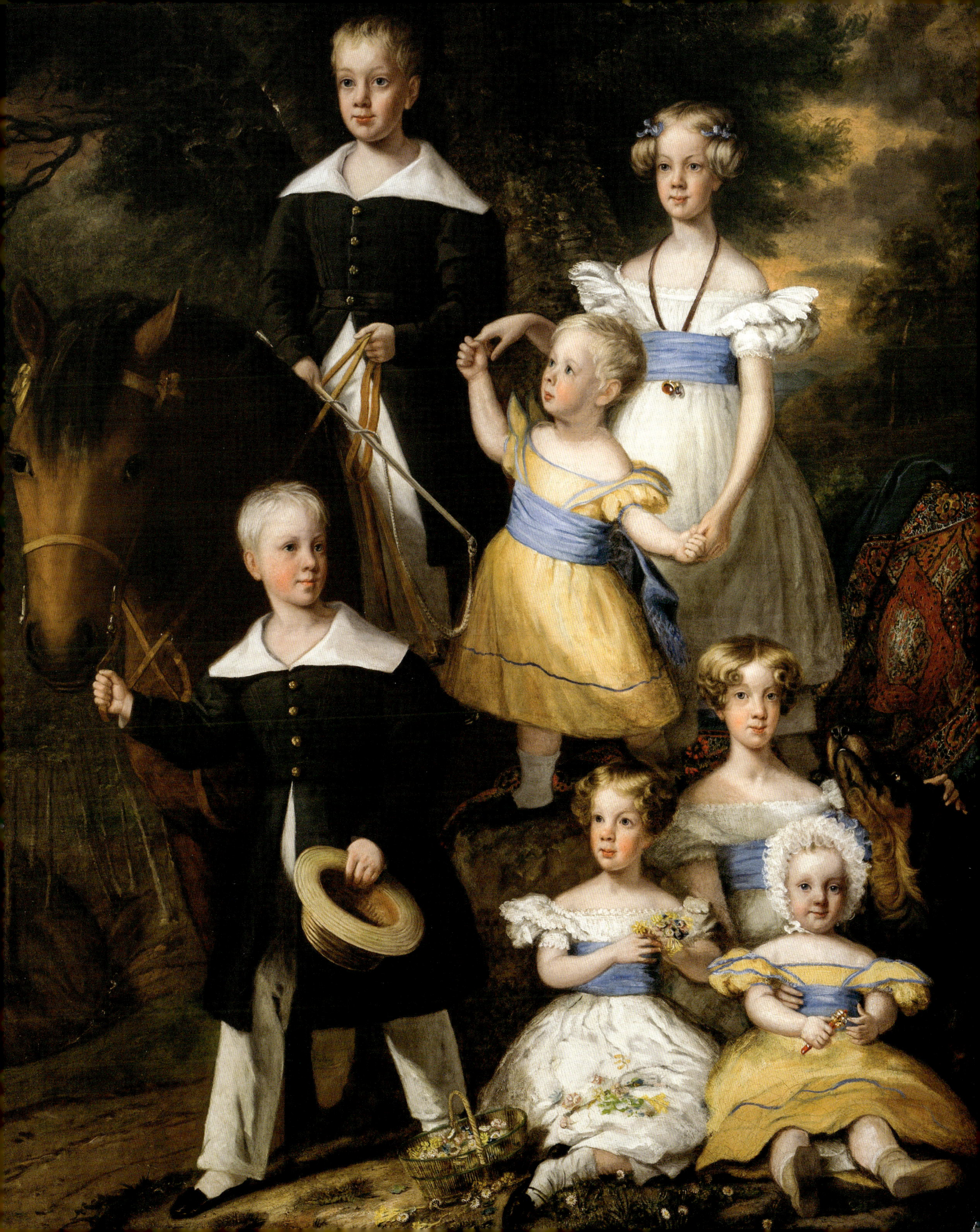

painted both copy portraits and originals. He exhibited at the Royal Academy, notably in 1819 with an interpretation of the Last Bard theme, and in a curious closing of the circle, in 1830 he was commissioned to add a further three portraits to the Erddig servant series, begun in the 1790s by the artisan John Walters. Jones painted the additional pictures in a self-consciously loose style, that did not reveal his academic training.[38] The exiled William Jones maintained contact with Welsh intellectuals throughout his life. Early on he painted portraits of the poets Dafydd Ddu Eryri, and Richard Llwyd, 'Bard of Snowdon'. Over forty years later, he was a competitor at the National Eisteddfod, when it was held in Chester. He was observed there by the young painter William Morgan Williams, 'Ap Caledfryn':

> I met Jones of Chester in 1866 at the Eisteddfod exhibition when I took the first prize and silver medal. There were 17 competitors and amongst them this old gent – quite the old fashioned gentleman dressed in good black cloth, his hair was as white as snow.[39]

38 The authorship of the paintings was revealed by a notice in a Wrexham newspaper, given in 'A Mystery Solved', the *National Trust Wales Newsletter*, Spring 1996, unpaginated.

39 NLW MS 6358B, unpaginated. William Morgan Williams was the son of the Independent minister William Williams, Caledfryn, a close friend of Hugh Hughes. As a child, Ap Caledfryn had received his first drawing lessons from Hughes.

188. Hugh Jones of Beaumaris, *Revd John Elias*, 1838, oil, 74.5x61.5

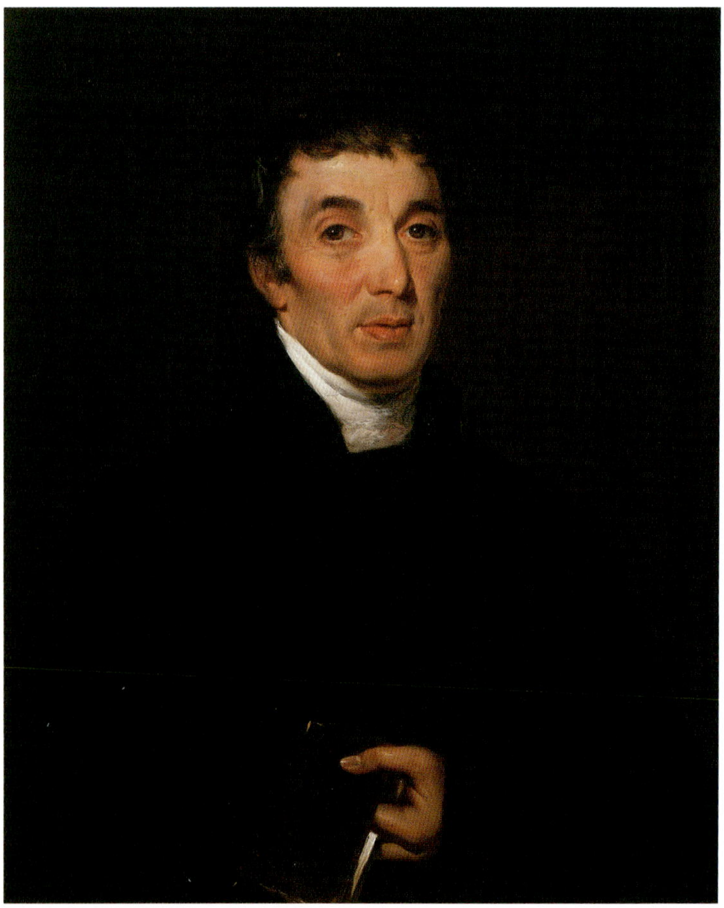

189. William Jones of Chester, *The Last Bard*, 1819, oil, 75x61

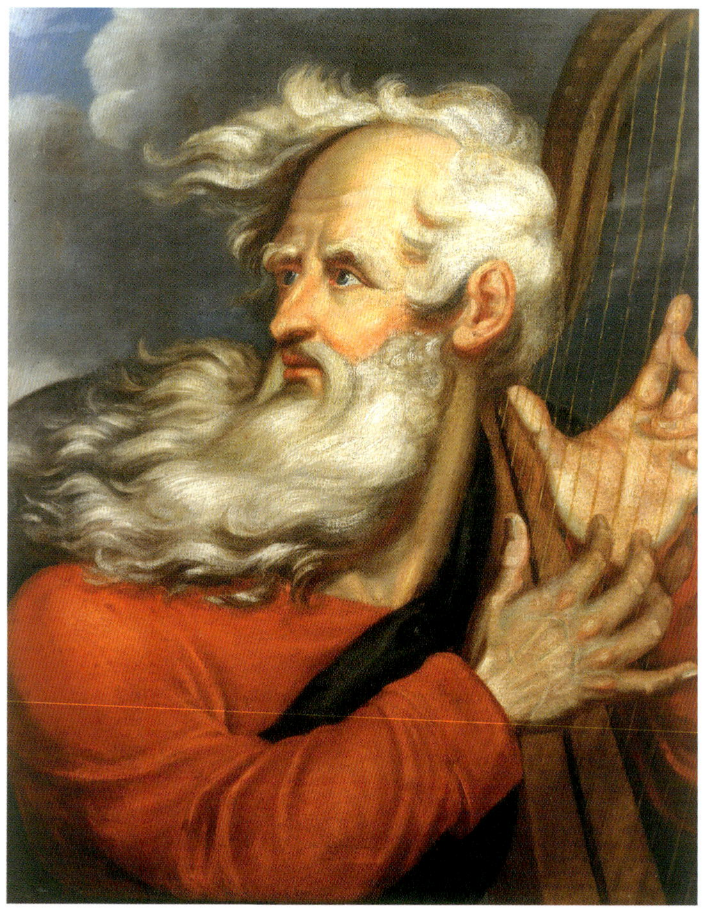

190. William Jones of Chester, *Dr Edward Johnes, Garthmyl*, c.1830-40, oil, 76.9x63.9

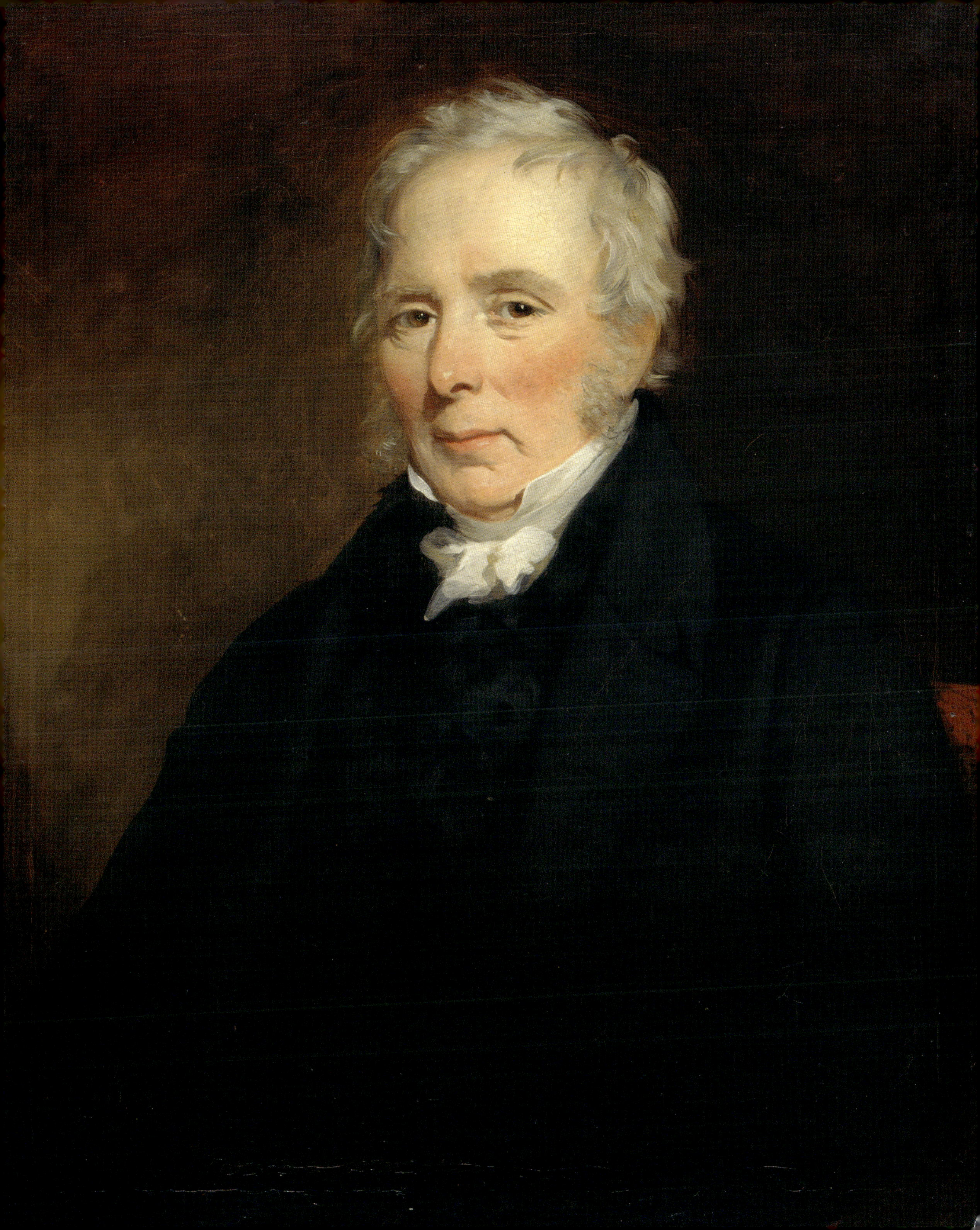

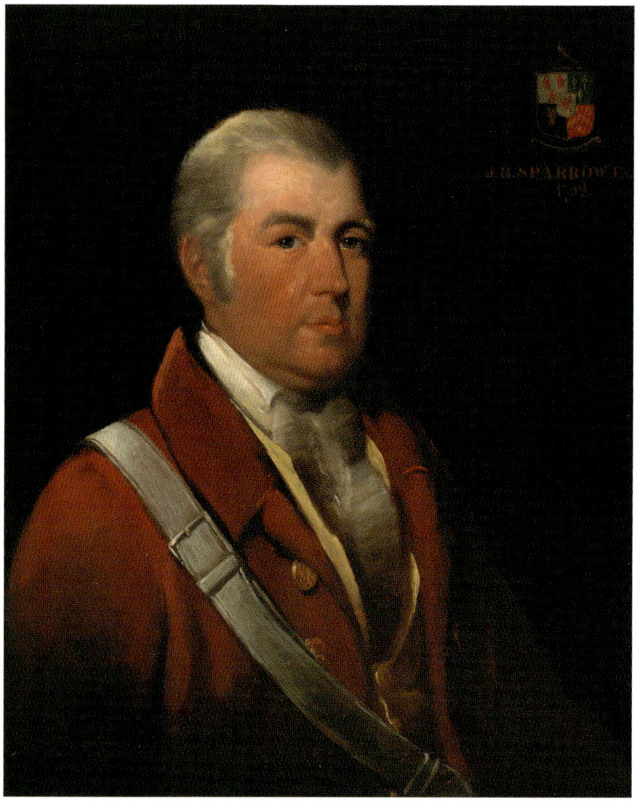

It would seem that as a young man William Jones had passed on something of his training to Hugh, his younger brother. Hugh took over the Beaumaris artisan business from his father, but also painted portraits and landscapes. The most celebrated would be his depiction of the Calvinistic Methodist leader Revd John Elias, since it was reproduced as an engraving and reinterpreted many times by other engravers, by the Staffordshire potteries, and indeed as an oil painting (masquerading as his own) by William Roos. The most substantial commission gained by Hugh Jones was, however, the result of gentry patronage, significantly given 'for the encouragement of native talent'.[40] Between 1830 and 1839 Jones painted at least twenty portraits of the Comptrollers of the Anglesey Hunt, which were hung in the rooms frequented by the society at a Beaumaris inn. Several portraits depicted deceased individuals, adapted from earlier paintings. In the case of John Bodychan Sparrow, Hugh Jones adapted an original of the sitter in military uniform that had been painted by his brother, William, some twenty years earlier.

191. Hugh Jones of Beaumaris, *John Bodychan Sparrow*, 1835, oil, 75.5x60.5

opposite
192. Thomas Brigstocke, *Study for a Portrait of Edward Matthew Ward*, *c.*1844, oil, 69.2x58.4

In Carmarthen, the origin of the career of the painter Thomas Brigstocke had much in common with that of William Jones in Beaumaris. The family was Wesleyan, and Brigstocke's father, David, ran a painting and decorating business, his clientele extending to the ranks of the gentry.[41] Thomas was sent to train under a London painter and attended the Royal Academy Schools in 1825-6, early enough to acquire a taste for Byronesque Romanticism, which he expressed in the portrait of his friend, the young English painter Edward Matthew Ward. Sufficient funds were available to enable Brigstocke to travel on the Continent for some eight years, though whether these were entirely the family's own or were supplemented by patronage from higher up the social scale is unclear. Brigstocke had been provided with a letter of introduction to John Gibson in Rome, which informed the great man that 'Mr Brigstocke will be able to "siarad Cymraeg" with you.' Many years later, Brigstocke recalled being struck by 'Gibson's genuine sincerity and simplicity of manners, which won for him the esteem of all who knew him. His strong Welsh accent was much more marked than that of Penry Williams ...'[42]

Like William Parry before him, while in Rome Thomas Brigstocke copied Raphael's *Transfiguration*, a picture that, on his return, was exhibited in Carmarthen and then purchased for the new Christ Church at Albany Street in London. He developed a

40 Anglesey Archives, MD/1/1.

41 An invoice of 1815 shows that David Brigstocke was also an artists' colourman, supplying 'Oils & Colours, Brushes, Pencils &c.'

42 Letters quoted in T.H. Thomas, 'Life and Work of Thomas Brigstocke', *Carmarthen Journal*, 8 June 1888, p. 5.

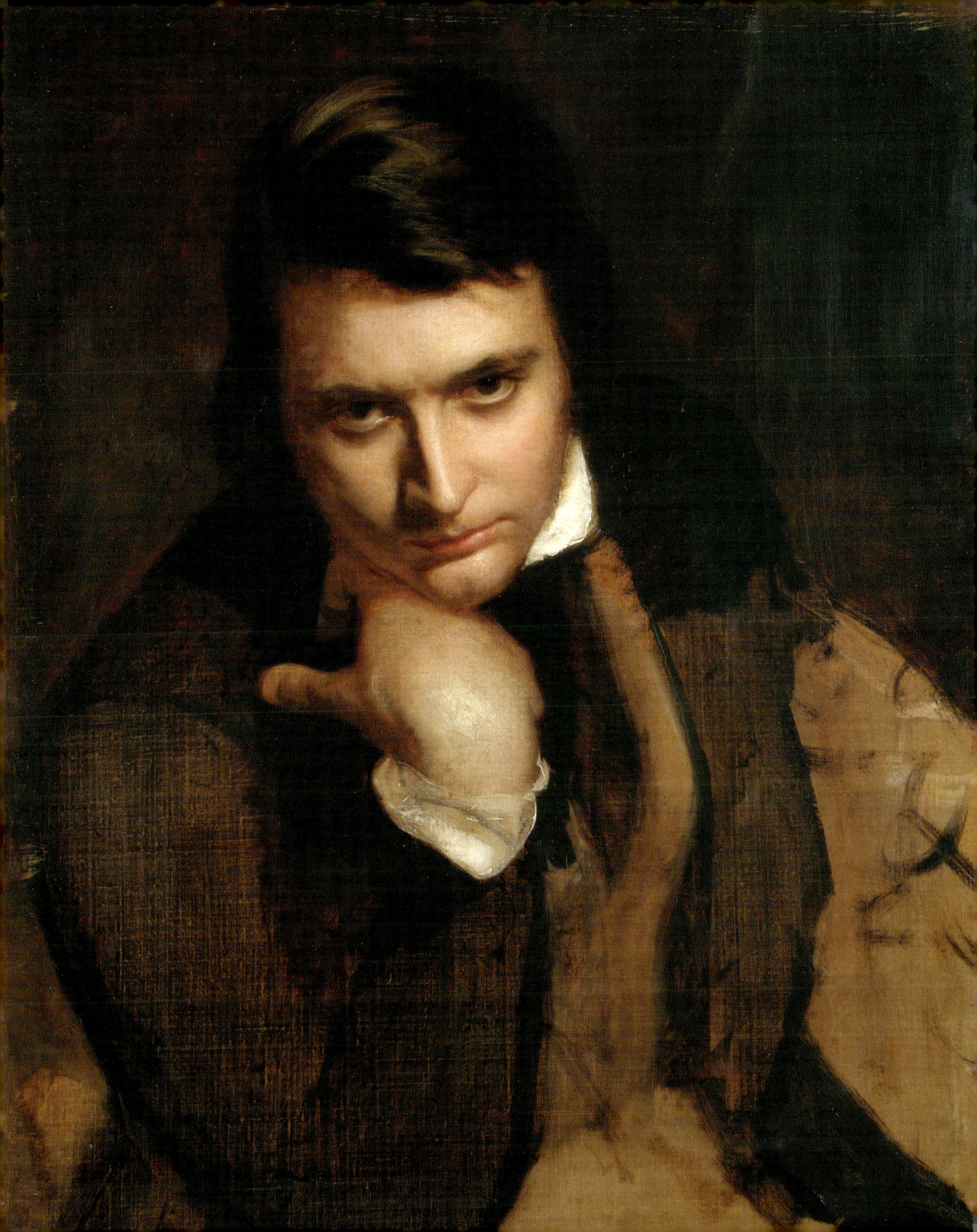

relationship with the Oriental Club, and was able to gain commissions to paint a number of individuals associated in one way and another with British imperial enterprise. Among the most exotic of his sitters were those painted during a stay in Egypt, between 1847 and 1849. His letters home to his family and friends in Carmarthenshire described in detail the circumstances of his painting portraits of the increasingly senile Muhammed Ali, the Turkish-speaking ruler of Egypt, and founder of a dynasty that lasted until the mid-twentieth century: 'I go to the palace every morning and the old boy sits very patiently to the great surprize of everybody ... he has been most condescending to me – for he has sat about 20 times for two portraits.'[43] On his return, Brigstocke took up residence in London, where he moved in Welsh circles. He developed a career as a portrait painter and also as a painter of animals, exhibiting at the Royal Academy and other venues.

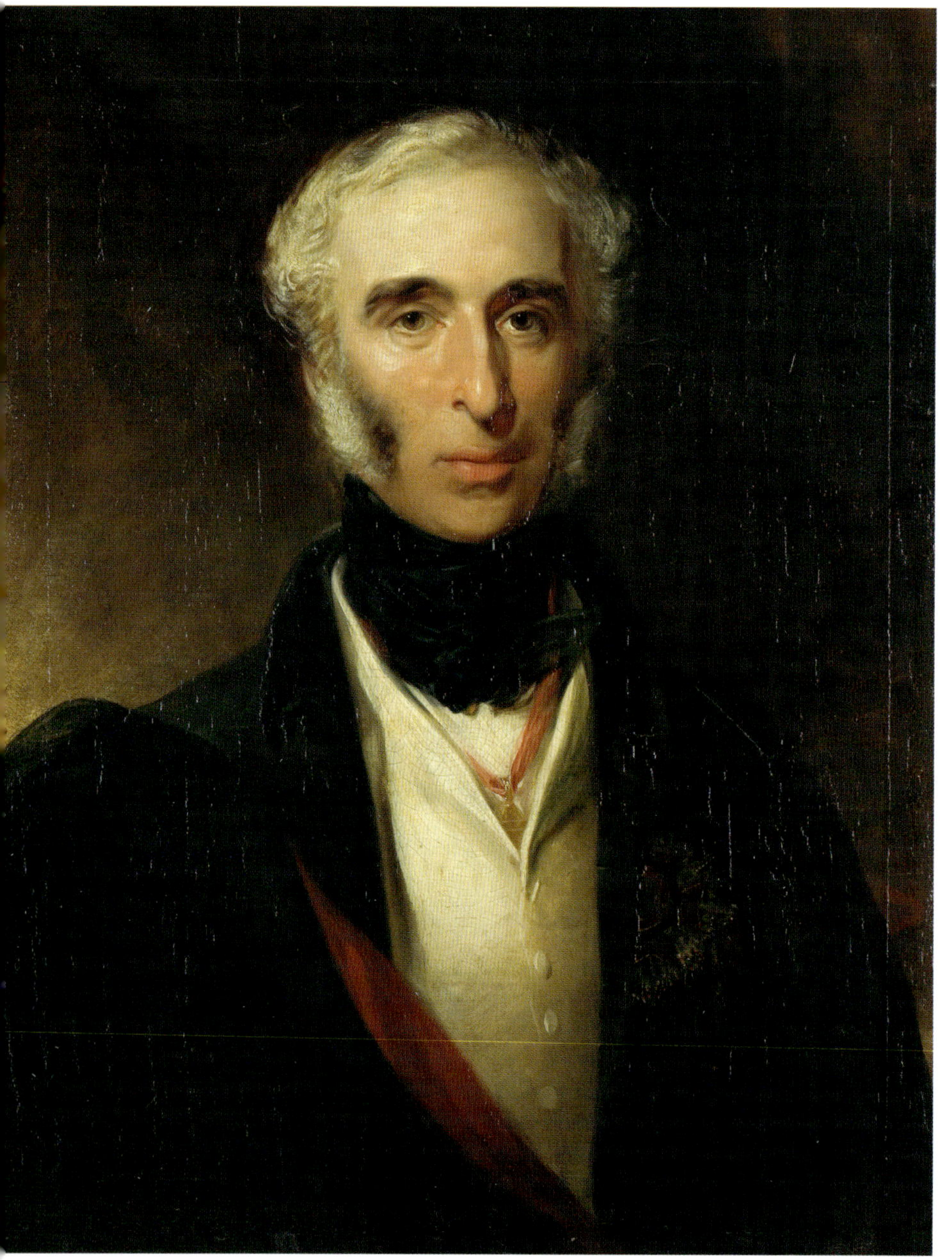

193. John Deffett Francis, *General Sir William Nott*, 1845, oil, 76.8x63.8

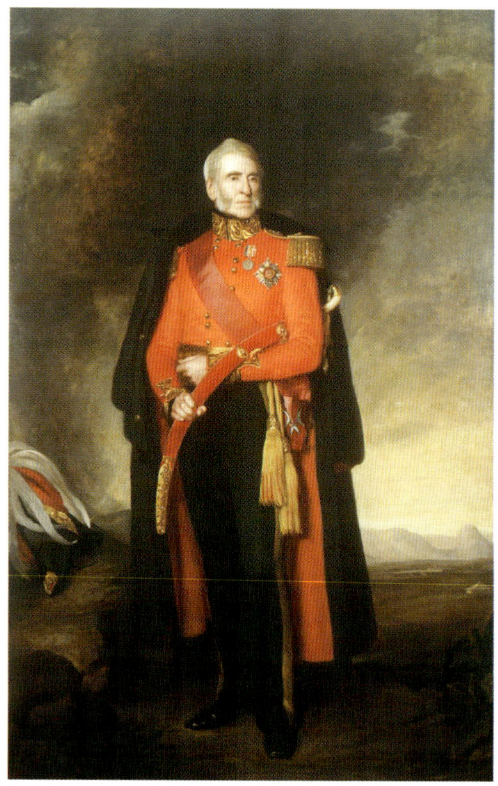

194. Thomas Brigstocke, *General Sir William Nott*, 1845, oil, 220x150

Welsh families figured prominently among his patrons throughout his career, though his most notable public work was completed early, before his visit to Egypt. On his return from service abroad General William Nott gave Brigstocke permission to paint him for the town of Carmarthen. Nott was born near Neath, but was considered a son of Carmarthen, since his father kept the Ivy Bush inn. He was celebrated for his campaign of 1842 in the vicious Anglo-Afghan War. Unfortunately, the portrait commission resulted in an unpleasant public dispute between Brigstocke and the Swansea painter John Deffett Francis, about engraved versions of their respective performances. The general died shortly after his return home, whereupon Francis somehow obtained permission to make a death mask, from which he painted his portrait. Irritated by the unexpected emergence of this rival depiction of 'the Hero of Cabul', in the *Carmarthen Journal* Brigstocke accused Francis of unethical behaviour – the likeness was drawn 'from an indifferent cast, taken three days after death ... in direct opposition to the wishes of Sir William Nott's family', he alleged. At copious length, Francis responded to Brigstocke's 'disingenuous and illiberal attack'. The spat enlivened the newspaper for three months, culminating with the publication by Deffett Francis of a parody of Brigstocke's original advertisement for his engraving:

> The only Vegetable Pills
> (Patronised by the Medico-Humbug Society)
> Prepared by Thomas Brigstocke Esq.
> None others are genuine ...[44]

At this point, Brigstocke retired from the fray, presumably secure in the knowledge that it was his original portrait and not that of his impertinent rival that would grace the Town Hall.

Within a few years, the public square near the Town Hall would also display an image of General Nott. Like Brigstocke, Edward Davis, the sculptor chosen to create a bronze statue of the General, had strong local connections. Though he worked in London, he came from a Carmarthen family. The commission signified the emergence in mid-century of a civic pride which, by the beginning of the Great War, would have generated commissions for public sculpture all over the country. Initially, Welsh involvement in British imperial power provided the predominant subject matter. In this respect, Carmarthen had led the way. Twenty years before the Nott statue, in 1824 the early connection between John

43 Privately held archive of Brigstocke letters.

44 *Carmarthen Journal*, 28 March 1845, and reports in preceding issues beginning 7 February 1845. Brigstocke repeated his portrait for the Oriental Club in London and for the Town Hall in Calcutta.

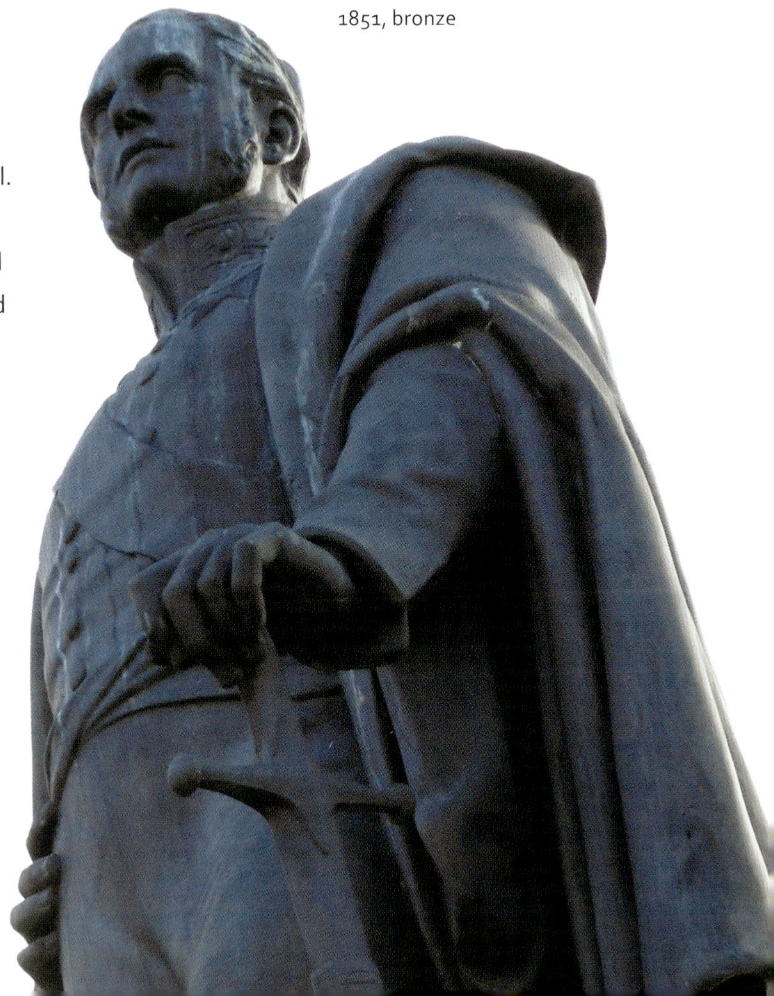

195. Edward Davis, *General Sir William Nott*, 1851, bronze

Nash and the town had been re-established in the form of the architect's design for a memorial to that 'rough, foul mouthed devil' Sir Thomas Picton.[45] It included a large relief carving by Edward Hodges Baily of the death of the General at Waterloo. At the same time, Nash and Baily were engaged together on creating the Marble Arch in London. Edward Davis, sculptor of the Nott memorial, trained in Baily's studio.[46]

The revival of sculpture and Welsh historicism

William Roos, painter of tradesmen and ministers, and Thomas Brigstocke, painter of gentlemen and generals, were born in successive years, but the social rise of Brigstocke placed him in a parallel universe of Welshness that was only rarely entered by the artisans. By mid-century, a combination of emerging civic patronage and industrial wealth began to expand opportunities not only for painters, but also for sculptors in this elevated social stratum. In 1810, a year after Brigstocke, John Evan Thomas was born in Brecon. At the age of 14 he was sent to train in the London workshop of Sir Francis Chantrey. He visited the continent, and on his return soon proved himself remarkably adept at the exploitation of the new patronage. As early as 1831 he appears to have attracted the support of the industrialist Bailey family, and a year later he was fulsomely praised in *The Cambrian Quarterly Magazine* for 'a grandeur of composition, a grace in grouping and a flow in his draperies.'[47] In 1838 he showed a work for the first time at the Royal Academy. The list of his many subsequent exhibits would be dominated by commissions undertaken for Welsh patrons – Sir Joseph Bailey (grandson of Richard Crawshay), the Wynns of Wynnstay, the Morgans of Tredegar Park, the Butes of Cardiff, the Halls of Llanover, the de Wintons of Maesllwch and the Clives of Powis Castle.

45 As Governor of Trinidad, Picton was a particularly brutal slave owner. Wellington's opinion was, nevertheless, moderated by the fact that 'he always behaved extremely well' in battle. Like General Nott, Picton's portrait, painted in heroic style by Martin Archer Shee, hangs in Carmarthen Town Hall. He was painted at least twice by Shee, and also by Lawrence.

46 The monument was completed in 1828, but due to the poor quality of the materials employed, it was demolished in 1846.

47 *The Cambrian Quarterly Magazine* (1832), pp. 147-8. Thomas is recorded in 1831 as the sculptor of a memorial to William Bailey at Mitcham in Surrey: see Rupert Gunnis, *Dictionary of British Sculptors 1660–1851* (London, 1951).

196. Edward Hodges Baily, *The Death of General Sir Thomas Picton at Waterloo*, 1827, Portland stone, 156x514

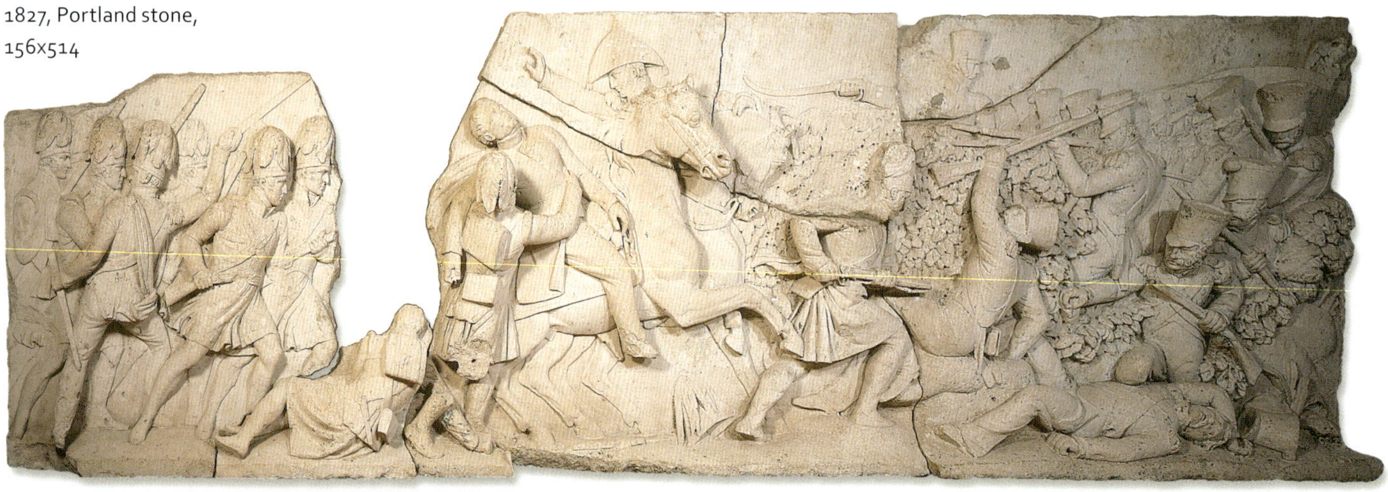

By the mid-1840s, five more Welsh sculptors were working in London, in addition to John Evan Thomas, who by this time had been joined by his brother, William Meredyth Thomas. Remarkably, all five came from Merthyr. Joseph Edwards, son of a stonemason, was the first to arrive in 1835. Two years later he entered the Royal Academy Schools and in 1838, like Thomas, exhibited for the first time at the Academy. Shortly afterwards, William Lorando Jones arrived, and worked for a time in Edwards's studio. He was followed by his brother, Watkin D. Jones. In 1842, William Davies established himself in the metropolis, where he was also later joined by a younger brother, David.[48] The Merthyr sculptors all moved in London Welsh circles, of which William Davies (who came to be better known by his bardic name of Mynorydd), would in due course become a leading light.

48 Similarly, John Gibson had been joined in his Rome studio by his brother Benjamin, who worked closely with him. Benjamin executed a bust of Queen Victoria that had been initially modelled by his brother. Now in the Government Art Collection.

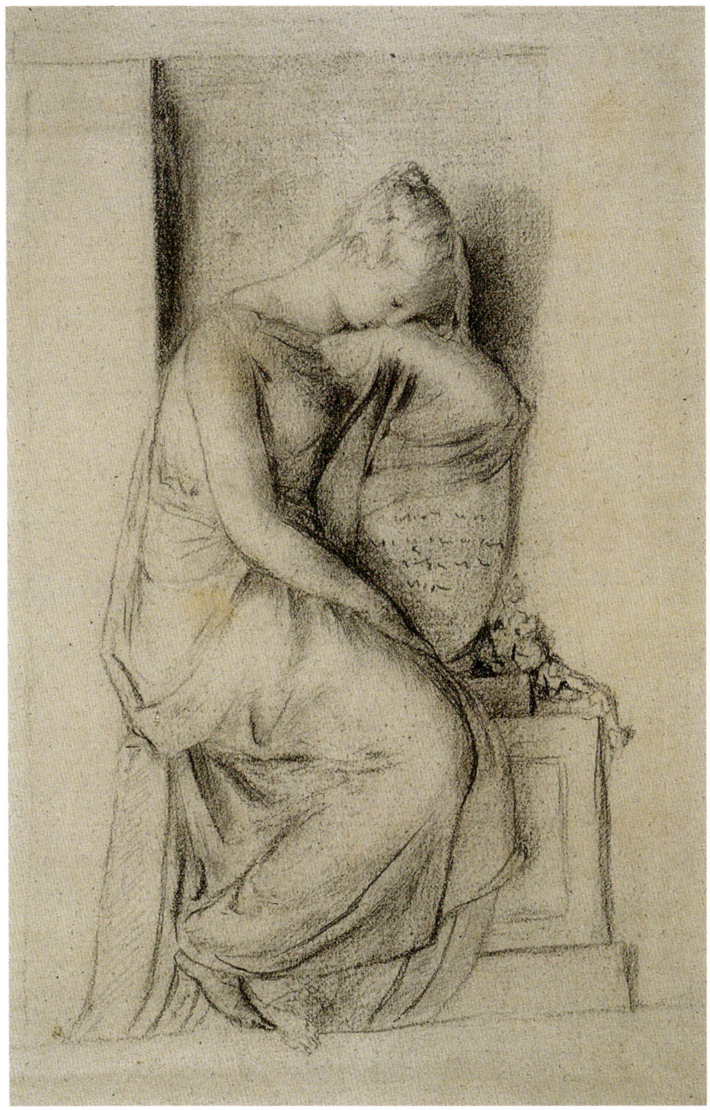

197. Joseph Edwards, *Drawing for sculpture*, c.1850-60, pencil, 32.2x26.2

The Thomas brothers of Brecon seem to have stood a little apart from their Welsh contemporaries, but in terms of public commissions, they made the most lasting impact. Following a fire in 1834, the rebuilding of the Palace of Westminster in London was undertaken on a grand scale, providing a stimulus to the creation of historicist sculpture. In 1844, an exhibition of pieces submitted for the consideration of the Fine Art Commission, charged with the adornment of the new building, generated unprecedented public interest. John Evan Thomas was awarded two commissions for the Palace – the statues of Henri de Londres and the Earl of Pembroke, signatories to Magna Carta.

Perhaps surprisingly, the most famous Welsh sculptor, John Gibson, was not involved in the Westminster project at this stage, though his first visit to England since 1817 coincided significantly with the 1844 exhibition. Whilst in London, Gibson displayed his unpretentious character by calling on the young Joseph Edwards. He arrived at Edwards's studio in the company of Penry Williams, who had travelled with him from Rome:

49 William Davies, 'Joseph Edwards, Sculptor', in *Wales*, ii (1895), p. 278.

50 NLW MS 20566–7E, letter dated 17 December 1846. See Elisabeth S. Darby, 'John Gibson, Queen Victoria, and the idea of Sculptural polychromy', in *Art History*, 4 (March 1981), pp. 37–53.

> October 8th; had the unexpected pleasure of seeing Mr Gibson the sculptor, and my talented townsman Penry Williams the painter, – both living at Rome. Took luncheon with them ... It was most gratifying to me, as I had never seen Mr. Gibson before ... Their condescension in calling at my humble place inspired me with an earnest desire and a strong determination to strive and be worthy of the honour they conferred upon me.[49]

Gibson's purpose in visiting London was to prepare material for a marble statue of Queen Victoria, that he would execute on his return to Rome. Although his work appealed greatly to Albert, the Prince Consort (and arbiter of fashionable taste in the period), his neo-classical style was not universally celebrated. He was criticised in some quarters for the 'absurdity' of clothing in classical robes the queen and other individuals that he memorialised. Furthermore, on his statue of the queen, Gibson first publicly displayed his controversial belief in the colouring of white marble, adding fuel to a debate among connoisseurs that would persist for many years. The practice was promoted by Gibson on the grounds that, contrary to the received wisdom, the Greeks and Romans had also painted their nude statuary:

> Since my return to Rome I have given myself up body and soul to finishing the Queen's statue, and have wrought her up as high as possible. My enthusiasm has also carried me beyond the practice of sculptors, for I have added colour. The diadem, sandals and borders of drapery, are tinted with blue, red and yellow.[50]

The Prince Consort was chairman of the Fine Art Commission and, therefore, it is not surprising that by 1849 Gibson had been awarded the most prestigious of all the Westminster Palace commissions. The group of *Queen Victoria between Justice and Clemency* dominated the Prince's Chamber, the ante-room to the House of Lords and the most intensively decorated of all the spaces in the new building.[51]

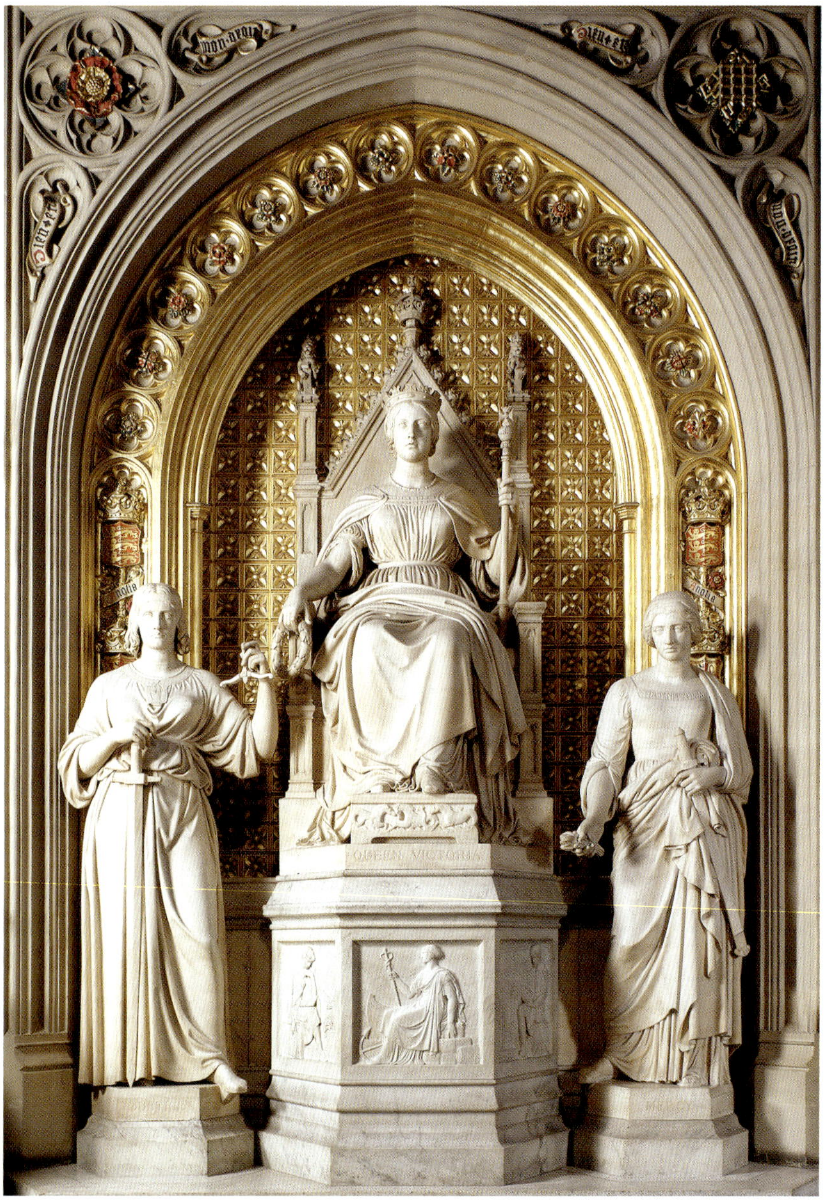

198. John Gibson, *Queen Victoria between Justice and Clemency*, 1855, marble

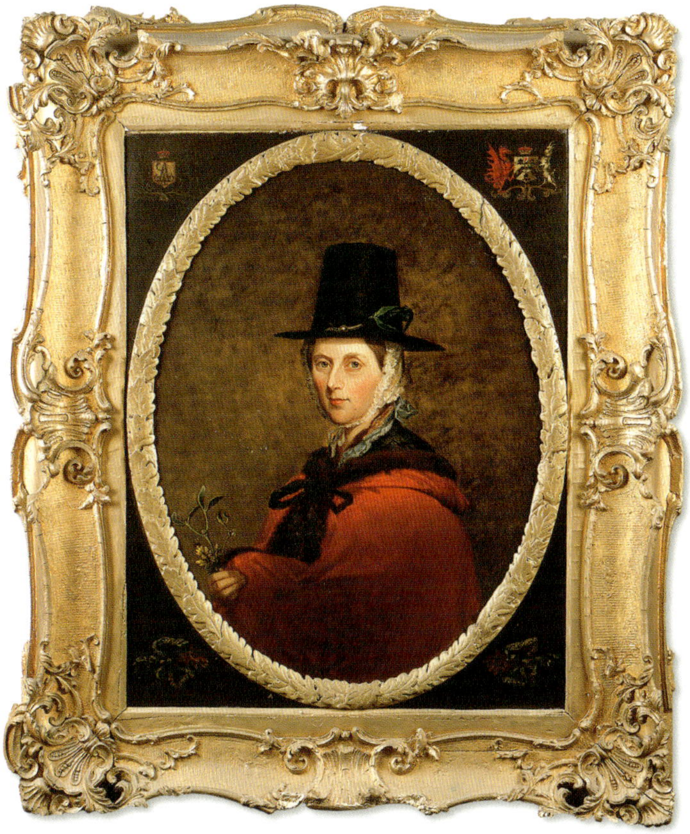

199. Charles Augustus Mornewicke, *Augusta Hall, Lady Llanover*, 1862, oil, 81.3x49.5

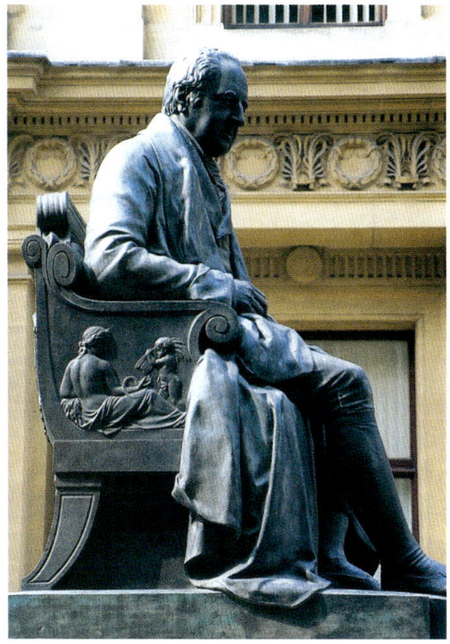

200. John Evan Thomas, *Sir Charles Gould Morgan*, 1848, bronze

While Gibson was engaged in London and Rome on the Westminster commission, John Evan Thomas turned his attention to further work in Wales. In 1848 he showed at the Academy his proposal for the statue of General Nott in Carmarthen. No doubt his failure to secure the commission was a disappointment, but he was engaged already on two other projects of public interest that he would bring to a successful conclusion. The first was the design of a memorial to the recently deceased Sir Charles Morgan, for a site in the centre of Newport. The bronze, depicting Sir Charles seated in a classical-style chair, was unveiled two years later. The second project signified a re-emergence in the visual culture of the interest in ancient British history and myth that had so excited the antiquarians of the eighteenth century. Signs of revival had been evident for a few years. In 1843, William Lorando Jones exhibited at the Academy a statue of Caswallon, the British leader who had resisted the Roman invasion.[52] Jones failed to win a commission for Westminster Palace the following year, though he found employment under successful sculptors carving the statues that decorated the exterior facades of the building.[53] Undaunted, he exhibited again at the Academy in 1845, showing a statue of *Taliesin Penbeirdd*. By this time his work had come to the attention of Augusta Hall, Lady Llanover, whose patronage of the triennial eisteddfodau at Abergavenny provided an opportunity for Jones to present his work at home. Under the leadership of Lady Llanover

51 The overwhelming presence of the work, installed in 1855, resulted in a dispute with the architect, Barry, as a consequence of which Gibson returned to Rome before he was able to paint the queen's image and its flanking figures, as he had intended. The Secretary of the Fine Art Commission was Sir Charles Eastlake, who was married to the art historian and critic Lady Elizabeth Eastlake. In 1870, Lady Eastlake would publish the *Life of John Gibson RA, Sculptor*, the first full length monograph about a Welsh artist.

52 Cassivellaunus led British opposition to the Romans in 54BC. He appears in the *Mabinogion* and other Welsh sources as Caswallawn, son of Beli Mawr.

53 John Howells, 'Reminiscences of Merthyr Tydfil', in *The Red Dragon*, ii (1882), p. 343. Howells reported that William Lorando Jones also worked cutting marble for Henry Weekes and Raffaelle Monti.

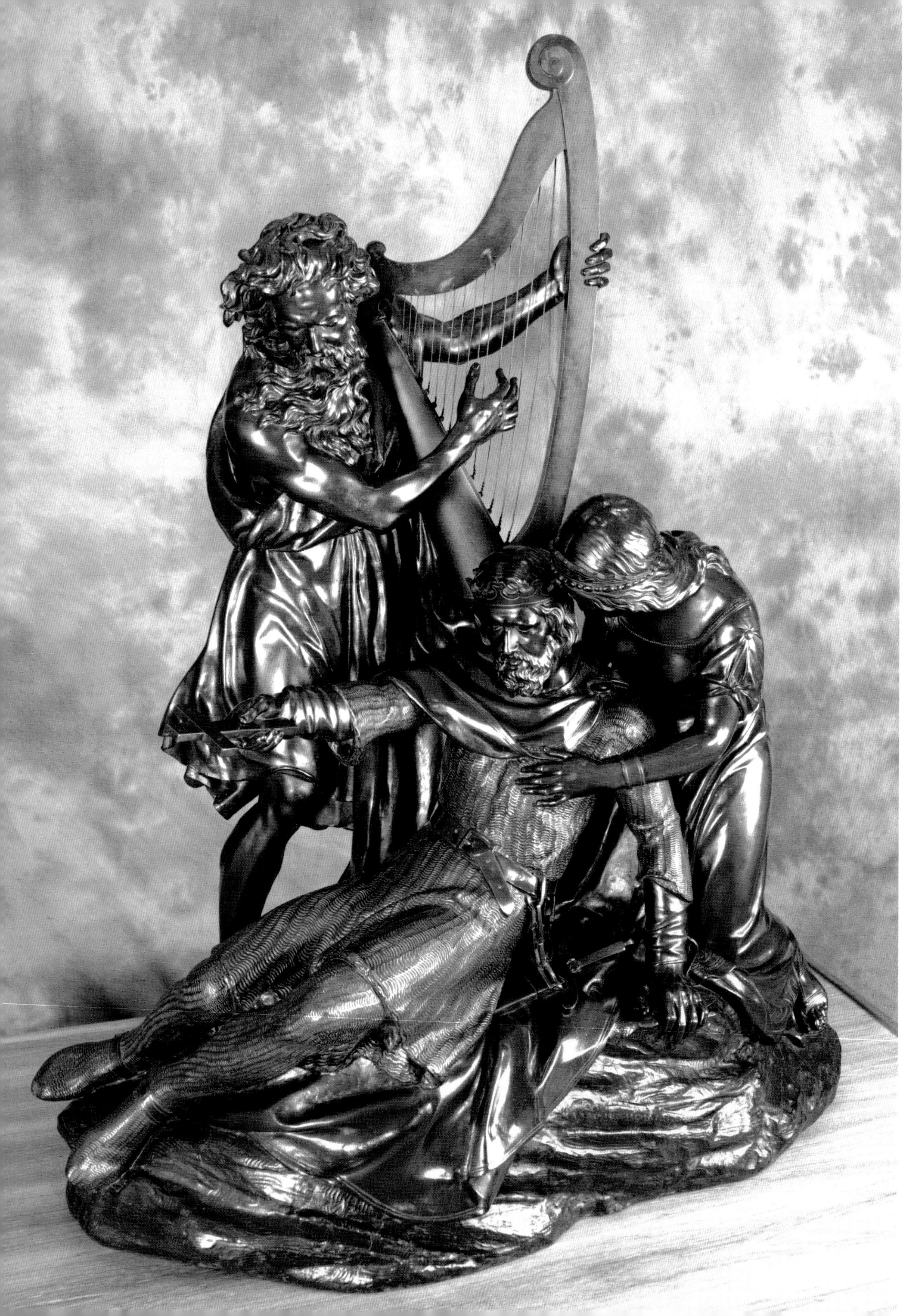

201. John Evan and William Meredyth Thomas, *The Death of Tewdrig*, 1848, h.167, electrotype

and the Revd Thomas Price, 'Carnhuanawc', by 1845 the Abergavenny eisteddfodau had become an important focus for intellectuals in Wales. They promoted not only Welsh literary endeavour, but also Lady Llanover's concept of national costume and the revival of traditional industries, especially weaving. Reflecting the success of the Westminster Hall exhibition of the previous year, the 1845 meeting extended the range of its activities to promote visual art. Addressing the assembled ladies and gentlemen, Carnhuanawc pointed out that

> as well as publishing books, we patronise the loom of the weaver, and endeavour to cultivate the taste for music; and in addition to this, we now have evidence before us that the fire of patriotism has even awakened the chisel of the sculptor. He has dared to gaze at the visions of glory which oppressed the aching sight of many an ardent Welshman; and has called even the great Taliesin from his grave ...[54]

Encouraged by the attention gained by the exhibition of the Taliesin statue, the Abergavenny Cymreigyddion Society (organisers of the eisteddfod) announced both a sculpture and a painting competition for its next meeting, in 1848. A list of subjects was published, from which the winners of the sculpture competition, the Thomas brothers, chose a theme with local resonance – the death of Tewdrig, King of Gwent, in battle against the Saxons. The sculpture was a remarkable symbolic assemblage that played on both Christian and pre-Christian tradition. It took the form of a Pietà, with Jesus and the Virgin replaced by the dying king and his daughter, Marchell. Reinforcing the Christian reference, the king held a cross in his hand, which he pointed at the pagan Saxon invaders to suggest the primacy of Welsh Christianity over the English adoption of the faith. Yet the dominating figure was the pre-Christian bard, rooted firmly in the eighteenth-century tradition of representations and emphasising another layer of Welsh primacy over the English, as the 'original inhabitants' of the islands of Britain.[55]

The Death of Tewdrig carried the signature of John Evan Thomas but it was modelled by William Meredyth Thomas, whose exhibited works, over the years, would demonstrate a greater interest in Welsh subject matter than that shown by his brother. William Meredyth exhibited a *Welsh Harper*, and the subject pieces *The Lament of Llewellyn over his Dog Gelert* and *Sabrina Rising from the Severn*. Sadly, in the absence of patronage to turn these plasters into bronze and a national public building to house them, the only surviving 'national' work that exemplifies the ability of the sculptor is his posthumous portrait bust of Carnhuanawc. In contrast, John Evan proceeded from strength to strength, producing

54 *The Illustrated London News*, 25 October 1845, p. 265.

55 The banner of the Cymmrodorion Society of 1751 had also combined pagan and Christian elements, the arms being flanked by images of a druid and St David. Samuel Rush Meyrick, author of the influential volume *The Costume of the Original Inhabitants of the British Islands* (1810), was an active member of the Abergavenny Cymreigyddion.

202. William Meredyth Thomas, *Thomas Price, Carnhuanawc*, 1848, plaster

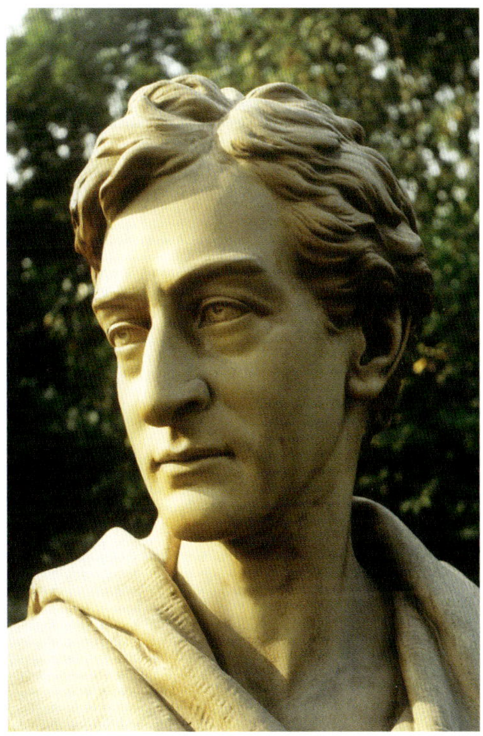

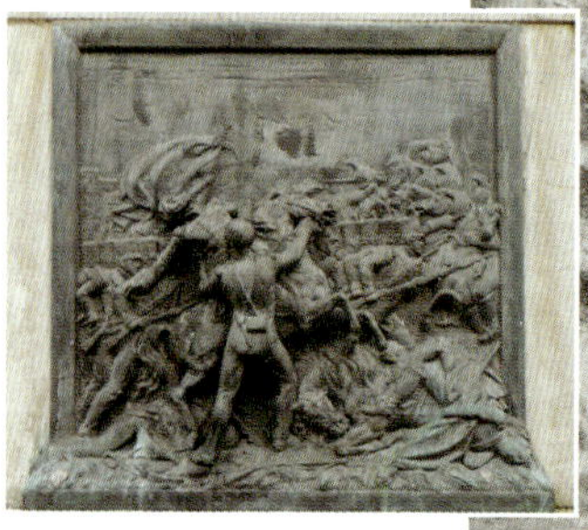

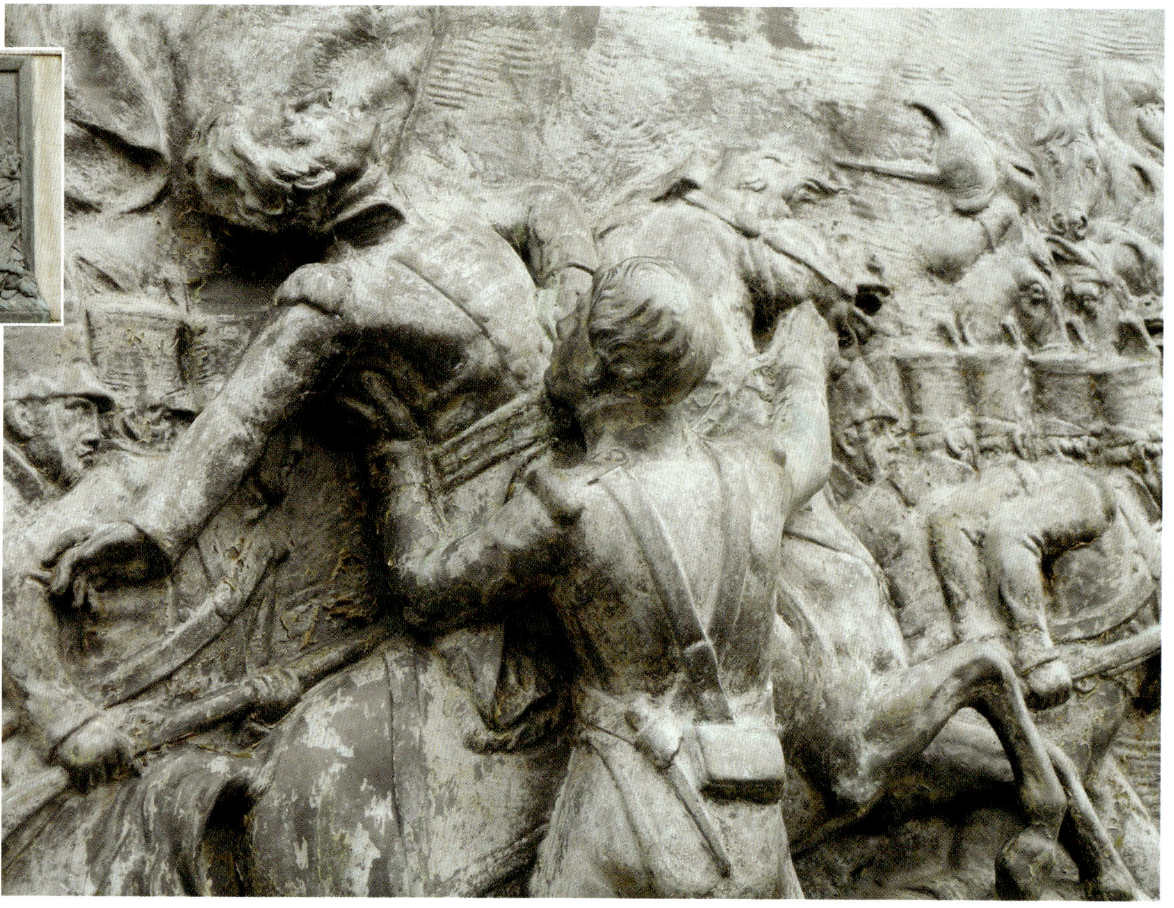

203. John Evan Thomas, *The Death of Sir Thomas Picton at Waterloo*, relief from the Wellington Memorial at Brecon, 1854, bronze

large-scale statues of the Marquess of Bute for Cardiff, Prince Albert for Tenby, and the Duke of Wellington for his own home town of Brecon. The Wellington statue crystallised a sense of identity manifested by many of those aroused by the patriotic spirit of the period. It combined the celebration of British military power in the person of the Duke with a specifically Welsh contribution, represented in a relief panel on the plinth by a repetition of the subject of the death at Waterloo of Sir Thomas Picton, that had been portrayed earlier by Baily at Carmarthen. The Brecon memorial was in place by 1854. Seven years later, the monumental statue of another celebrated Welsh soldier at Waterloo, the 1st Marquess of Anglesey, was placed at the top of the tall column that dominated the entrance to the island. Although attributed to the London sculptor Matthew Noble, it was modelled by Joseph Edwards. Enhanced by the first solo exhibition of works by a Welsh artist, held at the Royal London eisteddfod of 1855, Edwards had gained a reputation among Welsh intellectuals as a master craftsman of mystical inclination. However, in the competitive metropolitan art world, his other-worldliness had not helped his career to prosper. Latterly, he had earned his living working in Noble's studio.

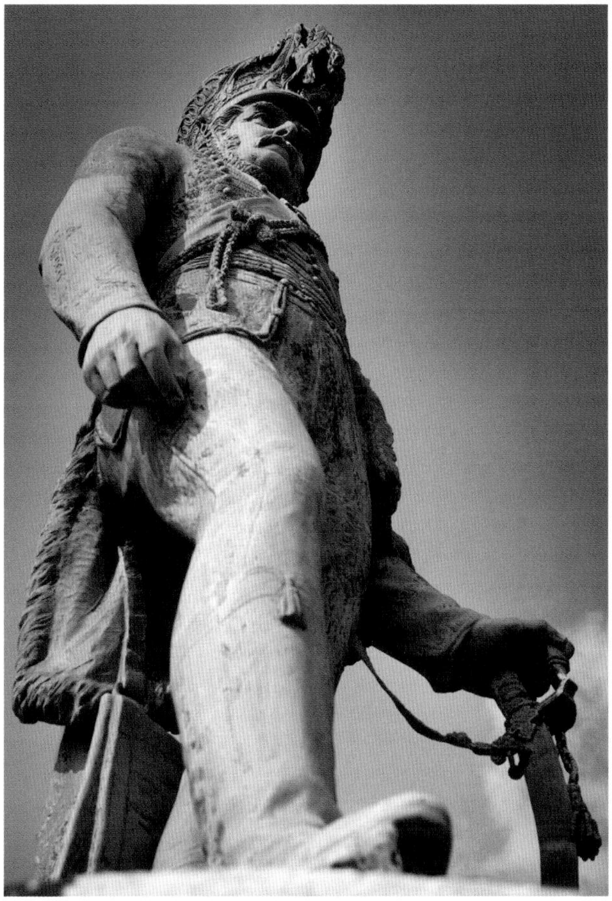

204. Joseph Edwards, *Henry Paget, 1st Marquess of Anglesey*, 1861, bronze

The patriotic *Death of Tewdrig* would be exhibited at Abergavenny in the context of an upsurge of national feeling throughout Europe. The year of 1848 saw risings in many countries against the imperial hegemonies that had dominated the continent since the fall of Napoleon. John Gibson was an eye witness to the occupation of Rome by republican supporters of the unification of Italy, led by Garibaldi. On the arrival of French forces, who retook the city, Gibson had departed in haste: 'I ran away and left my companion to his fate, as well as all my statues to take their chance', he observed, with characteristic simplicity.[56] 'The muses are said to be silent amidst the clash of arms.'[57] At the same time in Wales, the first stirrings of national assertiveness were disrupted not by force of arms but by the psychological impact of a damning government report on the state of education in the country. It came to be known as 'the treachery of the Blue Books' – a description significant for conveying the sense of betrayal by the English of Welsh contributions to British imperial history exemplified by the imaging of Picton at Carmarthen and Brecon.

By 1847 the evolution of the establishment that largely set the Nonconformist middle class in place of the Anglican gentry had proceeded quietly enough, to the extent that a complacent self-image of mildly progressive piety had taken root. The publication in that

56 Thomas Matthews, *The Biography of John Gibson R.A., Sculptor, Rome* (London, 1911), p. 130. Gibson's 'companion' was the sculptor Wyatt, whose studio was close to his own. Among the incomplete statues that Gibson deserted was that of Queen Victoria.

57 Matthews, *John Gibson*, p. 113.

year of the 'Blue Books' report, written by the government's Commissioners for Education, severely disturbed the complacency. The report attacked precisely the two aspects of Welsh cultural achievement most cherished by the Nonconformist intellectual community – the educational and moral progress of the people – and was perceived in particular as an attack on the Welsh language. The reaction was complex – indignant among radicals, pained and hurt among those of less combative inclination. As Gibson contemplated the movement for Italian unification in Rome, his contemporary at home, Hugh Hughes, attacked the London commissioners in a series of satires, each consisting of a picture and a bilingual text, published under the title *Pictures for the Million of Wales*. In the same year, the painter Evan Williams wrote the first of a series of detailed discussions of aspects of visual culture that would be published in the Methodist periodical *Y Traethodydd*. They pioneered the discussion of aesthetics in the Welsh language. In his opening remarks Williams made quite clear that his writing had been stimulated by the accusations of endemic ignorance in Welsh-language culture made by the Commissioners of Education:

> If better late than never, let us now commence with some simple lessons in those arts that are not yet familiar to the Welshman in his own language ... These days, as we know, there are some who seek to defame our character as a nation, and accuse us of being far behind other nations in every sense; but we know that this is a great untruth, and that we are, fortunately, much above our neighbours in religion and morals, if not in general knowledge.[58]

Though not immediately perceptible to the majority of Welsh people, among intellectuals the publication of the Blue Books came to be understood as a pivotal point of change. It was a setback for national confidence, the implications of which took many years to resolve. At the 1860 Denbigh eisteddfod, John Francis expressed the frustration felt by those patriots excited by the ongoing intensification of national sentiment in other parts of Europe. His speech was reported by the *Carnarvon and Denbigh Herald*:

> It was evidence of decay when nations or peoples forget the great men whom God had risen up to be their protectors and deliverers, and it was the best possible proof of the strength and vitality of a people when it could be seen that they revered, and honoured the memory of their noble dead (applause). Numbers of such monuments recently had been seen by him in France and Belgium – many of them often repeated – to those who had brought honour and fame to their country. How were we on this point? We ought to have monuments to Caractacus, to Boadicea, to Arthur, to Cadwalladr, to Llewelyn (cheers), and to Owen Glyndwr (loud applause), as well as to other worthies; Lewis Morris, Goronwy Owen, Charles of Bala, Twm o'r Nant, and many more than he could think to enumerate (loud applause).[59]

58 Evan Williams, 'Y Gelfyddyd o Arlunio', *Y Traethodydd* (1848), pp. 423–4, my translation from the Welsh.

59 *Carnarvon and Denbigh Herald*, 11 August 1860. Francis might also have cited the example of Scotland, for his speech was made shortly after the commissioning of the monumental Wallace Memorial at Stirling.

60 Eastlake, *John Gibson*, p. 239.

Though it was not manifested in his art, national sentiment stirred even the other-worldly John Gibson at the last. Shortly before his death in 1866, to a proud summary of his success in the art world – 'I am now a member of eleven Academies, also of the Legion of Honour' – he added the unequivocal statement: 'I am a Welshman'.[60] It was a significant affirmation, of a kind made by none of his eighteenth-century precursors in Rome. In 1862, on a visit to London where his most celebrated work, *The Tinted Venus*, was on display, he had troubled to visit William Davies, 'Mynorydd' – as he had Joseph Edwards, many years before. It would fall to Mynorydd finally to fulfil the aspiration to celebrate in the form of public sculpture one of the worthy Welsh leaders proposed by John Francis. Twelve years after his appeal, in 1872, a statue of Thomas Charles was installed outside his chapel at Bala. For the face, the sculptor relied on the simple image of the Methodist leader that had been painted in miniature, sixty years earlier, by Gibson's forgotten contemporary, the artisan Hugh Hughes.

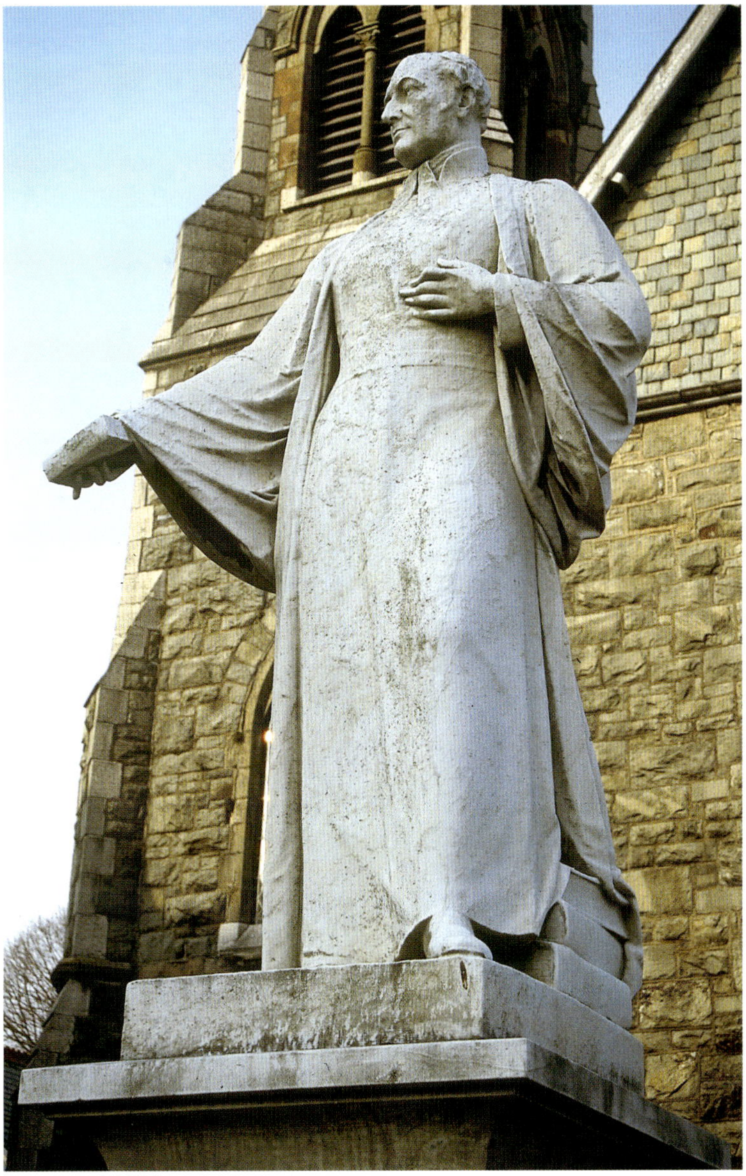

205. William Davies, *Thomas Charles of Bala*, 1872, stone

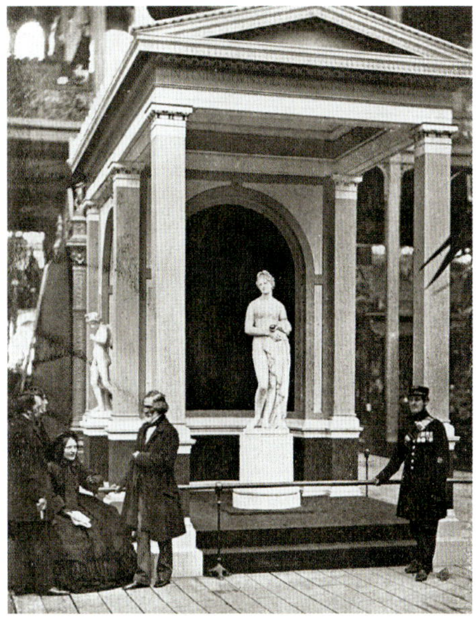

206. *John Gibson at the London Exhibition with his patrons Mr and Mrs Preston*, with the sculptor's *Tinted Venus* in the pavilion designed by Owen Jones, 1862

The Artists' Colony at Betws-y-Coed

In 1841, the amateur painter Calvert Richard Jones took a photograph of Margam Castle using the Daguerreotype process that had been revealed to the world only two years earlier. The technical and aesthetic development of the photograph proceeded with extraordinary rapidity, having a profound impact on the way the world was seen.[61] Among its most immediate effects on visual culture in Wales was to bring the brief golden age of the artisan portrait painters to an end. Their middle-class patrons deserted them for the photographers, who toured at first, like their painting precursors, but soon were to be found installed in the High Street of every town. William Roos adopted a strategy of diversification, but did not fare well. In 1873 he summed up his situation in a letter to his friend, the musicologist Nicholas Bennett: 'I have taken to Animal & Landscape painting for the last few years, this is the only thing in art Photography can't do ...', he observed.[62] Roos was last recorded in 1877, in the churchyard at Oswestry where he was seen tinting photographs of the church to sell for a few shillings. He died in poverty the following year.

61 Margam Castle was the elaborate historicist mansion of C.R.M. Talbot, first cousin to Henry Fox Talbot, the pioneer English photographer. Calvert Jones, Emma Talbot and John Dillwyn Llewelyn, all youthful members of wealthy Swansea industrialist families, made a significant contribution to the early development of photography. For Calvert Richard Jones, see Penny Cotter, *Calvert in Camera* (Cardiff, 1990) and for John Dillwyn Llewelyn, see Richard Morris, *John Dillwyn Llewelyn, 1810–1882, the first photographer in Wales* (Cardiff, 1980).

62 NLW MS 584B, item 95.

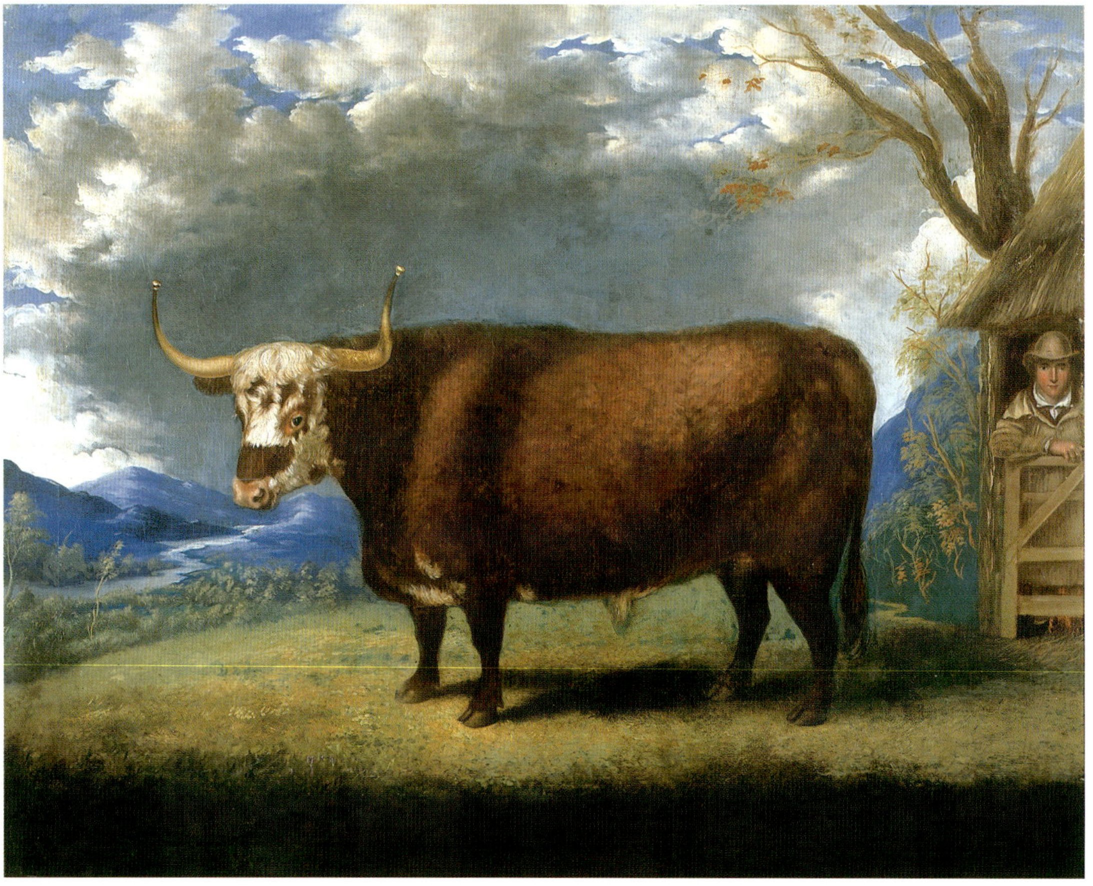

207. William Roos, *Hereford Ox*, 1844, oil, 71x91

The revival of the artisan painter as a portrait specialist had proved to be an evolutionary cul-de-sac. Only John Cambrian Rowland was able to adapt fully to the new situation. Initially he had travelled in Cardiganshire and Pembrokeshire from a base in Aberystwyth, painting in a simple, flat style. However, by the 1850s his technique had evolved considerably, enabling him to respond to the collapse of the market by diversification. His most successful venture was into the production of Welsh costume engravings. Based on drawings made in his native mid-Wales but relocated against Snowdonian backgrounds, they would have a long shelf life, reproduced on many forms of tourist kitsch. Rowland would eventually become the respectable headmaster of the first government art school in Caernarfon.

As the memory of the artisan portrait painters rapidly faded, in the second half of the nineteenth century the mainstream of Welsh painting returned to its eighteenth-century course, depicting the landscape and people of rural and upland Wales. Notwithstanding the attempts of Hugh Hughes, Hugh Jones, William Roos and Evan Williams to broaden their appeal by entering this market, for a time most exponents of the genre would continue to come into the country from outside. However, developments in the 1840s provided the beginnings of a domestic focus for their activities. In the Conwy Valley, centred at Betws-y-Coed, some of the visitors became residents, forming the earliest artists' colony in Britain. Links with indigenous practice were few – only Hugh Hughes's pupil, Ap Caledfryn, went on to train there. Nevertheless, by the end of the nineteenth century, the Betws-y-Coed painters would have contributed substantially to the development of what for the first time could truly be described as a Welsh art world.

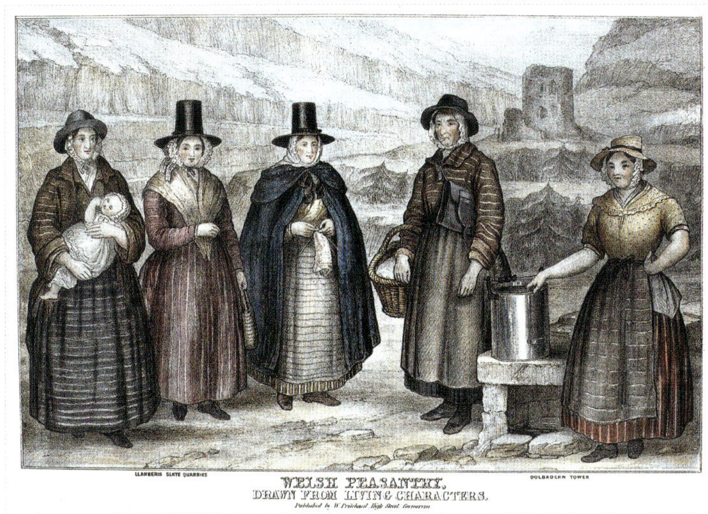

208. John Cambrian Rowland, *Welsh Peasantry Drawn from Living Characters in 1850*, c.1850–60, lithograph, 24x37.5

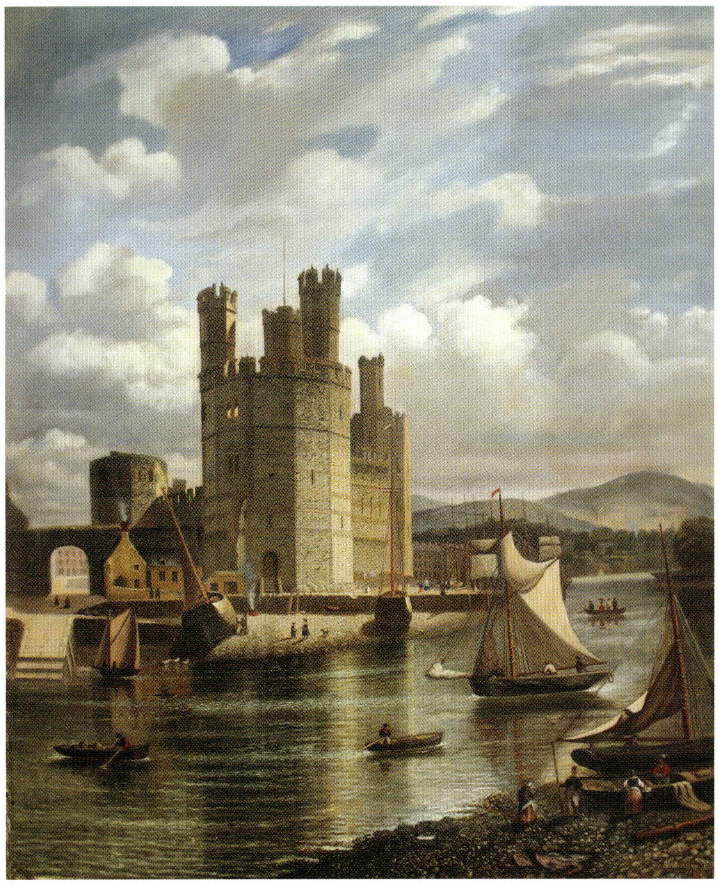

209. Evan Williams, *Caernarfon Castle*, c.1860, oil, 61x51

The catalyst for the development of the artists' colony at Betws-y-Coed was the annual appearance during the summer of David Cox – a painter who, by the 1840s, was second in reputation in England only to Turner. Cox had visited Wales early in his career, but his work in illustrating a new guide book, *Wanderings and Excursions in North Wales*, written by Thomas Roscoe – son of the first patron of John Gibson – seems to have initiated a particular interest in Betws-y-Coed. Roscoe's guidebook, which also contained engravings by Cox's rival Thomas Creswick, was first published in 1836 and soon became the most successful of its kind. It included a paragraph about the village, but a second and enlarged edition, published in 1844, extended the paragraph into a eulogistic chapter. Cox took up residence in the village for the summer season for the first time in the same year, and the combined effect was remarkable. The census of 1841 reported no artists resident in the area. By 1851, however, Betws-y-Coed was home to a substantial group, augmented by a seasonal influx of both professional and amateur painters who arrived, drawn by the presence of Cox, during the summer. Among them was William Hall, who would also become Cox's biographer. He reported that as early as 1846, 'During the sketching season, Bettws, as it became known, was often filled to overflowing with amateurs and artists':

> Their white tents and umbrellas, to be seen in whichever direction the eye turned, suggested to the visitor the encampment of an invading army. In every road or lane, on every eminence or river-bank, the artist was encountered, bearing his paraphernalia to or from the sketching-ground, or beheld busily at work transferring to canvas the beautiful objects before him; whilst in the evenings, after the labours of the day, he was seen chatting with his fellows at the inn door, smoking pipe or cigar, and enjoying the delicious calm of the closing day.[63]

The inn to which Hall referred was the Royal Oak, near Pont y Pair, the medieval bridge at the centre of the village which previously had been the only object of interest to artists, since it was the most northerly road crossing of the River Conwy.

Among the earliest residents, the watercolourist William Evans established a reputation beyond Betws that was enhanced, in best romantic tradition, by his early death from tuberculosis. His biographer was of the opinion that his living conditions at Ty'n-y-Cae, a 'hovel ... swarming with rats, which are said to have continually disturbed him by coursing over his bed in the night', were the cause of his demise.[64] Evans's contemporary, Richard Sebastian Bond, fared better. Bond had visited Wales from his Liverpool base as early as 1830, but seems to have established himself at Betws in about 1846.[65] He made his home not far from Evans but in the more substantial cottage of Wernfawr. It was described by the Welsh amateur sketcher George Whitwick:

63 William Hall, *A Biography of David Cox* (London, 1881), p. 85.

64 Royal Watercolour Society Archive, quoted in Peter Lord, *Clarence Whaite and the Welsh Art World. The Betws-y-Coed Artists' Colony* (2nd edition, Llandudno, 2009), p. 53.

65 Bond showed a landscape at the British Institution in London that year, and his son's birth was registered in Llanrwst parish.

66 George Whitwick, description in his 1856 volume of drawings and texts entitled 'A Week's Sketching in North Wales', NLW DV17. Sarah Bond was the daughter of a minister at Ro-Wen in the Conwy valley, to which artists had been guided by Edward Pugh in *Cambria Depicta*. Another early resident painter at Betws, George Harrison, also married a local woman and spent the rest of his life in the village. See Lord, *Clarence Whaite and the Welsh Art World*, pp. 67–8 and 167–8.

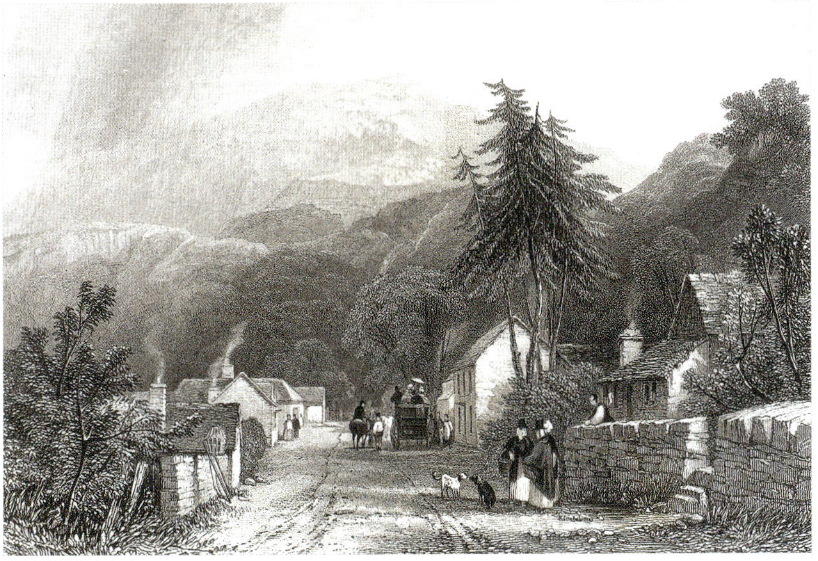

210. William Radclyffe after Thomas Creswick, *Bettws y Coed*, from Thomas Roscoe, *Wanderings and Excursions in North Wales*, 1836, engraving, 95x142

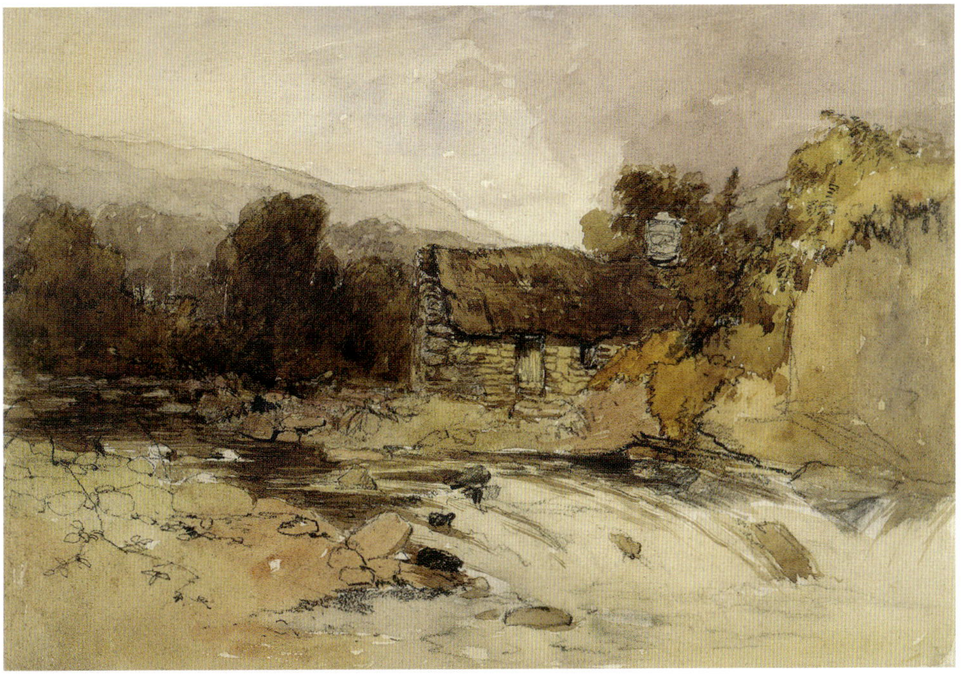

211. William Evans, *Cottage near Betws-y-Coed*, c.1844, watercolour, 17.7x25.4

Here lives the ... 'Landscape Painter', with the finest woman I ever saw in Wales for a wife, and three children 'beautiful exceedingly'. The Lady brought me out a chair, whereon to sit and take these views. The Gentleman fed me with oat-meal cakes, rendered delectable by butter, and facilitated by Whiskey. The Lady is of the blood of Glendower, – 'serene, imperial'. The Gentleman is an Englishman, blessed in his wife at all events, though I opine, rather content with his fate, than favoured by Fortune, in respect of what should be the monied estimate of his skill and feeling as an artist.[66]

67 Cardiff Central Library MS Cardiff 1.194 (4/6), no. 31. I am grateful to Professor Geraint H. Jenkins for this reference.

68 Roscoe, *Wanderings and Excursions*, 1844 edition, p. 214.

69 John Walter Cross, *George Eliot's Life as related in her Letters and Journals* (London, 1887), p. 281.

70 The precise dating of the several versions of *A Welsh Funeral* is not clear.

71 Letter dated 15 July 1844, quoted in N. Neil Solly, *Memoir of the Life of David Cox*, (London, 1873), p. 172.

It was to Bond that Ap Caledfryn was engaged 'as a pupil in landscape and figure painting'. He recalled that 'I had to start at once from nature. I had the advantage of seeing the renowned David Cox work ... I had to study from the antique at the same time and from models [and] in about twelve months Mr. Bond pronounced me able to make my own living ...'[67] Ap Caledfryn almost certainly met Cox directly as a result of his teacher's relationship with Bond, since the two English painters were friends, and worked together.

In 1848, David Cox painted the first versions of *A Welsh Funeral*, the picture that more than any other would come to represent Wales in the English Victorian psyche. It was inspired by the funeral of the young daughter of the innkeeper at the Royal Oak. The painter inserted himself in the scene, at the back of the group who moved slowly towards the church. Cox was a devout Christian and though an Anglican, like Roscoe, he was moved by what he perceived to be the piety of the largely Nonconformist common people at Betws. Roscoe had made the point strongly in *Wanderings and Excursions in North Wales*, with a lengthy description of a prayer meeting in the Welsh language at the Royal Oak.[68] The pathos of the funeral touched a public imagination predisposed by such literary equivalents to empathise with the scene, and the picture became well known. Cox produced several versions to meet the demand. After his death, in 1862 one of these was reproduced as an engraving that

212. Richard Sebastian Bond, *Driftwood after a Storm, Betws-y-Coed*, 1870, oil, 118.1x168.9

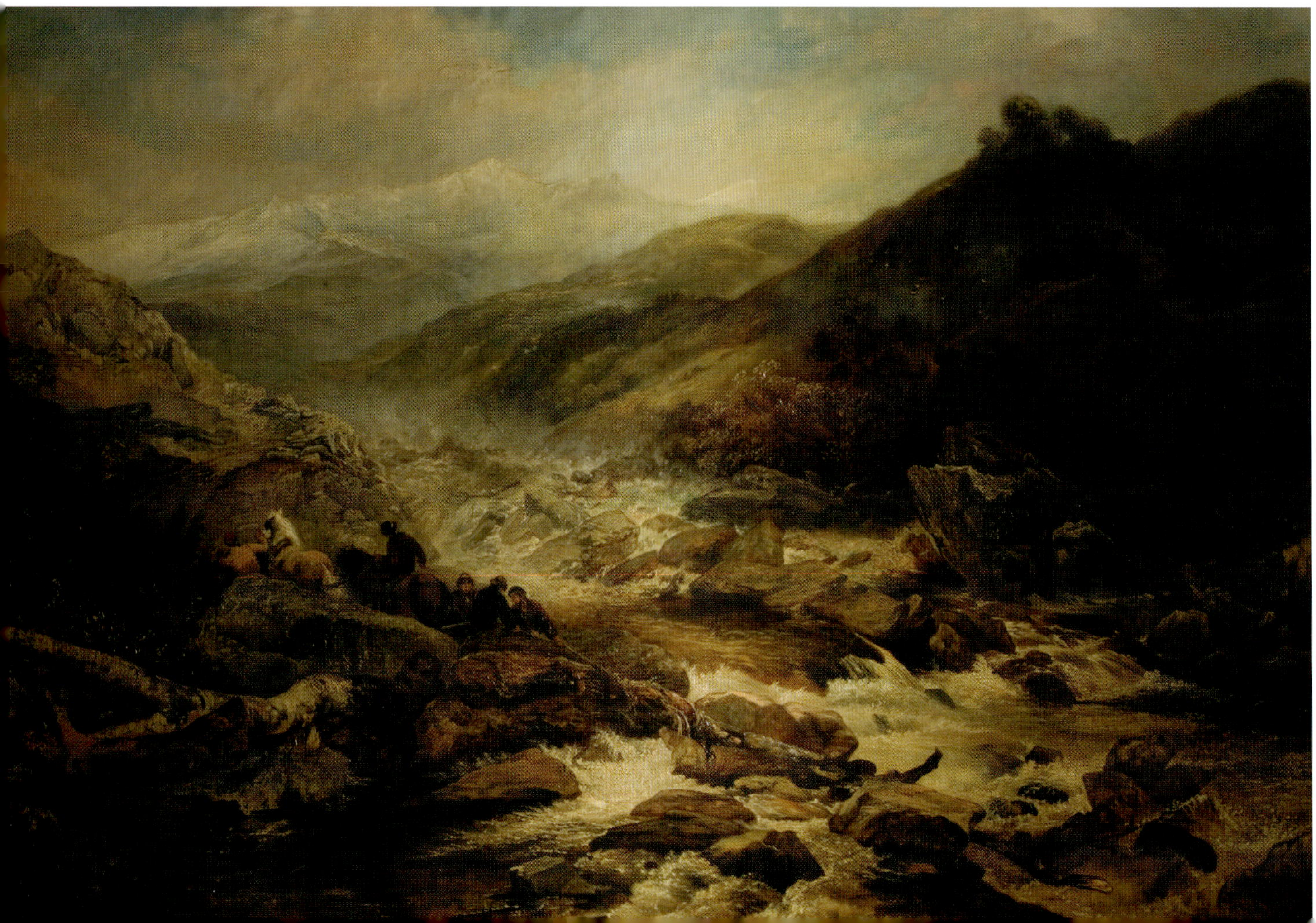

extended its celebrity even further. On a visit to Leeds, where one of the versions was hanging, the novelist George Eliot particularly remarked upon it: 'Certainly there was nothing finer there in landscape than that Welsh Funeral', she wrote to a friend.[69] The picture spawned a genre of funeral and churchyard images which played an important role in reasserting the idea of Welsh piety that the Commissioners for Education had sought to undermine just a year before Cox painted his seminal work.[70]

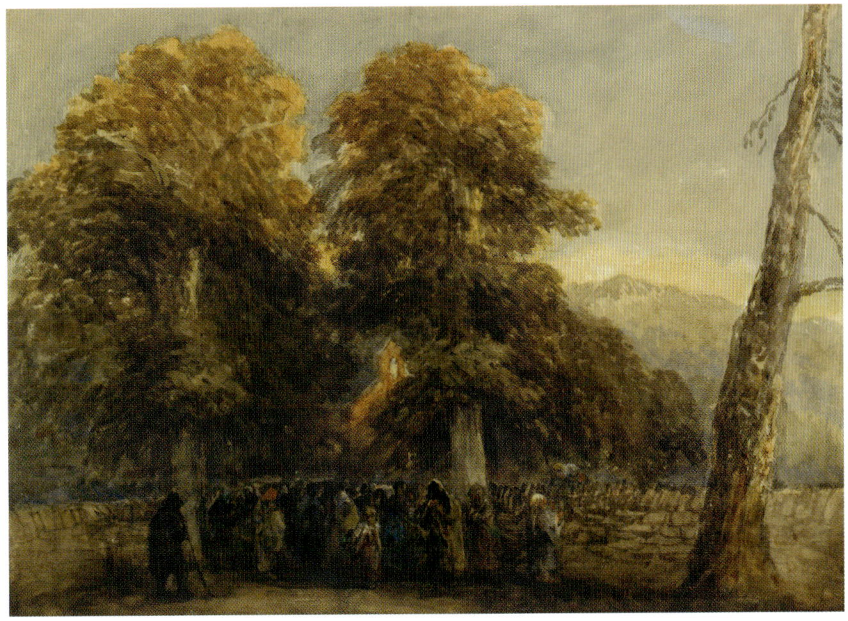

213. David Cox, *The Welsh Funeral*, 1848, watercolour, 60x85.5

George Popkin, an early resident among the Betws-y-Coed artistic community, reported hearing 'French, German, Hungarian, English, and Welsh flowing on like a polyglot stream' in the parlour of the Royal Oak.[71] To add to these languages, in 1862 Hans Fredrik Gude, who would become the most celebrated Norwegian painter of landscape in his period, arrived in the village with his family. He worked there for two years and later wrote that his

214. Hans Fredrik Gude, *Bridge in North Wales*, 1863, oil, 41.5x55.5

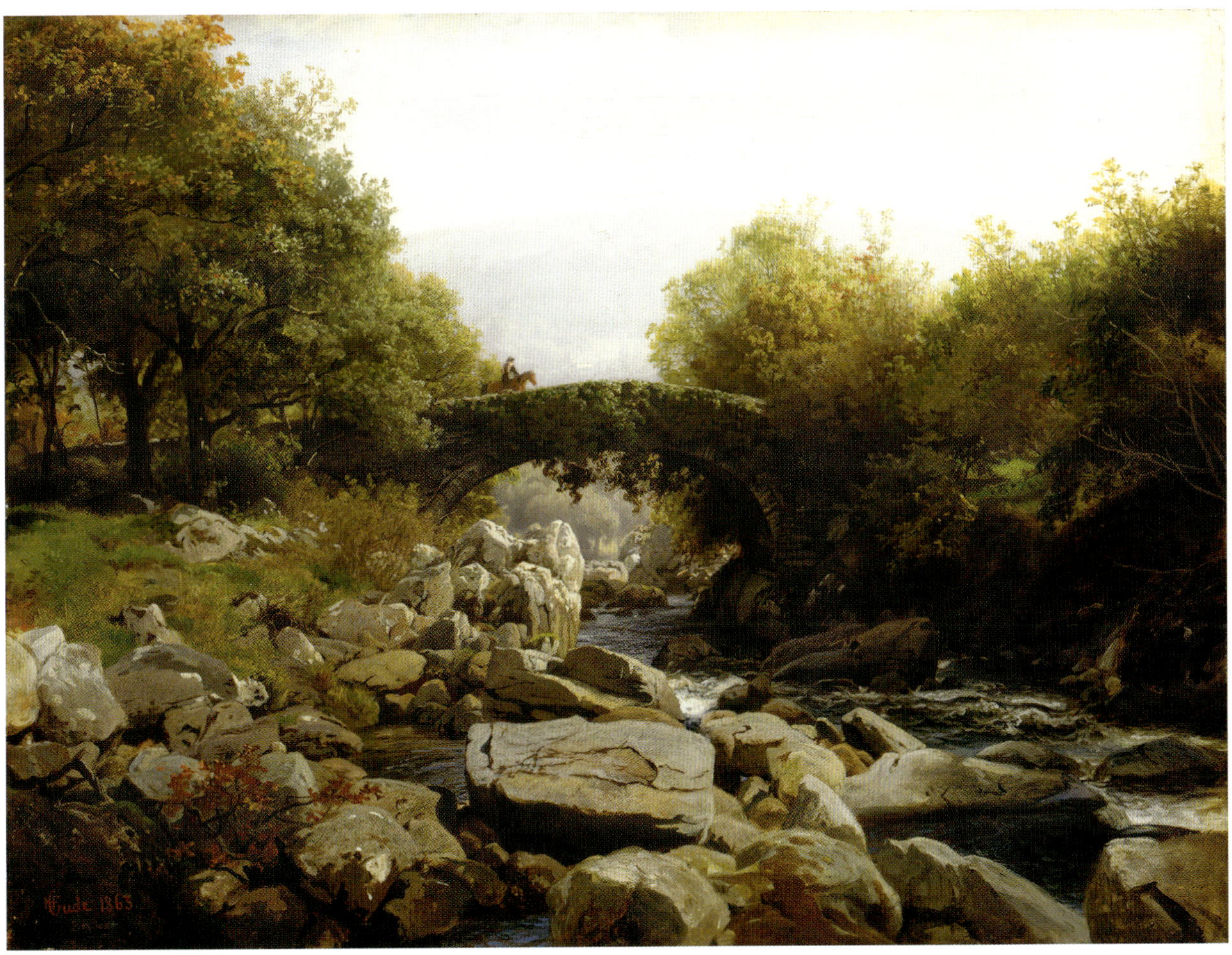

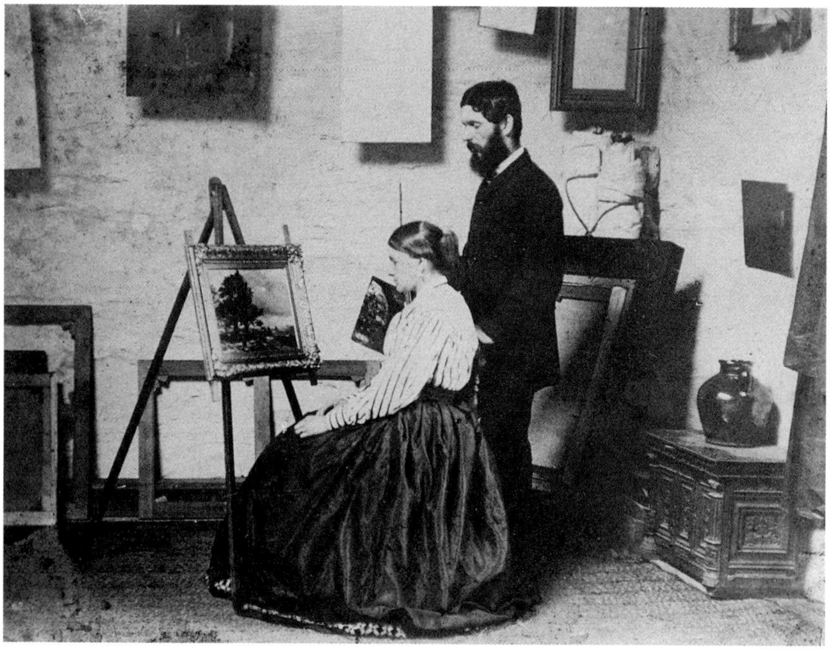

215. *George and Catrin Harrison in the studio at Betws-y-Coed, c.1865.*

stay had been 'of great benefit to me in that I freed myself from many of the prevailing studio maxims by being alone in a landscape so new to me that it forced me to observe more keenly.'[72] Young painters in many parts of Europe were reacting against academism. As early as 1856, the critic J.J. Jenkins made a comparison between the artists' colony at Betws and its contemporary at Barbizon, outside Paris.[73] The 1860s were years of experiment and liberation from the studio, and at Betws in particular for the painter Henry Clarence Whaite, whose engagement with his work was perhaps the most intense and sustained of all those who worked there. Whaite would become the leading figure in Welsh landscape painting through the second half of the nineteenth century, and also played an important role in institutional development in the visual arts. He was born in 1828 into an artisan painting family in Manchester, and trained there. He first came to Betws in 1851 and returned the following year when he met Cox, who 'expressed his delight' at the work shown him. From this point on Whaite was drawn increasingly to the area, coming to know residents including George Harrison from Kent and James Whittaker, who had also been attracted to Betws from Manchester. A letter written to his father by Whaite 1862 revealed something of the artistic community:

> I was at Bettws yesterday in the afternoon – the morning was wet, so did not go to church but attended the Welch at Capel Curig. I called to see Whittaker ... I dined with my friend Mr Luke at the Oak – I called to see some drawings by Mr Eddington and met five Manchester artists at his house, or rather four, for I made the fifth and another from Cheshire – so you see Manchester is well represented at Bettws.[74]

By this time Whaite was more than a fair-weather summer visitor. The letter was written in December, and he would in due course marry a local woman and became a permanent resident in the Conwy Valley, though he retained his interest in the arts in Manchester, benefitting throughout his life from patronage in the city. He also became a prominent figure in the Royal Watercolour Society in London. Reflecting the mid-century flush of interest that manifested itself in the contemporary work of Welsh sculptors, in 1854 Whaite exhibited *Ancient Britons Surprised by the Romans* at the Royal Academy. Five years later, he was awarded the crucial accolade of being noticed at the summer exhibition by John Ruskin, who approved *The Barley Harvest*, albeit with some reservations. Whaite became a member of the Hogarth Club, of which Ruskin was also a member along with G.F. Watts and the Pre-Raphaelites Dante Gabriel Rossetti and Ford Madox Brown. It was at this time, in 1861, that he began work on what would become his most celebrated painting, *The Rainbow*. Notwithstanding the large size of the picture, Whaite worked directly from the view that he depicted, looking west towards Moel Siabod and Snowdon from a position on the old road between Betws-y-Coed and Capel Curig. Lodging nearby, he worked for two seasons on the picture in a specially constructed studio. In one respect, *The Rainbow* was characteristic of its period, since it presented landscape incorporating a moral narrative. The undefiled mountains and stream, like the innocence of the children in the foreground group, suggested the closeness of God, while the rainbow and the lamb symbolised the eternal cycle of nature. A mystical view of the natural world would permeate Whaite's work throughout his life, against a trend perceived by one critic towards 'nature pure and simple'.[75] On the other hand, *The Rainbow* was indisputably radical in technique. It was painted under the influence of the French chemist M.E. Chevreul, whose work had been published in English in 1854 as *The Principles of Harmony and Contrast of Colours, and Their Applications to the Arts*, and which Whaite had studied. The luminous effect of the painting was achieved by the interaction of the thousands of tiny specks of colour from which it was built. It would be twenty years before Chevreul's work informed the pointillist painting technique of Georges Seurat and others in France.

72 See Henry Holiday, *Reminiscences of My Life* (London, 1914), p. 87. For the life of Gude, see Frode Haverkamp, *Hans Gude* (Oslo, 1992).

73 See J.J. Jenkins, 'An Artist's Haunt', *Brighton Gazette*, 23 (October 1856), quoted in Lord, *Clarence Whaite and the Welsh Art World*, p. 61.

74 NLW H. Clarence Whaite Papers, HPB5/2, December 1862.

75 The critic of the *Manchester Examiner and Times*, 3 April 1865, regarded Whaite's picture *The Penitent's Vision* as 'in somewhat questionable taste ... Now-a-days, most people prefer landscape pure and simple'. *The Penitent's Vision* set an incident from Bunyan's *Pilgrim's Progress* in a landscape characteristic of Betws-y-Coed.

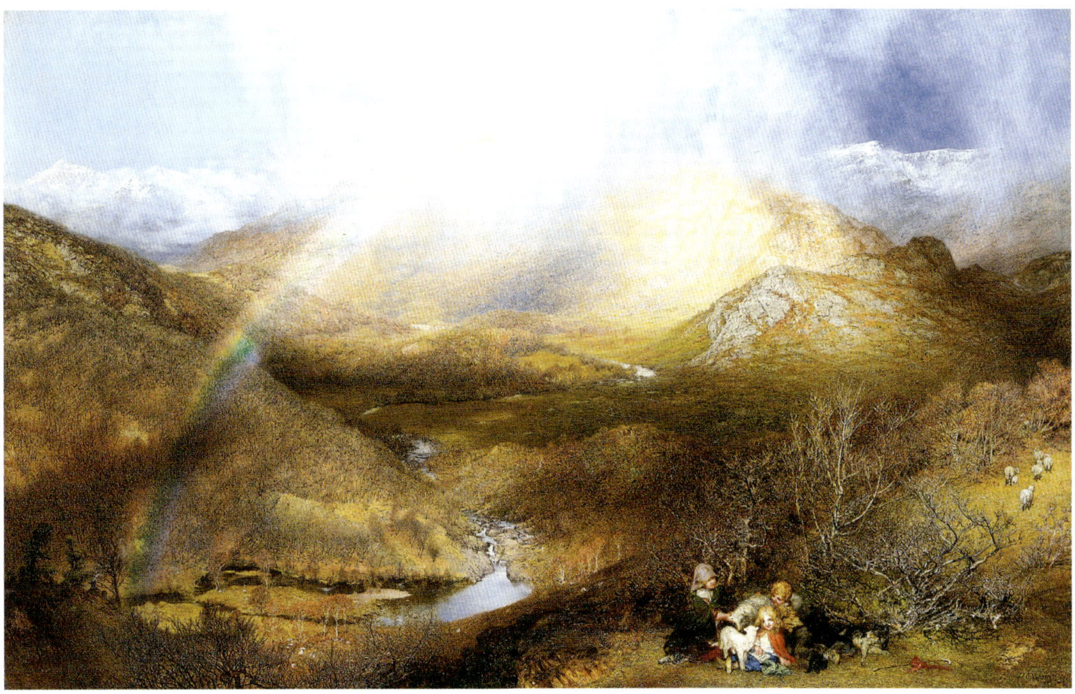

216. Henry Clarence Whaite, *The Rainbow*, 1862, oil, 139.7x241.6

217. Henry Clarence Whaite,
Old Woman on the Quay at Conwy, 1869,
watercolour on paper,
19x28

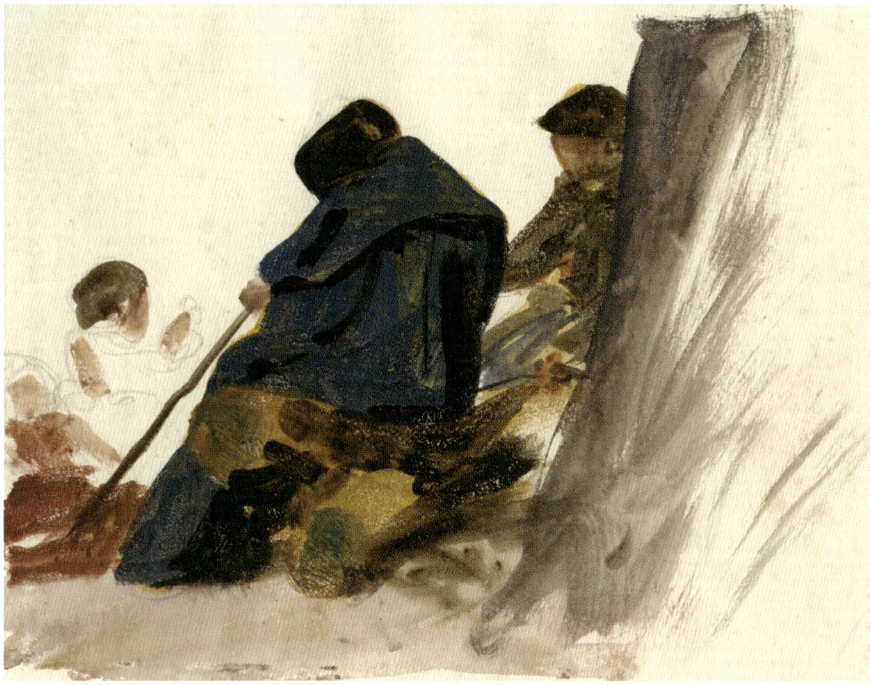

218. Henry Clarence Whaite,
Snowdon, 1910–11, oil,
145.4x245.0

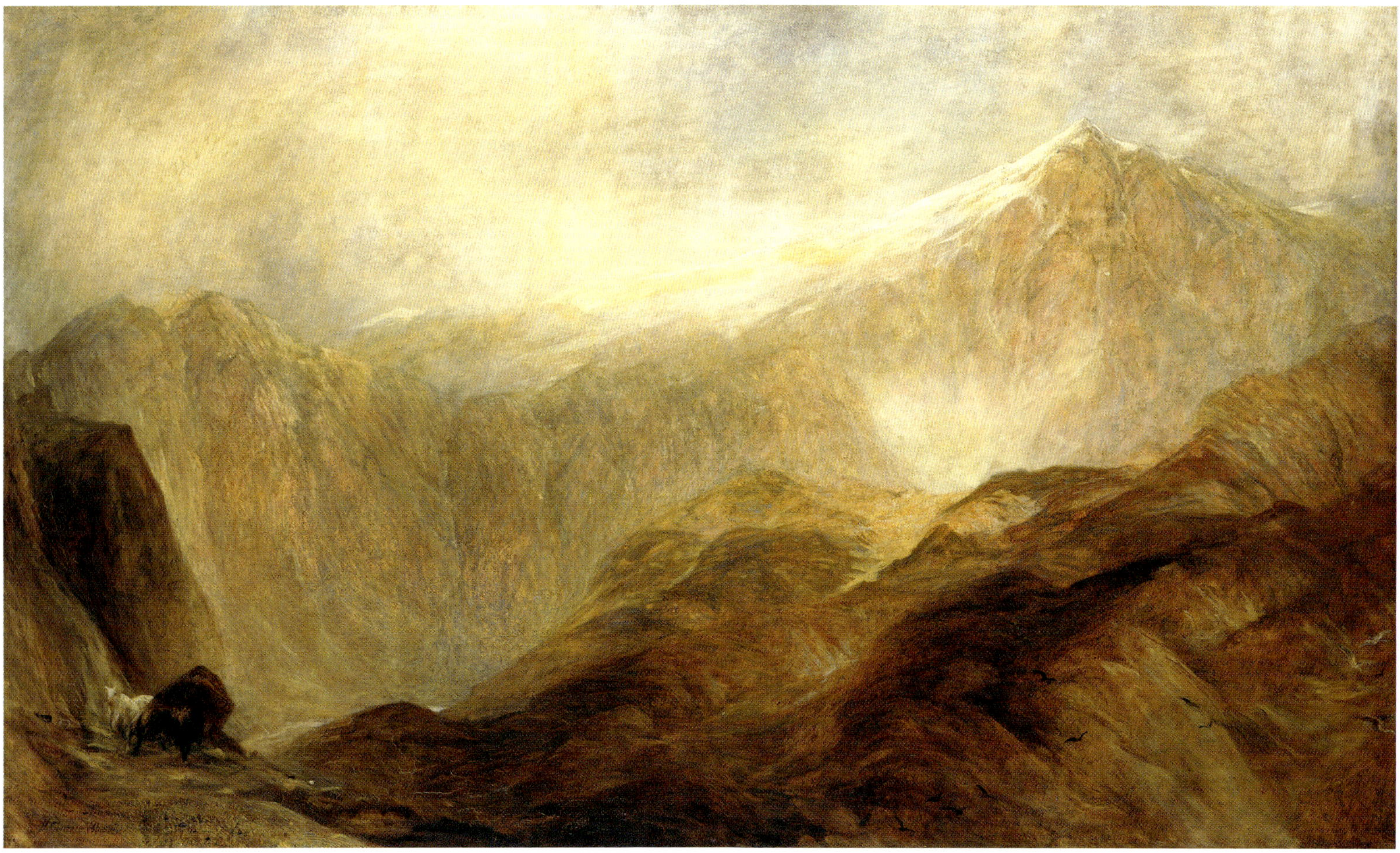

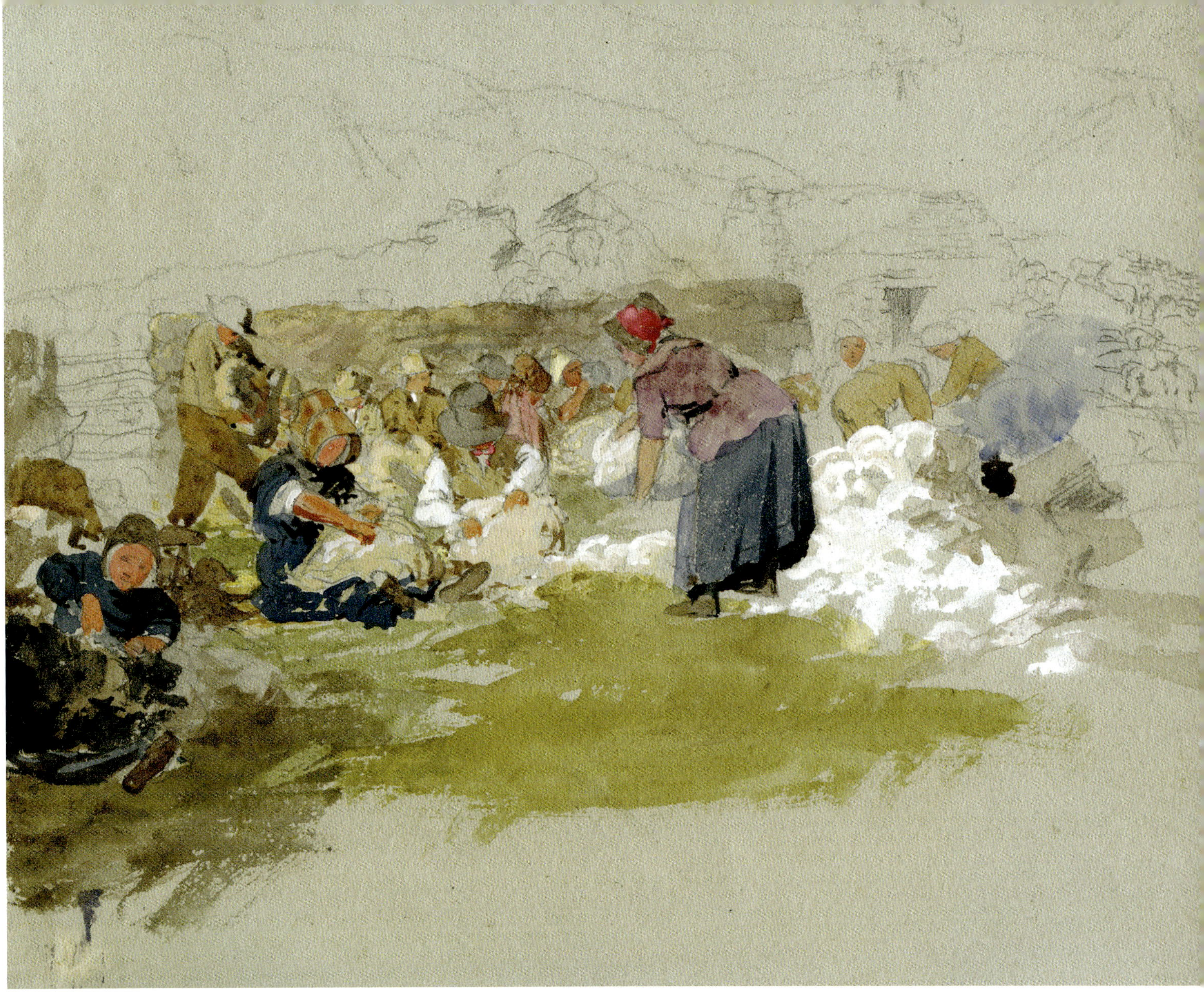

219. Henry Clarence Whaite, *Shearing Sheep*, 1862, watercolour on paper, 23.3x28.7

The Rainbow was greeted with approval when exhibited in 1862. However, the painter's equally remarkable preparatory works were not seen by the public. Through the 1860s, Whaite made countless drawings and watercolours in small sketchbooks, noting both the common people at work and the atmospheric conditions as they affected landscape. In the most free of these works material subjects dissolved under the atmospheric effects of rain and light. Much later in his career Whaite brought these elements together in the large scale mystical landscapes *Mountain Mist, Sunrise* (1892), *The Snowdonian Shepherd* (1906-7), and *Snowdon* (1910-11), in praise of which a contemporary critic was moved to quote Dafydd ap Gwilym for the way in which the painter had conveyed 'the might of the mountain, the snow-terror to the mountain-dweller, and the awesome beauty of the snow on the dismal precipices ...'[76]

76 Thomas Matthews, 'Celf yng Nghymru', *Cymru*, ed. O.M. Edwards (1911), p. 15, my translation from the Welsh, though the poem that Matthews proceeded to quote is no longer believed to be the work of Dafydd ap Gwilym.

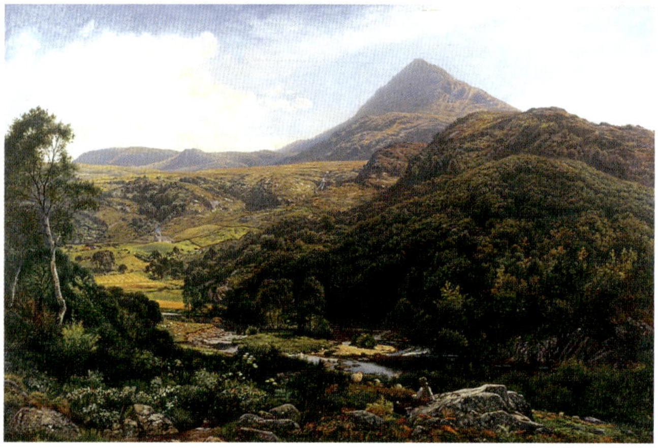

220. Benjamin Williams Leader, *A Quiet Valley amongst the Welsh Hills*, 1860, oil on canvas, 71.0x108.5

Fifty years earlier, in his formative days, the progress of *The Rainbow* had been a cause of much interest to artists at Betws. Amongst those who visited Whaite in his studio at that time was Benjamin Williams Leader, an up-and-coming young painter from Worcester. He had first painted at Betws in 1856, and by 1860 was a regular summer visitor at the Royal Oak. The minute attention to detail evident in his pictures painted into the early 1860s suggests that Leader was mindful of the commercial and critical success of the Pre-Raphaelites, but in 1867 he visited Paris, where he 'studied the French school of landscape, took notes, & felt that ... [he] ... had learnt much.'[77] The work of the Barbizon painters that he saw in France seems to have resulted in a loosening of his technique, evident in pictures such as *Betws-y-coed*. His experiences in France would certainly have been discussed by the artistic community in the village.

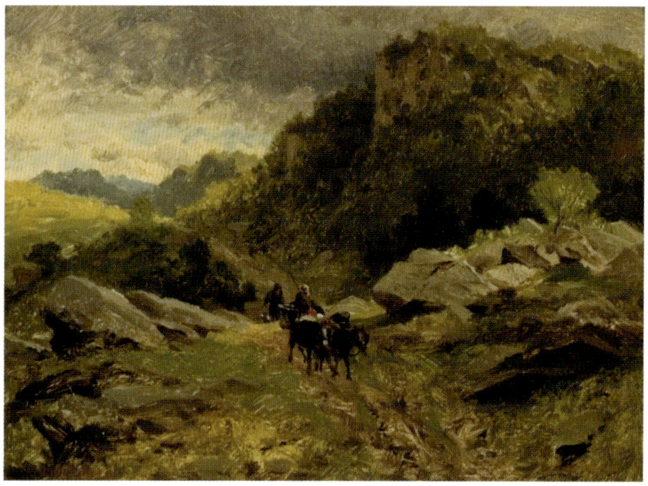

221. Benjamin Williams Leader, *Betws-y-Coed*, mid-1860s, oil, 16.2x23.2

Leader continued to visit Betws-y-Coed during the season until 1889, and utilising his earlier sketches, he produced and exhibited Welsh pictures at the Royal Academy for another thirty years, but in terms of the number of artistic visitors, by the 1880s the village had probably reached the height of its activity. Visitors came in droves, both to paint and to observe the painters. Their arrival was facilitated by a railway and their stay made comfortable by gas lighting in the streets and the construction of a commodious new English church.[78] In fact, the railway line at Betws was reaching towards Blaenau Ffestiniog, in order to carry the lucrative traffic in slate produced in the town – whose dramatic industrial landscape appears to have been entirely ignored by the painters so active ten miles away. However, industrialisation in other parts of Wales was having an effect on the art world, which would indeed touch the activities of the artists' colony by a circuitous route in the early 1880s. For many painters, including Clarence Whaite, patronage in the manufacturing towns of England was of fundamental importance in sustaining their activities. Increasing prosperity among the middle class and the industrial elite within Wales itself facilitated the implementation of aspirations to improve public access to the arts, both through civic development and national institutions.

Stimulated by the success in London of the Great Exhibition of 1851, Clarence Whaite's home town of Manchester staged an ambitious art exhibition in 1857. Together, these confident demonstrations of the state of English art and industry set an example that would be imitated on a smaller scale in Wales, over the next few decades.[79] In its various manifestations, the eisteddfod, as the only national institution in the country, made stuttering attempts to show visual art. At the 1858 eisteddfod at Llangollen, the 'Last Bard' image resurfaced, painted by William Edward Jones of Merthyr, who in due course would paint other national subjects, as well as portraits. Through the following decade, a reformed National Eisteddfod movement, led by the London Welsh, organised small exhibitions, beginning at Caernarfon in 1862, where the work of Mynorydd was shown. A few weeks later, the sculptor was favoured with the visit to his London studio by Gibson. The most comprehensive effort of this group was made at Aberystwyth in 1865, when an art and industrial exhibition was shown in two locations in the town, and a catalogue was published. As ever, the example of Gibson was cited from the stage as a model of Welsh potential in the field. Among the exhibitors in the fine arts at Aberystwyth were William Jones of Chester, Thomas Brigstocke, and Ap Caledfryn. However, it was a small and eccentric affair. It would require the energy and extensive art world contacts of an individual rather than an eisteddfod committee to produce an exhibition that would stand comparison with those being staged in England. This was an important consideration in the contemporary mind, given the continuing legacy of abuse from over the border that confronted these progressives. In response to their efforts at the 1866 eisteddfod, an editorial in *The Times* had observed that 'This is an age of exhibitions, and insofar as it affords any pleasure to Welshmen to make this exhibition of themselves and their antiquated customs, we have nothing against it':

> A bare existence on the most primitive food of a mountainous race is all that the Welsh could enjoy if left to themselves. Under such circumstances, what could be more out of place than an exhibition designed to foster satisfaction with Welsh productions and Welsh virtues? All the progress and civilisation in Wales has come from England, and a sensible Welshman would direct all his endeavours towards inducing his countrymen to appreciate their neighbours instead of themselves ...'[80]

In association with the 1868 eisteddfod at Ruthin, William Cornwallis West of Ruthin Castle brought together over 800 *objets d'art* to form by far the largest fine art exhibition held in Wales to that time. For his paintings and sculpture, Cornwallis West was able to draw both on gentry collections and on contemporary painters that he knew personally, including

77 The diary of Benjamin Williams Leader, 3 July 1867, quoted in Ruth Wood, *Benjamin Williams Leader RA 1831–1923. His Life and Paintings* (Suffolk, 1998), p. 39.

78 An indicator of the class of persons attracted there was the distinguished stained glass inserted in the windows of the new church. In 1880, the English painter John Samuel Raven, who worked at Betws and died at Harlech, was commemorated with glass made by Henry Holiday on the subject of 'Faith, Hope and Charity'. See Martin Crampin, *Stained Glass from Welsh Churches* (Talybont, 2014), p. 168. Holiday met his wife, Catherine Raven, sister of the painter, at Betws in 1861. Catherine Raven was an embroiderer who worked for William Morris and Co. Early in his career, John Samuel Raven had worked at Fontainebleau, another contact between Betws painters and Barbizon.

79 The Manchester exhibition was reviewed in Welsh periodicals by the painter Evan Williams, among others. Charlotte Guest had led a workers' excursion to the Great Exhibition, that took about a hundred 'good honest-hearted Welshmen' to London. See Revel Guest and Angela V. John, *Lady Charlotte. A Biography of the Nineteenth Century* (London, 1989), pp. 160–1.

80 *The Times*, 8 September 1866 and 14 September 1866.

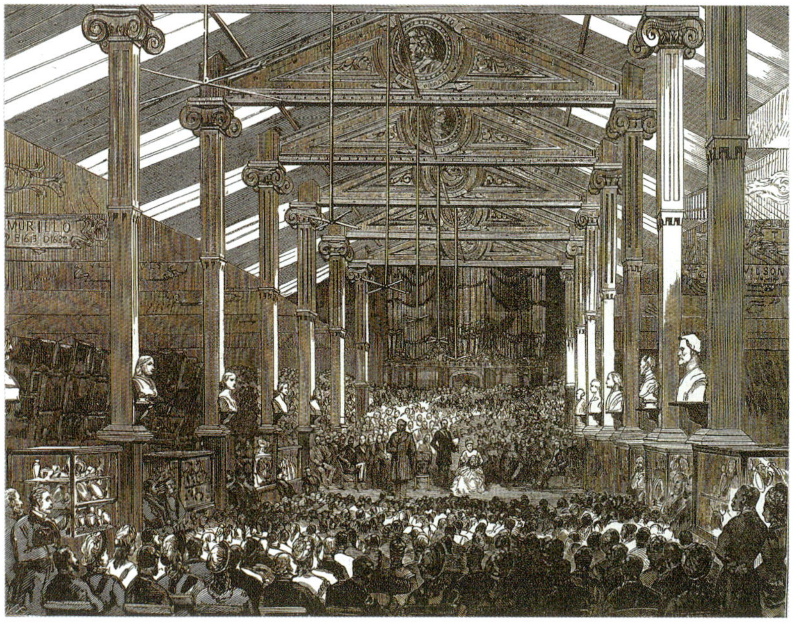

222. *The Art Treasures Exhibition*, Wrexham, 1876, woodcut

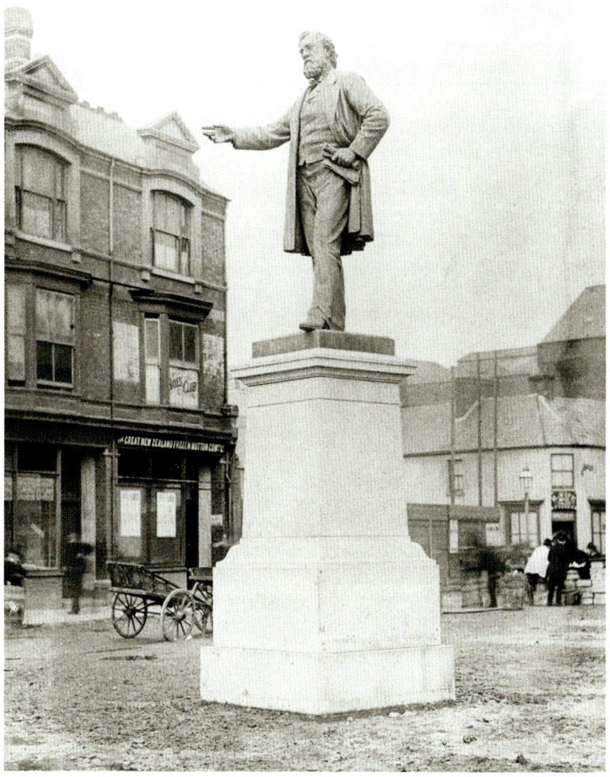

223. Milo ap Griffith, *John Batchelor*, Cardiff, 1886, bronze, photographed *c.*1890

G.F. Watts and Frederic Leighton. The gentry collections yielded portraits and subject pictures by Romney, de Loutherbourg and Benjamin West, as well as the three large portraits painted by Reynolds for Sir Watkin Williams-Wynn.[81]

Standing alone, the eisteddfod movement was not able to replicate this successful riposte to English sarcasm, and six years later Cornwallis West again intervened. At Wrexham, he financed and organised an art and industrial exhibition on an even larger scale, spending £3,000 on the construction of a gallery to house the work. His motives were truly altruistic – a notable expression of the high-minded and patriotic spirit that moved some among the privileged to use their wealth in the interests of 'raising up the common man':

> I believe that an immense deal of humanising good can be done to every single man in Wales if he can only find time to visit the exhibition to see the wonderful produce of industry and mental power which is to be seen there.[82]

The ambition of Cornwallis West was 'that the people of this country should, as the people of other countries, have an opportunity of seeing the beautiful in form, and colour, and design ...'.[83] Though it made a financial loss, some 77,000 people visited the exhibition.

In the meantime, between the two exhibitions organised by Cornwallis West, a similar spirit was moving in the south of the country. In 1870, a fine art and industrial exhibition was organised to aid the financing of a free library and gallery in Cardiff. Among the exhibitors were the Thomas brothers of Brecon and a sculptor of a younger generation, Milo ap Griffith. Following the exhibition, ap Griffith donated works to the town's nascent collection. Achievement of the organisers' aim was frustrated for a decade by enmity between the Liberal-dominated town council and the Tory Bute family estates. Shortly after the library was finally opened, ap Griffith was awarded a commission to commemorate the ship builder John Batchelor in the form of a statue at the side of the building. Batchelor, 'the Friend of Freedom', had been prominent among the civic activists, and the statue was clearly perceived by Tories as a provocation. It was defaced three times in three weeks, and on a fourth occasion defacement was accompanied by a threat to blow it up with dynamite.[84]

The Cardiff library building was designed by Edwin Seward, one of a group of intellectuals in the town with a particular interest in the arts, for whom the Cardiff Naturalists' Society, founded in 1867, provided a focus. Among the most prominent members was Thomas Henry Thomas, son of the Principal of the Pontypool Baptist Theological College. As a young man Thomas had trained in art at Bristol and the Royal Academy Schools, then travelled on the continent. In Rome he paid the ritual Welsh person's obeisance at the studios of John Gibson and Penry Williams. Subsequently, he worked in London as an illustrator and lecturer but in the late 1870s returned to Wales to live in Cardiff. He would become the leading figure in the promotion of Welsh art until his death during the Great War. Among the first ventures with which he was involved, along with Edwin Seward, was a substantial art exhibition organised at Merthyr Tydfil in 1880. Penry Williams's painting of the disturbances of 1816, and John Petherick's remarkable images of the Egyptian furnaces at Rhymney, were shown, but the exhibition was dominated by benign rural landscapes. An important source of these works was the collection of William Menelaus, a managing partner at Dowlais iron works but also a man who had begun life on the shop-floor, as a carpenter. Menelaus lent oil paintings by Constable and Millais, and watercolours by Cotman and Cox, from a collection that would continue to expand for many years.[85] Images of industrial society, to which the working people of Merthyr might have been expected to relate, were scarcely in evidence. Furthermore, the exhibition drew criticism from Cleopas Harris, father of the painters George Frederick and Albert Harris, for ignoring the work of local artists – such as his sons: 'Perhaps they fondly imagine in this conceit that they can stifle or keep back talent from coming to the front. They may as well imagine they can keep back the tide ...'[86] Combining the business with

81 Artisan painters were represented by a single picture – the portrait of Dic Aberdaron painted by William Roos. Unusually, the portrait was in a gentry collection, at Kinmel.

82 NLW XAS 36 (1876).

83 *Byegones*, November 1876, p. 162. See Lord, *Y Chwaer-Dduwies*, pp. 29–48.

84 A Bute Dock foreman was prosecuted under the Damages of Works of Art Act. See John R. Wilson, *Memorializing History: Public Sculpture in Industrial South Wales* (Aberystwyth, 1996).

85 The collection was catalogued by Edwin Seward and T.H. Thomas, and was given to the Cardiff Museum, from where it entered the National Museum.

86 *Merthyr Express*, 29 May 1880, p. 7.

photography, G.F. Harris in particular had succeeded in finding patronage for oil-painted portraits of middle-class sitters and decorative pictures for the Victorian parlour, at a time when other artisan practices had failed.

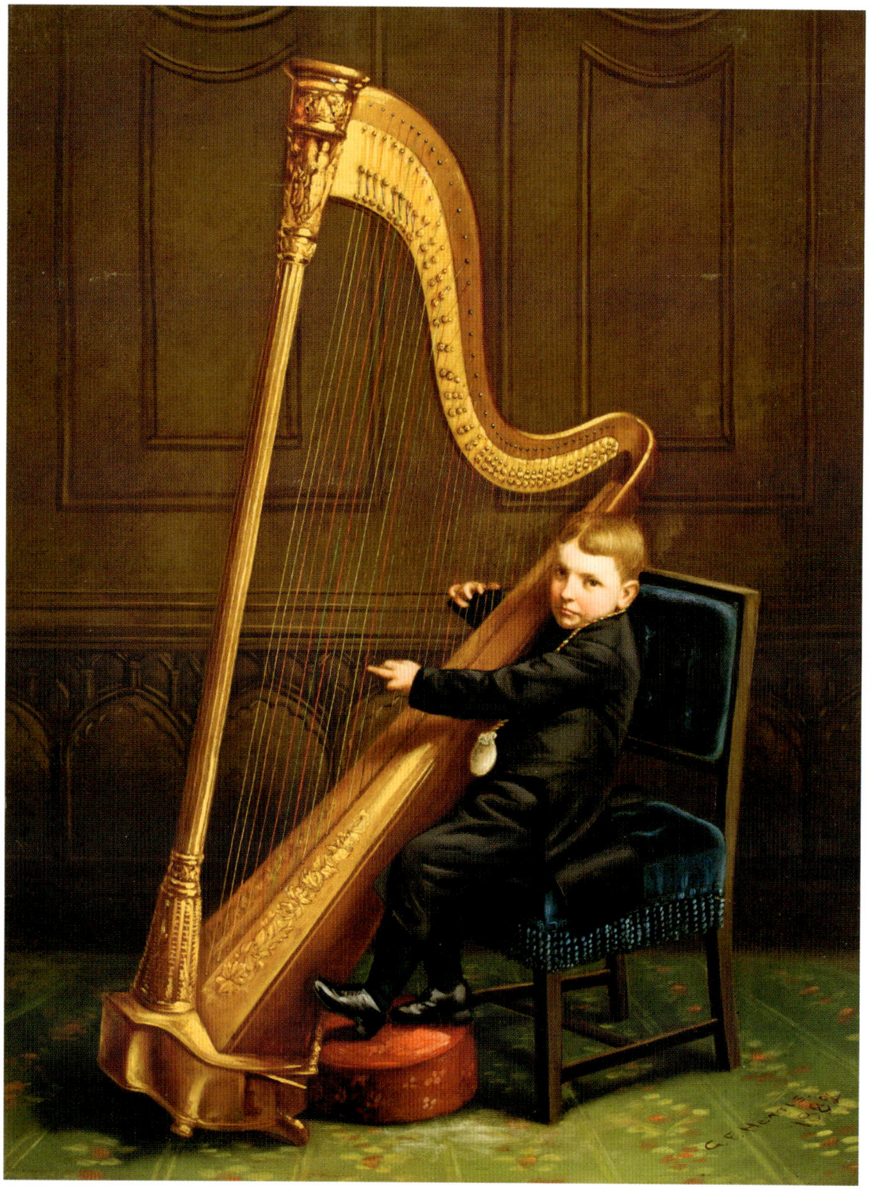

224. George Frederick Harris, *Boy with a Harp*, 1882, oil, 92x71

The Merthyr show, like the even bigger art and industry exhibition that followed a year later in Cardiff, drew large crowds, but it is difficult to tell in what ways the working people who attended were affected, if at all, by the promoters' aspirations to widen the horizons and improve the taste of their benighted social inferiors. At Ruthin, in 1868, the middle classes had been insulated from contact with the *hoi polloi* by a differential in admission prices between morning and afternoon. Contemporary comment on the Cardiff exhibition demonstrated the continuing perception of the relationship between art and society through a lens of class consciousness:

> A tide of excursionists swept me the other day into the exhibition ...
>
> The decorated walls become of secondary interest; you are wedged between stout humanities, hustled, pushed, have your corns trodden upon, until, getting into a little haven, you can console yourself by sketching the living sea that throngs by. No demure utterances, no amateurish comments, no looking-through one's hands, or inclining the head to an horizontal position, just as it is conventional to do at the Royal Academy; but the hearty, unconventional expression of the collier and his sweetheart, of the tin-plate worker, of the farmer, of the dock labourer, and the class generally whose avocations are 'the drawing of water and the hewing of wood'.[87]

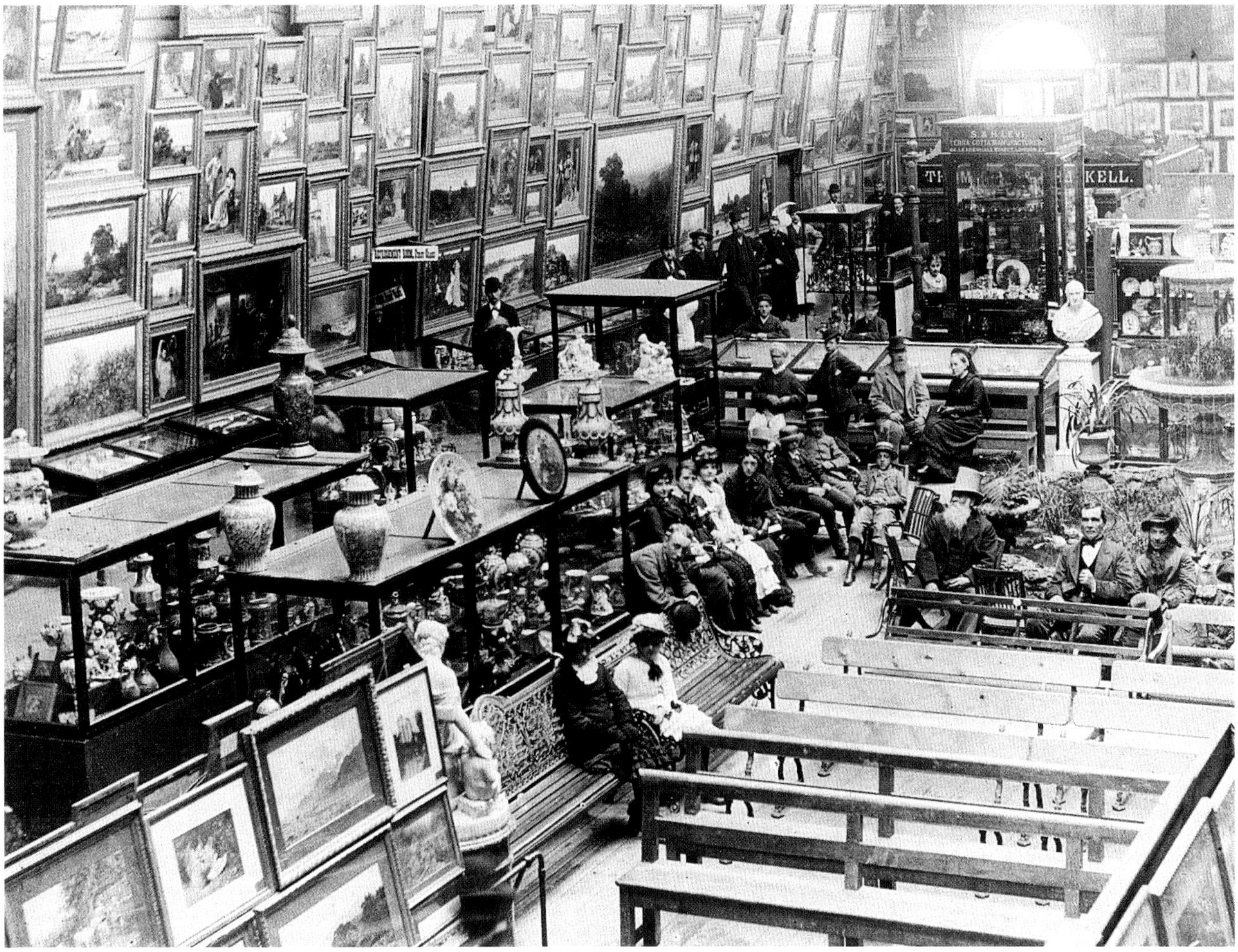

Fed by economic growth, a sense of confidence returned to Welsh intellectual life in the 1880s. As the Cardiff exhibition drew to its close, a group of Betws painters met together at the Llandudno Junction Hotel, with the aspiration to create a Welsh academy of art. The railway location was convenient because, remarkably, three of the promoters lived in Manchester. Only William Lawrence Banks considered himself Welsh, though he too had been born over the border, at Kington.[88] Nevertheless, their aspirations were genuinely national:

> The Royal Academy and other institutions of a similar character have long been established in England; the Royal Hibernian Academy in Ireland, the Scottish Academy in Scotland, but Wales has hitherto felt the want of a kindred society of its own.
>
> It has therefore been resolved to establish 'The Cambrian Academy of Art' in the hope that such an institution will give impetus to the further development of Art in the Principality.[89]

225. *Cardiff Fine Art and Industrial Exhibition*, 1881

87 *Western Mail*, 16 September 1881, p. 4.

88 Banks had settled at Llanfairpwll in Anglesey from where he had competed in various eisteddfod competitions. In 1874, at Bangor, he had been awarded a prize by the adjudicator, the Caernarfon painter J.J. Dodd.

89 NLW Royal Cambrian Academy (RCA) Art Records, Minute Books, 26 November 1881.

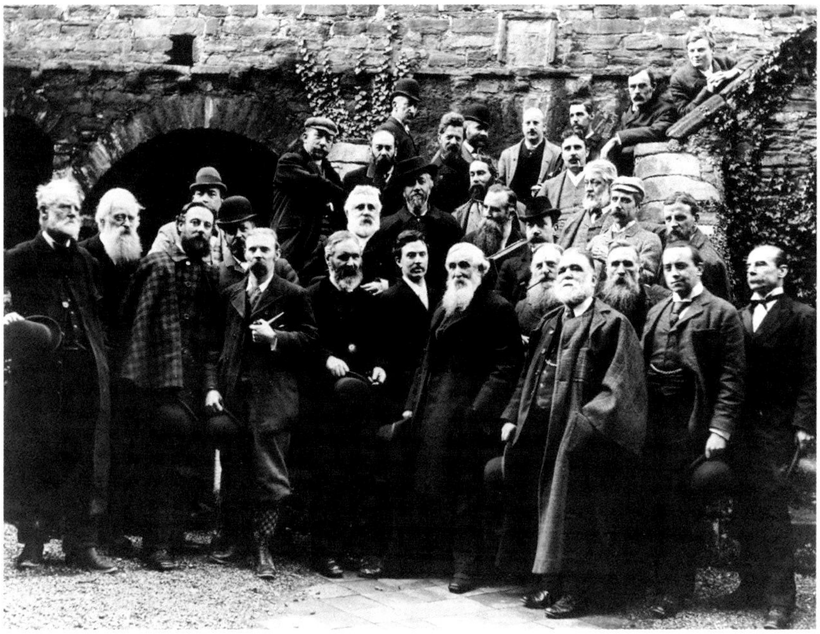

Membership was to be limited to fifty. An application from Carrie Walker provided a troublesome distraction, since the committee had 'not yet come to any determination as to the admission of Ladies'.[90] Shortly afterwards they did indeed determine to exclude women painters – a decision that would have radical consequences. Apart from this minor irritation, matters proceeded well. Patrons, including Cornwallis West, were forthcoming, and the Welsh connections of Mr Gladstone, the Prime Minister, seem to have facilitated the granting of royal patronage.

226. *Royal Cambrian Academicians at Plas Mawr*, Conwy, *c.*1897. Front row, fourth from left, George Harrison; sixth from left, Henry Clarence Whaite

opposite
227. Joseph P. Knight, *Lifting Mist*, 1883, oil, 137.5x91.8

The Academy organised its first exhibition, in less than satisfactory rooms over a 'photographer's establishment' in Llandudno. Reaction in England was predictably uncomplimentary, but response in the Welsh language press was more nuanced. Notwithstanding the matrimonial ties established by several of the expatriate Betws-y-Coed painters, interaction with Welsh-born artists had remained remarkably limited. However, writing in *Y Genedl Gymreig*, O.E. Hughes, 'Crafnant', indicated the potential of the Academy to further indigenous Welsh practice. Crafnant concentrated his critical attention on Clarence Whaite, whom he knew personally, and the more recently arrived Joseph Knight, a successful English painter. Knight's distinctive and somewhat melancholic landscapes did not please all the critics, but his professional prosperity enabled him to build a substantial house and studio on the river bank above the Waterloo Bridge in Betws. Crafnant also knew the young Welsh painter Samuel Maurice Jones, the earliest Welsh-born applicant to join the Academy, who had been granted associate membership in 1882. Jones was fired with ambition for Welsh painting and saw the Academy as a vehicle for its promotion. In the summer of 1882, he floated the idea that the Academy, if it were to be truly national, must extend its activities to the south of Wales.[91] By the end of the year, the Council of the Academy had agreed to enter discussions with the civic authorities in Cardiff and Swansea, and in the spring of 1883 it was resolved that Cardiff become 'the head quarters of the Academy and that the permanent gallery and schools be established and the annual exhibition held there.'[92] This far-sighted initiative created a lasting personal bond between some of the painters in the north and south, in particular between T.H.Thomas and Clarence Whaite.

90 Ibid., 4 February 1882.

91 *Y Genedl Gymreig*, 12 July 1882.

92 NLW RCA Art Records, Minute Books, 21 April 1883.

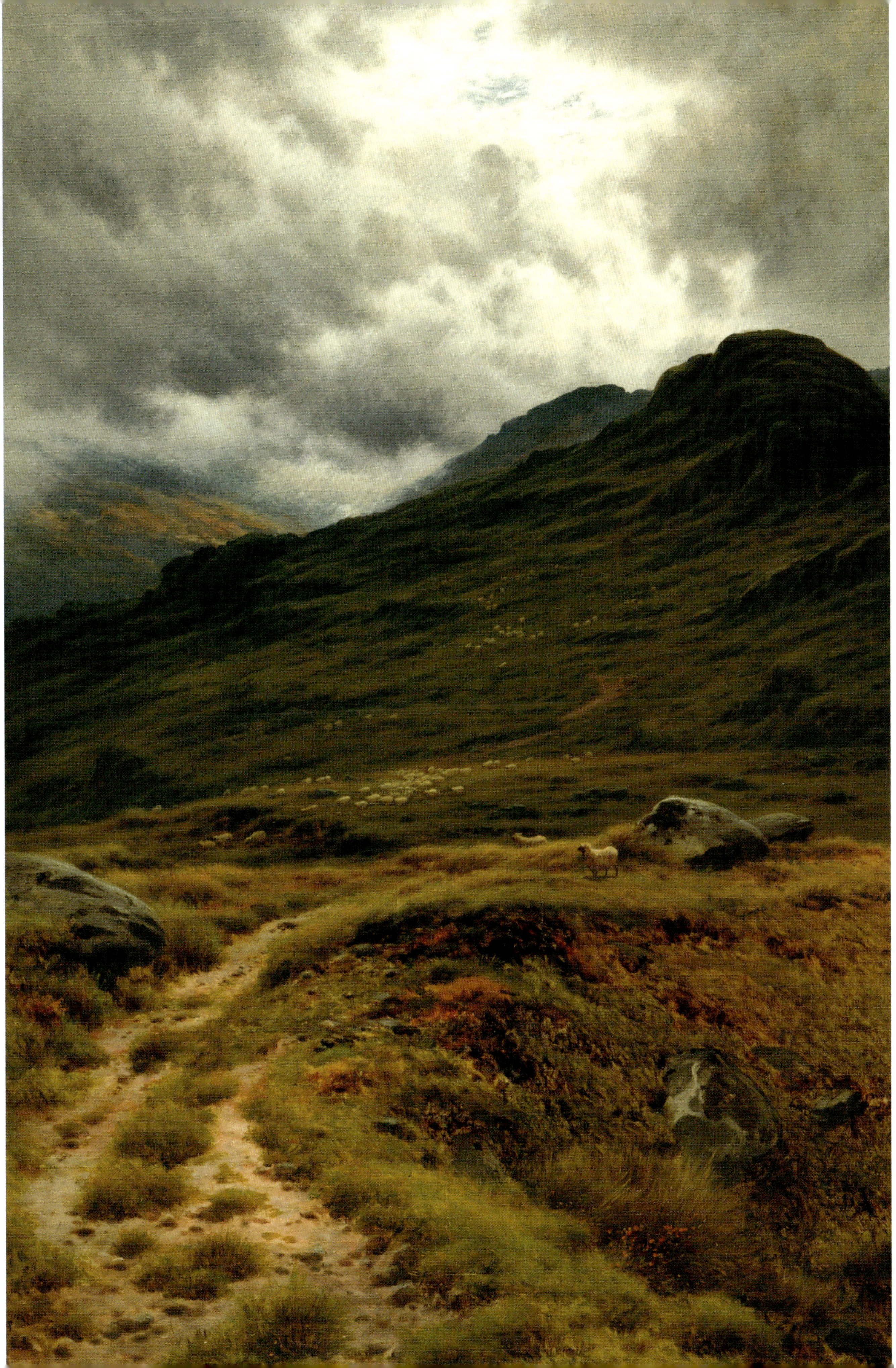

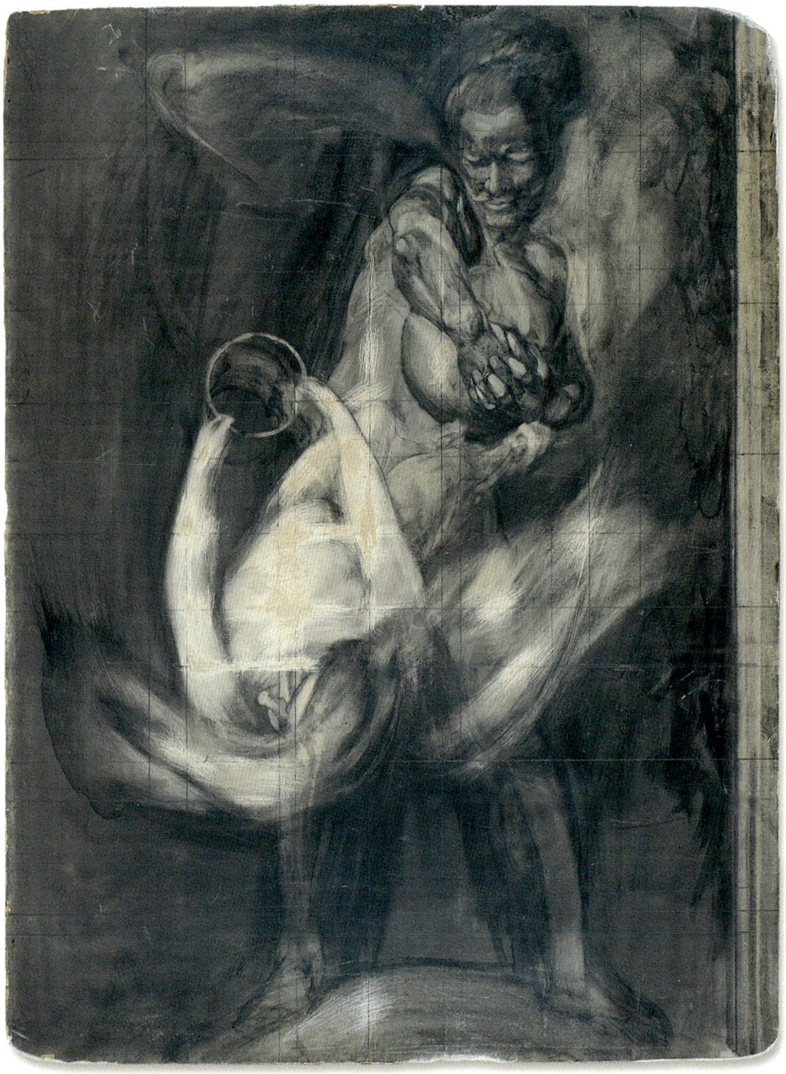

T.H. Thomas was deeply involved at this time in organising a large exhibition for the National Eisteddfod in Cardiff. Unlike the historical exhibitions organised by Cornwallis West, it showed new work ranging over a wide spectrum of arts and crafts. Thomas was able to attract commercial sponsorship and a major figure from the London art world, Lawrence Alma-Tadema, as adjudicator in the painting competition. Among the competitors who attracted his attention was a part-time student at the Cardiff School of Art, Edgar Herbert Thomas. Through the patronage of the Marquess of Bute, the eisteddfod President for the year, Thomas was enabled to study with Alma-Tadema and subsequently in Antwerp and in Paris. The winner in the sculpture section was Milo ap Griffith who, along with the Cardiff-born painter Barnett Samuel Marks, was invited to address the Cymmrodorion Society. The sculptor was less than complimentary on the state of art in Wales, suggesting that a lack of patronage might well render futile any efforts made by the nascent Academy to train young painters. As part of a programme to improve matters he appealed for the establishment of a national gallery:

228. Edgar Herbert Thomas, *Study for 'The Birth of Light'*, 1899, pencil and watercolour, 62.2x47.1

> If we intend the arts to be a success here in Wales, something should be done, besides establishing institutions for teaching, to collect the works of art of our living artists into a gallery, and if we can, make it into a national one.[93]

Nevertheless, enthused by the success of the 1883 exhibition, the promoters of the Academy idea proceeded to organise fund raising exhibitions in 1884 and 1885. At the outset, their optimism was expressed by the Mayor of Cardiff, for whom the objective was

> to give the toiling thousands of our race the opportunities of coming in contact with the productions of the best painters and artists – a privilege now enjoyed by the few who can afford to travel long distances in order to gratify their taste and fancy ... I believe in the elevating power of true art.[94]

93 *Western Mail* 10 August 1883, p. 4.

94 *Western Mail*, 15 February 1884, p. 5.

Sadly, both exhibitions were financial failures and over the next few years, largely scuppered by Cardiff parochialism, the Academy scheme failed. Under the presidency of Clarence Whaite, the members retired to a quiet life at Plas Mawr in Conwy, though individuals continued to engage with the painters in the south, especially through the South Wales Art Society, founded by T.H. Thomas, Edwin Seward and their associates, who held their first exhibition in 1888.

In its inconsistent and erratic way, periodically the National Eisteddfod continued to engage the public in visual culture through the efforts of highly motivated individuals. The most unlikely of these was the German-born artist and craftsman Hubert Herkomer. It was the painter Charles Mansel Lewis of Stradey Castle, Llanelli, who introduced Herkomer to Wales. In 1872 he had become a crucial early patron of the Bavarian, and they would remain lifelong friends. However, it was at the behest of Cornwallis West that Herkomer first appeared on the eisteddfod stage, a decade later at Denbigh. It appears that his interest in the area at this time was not entirely motivated by a devotion to the progress of national art, since in 1873 he married Lulu Griffiths of Ruthin, following whose premature demise he married her sister.[95] His relationship with Mansel Lewis continued to flourish and he was persuaded in 1895 to act as adjudicator at the ambitious Llanelli eisteddfod art competition, organised by the Welsh painter. Herkomer was by this time a major force in English art, and so the devastating criticism that he expressed from the stage – the competition was 'next to a disaster' – caused more than a ripple of concern.[96] Herkomer continued his engagement with the eisteddfod at Llandudno in 1896. He repeated his criticism, but at the same time demonstrated a positive commitment to the cause. He had become fascinated

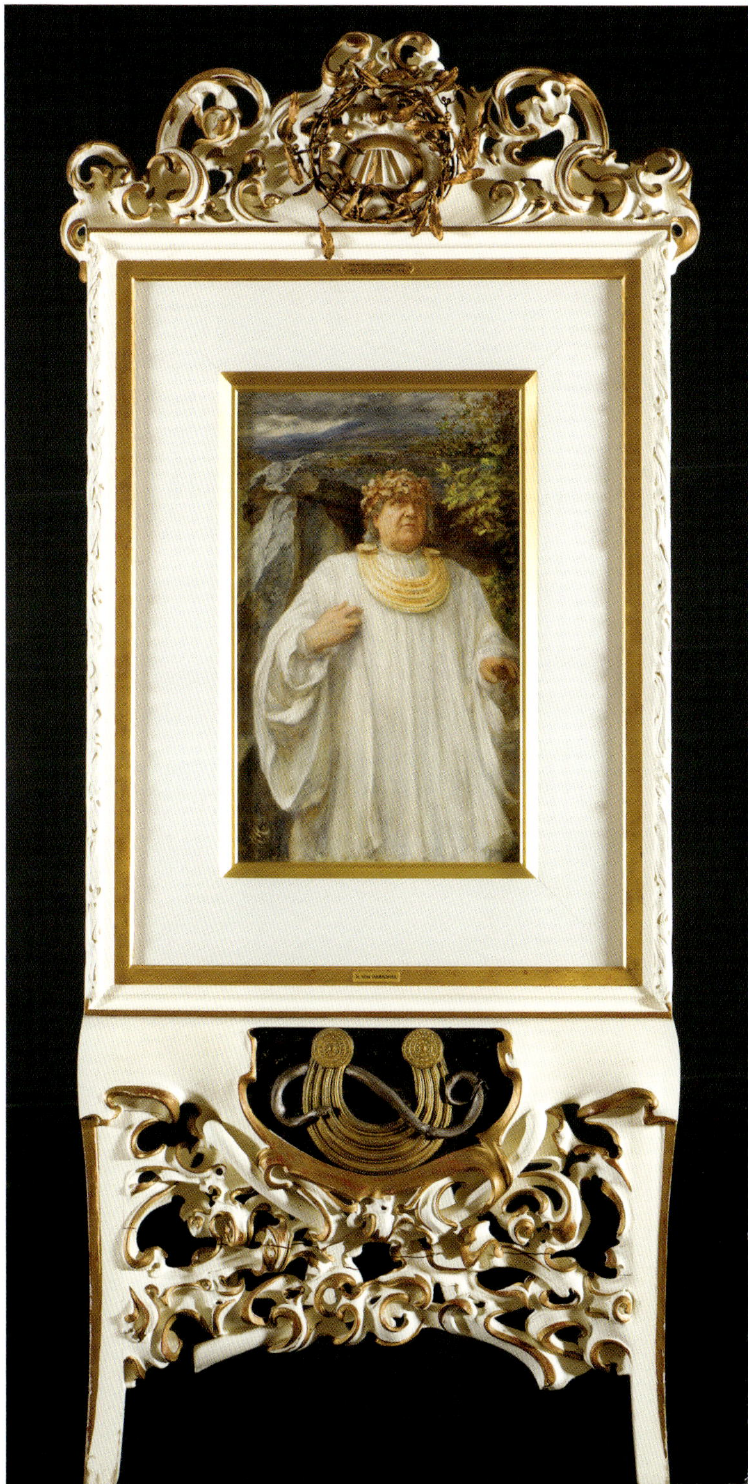

229. Hubert Herkomer, *Hwfa Môn*, frame with Gorsedd symbols, 1896, mixed media

95 Herkomer's matrimonial progress was complicated by the fact that a second marriage to his first wife's sister would have been illegal. In order to surmount this difficulty, he reclaimed his German citizenship.

96 *Carnarvon and Denbigh Herald*, 2 August 1895, p. 8. There were several public responses to Herkomer, among the most considered of which was that published in *Young Wales*, 1 (September, 1895), pp. 204–6 .

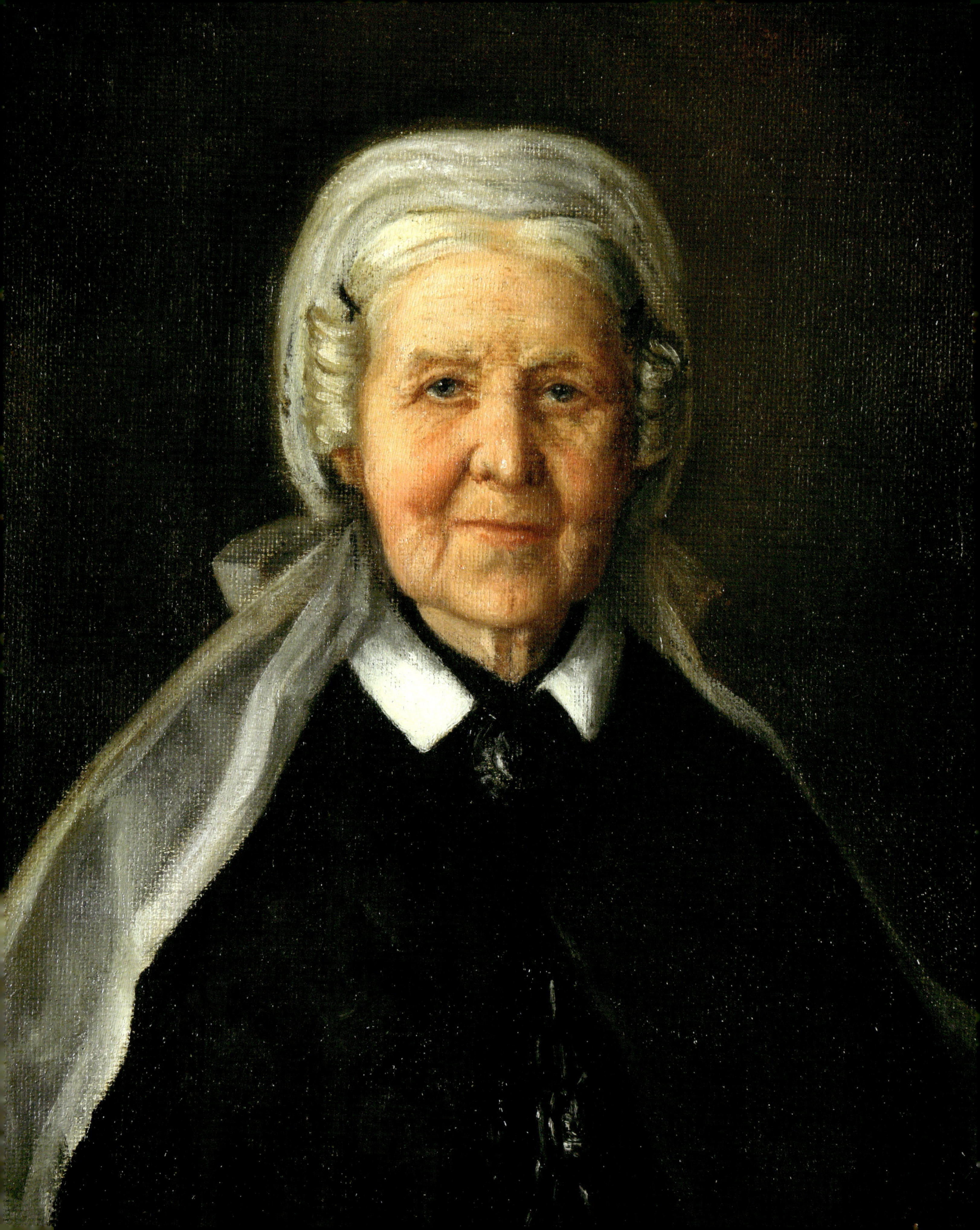

left
230. Gwenny Griffiths,
Mrs Octavia Howell, Founder of the Swansea Orphan Home,
oil, *c.*1900, 69.2x57

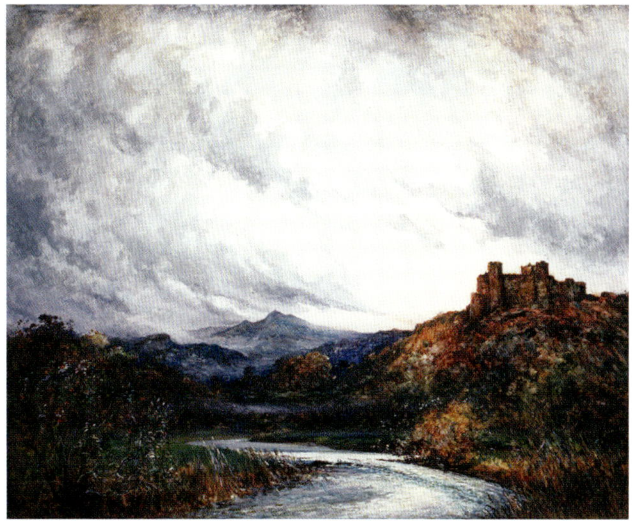

231. Clara Knight, *Harlech Castle*, watercolour, 78.5x99

with the faux-Celtic ritual of the Gorsedd, which centred on the charismatic figure of the Archdruid, Hwfa Môn, whom he drew first in 1895. Herkomer redesigned his robes and created the gold torque and tiara in which he appeared the following year, and in which he was painted, standing before a cromlech.[97]

The location of the 1896 National Eisteddfod at Llandudno had inevitably involved the Mostyn family, the dominant landowners in the area, whose collection of paintings, though unknown to the public, was rivalled in Wales only by that of Sir Watkin Williams-Wynn.[98] Lady Augusta Mostyn had become actively involved in contemporary art the previous year as patron of the Gwynedd Ladies Art Society, established in the face of the continuing refusal of the Royal Cambrian Academy to admit women painters. The situation persisted despite the fact that two of the many women who worked in the Betws-y-Coed area were Lily Whaite and Clara Knight, daughters of prominent academicians.[99] Augusta Mostyn chaired a special women's committee at the eisteddfod and subsequently, in a remarkable act of patronage, funded the building of a permanent art gallery on the site of the eisteddfod pavilion. The Mostyn Art Gallery was opened in 1902 for the explicit purpose of showing the work of women artists, and appears to have been the first gallery in Europe built with that intention. Sadly, the initiative did not expand to a national scale. The most successful young Welsh woman painter of the period, R. Gwenny Griffiths was showing her work with the Women's International Art Club in London by 1908, but she did not exhibit at the Mostyn Gallery.[100]

In the meantime, the ideas and energies of the Cardiff group of artists and patrons, frustrated by the loss of the Academy project, were redirected into the development of the Cardiff Museum and towards the creation of a national museum that would incorporate a collection of visual culture.[101] The twenty-year campaign to achieve that end proved no less contentious than its predecessor. In 1901, exasperated by arguments about the location and scope of the museum, T.H. Thomas wrote that

97 T.H. Thomas had written to Herkomer in 1895 on the subject, but in his reply the latter stated that work had already commenced on his own initiative and that of Mansel Lewis, 'bearing all the expenses together'. NLW MS 17345C, item 20, Herkomer to Thomas, 19 August 1895.

98 Though the Wynn collection had been severely reduced by the fire that swept through Wynnstay in 1858.

99 Joseph Knight, Clara's father, adjudicated in the painting competition at Llandudno.

100 Griffiths trained under Alphonse Legros, Slade Professor of Art at University College, and at the Académie Julian in Paris, before developing her career mainly as a portrait painter, based in London. See Ronald Austin and Ellie Dawkins, 'Miss R. Gwenny Griffiths 1867–1953' in *Swansea History Journal/Minerva*, 21 (2013-14), pp. 56–9.

101 The failure of the Cardiff scheme is described in detail in Lord, *Clarence Whaite and the Welsh Art World*, pp. 114–137.

> Probably no Welshman would disagree with the statement that the present position of the question of a national museum for Wales is a disgrace to our country ... Nothing prevents Wales obtaining a national museum within a very measurable period except Wales herself.[102]

The museum was finally granted its charter in 1907. Edwin Seward, who had campaigned tirelessly alongside Thomas for its establishment, and who had prepared the original drawings for a building in Cathays Park, was soon eased aside in favour of London architects by the body set up to realise the scheme, the Council of the National Museum of Wales.[103]

Notwithstanding the frustration felt at the time by Seward and his friends, the arguments surrounding both the museum project and the Academy, and also the question of standards at the National Eisteddfod, should not be viewed in an entirely negative light. They indicated that visual culture was on the public agenda and they provided a focus for an expanding range of Welsh artists, some working at home and others, like B.S. Marks and Charles Jones, developing their careers primarily elsewhere. In a letter to a friend, Christopher Williams from Maesteg, then training as a painter in London, observed that 'Wales seems to be taking great interest in Art now...'[104] His own work and that of his contemporaries increasingly became the subject of critical attention in the periodical press, especially in the Welsh language. Writing about Welsh art was facilitated by the success of the periodical *Cymru*, founded by Owen Morgan Edwards in 1891. While a student at Oxford, Edwards and his contemporary T. E. Ellis had been impressed by the lectures of John Ruskin, and had also heard William Morris speak. As editor, Edwards provided space in *Cymru* for the discussion of art, and in the period leading up to the Great War, Thomas Matthews of Llandybïe emerged as a sophisticated critic of romantic temperament and nationalist convictions who was able to add a new dimension to an increasingly assertive Welsh art world. Also at this time, the first attempt was undertaken to locate that contemporary world in a historical context. *Welsh Painters, Engravers and Sculptors* was compiled by T. Mardy Rees, though it drew on the researches of a wider circle of art enthusiasts. Guided by current notions of ethnicity, the selection of artists was determined by Welsh birth or ancestry, leading to extensive discussion of figures such as Burne-Jones and G.F.Watts, who 'himself confessed that he was of Welsh extraction'. Contemporary painters, including Clarence Whaite, not born in Wales, were omitted however great their contribution to the culture. Nevertheless, the researches of T.H. Thomas and T.C. Evans (Cadrawd) were the first step towards the reclamation from obscurity of important figures, such as Thomas Jones of Pencerrig and Hugh Hughes.

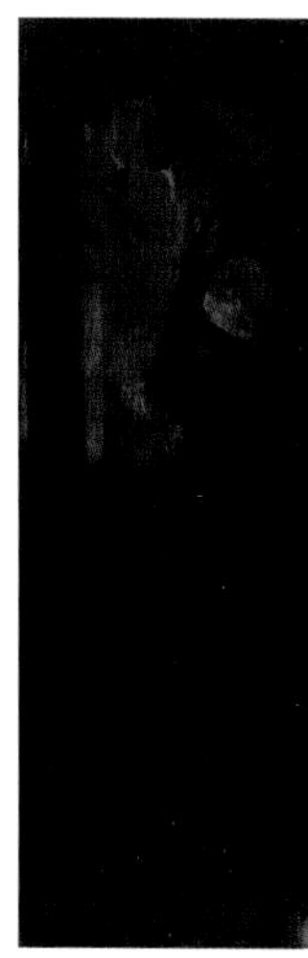

102 *Western Mail*, 20 August 1901, p. 4.

103 The Museum building was designed by Arnold Dunbar Smith and Cecil Claude Brewer. Their archive, which includes the National Museum drawings, is held by the University of Texas in Austin. Seward's exclusion was noted by T.H. Thomas, 'Art in Wales', in T. Stephens (ed.), *Wales To-day and To-morrow. 80 Writers 80 Portraits* (Cardiff, 1907), p. 357.

104 Christopher Williams to Sarah Parry Jones, 31 March 1895, quoted in Robert Meyrick, *Christopher Williams '... an artist and nothing else'* (Aberystwyth, 2012), p. 12.

105 NLW Dr Owen Thomas Papers, 11a, Josiah Thomas to John Ogwen Jones, 10–14 June 1852.

The Welsh art world that emerged in the 1880s was dominated by manifestations in various forms of the nationalist spirit that also reached its political apogee in that decade, under the leadership of T.E. Ellis. Nationalist intellectuals were enthused by the example of political and cultural movements elsewhere, and in particular *La Giovine Italia*, whose activities had disturbed Gibson's Roman idyll in mid-century. As early as 1852, 'Young Italy' had suggested 'Young Wales' – *Cymru Fydd* – as the title for an equivalent movement in Wales.[105] In the same way, the products of Welsh artists would come to reflect those of painters and sculptors in other European nations similarly excited by national sentiment. Images of national leaders, of historical and mythological subjects, and more obliquely of landscape as the home of an idealised folk culture that embodied a national ethos, combined to form a new mainstream of Welsh imagery.

In parallel with the romantic nationalism of the exponents of high art forms, there developed at the same time a body of visual documentation of a society that in reality was far from the ideal, in either its industrial or rural manifestations. During the second half of the nineteenth century there had emerged in England a body of painting that appealed to the Victorian social conscience, if it was not simply to vacuous sentiment. A notable Welsh contributor to the genre had been B.S. Marks. In 1868, the year after he left Wales, he exhibited at the Royal Academy *A Reminiscence of a Court Quarter Sessions*, in which the image of a bemused child summonsed in court, presumably for theft, expressed his increasing engagement with social questions relating to children. In the two panels of *Saved from the Streets*, Marks presented images of homeless boys sent from London

232. Barnett Samuel Marks, *Saved from the Streets: Portraits of Boys on Board the 'Chichester' Training Ship: In Deep Mire Where there is No Standing*, and *Escape as a Bird out of the Snare of the Fowler*, 1870, oil, 38x72.3

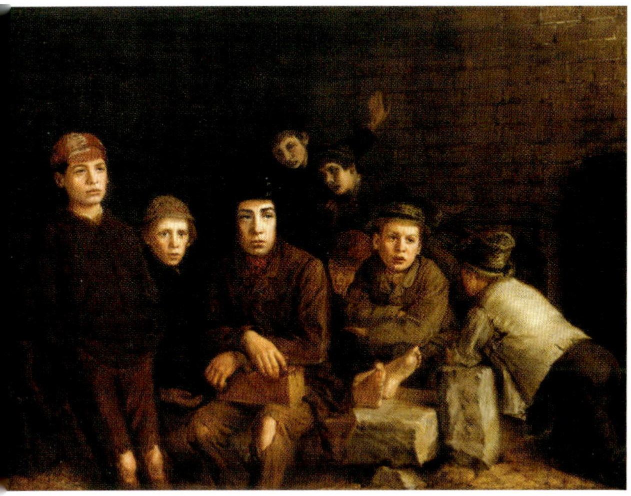

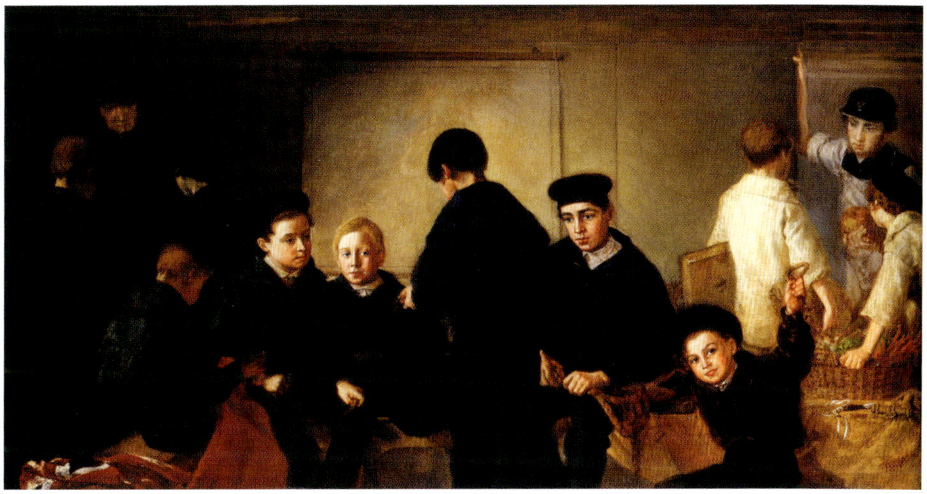

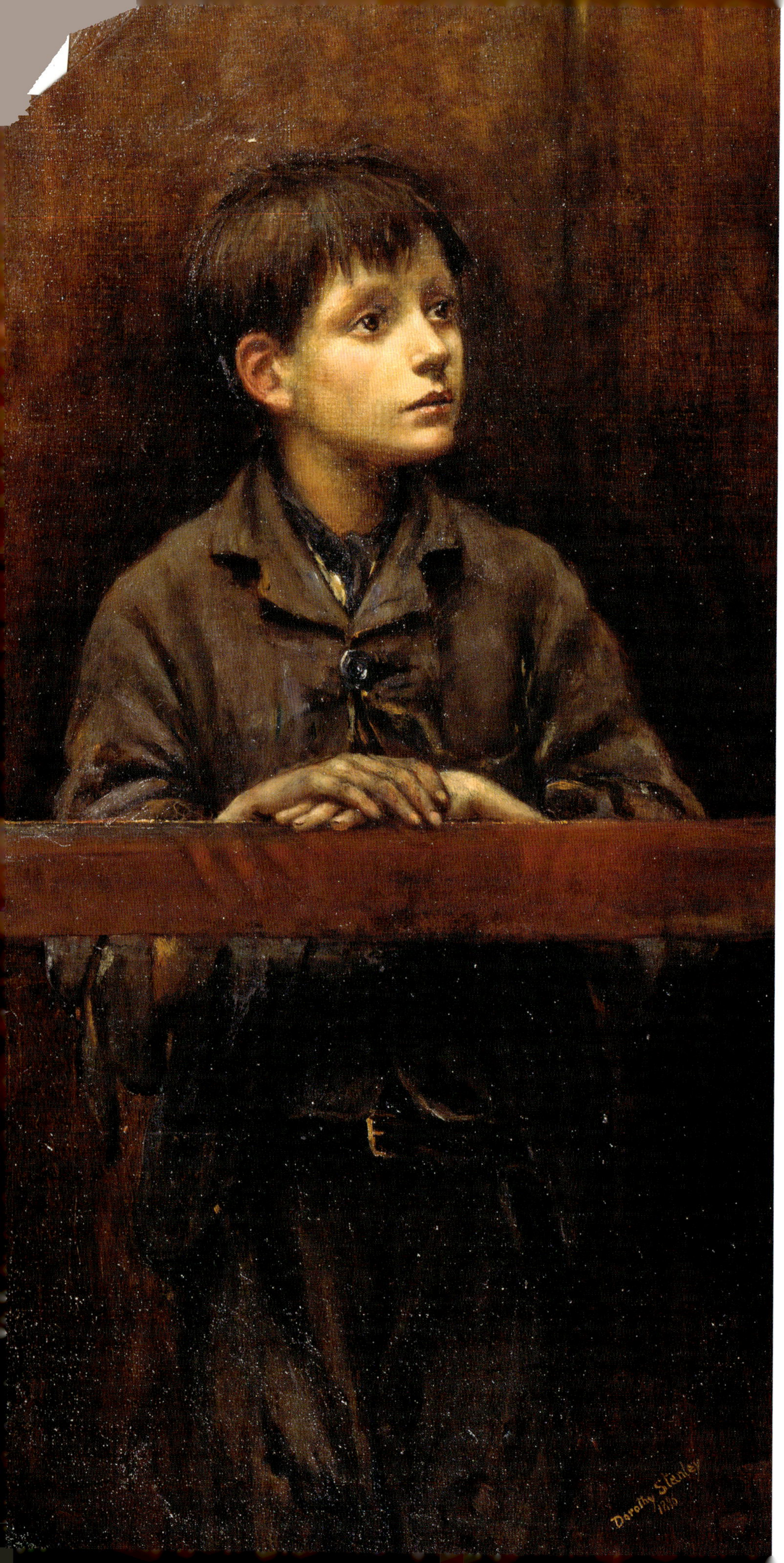

233. Dorothy Tennant, *His First Offence*, 1896, oil, 62.9x34.3

refuges to the former naval vessel, the Chichester, where they were trained in maritime skills. Dorothy Tennant, the daughter of a south Wales industrialist, also established a reputation based on her paintings and drawings of London street children. Tennant trained at the Slade School of Art, and in 1896, her picture, *His First Offence*, which repeated the subject painted by Marks, nearly thirty years earlier, was bought by Sir Henry Tate.[106] In 1911, Christopher Williams contributed his painting *Why?* to the genre. It depicted 'the outcasts of society – the poor folk who sleep on Thames Embankment at night time.'[107] Yet, remarkably, none of these academically trained Welsh painters engaged in their art with questions of social deprivation at home. It was left to T.H. Thomas, who emerged from the tradition of the illustrator, to break new ground by drawing and painting the working people of Welsh urban industrial society. The visual journalism in which Thomas worked had been pioneered by the *Illustrated London News*, established in 1842. The weekly newspaper printed pages of woodcut engravings of current

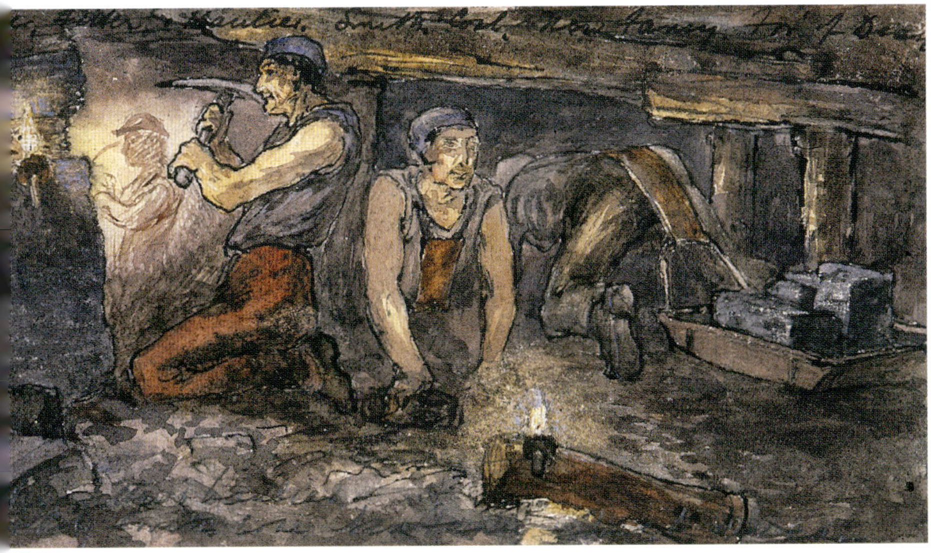

234. Thomas Henry Thomas,
Cutter, Fitter and Haulier Underground,
*c.*1875, watercolour, 8.8x16.3

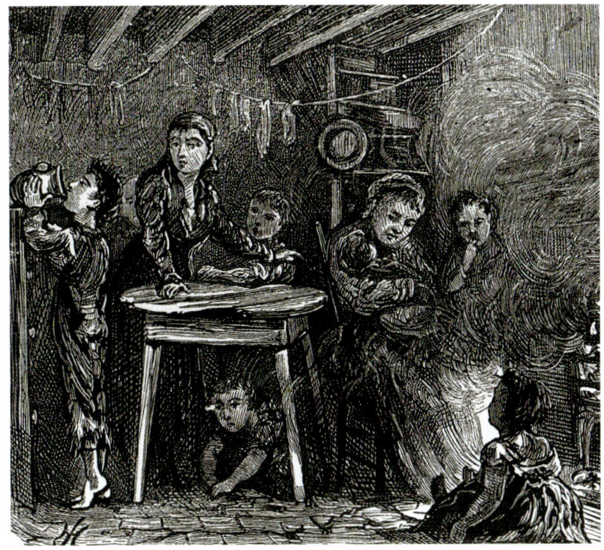

235. Herbert Johnson,
A Miner's Home in Gas Row, Dowlais,
1875, wood engraving, 9.9x11.1

affairs based on drawings made by reporter-artists and, later, by photographers. Attracted by accounts of the dire social consequences of strikes and lock-outs in 1873 and 1875, both the *Illustrated London News* and its rival *The Graphic* published striking images of the living conditions of working people in Merthyr. The sight of women and children scratching for waste coal on the tips particularly fascinated visiting illustrators. Herbert Johnson and his colleagues brought such scenes to the attention of a wide public. At about the time that Johnson's shocking images of Merthyr appeared in *The Graphic*, T.H. Thomas, who had also illustrated for the paper, became the first Welsh artist to paint underground in the mines.[108]

Visual images of accidents in the coalfield made a particular impact on the middle class readership of the illustrated newspapers. In 1877, events at the Tynewydd pit at Porth, in the Rhondda, attracted unprecedented attention not only throughout Britain but also in the United States over a ten day period, at the end of which a group of trapped miners was released. Visual documentation and melodrama became confused in reporting that reinforced, in the context of industrial society, the pious image of the common people of Wales:

> When the swarthy workman leaves his humble cottage after kissing his wife and children, and shoulders his pick and shovel for his spell of labour in the gloomy bowels of the earth, he knows not whether he shall ever again see their loved faces and the glorious golden sunlight, or whether his mangled and blackened corpse may not in a few hours be drawn up the shaft, and borne home to his bereaved widow and weeping babes. It is perhaps this awful sense of standing as it were in the immediate presence of Death, that makes the collier, especially the Welsh collier, so susceptible to the influence of religion, and so unswerving in his faith ...[109]

106 Dorothy Tennant became Lady Stanley on her marriage to the Welsh explorer H.M. Stanley. Her sister Eveleen, developed a career as a portrait photographer. See Peter Lord, *Winifred Coombe Tennant. A Life through Art* (Aberystwyth, 2007), pp. 15–20.

107 Originally titled 'Wealth and Waste'. Cardiff Central Library, MS Cardiff 1.194 (2–6), item 37, Christopher Williams to Cadrawd, 22 January 1911.

108 Yet, reflecting the unease with which his more academic colleagues regarded subject paintings from Wales that fed into current debates about the employment of women and children in heavy industry, even Thomas seems only once to have produced an exhibition work of this sort. *'Sackcloth and Ashes', Tip Girls Leaving Work, South Wales Coal District*, was shown at the Merthyr exhibition of 1880.

109 *The Graphic*, 27 April 1877, p. 386. For perceptions in Wales and beyond of the events at the Tynewydd pit, see Hywel Teifi Edwards, *Arwr Glew Erwau'r Glo: Delwedd y Glöwr yn Llenyddiaeth y Gymraeg 1850–1950* (Llandysul, 1994), and Ken Llewellyn, *Disaster at Tynewydd* (Cardiff, 1975).

Ten years later, T.H. Thomas would document in *The Graphic* an explosion at the Cwtch colliery, also in the Rhondda, for which his original drawings survive – an unusual circumstance, since it was the practice for originals to be dispatched to London immediately after they had been made for copying by the paper's engravers.

Thomas was a remarkable individual in many ways, but in particular as perhaps the only painter among his contemporaries whose images encompassed both the harsh realities of life for the common people of industrial Wales and the romantic optimism of the nationalist. In contrast with his images of the colliery explosion in the Rhondda, Thomas painted *John Elias Preaching at the Association at Bala*, which in 1892 was reproduced as one of the earliest coloured prints of a Welsh cultural subject for the mass market.[110] The image developed both the iconisation of Welsh spiritual leaders and the idea of the piety of the *gwerin Gymraeg* – the Welsh-speaking common people of upland Wales, that Cox's *Welsh Funeral* had promoted earlier. The idealisation of the *gwerin* became a cornerstone in the nation-building agenda of visual artists, often working in co-operation with writers. Samuel Maurice Jones illustrated essays written by O.M. Edwards about the homes of celebrated figures such as the hymn-writer William Williams of Pantycelyn, which reached a wide audience initially in the periodical *Cymru*, and then as a published collection. The title, *Cartrefi Cymru* ('The homes of Wales'), carried with it a suggestion that these places represented more than the dwellings of notable individuals, but also the source of national identity and ethos. T.H. Thomas was also responsible for the illustrations to the most overtly propagandist manifestation of the genre. *Echoes from the Welsh Hills*, written by the Baptist minister David Davies, was notable not only for the fact that it was published in English, but that it addressed the English people:

> My aim has been to illustrate in popular form the religious and social life of the Welsh people, their generous hospitality, ardent loyalty and patriotism, as well as the quaint humour, the poetic fancy, and rich pathos of their religious leaders.[111]

Alongside their landscapes, several artists at Betws-y-Coed, including Richard Bond and Frank Topham, had found a market for images of the common people but few Welsh-born painters seem to have interested themselves in the subject, and there was little continuity or development of tradition through teaching at Betws.[112] Hugh Hughes painted two pictures among coracle fishermen, probably in north Pembrokeshire, and it was also in the south that Carey Morris found the sitters for his striking image, *The Welsh Weavers*, painted in 1910. However, the picture owed as much to experience outside Wales as within. In 1902, Morris, then twenty years old, went to Newlyn in Cornwall to train with the English painters

opposite
236. Thomas Henry Thomas, *John Elias Preaching at the Association at Bala*, 1892, lithograph, 48x38.5

110 For his depiction of John Elias, T.H. Thomas had depended on the portraits made by Hugh Hughes and Hugh Jones. Surviving copies of the print suggest that it was distributed in the form of customised almanacs.

111 David Davies, *Echoes from the Welsh Hills* (London, 1883), Preface. The book proved a remarkable success, going through several printings and spawning a sequel. Thomas used his illustration to the chapter entitled 'The Association' as a prototype for his coloured print of John Elias preaching.

112 The attempts of the Royal Cambrian Academy to develop teaching at Conwy met with little success.

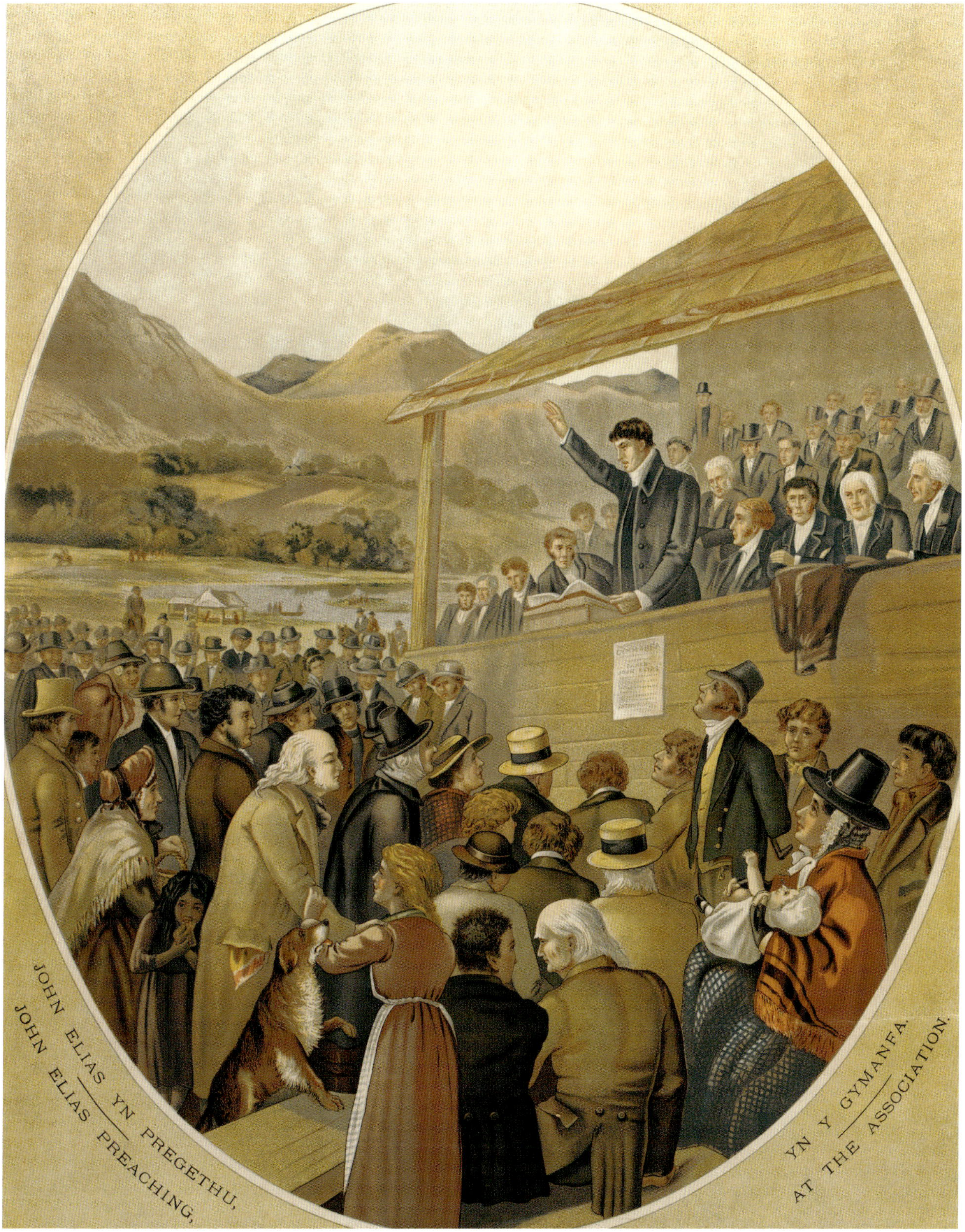
JOHN ELIAS YN PREGETHU,
YN Y GYMANFA.
JOHN ELIAS PREACHING,
AT THE ASSOCIATION.

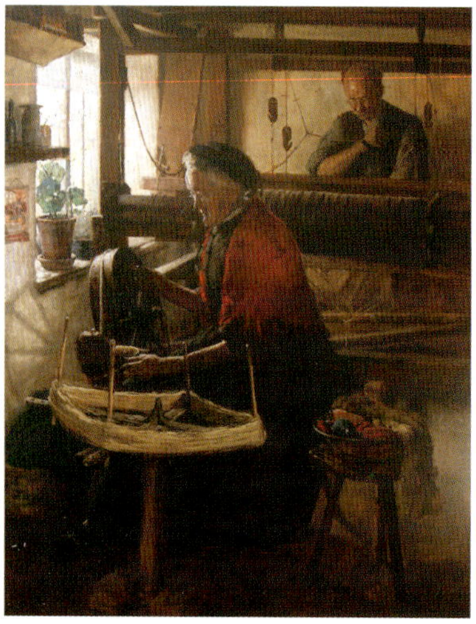

237. Carey Morris, *The Welsh Weavers*, 1910, oil, 142x112

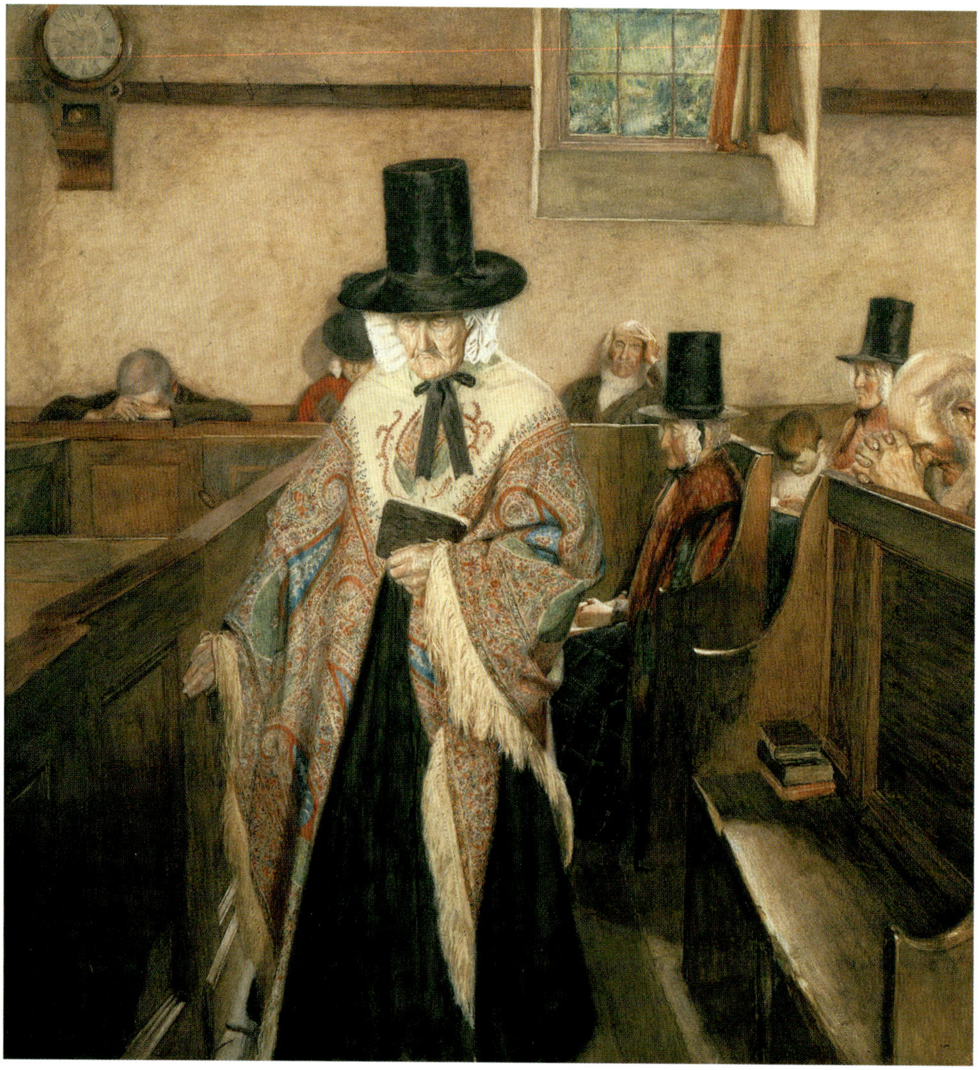

238. Sydney Curnow Vosper, *Salem*, 1908, watercolour, 70x72.5

Walter Langley and Stanhope Forbes. Langley's commitment to painting the common people had a great influence on him at this time. After his training, Morris continued to paint landscapes and portraits in Cornwall, but he also worked in Wales. He produced at least two large-scale pictures in the Newlyn manner, *A Welsh Fisherwoman*, painted in 1906 at Llangwm in Pembrokeshire, and *The Welsh Weavers*, which was painted near his home at Llandeilo. Both were exhibited at the Royal Academy, yet although *The Welsh Weavers* was reproduced in colour as a calendar image, it seems to have made little impact on the public.[113] The effect of a modest watercolour depicting chapel goers in Dyffryn Ardudwy, painted in the same period, was remarkably different. *Salem*, the work of the moderately successful English artist Sidney Curnow Vosper, became by far the most celebrated image ever created of the common people of Wales and, indeed, came to exemplify a particular

113 See Glyn Rhys, *A Celtic Canvas. The Life, Work and Times of Carey Morris, Artist, 1882–1968* (Talybont, 2013).

114 For the Salem myth, see Tal Williams, *Salem. Y Llun a'r Capel/ Painting and Chapel* (Barddas, 1991). A rival company to Lever Brothers, A. & F. Pears, had used Millais' picture *Bubbles* at an earlier date as a marketing tool.

perception of their character. In the wake of a nationwide religious revival in 1904, the picture itself and its associated mythology entered Welsh homes and folk memory. Coloured prints of *Salem* were given away as a marketing stratagem by the soap makers Lever Brothers, whose owner, Lord Leverhulme, had bought the picture at the Royal Academy. The simple building and the humility of the other worshipers contrasted suggestively with the richness of the shawl worn by the main character, Sian Owen. Though unintended by the painter, pious observers perceived a devilish face, concealed in the folds of the shawl, that they interpreted as a reminder of the sin of pride that she committed by dressing in an extravagant manner to attend chapel.[114]

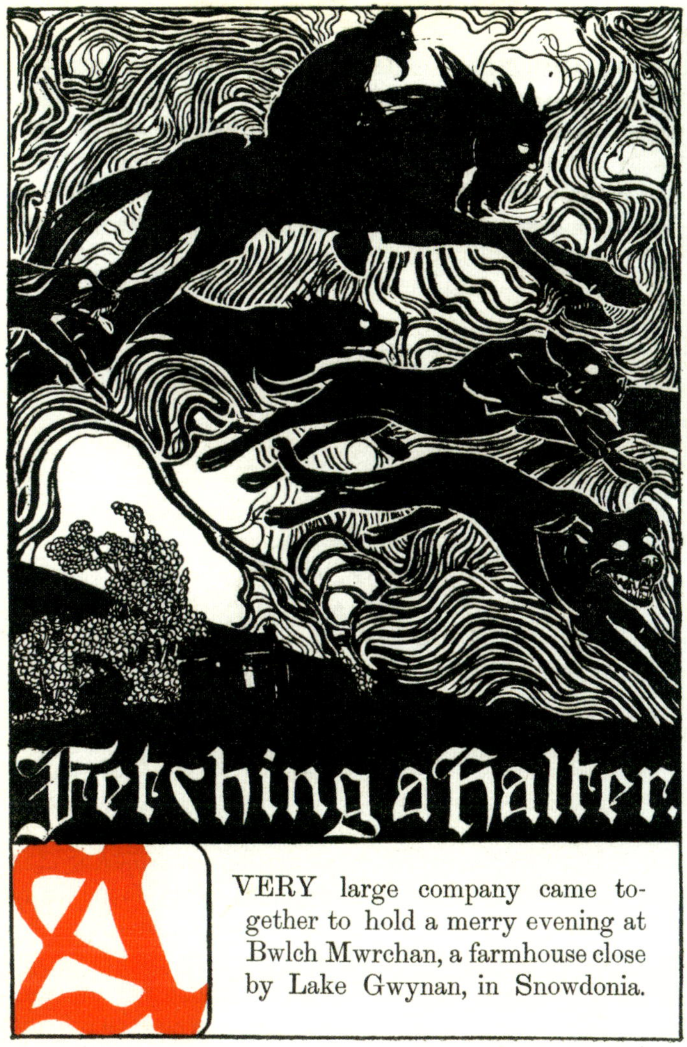

239. Willy Pogány, *Fetching a Halter*, from W. Jenkyn Thomas, *The Welsh Fairy Book*, 1907, 15.4x10.3

The development of ideas of 'the folk', that was central to national revivals throughout Europe, was facilitated by the development of academic research. Folk studies, pioneered as a discipline in Germany, were employed to legitimise romantic mythologies in Wales, as elsewhere. The reference made by David Davies in *Echoes from the Welsh Hills* to the 'poetic fancy' of his imagined common people alluded in particular to the persistence in rural areas of story traditions that had become the subject of study by folklorists. As early as 1879 T.H. Thomas had illustrated *Welsh Goblins*, a volume of retellings of traditional stories by his American friend Wirt Sikes. Thomas's illustrations were straightforward, but nearly thirty years later, in 1907, one of the most sophisticated publications of the period elevated the redaction of folk tales to a new level. Repeating the pattern exemplified by Tom Ellis, W. Jenkyn Thomas, author of *The Welsh Fairy Book*, was born near Llyn Tegid in Merionethshire, but 'rose' in the classic manner of the *gwerin* myth to be educated at Cambridge and return to teach at the university in Bangor. The elegant black and red illustrations of *The Welsh Fairy Book*, and its painted frontispiece, were made by the Hungarian Willy Pogány. The work did much to establish his reputation. He would become one of the most sought after illustrators and designers of his period, first in London and subsequently in New York.

In the same way, academic study of early Welsh history developed alongside more overtly politicised work. *Flamebearers of Welsh History*, by Owen Rhoscomyl, published in 1905, was the first popular history of Wales to be illustrated in colour. Following the militaristic inclinations of the author, the text emphasised not Welsh piety and loyalty, but themes of resistance to invasion, from the Celtic period to Owain Glyndŵr.[115] Again, T.H. Thomas was involved, though on this occasion not as illustrator but as the patron who had commissioned the pictures from the Merthyr painter Thomas Prytherch.[116]

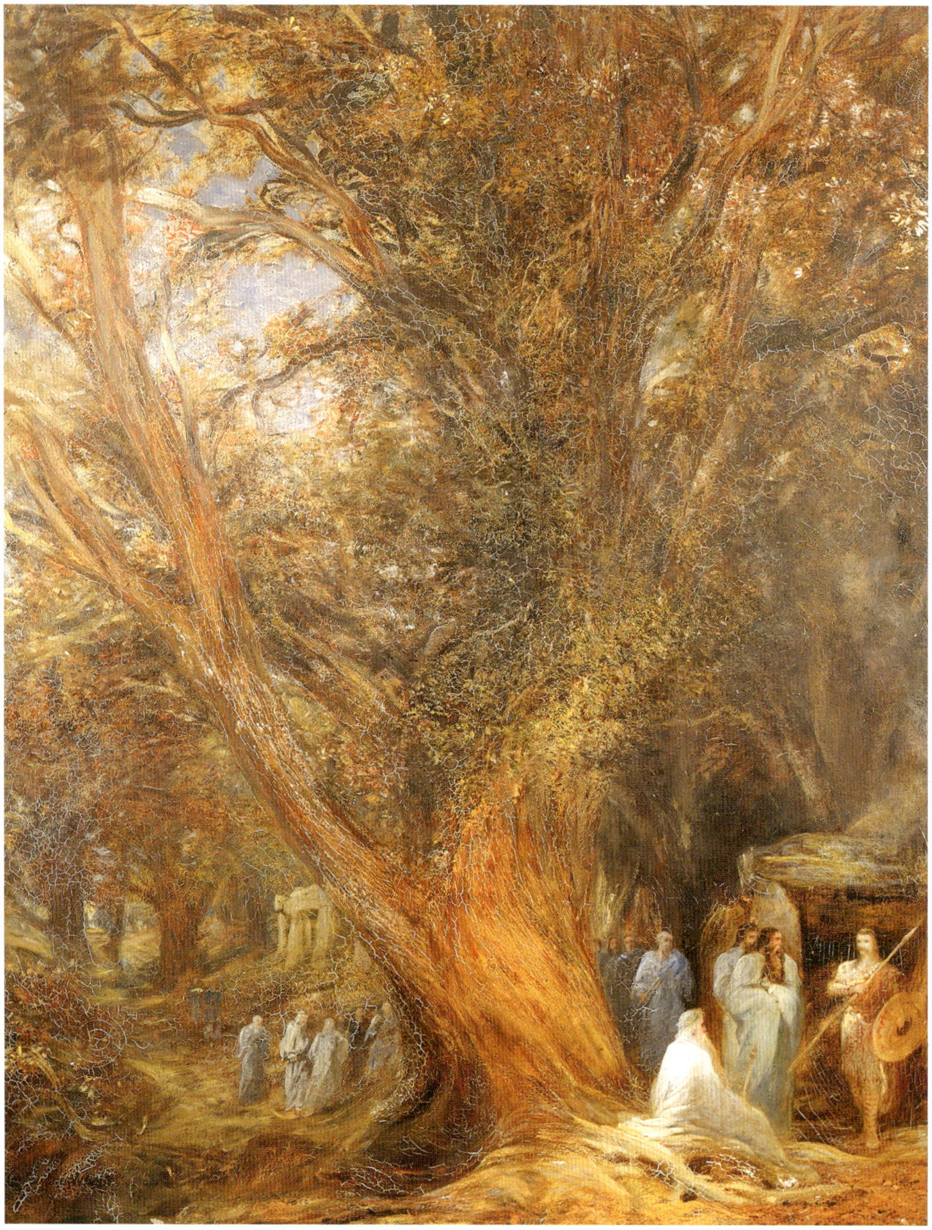

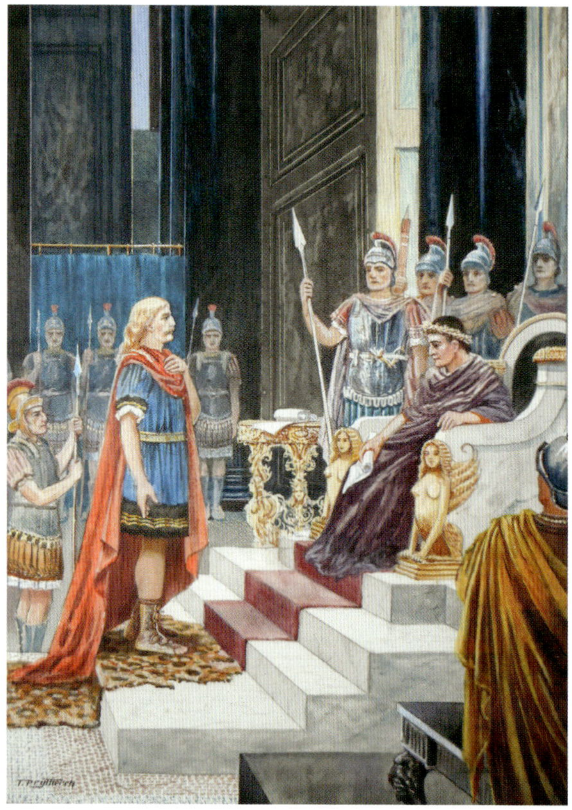

241. Thomas Prytherch, *Caradoc before the Roman Emperor*, 1905, watercolour, 30x22

240. Henry Clarence Whaite, *The Archdruid: A Throne in a Grove*, 1898, oil, 126x100

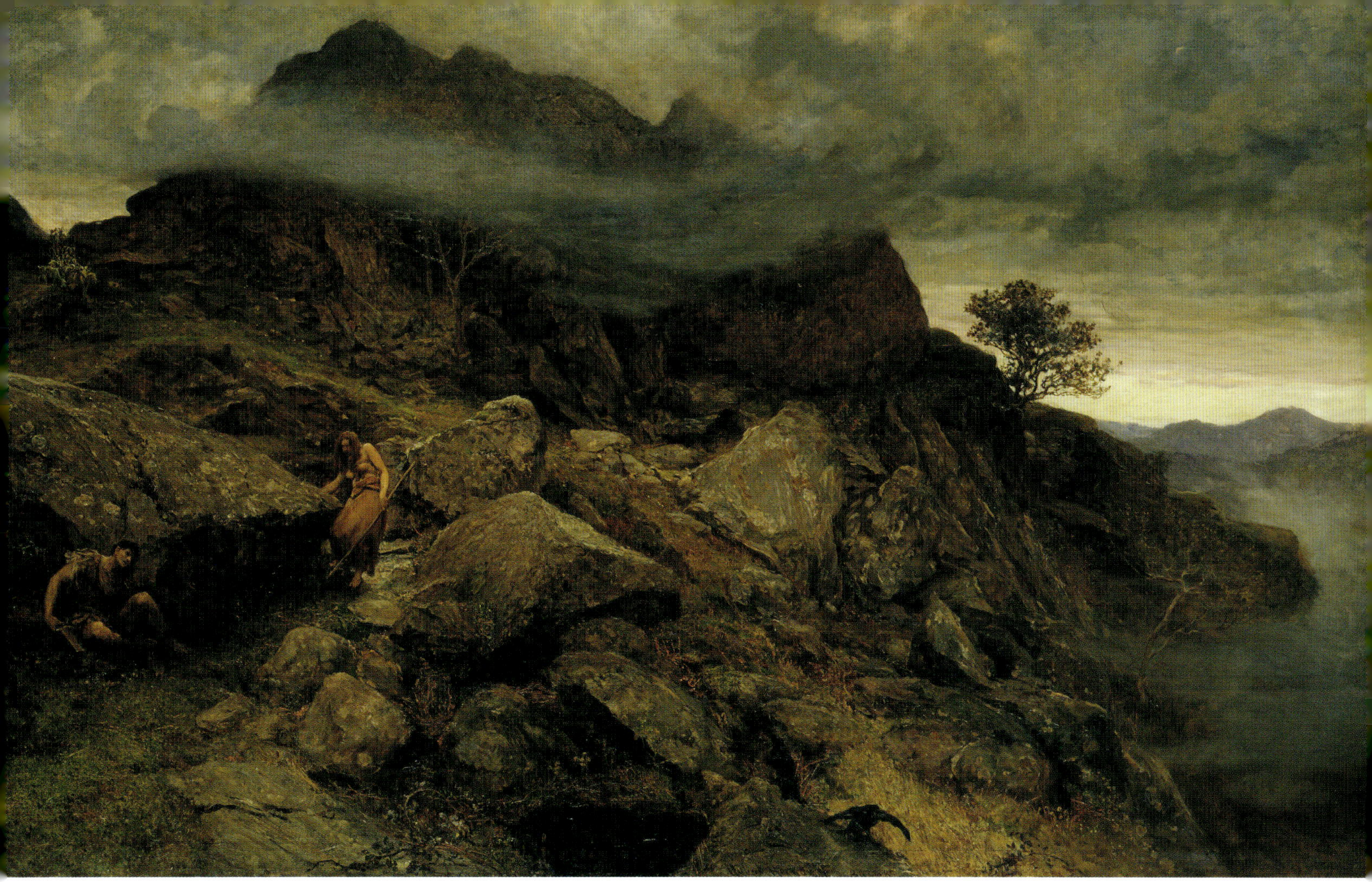

Among Prytherch's images, *Caradoc before the Roman Emperor* repeated one of the most popular of all Ancient Britain subjects.[117] In the last decade of the eighteenth century the London Welsh 'Caradogion Society' had named itself in the hero's honour and conducted its meetings beneath his portrait. Blake, Fuseli and Watts had all imaged Caradog, and at the opening exhibition of the Royal Cambrian Academy the Betws painter Edwin Arthur Norbury exhibited *Caractacus Leaving Britain a Prisoner.* Edward Elgar interpreted the theme musically in 1898, the same year in which Clarence Whaite returned to Celtic subject matter in his picture *The Archdruid: A Throne in a Grove*. It was inspired directly perhaps by the celebrity of Hwfa Môn, who had become Archdruid four years earlier, but the essentials of the image had changed little in the century and more that had elapsed since Wilson painted *Solitude*. Similarly, Herkomer's Celticist picture, *Found*, was set in the upland landscapes to the west of the Conwy valley where he painted in the company of Mansel Lewis.[118] By the turn of the century, a Celtic Revival expressed in visual culture, literature and music, was in full swing. Again, it combined sober developments in academic research with application to contemporary issues of national identity. The work of John Rhys, Professor of Celtic at Oxford University, provided a more legitimate foundation for the Celticism of the Cymru Fydd romantics than had been available to earlier enthusiasts,

242. Hubert Herkomer, *Found*, 1884, oil, 137.2x230.5

115 Academic research would lead to the publication in 1911 of J.E. Lloyd's *History of Wales to the Edwardian Conquest*.

116 T.H. Thomas, 'Art in Wales' in T. Stephens (ed.) *Wales Today and Tomorrow*, pp. 356–7. Thomas refers obliquely to the patronage of 'an earnest patriot' – almost certainly himself.

117 Owen Rhoscomyl, *Flame-bearers of Welsh History* (Merthyr Tydfil, 1905), facing p. 21. Prytherch's interpretation draws heavily on an engraving of the subject published in 1800. Later, he would illustrate in a similar manner, but in black and white only, Abel J. Jones and David R. Jones, *Chwedlau Cymru Fu* (Cardiff, 1909).

118 See also his *Watching the Invaders*, 1902, National Museums, Liverpool.

119 As 'Arlunydd Penygarn', T.H. Thomas was a prominent member of the Gorsedd. Inviting him to open a shopping arcade that he had designed in Cardiff utilising Celtic motifs, Edwin Seward wrote: 'The launching of anything whatever, – whether abstract or realised in Wales, which touches the Celt and his contact with art, is altogether incomplete without you.' NMW, T.H. Thomas Archive, 2435/188. The 'Celtic Corridor' on Newport Road was opened in 1905, but was destroyed by bombing during the Second World War.

120 Christopher Williams to his wife Emily, 1905. A.D. Fraser Jenkins, *Christopher Williams Centenary* (Cardiff, 1973), p. 7.

compromised by the inventions of Iolo Morganwg. Furthermore, Rhys taught a particularly brilliant generation of students that included O.M. Edwards, Tom Ellis and John Morris-Jones. In 1904, the Celtic Congress was held at Caernarfon, bringing together representatives with a variety of cultural and political agendas from all the Celtic nations. Among artists, T.H. Thomas, Samuel Maurice Jones, Christopher Williams and the young painter John 'Kelt' Edwards, were all in attendance.[119] Some, like Edwards, who had travelled in Brittany and knew the leading Breton nationalist, François Jaffrennou, 'Taldir', were already committed Celticists, but for Christopher Williams the Caernarfon meeting was a revelation:

> So here I have been with two really great men, Celts among Celts, and I have been steeped in Celtic ideals, flooded with early Welsh history and pre-Arthurian tales and mythology. The Mabinogion has been in constant use, so also has Lady Charlotte Guest's Red Book and the Black Book of Carmarthen. I have plenty of subjects for painting, three of which I shall soon tackle. It is a gold mine untouched and full of Welsh fire and imagination.[120]

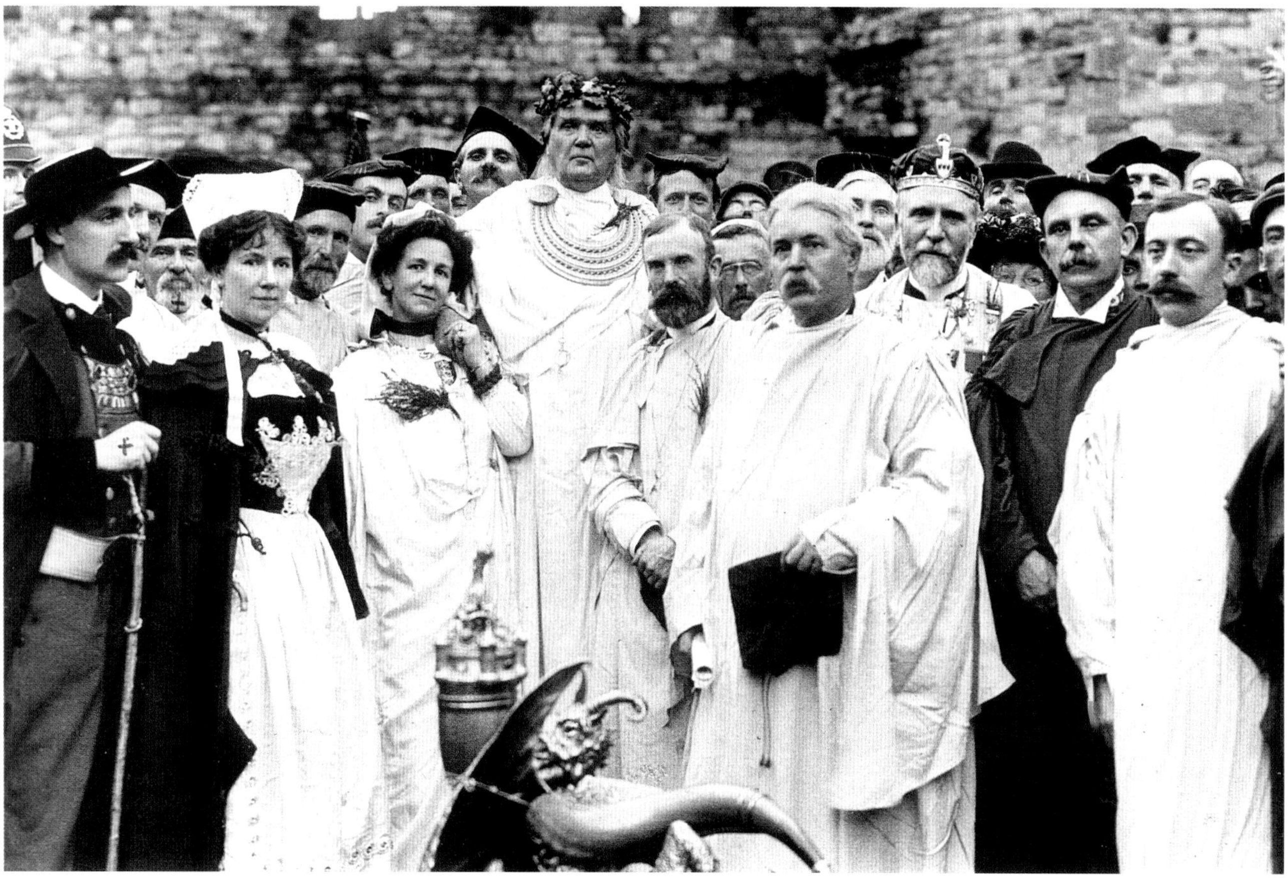

243. John Wickens, *The Celtic Congress, Caernarfon*, 1904. Centre, Hwfa Môn with Gwyneth Vaughan; second row, fourth from right, Samuel Maurice Jones; extreme right, Christopher Williams.

Williams had already painted his imposing depiction of Hwfa Môn, in full Herkomer regalia, and was now engaged on a portrait John Morris-Jones, but the three subject paintings to which he referred – probably *Ceridwen*, *Branwen* and *Blodeuwedd* – would emerge more slowly than anticipated. The first of them, *Ceridwen*, was shown at the Royal Academy in 1910. The following year, Williams conceived the picture that he intended as a summation

244. Christopher Williams, *Hwfa Môn*, 1904, oil, 134x108

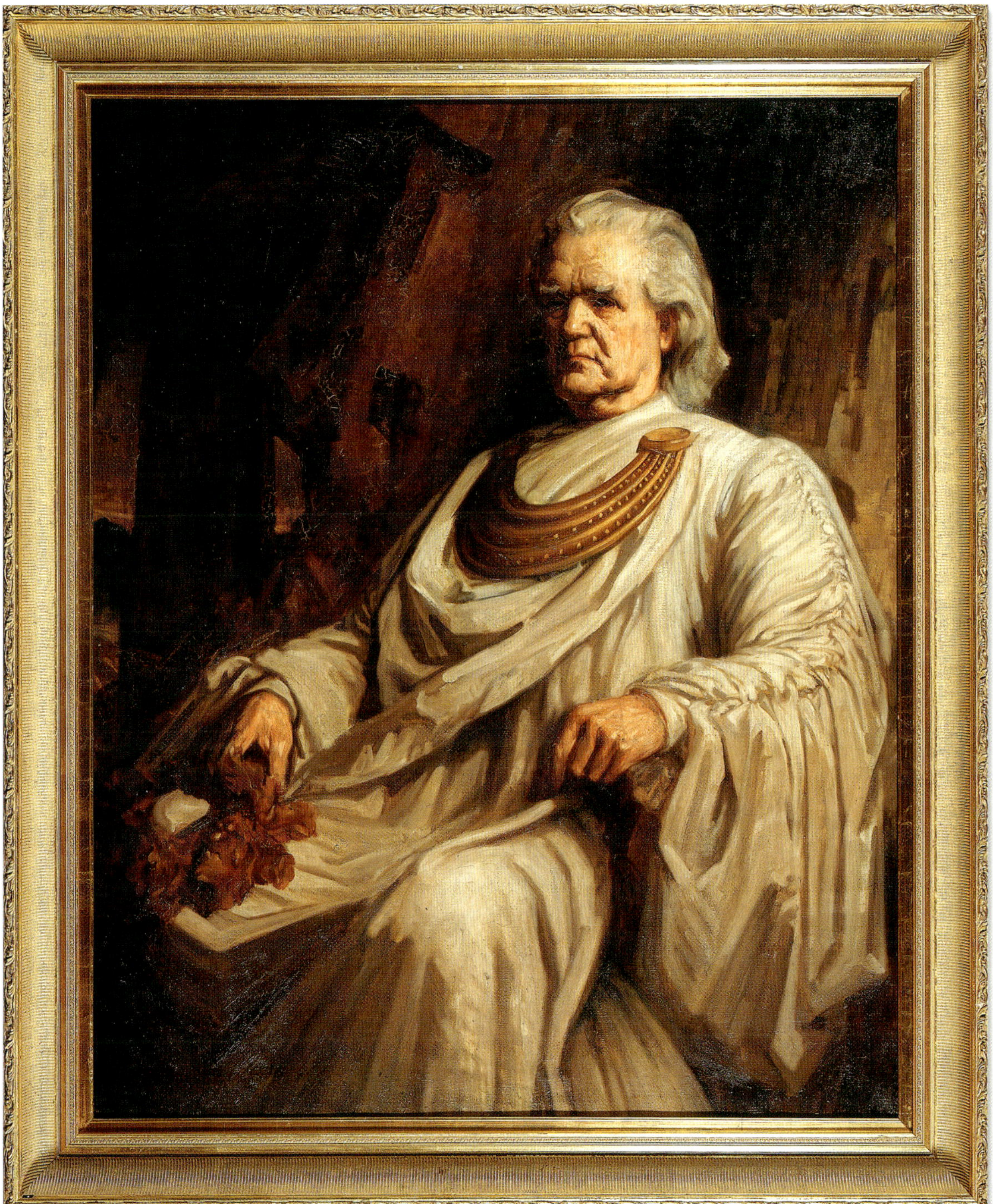

opposite
245. Christopher Williams, *Wales Awakening*, 1911, oil, 272x130

of the national revival, *Wales Awakening*. Williams portrayed a mythologised version of the story of Gwenllian, daughter of Llywelyn, last native Prince of Wales, who was incarcerated in a nunnery in England to ensure that there would be no direct succession in the line of the princes of Gwynedd. Gwenllian had not died there but merely slept, awaiting her country's revival. Writing in *Cymru*, the picture was interpreted by the painter's close friend, Thomas Matthews – a schoolmaster by profession:

> The national spirit of Wales slept, but after seven centuries, under the influence of the new light of education, she awoke ... Cymru Fydd is no longer in its infancy, but her gentle fair face and bearing are seen awakening to the white light of dawn. She is older than England; but because she has slept so long, she is yet young, and sees new hopes, – new and limitlessly high – in the fields of song and art.[121]

Williams may well have conceived *Wales Awakening* at Caernarfon, in the company of the Welsh intelligentsia who had gathered there for the investiture of the Prince of Wales in 1911. In the course of the proceedings, a high point for the artists among them was the knighting of the sculptor William Goscombe John, who had designed the regalia. John's rise from artisan origins in Cardiff had coincided precisely both with cultural revival in Wales and a wider renewal in the particular practice of sculpture. The extensive Welsh patronage that facilitated his art education and early career was crucial to his establishment as a leading figure in the New Sculpture movement, that directed the practice of many younger sculptors in London. John was born in Cardiff in 1860, and worked with his father, a woodcarver who was employed on the rebuilding of Cardiff Castle undertaken by the Marquess of Bute. Graduating through London workshops, he completed his training at the Royal Academy schools, winning a gold medal and travelling scholarship in 1889. He worked in Paris, studying Rodin's methods in his studio, and on his return was immediately in receipt of further Welsh patronage, gaining a commission to make the altarpiece for the Church of St John in Cardiff. In London his reputation grew yearly as the result of his exhibits at the Royal Academy, where the naturalism of his simply formed nudes made a particular impression. In 1894, the art critic Edmund Gosse, who coined the term 'New Sculpture' to describe such work, observed (in a tradition of cultural appropriation that extended back to Wilson) that John was 'the most distinguished English sculptor outside the Royal Academy' – a situation rectified five years later when he became an Associate of the institution.

John worked in London and carried out major commissions all over England, but he never became a token Welshman. His engagement with Wales was active and of importance both to his own career and to the development of the visual arts at home. Somewhat to the

121 Thomas Matthews, 'Celf yng Nghymru', *Cymru*, XI, (1911), p. 19, my translation from the Welsh. Robert Meyrick points out that *Wales Awakening* can also be read as an *homage* to Frederic Leighton's painting *Perseus and Andromeda* (1891), that had a crucial influence on his decision to become a painter. Robert Meyrick, *Christopher Williams*, pp. 16, 32.

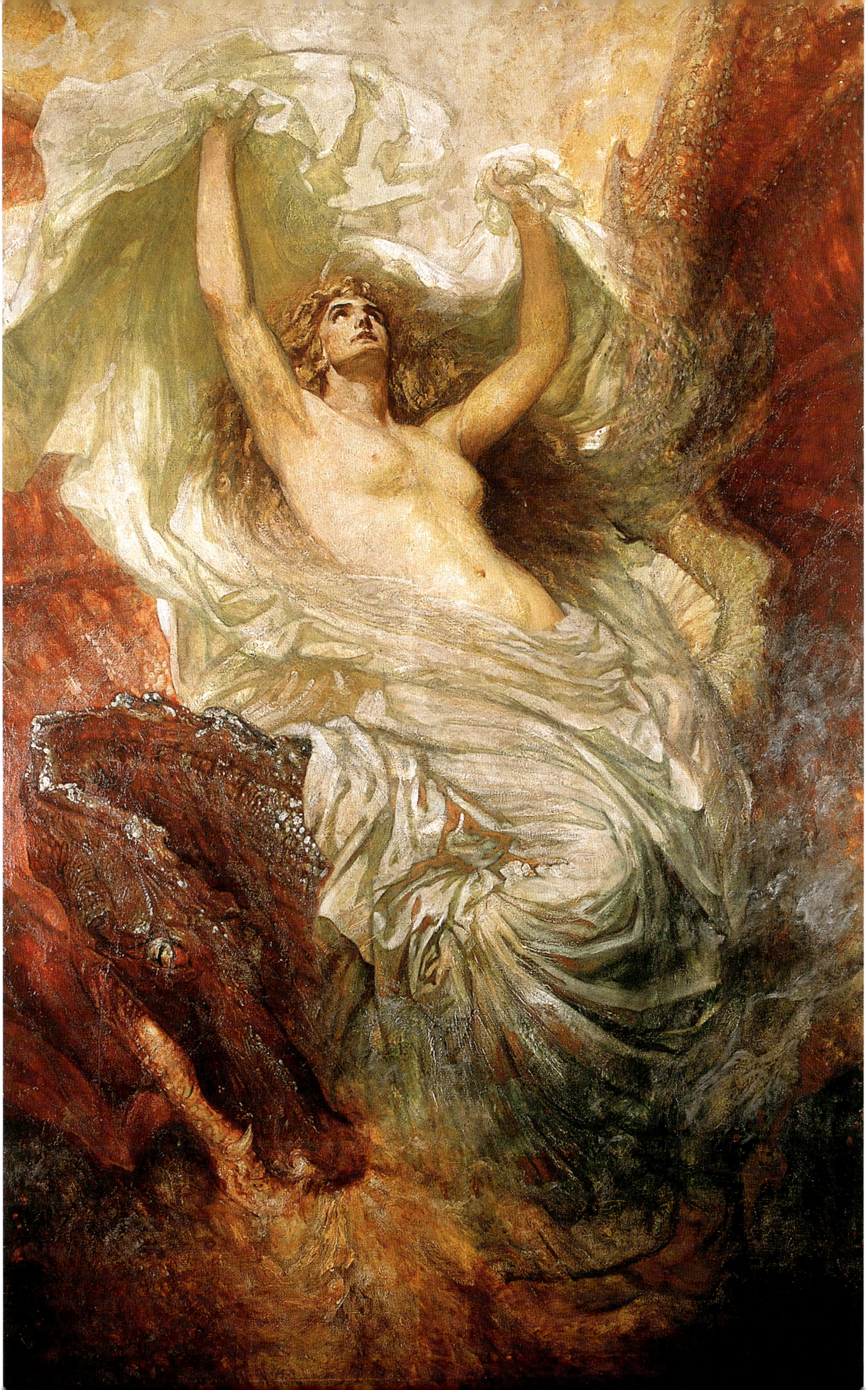

irritation of T.H. Thomas, who had made the original proposal, in 1898 he was commissioned to make the Corn Hirlas that completed the Gorsedd Regalia, and also the medal of the National Eisteddfod Association, for which he drew on the long tradition of bardic imagery. He also ventured occasionally into Celticist territory in statuary, notably in 1902 with his *Merlin and Arthur*. Significantly, the work coincided with T. Gwynn Jones's *awdl* 'Ymadawiad Arthur', which won the chair at the National Eisteddfod at Bangor in that year. Reflecting the grace and fluidity of the John sculpture, the poem treated its mythic subject matter with an ease and sophistication that exercised a profound influence on contemporary Welsh-language poetry.

It was in a literary context that John also made the clearest expression of his naturalism in sculpture. His memorial to a group of poets associated with Llansannan in Denbighshire exemplified the freshness sought by the New Sculpture movement:

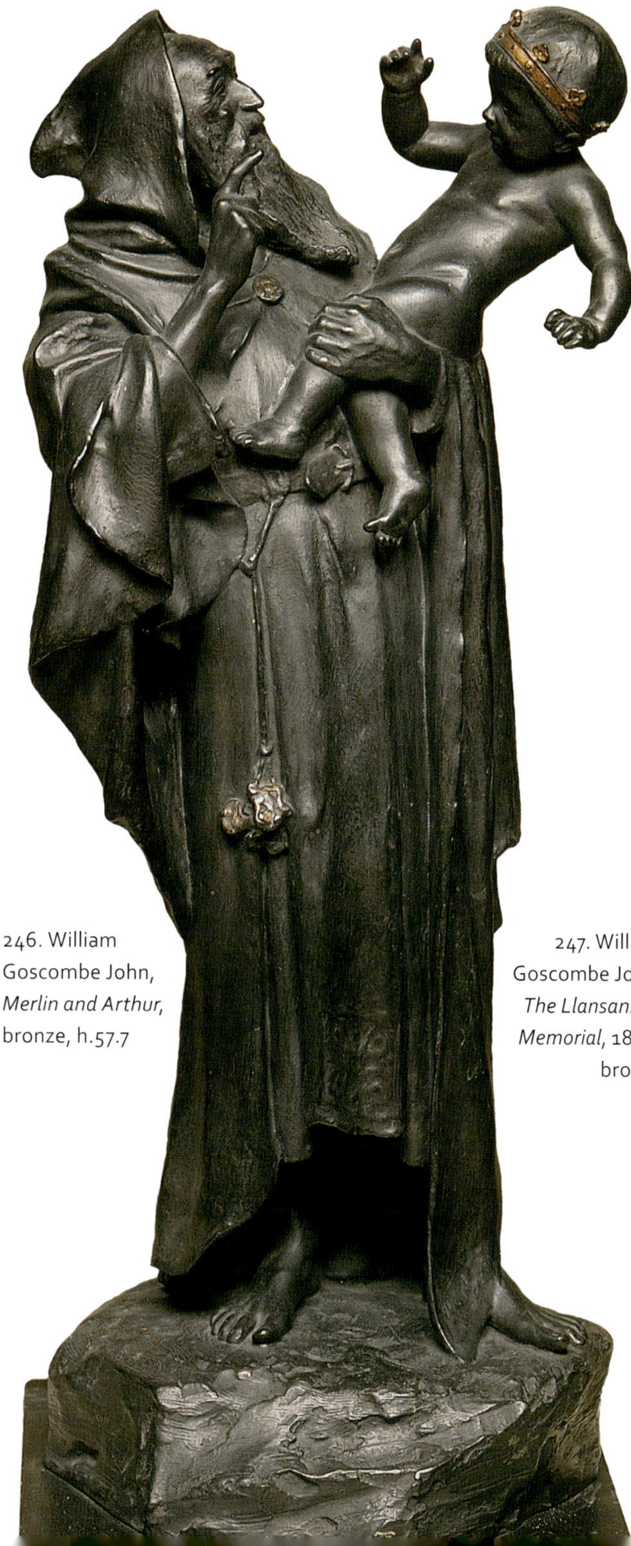

246. William Goscombe John, *Merlin and Arthur*, bronze, h.57.7

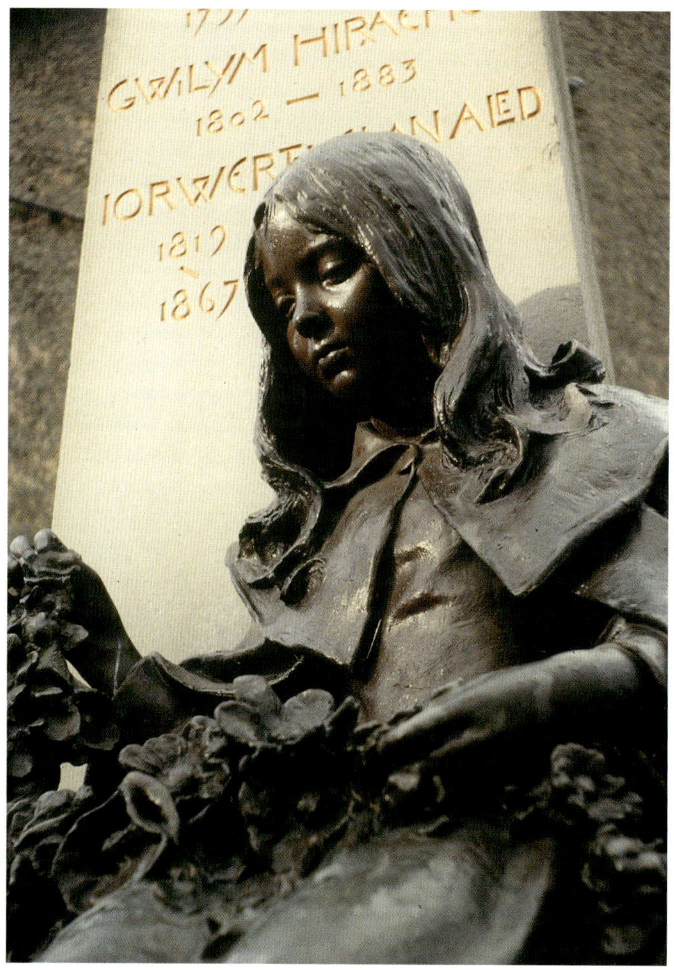

247. William Goscombe John, *The Llansannan Memorial*, 1899, bronze

> I felt that any *Academic* or *conventional* representations would have been out of place in an out of the world mountain village, something that would go with the surroundings & be understood by the *villagers young & old* struck me as being most fitted, so the idea I have worked on is ... a little girl, a village girl, in *modern village costume*, with *Welsh cloak* over shoulders ... You will I hope glean a notion from all this it would be an embodiment *of the present-day* thinking.[122]

122 NLW T.E. Ellis Papers, 987.

John was writing to Tom Ellis, who had conceived the memorial in 1896. It was unveiled in 1899, the year of Ellis's death at the age of 40. As both the political leader and an influence on the formation of the ideas of the national movement, the loss of Ellis at an early age was regarded as a tragedy by many people, and immediately moves were made to create a memorial to him. John was selected to make the bronze statue which was unveiled in the presence of David Lloyd George, political successor to Ellis, in the main street of Bala in 1903. The four stone carved panels on the plinth expressed the notion of personal progress

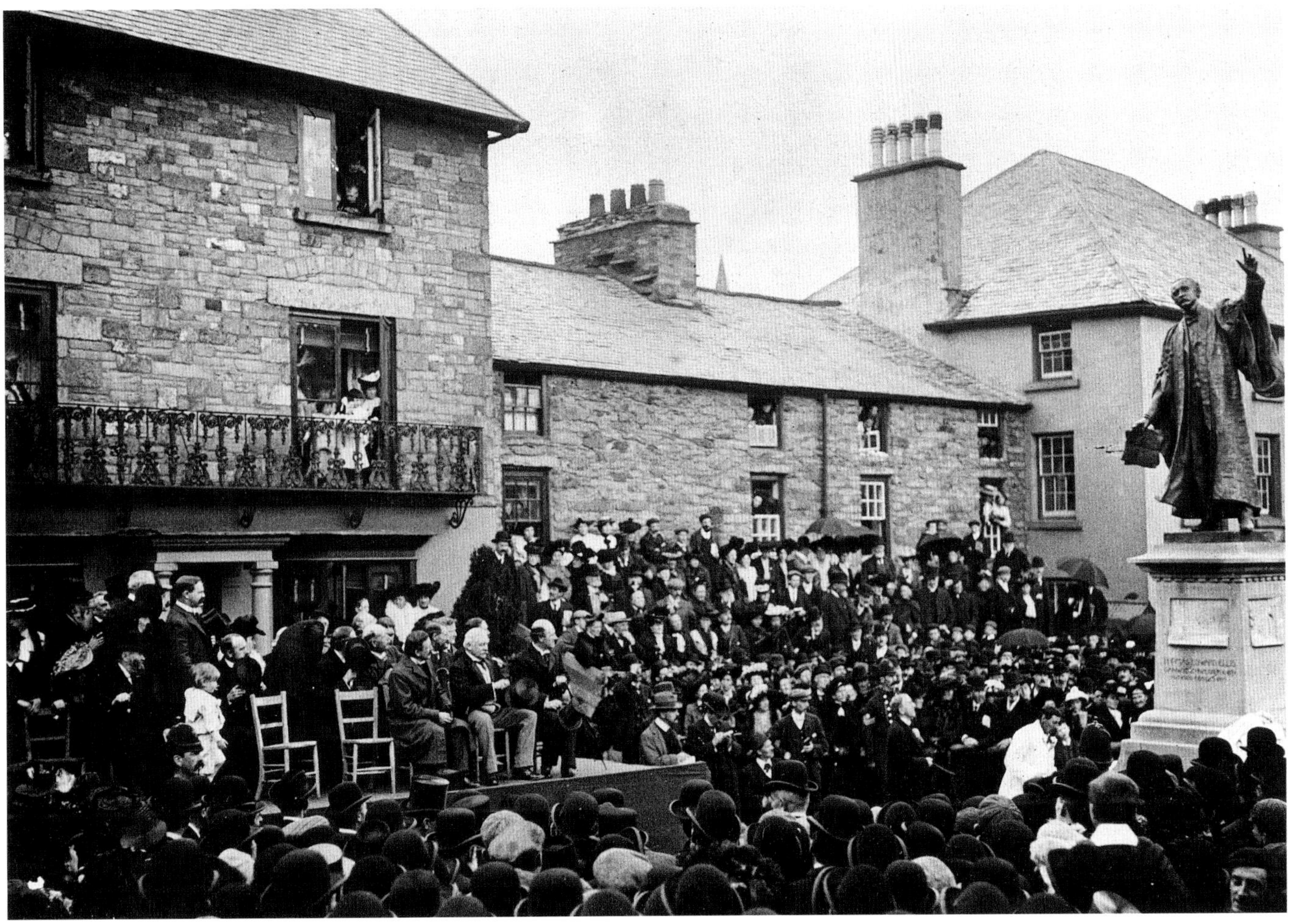

248. *The Unveiling of the Tom Ellis Memorial*, Bala, 1903

as a metaphor for national revival that the life of Ellis represented for his admirers. The rise of Ellis to the Houses of Parliament in London, through the universities of Oxford and Aberystwyth, had begun on the upland farm of Cynlas, where he was born:

> ... I feel that every cottage built on a Welsh hillside, and every generation reared within it, contains new possibilities for Wales. For from such have come the leaders of Welsh thought and movements, the makers of our nation ...[123]

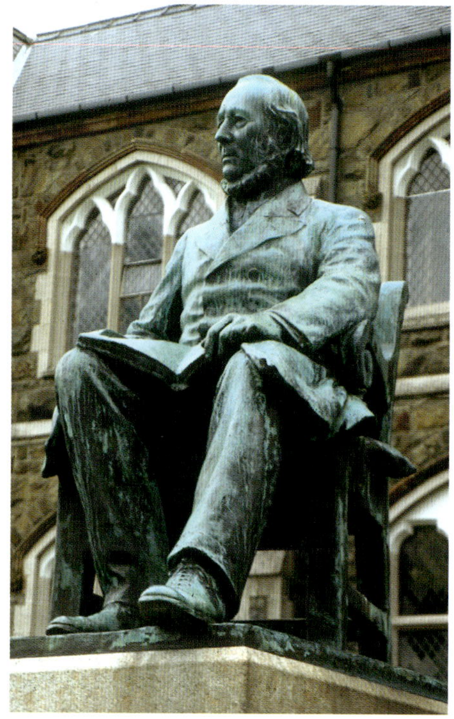

249. William Goscombe John, *Lewis Edwards*, Bala, 1911, bronze

Although constrained by the absence of buildings of national or even regional significance that might house statuary and painting, by the early years of the twentieth century important figures representing different aspects of Welsh life had been memorialised in the form of public sculpture. The centrality of Methodism in the culture, first celebrated at Bala with the statue of Thomas Charles, was reinforced by the unveiling of a memorial to Daniel Rowland at Llangeitho in 1883 and subsequently Lewis Edwards, again at Bala.[124] The novelist Daniel Owen and the educationalist Hugh Owen were celebrated at Mold and at Caernarfon, while in the south the industrialists Archibald Hood and Hussey Vivian were memorialised at Llwynypia and at Swansea. Casts of a statue of David Davies, entrepreneur of railways and builder of Barry Docks, were erected both at the entrance to the docks and in Davies's home village of Llandinam. The statue was modelled in 1893 by the English sculptor Alfred Gilbert but, albeit indirectly, this commission was certainly the most significant of the industrialist memorials for the visual culture of Wales. The immense wealth that Davies accumulated devolved equally on his three grandchildren, David, Gwendoline and Margaret. Advised by the museum curator and painter Hugh Blaker – brother of their childhood governess – in 1908 the two Davies sisters began to form a remarkable collection of paintings, initially buying works by Turner and Corot, and four years later adding the first of many Impressionist pictures, by Manet and Monet.[125] In 1913, the sisters agreed to loan their collection as the core of the first large scale exhibition presented by the National Museum of Wales. Hugh Blaker and another young artist in the Davies circle, the Scottish painter

123 From evidence given by Ellis to the Royal Commission on Land in Wales, 1893. For the evolution of the mythology of the Welsh Folk, see Lord, *The Meaning of Pictures*, pp. 76–121. For the ideas of Ellis himself, see *Speeches and Addresses by the late Thomas E. Ellis, M.P.* (Wrexham, 1912). For Ellis and the national movement, see Dewi Rowland Hughes, *Cymru Fydd* (Cardiff, 2006).

124 Edward Griffith, creator of the statue of Daniel Rowland, wrote an informative memoir, now NLW MS 21233C.

250. Alfred Gilbert, *David Davies, Llandinam*, Llandinam, 1893, bronze

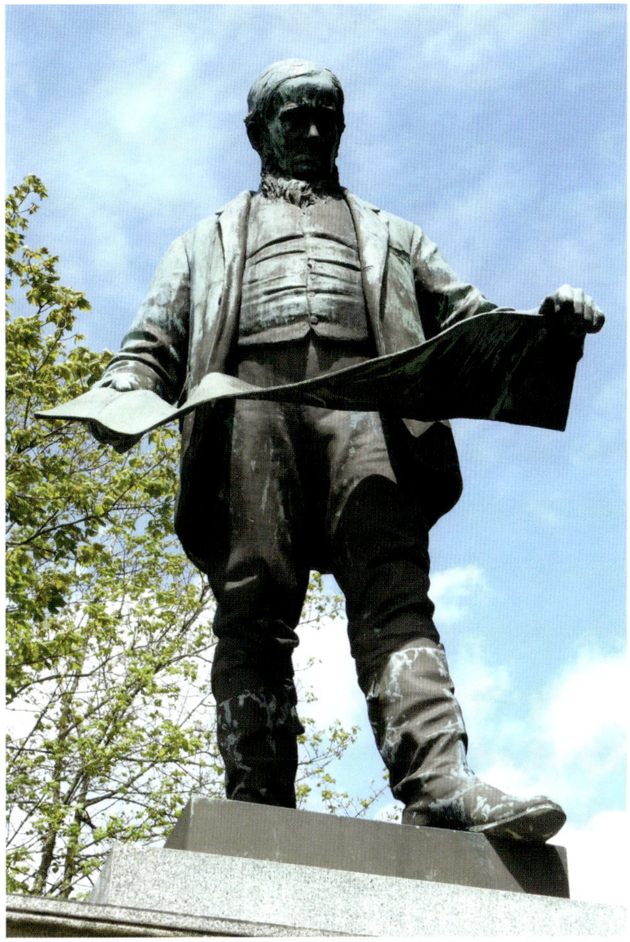

Murray Urquhart, were involved in the organisation of the exhibition, which was shown at Cardiff City Hall. It was interpreted as an essential part of the national revival in the arts – 'a milestone in Welsh artistic development', in Blaker's words – and it attracted over 26,000 visitors in less than two months.[126]

The exhibition of modern works from beyond Wales was followed by a companion exhibition that sought to mark the achievement of Welsh artists. However, the conception of this second exhibition, informed by the idea of Welsh ethnicity that had guided Mardy Rees in his *Welsh Painters, Engravers and Sculptors*, published in the previous year, seriously distorted the reality of the Welsh art world. The framework of 'certain Modern Artists of Welsh Birth or Extraction' enabled the organisers to include the likes of Frank Brangwyn, who had never worked in the country (but whose mother was Welsh), while excluding, for instance, Clarence Whaite, who had worked all his adult life in Wales but who had been born in Manchester. The exhibition developed the concept of Wales as both a distinct entity, whose people were defined by ethnicity, and as a contributor to a greater whole, in the form of the British empire. In this respect it stood firmly in the mainstream of nationalist thinking in the period, which by and large chose not to dwell on any potential paradox in the concept. Notwithstanding the memorialisation of prominent figures from the recent Welsh past, it is significant that the ambition expressed by John Francis at the National Eisteddfod at Denbigh in 1860 also

125 For the collecting of the Davies sisters, see Ann Sumner (ed.) *Colour and Light: fifty Impressionist and Post-Impressionist works at the National Museum of Wales* (Cardiff, 2005) and Oliver Fairclough (ed.), *'Things of Beauty': what two sisters did for Wales* (Cardiff, 2007).

126 The exhibition was funded by the Davies sisters who, the following year donated (with their brother) £5,000 to the National Museum building fund. The sisters had spent £120,000 on buying paintings by this time. See Fairclough, *'Things of Beauty'*, pp. 62–3.

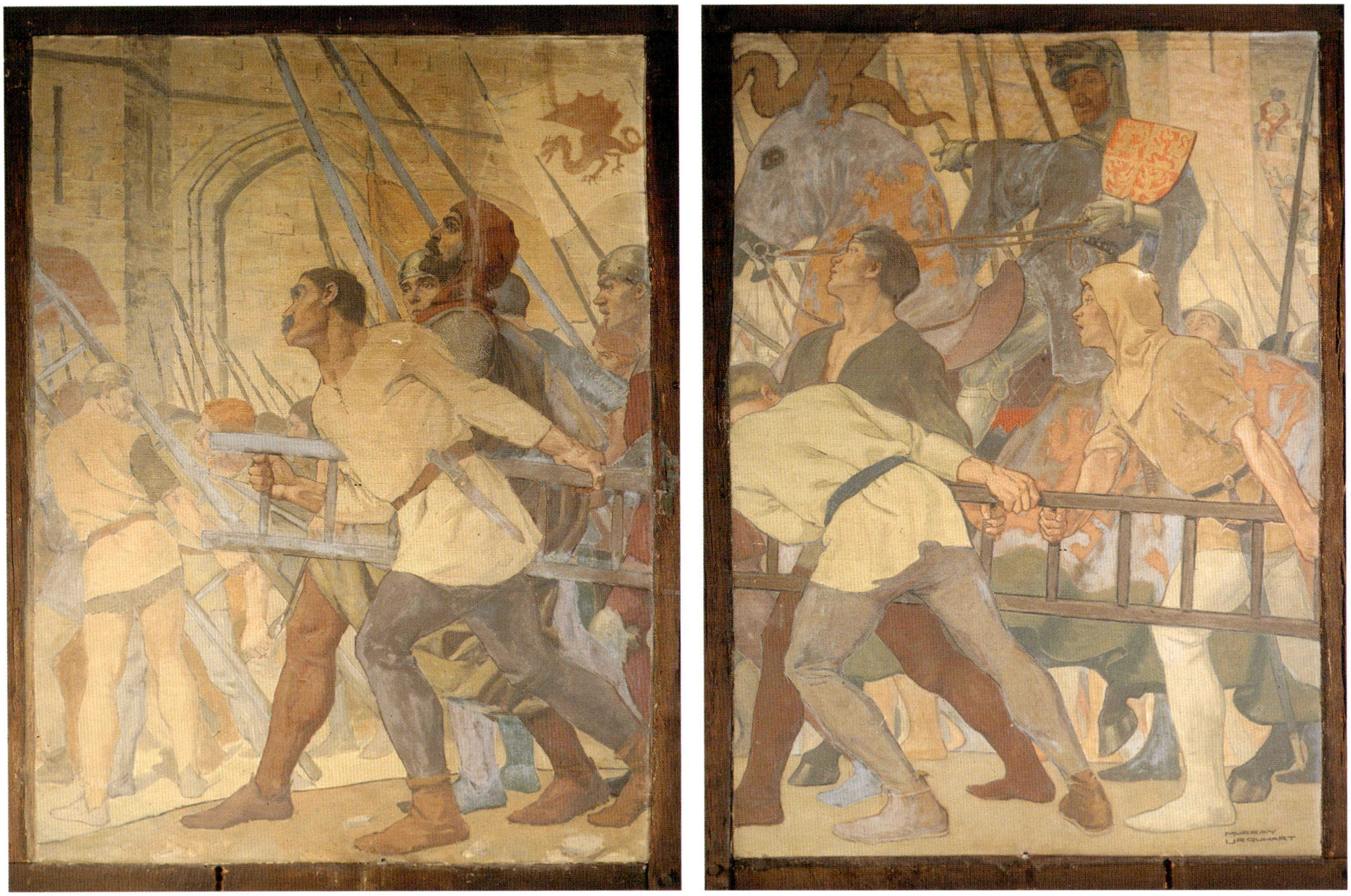

251. Murray Urquhart, *Mural at the Owain Glyndŵr Parlament House*, Machynlleth, 1912–14, oil, both 269x150

to memorialise deeper – and more problematic – Welsh history had made little progress. Ironically, it fell to the Scottish painter Murray Urquhart to image for the first time in a public space the subject of Owain Glyndŵr. The project coincided with the gift to the town of Machynlleth of the Glyndŵr Parliament House by the Davies family in 1912, but extended beyond their immediate circle. O.M. Edwards advised Urquhart on the iconography of the mural scheme of four panels, illustrating the life of Glyndŵr, that he had been commissioned to paint.

However, the most ambitious public art work of the national revival was undertaken at the Cardiff City Hall. The building, incorporating the concept though not the reality of a Pantheon of National Heroes, was opened in 1906. Ten years later, the installation of the eleven sculptures of the Pantheon, financed by the industrialist D.A. Thomas, was marked at a ceremony led by David Lloyd George. The sculptors had been selected by one of the

252. J. Havard Thomas, *Maquette for Buddug, Pantheon of National Heroes*, Cardiff c.1916, plaster

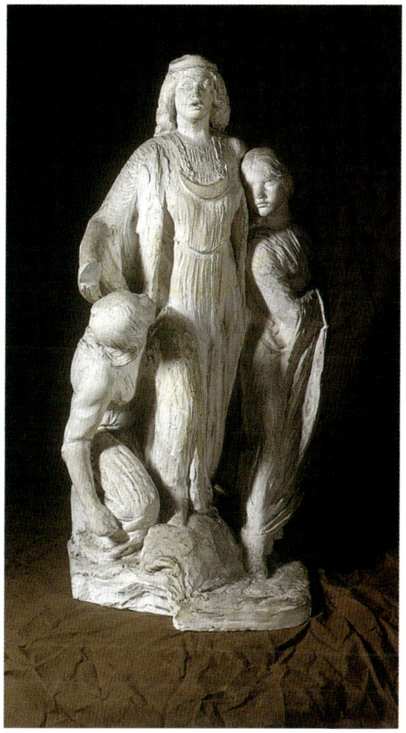

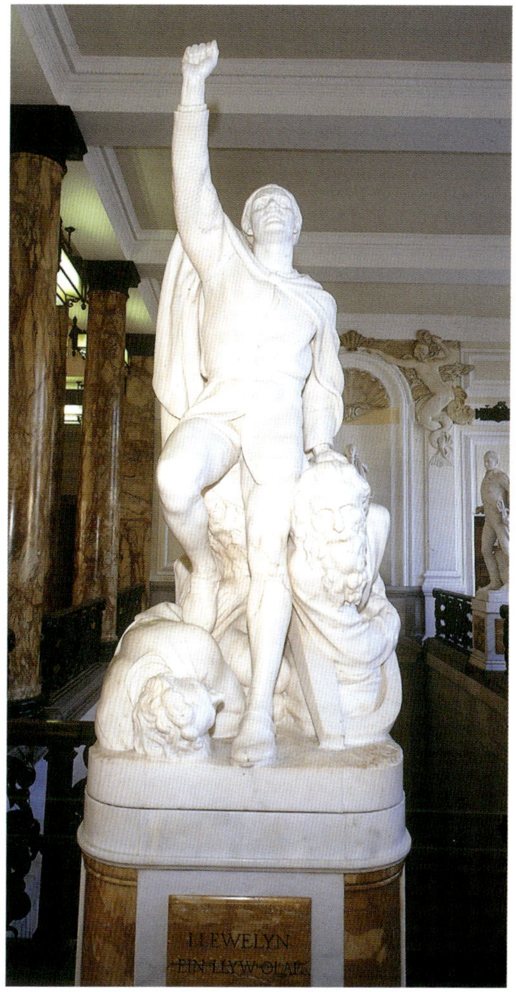

253. Harry Pegram, *Llywelyn ap Gruffudd, Pantheon of National Heroes*, Cardiff, c.1916, marble

participants in the 1913 National Museum celebration of modern Welsh artists, James Havard Thomas. In 1911 Thomas had become a teacher at the Slade School of Art, where he would soon become Professor of Sculpture.[127] Regarded as something of a modernist, the rejection of his nude *Lycidas* by the Royal Academy in 1905 had caused a considerable stir, which considerably enhanced his career prospects. Indeed, Thomas appears to have had a taste for controversy, and the decision not to organise a competition for the commissions in Cardiff led to the resignation of the council of the Royal Society of Sculptors in London. Further aggravation, in the context of pressure in the pre-war period for women's civil rights, was only narrowly avoided. It was pointed out that all the ten statues of the original Pantheon concept represented men. The figure of *Buddug and Her Children* was added to the list, and carved by Havard Thomas himself. The additional figure resulted in Goscombe John's *St David* being relocated to stand free of the staircase location of the other statues, in the centre of the Marble Hall. In addition to the token woman, the patron saint found himself surrounded by a varied company, that included both the odious rapist Sir Thomas Picton and William Williams, Pantycelyn. The statue of Llywelyn ap Gruffudd, carved by Goscombe John's student, Harry Pegram, would prove to be the only one that impressed itself on the public imagination – the raised fist of the prince being much in evidence at meetings of the Welsh Language Society in the 1970s and 80s.

127 Thomas (1854–1921) was born in Bristol to Welsh parents. He studied in Bristol, at the Royal College of Art in London, and at the École des Beaux-Arts in Paris. Between 1889 and 1906 he worked in Italy.

254. Margaret Lindsay Williams,
Clara Novello Davies, 1915,
oil, 257.3x165.1

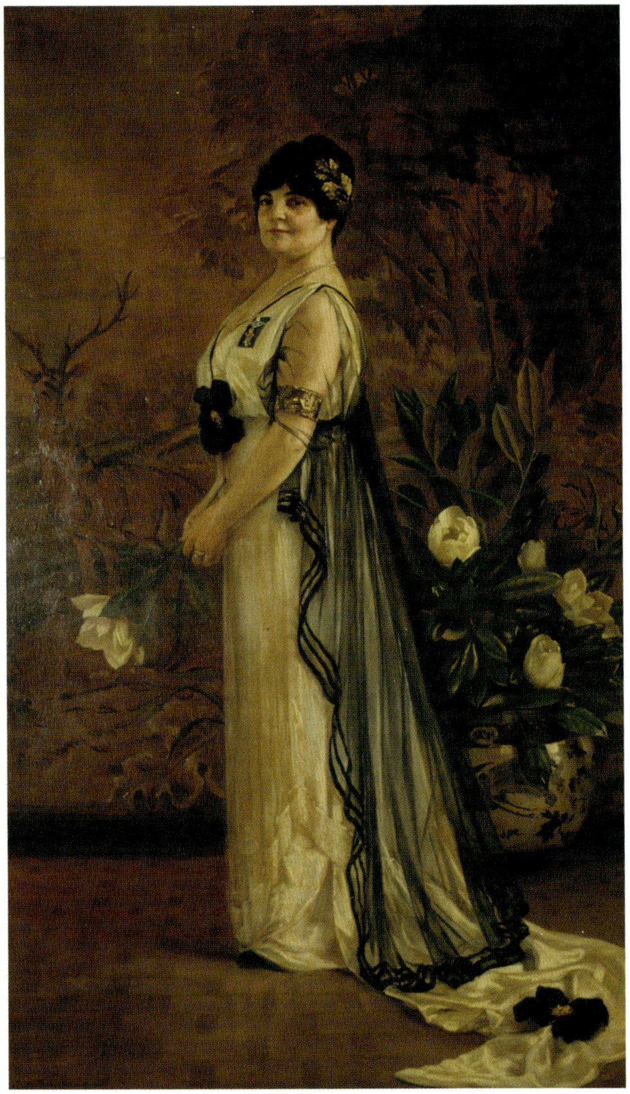

Modernists

The scene at the opening of the Pantheon of National Heroes in 1916 was painted on a large scale by Margaret Lindsay Williams for the civic authorities in Cardiff. Williams was born in the town in 1888, and like Goscombe John (whom she came to know) would benefit much from Welsh patronage, especially in the early development of her career. However, unlike John, she came from a prosperous middle-class background, and after a training that culminated at the Royal Academy, where she won a gold medal for her painting *The City of Refuge*, she was able to establish herself in a London studio, bought by her father. Nevertheless, her first substantial exhibition was at the New Galleries in Cardiff in 1914, and it attracted favourable critical attention in both the Welsh and the English language press.[128] Portrait commissions began to flow. Notable among her early sitters was the formidable Clara Novello Davies, famous as a choir leader and soon to be celebrated also as the mother of Ivor Novello, who modelled for Williams's picture *The Risen Soul* a year later, in 1915. The artist would continue to attract patrons for civic and society portraits which provided the basis for her long and successful career. On the other hand, her conservative aesthetics and also a personality inclined to privacy placed her outside a critical mainstream that became preoccupied with Modernism, both in London and in the United States, where she would also work.[129] In terms of her personality and also her relationship with the art world, Williams's career invites comparison with that of her older contemporary, Gwen John. Like Williams and, a little earlier, Gwenny Griffiths, John grew up in a middle-class Welsh

128 See Thomas Matthews, 'Celf Miss Margaret Lindsay Williams' in *Cymru*, XLVII (1914), p. 217, and *Welsh Outlook*, i, April 1914, pp. 149–50.

129 Angela Gaffney, *'Wedded to her Art': Margaret Lindsay Williams 1888–1960* (Aberystwyth, 1999).

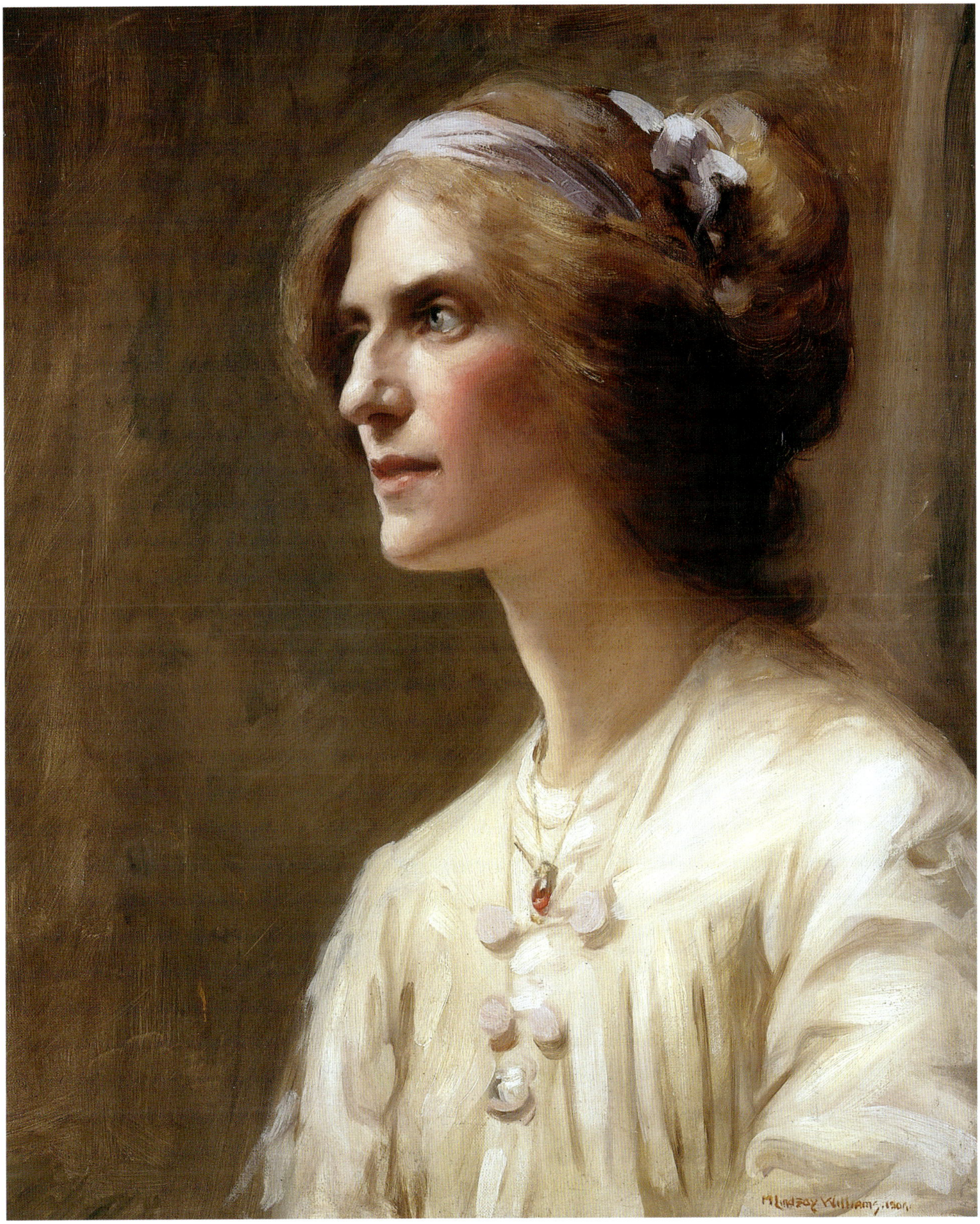

255. Margaret Lindsay Williams,
Self-portrait, 1909, oil, 60x50

home that financed her London art training, though she attended the Slade School rather than the more conservative Academy.[130] Her precocious younger brother, Augustus, had entered the Slade a year earlier, in 1894. For both brother and sister, the years immediately following their training involved travel on the Continent. Gwen visited Paris for the first time in 1898, and settled there in 1904, when she met Auguste Rodin, who became her lover for a time. Although she showed her work in London until 1911 with the New English Art Club, she lived in France for the rest of her life, where her work evolved slowly and privately. Her relationship with Rodin had initially placed her at the centre of the continental art world, but she withdrew into a meditative existence centred on her painting and the Roman Catholic faith that she embraced fully in 1913.

Gwen John did not engage intellectually, or, it would seem, emotionally with Wales, whereas her brother, notwithstanding feelings about his home country that were at best ambiguous, became involved during the most creative period of his life. Teaching at Liverpool in 1901, Augustus met John Sampson, the foremost English student of Romany tradition, though he was far from a conventional scholar. John adopted the bohemian Sampson's fascination with Romany life and language, and particularly its Welsh dialect, to the recording of which Sampson devoted much of his often alcohol-fuelled energy. John accompanied Sampson on expeditions into north Wales in search of Welsh Romany families, and toured England in a caravan with his rapidly growing entourage of Ida Nettleship (his wife), Dorelia McNeill (his lover), and an expanding family of children.

opposite
257. Gwen John, *Self-portrait*, 1902, oil, 44.8x34.9

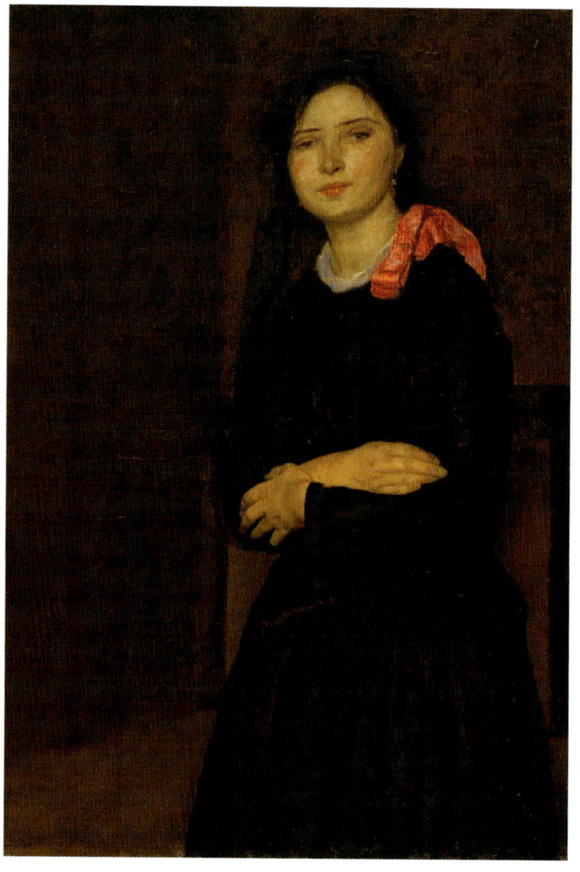

256. Gwen John, *Dorelia in a Black Dress*, c.1903–4, oil, 73x48.9

130 No evidence of contact between Gwen John and Gwenny Griffiths has been located.

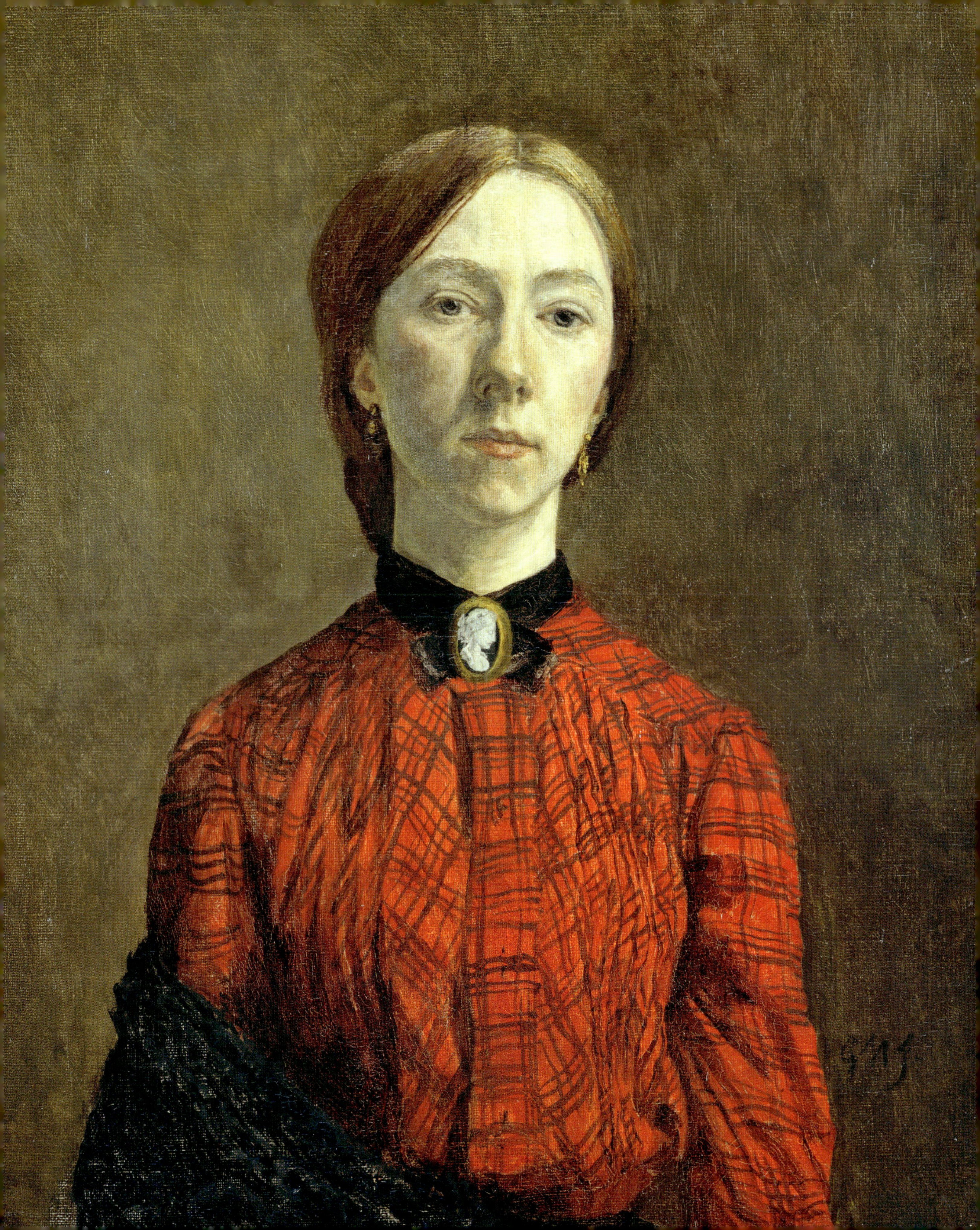

right
258. Augustus John, *Dorelia by the Caravan*, 1911, oil, 35.5x26.7

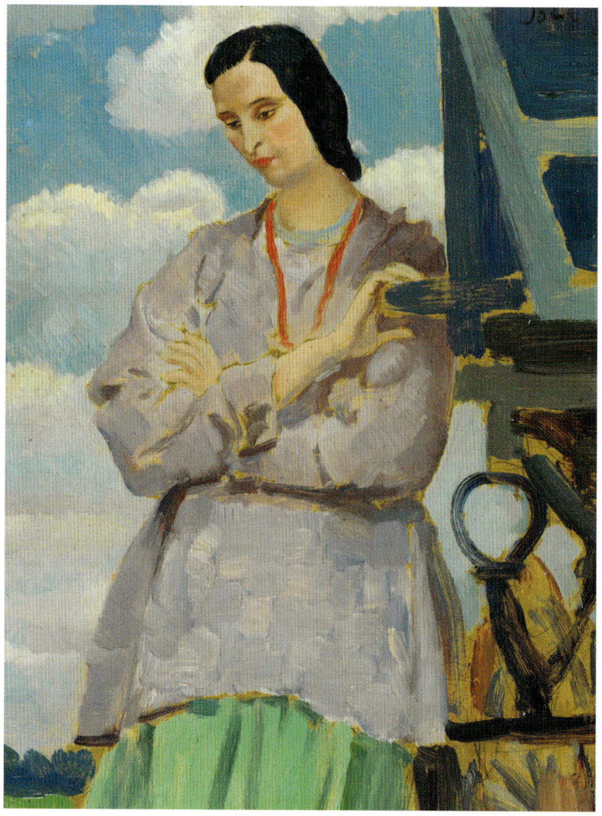

opposite
259. James Dickson Innes, *Girl Standing by a Lake*, 1911–12, oil, 38.1x29.2

In his painting, John rejected the laborious tradition of English academic training within which, at this time, his Welsh contemporary Christopher Williams continued to operate. As Williams was working on *Wales Awakening*, John was producing what seemed to many contemporaries to be startlingly simplistic portraits of Dorelia McNeill that clearly revealed the effect upon him of the Fauves painters. He moved easily between France and England where, like his sister, he showed his work in London with the New English Art Club. The radicalism of his pictures and his matching life-style brought him a celebrity that was not ignored by Welsh intellectuals, and he was occasionally drawn into public life at home. In 1907 he contributed to a volume of essays on Wales 'today and tomorrow' a diatribe on the artistic shortcomings of his compatriots, whose 'neglected sense of beauty evaporates in fits of yawning after periodical attacks of spiritual insomnia; their architectural sense is exhausted in the effort to construct New Jerusalem; their sense of design just suffices to render intelligible to them the scheme of the universe; – while form, colour, suggest ideas entirely trivial or vaguely diabolical.' Evidently, John had not been impressed by the eternal fruits of the religious revival of 1904. 'Yes! Wales must be barbarized!' he declaimed, from a safe distance, in Paris.[131]

Nevertheless, in 1911, John returned to Wales in the company of James Dickson Innes to paint landscape in the uplands between Bala and Blaenau Ffestiniog. The interaction between the two men facilitated the production, both in Wales and on their visits to France, of some of the most lyrical landscape painting of the period – small in scale, but intense in colour and mood. For Innes there was also urgency. Although he was some nine years younger than John, by this time he was aware that he was dying of tuberculosis. He had been born at Llanelli, trained first at Carmarthen and then at the Slade School. He met John in 1907 and in the following year, like his compatriot, he worked in France, though he favoured watercolour as a medium, whereas John worked more in oils. In 1910, the two painters were given successive exhibitions at the Chenil Gallery in London, and it was at

131 John in Stephens (ed.), *Wales Today and Tomorrow*, p. 349.

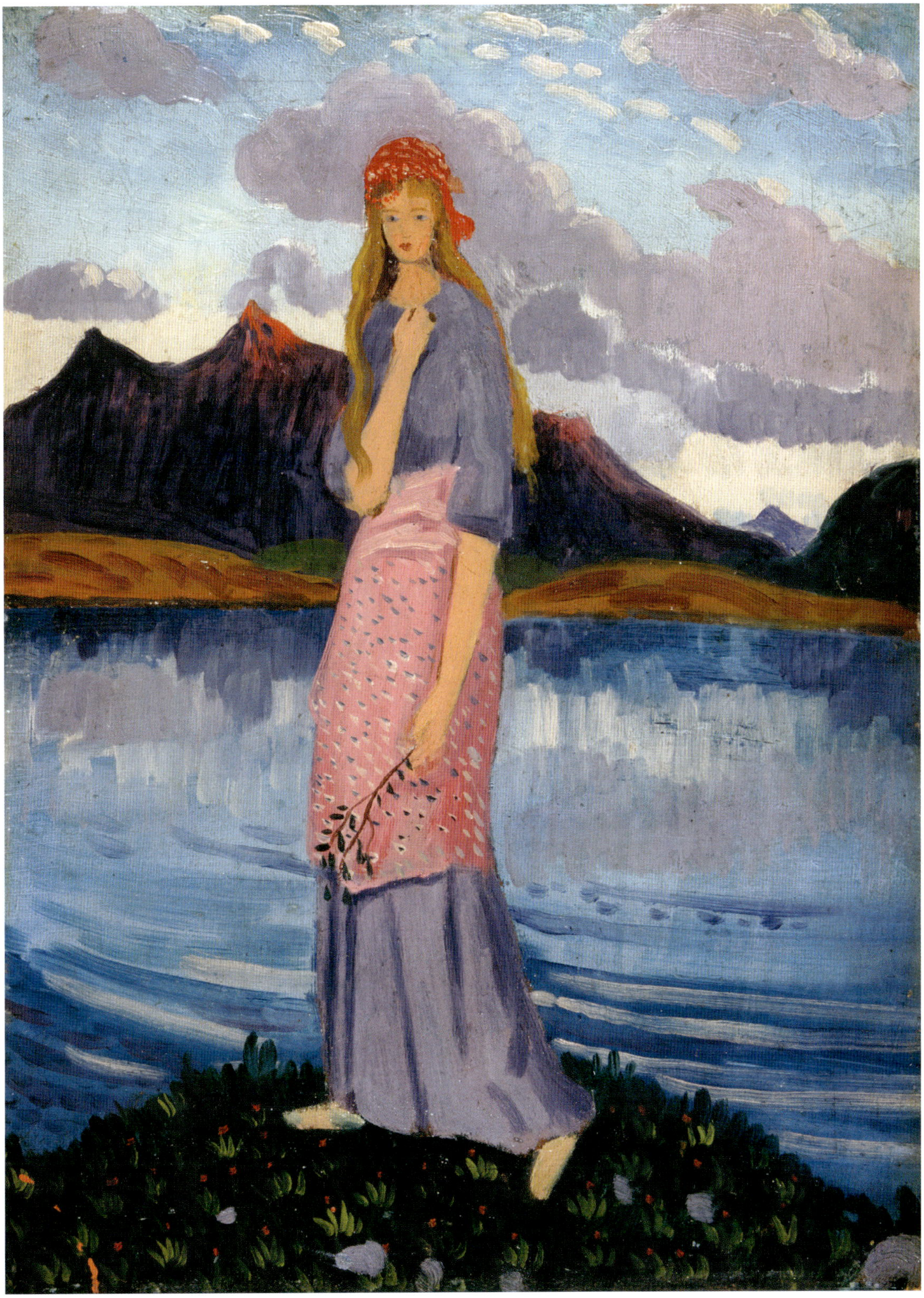

132 Quoted in Michael Holroyd, *Augustus John. The New Biography* (London, 1996), p. 354.

133 John, in T. Stephens (ed.) *Wales Today and Tomorrow*, p. 350. In a second essay on the subject of 'Art in Wales', published in the same volume, T.H. Thomas presented a long list of artists defined on the basis of 'Welsh birth or extraction', and made oblique reference also to Clarence Whaite and others in his situation, the 'many men of high repute in art who are Welsh by long residence and who paint Welsh subjects.' Gwenny Griffiths and Margaret Lindsay Williams were also named by Thomas.

this time that they became close. Earlier that year, Innes had found the motif that became of obsessive interest to him until his death – Mynydd Arenig – 'his sacred mountain' as John would later describe it.[132] Remarkably, at the same time, Clarence Whaite was painting with equivalent mystical intensity his huge *Snowdon*, a heroic work by a painter then in his eighty-third year. Ignorant of or indifferent to Whaite's work, John's opinion was that 'in Wales there is no Tradition, and no really old artists', from whom to learn.[133]

In the spring of 1911, John and Innes were installed together at Rhyd-y-fen – 'the most wonderful place I've seen', John enthused in a letter to Dorelia. They would return in 1912, and paint together again in Provence the following year. By this time, John's reputation extended as far as the United States. He had first shown a work there, his portrait of the painter William Nicholson, in 1910. Three years later, along with Innes and Gwen John, his work was selected for the exhibition at the Armory in New York that is regarded as having introduced European Modernism to the American public. Indeed, John showed more work than any other European painter, with the exception of Redon. Whether this remarkable Welsh imbalance owed anything to the fact that the instigator and one of the main selectors of the exhibition was Arthur Bowen Davies is unclear. Davies was born in

260. James Dickson Innes, *Cloud over Arenig*, *c.*1911, watercolour, 24.5x34.5

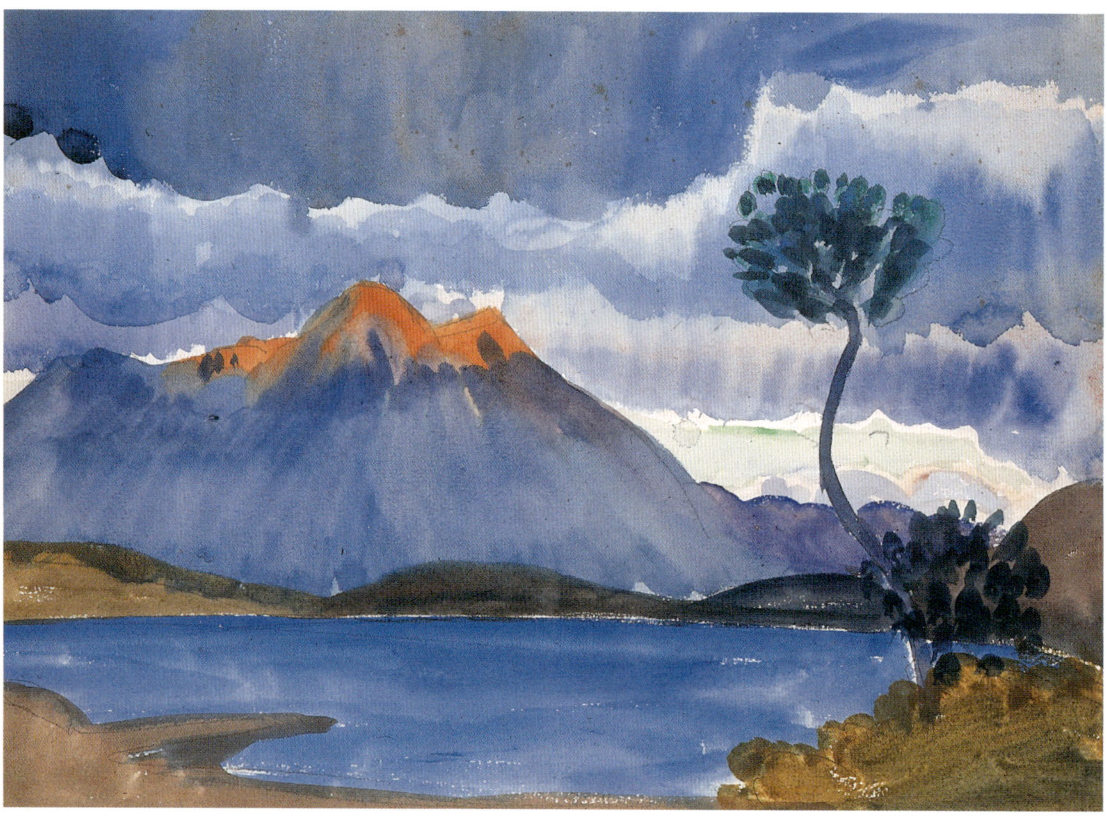

the United States, but his father hailed from Carmarthen.[134] Three years later, the magazine *Vanity Fair* would report that Augustus John was 'Britain's most conspicuous native painter' – a description in which the adjective was particularly apposite.[135]

Neither Gwen John nor J.D. Innes were represented at the National Museum's exhibition of painters of 'Welsh Birth or Extraction', late in 1913, but Augustus John showed five works, all of which had been recently seen at his Chenil Gallery exhibitions. The invitation to exhibit was probably the consequence of the particular interest in the painter of the exhibition's sponsor, Lord Howard de Walden, of Chirk Castle. De Walden had commissioned portraits of himself and Lady de Walden from John in 1912, though persuading the painter to complete the work proved to be a tortuous and lengthy process. At the exhibition, John's small, vivid and immediate pictures sat uneasily in the presence of Christopher Williams's massive narratives *Why* and *Ceridwen*, Margaret Lindsay Williams's *City of Refuge*, and Edgar Thomas's *Intellectual Blindness Following Old Thoughts*. Nevertheless, the critic Thomas Matthews rose to the challenge and sought to interpret John's painting to the Welsh public in the magazine *Cymru*:

> There is nothing more difficult than understanding the work of Augustus John – but the best way to understand it is to see that he is trying to protest against the smooth and finished style of academic painting, and instead give us painting in its bare simplicity ... In his romantic protest he tries to paint with the simplicity of primitive art.[136]

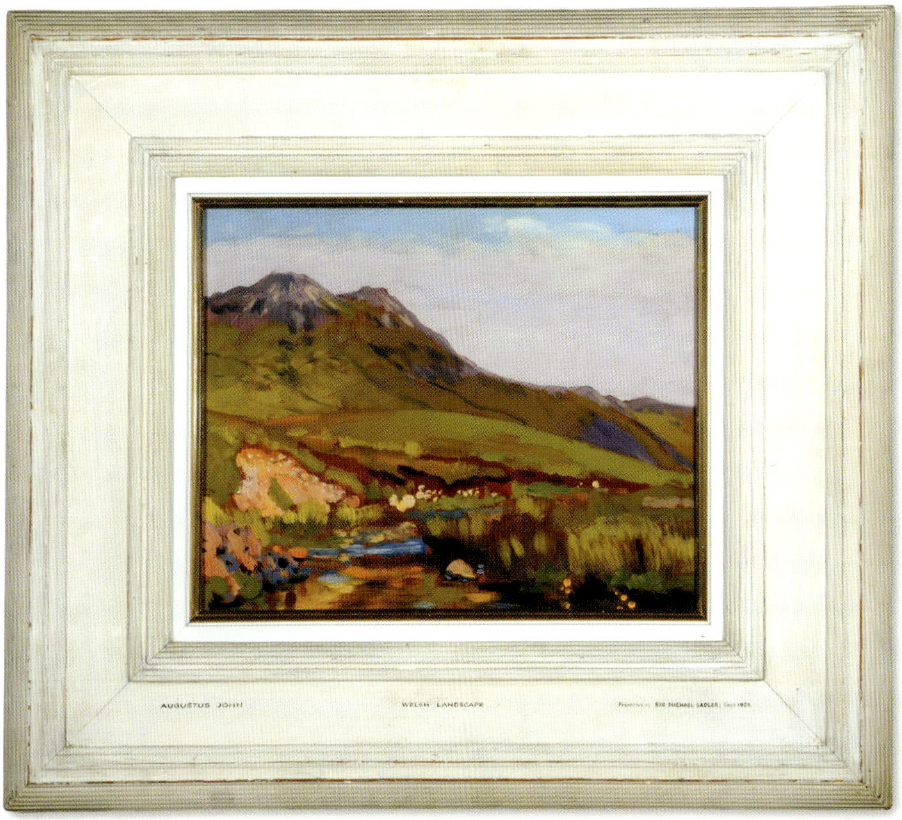

261. Augustus John, *Welsh Landscape*, 1911–14, oil, 30.5x38.1

134 Davies's father had grown up at Tynewydd, near Carmarthen, and entered the drapery business in London before emigrating to the United States and joining the Welsh community in Utica. He was described by his son as 'a man of high ideals, of an intensely religious nature, generous, hospitable, a leader in the temperance movement, devoted to his family, highly conscientious and of indomitable energy.' Bernard B. Perlman, *Lives, Loves and Art of Arthur B. Davies* (New York, 1998), p. 4.

135 Quoted in Holroyd, *Augustus John*, p. 488.

136 Thomas Matthews, 'Celf yng Nghymru: Arddangosfa'r Amgueddfa Genedlaethol', *Cymru*, XLVI (1914), p. 98, my translation from the Welsh.

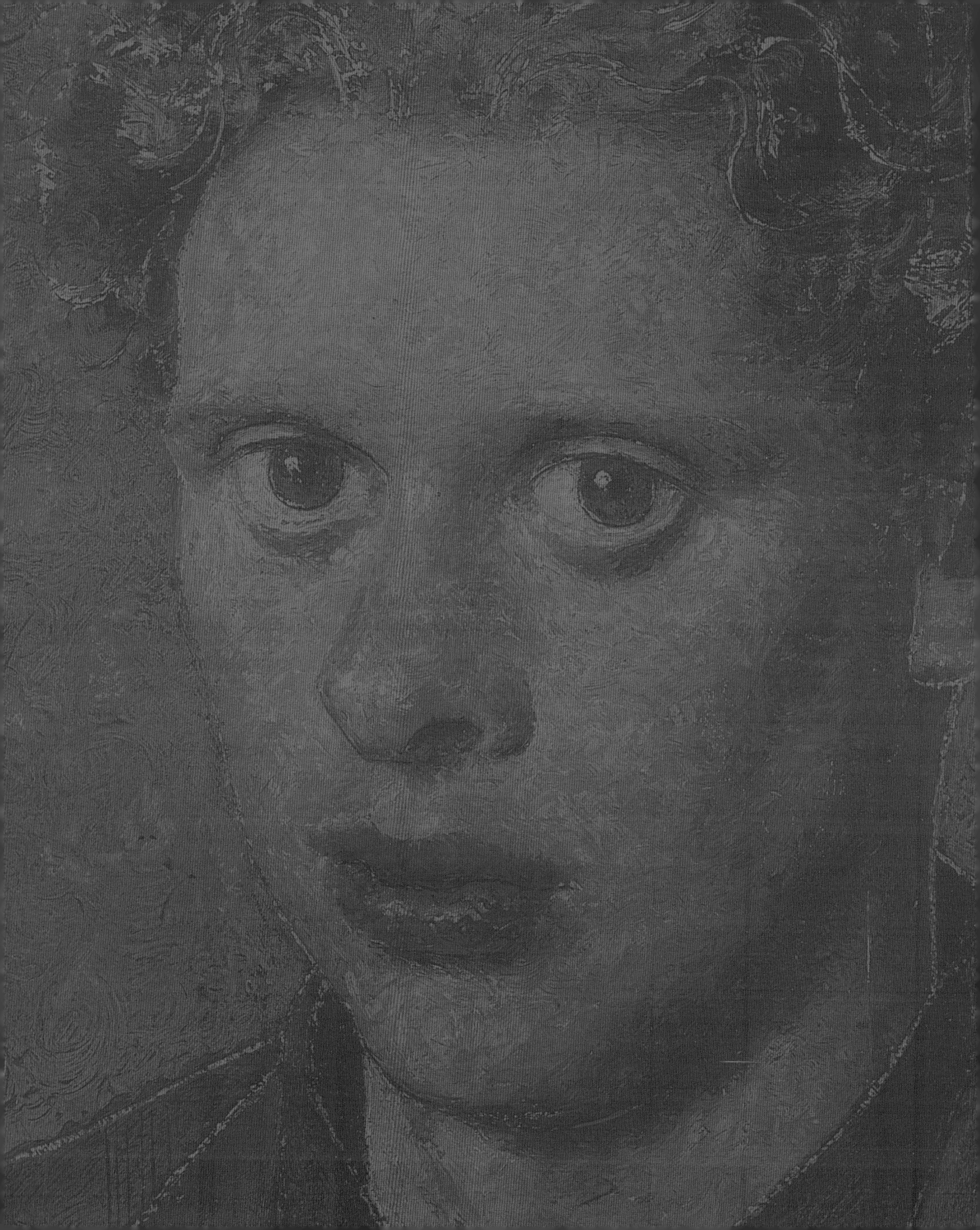

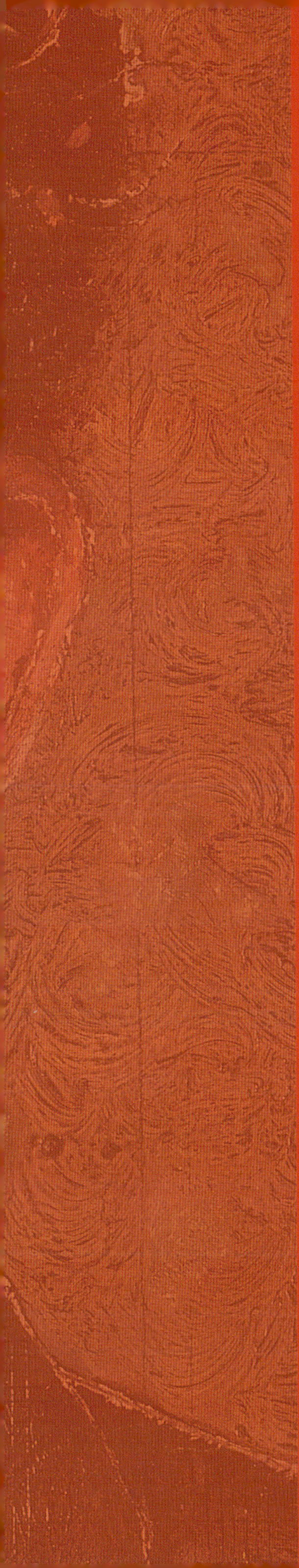

CHAPTER 4

1914–1939

CHAPTER 4 1914–1939

The Great War

By 1911, Welsh painters and sculptors were expressing in their work a wide diversity of vision, though almost all of them had been touched in some way by a sense of national revival. In that single year, Augustus John and J.D. Innes exhibited their small but radical north Wales landscapes, Clarence Whaite produced his huge mystical panorama of Snowdon, and Christopher Williams painted the grand allegory *Wales Awakening*. William Goscombe John's Investiture Regalia was seen at Caernarfon, and in Bala his statue of Lewis Edwards was unveiled. In London, Carey Morris showed a gentle portrait of his friend Walter Langley, which was his first success at the Royal Academy. However, for the future, certainly the most significant art product of 1911 was a small group of industrial landscapes, painted near Swansea, which was exhibited with the South Wales Art Society. Of the group, only the atmospheric depiction of *Cefn Cyfelach Colliery* is known to survive, but the painter, Evan Walters, would become a major figure in Welsh painting over the next forty years. Walters was unknown and just eighteen years old in 1911, but his work did not go unnoticed. An equally young reporter on a local newspaper, John Davies Williams, wrote of the exciting contrast the pictures made with the somewhat tiresome portrayals of the beauties of the Gower peninsula that surrounded them, and predicted accurately that 'Evan J. Walters is going to make a name for himself.'[1]

Behind the emergence of the young Evan Walters lay the teaching of William Grant Murray, Principal of the Swansea School of Art. Murray had arrived from his native Scotland in 1909, charged with developing both the art school and the new Glynn Vivian Art Gallery. However, the evolution of his ideas was interrupted after only five years by the outbreak of the Great War. Both through its effect on the psyche of the individual artists that it touched, and the upheaval that it caused to the social, political and economic context in which subsequently they functioned, the war changed everything. Two of the most prominent figures of the past would not live to witness the post-war era. Clarence Whaite died in 1912, and his friend

1 *Cambria Daily Leader*, 6 December 1911, p. 4.

2 Walters did not escape entirely, since he was conscripted into the American forces. However, he served only in the United States.

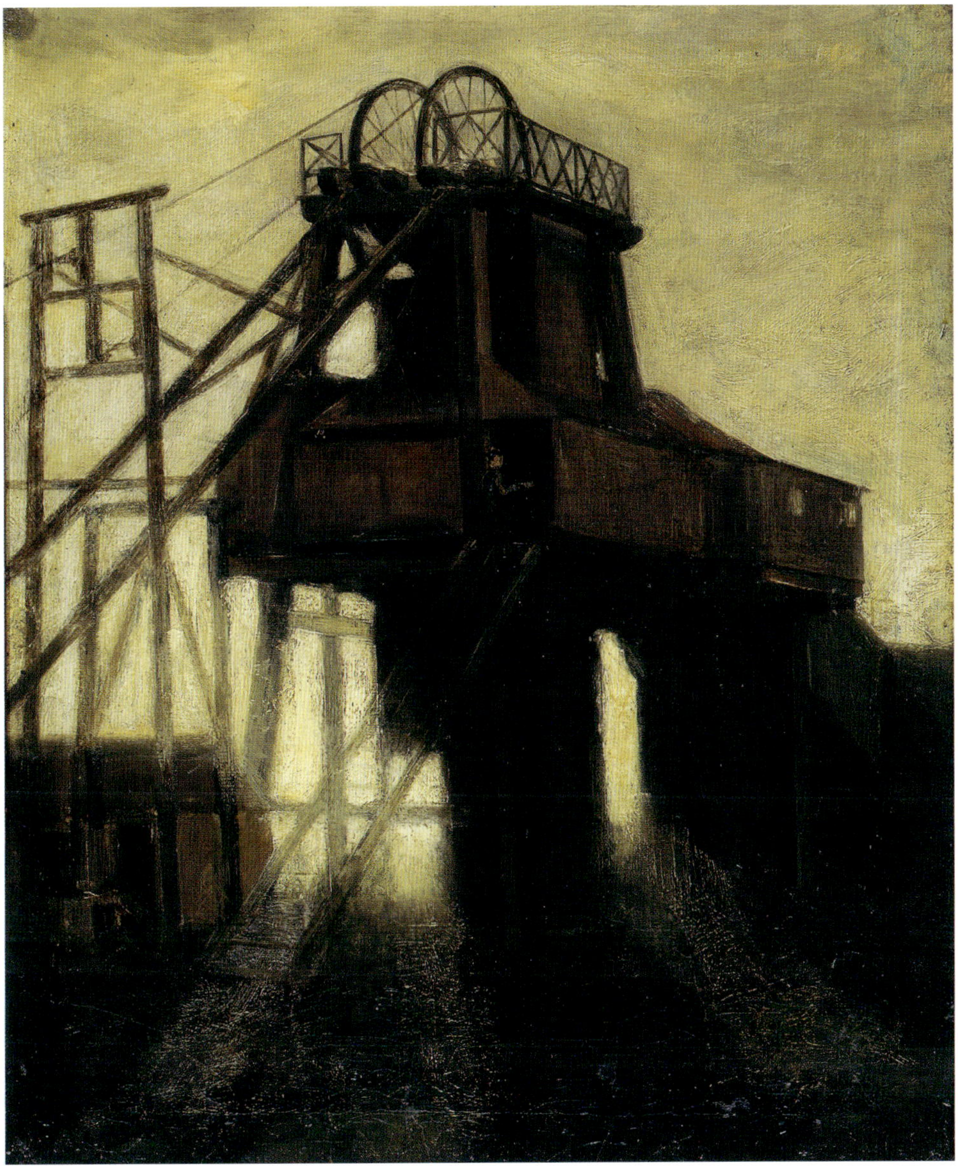

262. Evan Walters, *Cefn Cyfelach Colliery*, 1911, oil, 61.1x50.8

T.H. Thomas followed in 1915. The young J.D. Innes had succumbed to tuberculosis within a few weeks of the outbreak of the war in 1914. Of those who would survive, only Evan Walters was fortunate enough largely to escape its direct effects. With the aid of scholarships he had progressed from Swansea to train further at the Royal Academy Schools, and then left for New York before army conscription was introduced.[2] Others were not so fortunate. Carey Morris served in the trenches, where he witnessed distressing scenes, and was himself gassed. David Jones, who had begun his art training at the Camberwell School of Art, enlisted in 1915 and served with the Royal Welch Fusiliers. He was wounded in the terrible battle for Mametz Wood in the summer of the following year.

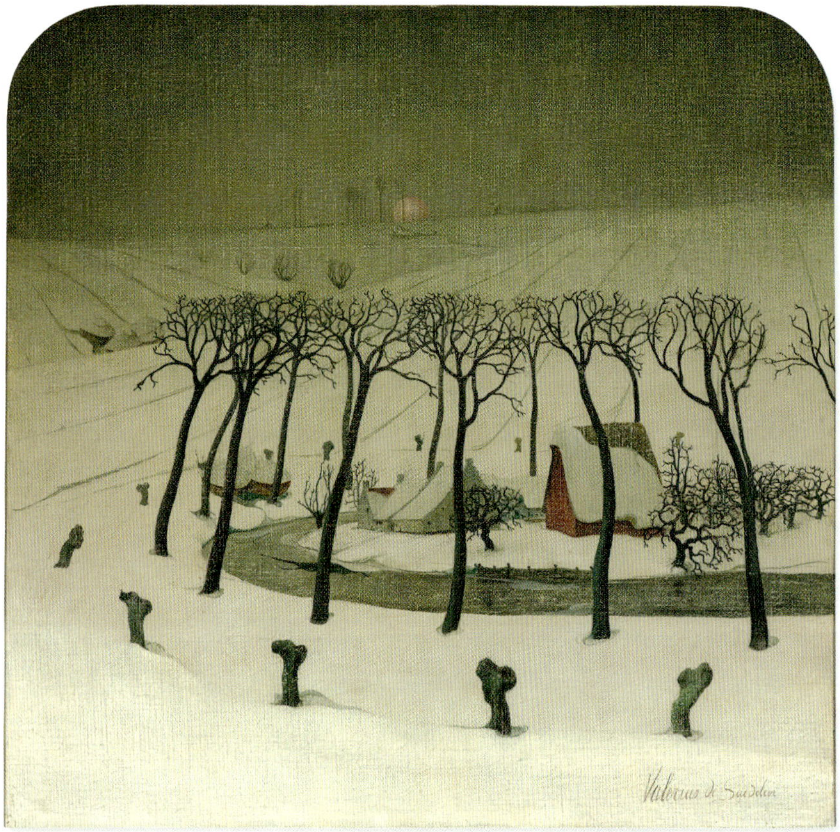

The invasion of Belgium by German forces in 1914 resulted in a massive exodus of refugees, many of whom fled to Britain. Among them were some sixty professional artists, and at the invitation of the Davies sisters of Llandinam, the sculptor George Minne, the painters Gustave van de Woestyne and Valerius de Saedeleer were settled with their families in mid-Wales. Later, the de Saedeleers were joined near Aberystwyth by Edgar Gevaert, who had been wounded in the fighting. Unsurprisingly, the work produced by these exiled artists in Wales was sombre in tone, though all but Minne sought to respond directly to their new environment. Valerius de Saedeleer painted mainly in the Rheidol and Ystwyth valleys, but presented a landscape that even in springtime rejuvenation he rendered devoid of people. Edgar Gevaert's studies of the natural world included suggestively symbolic animals and birds but, again, were unpopulated by humans.[3] It is clear that the Davies sisters and their associates hoped that the influx of these artists might contribute to the evolution of art culture in Wales.[4] Significantly, at the end of 1914, in a new magazine, *Welsh Outlook*, funded by the sisters' brother, David Davies, the editor, Thomas Jones, included the first of a number of essays about Belgian art and literature. Jones, whose early background had been the steel industry before he became an academic and civil servant, suggested that the realist strand of tradition, represented in painting by Eugène Laermans, and in sculpture by Minne and Meunier, might provide a model for young Welsh artists.

263. Valerius de Saedeleer, *Farmstead in the Valley*, *c*.1916, oil, 56.5x59

opposite
264. Edgar Gevaert, *The Bay of Aberystwyth*, *c*.1916–19, oil, 103x103

By this time, Christopher Williams and Augustus John, the two most prominent figures in Welsh painting, were in mid-career, and for both of them the war would prove a watershed. For John, it brought to an end a golden age of creative excitement. Perhaps he is not to be blamed for the insensitivity of his comment, made at the end of the first month of the war, that it 'probably makes France impossible for holidays', since the nature and duration of what was to follow was foreseen by very few people.[5] In 1914, wars were still regarded, on the whole, as a matter for professional soldiers fighting in unfamiliar distant lands.

3 *Art in Exile. Flanders, Wales and the First World War*, ed. Oliver Fairclough, Robert Hoozee & Caterina Verdickt (Ghent and Cardiff, 2002).

4 Moira Vincentelli, 'The Davies Family and Belgian Refugee Artists and Musicians in Wales', *National Library of Wales Journal*, XXII (1981), pp. 226–35.

5 John to Dorelia McNeill, 31 August 1914, NLW MS 22305D, ff. 118-19.

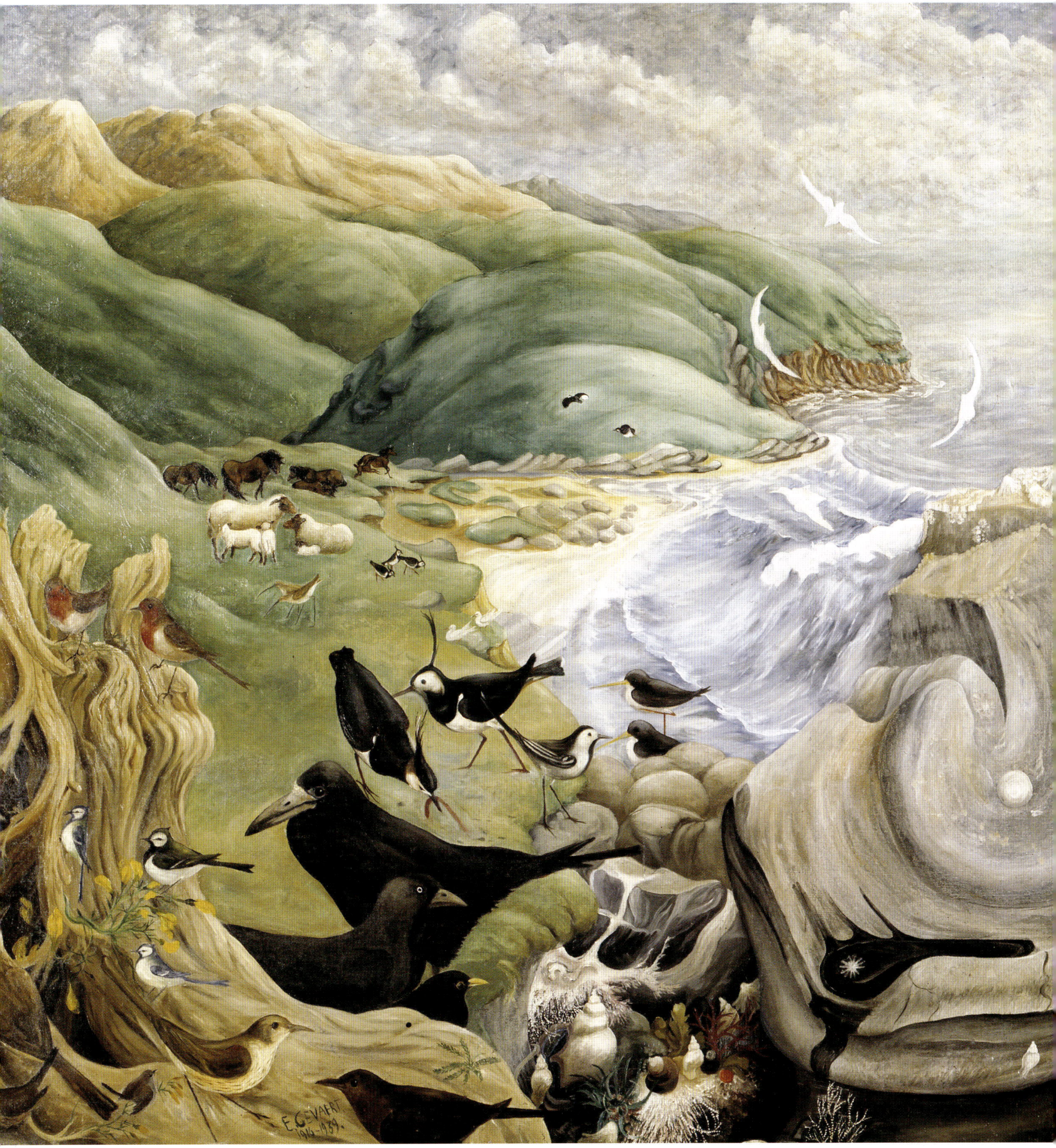
E.GEVAERT
1914-1939.

6 *The Times*, 27 November 1917 and Aitkin (subsequently Lord Beaverbrook), letter to F.E. Smith, quoted in Michael Holroyd, *Augustus John. The New Biography*, p. 426.

7 P.G. Konody, 'The Canadian War Memorials', *Colour* (September 1918). The fault was not entirely John's, since the building that was intended to house the mural was never constructed.

8 Williams did not travel as an official war artist. He was accompanied in France by the Scottish painter Muirhead Bone, who was in government employ.

opposite, top
266. Augustus John, *David Lloyd George*, 1916, oil, 91.6x72

opposite, bottom
267. Christopher Williams, *The Charge of the Welsh Division at Mametz Wood on 11 July 1916*, 1916, oil, 172.7x274.2

In contrast to his radical image as an artist, John soon came to take a conventional and patriotic view of the war, and indeed briefly considered enlisting. He had met David Lloyd George in Cardiff for the first time just before the outbreak of hostilities, and after his fellow-countryman's appointment as Minister of Munitions the following year, he was engaged to paint him. Equally charismatic and vain, the two men did not get on. The rise of Lloyd George continued through 1916, when he was instrumental in introducing conscription. By that time, nothing at home was unaffected by the war. John indulged simultaneously in the extravagant escapism of the London social elite, confirming his reputation as the archetypal Bohemian, and attempted to gain a commission that would enable him, as a member of the armed forces, to go to France and work. His chief Welsh associates, the de Waldens of Chirk Castle and the Morgans of Tredegar Park, followed his progress with interest. Alongside a steady trickle of military figures, among his Welsh sitters he began portraits of the de Waldens, and completed pictures of the eccentric Lady Tredegar and the writer W.H. Davies. In November 1917, many of these portraits, alongside earlier landscapes and figure groups, were brought together in his biggest exhibition to date. Indulging in its customary cultural appropriation, *The Times* declared John to be 'the most famous of living English painters'. Sir Max Aitkin, later Lord Beaverbrook, thought him 'the greatest artist of our time and possibly of any time'.[6] John himself was less sure, experiencing the lack of direction, the inability to focus, that would inhibit his subsequent career, in contrast with the increasingly intense vision of his sister. Gwen John had remained in Paris at the outbreak of war, moving subsequently to Meudon. Eventually Augustus was commissioned in the Canadian army, and travelled to France. Temporarily revived by this turn of events, the khaki-clad and well-trimmed officer drew and painted through to the Peace Conference of 1919. Among the Welsh in attendance there was T.E. Lawrence, of whom he painted what became the archetypal portrait, but his most important commission, given by Lord Beaverbrook to paint a mural scale work on the theme of *The Canadians Opposite Lens*, would never be completed. The cartoon was exhibited, exciting the prominent art critic P.G. Konody, who anticipated that the picture would express the 'epitome of modern war ... crowds of refugees ... detachments

265. Augustus John, *The Canadians Opposite Lens*, begun c.1919 but unfinished, oil, 370x1200

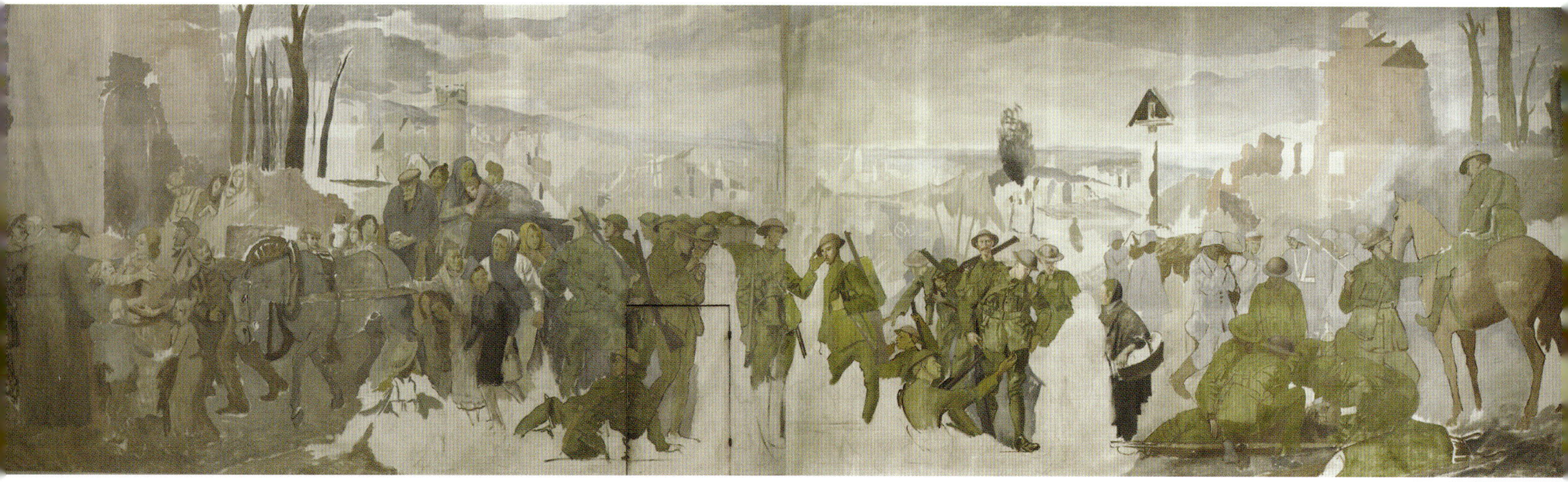

of soldiers … wounded sufferers and stretcher-bearers … all the destruction and desolation of war.' Sadly, the painting would languish unfinished in John's studio until his death.[7]

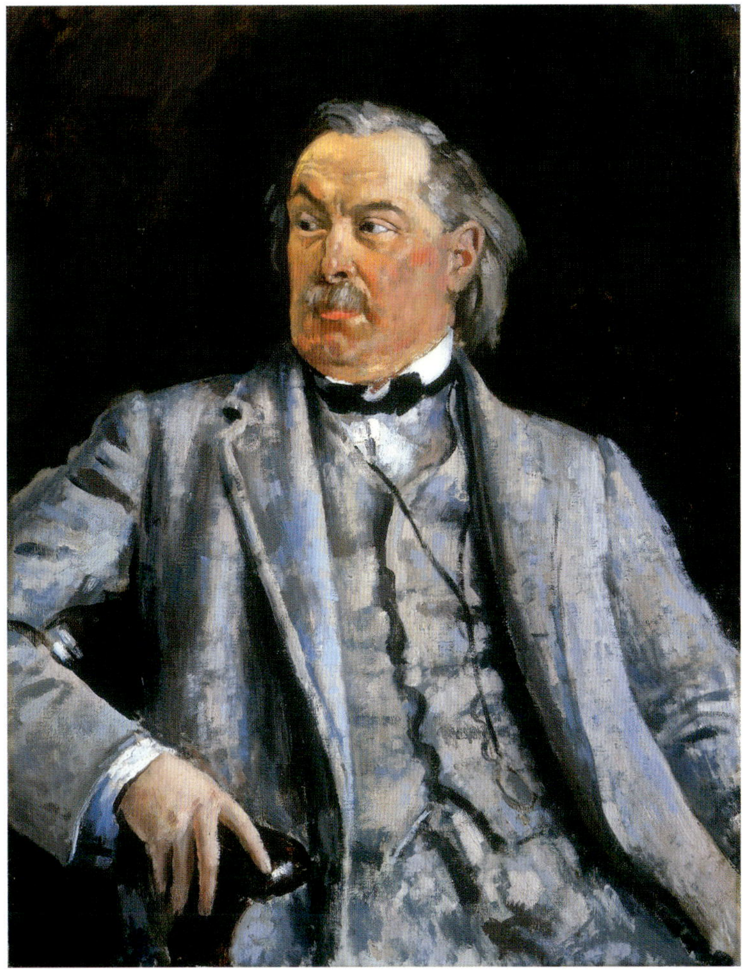

Overshadowed as a public figure by John, ironically it would fall to the aesthetically conservative Christopher Williams to paint the picture that truly expressed the horror of it all. Like John, though with more satisfactory results (in the mind of the sitter, at any rate), Williams documented the rise of David Lloyd George in portraits. In 1912 he painted him as Chancellor of the Exchequer, and in 1917 would do so again as Prime Minister. The previous year, in mid-ascent as Secretary of State for War, Lloyd George had arranged for the painter to visit France, with the intention that he should make a picture to memorialise the attack of the Welsh Division at Mametz Wood.[8]

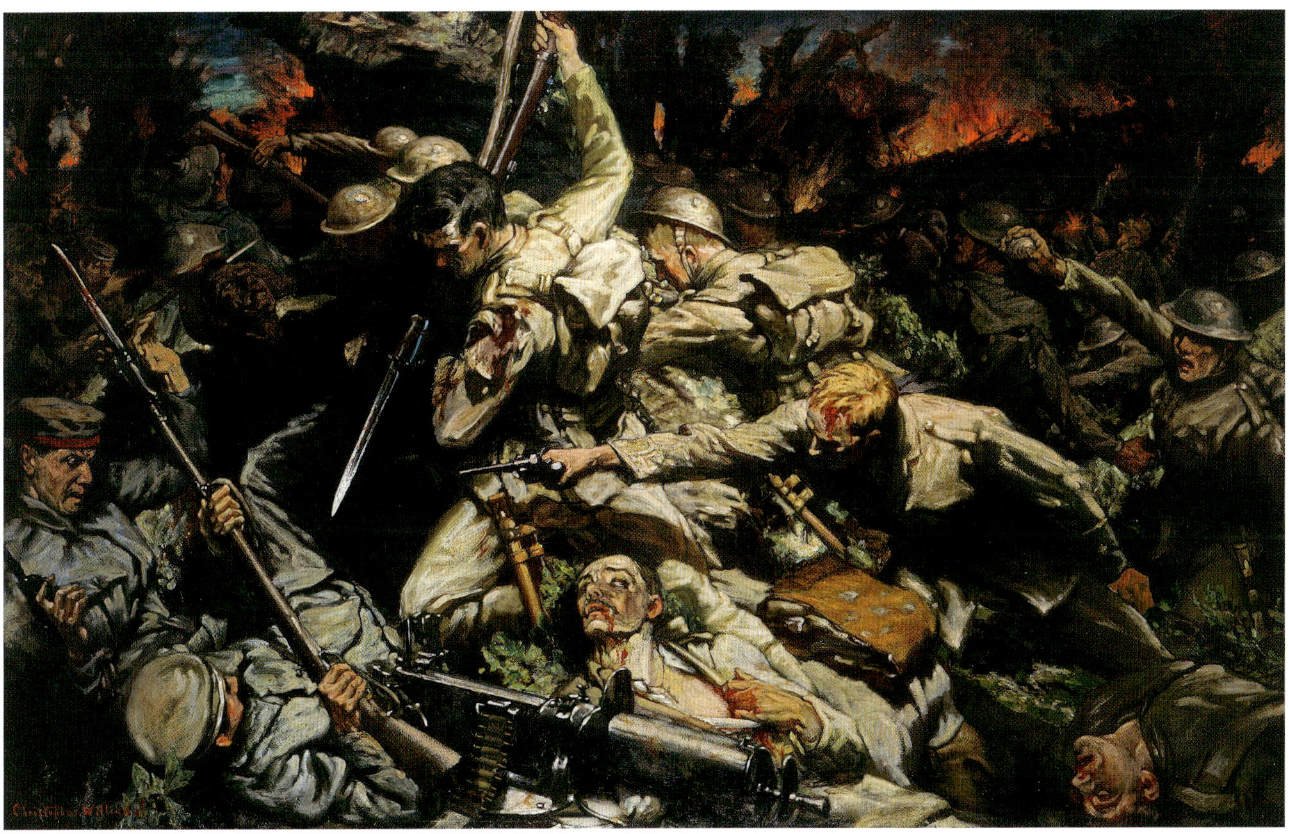

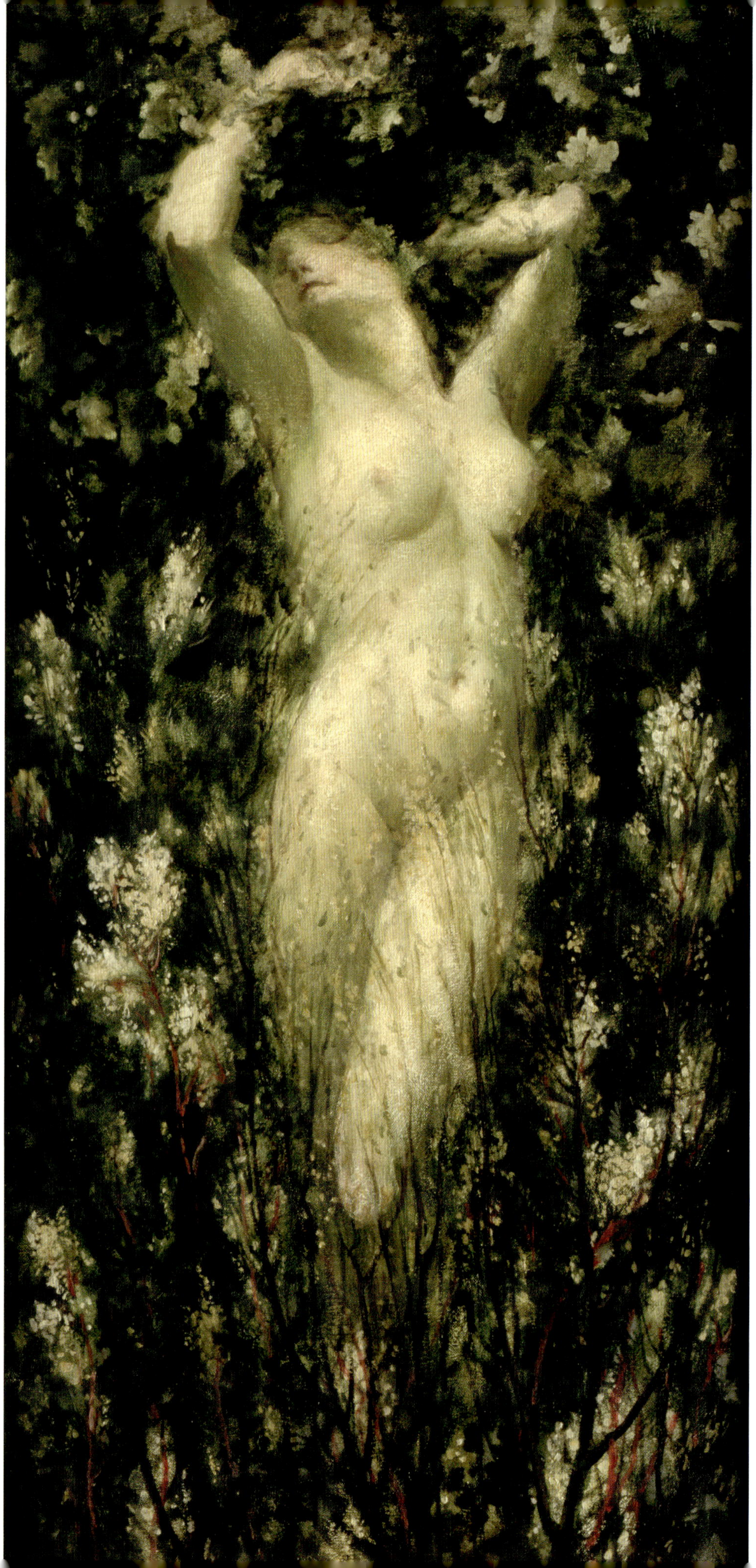

268. Christopher Williams, *Blodeuwedd*, 1925–30, oil, 110.5x51

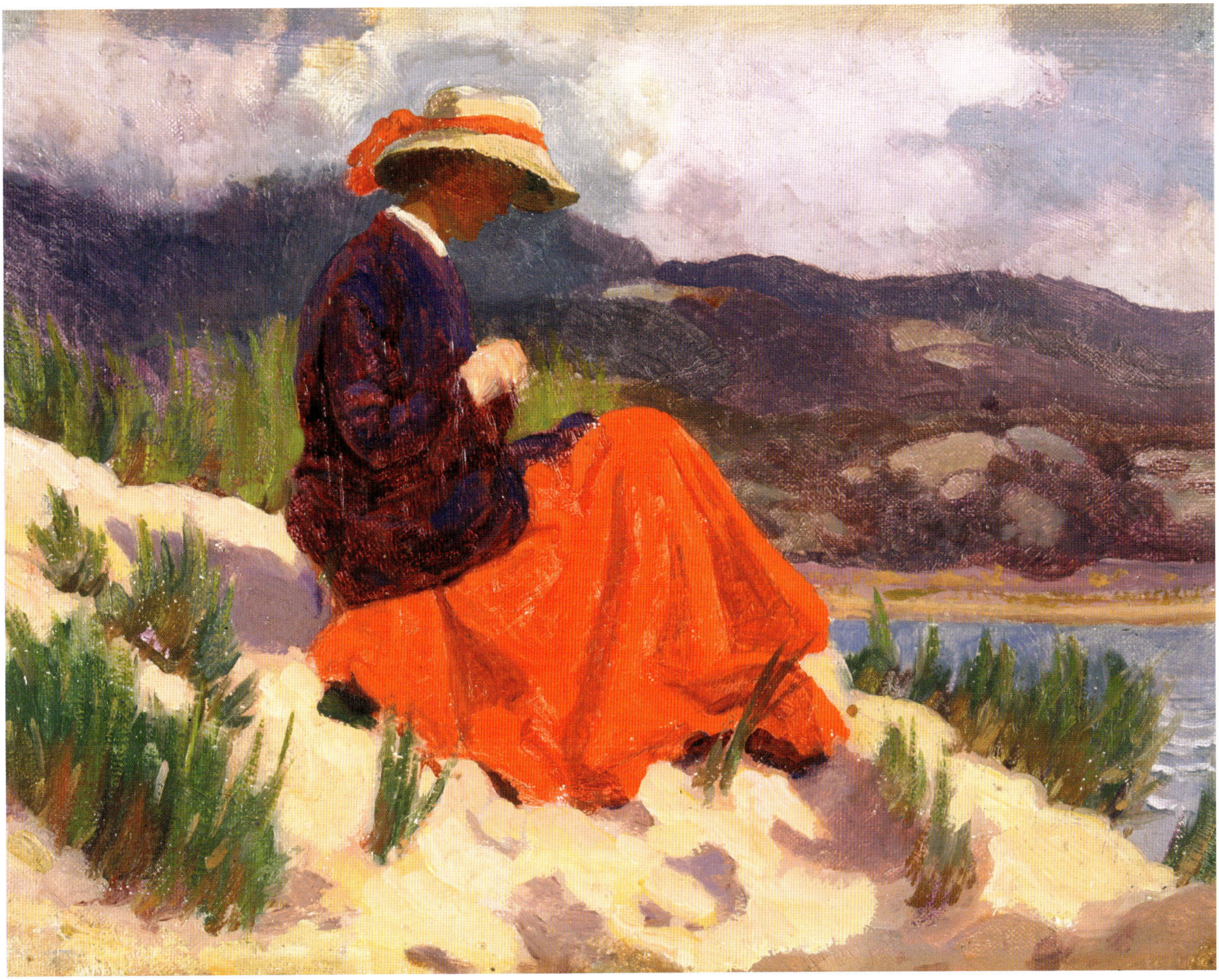

Some 4,000 men had been killed or wounded in the successive attacks on the German positions in July. As a pacifist, the response of Williams was a picture unequivocal in its condemnation of the savagery of the event.

269. Christopher Williams, *The Red Dress*, 1917, oil, 30.5x40.6

For Christopher Williams, the war marked the end of engagement with ideas of national revival. Only *Blodeuwedd*, the third painting in the Mabinogion series that he had begun to contemplate at Caernarfon in 1904, was painted afterwards. Perhaps the legend of a woman born from flowers now seemed appropriately pacific. Williams concentrated his work on portraits and small-scale landscapes, many set around Barmouth, the style of which suggests awareness of the pre-war works of John and Innes.

The response of Margaret Lindsay Williams to the war is more difficult to interpret. Her picture entitled *The Care of Wounded Soldiers at Cardiff Royal Infirmary* was commissioned in 1916 by a patron much involved with hospital charities and perhaps inevitably therefore the work emphasised compassion. A lost picture, *Onward and Upward*, was less oblique in its reference to the consequences of modern war, though its aesthetics appear to have harked back to the last vestiges of the symbolism of G.F. Watts, in whose tradition she was trained: '... the mother looks up and sees the spectre of her son being led onward and upward by the figure of an angel, both the latter being depicted in the nude'.[9] At the cessation of hostilities, Williams became one of many artists to benefit from commissions to memorialise the war. The massive group portrait of the *Welsh National War Service at Westminster Abbey* took her three years to complete, but it fell mainly to sculptors to image the nature of the war itself in their memorials. The process began early. Before the conflict, Goscombe John had been commissioned to make *The Engine Room Heroes Memorial* at Liverpool in memory of the 244 engineers who had drowned in the Titanic disaster of 1912, but since it was completed in 1916, inevitably it became more widely dedicated to seamen then losing their lives at war. Afterwards, John would produce many more memorials to those who died in battle, ranging from single figures to complex groups, and sometimes mixing allegory with his more characteristic naturalism. For Llandaf, he set a central figure, symbolic of defence and clad in Celtic apparel, between a student and a workman, whose youth was emphasised by the fact that, although they held weapons, they were not in uniform.[10]

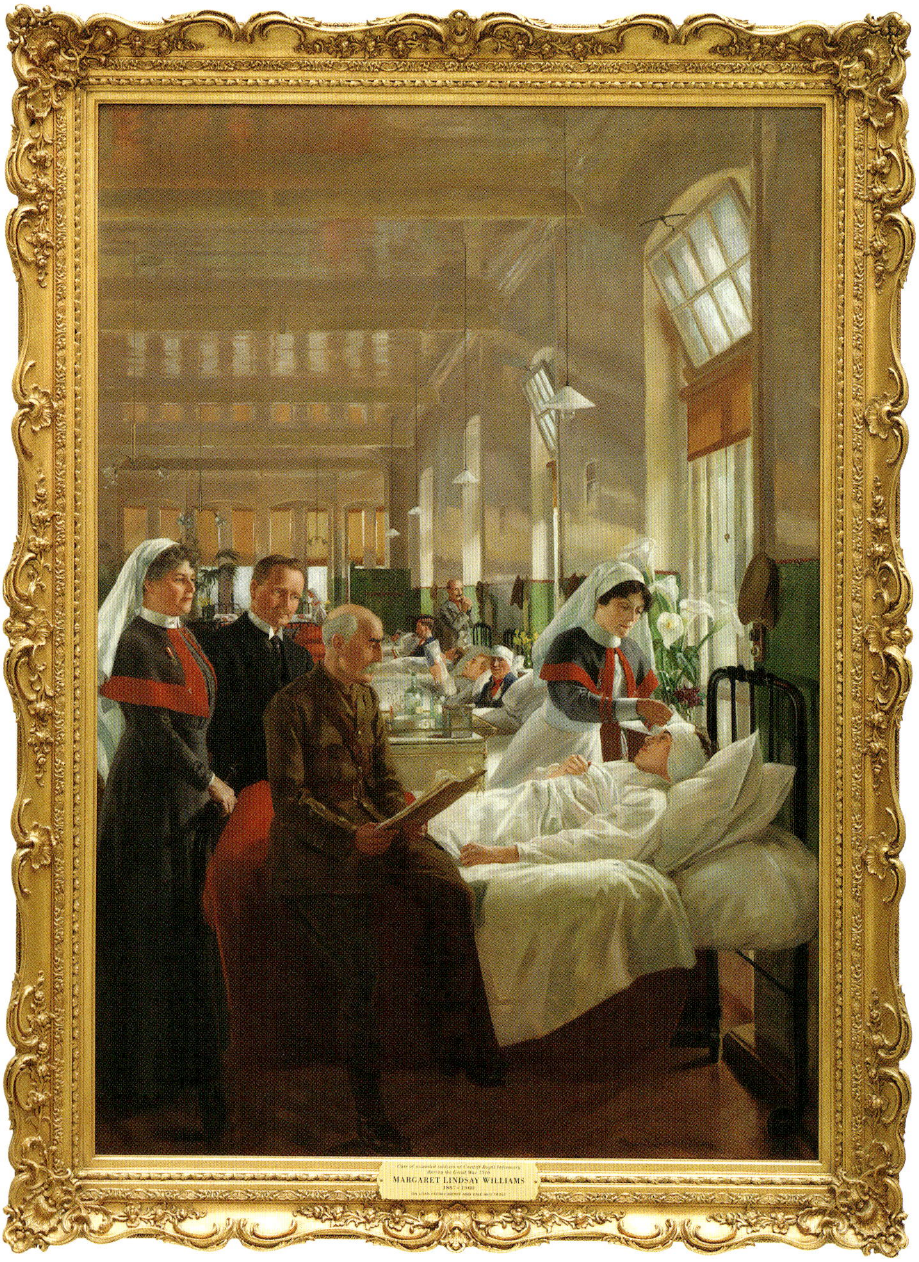

270. Margaret Lindsay Williams, *The Care of Wounded Soldiers at Cardiff Royal Infirmary during the Great War*, 1916, oil, 106.6x76.2

His most ambitious and complex memorial, among the largest commissioned, was made for Port Sunlight, near Birkenhead. The sculptor had previously worked for the patron, Lord Leverhulme, on the effigy of his late wife, Elizabeth, Lady Lever. In the art gallery that carried her name, close by the war memorial site, was hanging Curnow Vosper's *Salem*, the relic of a lost world. John's theme was, again, the defence of homeland, represented by a central group of woman and children, surrounded by an outer ring of relief plaques representing sailors, gunners and ambulance workers.

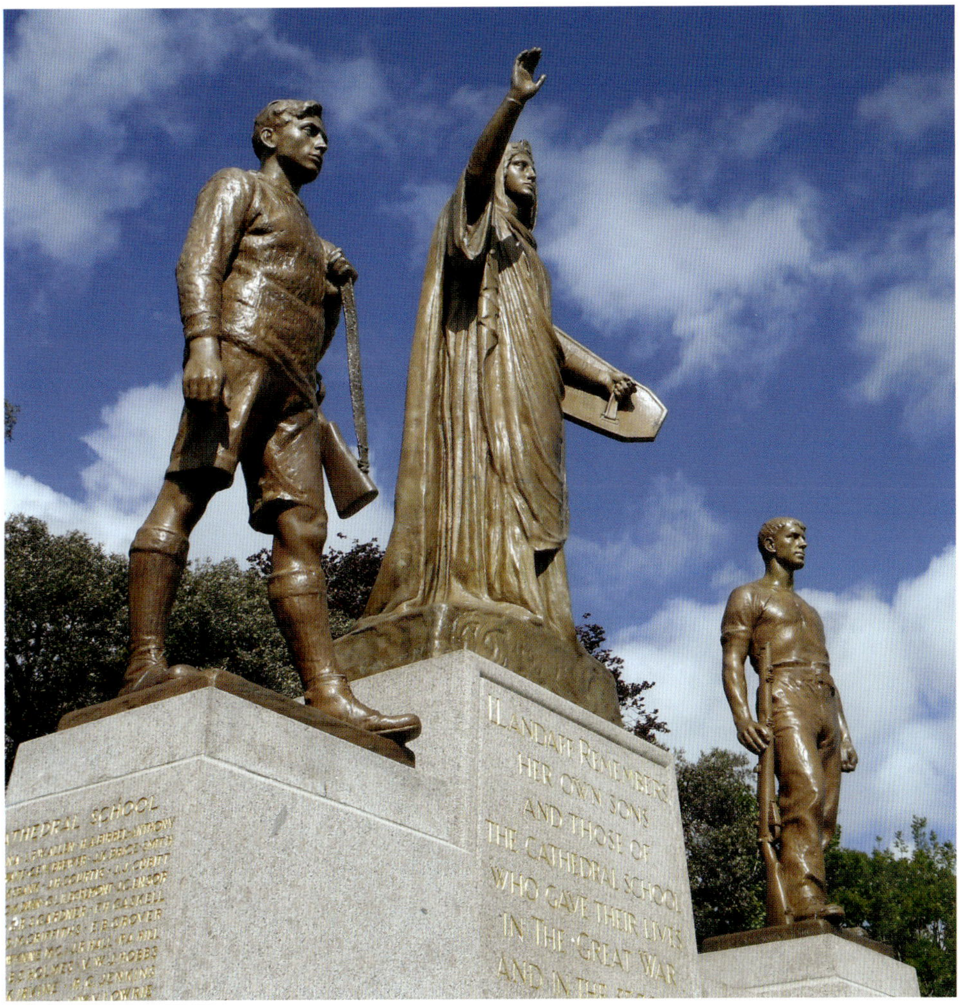

271. William Goscombe John, *The Llandaf War Memorial*, 1924, bronze

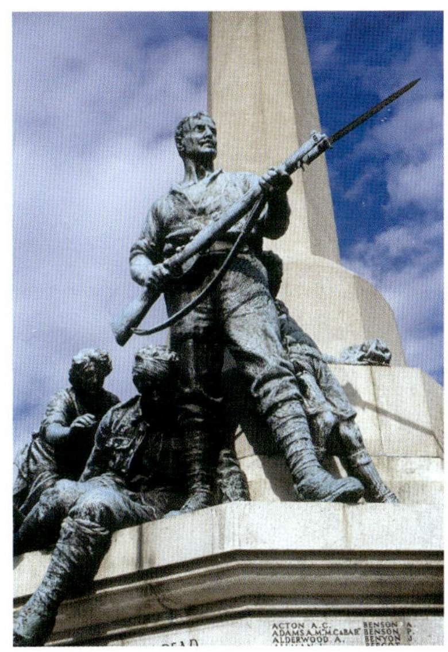

272. William Goscombe John, *The Port Sunlight War Memorial*, 1919, bronze

Goscombe John's use of Celtic reference in the Llandaf memorial reflected the perception of some Welsh intellectuals, who reached maturity in the atmosphere of the pre-war revival, that the conflict represented a struggle between nations with a contrasting national ethos – 'between the spirit of the Celt and the spirit of the Teuton', the one representing 'freedom and civilization' the other 'military arrogance and barbarity'.[11]

9 *Western Mail*, 18 March 1919, p. 4.

10 For this and other Welsh memorials, see Angela Gaffney, *Aftermath. Remembering the Great War in Wales* (Cardiff, 2000).

11 John Morris-Jones, foreword to *Gwlad fy Nhadau: Rhodd Cymru i'w Byddin* (London, 1915), p. v. The volume, published in English as *The Land of my Fathers. A Welsh Gift Book*, was notable for the reproduction in colour of the works of a number of Welsh painters, including Christopher Williams's *Wales Awakening*.

However, perceptions of the meaning of the war varied considerably, and resulted in disagreement about the nature of memorialisation on more than one occasion. None was as significant as the dispute over the statue of Hedd Wyn. The death of the poet at Pilckem Ridge in 1917, before his poem 'Yr Arwr' (The Hero) was awarded the Celtic-style 'black chair' at the National Eisteddfod at Birkenhead, quickly came to be regarded as a symbol of national loss, though not universally as of the wider futility of war.[12] Kelt Edwards's memorial painting,

12 The Black Chair was so named because of the cloth draped over it in mourning when the poet's name was called at the chairing ceremony. The chair itself, the work of the Belgian refugee Eugeen van Fleteren, was the first in a series of Celtic revival eisteddfod designs. The chair for 1919 would be designed by Kelt Edwards. See Peter Lord, *Y Chwaer-Dduwies: Celf, Crefft a'r Eisteddfod*, (Llandysul, 1992), pp. 73–5.

13 J. Dyfnallt Owen, 'Hedd Wyn', *Cenhinen Gŵyl Dewi* (1918), p. 16, my translation from the Welsh.

14 Toft was responsible for two other important commissions in Wales. In 1893 he had created the statue of Henry Richard at Tregaron, and in 1909 his Welsh National Boer War Memorial would be opened in Cardiff.

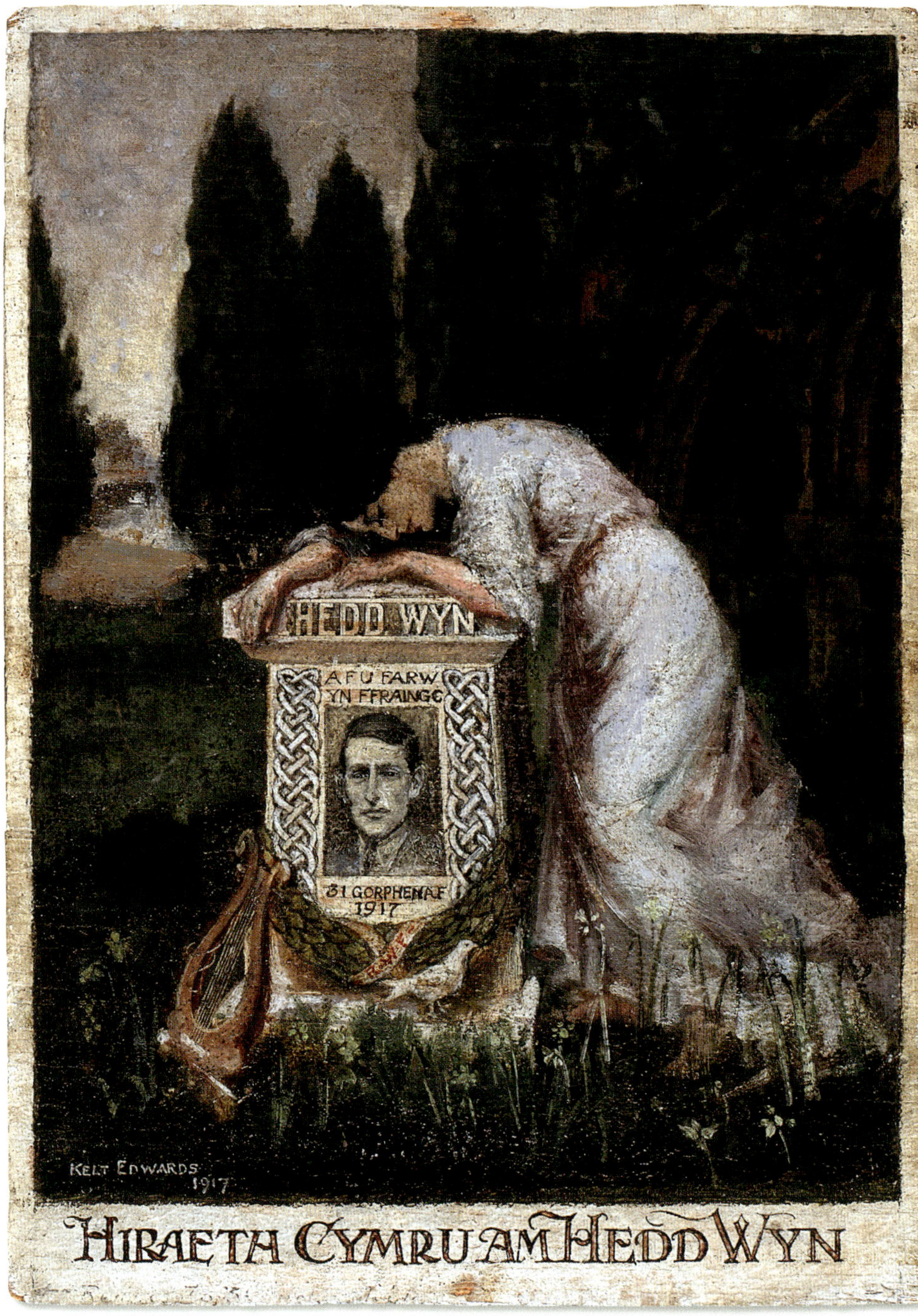

274. John Kelt Edwards, *Hiraeth Cymru am Hedd Wyn*, 1917, oil, 33x24

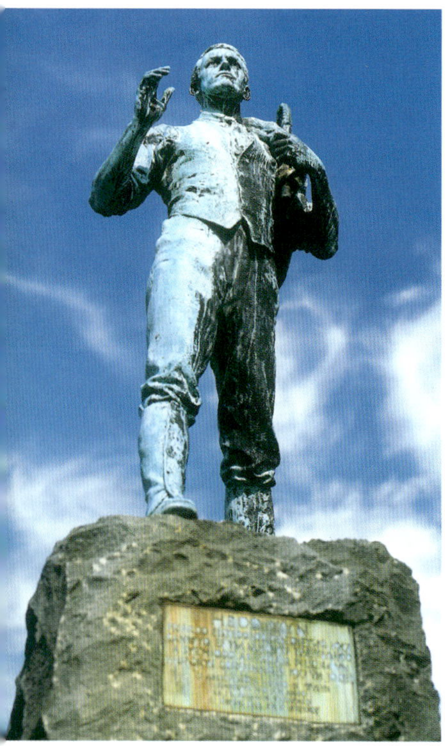

273. Leonard Merrifield, *Memorial to Hedd Wyn*, Trawsfynydd, 1923, bronze

disseminated in the form of a postcard reproduction and reinvented in black and white for the memorial volume of the poet's work, was celebrated by one critic as symbolic of the defence by 'the countries of the muse – France and Celtia, from the destruction of the Vandal on his accursed way.'[13] The poet was depicted in his army uniform. However, after the war, a dispute arose as to whether the memorialisation of the poet in the form of a statue should reflect this militant spirit, by portraying him again in uniform, or represent a spirit of pacifism, suggesting the immorality of war. Both the poet's bardic name, 'Hedd' and his work as a shepherd clearly suggested the potential potency of his death as a symbol of peace. The dispute was resolved in favour of the pacifist tendency, and Leonard Merrifield (a pupil of Goscombe John) was selected to create for his home village of Trawsfynydd the statue of the poet as shepherd.

In the aftermath

During the national revival of the late-nineteenth and early-twentieth centuries, the imaging of the common people of industrial society remained submerged beneath a sea of celebrations of the mountain landscape, of mythologised history, and of sculptural manifestations of civic pride. Only in forms marginal to academic art, such as trade union banners, were expressed the aspirations of industrial workers towards ownership and control of the resources that their labour made available. In public sculpture, it was not until 1902 that a pioneer of the labour movement was celebrated in Wales. The Co-operative Union funded the elaboration of the plain tomb of the utopian socialist Robert Owen at Newtown, his birthplace. The sculptor Albert Toft enclosed the tomb in elegant art nouveau railings, adorned with a portrait medallion and a relief depicting forward-marching workers. Two years earlier, Toft had made the statue of Owen for installation at New Lanark, site of the model manufacturing community that he had developed in Scotland.[14]

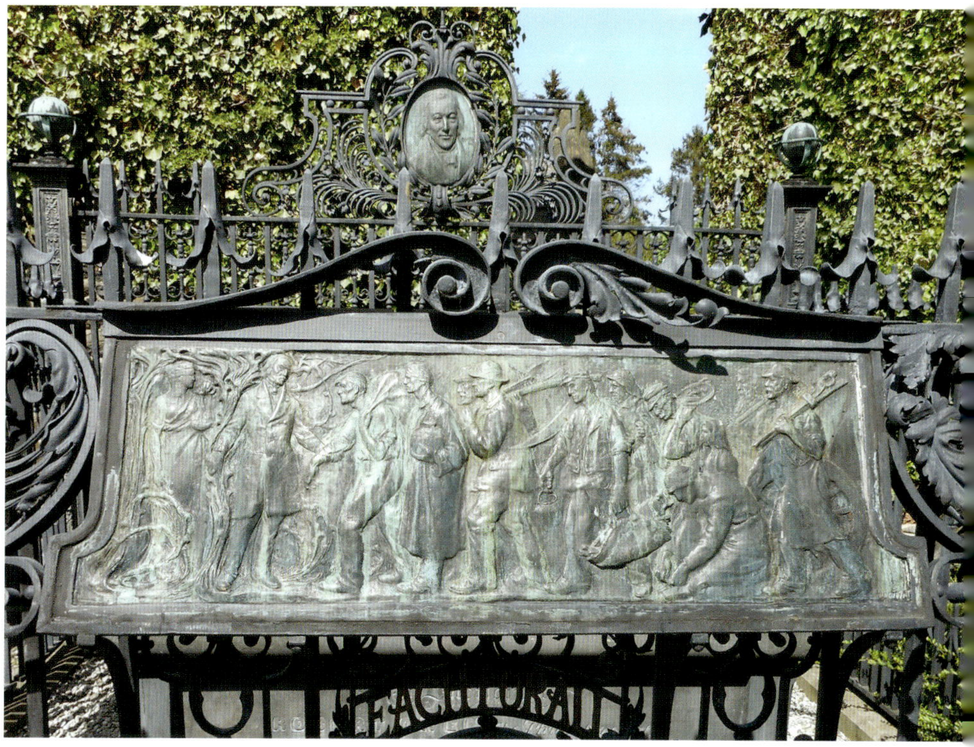

275. Albert Toft,
The Tomb of Robert Owen,
Newtown, 1902, bronze

In 1910, the year of *The Welsh Weavers*, Carey Morris's image of unchanging rural stability, the social cohesion which it implied visibly broke down in the other Wales, when property in the centre of Tonypandy in the Rhondda was smashed by angry and frustrated strikers. The events, and the government's response, which was to send in the army, were documented in a remarkable series of photographs taken by the local photographer, Levi Ladd. Some of Ladd's photographs were reproduced in the *Western Mail*, which also made use of the cartoons of J.M. Staniforth in its attempts to demonise the striking colliers. Imaging the case for the colliers was far more difficult, though voices were raised in support. In his poem 'The Strike', the socialist poet T.E. Nicholas – 'Niclas y Glais' – posed a question that would come to preoccupy intellectuals, including visual artists, after the war. How should a Christian react to immediate social crisis in the context of conventional dogma which taught that worldly tribulation was an expression of god's will, and that passivity in response would be rewarded by a heavenly after-life? It would become known as the 'Question of the Kingdom':

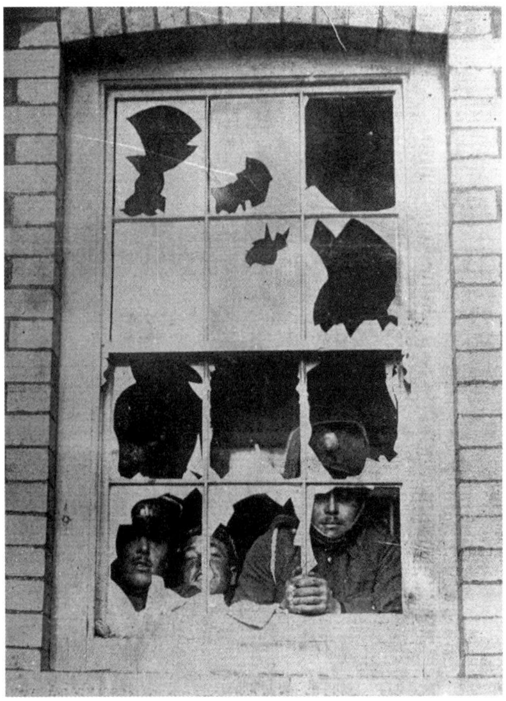

276. Levi Ladd,
Hussars at the Glamorgan Colliery, Tonypandy,1910

Ni soniaf am hawliau Duw
Nes cael bara ar fyrddau'r byd,
Ni soniaf am nefoedd tu hwnt i'r bedd
Nes cael y bythynod yn glyd.

Ofer yw son am Iawn,
A chanu am Galfari
Tra bryniau'r Rhondda yn goch gan waed
Diniwed fy mrodyr i ...

I will not speak of the rights of God
Until there is bread on the tables of the world,
I will not speak about heaven beyond the grave
Until cottages are warm.

Talk of Atonement is vain,
And songs of Calvary,
While the hills of Rhondda run red
With the blood of my innocent brothers ...

'The Strike' was published in 1912, in the collection *Cerddi Gwerin* (Folk Poems) with a frontispiece reproduction of the French painter Millet's celebrated symbol of labour, *Man with a Hoe*, and three didactic engravings. The next collection of the works of Nicholas, *Cerddi Rhyddid* (Songs of Freedom) displayed on its cover a characteristic image of the aspirations of working people, combining allegory and realism.[15] Chained workers – male and female – reach upwards to a winged figure of freedom, against a background of dark and smoking

15 T.E. Nicholas, *Cerddi Gwerin* (Caernarfon, 1912); T.E. Nicholas, *Cerddi Rhyddid* (Swansea, 1914), my translation.

chimneys. Little is known of the views on such matters of the young Evan Walters, whose industrial landscapes excited the interest of the critic John Davies Williams in 1911, but imagery of this kind suggests a context for the direction that his own work and that of some of his contemporaries would take after the interruption of the war.

During that remarkably creative year of 1911, a sixteen-year-old collier from Ystalyfera began attending part-time classes at Swansea School of Art. The family circumstances of Vincent Evans required that he continue to work underground, but he had been sketching what he observed there already for at least two years. In 1912, no doubt at the instigation of John Davies Williams, some of his drawings were published in the *Cambria Daily Leader*. By 1919, when Walters returned from the United States with the work of establishing his reputation all before him, Evans had already exhibited for the first time at the Royal Academy, and the South Wales Miners' Federation had bought his painting, *Toilers Underground*, for £60.

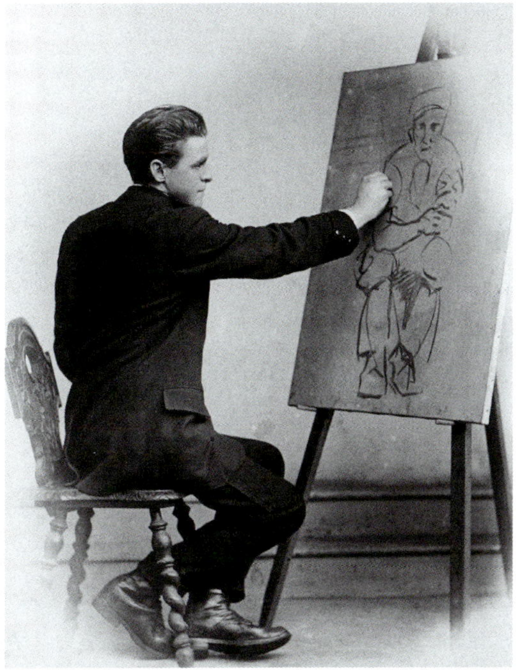

left
277. Chapman & Sons, *Vincent Evans*, *c.*1918

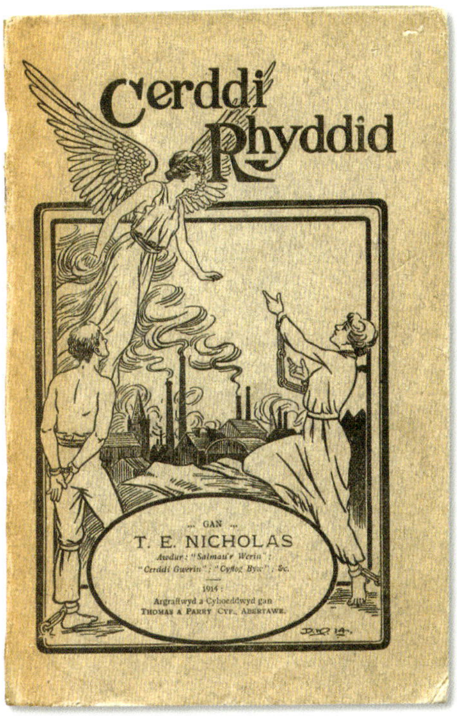

below left
278. Possibly D.J. Davies, cover illustration for T.E. Nicholas, *Cerddi Rhyddid*, 1914, 18x12

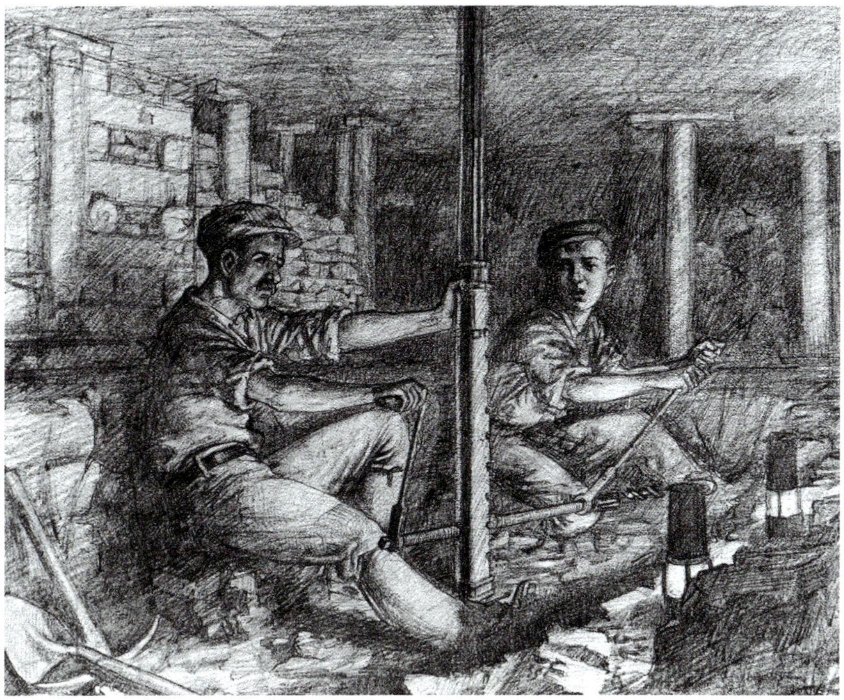

279. Vincent Evans, *Boring a Bottom Hole Underground*, 1919, pencil, 24.3x29.6

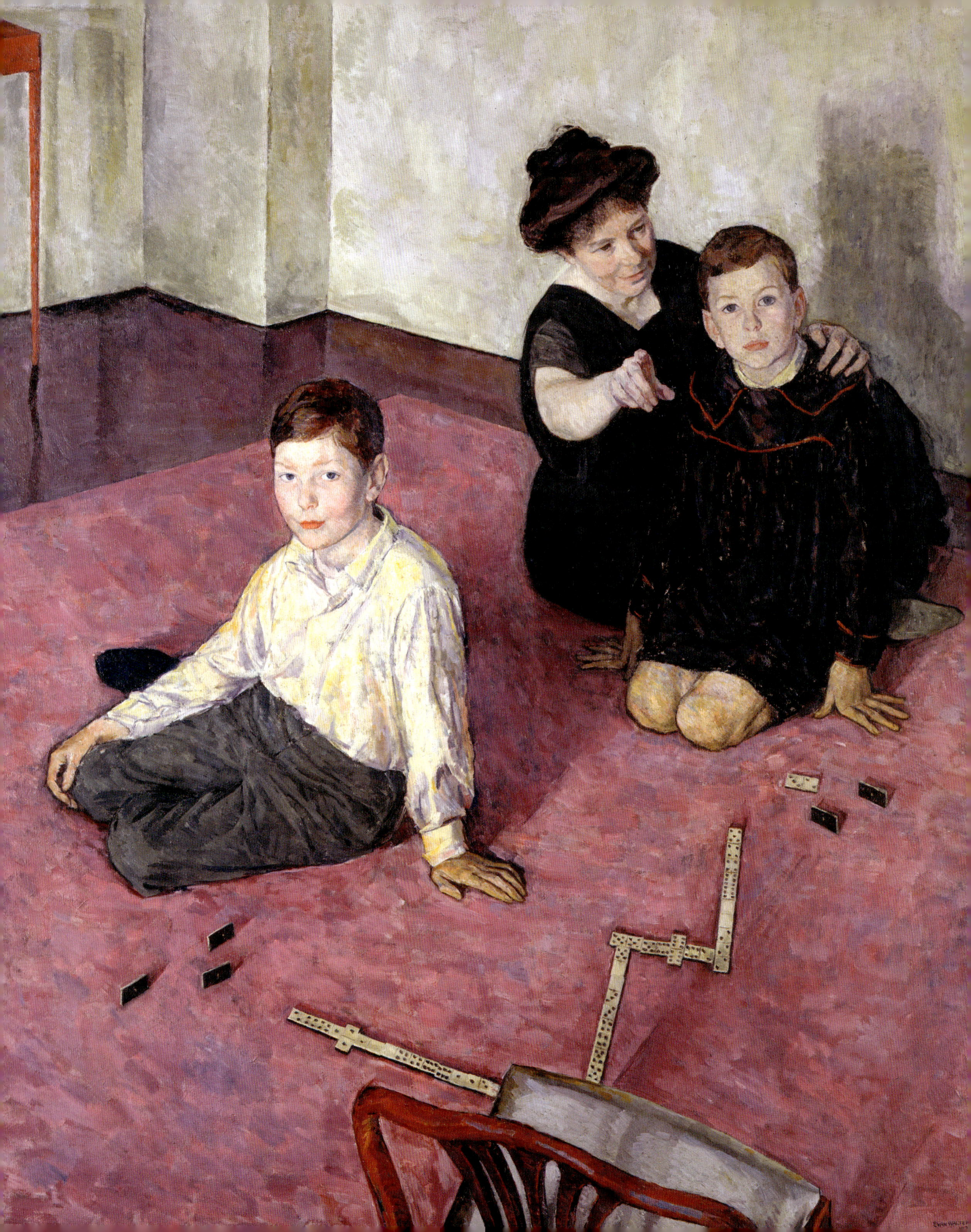

The following year Evans was granted a scholarship, on the advice of Goscombe John. The *Western Mail* reported the award and described the recipient as a 'collier artist', an epithet that would become something of a cliché with newspapers over the ensuing decade as several painters from backgrounds in the coalfields of England, as well as Wales, attracted the attention of the London press and intelligentsia.[16] Evan Walters would soon become a beneficiary of this attention, despite the fact that he had not worked in the coal industry. In fact, the exhibition that he was given by Grant Murray at the Glynn Vivian Art Gallery in 1920 contained only three works related directly to the mining community within which he had grown up.[17] Nevertheless, one of them proved to be fundamentally important in the re-establishment of his career. Among the visitors to his exhibition was Winifred Coombe Tennant, of Cadoxton Lodge in the Neath Valley. Coombe Tennant was a rising figure in Welsh Liberal Party politics, close to Lloyd George, and with a pre-war background in sophisticated London society.[18] She had begun to engage with young Welsh painters in 1911, when she first became aware of yet another student at Swansea School of Art, called Frank Alford. She commissioned a portrait from Alford in 1915, and although his career would take him away from Wales (he would become Frank Brangwyn's chief studio assistant), Coombe Tennant's close involvement with the development of Welsh visual culture would last until the end of her life.[19] When she saw Walters's painting *Mother and Babe* at the Glynn Vivian gallery, she perceived immediately the ability of the painter to combine sophisticated reference to European high art tradition with the immediacy of the local contemporary world. *Mother and Babe* was 'the typical Madonna and Child of Industrial Wales'. Soon afterwards she met Walters:

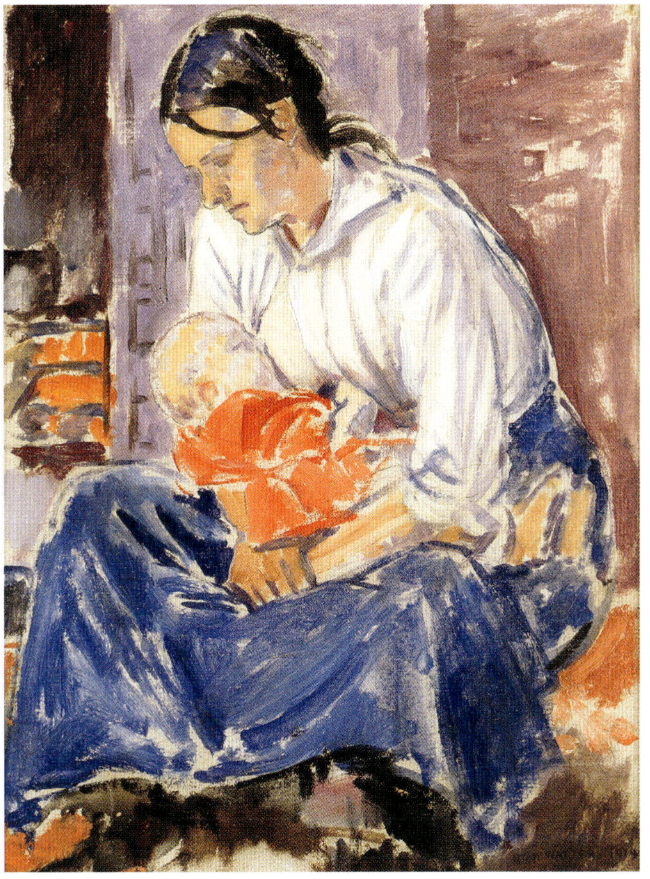

281. Evan Walters,
Mother and Babe,
1919, oil, 38x29

> A young dark typical Welshman. Very intelligent and pleasant. Had a long talk ... He will paint my portrait this summer – 15 to 20 guineas – and charcoal heads of the children would be 5 gns. He has genius. He then introduced me to the Director of the Gallery. Mr Murray and I had a long talk on Welsh Art, Augustus John, Eisteddfod exhibitions etc ... Oh! How refreshing to meet kindred spirits.[20]

The meeting established relationships with Walters and Murray that would be sustained by Coombe Tennant for thirty years. She immediately bought three works from the exhibition and commissioned not only her own portrait but also that of her husband and a group of herself with her two children, Alexander and Henry, playing dominoes.

16 For the English painters, see Robert McManners and Gillian Wales, *Shafts of Light: Mining Art in the Great Northern Coalfield* (Shoreham, 2002).

17 The pre-war *Cefn Cyfelach Colliery*, *The Haulier*, and *Mother and Babe*.

18 See Peter Lord, *Winifred Coombe Tennant: a Life through Art* (Aberystwyth, 2007), and *Between Two Worlds: The Diary of Winifred Coombe Tennant 1909-1924*, ed. Peter Lord (Aberystwyth, 2011).

19 For Alford, see *Brangwyn in his Studio. The Diary of his Assistant Frank Alford*, eds. Roger Alford and Libby Horner (2004).

20 Diary entry for 10 May 1920, *Between Two Worlds*, p. 291. Coombe Tennant's description of *Mother and Babe* is quoted from her retrospective observations on the rise of Evan Walters, *Cambria Daily Leader*, 25 November 1927, p. 4.

280. Evan Walters,
Dominoes, 1920,
oil, 152.5x127

In terms both of its structure and its psychological insight into the relationship between the sitters, *Dominoes* proved to be a remarkable picture. Isaac Williams, Keeper of Art at the National Museum, seeing it for the first time when visiting Coombe Tennant in 1924, thought it a 'great masterpiece'.[21]

As Walters developed his work, sustained by a steady supply of portrait commissions, Vincent Evans moved from Swansea to the Royal College of Art in London, where he was taught by the recently arrived Principal, William Rothenstein. However, on leaving in 1923 he decided to take up a teaching post in New Zealand. In retrospect, it was a decision that seems unfortunate, since he disappeared from the scene at precisely the moment when circumstances would combine to create an atmosphere favourable to the idea of the 'collier artist'. The rise of the political left, fed by economic depression and disappointed expectations following the war, provided a fertile context for the promotion of new artists who not only imaged working-class life, but themselves might be promoted by sympathetic intellectuals as expressions of a rising proletariat. A series of disputes in the coalfield culminated in the summer of 1926 in a stoppage that escalated into a general strike of industrial and transport workers throughout Britain. Coming less than a decade after the Russian Revolution, the strike polarised opinion as never before. It was defeated after ten days, but the title of Idris Davies's long poem on the subject crystallised the mood. It was 'The Angry Summer', though workers in the Welsh coalfield stayed out through the autumn of 1926 and into the following year.

282. *William Grant Murray greeting William Goscombe John at Swansea*, from the *Cambria Daily Leader*, 23 July 1926

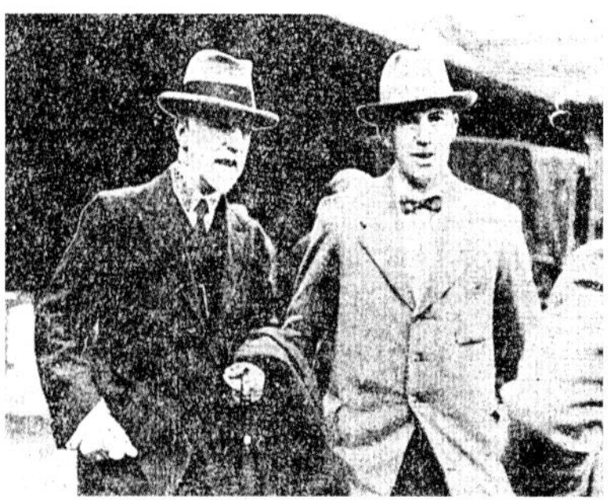

opposite
283. Evan Walters, *Poster for the National Eisteddfod at Swansea*, 1926, lithograph, 101.7x63.5

Late in July of the angry summer, against the background of the strike, the National Eisteddfod opened at Swansea. For a year, William Grant Murray had been organising what would be the largest art and craft exhibition yet seen in Wales. It included a loan section with historical pictures but its emphasis was firmly on the promotion of the work of contemporary artists and craftspeople, whom the audience was urged to patronise by pithy mottos printed in the catalogue: 'Purchase your pictures from living artists, the old masters do not require your support.' Further to this end, Grant Murray and his colleagues went to considerable pains to maximise publicity. Evan Walters created an unprecedented stir at the outset with his design for the eisteddfod poster, a striking image in black and red, whose sexual innuendo resulted in the entire edition being pulped. Winifred Coombe Tennant preserved what appears to be the only surviving copy. Surveying the exhibitions themselves, a newspaper reviewer provocatively observed that in 'Room 6 we meet the moderns who are in the dangerous stage of being accepted by the public.'[22] Among them was Augustus John, enlisted also as an adjudicator by Grant Murray with the clear intention of creating controversy, since he was to work with George Clausen, a man of conservative

21 The diary of Winifred Coombe Tennant, private archive, 19 and 20 November 1924: 'A hundred years hence that picture will be worshipped as a great masterpiece'.

22 'D.H.I.P.' in the *Cambria Daily Leader*, 3 August 1926, p. 3.

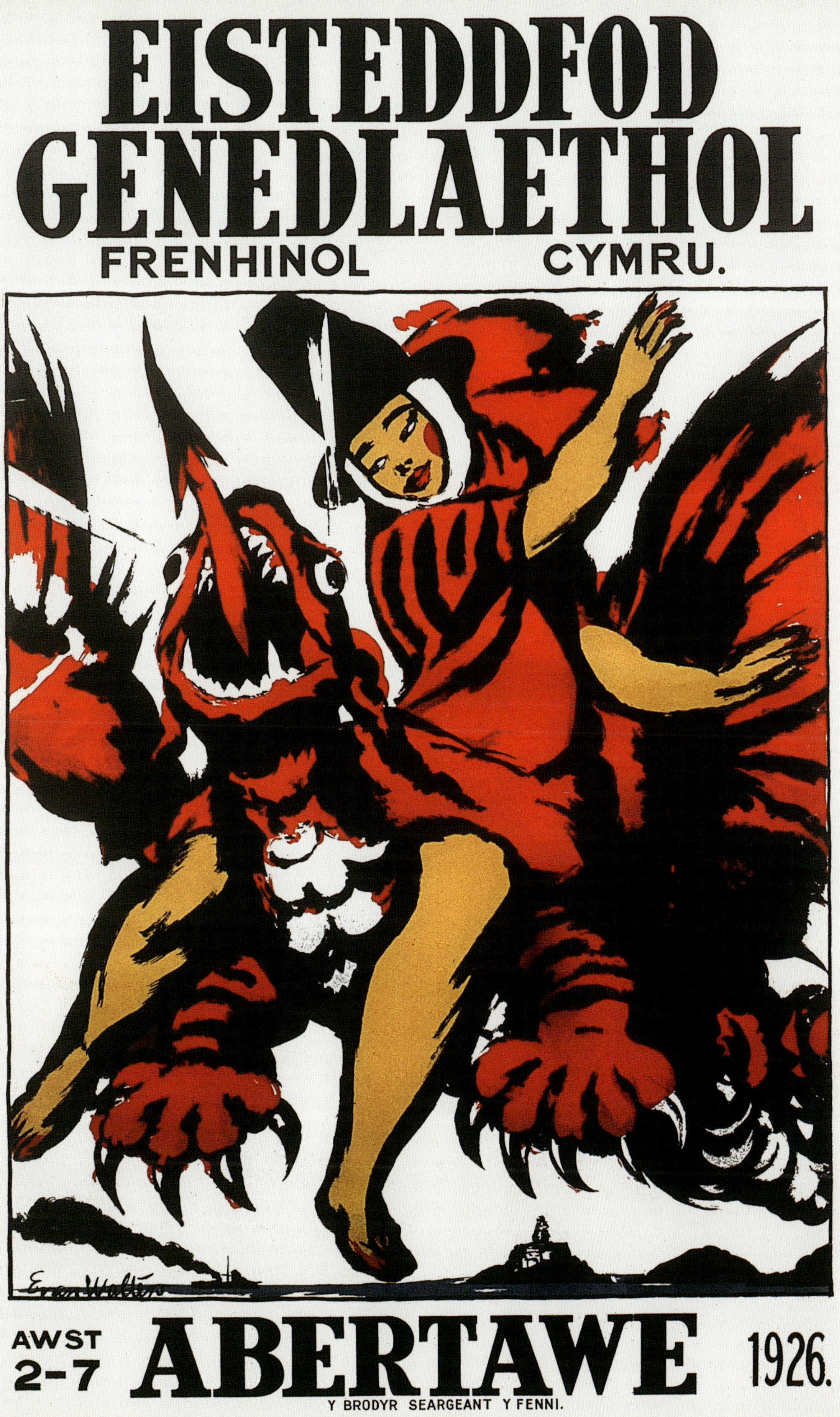
EISTEDDFOD
GENEDLAETHOL
FRENHINOL CYMRU.
AWST 2-7
ABERTAWE
1926.
Y BRODYR SEARGEANT Y FENNI.

23 He was to have stayed, with Clausen, at the home of Winifred Coombe Tennant. For the eisteddfod art exhibitions see Lord, *Winifred Coombe Tennant*, pp. 98–108, and Lord, *Y Chwaer-Dduwies*, pp. 84–92.

24 Letter from John to David Bell, Glynn Vivian Art Gallery Archive.

25 *Cambria Daily Leader*, 3 August 1926, p. 3.

26 The diary of Winifred Coombe Tennant, 1 May 1926, private archive.

aesthetic opinions. The two duly obliged by disagreeing in all competitions. John awarded Evan Walters three first prizes, though it was a judgement made in some haste, since he did not appear until 4 o'clock on the second day of adjudication, and retired to London later that night.[23] Subsequently, his memory of the event would be hazy, at best:

> I went down, I think, to Pontypridd to adjudicate at an Eisteddfod where I noticed a painting of a collier: At least, I took it to be a collier from the general blackness of the colour. This was by Evan Walters and gained a prize. I had then never heard of him.[24]

Ominously, Clausen had indeed heard of Walters, since he had taught him at the Royal Academy before the war. The work of Margaret Lindsay Williams, his student of a few years earlier, had been more to his taste.

opposite
285. Evan Walters, *Welsh Collier*, 1926, oil, 61.3x50.9

The portrait so vaguely remembered by John was titled simply *Welsh Collier*, but in the political context of the period in which it was painted – the weeks of the strike, immediately prior to the exhibition – the absence of the name of the sitter in the catalogue was surely significant. The collier, William Hopkins, stood for more than himself, in both the painter's mind and in the minds of the public who saw the picture. The critic of the *Cambria Daily Leader* asked the public to 'Look at the eyes alone of Evan Walters' collier and you read the coal trouble as plainly as you can war in Augustus John's "Canadian Soldier"', a picture shown in the loan exhibition.[25] Contrasting the 'peace and life' of her own privileged situation with that of people in the position of the striking Hopkins, Winifred Coombe Tennant confided her distress to her diary: 'The masses toil on, ill housed, unemployed, becoming unemployable, and so it goes on. Lord God of Hosts.'[26]

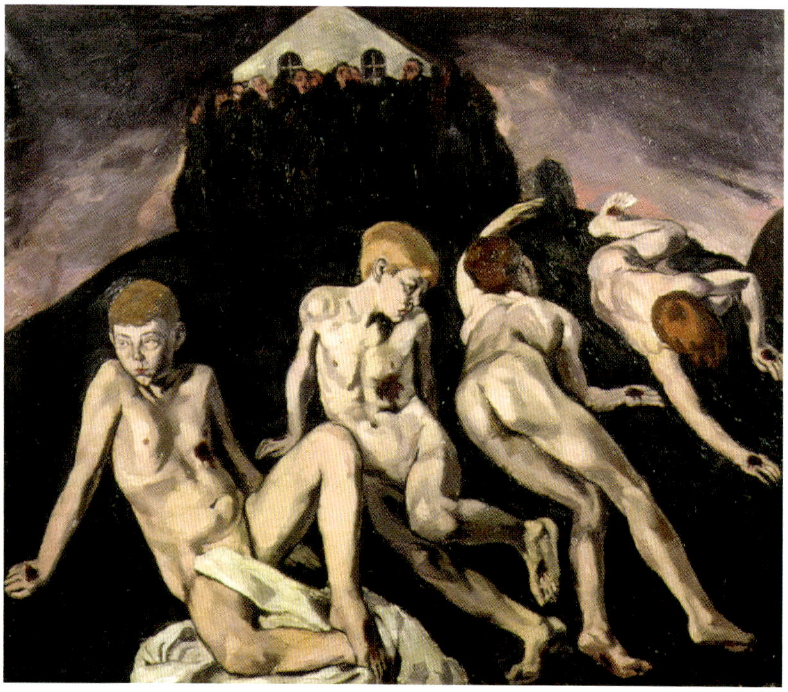

284. Evan Walters, *Bydd Myrdd o Ryfeddodau*, 1926, oil, 109x132

Beyond the constraints imposed by the set subjects of the painting competitions, Walters responded to the contemporary political and social context with one of the most remarkable images of twentieth-century Welsh painting, *Bydd Myrdd o Ryfeddodau*, the 'Welsh Funeral Hymn'. In the foreground Walters set four naked boys in transfiguration. They carry the stigmata, and lie on a coal tip. Above, and in the background, outside a chapel, a choir sings the funeral hymn in which is expressed the expectation of resurrection and release from the tribulations of

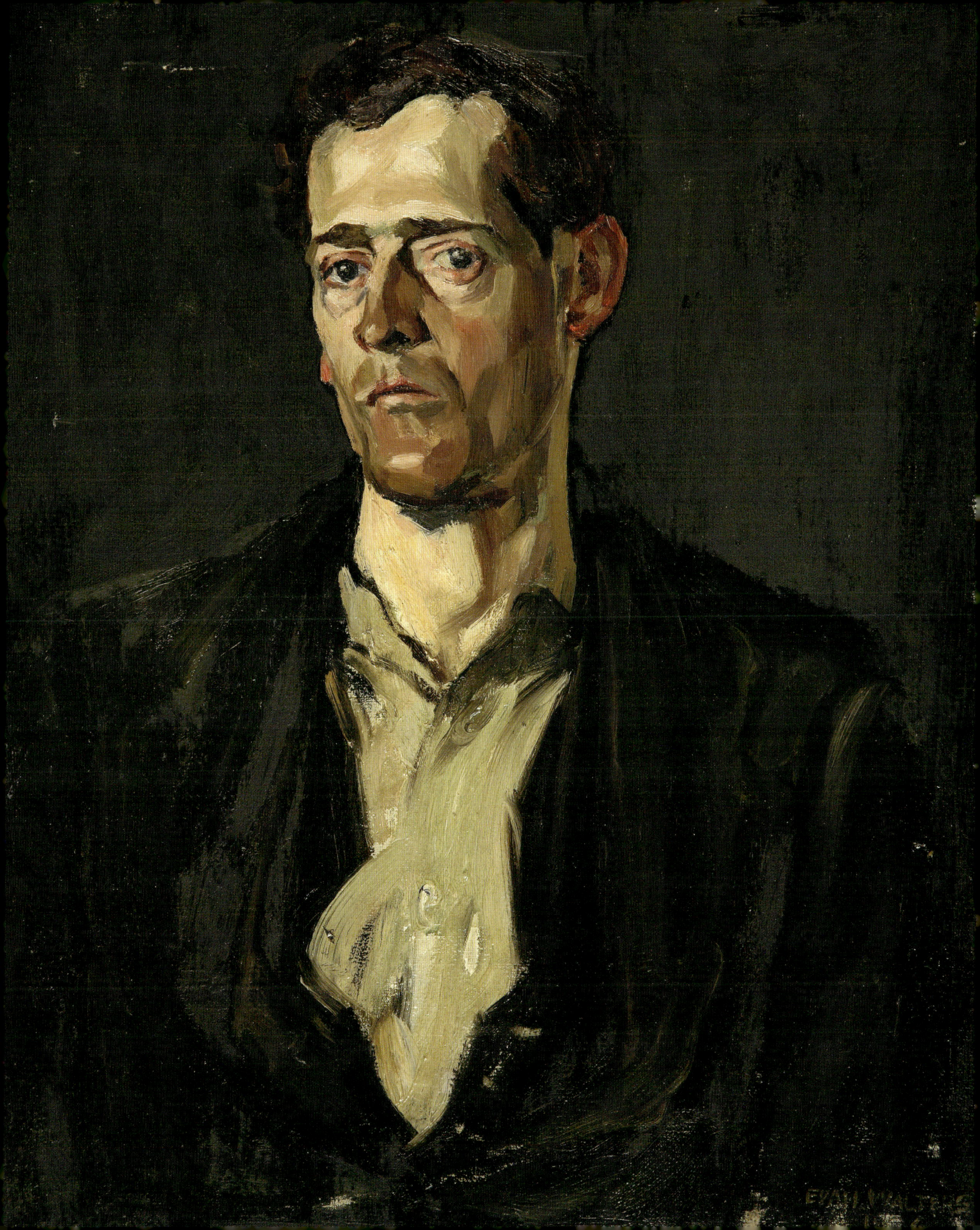
EVAN WALTERS

worldly life. The picture was considered problematic by many critics. Even Coombe Tennant thought it 'a weird queer thing' when she saw it in Walters's studio, five months before the eisteddfod, though the painter himself, seeking later to explain it to her considered it 'to be about my best work':

> There is no sign of happiness or resurrection in the singing. All is hopeless, dreary, dark, and it rends the hearts of the spirits as they hear it, so melancholy and mournful are the sounds.[27]

Most of the celebrated literature of the coal strike of 1926, including 'Angry Summer', would be written a decade and more in retrospect, when the outcome was known. Walters drew and painted as the events unfolded, in the uncertainty of revolution. The picture questioned the validity of the Christian understanding of human suffering as an expression of God's will, to be endured with patience in the expectation of resurrection into a putative other life.[28]

At the beginning of the year of the strike, two other young painters from the Swansea area, Archie Rees Griffiths and Ceri Richards, were attending the Royal College of Art in London. Like Vincent Evans, Griffiths, whose home was in Gorseinon, had worked underground before going to the local School of Art and on to London. Richards's father was a tinplate worker yet, curiously, while the progress of Griffiths's career was followed in the local newspapers as the local, working-class boy made good, Richards was rarely mentioned. At the Royal College, Richards worked in the Design School whereas Griffiths was classified as a painter, but they knew each other well. In the slightly attenuated style that he adopted as he tentatively moved towards abstraction, Richards painted a portrait of his friend. Both made an impression on their teachers – Richards as a draughtsman, and Griffiths, in particular on Rothenstein, as something of a mystic.

Though Richards sent pictures to the 1926 eisteddfod, Griffiths did not, perhaps preoccupied with examinations at the Royal College. However, his work was already familiar to Swansea people, since it had been reproduced in the *Cambria Daily Leader* extensively in 1924, and on his return from London, the paper published two further drawings, of striking colliers. By this time, the work of Griffiths was largely focussed on the mining community, but like Walters, the context of Christian belief in which he had been brought up,

27 The diary of Winifred Coombe Tennant, 2 March 1926, private archive, and a letter from Walters to Coombe Tennant, NLW Winifred Coombe Tennant Papers, A1/39, undated. An extract from the letter was published in the *South Wales News*, 16 November 1927, p. 7.

28 The notion of the uncertainty of revolution, and of artists working when 'everything was at risk' derives from the work of T.J. Clark on the 1848 revolution in Paris. For a fuller analysis of the meaning of Walters's picture and other works of the period, see Peter Lord, 'Biblical and Marxist rhetoric in the painting and literature of the Depression', in *Moment of Earth. Poems and Essays in Honour of Jeremy Hooker*, ed. Christopher Meredith (Aberystwyth, 2007), pp. 201–217.

29 *Western Mail*, 17 June 1927, p. 5. The picture had been selected by the critic R.H. Wilenski for inclusion in the Daily Express Young Artists Exhibition at the RBA Galleries in London in 1927. It was hung prominently and noticed in the London press.

286. Ceri Richards, *Archie Rhys Griffiths*, c.1924–8

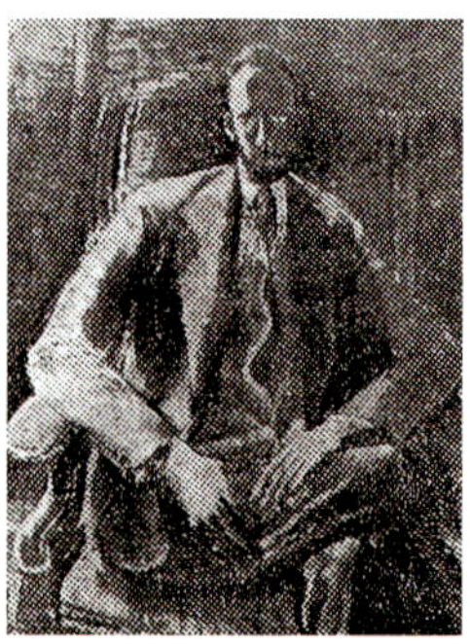

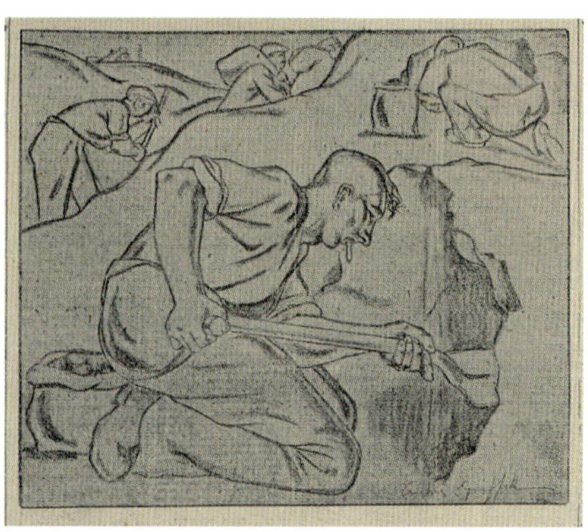

287. Archie Rhys Griffiths, *Digging for Coal in an Old Tip*, from the *Cambria Daily Leader*, 21 August 1926

inside a Welsh-speaking, Nonconformist family, took his response in his most considered works beyond the level of documentation. His diploma picture at the Royal College had been *Preaching in the Mines*. It depicted a group underground:

> ... a bearded man at the centre as the true follower, flanked by one who was trying to reason things out for himself, and a youth, as representative of a generation that adapts itself to anything, regardless of the consequences. In the background I placed an atheist, who sneers at everything, and this, with a horse and a rat – creatures who feel but cannot reason ...[29]

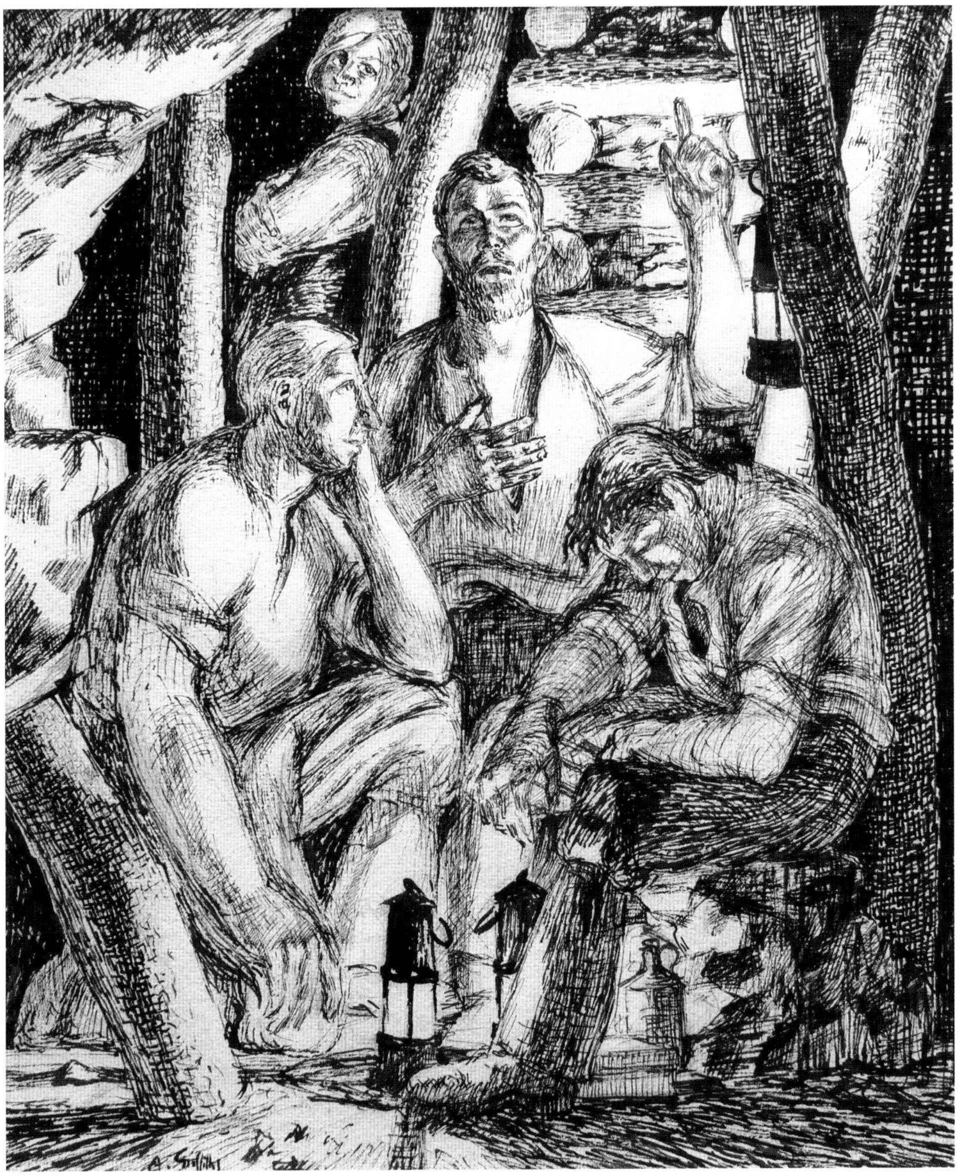

288. Archie Rhys Griffiths, *Preaching in the Mines*, *c.*1926–32, etching, 36.5x31.5

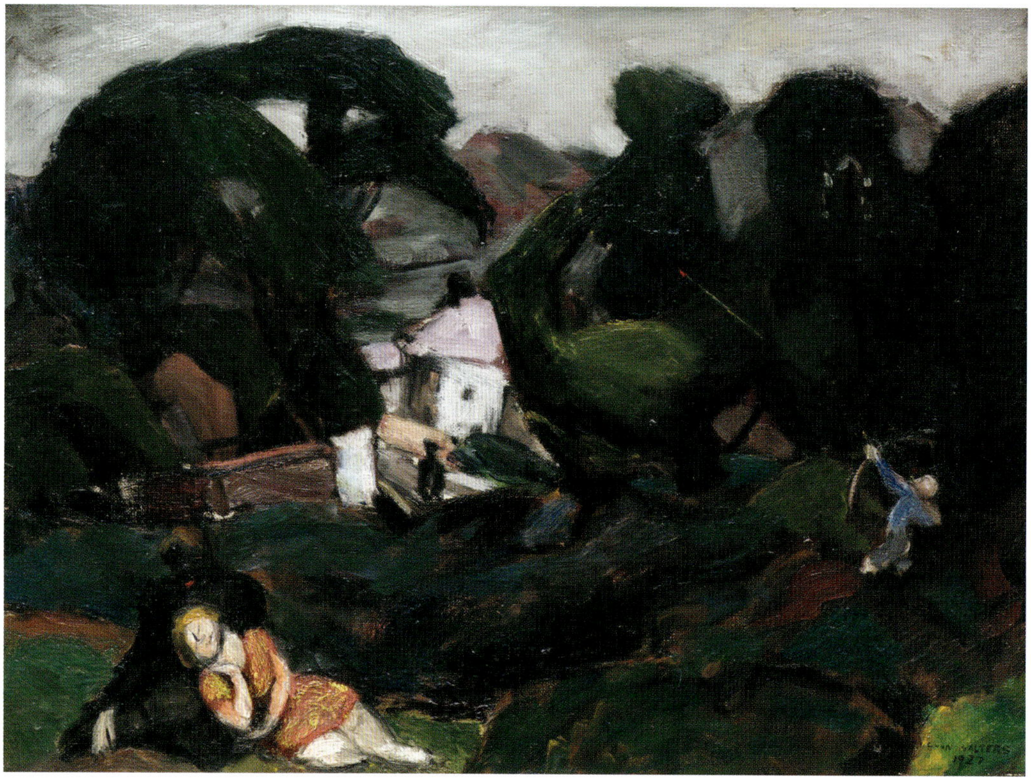

289. Evan Walters, *Courting*, 1927, oil, 50x67.5

30 *La Revue Moderne*, 15 February 1927, translated by Winifred Coombe Tennant. Walters was 'essentially and profoundly Welsh', and the reviewer drew attention to three works that she owned – *Dominoes*, and portraits of Lloyd George and Gerald Balfour. The review is unattributed, but Coombe Tennant was a regular visitor to French galleries in the mid-1920s and was a fluent French speaker. The other French essay appeared in *Revue du Vrai et du Beau*, 10 September 1927, p. 6.

31 *Daily Mail*, 15 November 1927.

32 Headline in the *South Wales News*, 16 November 1927, p. 7, above photographs of John and Walters.

33 Morris to Coombe Tennant, NLW Winifred Coombe Tennant Papers, A1/29, 5 December 1927.

34 The diary of Winifred Coombe Tennant, 8 September 1928, private archive. Griffiths acknowledged that the picture was 'the result of our talks'. It seems likely that they had discussed in particular *The Way of Rest* by Eugène Laermans, a picture that had been reproduced by Thomas Jones in *The Welsh Outlook*.

Griffiths followed this picture with a competition piece for the Prix de Rome on the subject of the expulsion from the Garden of Eden, which he again translated into a mining context.

It is not clear exactly when Griffiths met Walters for the first time, but it seems likely to have been either in 1926 or in the following year when the older painter broke through into the international art world. Two reviews of his work appeared in the art press in France, both drawing attention in particular to a combination of French-inspired Modernism and Welshness in his work. Their judgements were reinforced by extravagant comments attributed to Augustus John, who had pronounced Walters 'a child of nature, without artistic education, living somewhere in the Welsh mountains'.[30] Again, it was John who had a negligent hand in the crucial event which crowned the success of the painter at the end of the year. John's characteristic failure to meet a commitment to show at the Dorothy Warren Gallery in London presented Walters with the opportunity to fill the gap. The London exhibition, which included *Bydd Myrdd o Ryfeddodau* and the *Welsh Collier*, supplemented by new works set in the coalfield, such as *The Convalescent Collier Tom Rees* and *Courting*, caused considerable interest. P.G. Konody drew particular attention to *Bydd Myrdd o Ryfeddodau*, a picture of 'passionate intensity of realisation'.[31] It was reported that John had pronounced Walters 'a new genius'.[32]

The exhibition not only promoted Walters, but had the effect of creating a focus of attention for other, scattered Welsh artists and intellectuals. Survivors from the more coherent pre-war art world, including Christopher Williams and Goscombe John, had things to say about him, as did newly emerged figures like Cedric Morris, whose own London exhibition at the Tooth's gallery had preceded that of Walters. Morris wrote to Coombe Tennant that he 'was both surprised and very delighted to find how good' a painter he was – a comment whose patronising nature reveals the strength of the contemporary myth of Walters as a newly discovered naïve.[33] In fact, Morris was only four years his senior.

Coombe Tennant, observing Walters's transformation from 'a one legged ugly duckling' into a swan, provided a point of contact at home for several of these painters, including Morris. She had yet to meet Archie Griffiths who, although he had narrowly failed to win the Prix de Rome, had been granted a travel scholarship that enabled him to visit that city, via Paris. Informed by Grant Murray that on his return to Wales he would be 'penniless', Coombe Tennant wrote to invite him to stay at Cadoxton Lodge and work. She found him 'a tragic figure', and enlisted Walters to advise him on his development. In his opinion, Griffiths needed to 'slap on paint freely, caring nothing for detail, but putting down the strong facts of anything seen without a care of what the result was.' Among the most immediate results was the first version of Griffiths's image of *Miners Returning from Work*, clearly influenced also by an awareness of the Belgian Realist art promoted a decade earlier by Thomas Jones in *The Welsh Outlook*.[34] *Miners Returning from Work* was among more than 60 pictures in various media shown by Griffiths in an exhibition given him in November 1928 by Grant Murray at the Glynn Vivian gallery. Coombe Tennant bought the picture there, describing it as 'a rough strong thing of rough strong men'.

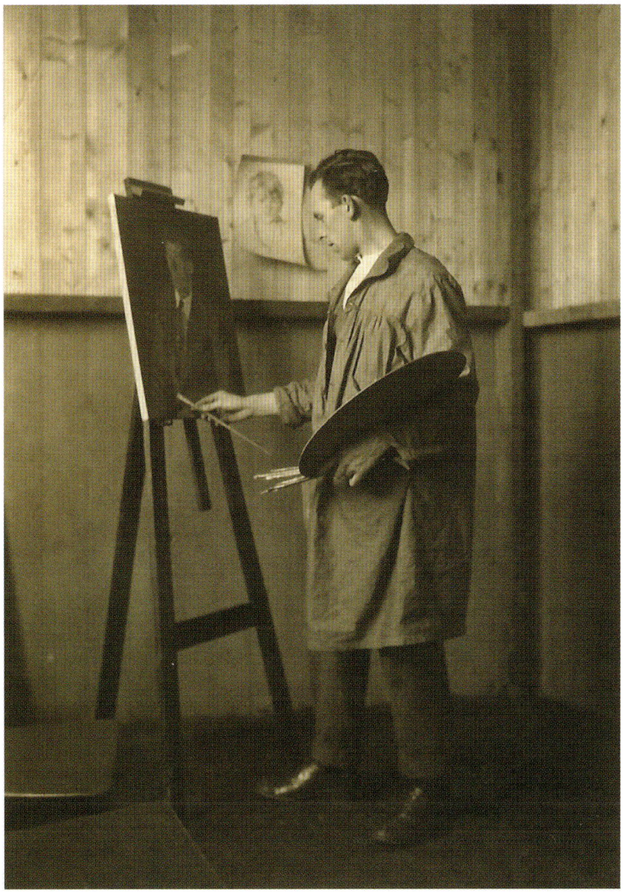

290. John Latimer Jones,
Archie Rhys Griffiths in his studio in Gorseinon, c.1928

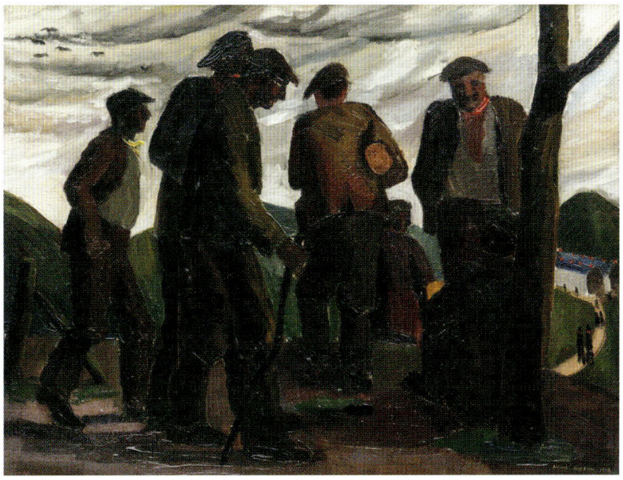

291. Archie Rhys Griffiths,
Miners Returning from Work, 1928, oil, 50x68

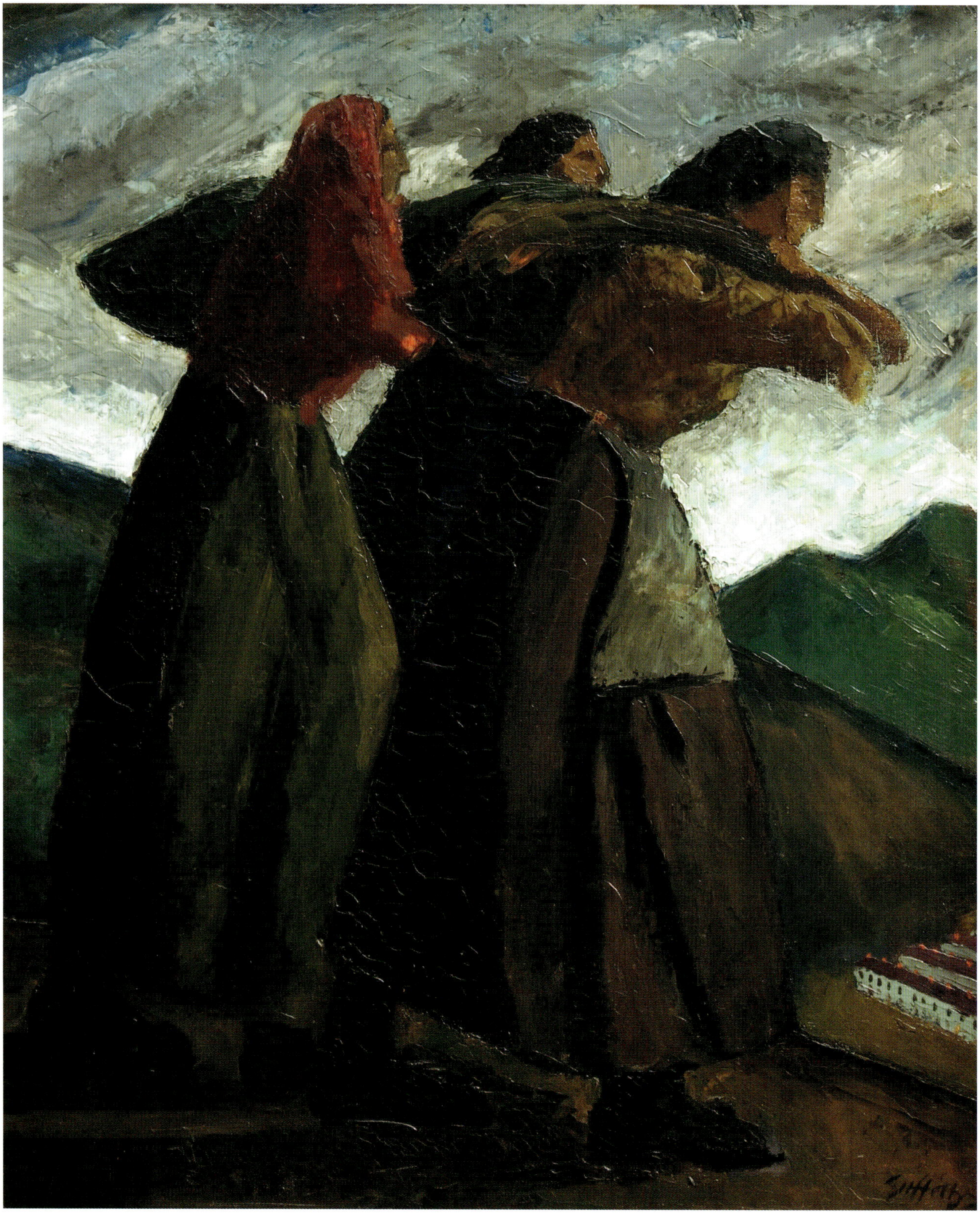

The exhibition proved popular with the general public, who clearly identified with Griffiths both as a local man and with his familiar imagery. The *cognoscenti* were equally impressed. In the exhibition catalogue, William Rothenstein praised the 'passionate element of sincerity in his figure compositions':

> The subjects showed an intimate knowledge of the miner's life; but objective though they were in treatment, one was always aware of an inner mystical spirit, which raised his designs far above mere illustration ...[35]

No doubt the sombre mood of much of his work reinforced Rothenstein's perception of depth in Griffiths. Although Griffiths was possessed of a melancholic personality, unlike that of Evan Walters, in their most serious work both men drew on the same deeply embedded cultural resources. The language of the pulpit and the Bible formed the grammar of their thought. After the Glynn Vivian exhibition, Griffiths painted *On the Coal Tips*, in which the superficial narrative of carrying coal scavenged from the waste tips above a mining village overlaid the biblical story of the three women who visited the tomb of Jesus after the Crucifixion, carrying spices. The women found the tomb empty, and were perplexed by the meaning of the circumstance – an allusion to the same questioning of Christian belief that had lain behind Walters's *Bydd Myrdd o Ryfeddodau*. Subsequently, Walters returned to the meaning of Christian faith in the context of materialist critiques in his picture *The Communist*. The obvious crucifixion resonance of the posture of the communist orator, who offers his own understanding of salvation, was reinforced by more subtle reference in the technique and structure of the painting to the work of the French painter Honoré Daumier. Walters alluded to *Ecce Homo*, Daumier's celebrated image of the presentation by Pontius Pilate of the scourged Jesus to the Jewish populace, prior to the Crucifixion.

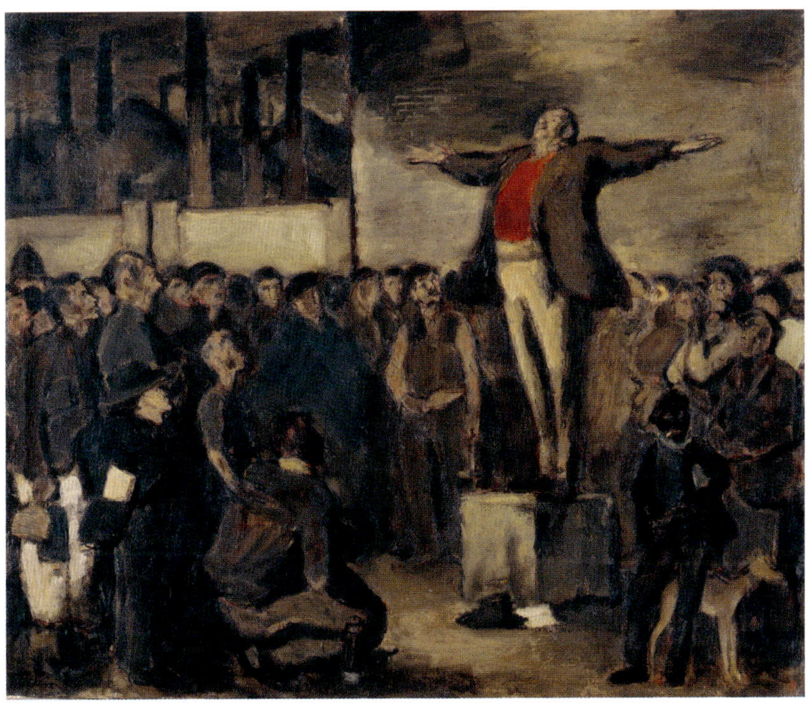

Walters could now sustain his career with portrait commissions, but Griffiths, less able in this work and unwilling to teach, struggled with increasing poverty and dependence on alcohol. Both Rothenstein and Thomas Jones attempted to come to his aid. A mural commission in London,

35 Curiously, in his catalogue essay, Rothenstein linked Griffiths to another former student, Charles Frederick Tunnicliffe, at that time not associated with Wales, but who, after the Second World War would live at Malltraeth in Anglesey.

opposite
292. Archie Rhys Griffiths, *On the Coal Tips*, *c*.1928–32, oil, 75x63

293. Evan Walters, *The Communist*, *c*.1932, oil, 76x92.1

gained for Griffiths by Rothenstein, again contrasted crucifixion imagery with contemporary life, but appears not to have been carried beyond the cartoon stage. However, at the Young Wales Centre in London in 1932, Griffiths was given an exhibition which was opened by Rothenstein. The pictures were hung by Griffiths and Walters together, and the two men were linked in press comment, some of which emanated from the journalist (and later novelist) Geraint Goodwin, a close friend of the painter at this time. Prior to the show, Goodwin had written in high romantic terms in *The Welsh Outlook* about their friendship, and about Griffiths's background and work.[36] However, despite the short-term success of this exhibition, Griffiths would disappoint his promoters. By 1935, personal problems had resulted in his disappearance from the art scene.[37] Shortly afterwards, the work of Evan Walters underwent a dramatic change of direction. Though he did not entirely abandon his engagement with subject matter related to his cultural origins, he became preoccupied with an aesthetic theory that perplexed many of his supporters.

36 Geraint Goodwin, 'An Artist of Vision – The Work of Rhys Griffiths', in *The Welsh Outlook* XIX (1932), pp. 78–80.

37 See Peter Lord, *The Meaning of Pictures. Images of Personal, Social and Political Identity*, (Cardiff, 2009), pp. 123–65, 'The Construction and Destruction of Archie Rees Griffiths', and Peter Lord, *Relationships with Pictures: an Oblique Autobiography* (Cardigan, 2013), pp. 209–22, 'On the Coal Tips'. The spelling of 'Rees' is that of Griffiths's birth certificate. In 1931–2 he adopted 'Rhys'.

Meanwhile, in another country ...

Welsh painting in the 1920s was characterised by a polarity of vision. Archie Griffiths and Evan Walters confronted the questions arising from the increasing gloom of the south Wales valleys, but most other painters – even those living in close proximity to the centres of the unfolding crisis – chose to present Welsh landscapes unaffected by industrialism or, indeed, by rural poverty. In 1927, the Newport bookseller, Ifan Kyrle Fletcher, drew the attention of Winifred Coombe Tennant to the work of David Jones. Fletcher thought highly of Jones, though he acknowledged that the style of his engraving, painting and sculpture might be difficult for a conservative audience: 'His exaggerated simplicity seems to repel at first, but I think all his detractors will have to admit themselves in error.' Fletcher invited Coombe Tennant to subscribe to Jones's 'great edition', of engravings on copper, illustrating Coleridge's poem *The Rime of the Ancient Mariner*, which he had just begun. Perhaps surprisingly, she did not respond, but Fletcher's estimation of Jones proved correct.[38]

The Ancient Mariner series had been conceived in the summer of 1927, towards the end of a period that Jones spent working predominantly at Capel-y-ffin, near Llanthony in Breconshire, in a Roman Catholic art and craft community established there by the sculptor Eric Gill. Jones had first met him in 1921 at Ditchling in Sussex, where Gill and friends had established an earlier community. Much impressed by his ideas, Jones became a Roman Catholic, and by early 1924 was engaged to the sculptor's daughter, Petra.[39] Gill's intention

38 Kyrle Fletcher to Coombe Tennant, NLW Winifred Coombe Tennant Papers, A1/13, 16 November 1927. Coombe Tennant's fascination with the early Christian church and with iconic art might have predisposed her to the work of Jones. Kyrle Fletcher had first discussed Jones with Coombe Tennant in early 1927, though it is unclear whether he was in direct contact with him, or had become acquainted with his work through Douglas Cleverdon, a fellow bookseller in Bristol. Cleverdon had visited Capel-y-ffin in 1926 and subsequently suggested the idea of *The Ancient Mariner* to Jones.

39 Nevertheless, Jones was never a disciple of Gill. In retrospect, he thought him 'a great man', but not a great artist. BBC Radio 3 broadcast, 1961, typescript held at the Humanities Research Center, University of Texas, Houston. For Gill, see Fiona MacCarthy, *Eric Gill* (London, 1989).

40 Gill Sans had its origins in the Johnston typeface, designed for London Underground by Edward Johnston, Gill's teacher.

in coming to Capel-y-ffin was to escape from an industrialised and secularised world to which he was spiritually unsympathetic. In fact, his new home was only a few miles from the eastern coalfield, but it might as well have been in another country. The period proved remarkably productive for Gill in terms of sculpture, engraving and typography. His erotic illustrations to *The Song of Songs* and *Procreant Hymn* caused some controversy among his friends in the Roman Catholic Church, and his more prosaic work in typography reached its peak as he designed what would become one of the most successful type-faces ever designed, Gill Sans.[40] However, the theoretical need for isolation that certainly was met at Capel-y-ffin was at odds with his professional development. His clients belonged predominantly to the very urban world he sought to escape. By 1927, he was working on a large stone carving, *Mankind*, in a Chelsea studio provided for him by Howard de Walden.

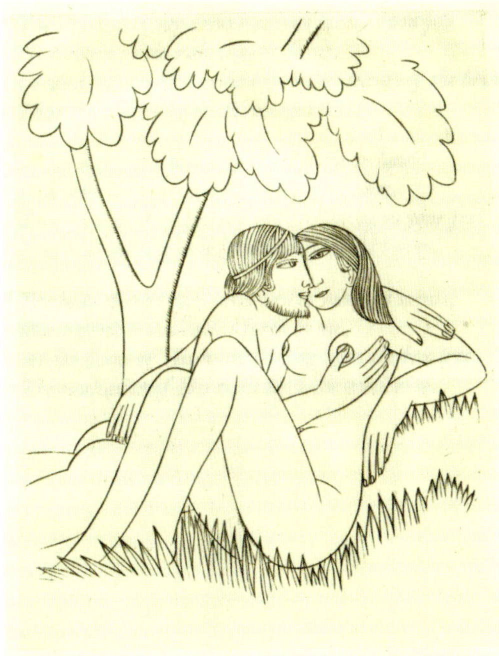

294. Eric Gill, *Dalliance*, from Edward Powys Mathers, *Procreant Hymn*, 1926, wood engraving, 11.1x8.6

Wales was of no particular cultural significance to Gill. His only work placed in the country was the war memorial at Chirk, which had been commissioned by de Walden before the move to Capel-y-ffin. On the other hand, Wales was highly significant to David Jones. It had been the land of his father and it became the land of his imagination. Although the three years he spent as a regular visitor to Gill's community, during which he also stayed several times at the Benedictine monastery on Caldey Island, would be his only experience of living in Wales, the country became bound into the complex web of erudite mythological, historical and literary reference that informed his engraving, painting and writing for the rest of his life.

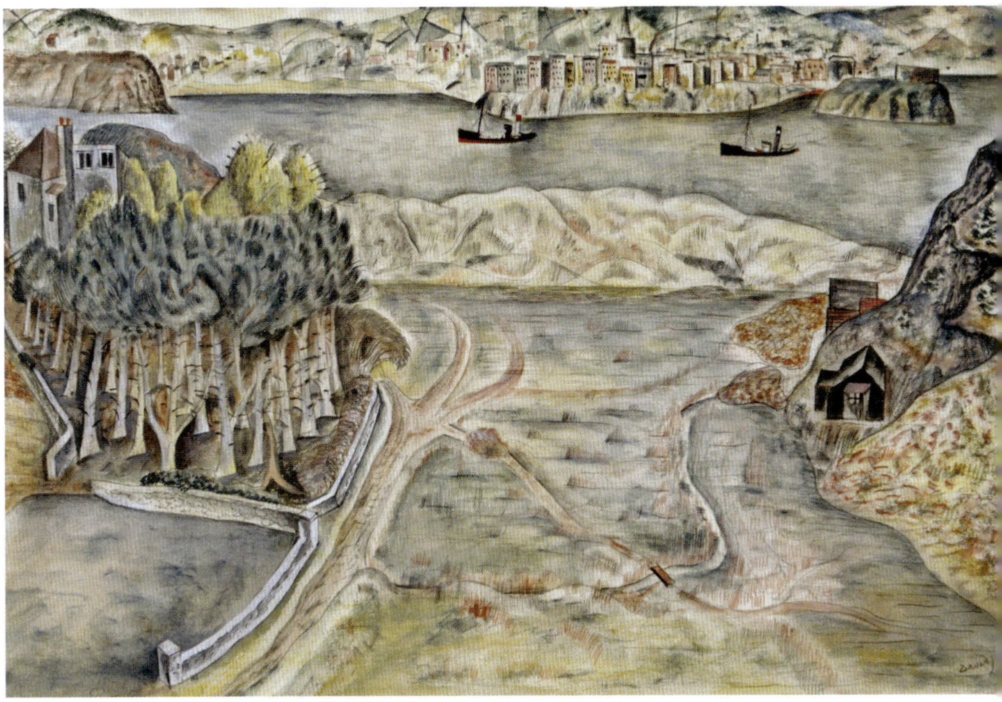

295. David Jones, *Tenby from Caldey Island*, 1925, watercolour and gouache, 34.3x52

opposite
296. David Jones, *Tir y Blaenau*, 1924–5, pencil, ink and watercolour, 57.1x38.1

At Capel-y-ffin Jones sought to respond directly to the landscape and through that to the mythology that he perceived beneath its surface. He worked in the open air in watercolour, drawing in particular the Twmpa, the prominent hill opposite Gill's home. In 1927 this work formed a substantial part of his first major exhibition in London, shared with Gill. The show was held at the St George's Gallery in Hanover Square, run by Arthur Howell.[41] The critical response to the exhibition was mixed, but some among the London avant-garde were enthused by the work. Proposed by Ben Nicholson, early in 1928 David Jones was elected a member of the Seven and Five Society. Yet it would be many years before the depth of the resonance for Jones of these watercolour images would be made clear, and then it would be in his writing. The landscape of *Tir y Blaenau*, recorded in a painting made shortly after his arrival at Capel-y-ffin, reappeared in the extraordinary weaving together of impressions that formed the text of *In Parenthesis*, his evocation of the Great War. 'Grey rain swept down torrentially. The water in the trench-drain ran as fast as stream in Nant Honddu in the early months, when you go to get the milk from Pen-y-Maes.'[42] Jones began to write *In Parenthesis* in about 1928, at the end of his Capel-y-ffin period, though it was not published until 1937. Thirty years later, in the poem 'The Sleeping Lord', the landscape came again to the surface:

> Does he cock his weather-ear, enquiringly
> lest what's on the west wind
> from over beyond the rising contours
> may signify that in the broken
> *tir y blaenau*
> these broken dregs of Troea
> yet again muster?[43]

Jones found the same resonant interaction of classical and ancient British mythologies in the wild ponies that he drew in *Tir y Blaenau* and other Capel-y-ffin landscapes. They evoked the horses left to roam after the slaughter of the Battle of Camlann, according to the Arthurian legends: 'And so their horses went where they would ...'. Jones saw them in 'their descendents, shrunken in bulk ... but holding themselves with breeding, black in colour, and primitive in contour, on a Brecon hill-slope ...'[44]

Jones had come to Capel-y-ffin known primarily as a wood engraver, and the period he spent there was notable for the many illustrations he made to editions of *Gulliver's Travels*, *The Book of Jonah*, and *The Chester Play of the Deluge*, all published by the Golden Cockerel Press in England. However, he also worked on one publication for the Gregynog Press. After the war, Gwendoline and Margaret Davies developed Gregynog, a house near

41 Arthur Howell was the son of the founder of the famous Cardiff department store. On several subsequent occasions Howell would again manifest a passing interest in the art and artists of his native country.

42 David Jones, *In Parenthesis* (London, 1937), p. 77.

43 David Jones, 'The Sleeping Lord' (1967), in *The Sleeping Lord and other fragments* (London, 1974), p. 95.

44 David Jones, 'The Myth of Arthur' (1942) in *Epoch and Artist* (London, 1959), p. 291.

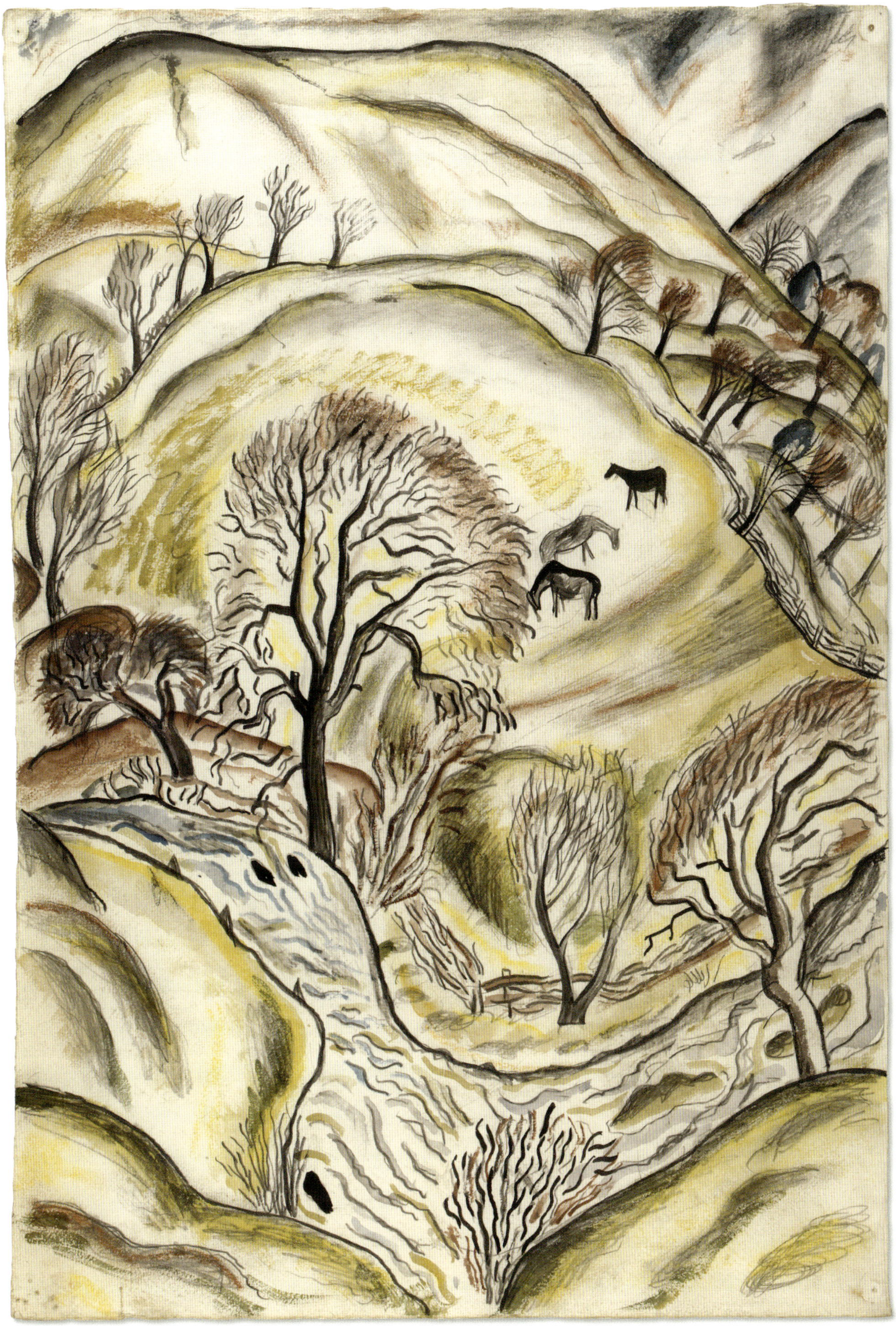

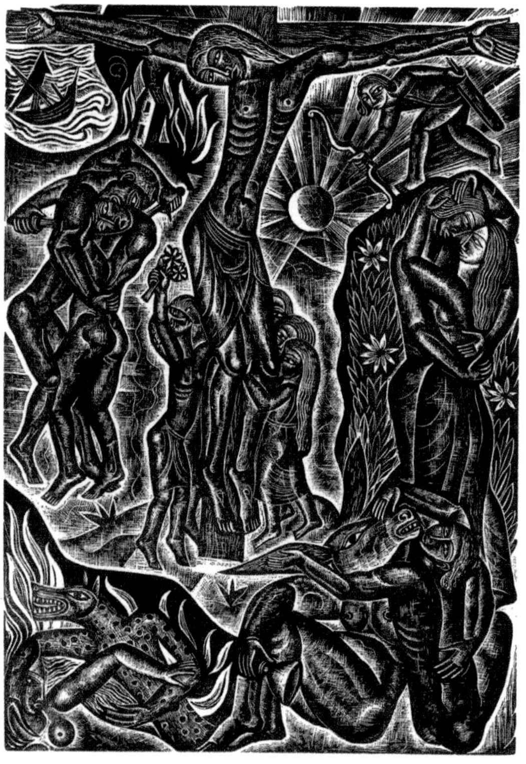

297. David Jones, Illustration for the Gregynog Press edition of *Llyfr y Pregeth-wr*, 1927, wood engraving 16.4x11.7

Newtown acquired by their brother during the war, as a centre for the visual arts and music, and for the discussion of ideas related to Wales. Thomas Jones and others of *The Welsh Outlook* circle were involved in developing the concept, which also owed something to the influence of the exiled de Saedeleer family. The Press, which was established in 1922, would prove the most productive of its several ventures.[45] Under its first Controller, the printmaker Robert Ashwin Maynard, Jones was commissioned in 1927 to make the frontispiece and an illustration for the title page of *Llyfr y Pregeth-wr* (the book of Ecclesiastes). Kyrle Fletcher reviewed the book for *The Welsh Outlook*:

> The small design of the title page is perfect. Not only has it exquisite beauty as a design, but it attunes the mind to the precise key of Llyfr y Pregethwr. Having allowed the beauty of its drooping curves to saturate the mind, the reader is prepared for the opening:
>
> 'Gwagedd o wagedd, medd y Pregethwr. Gwagedd o wagedd, gwagedd yw'r cwbl'.[46]

In the background to the frontis engraving (about which Fletcher was less enthusiastic) Jones set an image of murderous embrace, unusual in his work, perhaps related to his experience in the trenches and to the verse: 'Wisdom is better than weapons of war; but one sinner destroyeth much good.'[47]

Jones's fascination with Welsh imagery and identity was intense, but developed largely in the isolation of an inward looking personality, who lived in his imagination. Shortly after the publication of *In Parenthesis* he developed a relationship with Saunders Lewis but links with Welsh image makers in the 1920s and 30s were tenuous.[48] He was joined as a member of the Seven and Five Society in 1927 by Cedric Morris, but his awareness of other Welsh landscape painters of the period was probably minimal. However, between these other painters there were indeed links. Several of them were in direct contact, and their pictures hung together from time to time in exhibitions. Furthermore, although until 1935 they did not make any professional association on the basis of national identity or aesthetics, their pictures presented a coherent strand of lyricism in landscape imagery that flourished despite – or perhaps in denial of – the worsening economic situation. Only Evan Walters bridged the gulf between imaging the social trauma of industrial Wales and

45 Winifred Coombe Tennant was among visitors to Gregynog in 1921 as the project was being developed. She was enthusiastic about it, but by 1939 would feel that the press, indeed the Gregynog project as a whole, had failed. In her opinion it became a 'rich man's toy' and did not contribute to raising standards of design as they affected the ordinary people of Wales. See Lord, *Winifred Coombe Tennant*, pp. 64–5 and 161–2.

46 'Vanity of vanities, sa'ith the Preacher, vanity of vanities; all is vanity.' *The Welsh Outlook* 15, No 1 (January 1928), pp. 15–16.

47 Ecclesiastes, 9.18. See Jonathan Miles and Derek Shiel, *David Jones, The Maker Unmade* (Bridgend, 1995), p. 146.

48 Geraint Gwilym Evans, '*The Correspondence of Saunders Lewis and David Jones*' (unpublished MA thesis, Swansea University, 1987).

the countryside. The Modernist angularity and dark colour of his landscapes of 1926 and 1927 contrasted starkly with the benign views painted by Morris and by Will Evans, John Cyrlas Williams and Edward Morland Lewis, all of whom emerged with him in the post-war period. The summer vision of these painters was associated primarily with the south and west, but extended also to the north of Wales in the work of Harry Hughes Williams.

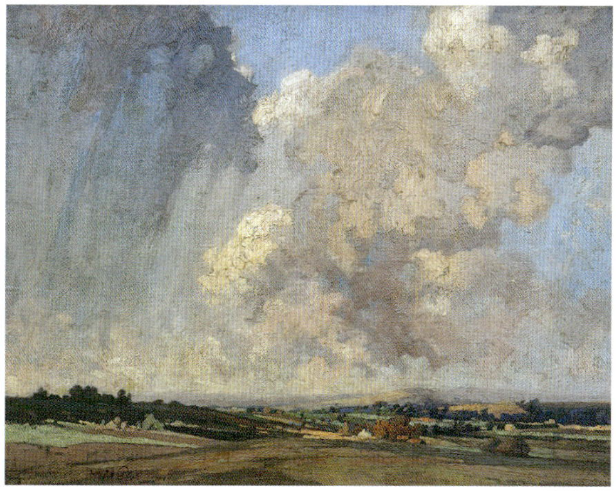

298. Will Evans, *Stormy Down*, oil, 48.2x63.5

The 1926 eisteddfod at Swansea had drawn entries from all these painters but Cedric Morris, who had only recently arrived in London from Paris. Will Evans was the oldest of them, and the most familiar to the local audience, as he had shown regularly with the Swansea Art Society since just before the war. He had been an early part-time student of Grant Murray at the School of Art before pursuing a career in commercial lithography in the tinplate industry. Later, he would become known throughout Wales, working also in the north and exhibiting with the Royal Cambrian Academy. He exhibited there alongside Harry Hughes Williams, with whom his pictures had much in common.

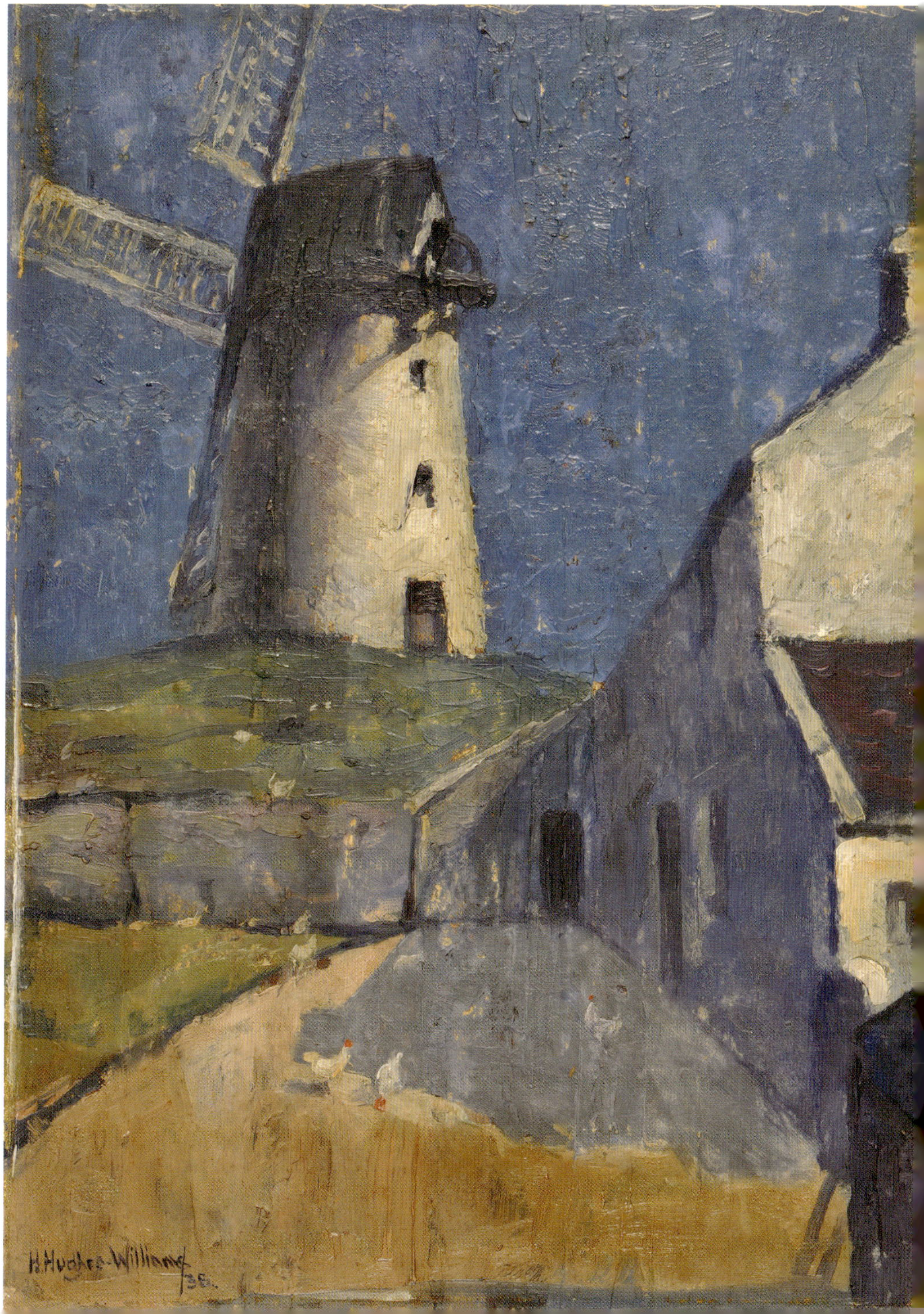

299. Harry Hughes Williams, *Stanley Mill*, 1938, oil, 39x31

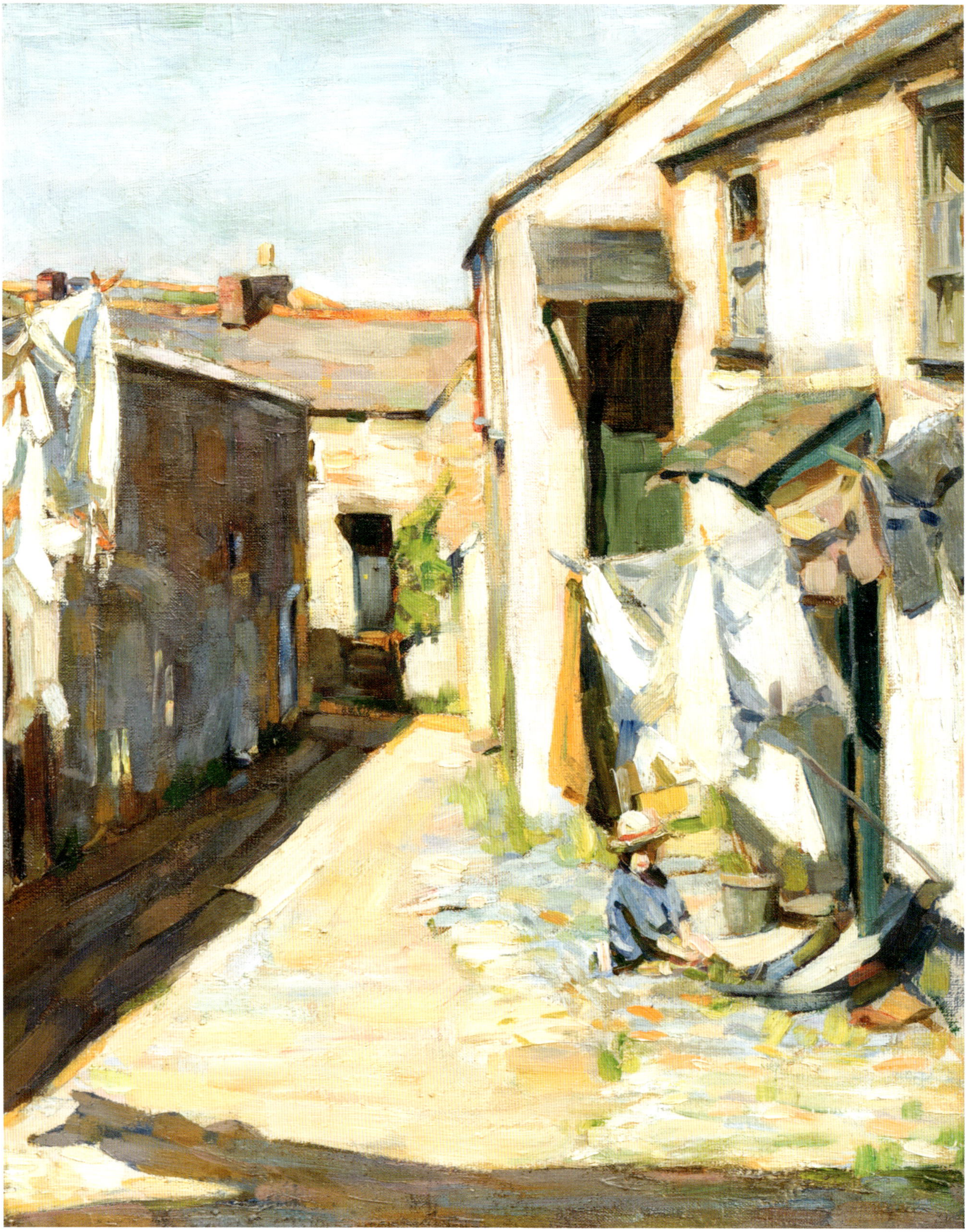

Both painters worked in an Impressionist manner to present the open landscapes so familiar to them – Gower in the south and Anglesey in the north. Williams had trained at Liverpool and at the Royal College of Art, but was unable subsequently to travel, as many of his immediate predecessors had done, because of the war. Though in terms of the avant-garde of the period, Harry Hughes Williams was a conservative, he became a master of his technique, producing vibrant landscapes of remarkable luminosity. Like Evans, he would eventually sustain his work by teaching, though in his case in a secondary school. Evans returned to Swansea School of Art to teach lithography.

Harry Hughes Williams and Will Evans were a crucial decade older than John Cyrlas Williams and Edward Morland Lewis, both of whom were born in 1902 and so escaped entanglement in the war. They were also, therefore, the exact contemporaries of Archie Griffiths and indeed, like Griffiths, Cyrlas Williams was born into a family of colliers. However, his father had become the owner of a mine at Pontyrhyl, north of Bridgend, and prospered sufficiently to re-locate the family in the salubrious surroundings of Porthcawl – a move which, clearly, had a profound effect upon John's life experience and thence on his work. He began to paint at the age of 16, and his comfortable family circumstances enabled him to train privately with Stanhope Forbes at Newlyn. When he arrived, Cedric Morris had just left the village, after two years, for the rather different environs of the Paris *ateliers*. In 1922 a personal crisis arose in Williams's private life that resulted in his living for four years in Australia, but on his return he sent paintings to the 1926 eisteddfod, one of which was bought by Winifred Coombe Tennant. Recognising his talent, she sought to encourage him, though it would be nearly two years before they met, on which occasion she bought more pictures. In the meantime, Williams had again followed in the footsteps of Cedric Morris, this time to work in Paris. From there he had gone south to Martigues, in pursuit of Augustus John, but the great man had left his beloved French studio shortly after Williams arrived. In 1928 Coombe Tennant arranged for Williams to meet both Morris and Evan Walters in London. The meetings took place, but little came of them. Unbeknown to Coombe Tennant or Grant Murray, who had also interested himself in the young painter, Williams suffered from alcoholism and depression. Seen in this light, the urgency of his substantial output of pictures, painted in bursts of intense activity, seems especially poignant. They reveal a remarkable level of ability, but after 1932, he would not paint again.[49]

opposite
300. John Cyrlas Williams, *The Cat on the Wall*, c.1922, oil, 56x45.5

The career of Edward Morland Lewis, also competing at the Swansea eisteddfod, took a different course, though it too would be tragically short. He was the son of a well-known amateur painter, B.A. Lewis – a friend of Christopher Williams, who painted with him on his visits to Carmarthenshire. Morland Lewis attended Carmarthen School of Art and then the

49 Coombe Tennant did not meet him again until 1952: 'I felt an ailing mind. He was surprised at the warmth of my welcome. He had it in him to be a very considerable painter …' The diary of Winifred Coombe Tennant, private archive, 25 May 1952. For Williams, see Peter Lord, A Brief Flowering', *Planet* 199 (2010), pp. 79–92, and Lord, *Relationships with Pictures*, pp. 223–40.

Royal Academy schools, where in 1924 he met the German-born painter Walter Sickert. He chose to continue his training in Sickert's studio, and remained closely associated with him until the end of the decade. He adopted some of his master's techniques, working over a subdued under-painting as a consequence of which the tonal values of his pictures were often more restrained than those of Cyrlas Williams and Harry Hughes Williams. However, although the landscapes and townscapes of south-west Wales would remain central to his subject matter, unlike those painters, he became known to the metropolitan art world. He exhibited with the London Group of artists from 1929,[50] and was given his first one-person exhibition the following year. He would go on to teach at the Chelsea School of Art where among his colleagues would be Graham Sutherland. The development of his career proceeded quietly and steadily. He was held in some esteem by his contemporaries, but died of malaria in 1943 while serving with the army in north Africa during the Second World War.

opposite
302. Cedric Morris, *Self-portrait*, 1919, oil, 38x27.9

In terms both of reputation in the English art world and engagement with art affairs in Wales, Cedric Morris would achieve the highest profile among these contemporaries. Morris was descended from John Morris, the founder of Morriston, near Swansea, and so belonged by birth to industrial Wales. The wealth of his family had enabled him to begin his training as a painter in Paris before the outbreak of the war, from which he escaped active service on medical grounds. His return to the London art world from post-war Paris in 1926 was marked also by a reawakening of his interest in Wales. His meeting Evan Walters may,

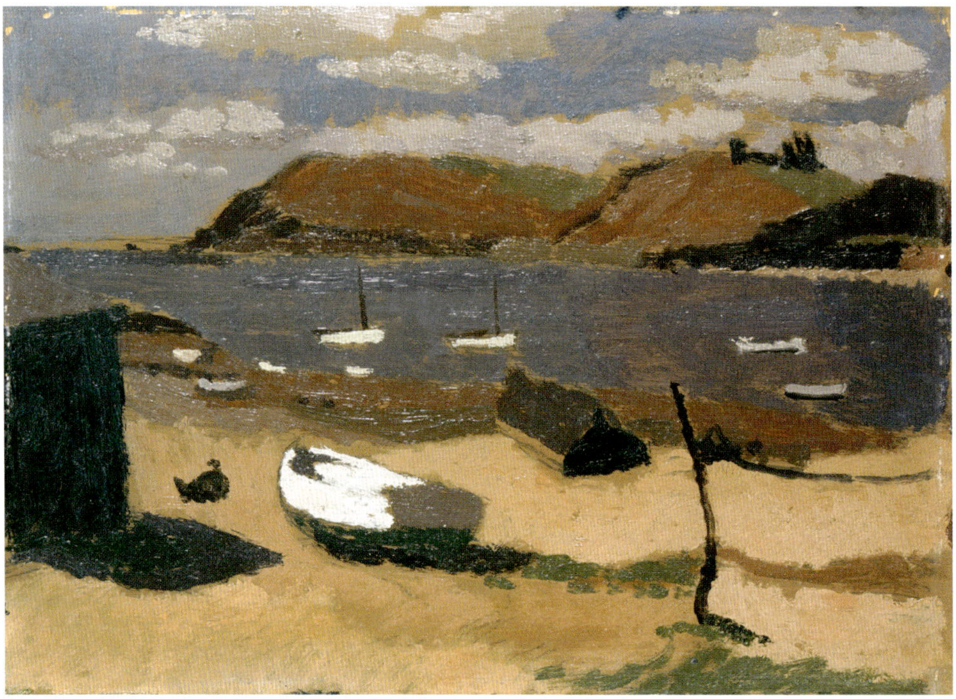

301. Edward Morland Lewis, *Carmarthen Bay*, c.1925-35, oil, 19x27

50 Sickert was a founder member of the London Group, established in 1913.

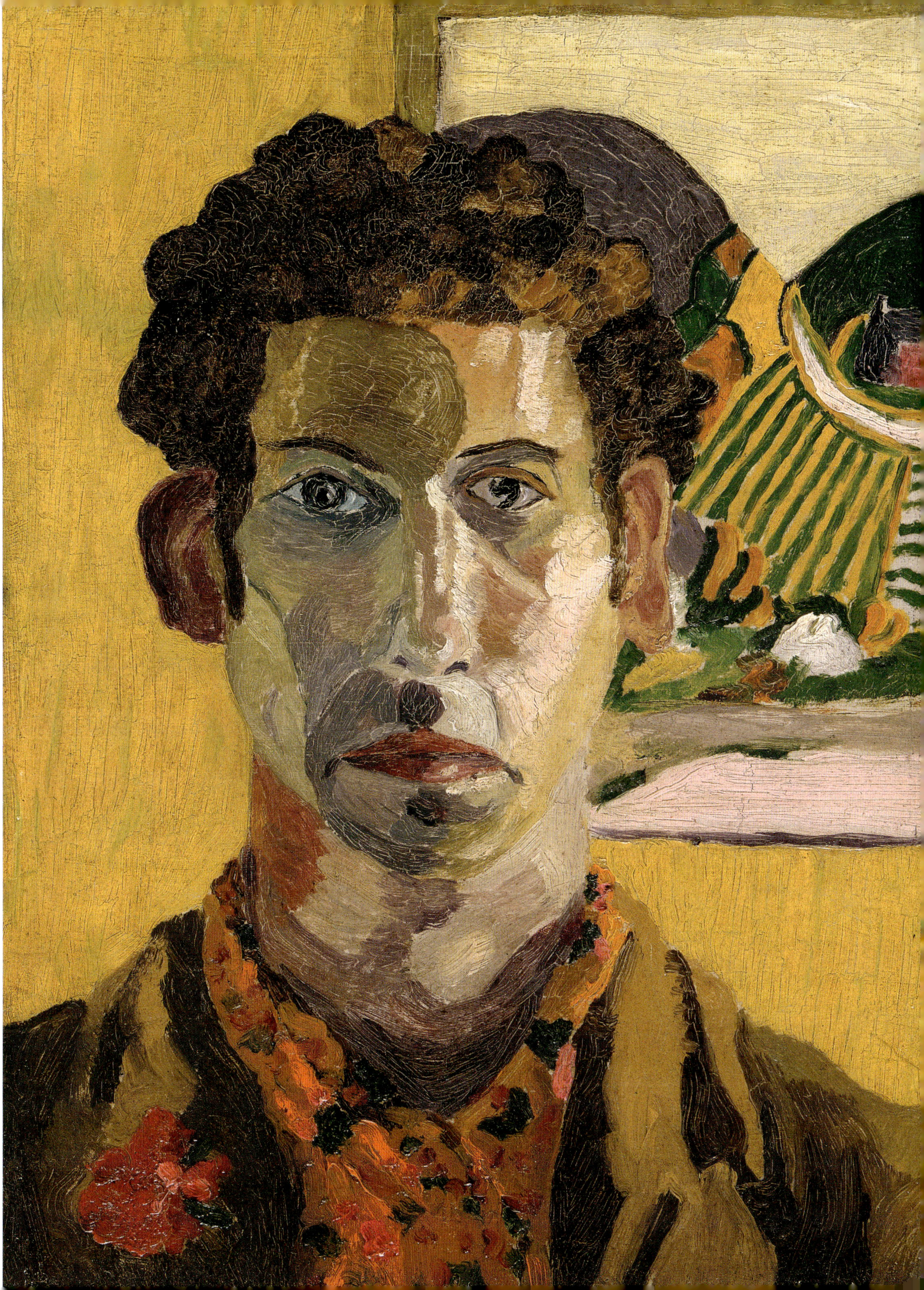

perhaps, have been partly responsible. In 1927 Walters introduced him to Winifred Coombe Tennant, with whom he developed an initially uneasy relationship. Nevertheless, Morris began to paint landscape at home, especially in Gower. Moved by this return to places familiar from his early childhood, he wrote in July 1928 to his partner, the painter Arthur Lett Haines, who had remained in London:

> I always said this was the most lovely country in the world and it is – it's so beautiful that I hardly dare look at it – and I realise now that all my painting is the result of pure nostalgia and nothing else – I thought I was homesick for England but not at all – dirty grimy little market garden – it was this I wanted …[51]

Like David Jones, Morris sensed the mythic associations of the landscape that he painted. Continuing his letter to Lett Haines, he described Cefn-y-Bryn, 'the highest point hereabouts [which] used to be a place of great mystery to me with Arthur's Stone on the top – you will

303. Cedric Morris, *Rhossili Down*, 1928, oil, 54×84

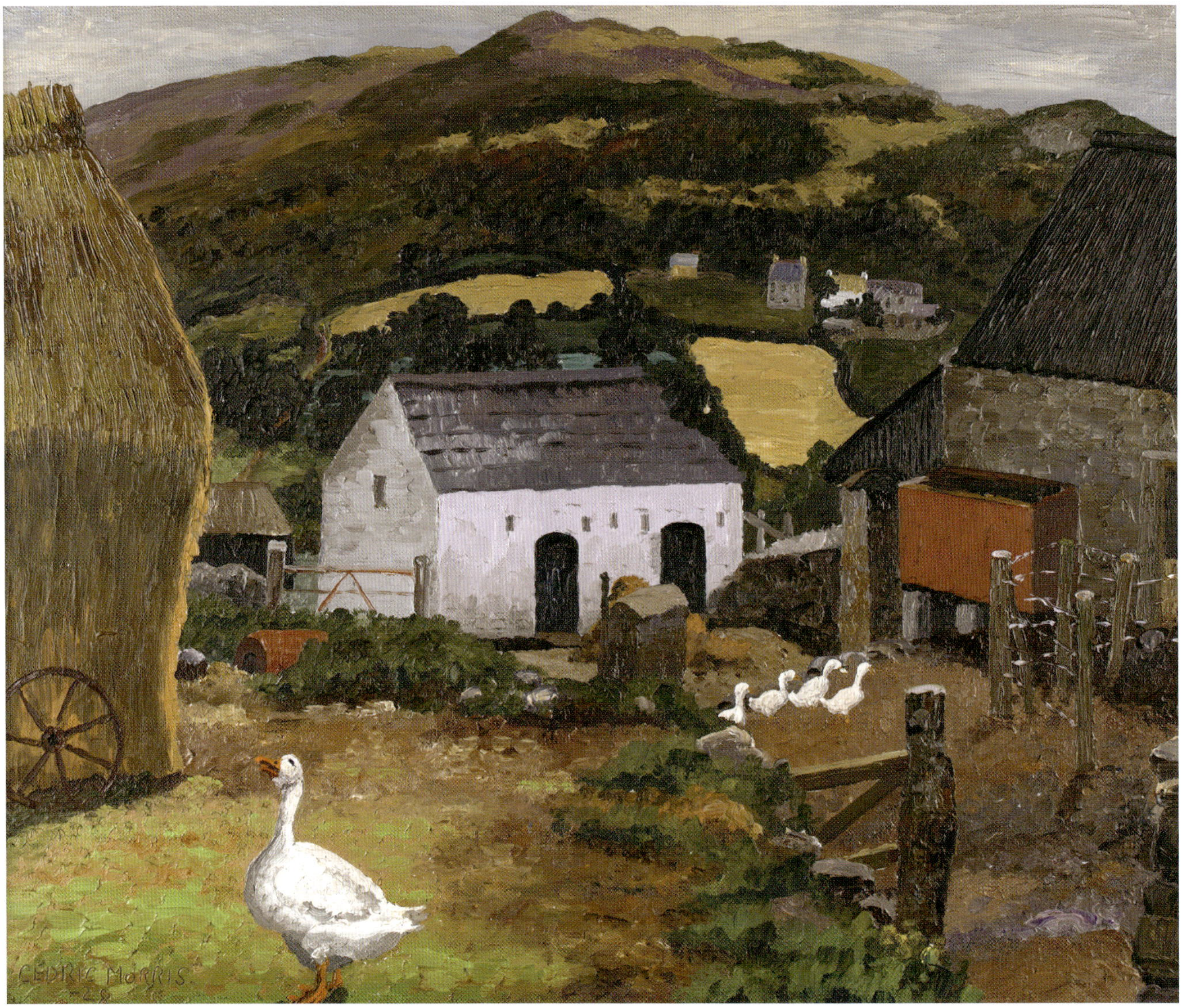

have to climb up and pay your respects to your namesake – he sat there when he read out the laws.' Morris drew attention also to the 'hundreds of wild ponies still here', and later he would use the word 'primeval' to describe his sense of it.[52] Certainly, the paintings of birds made by Morris in this period have that quality, sometimes verging on the surreal, but his landscapes seem to have drawn from him a more lyrical response to the visual qualities of place, rooted in the familiarity of childhood. Morris imaged the land with the faux primitive simplification of a sophisticate.

Gradually, Morris established contact with other Welsh painters and intellectuals. In 1932 he wrote to Coombe Tennant about Morland Lewis – 'a journeyman from Carmarthen – I think he is good (or will be).' His patrician tone expressed one side of a conflicted character, equally liable to complain of snooty narrow-mindedness among his county peers in Glamorgan and Carmarthen, and to reveal a deep sense of class-conscious and metropolitan snobbery in

51 Tate Gallery Archives, Cedric Morris Papers, 8317.1.4, item 52.

52 Morris used the word in attempting to describe the essence of Welshness in art. BBC radio script, 'Welsh Forum, Art in Wales', broadcast 21 February 1947, Tate Gallery Archives, Cedric Morris Papers 8317.3.1.2.

304. Cedric Morris, *Shags*, oil, 91.4x122

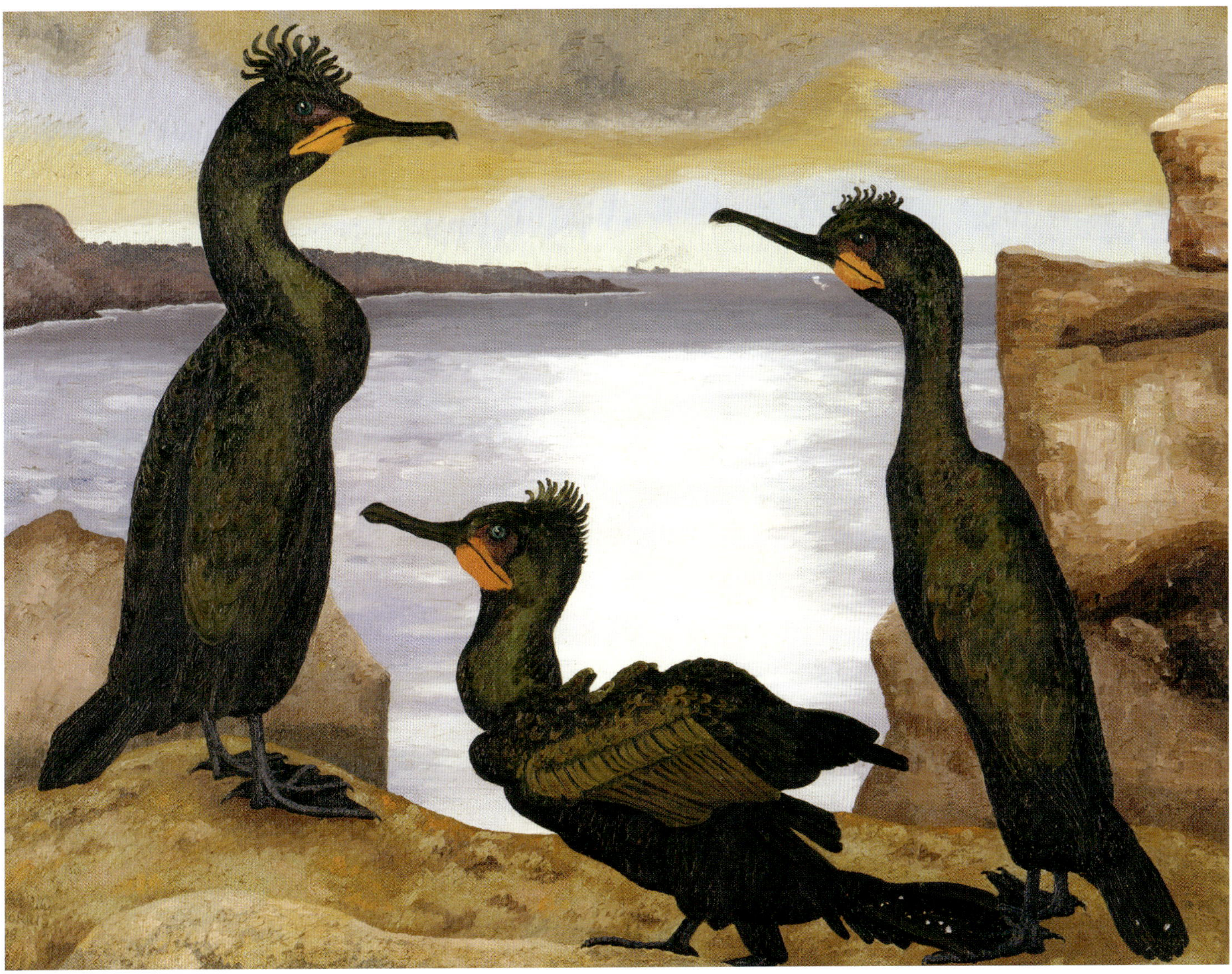

his own attitude to his Welsh colleagues: 'I don't quite like this idea of Evan W[alters] becoming prosperous and portly ... but this has been coming for some time I fancy – financial success is irresistible to the peasant mind unfortunately and most other minds also for that matter ...'[53] Given to periodic outbursts of slumming, in the summer of 1934 he tramped and painted in the rural south west, writing to let Lett Haines of being 'nearly frozen to death sleeping by the roadsides', but soon afterwards a distinct change occurred. To that point, Morris had revealed little concern with the social deprivation and political tensions that increasingly afflicted those he himself described as 'my people'. After 1935, pictures and letters reveal a shift that would result in a decade of close involvement in the relationship between art and the common people of industrial Wales: 'Am staying here in an out of work miner's cottage – all extremely uncomfortable and filthy food, but nice people and clean and it is the landscape I want ...It is really heartbreaking the way they have to live ...'[54] By 1936, back in London, Morris revealed his anger at the indifference of the metropolitan English to the distress of his own country:

> I don't think I can go on living in England ... I have never in my life felt anything like this.
>
> Surely this is the last blot on an infamous history and the sooner this stinking old whore of a country is blown into the sea the better – except that it would dirty the sea. If only there was something one could tie oneself onto that was against all this but there is nothing – fat complacency everywhere – perhaps in a few half-starved, frightened miners who have got to be murdered anyway to make room for more complacency ...[55]

53 Morris to Coombe Tennant, NLW Winifred Coombe Tennant Papers, A1/29, 20 February 1932 and undated c.1932.

54 Morris to Lett Haines, 30 July 1935, Tate Gallery Archives, Cedric Morris Papers, 8317.1.4.92.

55 Morris to Lett Haines, 15 December 1936, Tate Gallery Archives, Cedric Morris Papers, 8317.1.4.106.

56 Quoted in Eirene White, *The Ladies of Gregynog* (Cardiff, 1985), p. 41.

57 See Wal Hannington, *The Problem of the Distressed Areas* (London, 1937), p. 214.

The 1930s: politicised understandings of Wales in the Depression

The social concern revealed by Cedric Morris in the mid-1930s was characteristic of a wider awakening among artists and intellectuals to the consequences in both industrial Wales and in the industrial north of England and Scotland of the world-wide slump that followed the Wall Street crash of 1929. Unemployment would reach nearly 40% in Wales in 1932, and much higher levels in parts of the south Wales valleys, where the slump represented merely the acceleration of a decline in the coal and steel industries that was already resulting in mass unemployment and social deprivation. In the decade following 1921, the Rhondda lost 22% of its population. By 1929 the Davies sisters of Gregynog were directing their money into relief efforts. In that year, Margaret Davies wrote to Thomas Jones asking him to exert his influence in political circles in London: 'The enemy Despair is gaining ground daily', she told him, complaining that the government's policy of 'transference' – resettling large numbers of unemployed workers from the Valleys in the south-east of England – 'cannot cope with the situation'.[56]

The response of such liberal-minded philanthropists took the form both of palliative measures and the encouragement of what was described as 'self-help'. The first of several educational settlements was established by the Society of Friends at Maes-yr-haf in the Rhondda in 1927, and in the following year what became known as 'The Bryn Mawr Experiment' was initiated in Monmouthshire. Loans and advice were given to enable groups of unemployed workers to start small businesses. The spiritual needs of those who had on their hands what was euphemistically referred to as 'spare time' or even 'the new leisure', were to be met by the encouragement of literary, musical and artistic activities. Bryn Mawr became the most celebrated of these initiatives as a result of the success of its furniture manufacturing business in the 1930s. The products of the factory combined the attraction of the hand-made artefact, in the Arts and Crafts tradition of William Morris, with the spare, modern designs of Paul Matt. Considered from a different perspective, the production of up-market consumer goods at the instigation of middle-class do-gooders by workers who could never afford to buy such products for their own homes drew the contempt of some inside the working-class movement. The prominent communist, Wal Hannington, regarded such projects as the attempts of a frightened ruling class to contain the increasing radicalisation of working people.[57]

305. *Advertising Poster for the Bryn Mawr Furniture Company*, mid-1930s

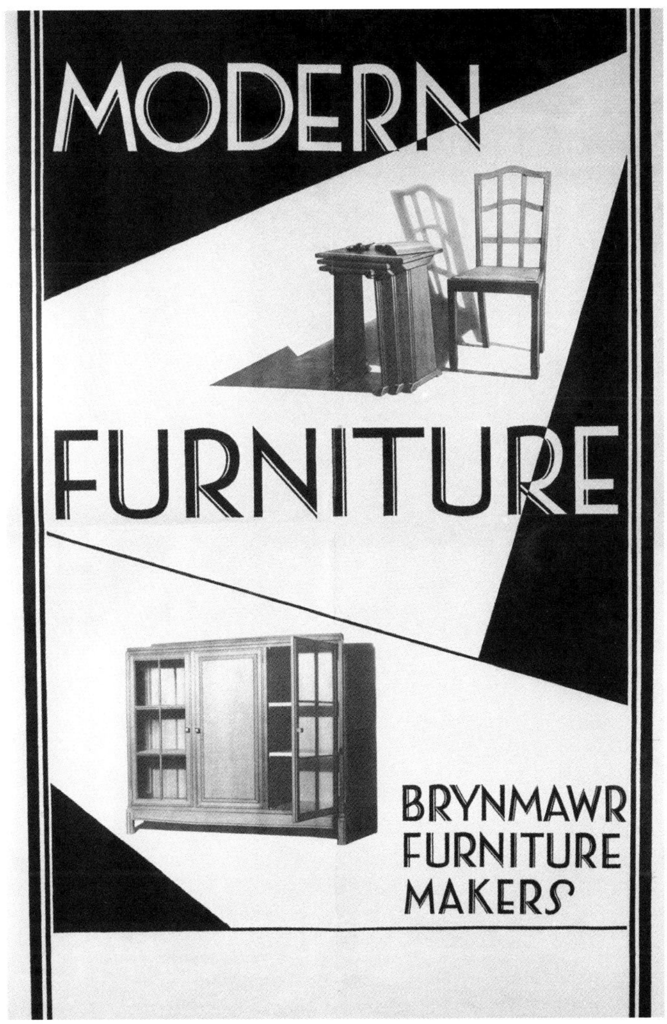

The high point of unemployment in 1932 – the year that also marked the introduction of the Means Test, which reduced benefit payments to thousands of already impoverished families – proved to be a turning point in the response of artists to the crisis. Over the ensuing five years mining communities came under the scrutiny of a flow of radical image makers from beyond Wales such as had not been seen since the 1870s. The Dutch-born

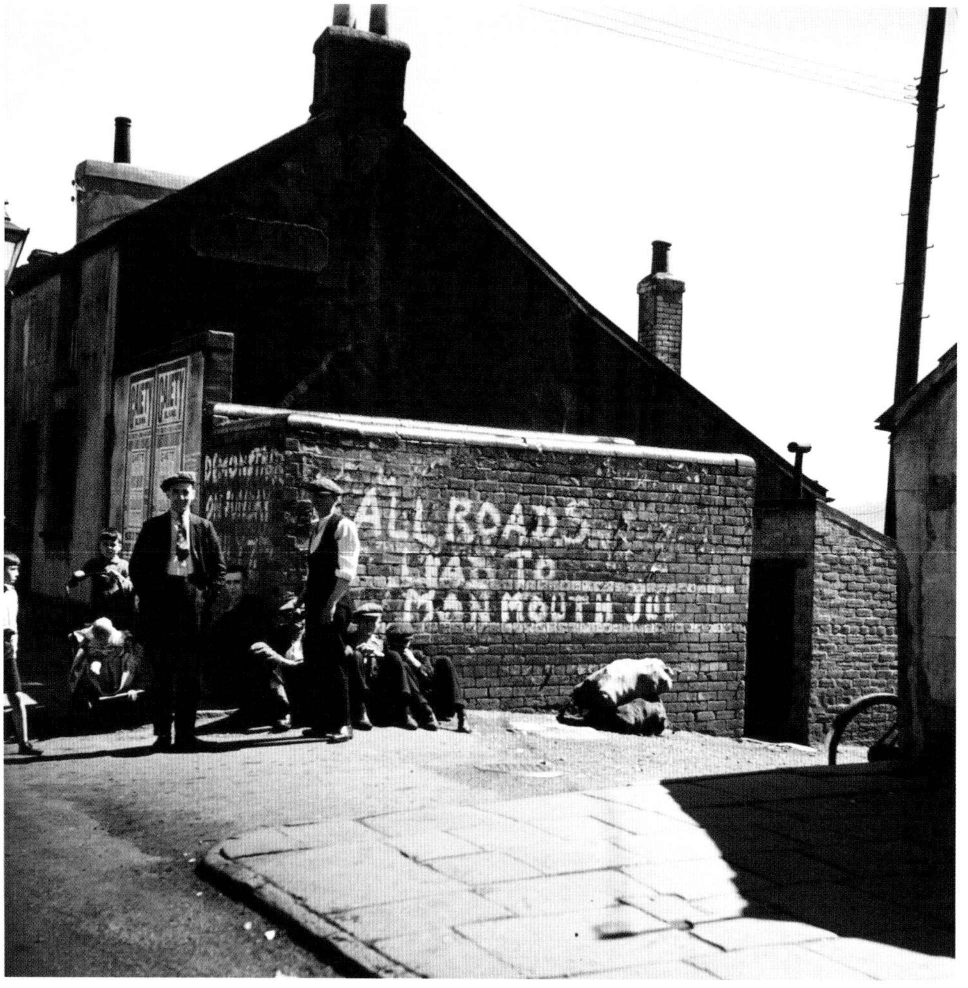

306. Edith Tudor-Hart, *Unemployed Workers, Abertillery*, 1935

opposite
307. Albert Houthuesen, *The Collier*, 1933, oil, 67.3x49.3

painter Albert Houthuesen, contemporary of Archie Griffiths and Ceri Richards at the Royal College of Art, came to the north-east coalfield for the first time in 1933, but it was the south Wales valleys that most attracted outsiders.[58] Among the first to arrive, and perhaps the most remarkable of them, was the Austrian photographer Edith Tudor-Hart. She had trained at the Bauhaus and had already achieved a distinguished body of documentary work in her own country, when in 1933 she came to the Rhondda, where her husband established a medical practice.[59] Her work was dedicated to the achievement of clear political ends. As she was a communist, Tudor-Hart's photography in Wales (as in other deprived areas), was intended to raise consciousness about the immorality of capitalist society, and to undermine it.[60] Her photograph of unemployed workers at Abertillery relaxing in the sunshine combined the informality of many of her images of everyday life in the Valleys with a reference to a specific political cause célèbre – a slogan chalked on a wall behind the group, 'All roads lead to Monmouth', placed the image in the aftermath of the 'Blaina Riot', when police violently dispersed a demonstration against the Means Test on 21 March 1935. The arrested men were tried at Monmouth.

58 Houthuesen became friendly with Richards, in particular, since both were in the same year. See Peter Lord, *The Visual Culture of Wales: Industrial Society* (Cardiff, 1998), pp. 214–15, and James Huntington-Whiteley, *Albert Houthuesen 1903-1979. An Artist in Wales. Paintings and Drawings from the 1930s* (Cardiff, 1997). William Rothenstein was enthusiastic about Houthuesen's work, and the portrait, *Painted in a Welsh Village*, made in 1933, was acquired by the Tate Gallery as early as 1938.

59 Edith Suschitzky had married Alex Tudor-Hart in Vienna. Alex Tudor-Hart would leave the Rhondda to fight on the Republican side in the Spanish Civil War between 1936–8.

60 Edith Tudor-Hart worked as an agent for the KGB, and was instrumental in the recruitment of the Cambridge spy-ring.

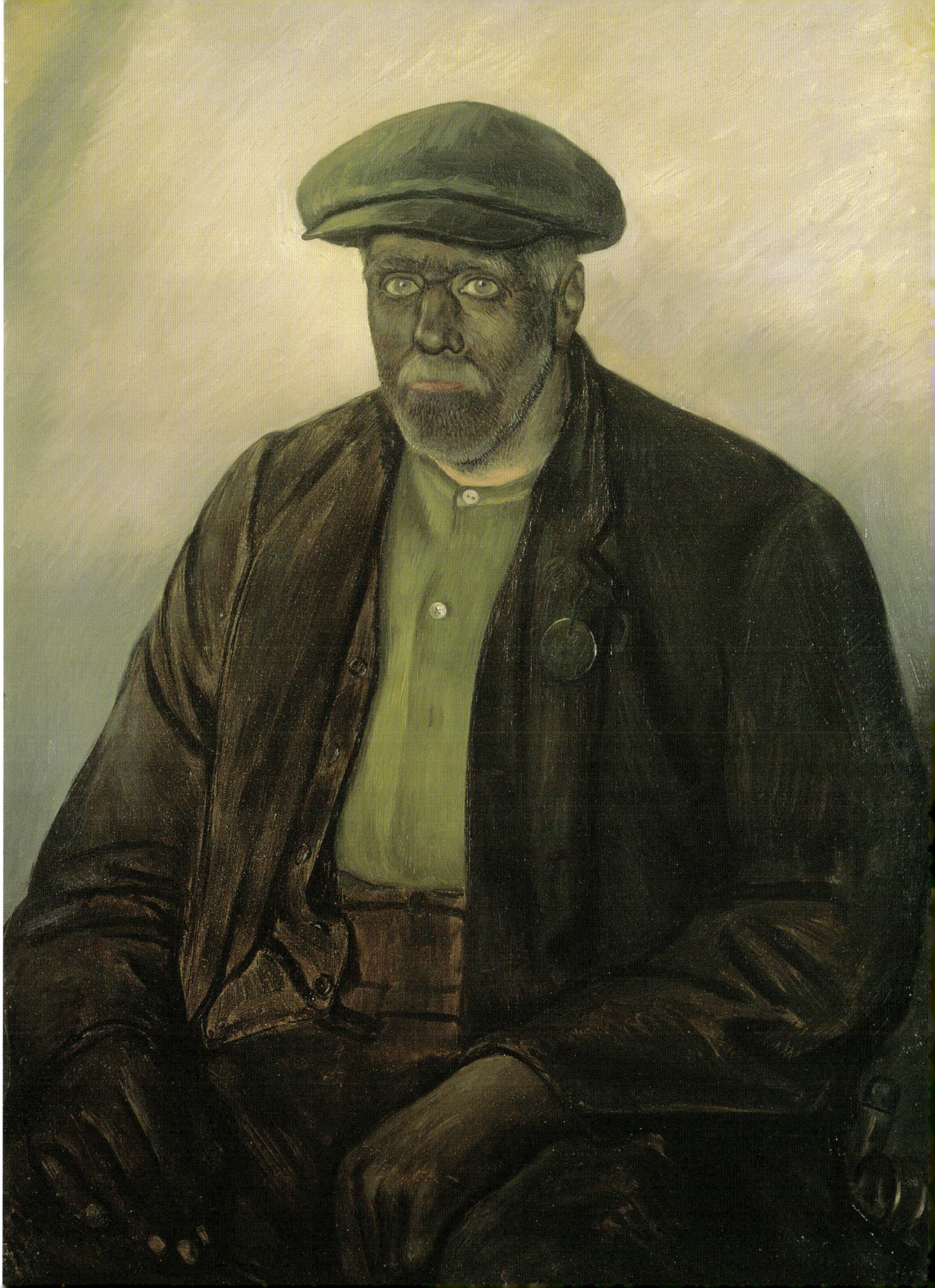

It was difficult for Tudor-Hart to reach her audience. Showing her work with the Workers Film and Photo League was to preach to the converted, but only occasionally was she able to publish her photographs in periodicals with a large circulation. In 1935 her work was used in association with an article about Bryn Mawr in *The Geographical Magazine*, but this was a rare exception.[61] Similar obstacles were faced by left-wing film makers. Ralph Bond, also associated with the Workers Film and Photo League, produced workers' newsreels that found an audience in some miners' institutes, but on the whole the institutes showed commercial film as the mainstay of their programmes through the 1930s.[62] In 1936 Bond's *Today We Live* did achieve a wider audience, but his radicalism had been constrained by the fact that the film was commissioned by the National Council of Social Service, a liberal-minded organisation involved in palliative work in education and the arts.[63] Nevertheless, with its comparison between rural life in Gloucestershire and the mining community of Pentre in the Rhondda, the film attempted to present a view of industrial society from the inside, and it was narrated by local people. Its striking imagery of idle railway yards and pit-head gear was reinforced by the insertion of one of the most remarkable film sequences of the period, shot the previous year by Douglas Alexander for a short called *Rhondda*. Alexander had been 'appalled' by what he found there: 'It was a devastating experience', he remembered.[64] His image of men digging for coal on a waste tip in swirling clouds of dust was the powerful culmination of a sequence that may be traced back through the work of Archie Griffiths and T.H. Thomas to the woodcuts published in the *Illustrated London News* and the *Graphic* in the 1870s. In 1937, Alexander made *Eastern Valley*, a film partly sponsored by the Society of Friends, about a self-help collective at Cwmavon in Monmouthshire. The visual imagery of the film stressed the desperate legacy of failed industrialism in the valley, but the commentary, provided by the members themselves, made clear their ambiguity of feeling about the venture. The members of the collective worked for nothing, to provide food and manufactures at reduced prices to their fellows.

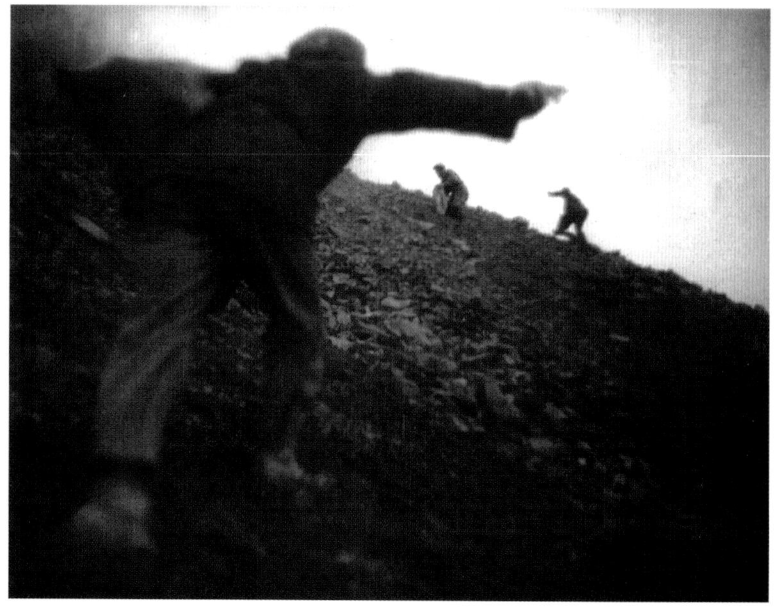

308. Douglas Alexander, frame enlargement from the Ralph Bond film *Today We Live*, 1936

61 *The Geographical Magazine*, ii, No. 5 (1935), pp. 372-386. The author of the text, Miles Davies, worked at the Maes-yr-haf educational settlement. The article also included photographs from other sources, including the work of Albert Davies.

62 See David Berry, *Wales and Cinema. The First Hundred Years* (Cardiff, 1994), pp. 127–45.

63 The Council was a non-governmental body but one with high-powered connections. The Secretary to the Welsh Department of the Council was the former senior civil servant Percy Watkins, a close associate of Thomas Jones and others of the Liberal circle of *The Welsh Outlook*. See Richard Lewis, 'The Welsh ideal of a democratic popular culture', in *Liberals, Radicals and Collective Identities in the British Isles, 1865–1931*, ed. Eugenio F. Bagini, (Cambridge, 1996), pp. 339–40.

64 Interview with Dave Berry, 1985, quoted in Berry, *Wales and Cinema*, p. 138.

Photography and film dominated the politically motivated art of the period made in or about Wales.[65] Notwithstanding the powerful influence of communist ideology and widespread admiration for the Soviet Union in the period, no Welsh painter adopted Socialist Realism as a medium of expression in a way equivalent to that in which Lewis Jones wrote his didactic political novels, *Cwmardy* and *We Live*.[66] In London, the English painter Jack Hastings created, with a strong Welsh content, a mural depicting the fall of capitalism. The massive torso of the central figure, staring like a Roman god from within

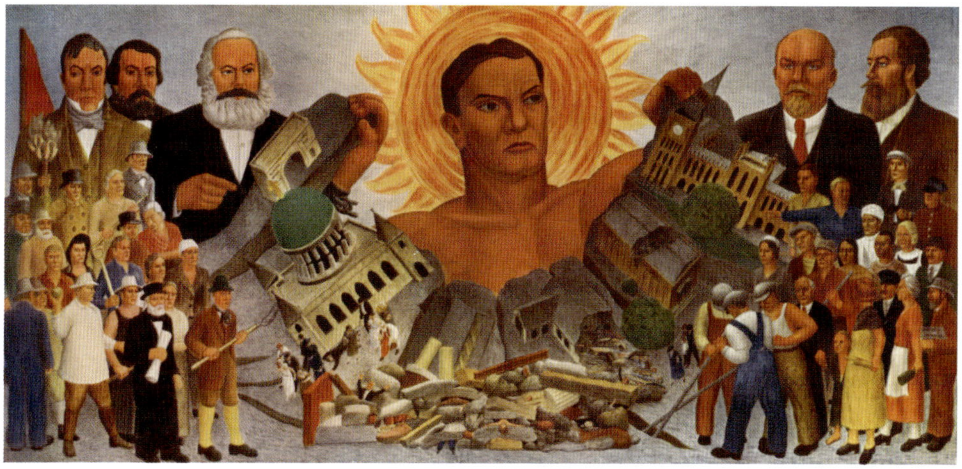

309. Jack Hastings, *Mural at the Marx Memorial Library*, London, 1935, fresco, 302.4x602.8

the halo of the sun, represented a Welsh miner. He was flanked by portraits not only of Marx and Lenin, but also of Robert Owen and William Morris. Hastings had recently returned from working in San Francisco with the communist painter Diego Rivera, whose influence dominated the conception of the picture. However, it did not establish a widely followed precedent. Neither did Social Realism, the supposedly documentary rather than didactic manifestation of political principle in painting, make an impact equivalent to that of the remarkable body of literature that emerged in the period.[67] Curiously, the most substantial contribution to the genre in Wales was made immediately after the filming of *Eastern Valley* and very close by, though apparently in ignorance of the film. Nevertheless, it was as a result of his awareness of what he described as the 'desolate parts' of the Valleys that in August 1937 Maurice Sochachewsky, a young painter from the Jewish community of east London, came to the area.[68] His contact with the mining village of Talywain was made through Arthur Jenkins, the Member of Parliament for Pontypool, who found him lodgings with a collier's family. Over the ensuing four months, and again in 1938, Sochachewsky drew and painted scenes by which he was profoundly shocked: 'Hell I think must be a more heavenly place

65 Commercial cinema also became marginally interested in the coalfield as a background for drama, notably in *Proud Valley*, which emerged in 1940 as a vehicle for the singing of Paul Robeson. The original screenplay was written by Herbert Marshall, though his treatment was subsequently rejected in favour of a script to which Jack Jones contributed. During the development of the film, Robeson was sculpted by Alfredda Brilliant, who was married to Marshall, and the process was recorded in a memorable photograph taken by Edith Tudor-Hart. The image demonstrates the close relationship that existed between communist artists in the period.

66 First published respectively in 1937 and, posthumously, in 1939. Jones described portraits of men who had fought in the Spanish Civil War painted by 'Artists belonging to the Party', but no work of this kind is known to survive. Lewis Jones, *Cwmardy and We Live* (new edn., Cardigan, 2006), p. 871.

67 For the relationship between the painting and literature of the period, see Lord, 'Biblical and Marxist rhetoric in the painting and literature of the Depression', in Meredith (ed.), *Moment of Earth*, pp. 201–17.

68 Maurice Sochachewsky is quoted from his letters, written from Wales in 1937–8 to his family in London, private archive. For the painter and his Welsh work, see Lord, *Relationships with Pictures*, pp. 259–78.

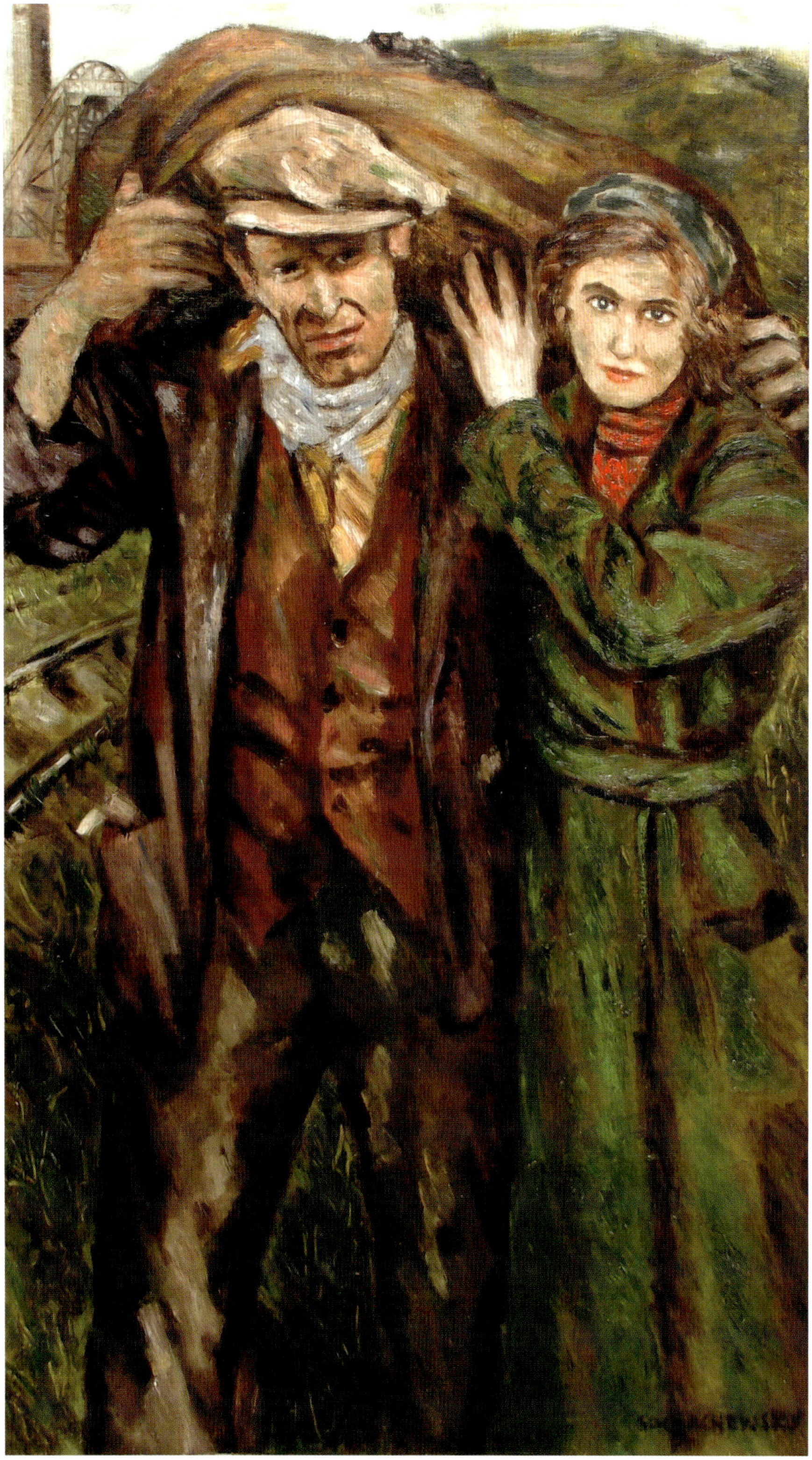

than this', he wrote after going underground for the first time. Later, he was welcomed at the collective in Cwmavon that had been filmed by Alexander, where he found a German painter already established and running art classes. Through his father's contacts, Sochachewsky was able to work towards an exhibition of his paintings that aspired to 'open the eyes of London's complacent, often unbelieving people'.[69] The exhibition took place at the Bloomsbury Gallery in 1938, and among the twenty-five works exhibited was *Their Burden*, a picture that yet again presented the image which had encapsulated for generations of artists the essence of the degradation of working people by Capitalism – men and women collecting waste coal from the tips.

However closely he identified with the people of Talywain, Maurice Sochachewsky's London exhibition presented the attitudes of an outsider. It is clear that many local people developed an affection for the young painter, but perceptions of the sudden interest among intellectuals from outside in working-class communities in the deprived areas were not always

310. Maurice Sochachewsky, *Their Burden*, 1937, oil, 115x66.5

so benign. In 1937, the writer James Hanley published *Grey Children*, an account of conditions in the Valleys, largely based on interviews. Hanley opened his book with the words of an unemployed collier: 'We're about fed up with people coming down here looking us over as though we were animals in a zoo. Put that in the headlines for a change.'[70]

The development of outsider art in the Valleys coincided with the end of the career of Archie Griffiths and the change of direction in the work of Evan Walters that largely took him away from imaging the coal field. The last review of Griffiths' work was published in 1934 by John Davies Williams:

> 'Disused Colliery' ... may repel you at first, but if you go back to it you will get to see that this Gorseinon artist has painted the whole hopeless tragedy of the Welsh coalfield. Here is the artist indeed taking the role of prophet. Mr Griffiths has never done anything so big. It is sombre – but it is Wales in 1934.[71]

In fact, the picture had been painted two years earlier, at the height of the Depression and in the year in which Griffiths's older contemporary, Vincent Evans, returned from his teaching post in New Zealand. Evans took up the imaging of the coal industry where he had left off, a decade earlier, and became the only insider to produce a substantial body of work in the 1930s. In 1933 he showed pictures at the Cooling Gallery in London, where they were viewed by William Rothenstein, and in 1936 he had two major works depicting workers underground – 'essentially from Welsh inspiration and of Welsh life' – accepted at the Royal Academy.[72] Yet, apart from the South Wales Miners' Federation, he seems to have found no patrons in Wales. Even Winifred Coombe Tennant did not buy his work, annoyed by what she regarded as an arrogant personality.[73]

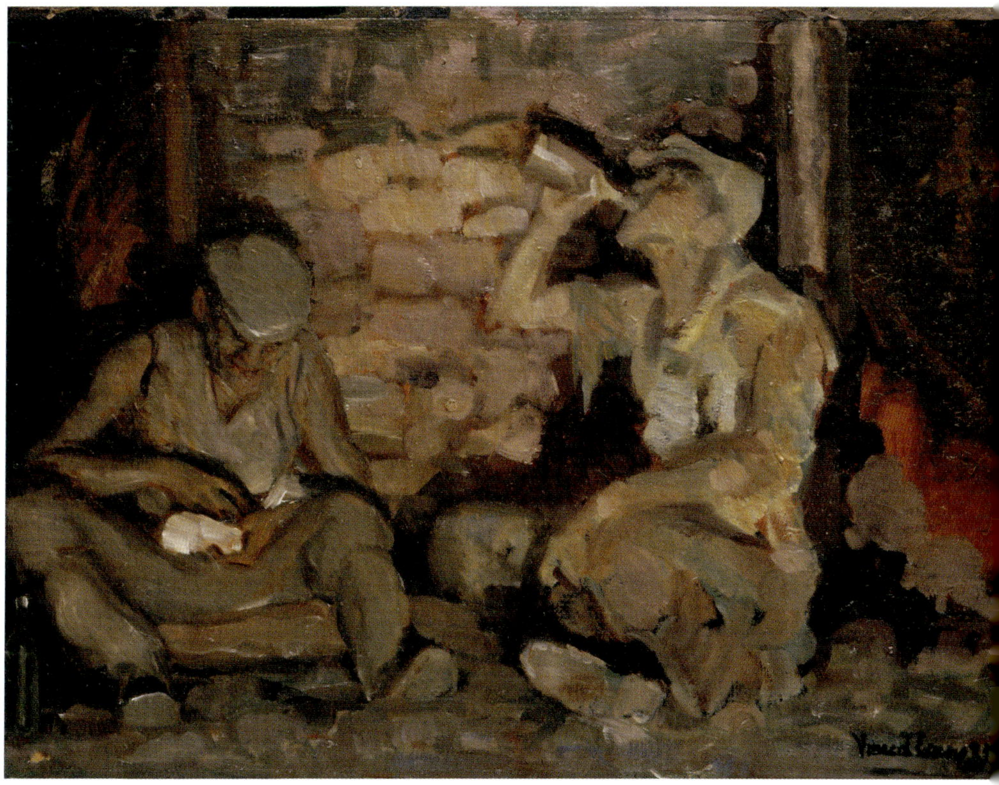

311. Vincent Evans, *A Snack*, 1935, oil, 29.5x39.5

69 *Daily Herald*, 7 December 1937. Sochachewsky did not fully name the German painter working at Cwmavon, referring to him as 'Mr Mach', and as a 'Futurist and Surrealist'. He remains unidentified.

70 James Hanley, *Grey Children. A Study in Humbug and Misery* (London, 1937).

71 *Herald of Wales*, 11 August 1934, p. 1.

72 Evans, letter to the National Museum of Wales, 26 June 1936, NMW Artists' Files.

73 Coombe Tennant visited Evans in London in December 1935, but found him 'little gifted and loquacious'. She did not like 'the impression his accumulated work made on me', and did not buy a picture. Diary of Winifred Coombe Tennant, 31 December 1935, private archive. The tone of Evans's correspondence with the National Museum, when he offered pictures to them between 1936–8, and again in 1948, was often somewhat hectoring.

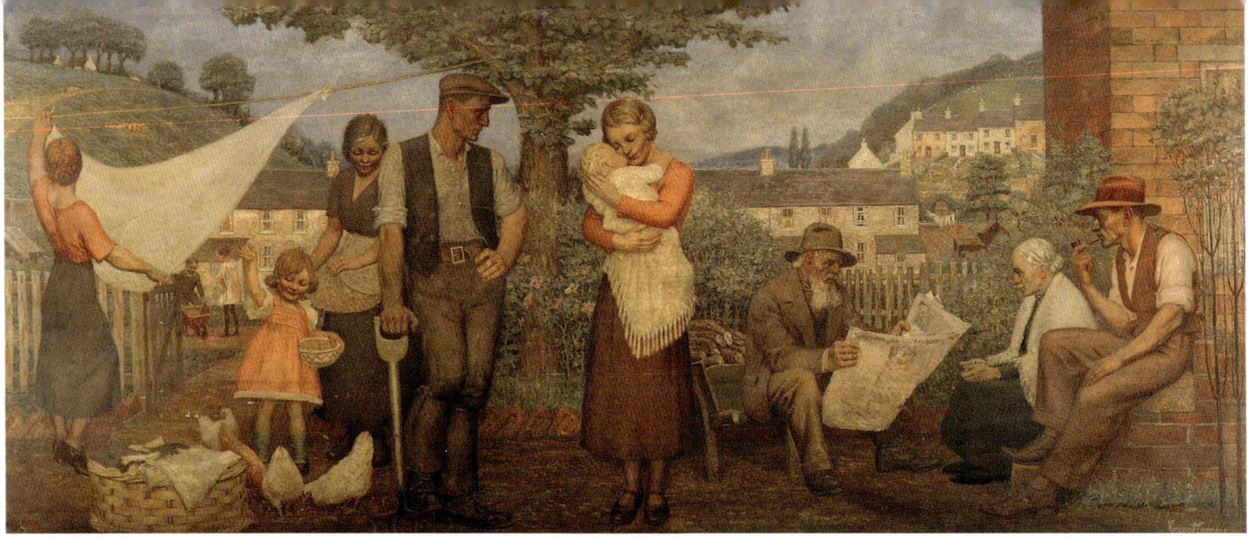

312. Vincent Evans, *A Welsh Family Idyll*, c.1936, oil, 141.5x321.2

The political views of Vincent Evans, and to what extent they were expressed in his imagery and so affected the attitude of his potential patrons, are unclear. He was certainly closer to the formal labour movement than Griffiths or Walters, and he became a friend of Jim Griffiths, the President of the South Wales Miners' Federation. He painted the scene of a union meeting held underground, which may also have carried, as a sub-text, ironic comment on the earlier imaging of the underground prayer meetings that took place following the religious revival of 1904. Yet although the monumentality of his larger works in the 1930s superficially suggested an awareness of Socialist Realism, its origin is more likely to be identified in the Classicism of the French painter Puvis de Chavannes. In about 1935, Evans conceived and began work on his most ambitious picture – an attempt on mural scale to image what he conceived as the characteristic values of the community from which he had emerged in Ystalyfera, on the western edge of the coalfield. The title of the picture was significant. *A Welsh Family Idyll* was intended as a statement of national cultural values, rather than of the concept of international working class solidarity that was so important to artists inspired by communist ideology.[74]

Modernism in the 1930s

During the 1930s, artists connected with Wales exhibited the same dichotomy in their responses to the state of the world as they had in the previous decade. The work of those like Tudor-Hart and Sochachewsky, who chose to address directly the crisis of industrial society, contrasted starkly with the work of others who were, apparently, untouched by its unpleasant realities, or who sought escape from them.[75]

In London, by the early 1930s, an internationally oriented core of radical artists were experimenting with various forms of abstraction, most of them derived from the works of the Paris avant-garde. Evan Walters, whose studio was in Hampstead at this time, was

74 Evans also referred to the picture as 'Welsh Family Life'.

75 'It passed me by', was the reflection of the painter and writer Mervyn Levy, when questioned in 1995 about the social trauma of the Depression. 'What we wanted to do was to go to London and if possible go to Paris and somehow or other to identify ourselves with the French and continental avant-garde.' Interview with Peter Lord, NLW, National Screen and Sound Archive, Visual Culture of Wales Research Project Deposit, DT000045.

surely aware of these experiments, and they may well have played a part in his decision to change the nature of his own work. Nevertheless, he did not align himself with any movement or group of artists, choosing rather to plough his own Modernist furrow. He became fascinated by the mechanics of seeing – by the paradox of the binocular vision of the painter and the monocular recording of things seen in paintings. In 1936 he exhibited a group of pictures in which the double images received from the eyes, and normally resolved by the brain into a coherent vision, remained separated. Most of his supporters were unimpressed. Winifred Coombe Tennant did not patronise him again until 1950, and then it would be on condition that there was 'no nonsense about double vision'. The painter's new portrait of Winifred was to be 'straight painting'.[76] In an attempt to clarify his intentions, Walters wrote a thesis on the subject, that he called 'The Third Dimension', and in his painting pursued his theory to the end of his life.[77] In 1951, his last work, the unfinished *Primavera*, revealed the painter endeavouring to combine – as he had done in a different way in the 1920s – his personal vision with a theme drawn from the deep traditions of European high art.

76 Coombe Tennant to Augustus John, NLW Winifred Coombe Tennant Papers, A1/20, 9 November 1950. The result of her patronage on this occasion was one of Walters's finest portraits, for which see Lord, *A Life through Art*, p. 184.

77 'The Third Dimension', *c*.1937, was not published, and survives in a number of illustrated typescript copies.

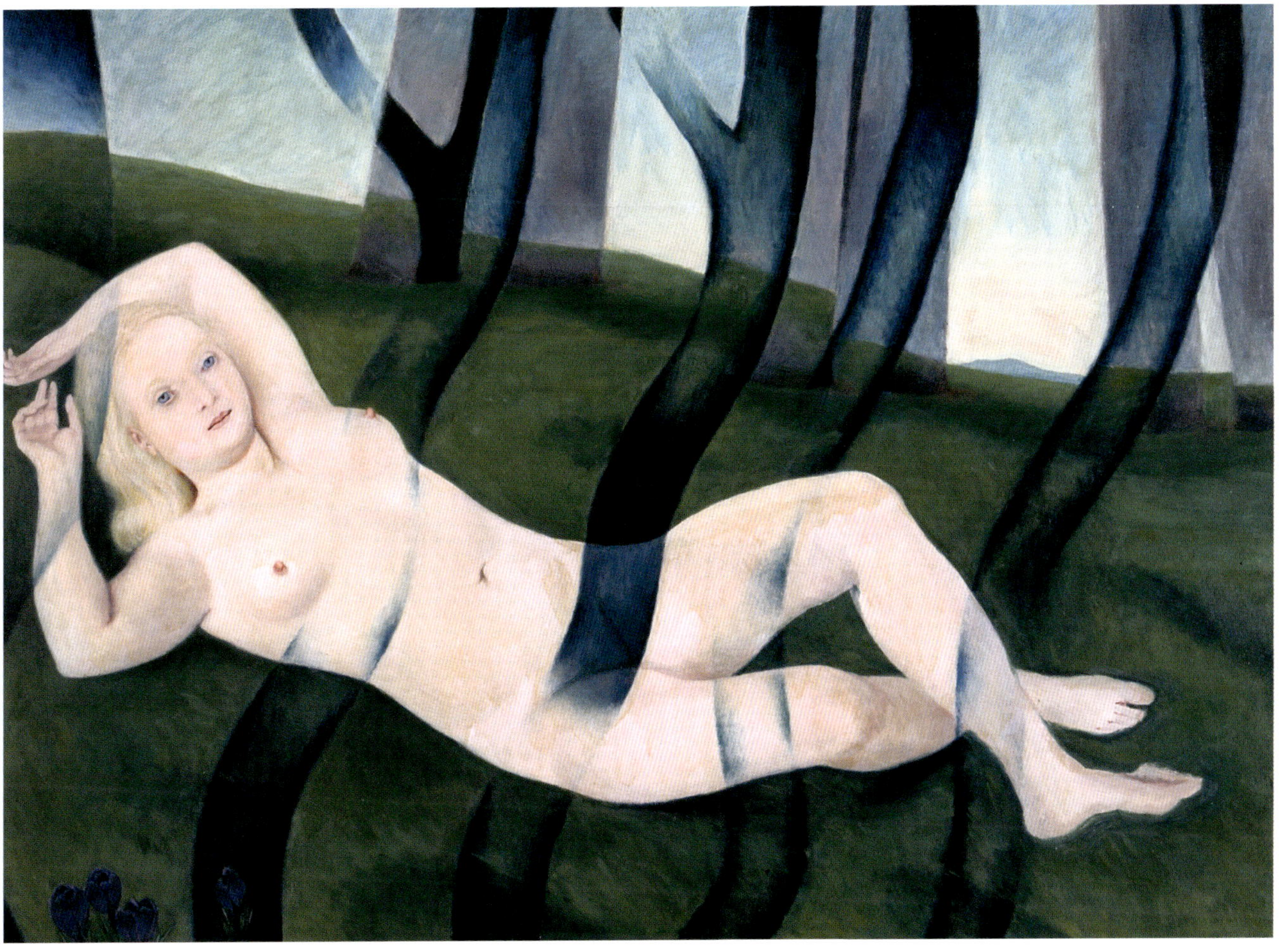

313. Evan Walters, *Primavera*, 1951, oil, 76.2x106.7

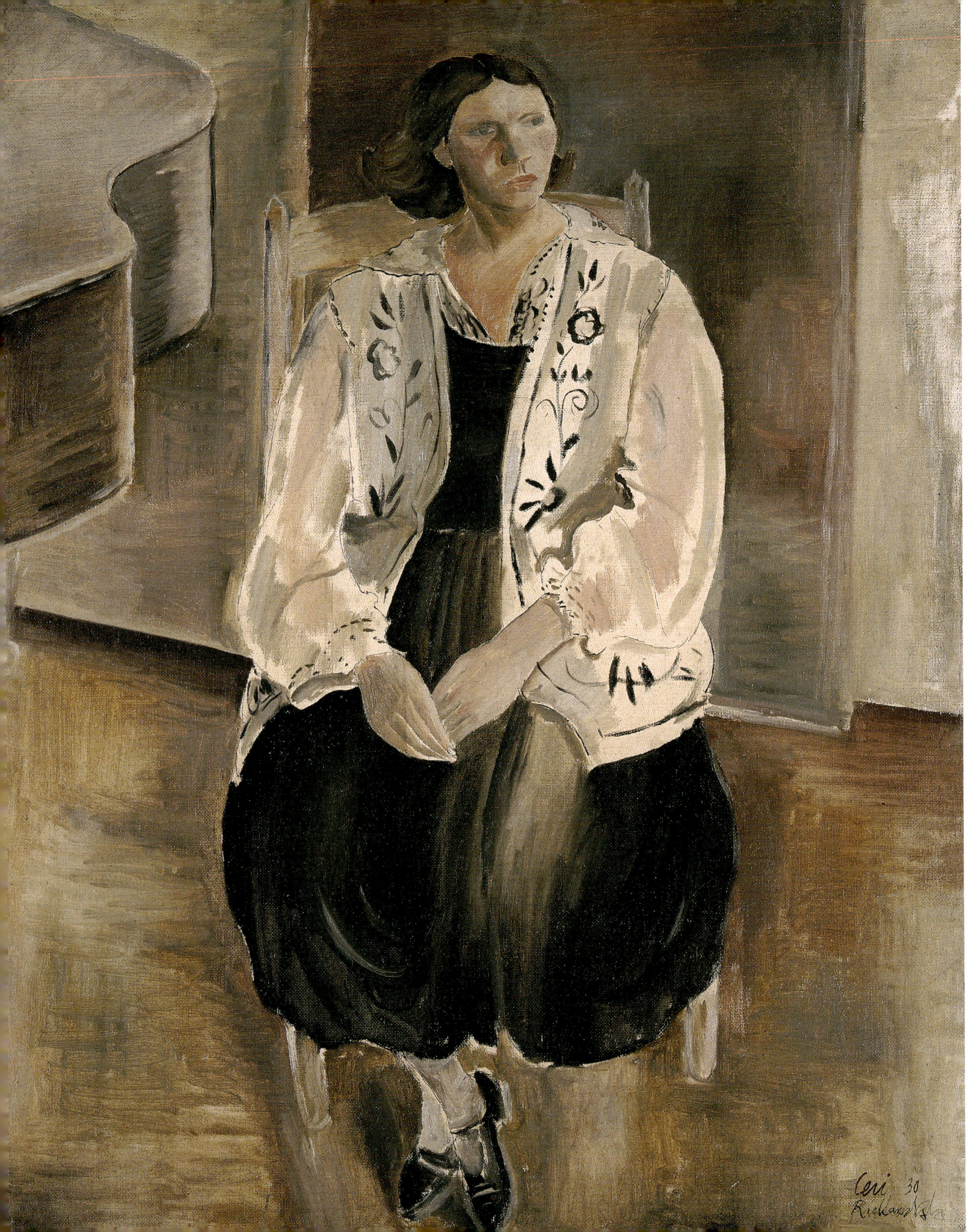
Ceri 30

Ceri Richards, also in London, responded to the stimulus of new ideas around him by engaging directly with Modernist movements. His first contact with French art had been at Gregynog where, in 1923, he attended a summer school run by Hugh Blaker during which he saw the Davies sisters' collection. Notwithstanding remarkable talent as a draughtsman, after leaving the Royal College in 1927 he moved steadily towards abstraction. A group of his portraits, including that of Archie Griffiths, was included in his first one-person exhibition, given him by Grant Murray at the Glynn Vivian gallery in 1930. Four years later he had established a sufficient presence among the metropolitan avant-garde to be shown alongside the Objective Abstraction Group in London. He exhibited Cubist-inspired montages that integrated painting with shallow wooden shapes and pages of found text and music, though he made no formal commitment to any of the groups that frequently appeared and disappeared beneath the shifting sands of aesthetic allegiance in that period of intense artistic debate.[78] He was among the thousands of visitors to the International Surrealist Exhibition in London in 1936, which injected a further stylistic influence into his work. The exhibition had been opened to huge publicity by André Breton, with Salvador Dalí in attendance, clad in a diving suit.

opposite
314. Ceri Richards, *Black and White Figure (Portrait of the Artist's Wife)*, 1930, oil, 76.6x61.5

78 In this period, between 1933–5 Richards and his family shared a house with the family of Richard Llywelyn Huws, who had studied with Bauhaus teachers at Vienna between 1927–30, at the same time as Edith Tudor-Hart was working in the city. See Lord, *Imaging the Nation*, pp. 381–2.

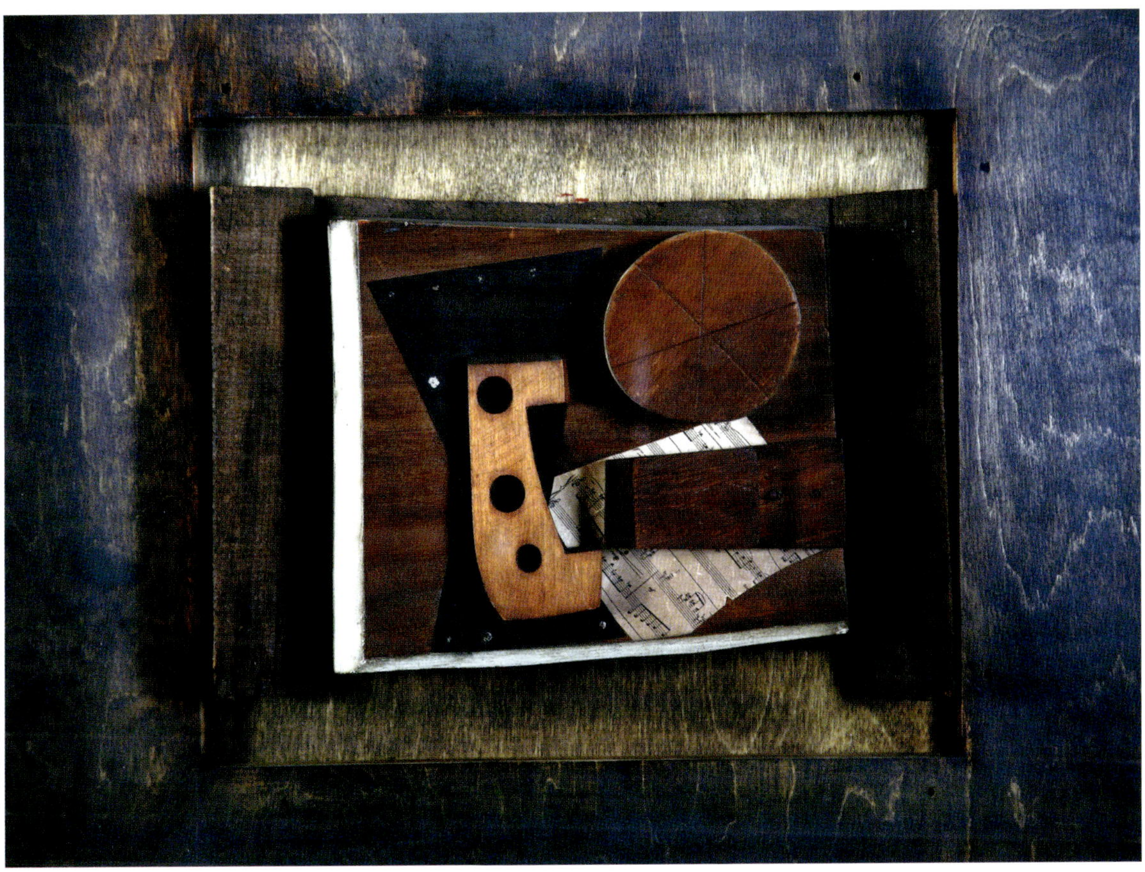

315. Ceri Richards, *Relief Construction with Fragment of Music*, 1934, mixed media, 18.5x28

79 Diary of Winifred Coombe Tennant, 26 June 1932. Kenneth Hancock established the closest relationship with Coombe Tennant, keeping her in touch by letter with Swansea life.

80 Interview with Peter Lord, 1995, NLW Welsh Visual Culture Research Project Deposit, DT000045.

81 John Petts in *Artists in Wales*, 3, ed. Meic Stephens (Llandysul, 1977), p. 177.

82 The Newbridge Institute also included a small element of mural painting, though the history of this part of the project remains obscure.

The celebrity of the continental avant-garde also attracted the next generation of Swansea painters. Alfred Janes and Mervyn Levy, both initially trained by Grant Murray, were studying at the Royal Academy and the Royal College of Art, and later they were joined by James Govier. Winifred Coombe Tennant, who herself moved to a London flat in 1931, pursued their careers:

> Not out all day, but a pleasant Bohemian supper party – Evan Walters and Morland Lewis the young painter from Carmarthen, and Hancock and Janes the Swansea art students. They came at 7.00 and left at 11. Much interesting talk.[79]

Clearly, Coombe Tennant was well aware of the life-style pursued by these young men when not on their best behaviour in her, by now, matronly company. Levy would remark later of this period that Augustus John was their 'lode star'. It was all 'tremendous fun'.[80] The Welsh company was augmented by Brenda Chamberlain, who drew in her lover, John Petts, whom she would later marry. Both were studying at the Royal Academy. Like Levy, Petts would later recall the excitement of life in this Bohemian circle, one of the characteristics of which was the interaction of painters and writers. Evan Walters was a good friend of the Irish playwright Seán O'Casey; Levy and Janes lived with Dylan Thomas, and Vernon Watkins was in close attendance:

opposite
317. Alfred Janes,
Dylan Thomas, 1934,
oil, 40.6x30.5

> Voices from Wales sounded clear above clipped English monotones: blonde Fred Janes from Swansea, enthusiasm sparkling through his round specs; tense Bromfield Rees from Sospan Fach, Brenda Chamberlain from Bangor, soft sandals pacing the cloister-corridor, a smiling novice in the long, white smock. Dylan Thomas called in, taking his pork-pie hat off, with Mervyn Levy from the Royal College. Ankle-deep in cigarette cartons, they shared a flat with Fred.[81]

Alongside the experimentalist and Bohemian avant-garde, Modernism in England encompassed a more democratic philosophical strand that, in an oblique manner responded creatively to the social upheavals of the period. It penetrated Wales most obviously in architecture, especially in the use of the Art Deco style in the design of places of popular entertainment, such as cinemas, lidos and piers. The Odeon chain built notable Modernist cinemas with Art Deco styling at Newport and Rhyl, for instance. The dramatic interior of the Memorial Hall of the Newbridge Workingman's Institute was designed in 1924 in the same manner. Five years later, Penarth Pier was rebuilt in the Art Deco fashion, as was the Victoria Pier at Colwyn Bay, where the scheme included interior mural decorations carried out by Eric Ravilious and Mary Adshead.[82]

316. Eric Ravilious,
Mural in the Tea Room,
Victoria Pier, Colwyn Bay,
1934

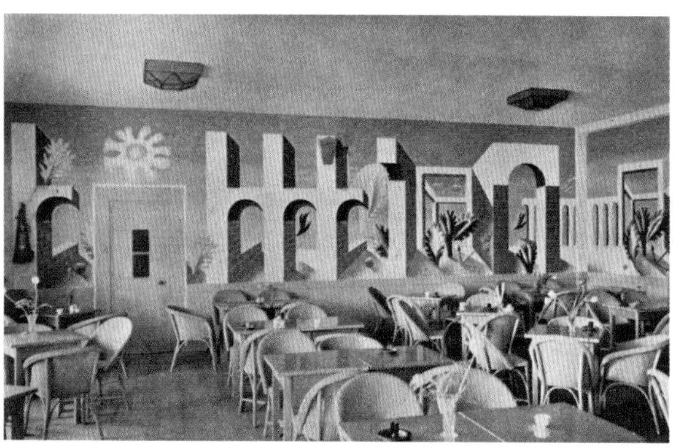

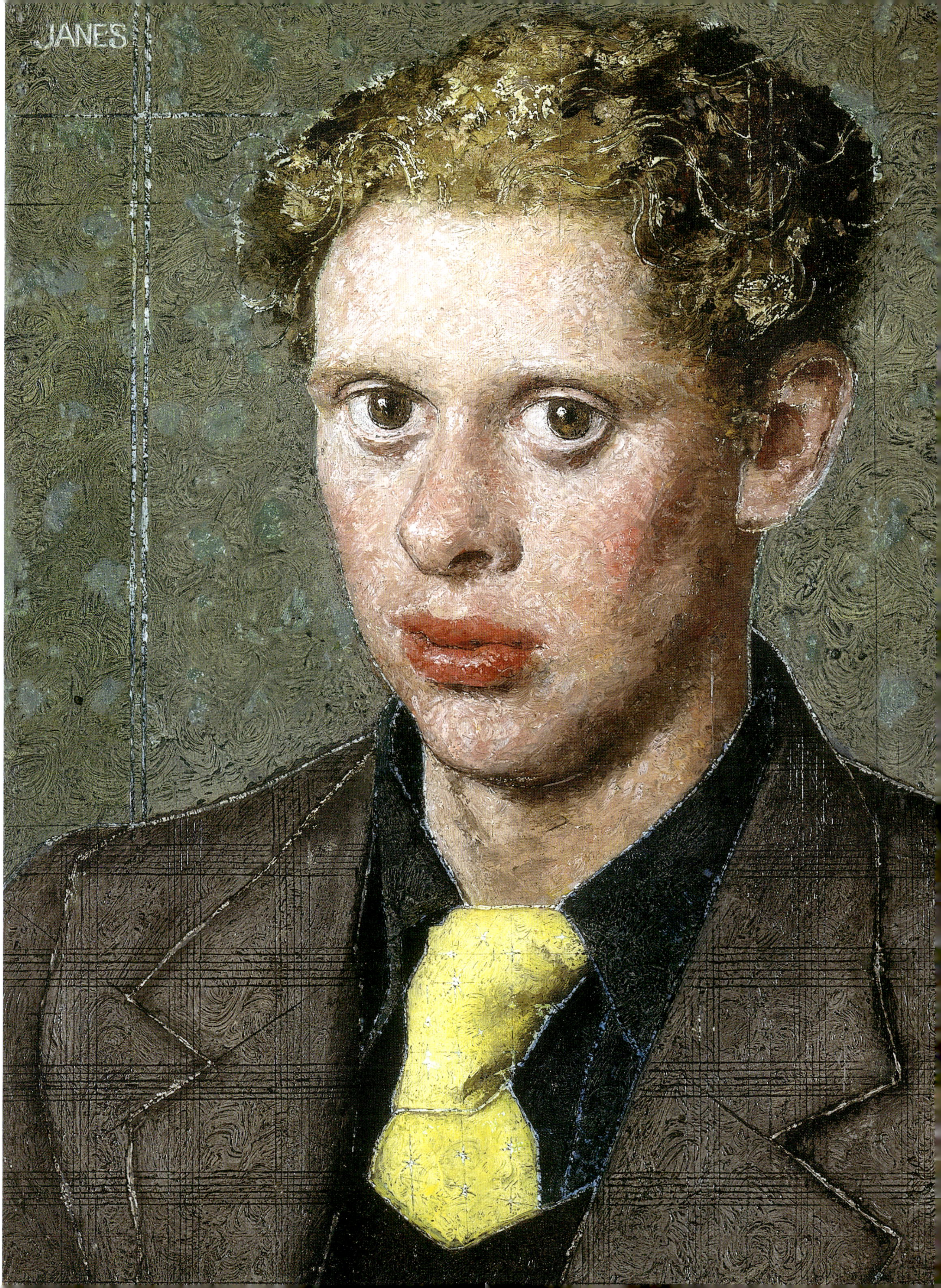
JANES

83 For the English Neo-Romantics, see Alexandra Harris, *Romantic Moderns. English Writers, Artists and the Imagination, from Virginia Woolf to John Piper* (London, 2010).

Ravilious was a central figure in a network of English Neo-Romantics, that included also Rex Whistler, who in 1936 undertook the largest domestic mural scheme of the period in Wales, at Plas Newydd, in Anglesey. The Plas Newydd mural presented an eccentric contrast with the gentle, even whimsical approach that characterised the public work of Ravilious. Responding to an act of gentry patronage on a domestic scale more characteristic of the eighteenth than the twentieth century, Whistler created a vast and fantastic harbour scene in a room overlooking the Menai Strait. In one of the smaller end panels he included a self-portrait.[83]

The Modernism of Neo-Romantics such as Ravilious coexisted with a paradoxical inclination to reclaim an imagined pastoral English tradition. Curiously, as in the eighteenth century, a part of the groundwork for that reclamation was laid in Wales. Following in the footsteps of Turner, the Neo-Romantic disposition drew into Wales two painters who would assume prominent positions in the English art world for decades to come. Nevertheless, though Graham Sutherland and John Piper are rightly considered as manifestations of the same

318. Rex Whistler, *Mural at Plas Newydd*, Anglesey, 1936, oil, l.1768

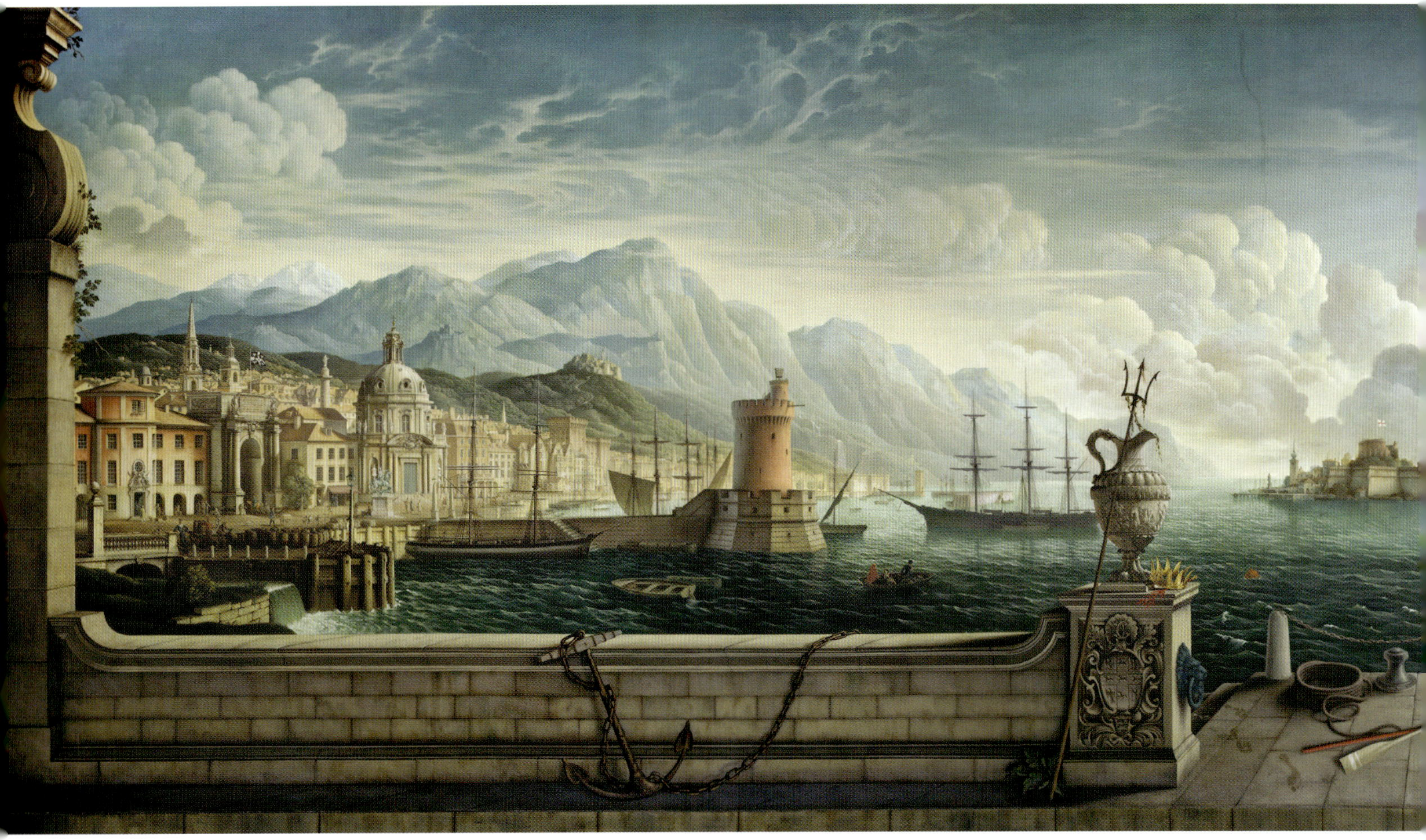

general tendency in English arts, they pursued different aesthetic trajectories. Sutherland made his first visit to Pembrokeshire in 1934, though like most of his eighteenth-century precursors from England, he would engage but little with the culture of Wales. On the other hand, the Welsh landscape became the most important source for his lifelong attempt to penetrate surfaces and express his sense of the fundamental building blocks and forces of nature. By the time of his first visit to Pembrokeshire, Sutherland's career, developed initially as a print maker, was well established. He was a participant in the 1936 Surrealist exhibition that impressed Ceri Richards, and indeed Richards's own concern with natural forces and with Christian subjects would in some ways develop in parallel with that of Sutherland. In 1938 Sutherland's first London exhibition as a painter was dominated by works made in Wales.

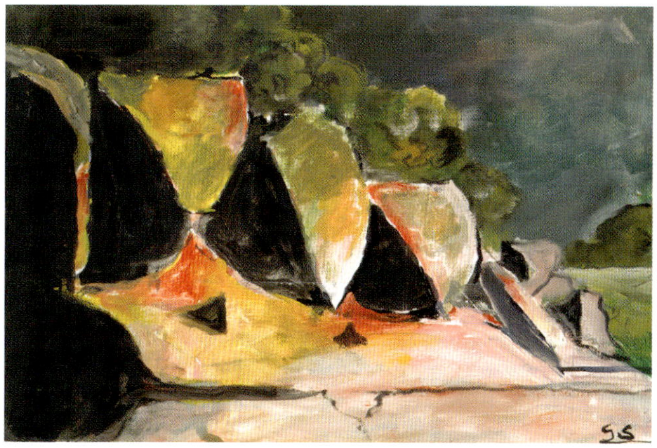

319. Graham Sutherland, *Estuary with Rocks*, 1937–8, oil, 27.1x41.5

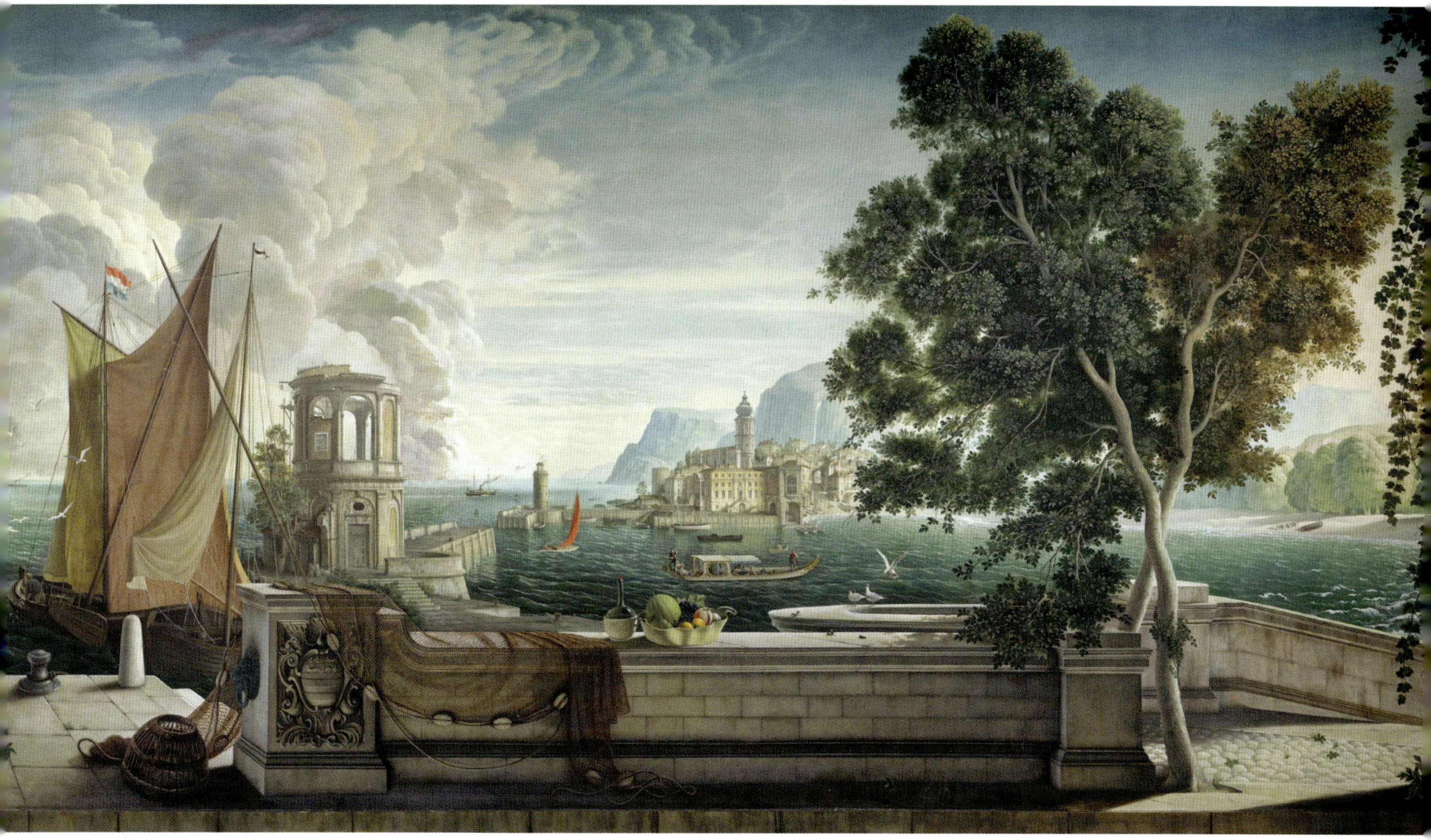

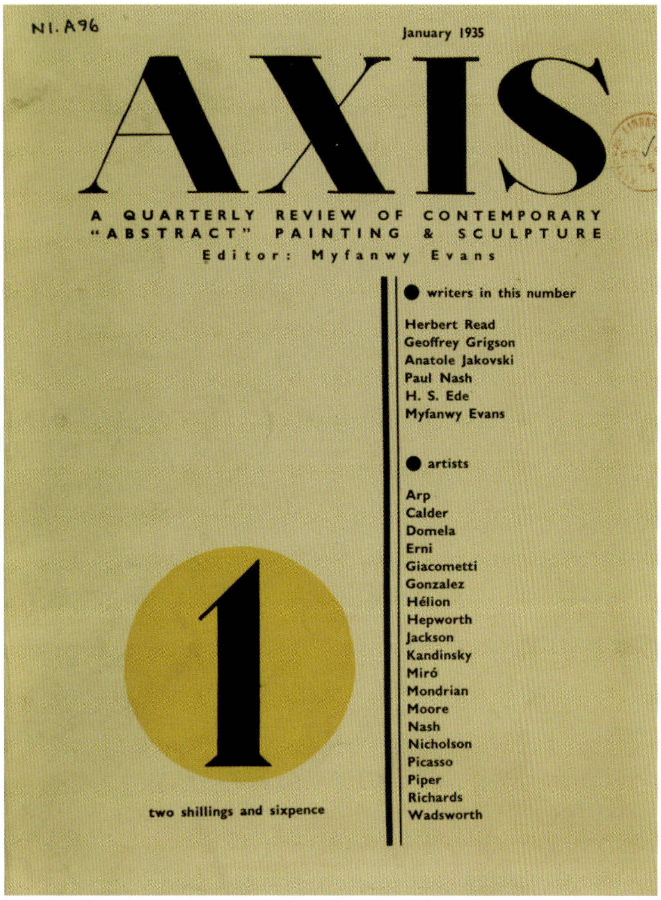

320. John Piper, Cover for the first issue of *Axis*, edited by Myfanwy Evans, 1935

Sutherland moved from representational imagery towards abstraction as his exploration of what he regarded as the fundamentals of nature developed. John Piper moved in the opposite direction. He became committed to non-figurative painting early in his career. Departing prematurely from the Royal College of Art in 1929, he was soon moving in the same circles as Ceri Richards. In 1934 he became a member of the Seven and Five Society, into which he sought to draw Richards, 'An excellent draughtsman, and he may do great things, and anyway he must be in 7&5'.[84] It appears that Richards had a brief dalliance with Piper's wife, Eileen, at the same time that Piper was becoming involved with Myfanwy Evans, an aspiring writer. Evans, who had grown up in a London Welsh family, was about to visit Paris, from where the Pipers had just returned.[85] With the help of introductions made through Piper, Evans met many of the Modernists working in the city – Mondrian, Brancusi, Kandinski, Domela, Giacometti and Arp. She too became a proponent of abstract art, and on her return was the prime mover in the establishment of *Axis*, a quarterly periodical intended to promote it, and of which she became editor. Ceri Richards was among the artists whose work she chose to illustrate in the first issue, in 1935. Myfanwy Evans married John Piper in 1937, the year in which he made his first working visit to Wales.[86] At Aberaeron on the Cardiganshire coast, almost immediately elements of the observed world began to infiltrate the abstract collages on which he worked. From that point his work became steadily more representational, though in a manner that was distinctively his own. Piper's abiding interest became the dramatic integration of buildings and architectural elements into landscapes coloured and shaped by his earlier investment in formal abstraction. Piper would paint all over Britain and the continent, but his engagement with the Welsh landscape remained particularly strong. In the 1940s he planned to emulate Edward Pugh's *Cambria Depicta*, which had become his guide to the north of the country.[87] Later he would follow Sutherland in finding inspiration in Pembrokeshire.

84 Quoted in Frances Spalding, *John Piper. Myfanwy Piper. Lives in Art* (Oxford, 2009), p. 59.

85 Evans's grandfather, Lodwig Evans, was a Baptist minister at Tenby. Her father was born at Milford Haven but worked as a chemist in London.

86 For her memories of the period, see Myfanwy Piper, 'Back in the Thirties', in *Art and Literature: An International Review* (Winter, 1965), pp. 136–43.

87 Piper described the book in *The Mountains* (New York, 1968), a volume on which he co-operated with R.S. Thomas and the wood engraver Reynolds Stone. Piper had worked in Wales with Stone in the late 1940s, when the plan for the new artists' guide, inspired by Pugh, was conceived. R.S. Thomas was brought into the project by Douglas Cleverdon, the early publisher of David Jones, see above, p. 272.

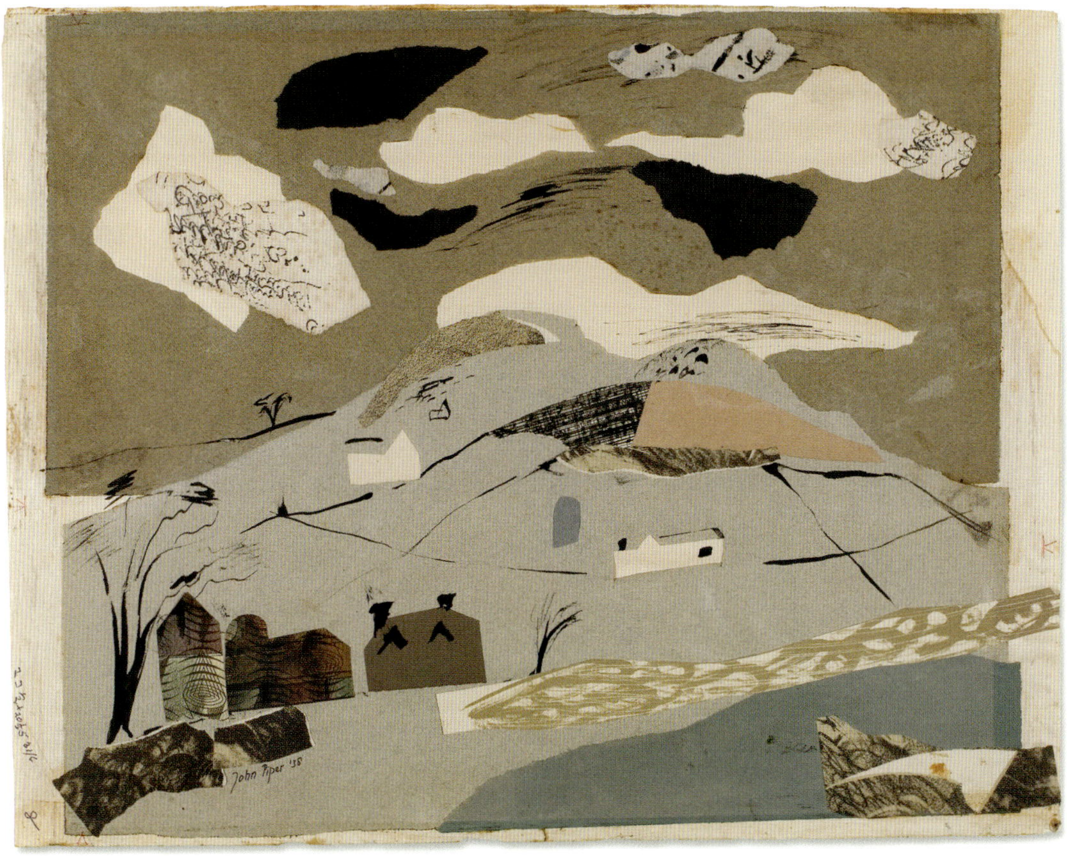

321. John Piper, *Grongar Hill*, 1938, mixed media, 40.7x53

Identifying a Welsh art

Throughout Europe between the two world wars, democratising inclinations, alongside a resurgence of the desire to identify national cultural characteristics, led intellectuals to interest themselves in the cultures of the common people. In Wales, it was significant, for instance, that Winifred Coombe Tennant both patronised young Welsh artists and simultaneously sought out the last vestiges of dying craft traditions. She was particularly interested in the work of hand-loom weavers, whose skills Lady Llanover had promoted a century earlier.[88] There was also institutional investment. The crisis of industrialism, so obvious in the south Wales valleys, suggested a return to what seemed to be the simpler and more sustainable ways of manufacture, practiced in some of the settlements.[89] In 1928 the National Council of Social Service set up an advisory service and a sales outlet in London for the products of such 'rural industries'. Most importantly, in 1932, the National Museum of Wales established a new sub-department of Folk Culture and Industries, under

88 Lord, *Winifred Coombe Tennant*, pp. 73–80.

89 In 1934, Coombe Tennant visited William Rothenstein at his Gloucestershire home. At this country retreat, Rothenstein, who had promoted the painting of industrial society by Archie Griffiths, lived a life inspired more by the ideas of William Morris: 'Their Cotswold cottage a place of peace and beauty. Morris hangings everywhere and simple waxed elm furniture, pleasant loggias in which to sit or sleep ... After lunch, talk in the garden and then Lady Rothenstein and I started for Chalford where one Waals, a Dane, makes beautiful furniture ...' Diary of Winifred Coombe Tennant, 24 and 30 August 1934, private archive. See Lord, *Meaning of Pictures*, pp. 148–9.

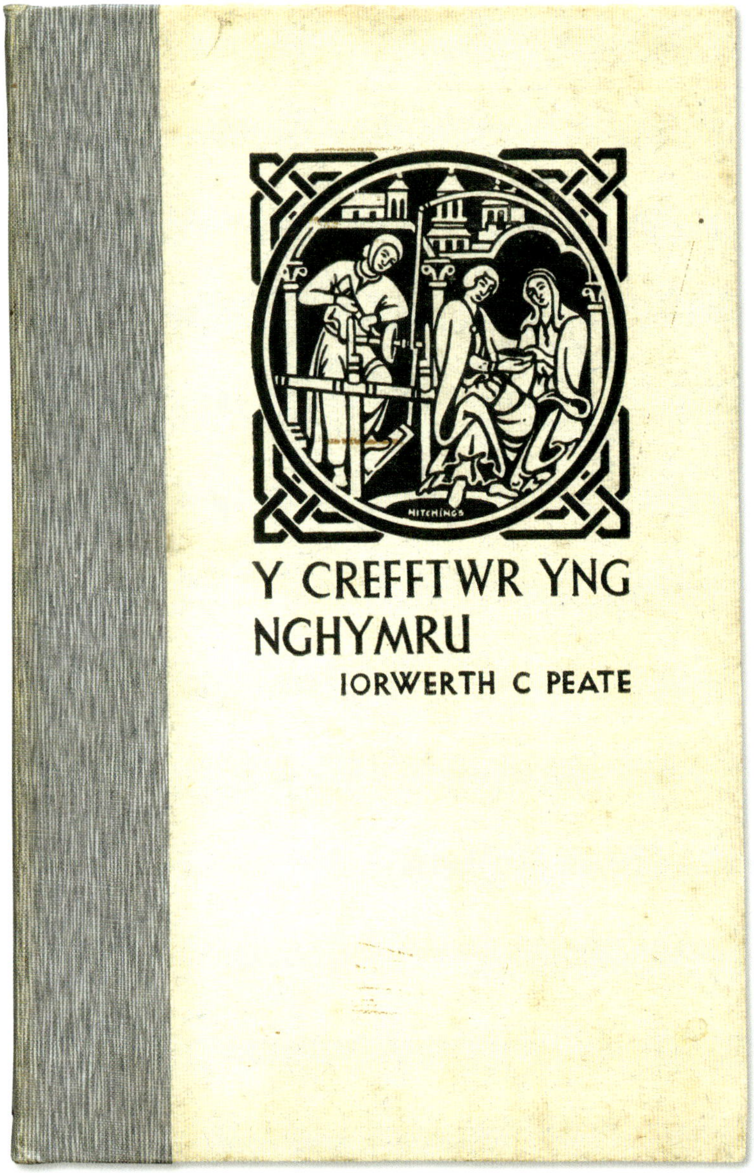

322. Unknown designer, Cover for Iorwerth C. Peate, *Y Crefftwr yng Nghymru*, 1933, 22.5x15

the curatorship of Iorwerth C. Peate. The following year, Peate's pioneering and influential volume, *Y Crefftwr yng Nghymru* (The Craftsman in Wales) was published.

To the intellectuals of the national revival of the late nineteenth and early twentieth centuries it had seemed important to demonstrate the existence of a shared spiritual essence that united the products of the Celtic artist. Iorwerth Peate was in the process of establishing a position from which he would argue that a distinct national visual culture could not be founded on traditions of high art, which were alien by their nature to his concept of Welshness. However, a modern tradition might be constructed on the basis of the buildings and handicrafts of the common people – the Welsh folk, *Y Werin Gymreig*. It was a position that reflected a fundamental tension between competing constructs of Welsh identity, and later it would prove angrily divisive. In the meantime, the first signs of an impending difference of opinion came in 1935, when moves were made in London to promote collectively the work of contemporary Welsh painters.

At a London party given by Lady Astor, in December 1934 Winifred Coombe Tennant had 'a long talk with Cedric Morris about pictures and painters'. Very shortly afterwards, Morris instigated – though without Coombe Tennant's knowledge – the creation of the Contemporary Welsh Art Exhibition. The organisers included the architect and conservationist Clough Williams-Ellis, the novelist Richard Hughes, who was newly installed at Laugharne Castle on the Carmarthenshire coast, and his friend Augustus John. Morland Lewis was also involved, but no doubt in the interest of securing a high profile for the event, John became the selector

90 Walters to Coombe Tennant, NLW Winifred Coombe Tennant Papers, A1/39, 19 August 1935 and *Cambrian News*, 19 July 1935, p. 6.

91 Murray to Coombe Tennant, NLW Winifred Coombe Tennant Papers, A1/30, 16 April 1935.

323. Augustus John, *Richard Hughes*, 1937, oil, 61x51.5

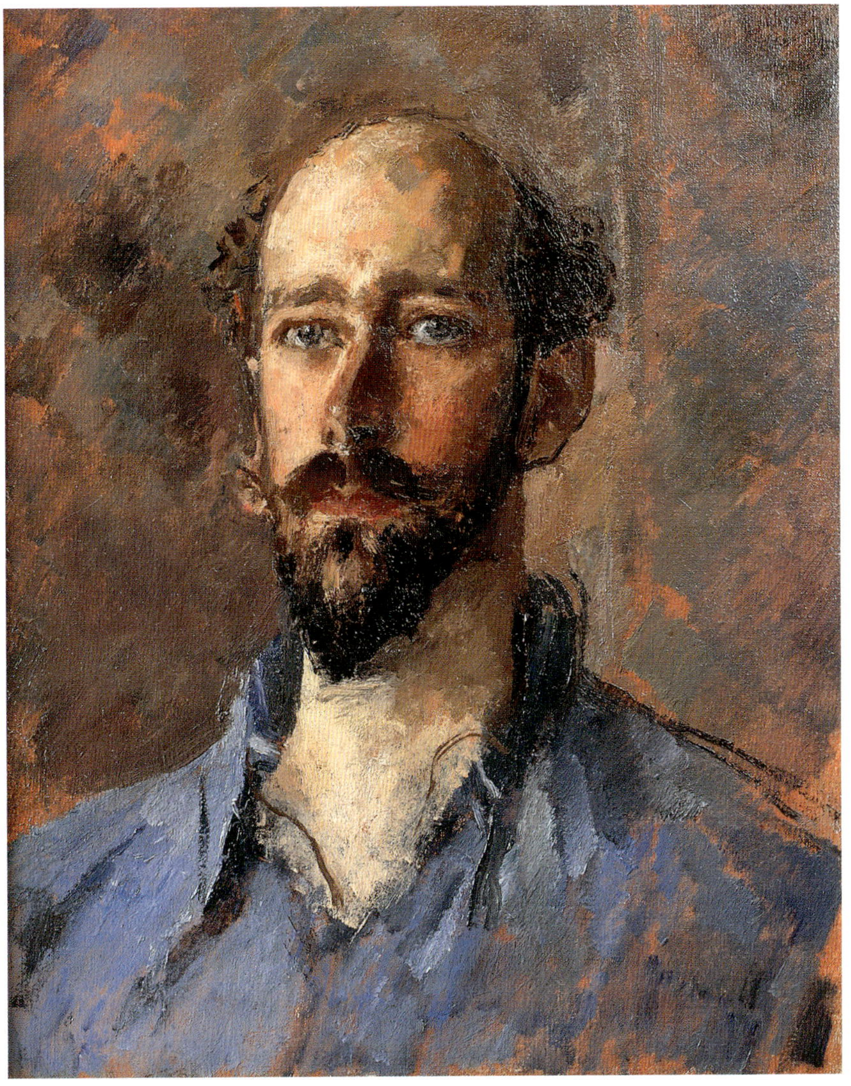

and the public face of the exhibition. Morris's motivation in forming the group had been straightforward and patriotic, in the nineteenth-century manner of Cornwallis West and others who had sought to bring art to the people for their spiritual benefit. The exhibition's first venue was the Gregynog Gallery of the National Library at Aberystwyth. The local newspaper reported the speech made by Williams-Ellis: 'The exhibition had been hatched in London and its purpose was to initiate Welshmen into their countrymen's work. It was felt that the Welsh were not conscious of what Welshmen had done and could do. The exhibition was literally an eye opener ...'.[90] Unfortunately, the fact that the exhibition had, indeed, been 'hatched in London', had led to bad feeling even before the Aberystwyth opening. Like Coombe Tennant, William Grant Murray had not been consulted:

> They think that the whole world of art lies within the little circle that encompasses them in London and that they are building up a sort of New Jerusalem for the painter and public. The conceit of it is comic – there is no other word for it. They don't seem to realise that novelty, in its crudest form, is not art; and so they go on living and working in a fool's paradise.[91]

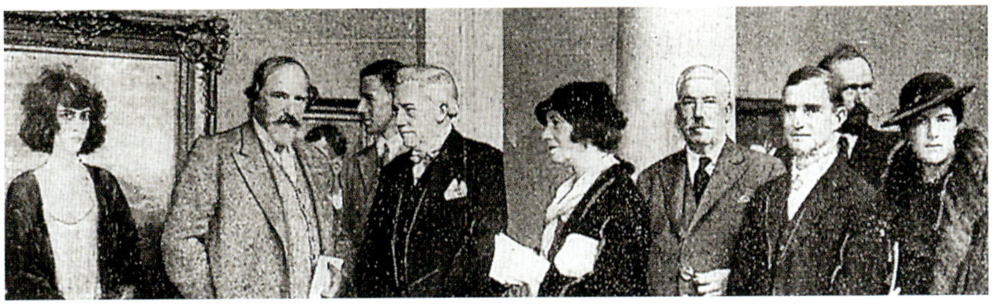

324. *The opening of the Contemporary Welsh Art Exhibition at the National Museum of Wales*, 1935. From left, Augustus John, D. Kighley Baxandall, J.B. Manson, Frances Byng-Stamper, Major Trehearne James, Sir Cyril Fox, Richard Hughes, Lady Fox.

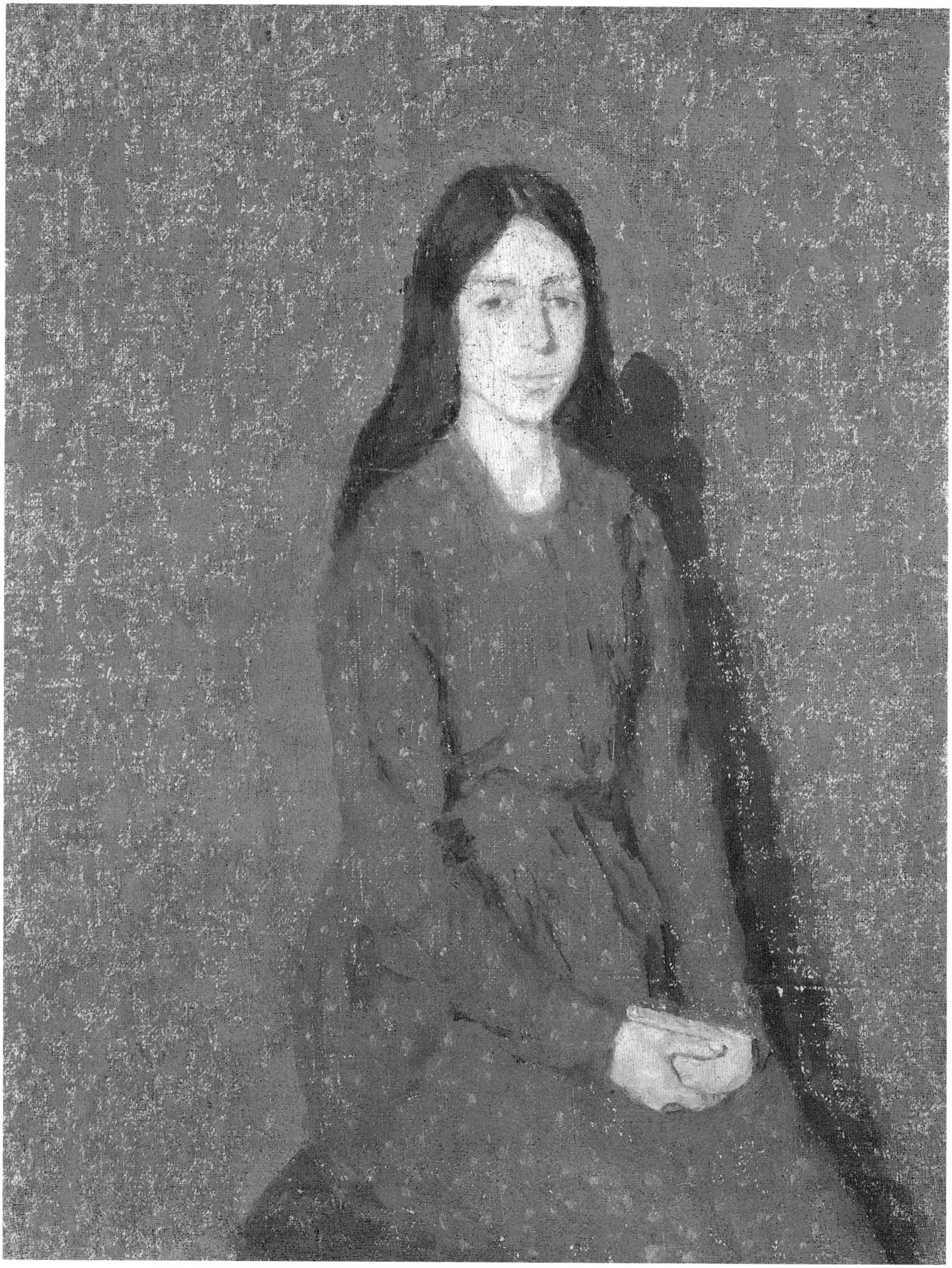

In fact, the most novel of the Welsh painters, Ceri Richards, was not included in the exhibition by John, whose own works dominated the proceedings – a 'most undignified' exercise in self-promotion, in the opinion of Evan Walters:

> What we have in Aberystwyth is English art by Welsh artists. Welsh art would express the ideals and soul of Wales – just as 'Bydd Myrdd o Ryfeddodau', 'Calon Lan', and 'Yn y Dyfroedd' are expressions of the very soul of Wales.[92]

325. Gwen John, *Girl in a Blue Dress*, *c.*1918-20, oil, 43.9x34.9, shown at the Contemporary Welsh Art Exhibition, Fishguard, 1936

Given the Modernist transformation that was about to overtake his own work, his comments are surprising, and were no doubt motivated by the same irritation at the clique-like nature of the organising group that upset other outsiders.[93] In fact, Walters had been invited to exhibit and showed six works, but he reported to Coombe Tennant that John had no less than 31 pictures in the exhibition.[94] Gwen, Edwin and Vivien John were also well represented, as was J.D. Innes, notwithstanding the contemporary premise for the exhibition. Archie Griffiths and Vincent Evans were excluded.

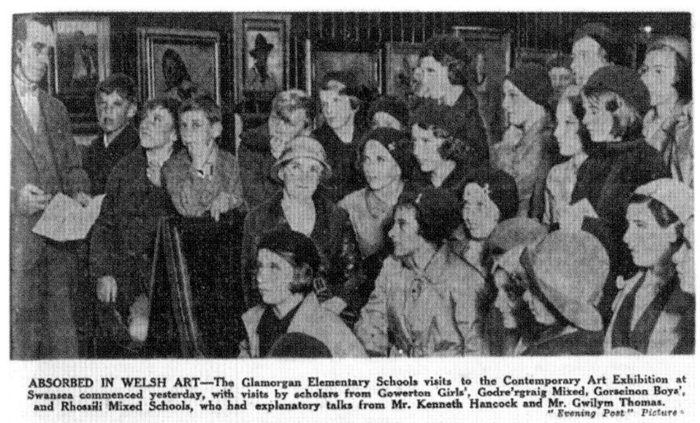

326. *Kenneth Hancock with schoolchildren at the Contemporary Welsh Art Exhibition*, 1935

The exhibition was well attended at Aberystwyth and at its subsequent showings. At Cardiff it was opened by John himself, and at Swansea the Council of Social Service organised educational visits for school children, led by Kenneth Hancock. Later in the year at Swansea, the Glynn Vivian Gallery presented an exhibition of its own painters, that included Ceri Richards and others not seen in John's show. Opening that exhibition, Winifred Coombe Tennant proposed the establishment of a Contemporary Art Society for Wales, presumably mindful of the pioneering English society, established a quarter of a century earlier. Although the London Welsh group organised a second exhibition to coincide with the National Eisteddfod at Fishguard in 1936, the following year it did, indeed, transform itself into the Contemporary Art Society for Wales (CASW), with Howard de Walden in the chair. The Society would succeed in providing a modest but consistent level of patronage to contemporary artists, that would enrich public museums and galleries by gift of its pictures and sculptures throughout the twentieth century.

Notwithstanding his role as instigator of the exhibitions and so, indirectly, of the Contemporary Art Society, Cedric Morris himself took a different direction. Before the first exhibition had finished its tour, he was already discouraged about its potential in the face of what he perceived as the comatose condition of people in the Valleys, overwhelmed by material and cultural deprivation:

92 *South Wales Evening Post*, 11 September 1935, p. 4.

93 The painter Timothy Evans felt that it was 'not for some half-English snobs like Clough Williams-Ellis and his cronies to control and chatter about art in Wales.' NLW J.W. Jones Papers, 3619, 13 September 1935, my translation from the Welsh.

94 Walters exaggerated somewhat – John showed 27 works. The exhibition included 18 pictures by Innes, reflecting John's high opinion of his friend. Among Walters's pictures were two coalfield subjects, both portraits of colliers, one of them lent by David Lloyd George.

... at least they dream in this sleep which is more than the English do and they are trying to wake but I'm afraid that a few pictures won't do it at all ... The reason I cannot get a room up the [Swansea] valley is because they all crowd together in the occupied houses to save the rent – there is no room and yet plenty of empty cottages – all this and much more in the 'fat vale of Glamorgan', plenty everywhere and the people have not enough to eat. Either I am going mad or the rest of the world is ...[95]

Morris decided to encourage the public understanding of art through practice, both by creating opportunities for amateurs to discuss and to make work for themselves, and by developing young painters in his own school. By 1937 he had become acquainted with the educational settlement run by Quakers at Dowlais Top, Merthyr Tydfil, where later he would establish art and craft classes under the patronage of the English philanthropist, Mary Horsfall. At the same time, he was in the process of establishing his own school of art at Dedham in East Anglia. A letter written by Morris in 1937 to the writer Keidrych Rhys, whose newly established magazine, *Wales*, was soon to become an important focus for Welsh writers and painters, indicated the degree of engagement of Morris with his own country – its politics as well as its arts – in this period, but also the strain of the emotional demands he felt it made upon him:

I have been hellishly busy with the school ... I am working myself to death and not making any money at it. Living is a bit frightening at times.

Have had no news of Saunders Lewis – gathered it was best not to write to him, as he is only allowed a certain number of letters and naturally wants those for his family first – No I have not forgotten the unemployment – my country. I never forget it and all the misery that goes with it. I hear from Miss Horsfall from Dowlais at times – I want to go to Wales, but I can't get away – perhaps later ... Write when you have time and cheer up – and don't get lost entirely – my love to Dylan if you see him and Janes.[96]

In December 1939, Morris had indeed returned to Merthyr, staying at Gwernllwyn House, Dowlais, where he painted and taught against the background of the first months of the Second World War. He wrote to Lett Haines:

Several factories are being started ... but for the rest the means test has been much tightened since the war causing some riots and much distress, but things are a bit better on the whole ... I am starting evening classes for various kinds of design and handicrafts – 2 nights a week and every afternoon ... We start with – wallpaper some Woolworth colours brushes pencils and some very good clay off the mountain ...

There are endless landscapes here and I can get as many models as I want.[97]

95 Morris to Lett Haines, Penclawdd, 13 August 1935, Tate Gallery Archives, Cedric Morris Papers, 8317.1.4, item 95.

96 NLW MS 22745D, f. 81. Saunders Lewis was in Wormwood Scrubs prison, following his conviction, along with D.J. Williams and Lewis Valentine, for the burning of the bombing school at Penyberth, Llŷn, in 1936. Morris had become aware of Janes while researching the 1935 exhibition, in which the young painter had been included. Morris showed a portrait that he had painted of Keidrych Rhys in an exhibition of his work in 1938.

97 Morris to Lett Haines, 1 December 1939, Tate Gallery Archives, Cedric Morris Papers, 8317.1.4.115.

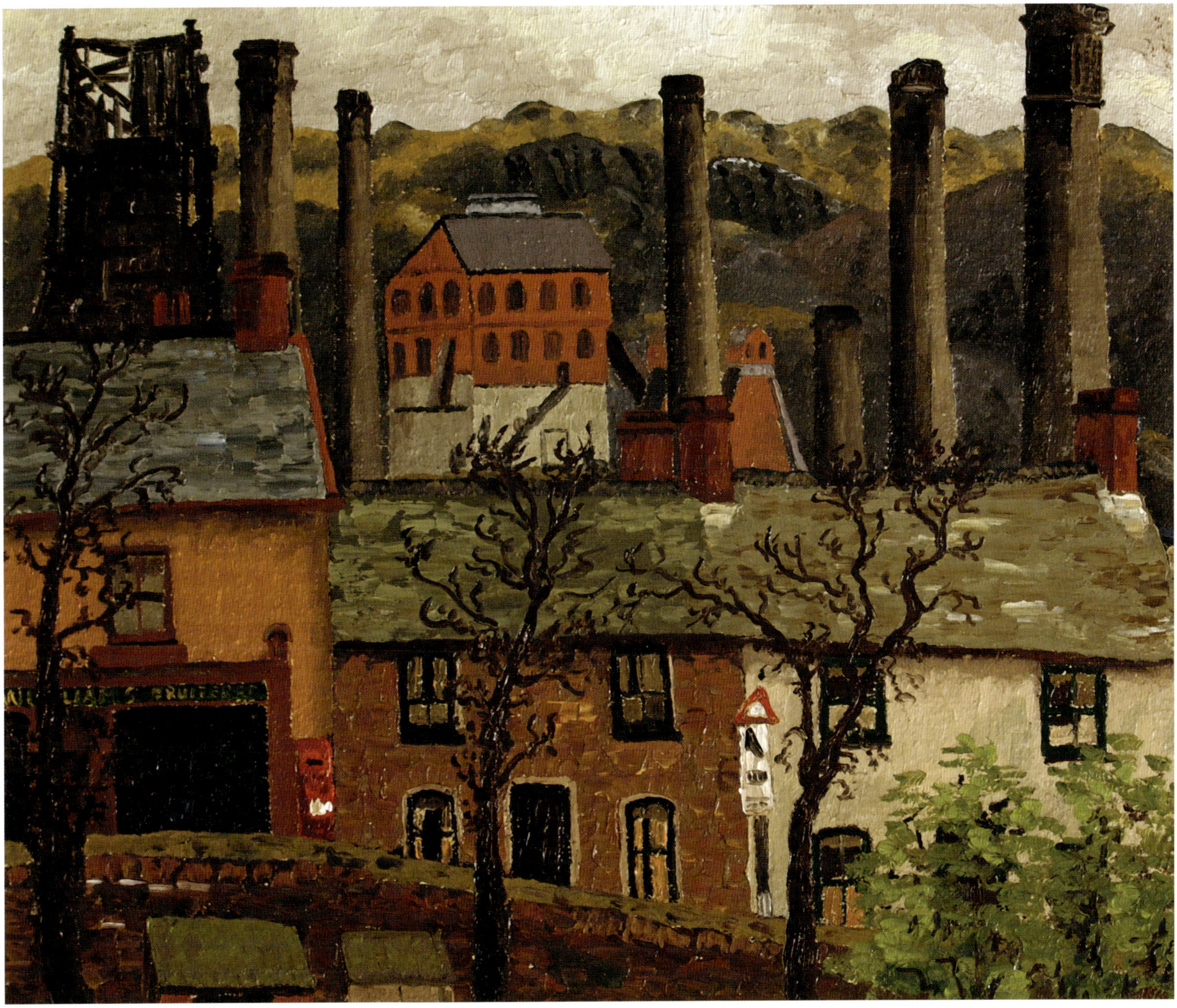

327. Cedric Morris,
Caeharris Post Office from Gwernllwyn House,
*c.*1939, oil, 62x25

Ironically, in the post-war period, Morris's commitment to amateur painting and crafts at Dowlais would prove to have its most important consequence in the development of professional art practice in Wales.

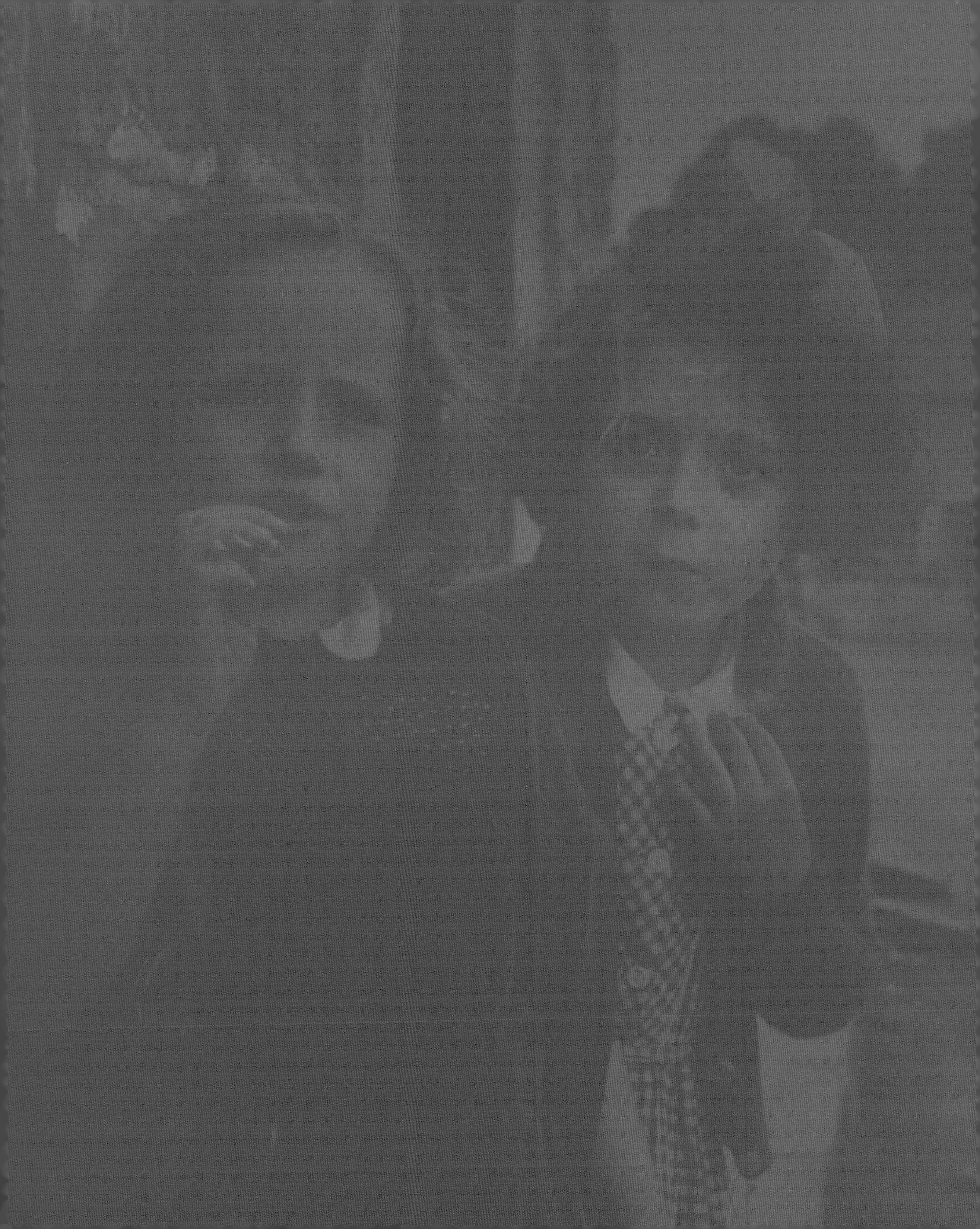

CHAPTER 5

1940–1990

CHAPTER 5 1940–1990

War art

Repeating the practice established between 1914–18, the government employed artists in an official capacity during the Second World War, though not only to record action at the fronts, but also daily life at home. Kenneth Clark, Director of the National Gallery in London, established committees to oversee two schemes. 'Recording Britain' was intended to create images of landscape and architecture, and although it began work in 1940 in the face of the immediate threat of destruction by bombing, its roots lay deeper, in the nostalgic Neo-Romantic agenda of English painters such as Eric Ravilious in the 1930s.[1] At the Royal College, Ravilious had been among those who taught Mildred Elsie Eldridge, who began her long relationship with Wales shortly before the war by designing stained glass for the church at Llanpumsaint in Carmarthenshire.[2] Her image of *Baptism in the River Ceiriog*, one of many she made in Wales during 1941 for the Recording Britain scheme, contributed to the presentation by English Neo-Romantics of the idea of Britain as a happy coalition of peripheral regions with charming characteristics.

The second of Clark's schemes, administered by the War Artists' Advisory Committee ('WAAC'), employed painters to record the war effort in industrial and military terms, and the effects of bombing. Ray Howard-Jones, who had grown up in Penarth and trained at the Slade School in London, was

1 The full title of the programme was 'Recording the Changing Face of Britain'. It was administered by the Committee for the Employment of Artists in Wartime, within the Ministry of Labour and National Service, and funded by the Pilgrim Trust. Clark's scheme reflected his awareness of the work of the Federal Art Project, that employed artists in the United States during the Depression. The collection of over 1500 commissioned works, now held by the Victoria & Albert Museum, was documented in a 4-volume catalogue, 1946–9.

2 The window was made by Muriel Minter. See Martin Crampin, *Stained Glass from Welsh Churches* (Talybont, 2014), p. 18.

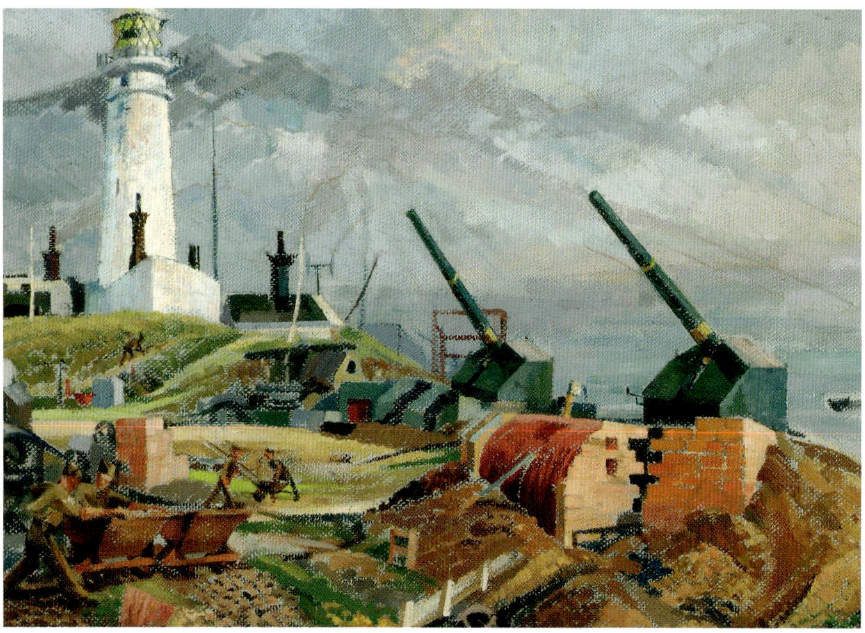

328. Ray Howard-Jones, *Fortified Islands (Building the North Battery, Flatholm, Bristol Channel)*, 1943, oil, 40.8x58.4

329. Mildred Elsie Eldridge, *Baptism in the River Ceiriog at Pontfadog, Denbighshire*, 1941, watercolour, 47x38.1

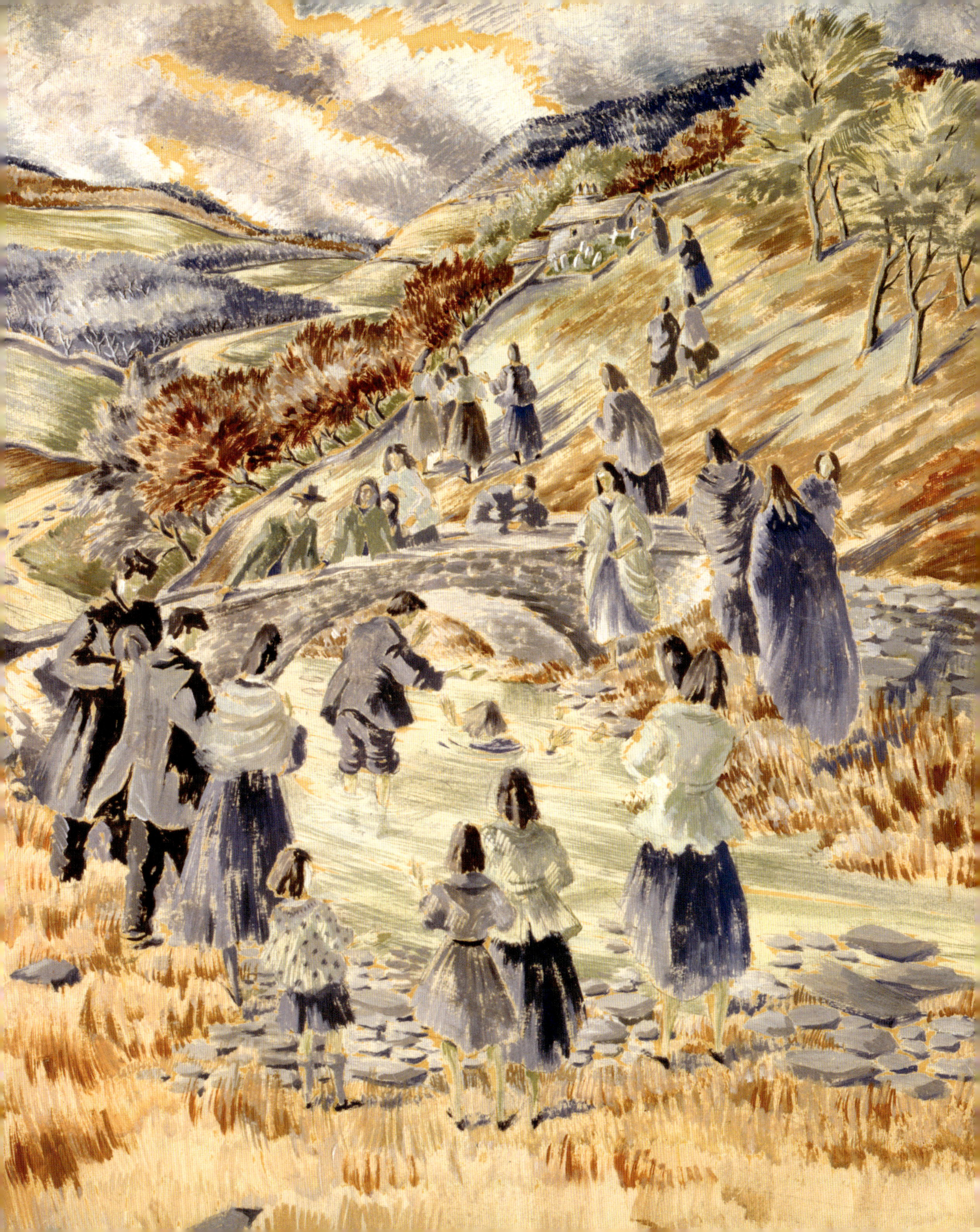

the most prolific of the Welsh painters involved. Her commissions included recording the construction of fortifications on the islands of the Bristol Channel – locations that predicted her later fascination with the island of Skomer, which would begin in 1949. Among those employed by the WAAC on a full-time basis, and who worked in Wales, was John Piper, though he regarded it as impractical to record, as requested, the storage and conservation in the Manod slate caverns at Blaenau Ffestiniog of pictures evacuated from public collections in London. Instead, he took advantage of his visit to pursue his own work in a series of paintings of rock formations in the mountain landscape. In fact, Piper had been preceded at Manod by the painter Mona Moore, working for

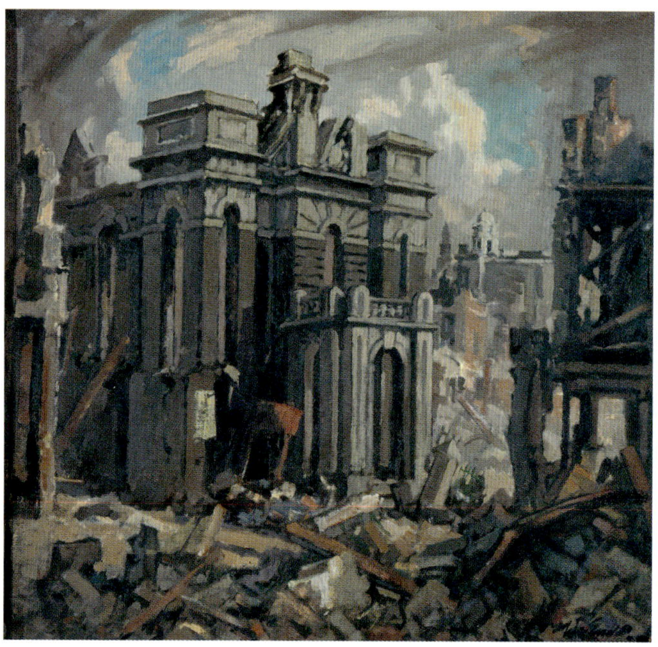

330. Will Evans, *Wesley Chapel Destroyed by Bombing*, 1941, oil, 58.1x63.6

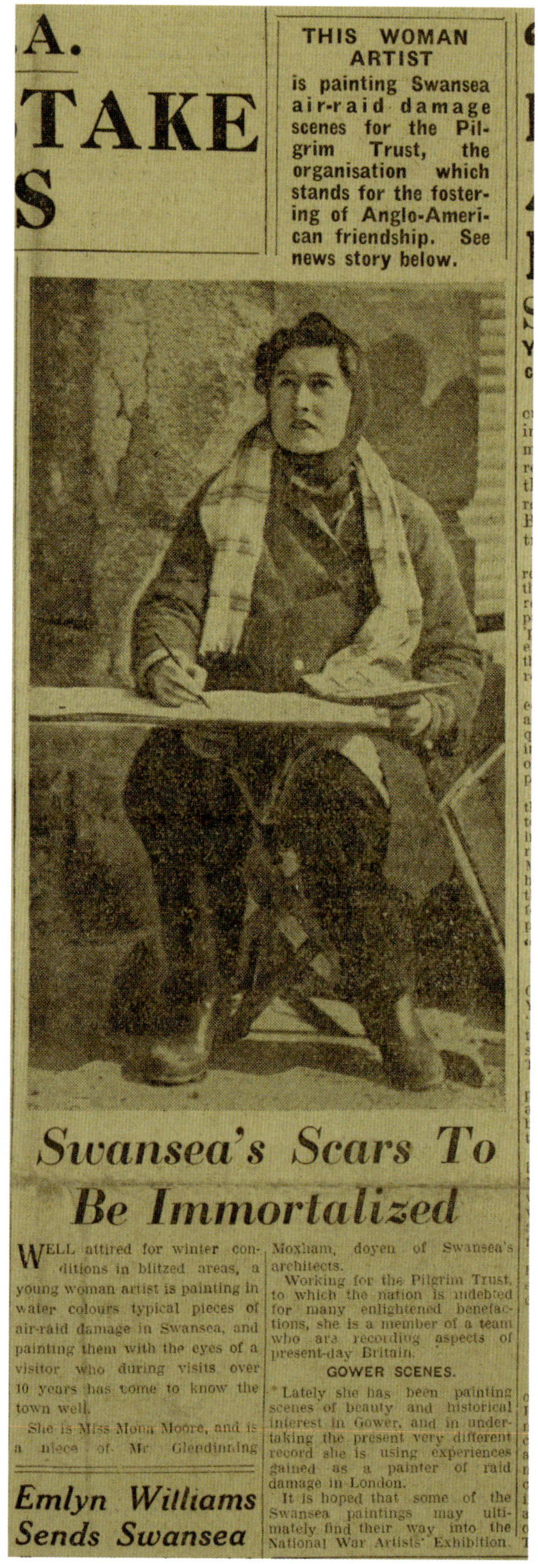

A.
TAKE
S

THIS WOMAN ARTIST is painting Swansea air-raid damage scenes for the Pilgrim Trust, the organisation which stands for the fostering of Anglo-American friendship. See news story below.

Swansea's Scars To Be Immortalized

WELL attired for winter conditions in blitzed areas, a young woman artist is painting in water colours typical pieces of air-raid damage in Swansea, and painting them with the eyes of a visitor who during visits over 10 years has come to know the town well.

She is Miss Mona Moore, and is a niece of Mr Glendinning Moxham, doyen of Swansea's architects.

Working for the Pilgrim Trust, to which the nation is indebted for many enlightened benefactions, she is a member of a team who are recording aspects of present-day Britain.

GOWER SCENES.

Lately she has been painting scenes of beauty and historical interest in Gower, and in undertaking the present very different record she is using experiences gained as a painter of raid damage in London.

It is hoped that some of the Swansea paintings may ultimately find their way into the National War Artists' Exhibition.

Emlyn Williams Sends Swansea

331. *Mona Moore drawing at a Swansea bombsite*, from the *South Wales Evening Post*, 18 March 1941

3 Maurice Sochachewsky, who had worked in Wales before the war (see above, pp. 290–1) joined the Royal Welsh Fusiliers at the beginning of the war and documented visually their activities until the Normandy landings, though in a private capacity, not sponsored by the WAAC. Sochachewsky lost an eye during the fighting in Normandy. The drawings are held in a private archive.

4 Evans was drawn to the attention of the Committee by Clark himself. They inspected his *Repairing Main Road* and commissioned him to paint a smaller version for the collection. They also purchased two monotypes. I am grateful to David George for this information, gleaned from the Imperial War Museum files.

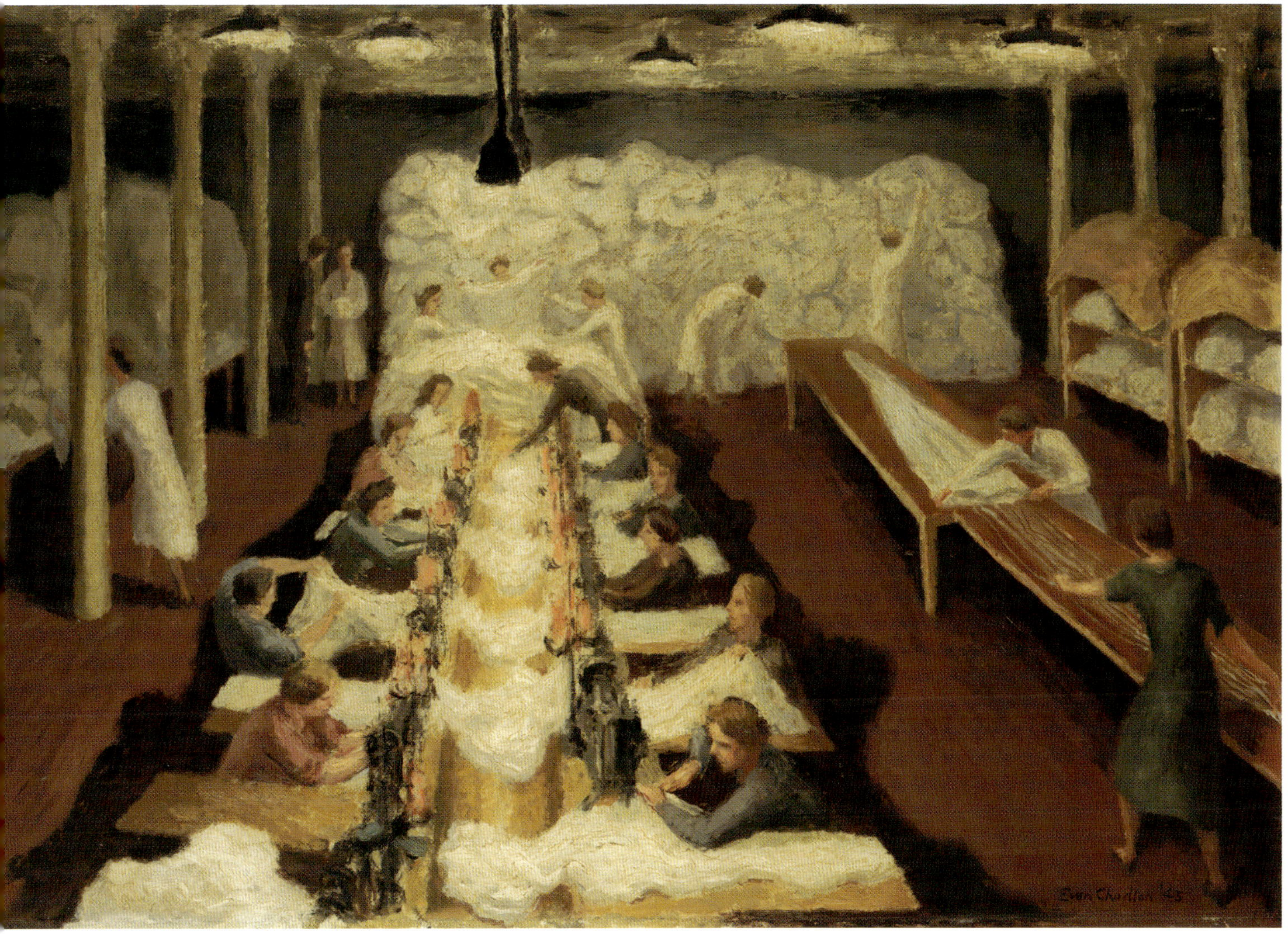

332. Evan Charlton,
A Parachute Factory, 1943,
oil, 51.1x76.2

Recording Britain. She had begun her series of Welsh landscapes, made for the project, on the Gower peninsula. As a consequence, she was on hand to record the bombing of Swansea in 1941, though it was Will Evans, working independently, who produced the most detailed record of the devastation.

The work of three Welsh-born painters was bought or commissioned by the WAAC – Vincent Evans, Evan Charlton, and Ceri Richards.[3] For Evans, drawing colliery workers underground, this involved no change in his imagery or his working processes.[4] However, for both Charlton and Richards, commissions required that they work in parallel with the flow of their personal imagery. Charlton had been appointed Principal of the Cardiff School of Art in 1938, and two years later appointed Richards to the staff as Head of

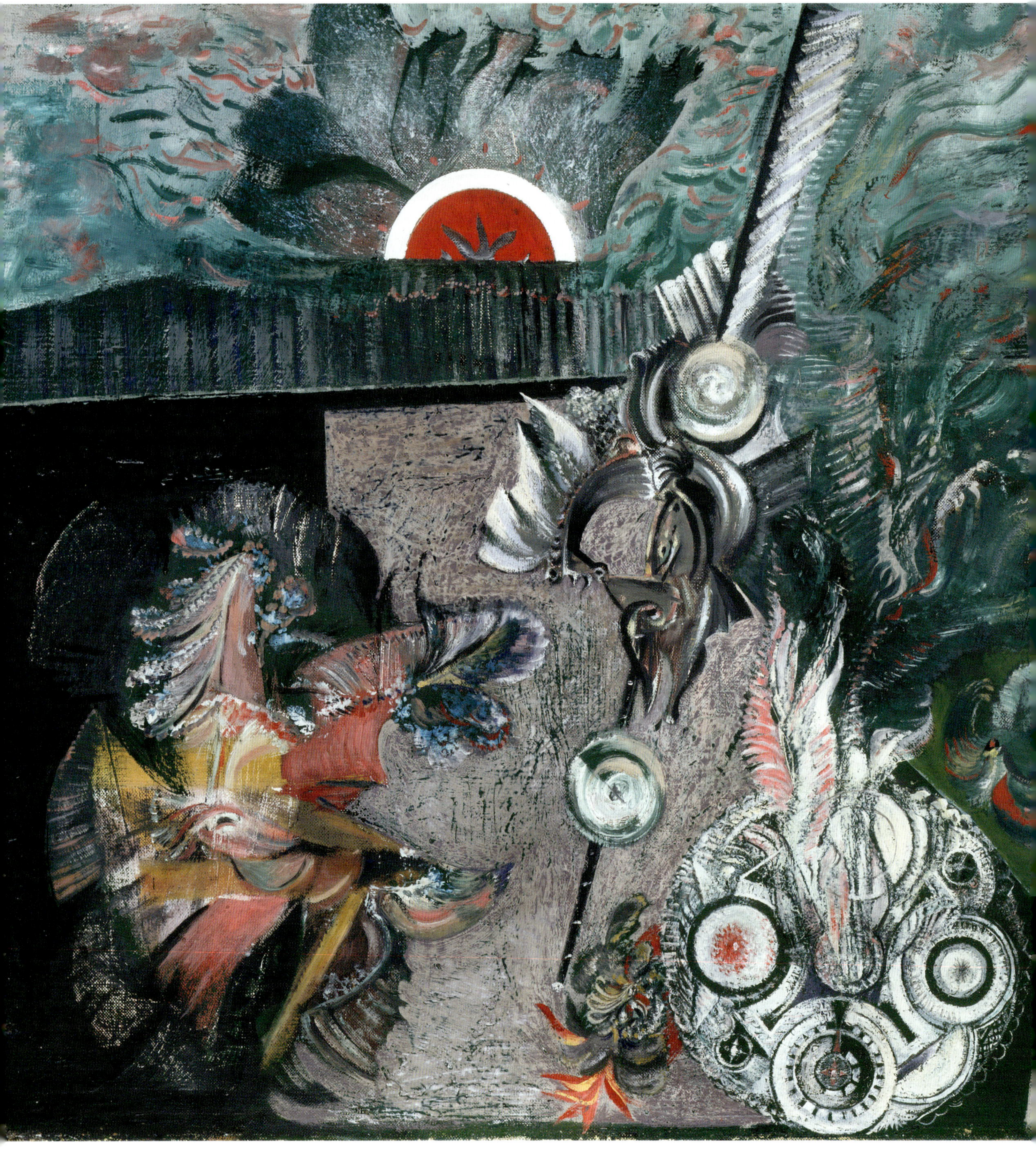

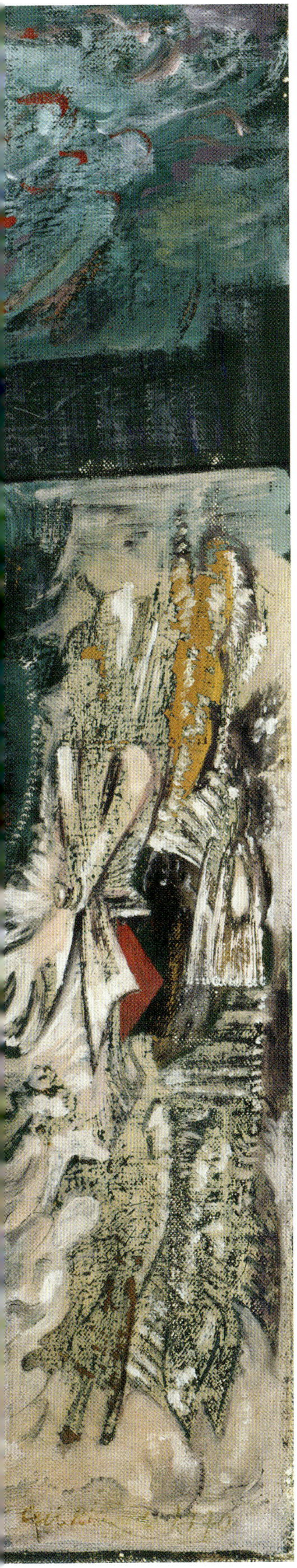

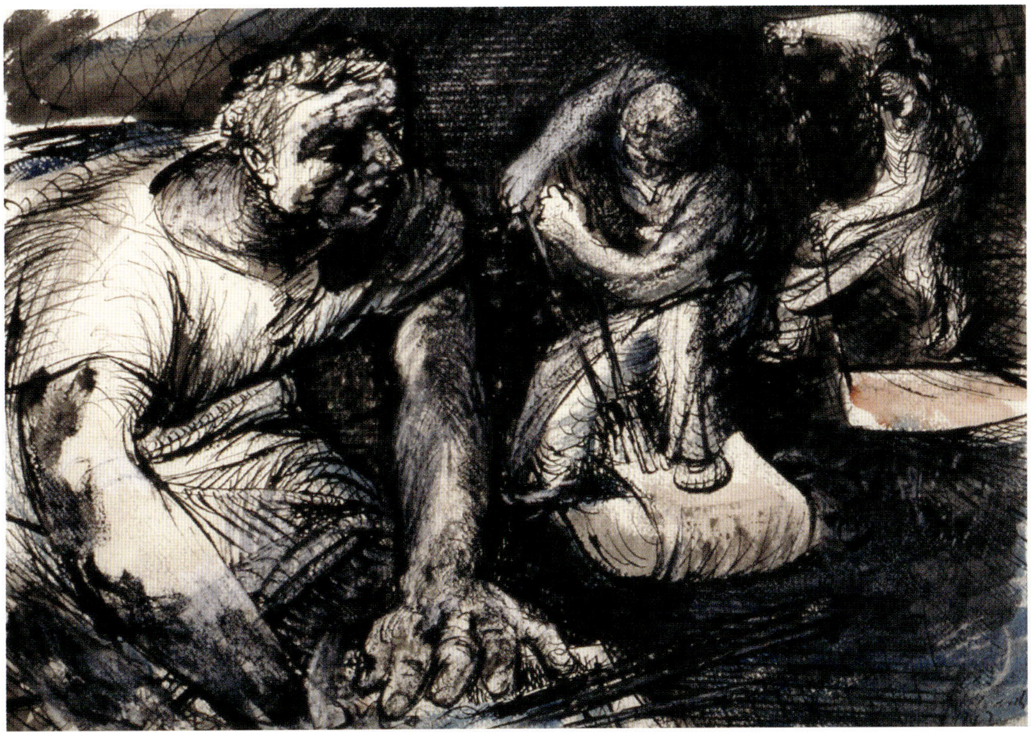

334. Ceri Richards, *Tinplate Workers*, 1942, ink and chalk, 52x75

333. Ceri Richards, *Blossoms*, 1940, oil, 51x61

Painting, after the Chelsea School of Art had closed for the duration.[5] In 1942, Richards was commissioned to draw and paint the tinplate works at which his father had been employed in Gowerton. The pictures he made were documentary, though their intense tone and agitated lines clearly corresponded with the less figurative pictures that he was painting independently, reacting to what he described as the 'chaos and waste' of the war. Their tortuous mixtures of surreal organic and mechanistic forms were informed by his observation of bombing in Cardiff. Richards would carry the visual vocabulary of these disturbed images forward into a long engagement with the poems of Dylan Thomas, that began to evolve in 1943 with his initial evocations of 'The force that through the green fuse drives the flower'.[6]

5 For Charlton's appointment of Richards and his war time paintings, see interview with Felicity Charlton in Tony Curtis, *Welsh Painters Talking* (Bridgend, 1997), p. 46.

6 For the evolution of these images see Mel Gooding, *Ceri Richards* (Dumfriesshire, 2002), pp. 64–76. Notwithstanding his fascination with the poetry, Richards would meet Thomas only once, immediately before the poet's departure for the United States, where he died. Gooding also notes the closeness of Richards's relationship, during the war, with the academic T.J. Morgan, another native of Swansea.

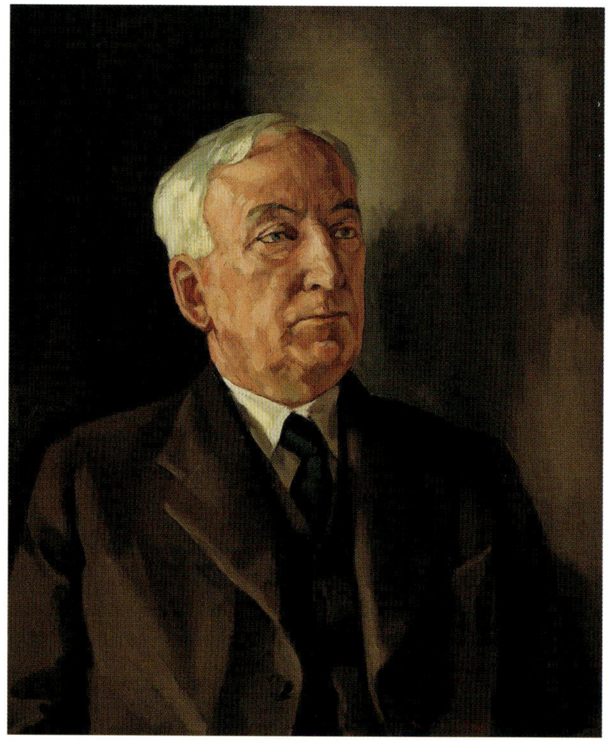

335. Ivor Williams, *Thomas Jones*, 1939, oil, 61.3x50.8

Welsh art and the British state

Ceri Richards would return to London at the end of the war, but his stay in Cardiff, working under Evan Charlton, coincided with the beginning of a sea-change in the nature of both professional practice and the public display of visual art in Wales. In the half century following the outbreak of the Second World War the art world underwent greater change at faster speed than in any earlier period. The war was not, in itself, the cause of this change, but rather it acted as the catalyst that accelerated a long-standing aspiration among the liberal-minded within the establishment to engage the common people with visual culture. It was the aspiration that had motivated Cornwallis West, creator of the art exhibitions of 1868 and 1876, the likes of William Grant Murray and Winifred Coombe Tennant, who had endeavoured in the inter-war period to enable talented individuals drawn from the working class to practice as artists, and most recently Cedric Morris, who encouraged amateur practice. However, the emphasis would shift in the decade 1940–50 from private initiative to public patronage. During the war, the need to create unity of purpose within Britain, both at a psychological level and in terms of economic organisation, deepened government involvement in every aspect of people's lives. Furthermore, just as enforced engagement in national life on the part of the people themselves during the Great War had intensified the demand for democratisation (most obviously achieved in the enfranchisement of women), during the Second World War the political aspirations of the people would be realised in substantial social and economic changes. They were initiated through the implementation of the Beveridge Report of 1942 on social security and the Butler Education Act of 1944 and, in the first year of peace, by a socialist government that nationalised major industries, services and transport. Although the political complexion of subsequent governments changed from time to time, a social-democratic consensus emerged that would not be effectively challenged until the 1980s. The huge expansion of government promotion of all the arts that developed in the post-war period was an essential aspect of the evolution of the Welfare State.

During its first decade, the process of change did not proceed without tension arising between competing visions of the future. In the 1930s, under the direction of its secretary William Emrys Williams, the son of a carpenter from Porthmadog and a farmer's daughter from Llandeilo, the British Institute of Adult Education, funded by charities, had been active in the visual arts. At the start of the war, it was superseded by a new organisation, the Council for the Encouragement of Music and the Arts, known by its acronym CEMA. Like its predecessor, CEMA was initially independent though also supported by government. It was funded by the Pilgrim Trust, administered by Thomas Jones, confidant of the Davies sisters. W.E. Williams's involvement continued as honorary Director for Art. The ideas of Williams and Jones, and the experience of the settlement movement in the Valleys, together exerted a considerable influence on the evolution of the new body.[7] Indeed, it was publicly acknowledged in 1943 that 'Wales is, in some ways, the cradle of CEMA'.[8] However, in a crucial change of principle, which would have far-reaching consequences, the government took over the funding and policy direction of the organisation. In the visual arts, the public became aware of its activities chiefly through the touring exhibitions and lectures that it organised at small venues, including settlements and public libraries.[9]

Meanwhile, the work of the voluntary sector was maintained in parallel. Though he was chiefly engaged with his art school in East Anglia, Cedric Morris continued to visit the Dowlais settlement, and there were interactions between the two projects. Volunteer teachers at Dowlais visited the school, now situated at Benton End, and Arthur Lett Haines was among visitors to Gwernllwyn House. In 1942, as the result of touring an exhibition of his paintings to the educational settlement at Pontypridd, Morris met two young teachers there, Esther Grainger and Arthur Giardelli. Grainger, who had trained at Cardiff School of Art, subsequently visited Morris at Benton End, and a close friendship developed between them. Morris's influence on Giardelli was even more fundamental, since it initiated his career as a practising artist.[10] Giardelli was a Londoner, who arrived in Merthyr when the girls' school at which he was teaching was evacuated early in the war. Dismissed because of his refusal to join the armed forces, he stayed to teach art history and appreciation at the Dowlais settlement.

7 For the attitude of Thomas Jones, see 'Art and the People' (1936), published in Jones's memoir *Leeks and Daffodils* (Newtown, 1942). See also Percy Watkins, 'Adult Education and the New Leisure in Wales' in *Welsh School of Social Service, 1934, School Addresses delivered at the Friends Meeting House* (1934) for a further Welsh contribution to the early development of quasi-public intervention in adult education.

8 CEMA *Monthly Bulletin*, 1943. When CEMA became a government organisation in 1940, the economist John Maynard Keynes was appointed Director.

9 A film about its exhibition activities, produced by CEMA with a script by Dylan Thomas, is profoundly revealing of prevailing attitudes, especially in terms of perceptions among the intellectual elite of naivety among the common people. A print is held by the Imperial War Museum, London.

10 Surprisingly, Giardelli's earliest memoir of this period of his life fails to mention the influence of Morris, though much later he would rectify the ommission. The influence is clear from Giardelli's letters in the Cedric Morris Papers (Tate Archives, London) and other published writings. See 'Arthur Giardelli' in *Artists in Wales*, ed. Meic Stephens (Llandysul, 1971), pp. 20–30.

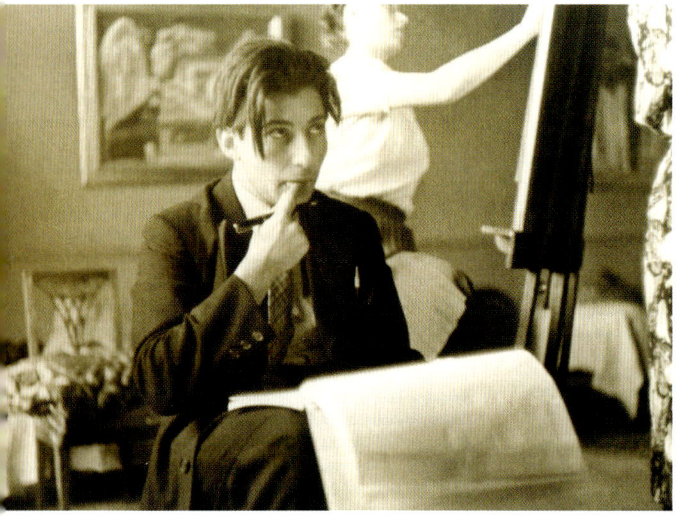

336. *Heinz Koppel in Martin Bloch's Painting School, London, c.1938*

Later, Giardelli would recall how, in 1944, a young man had presented himself at the Pontypridd settlement with the words 'I am told there are painters here'.[11] He was Heinz Koppel, who was visiting the family manufacturing business nearby. Koppel had left Germany in 1933, settling first in Prague and then in London. Grainger and Giardelli introduced him to Morris, who installed him at Dowlais as art teacher.

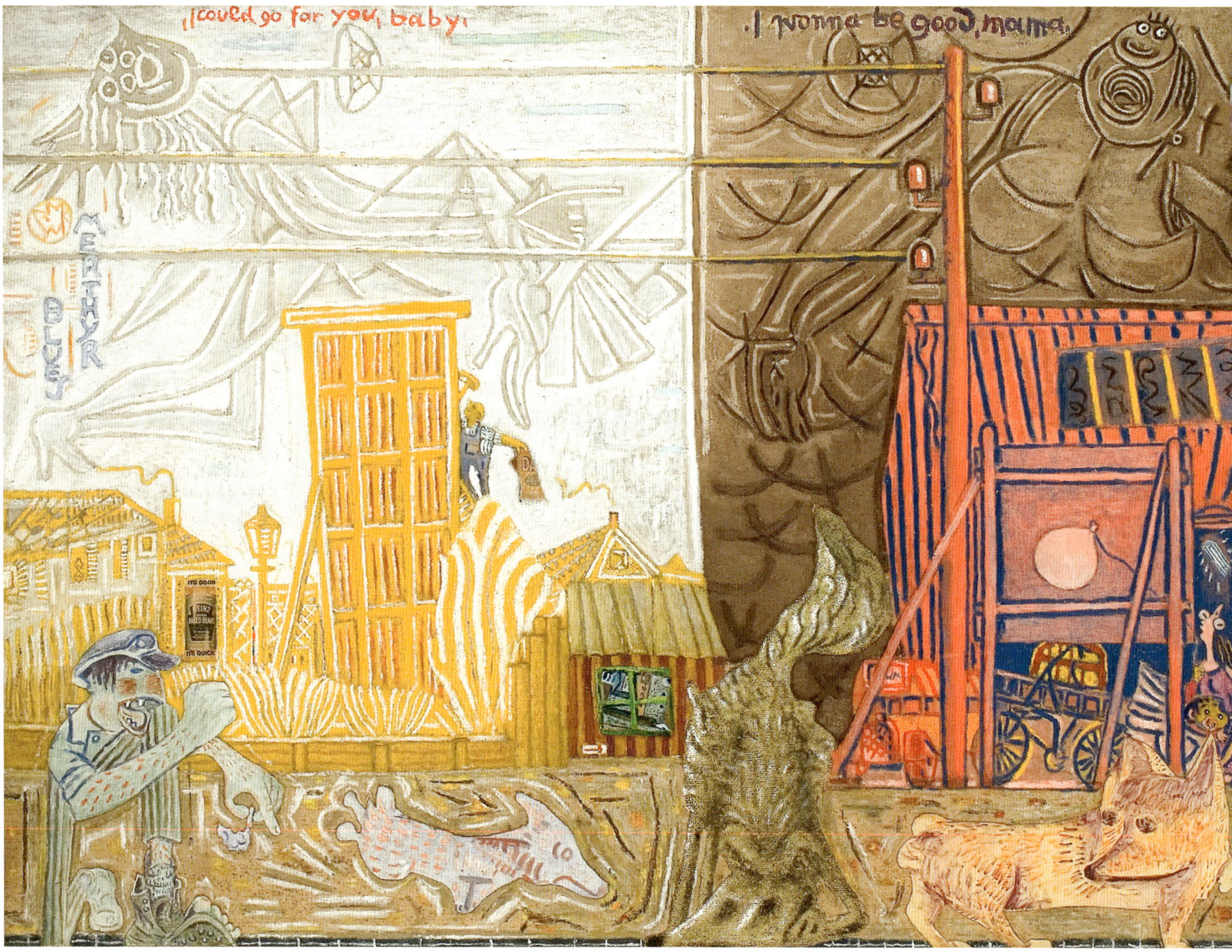

There Koppel further developed the Morris philosophy of blurring distinctions between amateur and professional practice. In July 1945, for instance, the Merthyr Art Society (which he founded) presented the work of local children side by side not only with paintings by Koppel himself, Grainger, Giardelli and Morris, but also original works by Kokoshka, Klee, Nolde and Chagall, borrowed through London connections. The exhibition reflected Koppel's interest in painting as a medium for the expression of deep psychological traits, which manifested itself in his own work in surreal imagery that combined, in a faux naive manner, observation of the Valleys world around him with expressions of internal trauma, rooted in the events that had so disrupted the life of his Jewish family in Germany.[12]

Together, this group of socially motivated individuals – Morris, Grainger and Giardelli – sought to co-ordinate the work of the settlements and others in the field in the south of the country by establishing a Federation of Welsh Music and

11 Ibid., p. 25.

12 See *Heinz Koppel, Ein Künstler zwischen Berlin und Wales*, ed. Chana Schütz and Hermann Simon (Berlin, 2009).

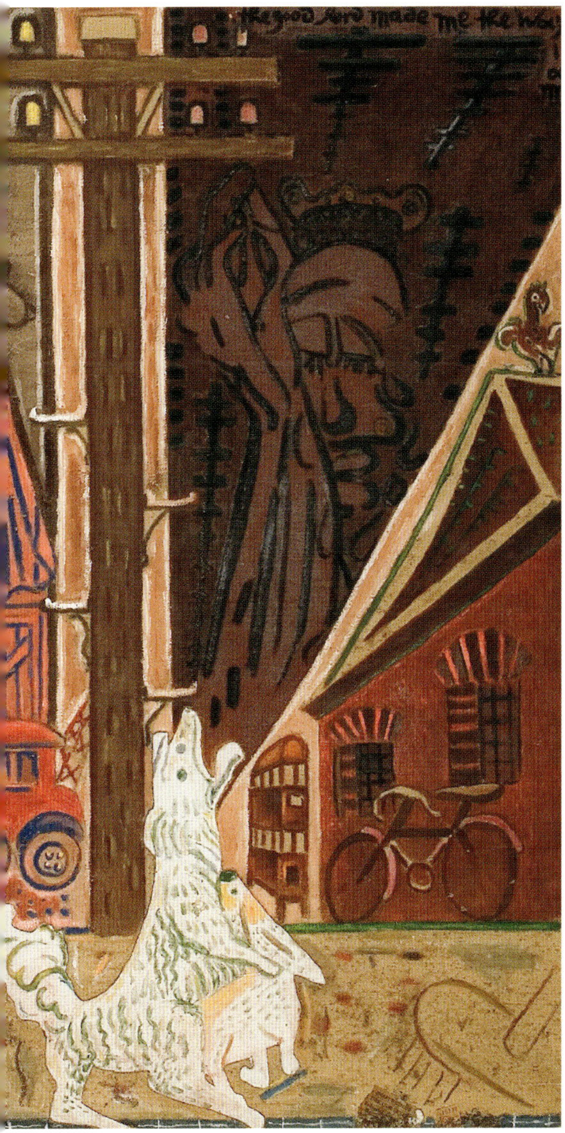

337. Heinz Koppel, *Merthyr Blues*, 1955, oil, 124x245

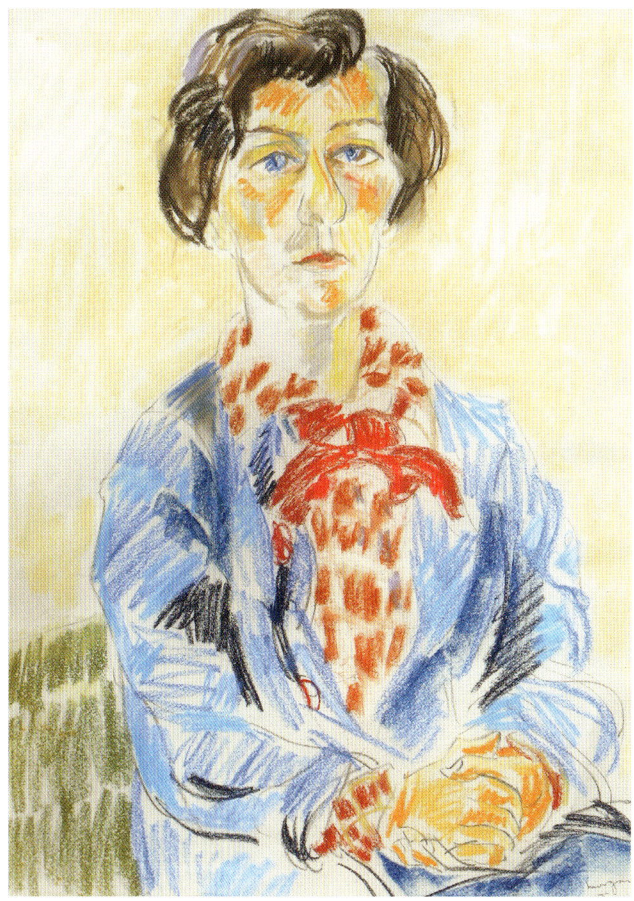

338. Glyn Morgan, *Esther Grainger*, 1955, pastel, 50x36.5

13 It appears that Georg Mayer Marton came to Wales initially as a lecturer with travelling CEMA exhibitions.

14 The Arts Council's Charter of Incorporation was granted in 1946 under the Atlee government, but the decision to create the Council had been taken under the previous administration led by Churchill.

15 Indeed, William Emrys Williams would hold the post of Secretary General to the Arts Council of Great Britain from 1951 until 1963.

16 Cedric Morris Papers (Tate Archives), 8317.1.1, item 1263.

17 *Western Mail*, 10 February 1956, p. 6.

18 Walter Dowding, 'The Music and Arts Clubs: What are they?', *Wales* (ed. Keidrych Rhys), 23 (1946), pp. 42–4.

Arts Clubs. Grainger worked as Secretary. Among their activities in 1945–6 was a joint travelling exhibition selected by Evan Charlton and the Hungarian painter Georg Mayer Marton.[13] However, by this time, rather than wind down the arts provision that had developed as part of the war effort, the decision had been taken in London to expand it. In 1946 CEMA was reinvented as the Arts Council of Great Britain.[14] With government funding already established, little change of principle was involved, except in one respect. The new organisation adopted a devolved structure, establishing Scottish and Welsh offices with appointed advisory committees, which perhaps reflected, once again, the influence of the two prominent Welsh administrators.[15] It soon become apparent to Grainger that this 'official' development might render the Federation superfluous. She wrote to Morris:

> One thing that has rather changed the situation is this appointment of David Bell – I expect that you've heard that the Arts Council has appointed more staff for Wales with David Bell as art officer. That's probably a good thing (I haven't met him yet). But if they are going to expand in Wales then there isn't much room for the expansion we foresaw in Federation work. They are the official people with the money and the staff to do the job, and it looks as if eventually they will do it.[16]

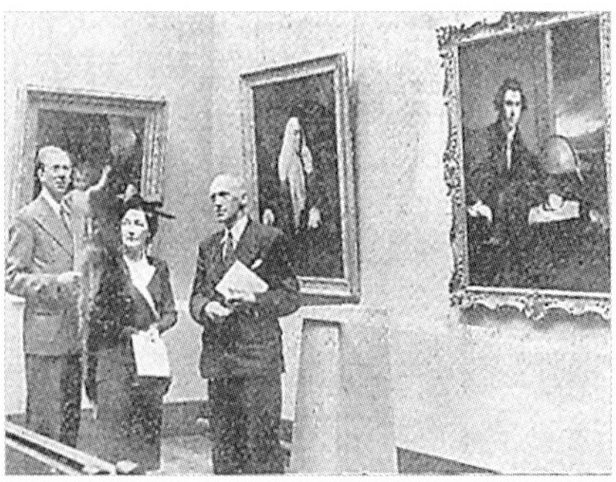

339. *David Bell with Myra Owen, Director for Wales of ACGB, and Wyn Griffith, chairman of the Welsh Committee, c.*1950

David Bell was the son of the literary scholar H. Idris Bell, and had been trained at the Royal College of Art. He began immediately on a five-year campaign to create a new framework within which a flourishing visual art practice might develop out of what he saw as a 'loose assortment of unattached art groups and societies'.[17] The idea of central planning permeated every aspect of public life in the period, and the arts were to be no exception. Bell's intention was to effect radical change both by 'direct provision' – creating exhibitions, giving commissions, purchasing art, publishing criticism and history – and by exerting influence, backed by money, on independent institutions. However, his centrist model did not appeal to all. In 1946, Walter Dowding of the Bryn Mawr Settlement warned of the danger of 'too much dependence on the Arts Council of Great Britain' on the grounds that it had been formed 'for the propaganda of English, *not* British, culture'.[18] Dowding sensed, correctly, not only that voluntary participation and amateur practice would be undermined, but that the new institution would promote metropolitan concepts of high art 'excellence'. In the following year, in the course of a discussion broadcast on the radio, Cedric Morris expressed similar patriotic concerns, and floated the idea of annual exhibitions generated within Wales by Welsh artists.[19] In 1948, the idea was taken up at a meeting between David Bell and William Grant Murray, and the South Wales Art Society was established as an exhibiting group. Consistent with the ideas of Cedric Morris, initially it brought together both professional artists and the art clubs and societies, but participation by professionals fell away as a result of what modernists among them regarded as the conservatism of the amateurs. Within ten years, and with Arts Council connivance, the society would reform itself into a professional organisation, though in the face of considerable recrimination.[20]

In a similar way, David Bell sought to use the National Eisteddfod to promote professional art practice on a metropolitan model. Here he met with stiffer and more high-profile opposition. In 1948 the status of the study of folk cultures in Wales, led by Iorwerth Peate at the National Museum of Wales, was greatly enhanced by the initiation of the open-air museum at Saint Fagan's, near Cardiff. With the support of the Museum director, Cyril Fox, who had visited the pioneering open-air museums of Scandinavia before the war, Saint Fagan's was established on land donated by Lord Plymouth. Peate's vision for the Museum was not simply retrospective. Also inspired by the Scandinavian model, he envisaged that the revelation of the rich history in Wales of architecture and hand-made artefacts in wood, metal, ceramic and textile would stimulate not only a revival of traditional practice, but the adoption by contemporary craftspeople and artists of Welsh design as the basis for new work.[21] Peate foresaw the projected open-air museum as 'a temple of the living muse'.[22] Inheriting notions rooted in the national revival of the late nineteenth and early twentieth centuries, Peate believed that the core values of Welsh life sprang from the culture of the *gwerin*, the common people of rural Wales. His belief that true national revival could only be built on these values marginalised the cultures both of the English-speaking industrial proletariat and of what he regarded as an Anglicised gentry. The orientation of many among the gentry towards metropolitan, high art traditions represented, from his standpoint, an alien influence in visual and material culture.

The patriotic motivation of Peate was clear, but it is certainly the case that David Bell was also motivated by the idea of national revival. For a time he was influenced by the democratising spirit of the settlement movement. In 1947 he organised a touring exhibition of the work of Koppel and his students at Dowlais, 'Pictures from a South Wales Town'. However, consistent with the mainstream of Arts Council policy at a British level and, indeed, with the tradition of nineteenth-century Welsh patriots, Bell's model reverted to that of 'enlightenment' percolating from the top down, on the basis that the culture of the socially and politically empowered represented excellence in all the arts.[23]

Both Peate and Bell employed the National Eisteddfod as a platform for the promotion of their contending ideas and institutions. At Mountain Ash in 1946, Peate organised exhibitions of craftspeople at work and at the opening pointedly referred to the 'Craft and Art' exhibition, reversing the customary order of priority.[24] Bell responded with showings of his touring exhibitions of painting, matching

19 The script of 'Art in Wales', a discussion in the *Welsh Forum* series, is held in the Cedric Morris Papers (Tate Archives), 8317.3.1.2. The participants were Morris, A.G. Tennant-Moon, Josef Herman, John Steegman and Ivor Williams (son of Christopher Williams).

20 The Society's transformation would be completed in 1975 when, as an exclusively professional organisation, grant-aided by the Arts Council, it was renamed 'The Welsh Group'. Peter Wakelin, *Creating an Art Community: 50 years of the Welsh Group* (Cardiff, 1999).

21 See Cyril Fox, 'Open-air Museums', *The Museums Journal*, 34 (1934–5), p. 113.

22 *'teml yr awenau byw'.* Iorwerth C. Peate, 'Diogelu ein Gwreiddiau', in idem, *Sylfeini: Ysgrifau Beirniadol* (Wrecsam, 1938), p. 102.

23 The ideas of Bell dominated Arts Council attitudes into the 1980s. Writing in the Council's 1978 publication *Art in Wales 2000BC–AD1850, an Illustrated History*, p. 11, John Ingamells observed that 'Throughout this book, only the new and most accomplished skills are represented, and hence folk art has been excluded.'

24 'We shall preserve and develop every significant traditional craft in Wales. We shall have craftsmen's workshops where Welsh craftsmen will work and there you will see all the year round what you see at this eisteddfod for one week ... Who can measure the influence of this revolutionary development on the whole future of Welsh craftsmanship?' *Western Mail*, 6 August 1946, p. 3.

340. *Tom David demonstrating thatching, National Eisteddfod at Mountain Ash*, 1946

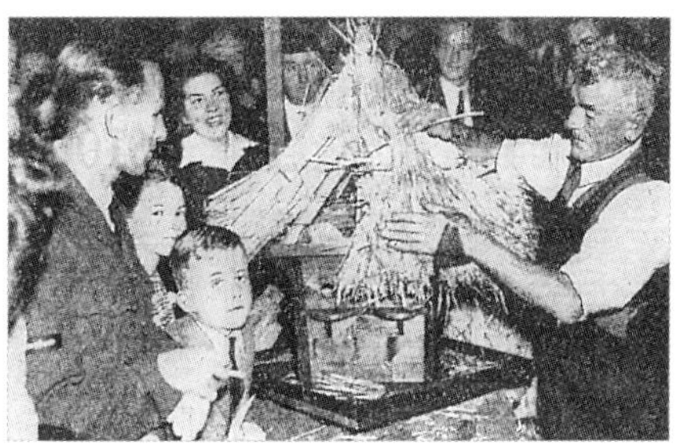

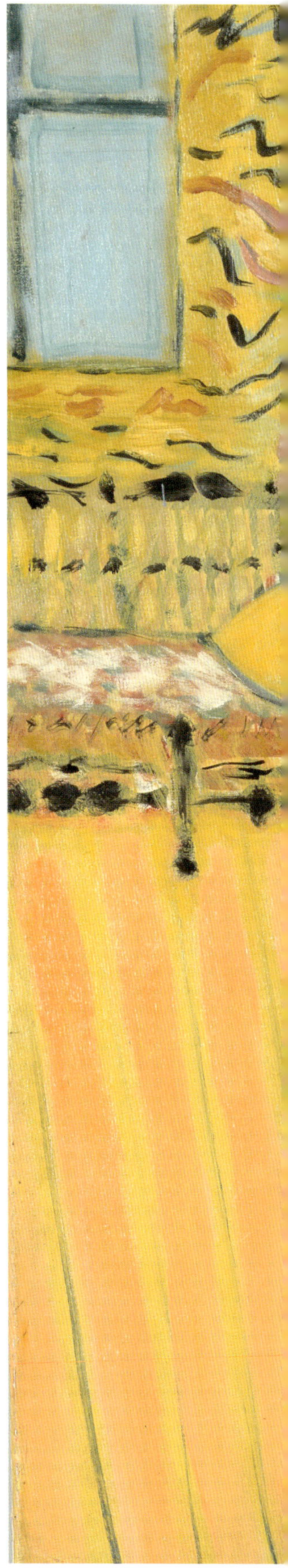

341. Ceri Richards, *Yellow Interior*, 1950, oil on canvas, 80x97

Peate's craftspeople with 'Masterpieces from Welsh Houses'[25] and 'Works by Contemporary Artists', in association with CASW. In the following year he arranged for a British Council exhibition of recent art from Czechoslovakia to be shown at Colwyn Bay. Such relatively quiet witness to contending ideas became a public controversy in 1950 at the Caerphilly eisteddfod. Peate was chairman of the art and craft department, but the exhibition sub-committee was led by Esther Grainger and the new Principal of Cardiff School of Art, James Tarr. Under Bell's influence, rather than a competition the committee organised an exhibition selected by Cedric Morris, Ceri Richards and Georg Mayer Marton, prompting Peate in his introduction to the catalogue to make disparaging reference to 'intellectual' critics, by whom he meant the London-educated Bell and his high art associates:

> We continue to depend excessively on critics and patterns of thought which are foreign to our tradition ... If the saying 'from a body of living crafts grows a living art' is true, it is equally the case, I believe, that a completely Welsh contribution to art will come from the work of Welsh people under the criticism of people who know about Wales.[26]

Bell's rebuttal, published the following year in *The Welsh Anvil/Yr Einion*, opened with the provocative remark 'There never has been in Wales any tradition of the fine arts.' It had become Bell's mission to create one, and based on the experience of Caerphilly, he was optimistic:

> There is in fact growing in Wales to-day a sense of community among practising painters and a consciousness among the public of the art [of painting] as a part of Welsh life ... what we are witnessing in Wales is the first stirrings of a new and vital interest in the fine arts, which will one day grow into a tradition of painting.[27]

Arts Council ascendency in the visual arts had been established, with the promotion of a principle of 'excellence' – undefined, but clearly understood to mean metropolitan high art – firmly embedded as its core philosophy. Until the end of the 1980s, the Council would dominate the funding of practice and the display of visual art in Wales.[28] Rather as the founding of the Royal Academy in London in the second half of the eighteenth century had established a stage for the presentation to the public of new work and for aesthetic pronouncements, whose 'authoritative' status conditioned metropolitan taste, so the financial support of the Arts Council in its Welsh

25 Welsh gentry houses had been periodically mined as sources of exhibitions of Welsh art by the eisteddfod since the nineteenth century, a practice that continued under the Arts Council. In 1951 'Pictures from Welsh Private Collections' was sponsored jointly by the Council and the National Museum. The chronic lack of visual art infrastructure at the time meant that it was shown only in Swansea and Cardiff: 'In spite of every effort, no adequate accommodation could be found for showing it in North Wales.' Catalogue to the exhibition 'Pictures from Welsh Private Collections' (Cardiff, 1951), p. 3.

26 Introduction to the catalogue *Eisteddfod Genedlaethol Frenhinol Cymru, Celf a Chrefft, Caerffili, 1950*, p. 5, my translation from the Welsh.

27 David Bell, 'Contemporary Welsh Painting', *The Welsh Anvil/Yr Einion*, III (1951), p. 17.

28 For the evolution of Arts Council policy in Wales, see Huw David Jones, 'Exhibiting Welshness. Art, Politics and National Identity in Wales, 1940-1994', unpublished PhD thesis, Swansea University, 2007. I have drawn extensively on the work of Dr Jones for this chapter, and I am greatly indebted to him for his enrichment of my understanding of the period.

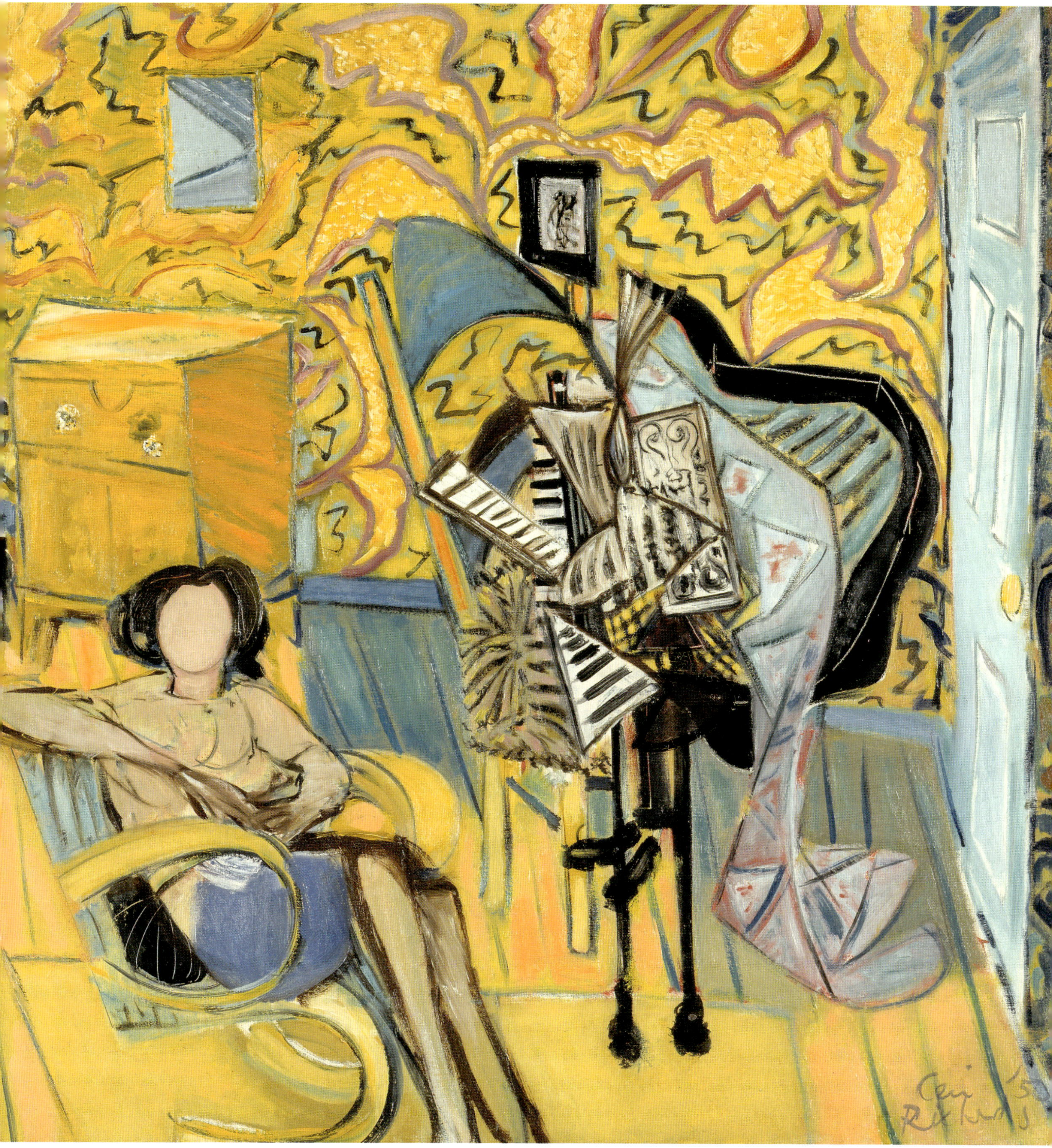

manifestation promoted a core of approved artists and guided debate on aesthetics. Despite being established as a body funded by government but independent of it – the 'arm's length' principle – in practice, at the peak of its activity in the visual arts, through its direct provision the Arts Council in Wales came close to being a ministry of culture. As such, its policy both reflected and reinforced the evolving political and social outlook of the Welsh establishment.[29] Nevertheless, it is certainly the case that its activities led a creative transformation of both the production and the public presentation of visual art in Wales in the four decades after 1950.

Professional art practice in the post-war decade: imaging the Valleys

There have always been painters and sculptors, even those well-connected in the metropolitan art world, who have stood on the margins of prevailing trends. After the Second World War, David Jones, for instance, would follow a unique path in his work right up to his death in 1974. Nevertheless, in Wales a distinct mainstream emerged in which a substantial number of professional artists swam. The imaging of the south Wales valleys was a prominent feature of the work they produced. Having emerged from the pre-war Depression, and following nationalisation of the coal industry and new investment in steel manufacture, the communities of the Valleys experienced a period of renewed cultural energy. Set in their unique built and natural environment, it both attracted artists from outside and was sufficiently strong to retain, for a time, young painters born in the area. They operated in a wider context of renewed creativity in the literatures of Wales, and of intellectual engagement with working-class life

29 'In examining, therefore, the role of the British State in relation to the visual arts we are looking at one of the ways in which the British State has become involved in developing and reproducing moral concepts and a moral authority.' Nicholas Pearson, *The State and the Visual Arts: A Discussion of State Intervention in the Visual Arts in Britain, 1760–1981* (Milton Keynes, 1982), p. 2.

30 Glyn Morgan, typescript memoir of Cedric Morris (1992), private archive. It seemed to Morgan that 'the creaking old house and the glorious garden were the only real life and the outside world was a sort of shadow-land.'

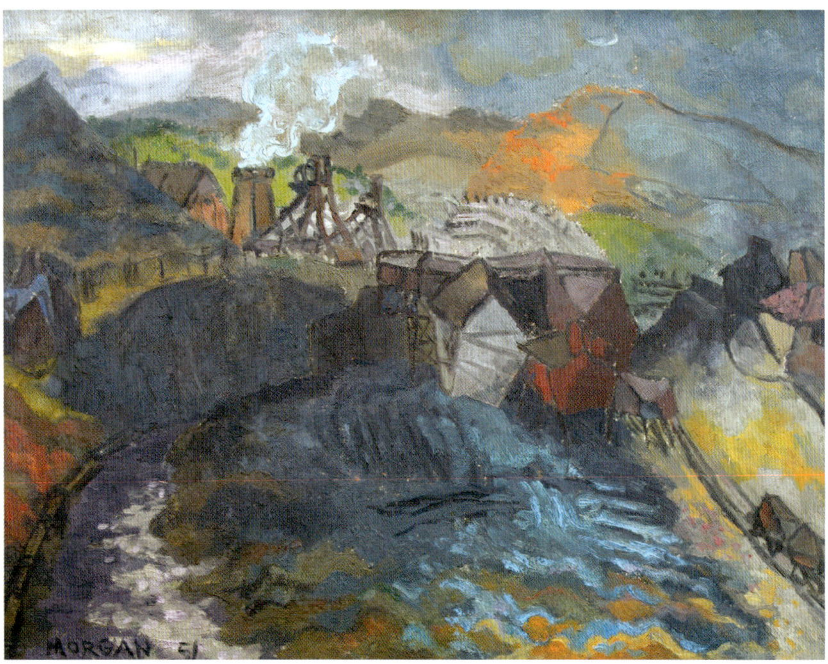

342. Glyn Morgan, *Tonypandy*, 1951, oil, 53x69

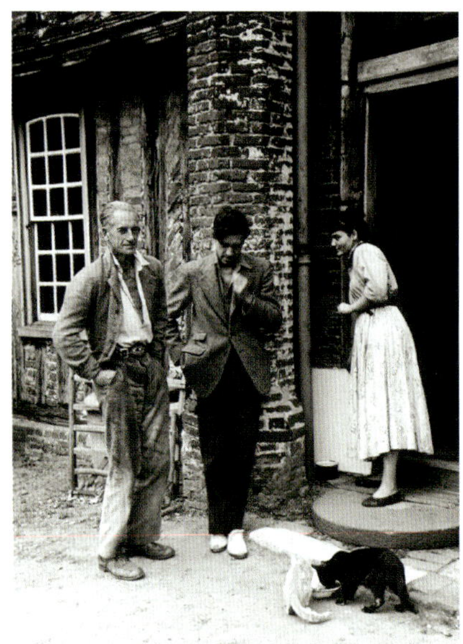

343. *Cedric Morris, Glyn Morgan and Renate Koppel at Benton End*, 1946

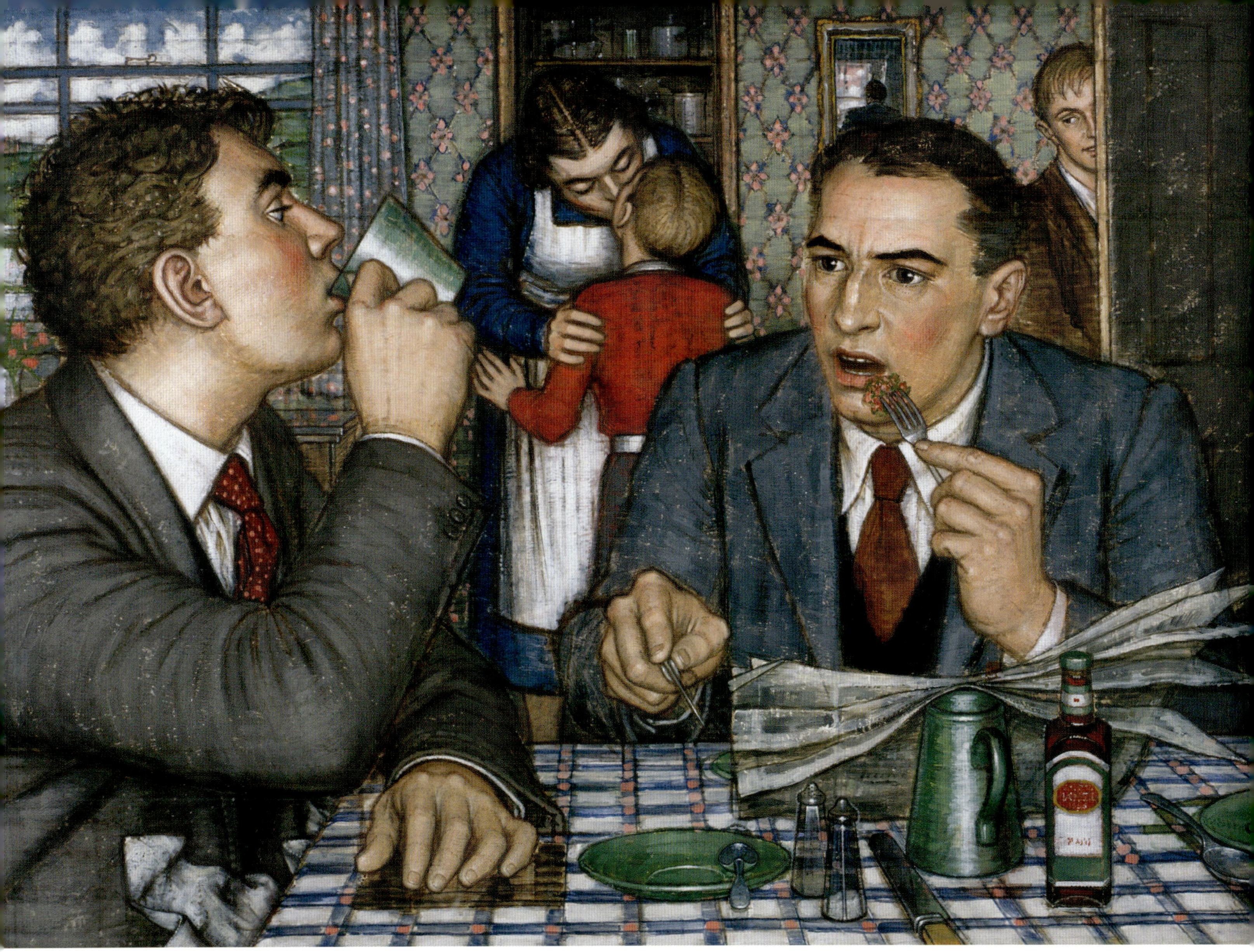

throughout Britain. The influence of Cedric Morris on Heinz Koppel and Esther Grainger extended to include Glyn Morgan from Pontypridd, then being taught by Ceri Richards. Morgan's paintings were noted by Morris at an exhibition in 1943. He worked at Benton End the following year – 'very young, very innocent, and more than a little terrified'.[30] Inspired by Morris, and influenced by his style, Morgan painted periodically in the Rhondda Valley into the mid-1950s: 'How can one mortal painter hope to put down all that mystery and dignity', he wrote to Winifred Coombe Tennant, who was, like Morris, still engaging with young Welsh painters, though now established in London.[31]

344. Alfred Janes, *Breakfast*, 1955, oil, 71x102

Among the other students that Glyn Morgan met at Benton End was Renate Fischl, with whom he fell in love – though the relationship did not prosper, since in 1948, on Morris's advice, Fischl travelled to Dowlais to meet Koppel. They married early the following year in London, on the occasion of an exhibition of Koppel's work that marked his growing reputation.[32]

31 Morgan to Coombe Tennant, NLW Winifred Coombe Tennant Papers, A1/28, 4 November 1950. The charisma of Morris eventually drew Morgan away to live in East Anglia, from where he has pursued a distinguished career.

32 Renate Fischl would develop her own career as a ceramicist at the side of Heinz under her married name, Pip Koppel.

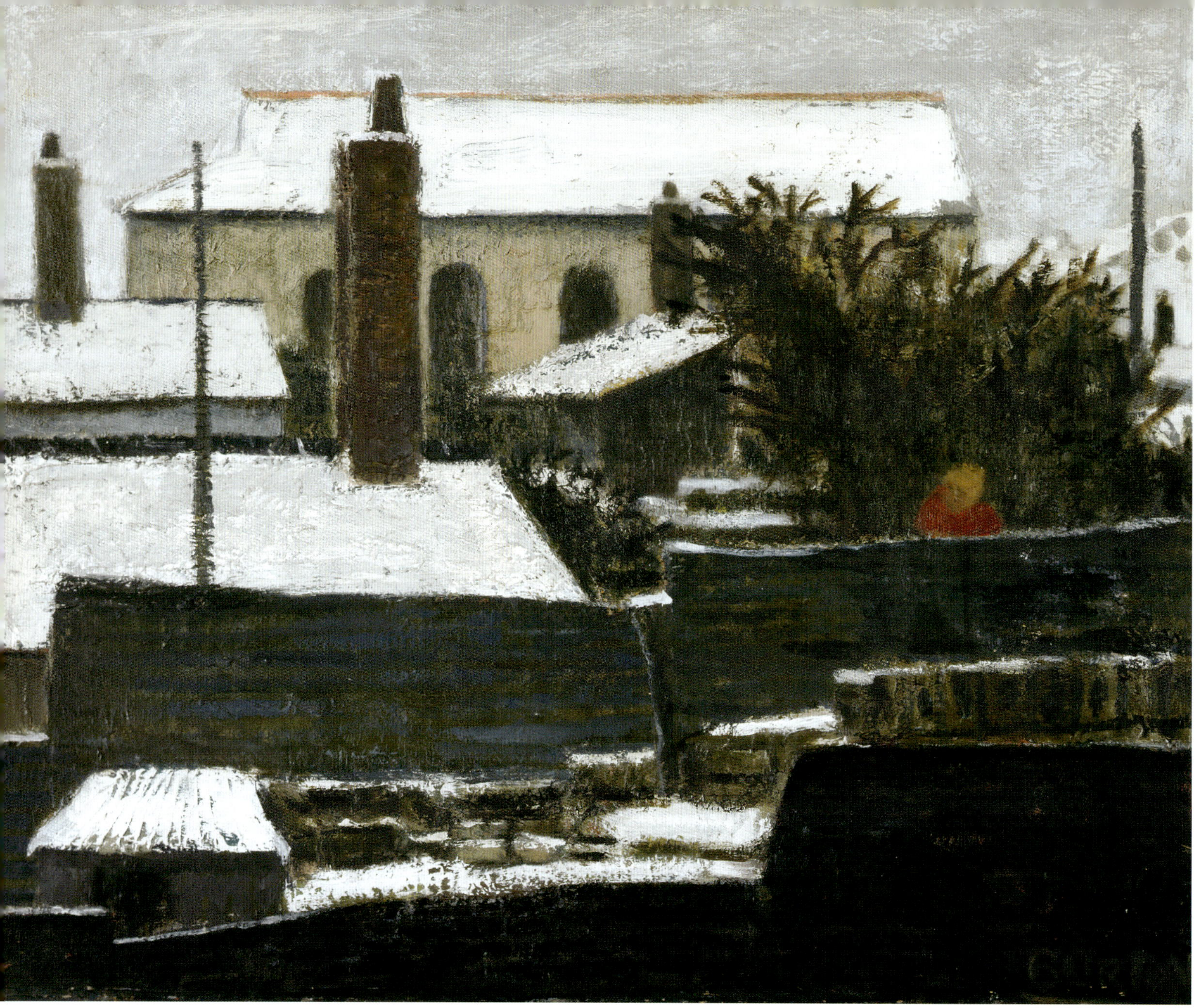

345. Charles Burton, *Snow in Treherbert*, *c.*1955, oil, 65.5x77.5

His presence a few miles from Cardiff attracted the attention of a new generation of students at the School of Art. Although he was a little older, Glyn Morgan noted the promise of this emerging generation, and planned to exhibit with them. They were 'all rather tired of art school procedure, all full of energy and vitality, and they want to get together (about 20 of them) with Janes, Esther Grainger, myself and possibly Cedric, and have an exhibition some time next year.'[33] The Cardiff students came to be associated together as the Rhondda Group, though it was never a formal organisation. They were united by their homes at various places in the Rhondda, from which they travelled together into Cardiff every day by train, and by their use of the landscape and community that was so familiar to them as the source of their imagery. Nevertheless, their perceptions of the meaning of that source differed. In retrospect,

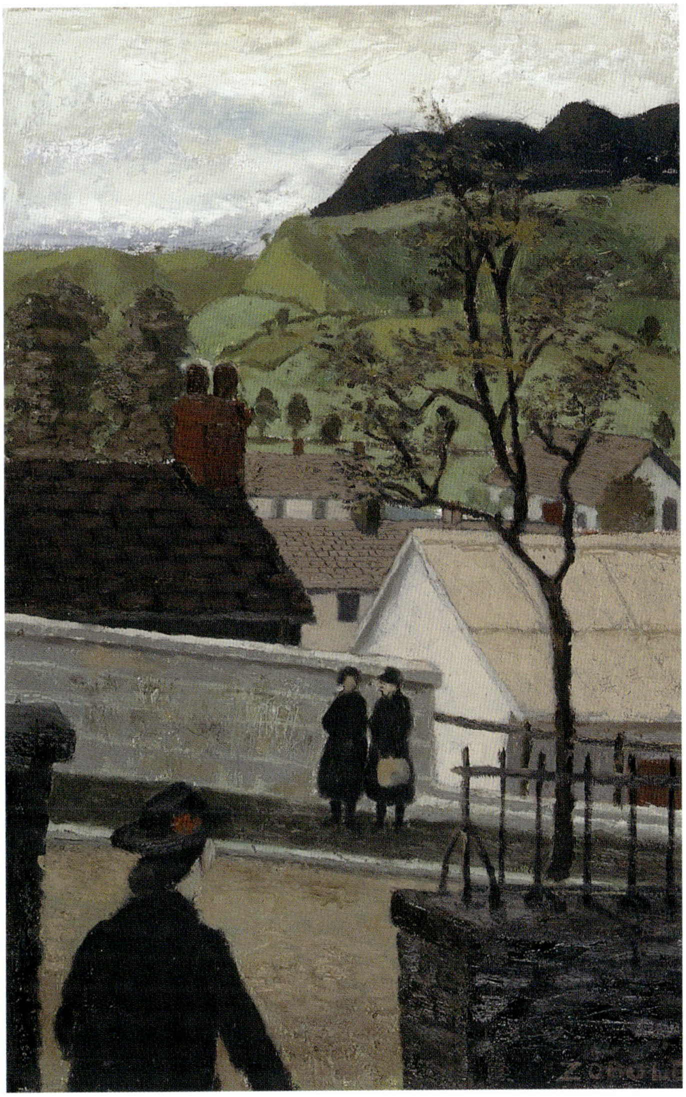

346. Ernest Zobole, *Penrhys*, 1951, oil, 60.0x39.5

Charles Burton would maintain that it had been merely a starting point for an exploration of the formal aspects of painting. For Ernest Zobole, inescapably it embodied a particular history: '... the whole landscape has always been made by people. The industry that was here ... It shaped the landscape and it shaped the people's lives as well, I mean the way they thought, politically. You can't help being touched by it, the social struggle people went through, the deprivation, the continuous fight for some kind of justice ...'[34]

Burton, Zobole and David Mainwaring all visited Koppel at Dowlais. Zobole was 'bowled over' by the experience of the studio, the paintings and by the painter himself, who 'with his foreign sounding name [and] guttural German accent' seemed an exotic figure to the

33 Morgan to Coombe Tennant, NLW Winifred Coombe Tennant Papers, A1/28, 31 October 1950.

34 Ernest Zobole, interview in Curtis, *Welsh Painters Talking*, p. 178.

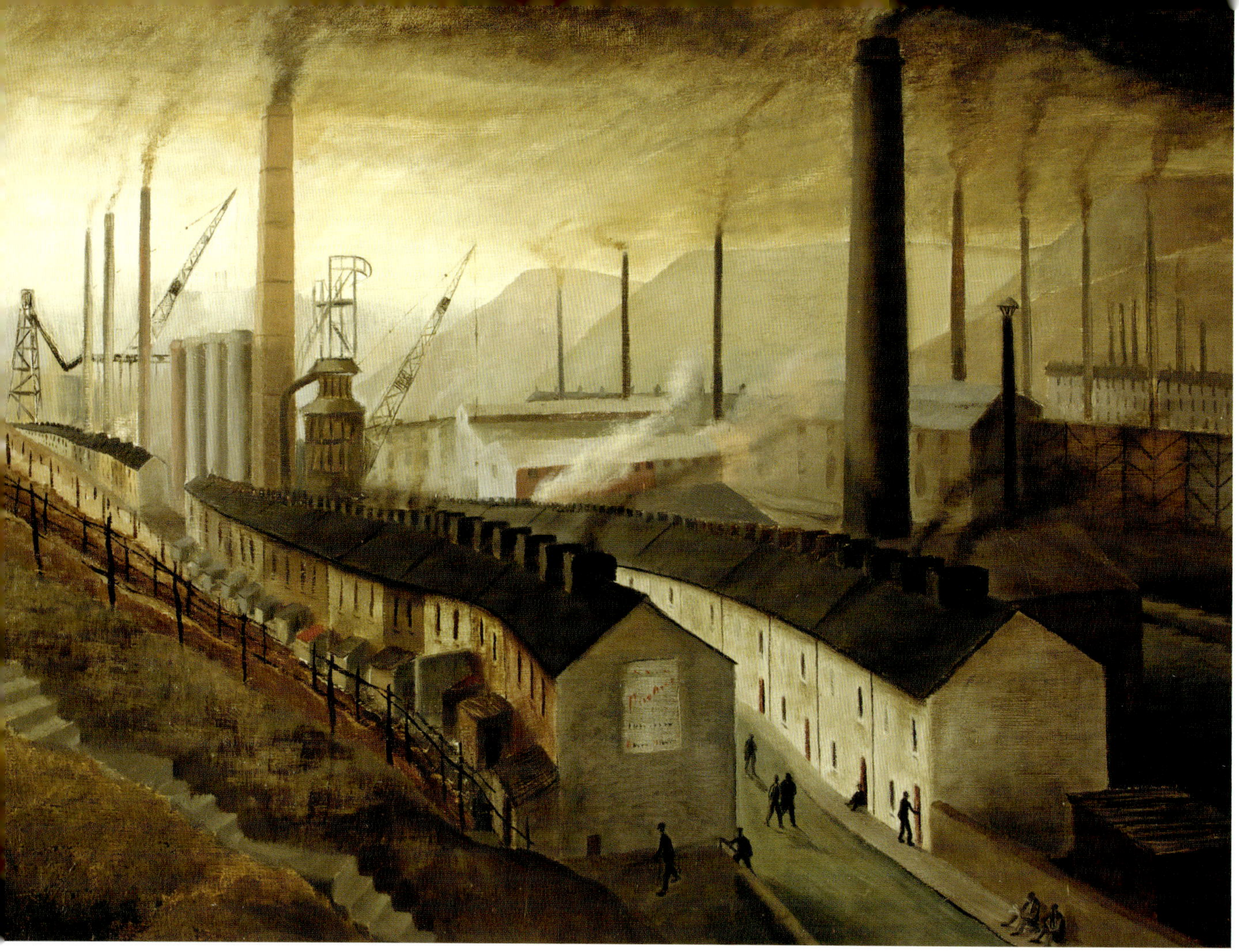

347. Nan Youngman, *Steelworks, Ebbw Vale*, c.1951-5, oil, 59.7x80

romantic imagination of the young student.[35] The work of Zobole came quickly to the attention of critics – he was among those shown, alongside Koppel, at the 1950 Caerphilly eisteddfod exhibition. Nevertheless, David Bell, writing shortly afterwards, was concerned about the ability of the young painters to develop their careers at home:

> What will happen to these painters as yet scarcely out of their teens in this harsh world where so much is set upon destroying the artist in a man no one would hazard a guess, but if Burton, Flower and Zobole and a few others can preserve their sensibility intact and their loyalty to the South Wales subject something very significant to Welsh painting may emerge.[36]

To further that end, encouraged by a discussion document co-authored by Evan Charlton, Bell initiated a purchase scheme at the Arts Council with the intention of creating a national collection of contemporary art. Zobole's *Penrhys* was among the first acquisitions. At the same time, Bell developed a second scheme intended both to assist artists and to raise the awareness among young people of Welsh painting. Inspired by an exhibition and purchase initiative established in England in 1947, Bell invited the painter and educator Nan Youngman

35 Ernest Zobole, interview with John R. Wilson, 1995, NLW National Screen and Sound Archive, Visual Culture of Wales Research Project Deposit. For Burton's relationship with Koppel, see Curtis, *Welsh Painters Talking*, p. 38.

36 Bell, 'Contemporary Welsh Painting', *The Welsh Anvil/Yr Einion*, iii (1951), p. 28. Nigel Flower exhibited at the National Eisteddfod, with the South Wales Group, and in 1952 at the Young Contemporaries exhibition in London. Later, he would develop his career as a graphic designer.

37 Esther Grainger, 'Nan and the "Pictures for Schools" Exhibitions' in *For Nan Youngman. Tributes on her 80th birthday, June 28 1986* (privately published, Cambridge, 1980), pp. 21–4. See also *Nan Youngman 1906–1995*, ed. Julian Rea (London, 1997). Published sources date the first meeting of Grainger with Youngman both to 1950 and 1951; Grainger herself dated it to the late 1940s.

38 See David Alston, *Lowry in Wales* (Swansea, 2002).

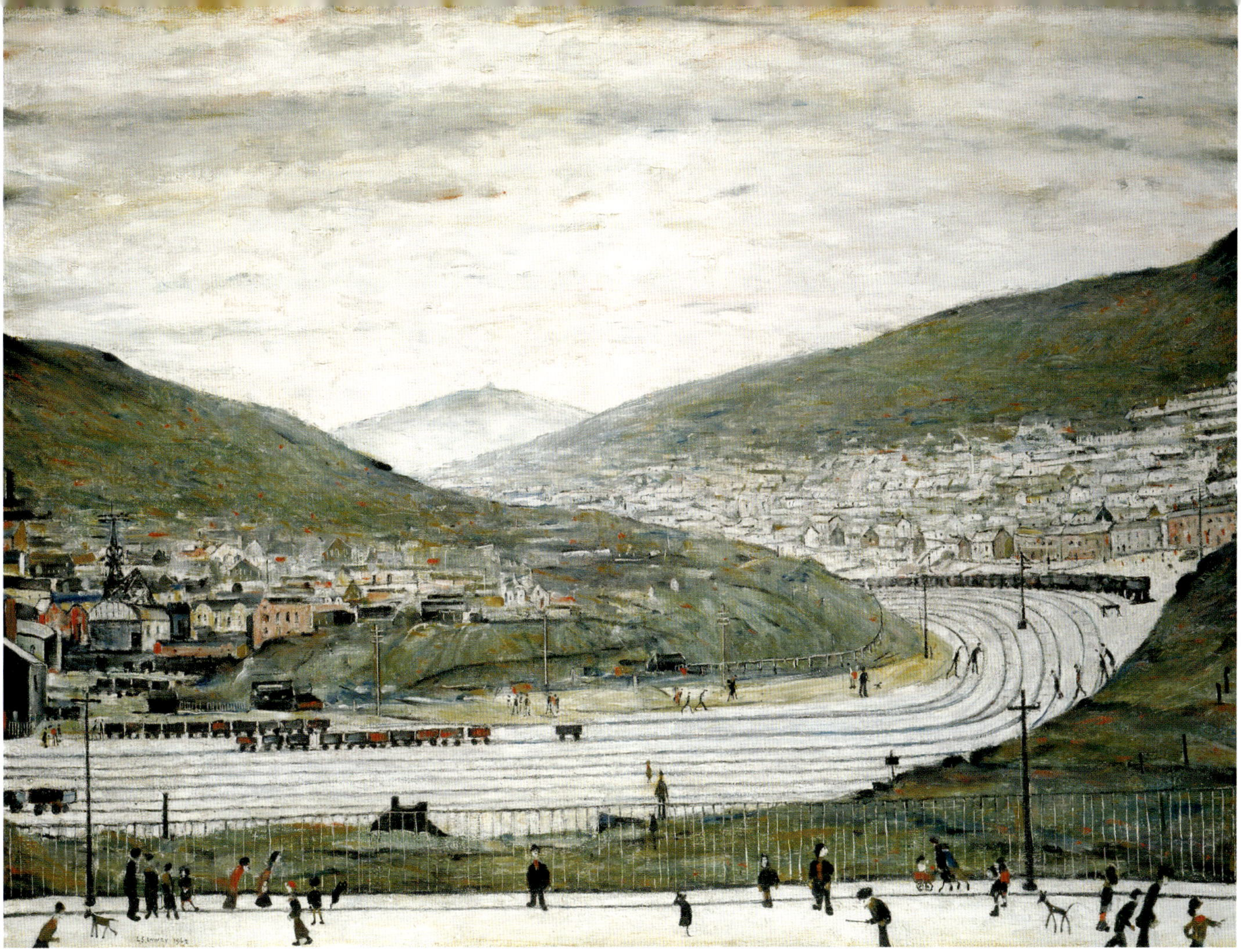

348. L.S. Lowry, *Six Bells, Abertillery*, 1962, oil, 132x169

to develop 'Pictures for Welsh Schools'. The first selected exhibition took place at the National Museum in 1951, from which works were purchased for display by education authorities. During the preparation of the scheme, Youngman met Esther Grainger and began a relationship that lasted for many years. Youngman came often to Wales to visit Grainger and to paint. Her images of the urbanised Valleys contributed to the growing sense that a mainstream and characteristically Welsh painting had emerged.[37] At the same time, in a wider context, as a left-wing activist with a pedigree reaching back to membership of the Artists International Association in the mid-1930s, Youngman extended the tradition of observation of Valleys' life by politically-conscious artists from outside. Notwithstanding the improvement in economic circumstances and morale that the people were enjoying, the physical environment, largely unchanged since the 30s, and the community, both in the towns and at work underground, continued to attract image makers. Two notable photographers, the American William Eugene Smith and the Swiss-born Robert Frank came in 1950 and 1951. Later, in 1958, the English painter L.S. Lowry would make his first visit, brought to Ebbw Vale by his Welsh patron Monty Bloom.[38]

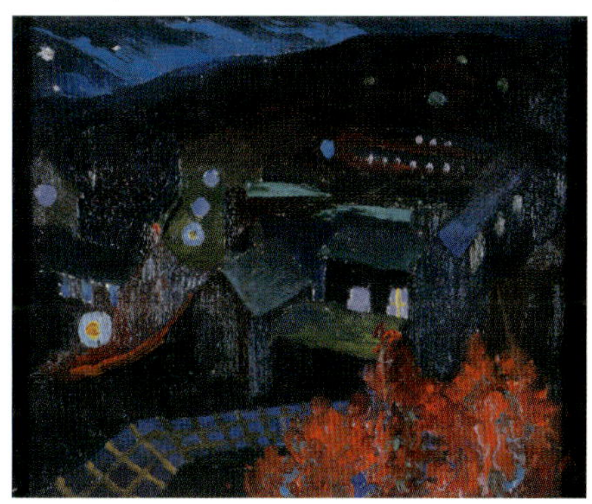

349. Esther Grainger, *Pontypridd at Night*, 1953, oil, 39.7x50

The new generation of Valleys painters flourished in the context of a second strain of industrial imaging that developed further west. Before he came to Wales, Heinz Koppel had worked in London, first as a student and then as a colleague, with the German painter Martin Bloch. After the war, Bloch too would come to Wales to work, though his choice of location would be a slate-quarrying district in the north-west. Nevertheless, returning to London from his initial visit there in 1947, he took a considerable detour in order to stay with another émigré friend, Josef Herman. Since 1944 Herman had lived and worked at Ystradgynlais in the Tawe valley. He had arrived from Poland, by way of England and Scotland, as the result a chance meeting with a colliery worker in 1944. From the first moment, he was deeply attracted by what he found:

> At first I spent entire days looking. I walked the small streets and the open hills where you can touch the sky. I also went down the mines, with a lamp on my helmet, a sketchbook in my hand, in a dirty mackintosh I borrowed from Sid ...
>
> One sleepless night I recalled how much I liked walking in the dark woods outside Warsaw. There I often felt that having a soul and a mind I needed little else. In the years of perfecting the painter's craft I lost that wonderful feeling. Now it is back ...

Herman 'arrived a stranger for a fortnight', and 'The fortnight became eleven years'.[39]

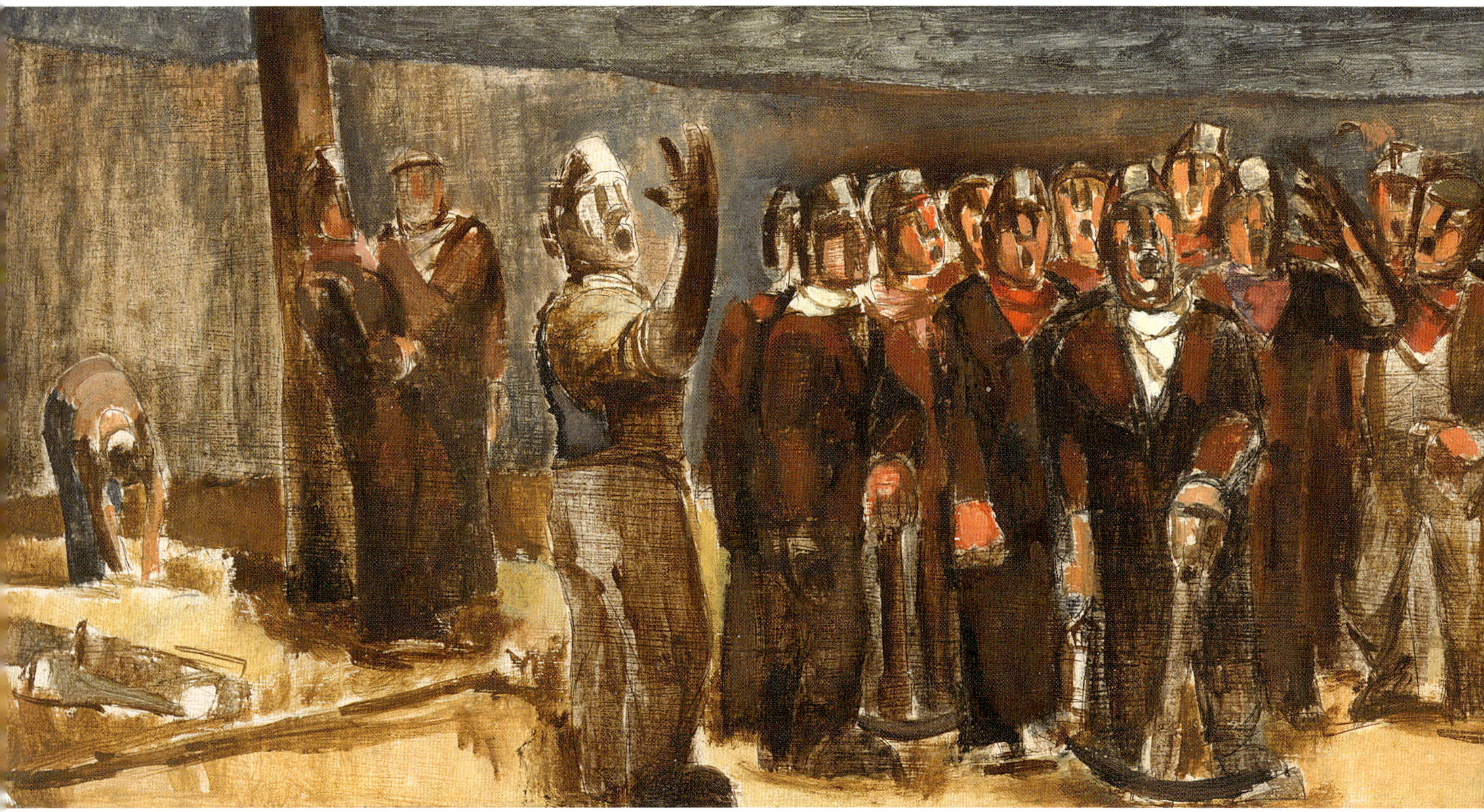

With a London reputation established before he came, Herman's new pictures would attract more attention than those of any other painter of the period working in Wales. He was regarded as a great asset by Welsh intellectuals, who wrote about him in terms that emphasised a familiarity with continental European painting that they believed he contributed to a nascent Welsh art world. Bell felt that 'when he has painted his neighbour in Ystradgynlais, the eye with which he has seen him has been sharpened by that familiarity.'[40] However, among the general public, the expressionist manner of Herman's painting aroused some hostility. The exhibition 'Miners at Ystradgynlais', organised by Bell, toured institutes, libraries and other small venues in the Valleys. Complaints that the pictures were 'monstrosities' and 'ghastly travesties of the present-day miner and his womenfolk' were published in the newspapers. Arthur Giardelli, interpreting the exhibition to the public at Ebbw Vale, found that local people 'were offended ... that their husbands, brothers or sons should be painted like that.'[41] Unease of another sort was expressed, though in retrospect, by the left-wing critic John Berger, who observed that 'Herman spent many years painting miners as if they were peasants instead of one of the most militant sections of the proletariat.'[42] Herman himself might not have dissented from this view, since for him the miners represented 'the embodiment of labour as a human rather than a merely industrial force, in fact the basic humanity that I have always sought and tried to express.'[43]

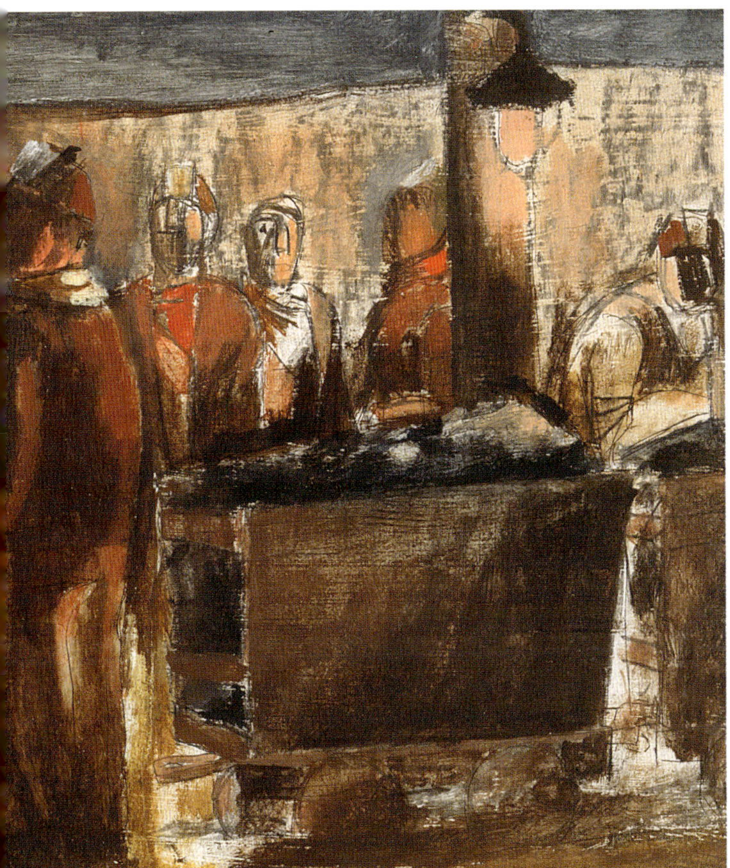

The network of émigré painters, born and trained in central Europe but working in Wales, proved more directly influential than the artificial implantation of Belgian artists had done in 1914.[44] In addition to the dynamic circle around Koppel at Dowlais, at Ystradgynlais Herman was joined by Will Roberts, a year older than the Polish painter though yet to establish a reputation. He had grown up at Ruabon in the north-east coalfield, but trained part-time at the Swansea school in the early 1930s.

350. Josef Herman, *Miners Singing*, 1950-1, oil and crayon, 43.5x121.6

39 Josef Herman, *Notes from a Welsh Diary* (London, 1988), pp. ii and xi.

40 David Bell, 'The Art of Josef Herman', *The Welsh Review*, vii, 2 (1948), p. 108.

41 Published comment on the exhibition was collected by the Arts Council, see NLW Welsh Arts Council Archive, Exhibition Files, A/E/11. Giardelli is quoted from Derek Shiel, *Arthur Giardelli: Paintings, Constructions, Relief Sculptures* (Bridgend, 2001), pp. 59–60.

42 John Berger, *Permanent Red* (London, 1960), pp. 90–4.

43 Edouard Rotiti, *Dialogues on Art* (London, 1960), p. 176.

44 In addition to those mentioned in the main text, the German painter Frederick Könekamp lived and worked in Pembrokeshire, and Fred Uhlman, also born in Germany, kept a house near Penrhyndeudraeth from where he painted extensively in the area.

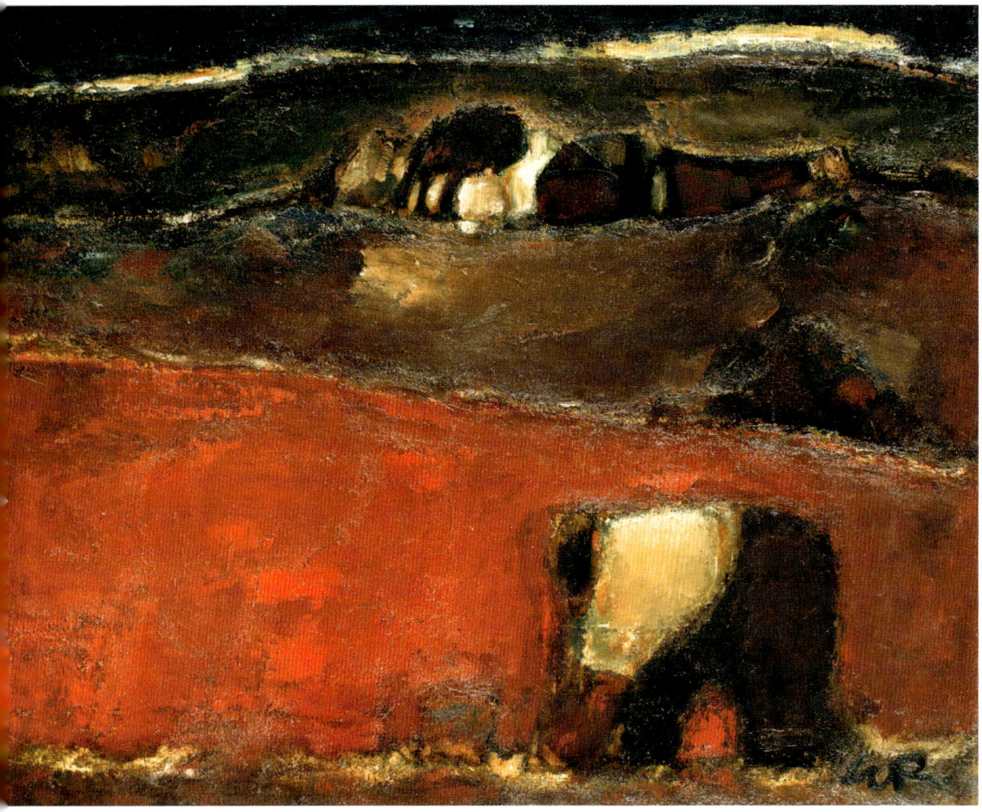

On leaving the airforce in 1945 he sought out Herman and 'learned much from him as his pupil'.[45] In 1950, Roberts was selected for the seminal Caerphilly eisteddfod exhibition. Herman would leave Wales in the mid-1950s, but Roberts stayed and his work became an important presence in Welsh art throughout the second half of the twentieth century. Evolving within the expressionist tradition represented by Herman and the early work of Koppel, his imaging of people and landscape reflected the mixed industrial and agricultural communities of the western edge of the coalfield.

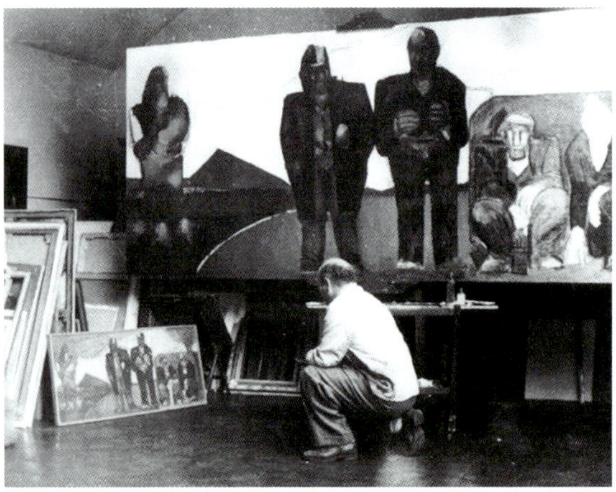

In 1951, the Festival of Britain presented a snapshot of British culture as perceived from London by the political and intellectual establishment. In the commissioned exhibition '60 Paintings for '51', Josef Herman was among the four painters who represented Wales. His high profile was reinforced by a second commission to paint a mural-scale work for the Pavilion of the Minerals of the Islands. *Miners Crouching* epitomised at the Festival an image of working-class industrial Wales that was emphasised by the work of Martin Bloch, who painted *Down from Bethesda Quarry*.[46] At home, urban Wales remained central to the imaging of the nation throughout the ensuing decade, reinforced in particular by the work of two English-born painters. George Chapman made his first visit to the Rhondda in 1953, and by 1957 had been awarded the Gold Medal for Art at the National Eisteddfod for one of the urban landscapes which established his enduring reputation. The following year, Denys Short, introduced to Wales as the result of his marriage to the embroiderer Eirian Short, was awarded the medal for a painting in the same genre. Initially through three-dimensional evocations of Valleys streets, Denys Short's work would evolve much further than that of Chapman, primarily into sculpture.

352. T.J.Davies, *Josef Herman in his studio at Ystradgynlais*, 1950

top 351. Will Roberts, *Hill Farm*, 1981, oil, 61.5x76.5

45 Roberts described his background and development as a painter in Meic Stephens, *Artists in Wales* 3 (Llandysul, 1977), pp. 98–111.

46 Although not representing Wales in an official capacity at the Festival, the English painter Frances Macdonald also imaged the Penrhyn quarry in her picture *The Welsh Singer*. At about the same time, the artist Mary Elizabeth Thompson also worked there, and described her experience in 'An Artist in the Penrhyn Slate Quarry', *The Highway. The Journal of the Workers' Educational Association*, 41 (May 1950), p. 161. The other Welsh representatives commissioned for the Festival of Britain exhibition were Merlyn Evans and Ceri Richards. The choice was not universally approved. See Peter Lord, *The Visual Culture of Wales: Industrial Society* (Cardiff, 1998), p. 239, and for an analysis of the significance of the exhibition from a Welsh perspective see Jones, 'Exhibiting Welshness', pp. 103–6.

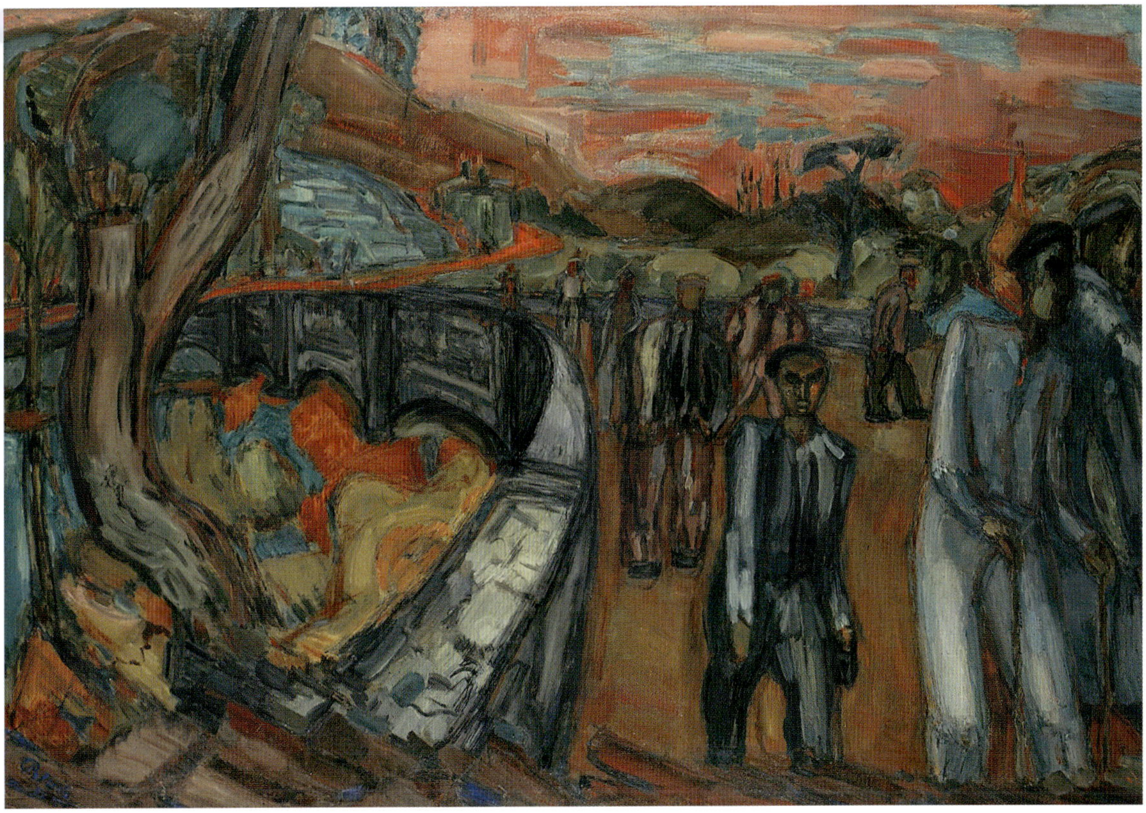

353. Martin Bloch, *Down from Bethesda Quarry*, 1951, oil, 122.4x182.7

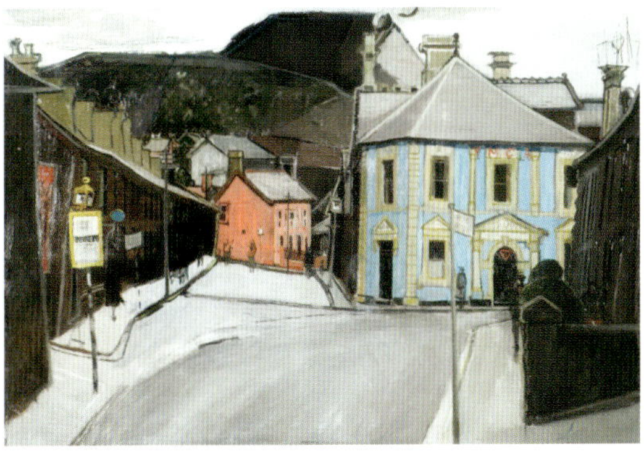

354. Denys Short, *YMCA, Porth*, *c.*1961, oil, 107x137

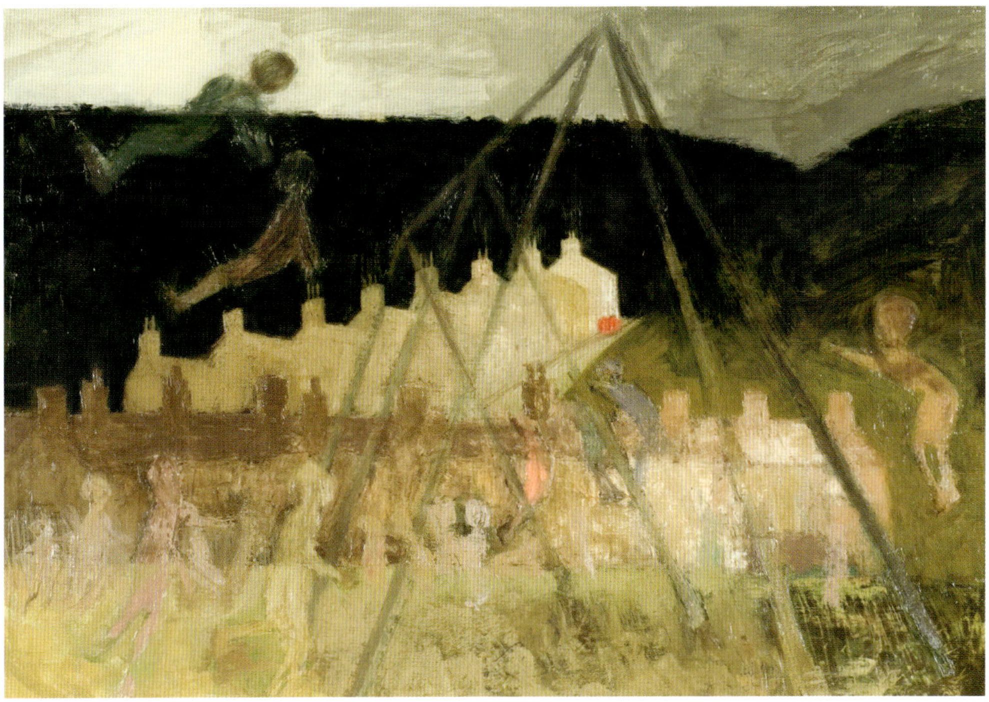

355. George Chapman, *The Red Van*, *c.*1960, oil, 109x149.2

Creating a parallel flow of images to those representing urban Wales, rural and upland landscape continued to attract painters as it had done since the eighteenth century. Alongside it, a further stream of painting became apparent that emphasised human interaction and which, perhaps, had fewer historical precedents. In the same year as the London Festival of Britain, the Llanrwst National Eisteddfod had instituted the award of the Gold Medal for Fine Art. The first winner was Brenda Chamberlain, and her picture, *Girl with a Siamese Cat*, was purchased for the national collection. One of the two buyers was John Petts, a coincidence that might perhaps have raised eyebrows, though the couple

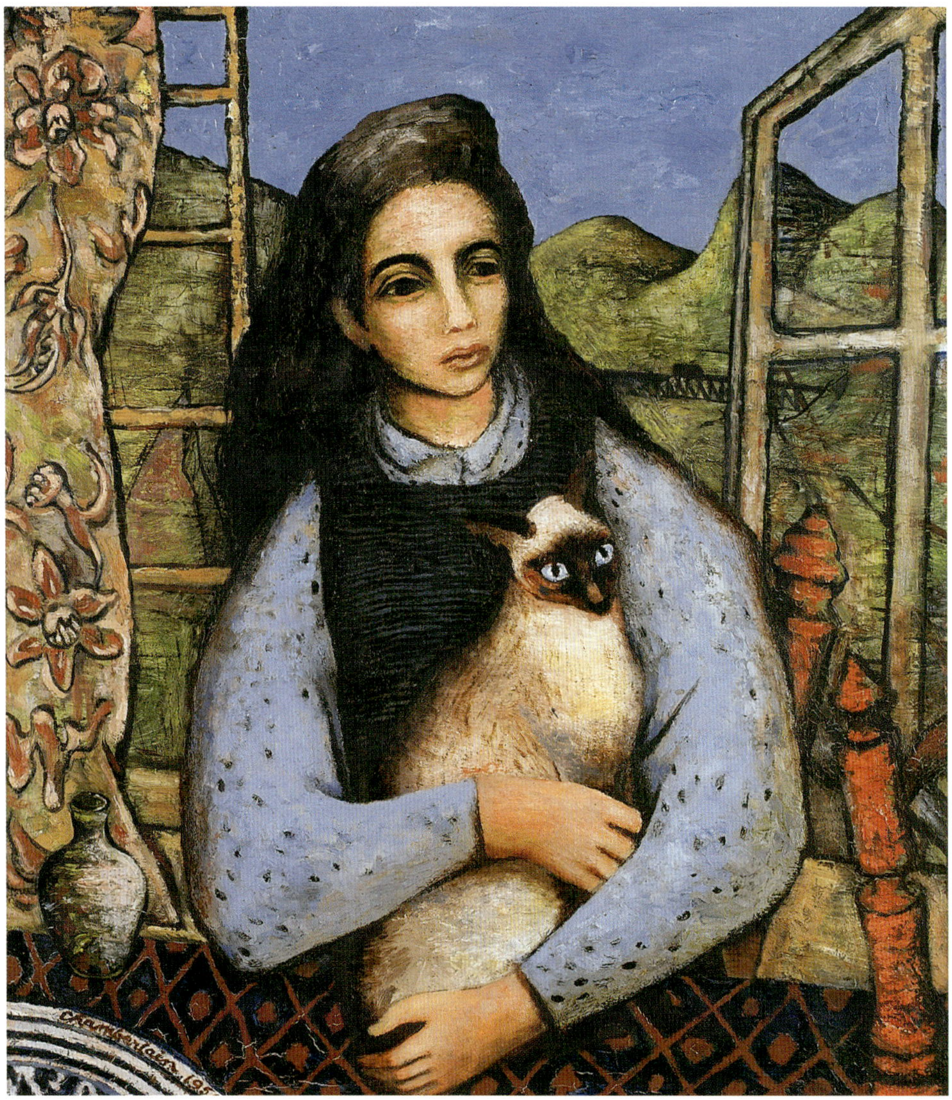

356. Brenda Chamberlain, *Girl with a Siamese Cat*, 1951, oil, 78x73.5

47 For the Caseg Press, and the Caseg Broadsheets, produced by Chamberlain, Petts and the poet Alun Lewis, see Jill Piercy, *Brenda Chamberlain, Artist and Writer* (Cardigan, 2013), pp. 61–102.

48 At Bristol, John Elwyn was taught by Evan Charlton, before Charlton was appointed Head of Painting at Cardiff. See the interview with Felicity Charlton in Curtis, *Welsh Painters Talking*, p. 48, and Robert Meyrick, *John Elwyn* (Aldershot, 2000), p. 21.

had separated some time previously. When first together, in 1938 they had established a private press – the Caseg Press – at Llanllechid in Caernarfonshire.[47] After the war, Petts re-established the Press at Llanystumdwy in Eifionydd, before moving to Cardiff as the Art Officer of the Arts Council. David Bell left to pursue his vision as curator of the Glynn Vivian Art Gallery, a post made vacant by the death of William Grant Murray the previous year. Chamberlain's painting was one of many that she made working on Bardsey, which she visited first in 1946, and where she soon after set up home. She would stay until 1962, painting and writing, though the period included also visits to Germany and later to Greece, where she lived for a time. Another of Chamberlain's Bardsey paintings was widely admired in the exhibition at the National Eisteddfod in 1952, and in 1953 she was again awarded the Gold Medal for her picture *The Cristin Children*. Chamberlain's success in the eisteddfod exhibitions in the early 1950s was remarkable in particular because it coincided with the emergence not only of the Rhondda painters, but also of two figures who would, along with Zobole and Roberts, eventually come to dominate figurative painting in Wales for a generation – John Elwyn and Kyffin Williams.

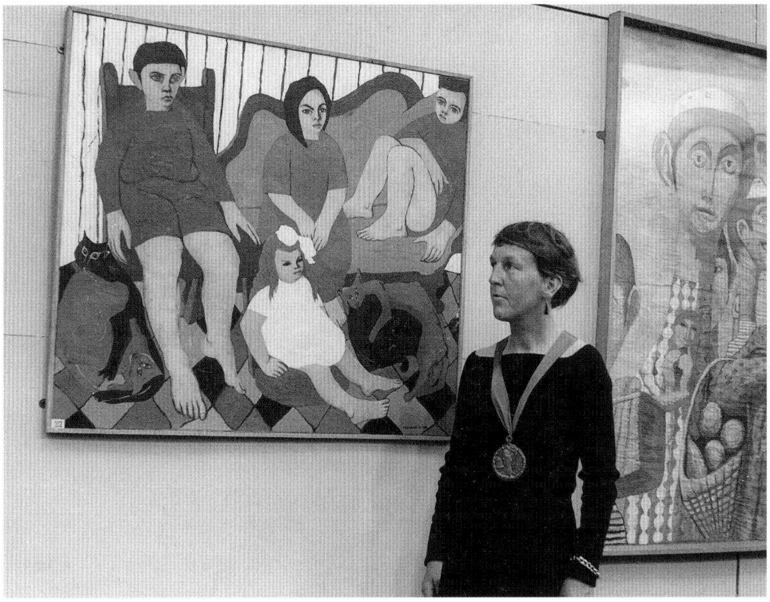

357. *Brenda Chamberlain with her picture 'The Cristin Children'*, 1953

John Elwyn was born in rural Cardiganshire into a family that suggests a realisation of the *gwerin* ideal of O.M. Edwards and Tom Ellis. His father was a weaver by profession and a poet by inclination, a man guided in morality by Christian conviction. John Elwyn trained as a painter initially at Carmarthen and Bristol, but his career at the Royal College of Art was interrupted by the outbreak of war.[48] Unsurprisingly, given his background, he registered as a Conscientious Objector and so in 1940 spent the first of four seasons working in forestry at Pont-Rhyd-y-Fen near Neath. He was able, however, also to enrol as a part-time student at Cardiff School of Art, where he was taught by Ceri Richards. For him, as for his teacher, the war manifested itself in his imagery, which became dark and intense. In 1946 he was able to resume his art education in London, and soon afterwards a single exhibited picture drew him to the attention of Winifred Coombe Tennant. Excited by what she saw, she wrote the first of some fifty letters to him, bought his work and encouraged others to do the same. Her vision for him, that he 'paint out of doors, paint in Wales, the life you know, paint small

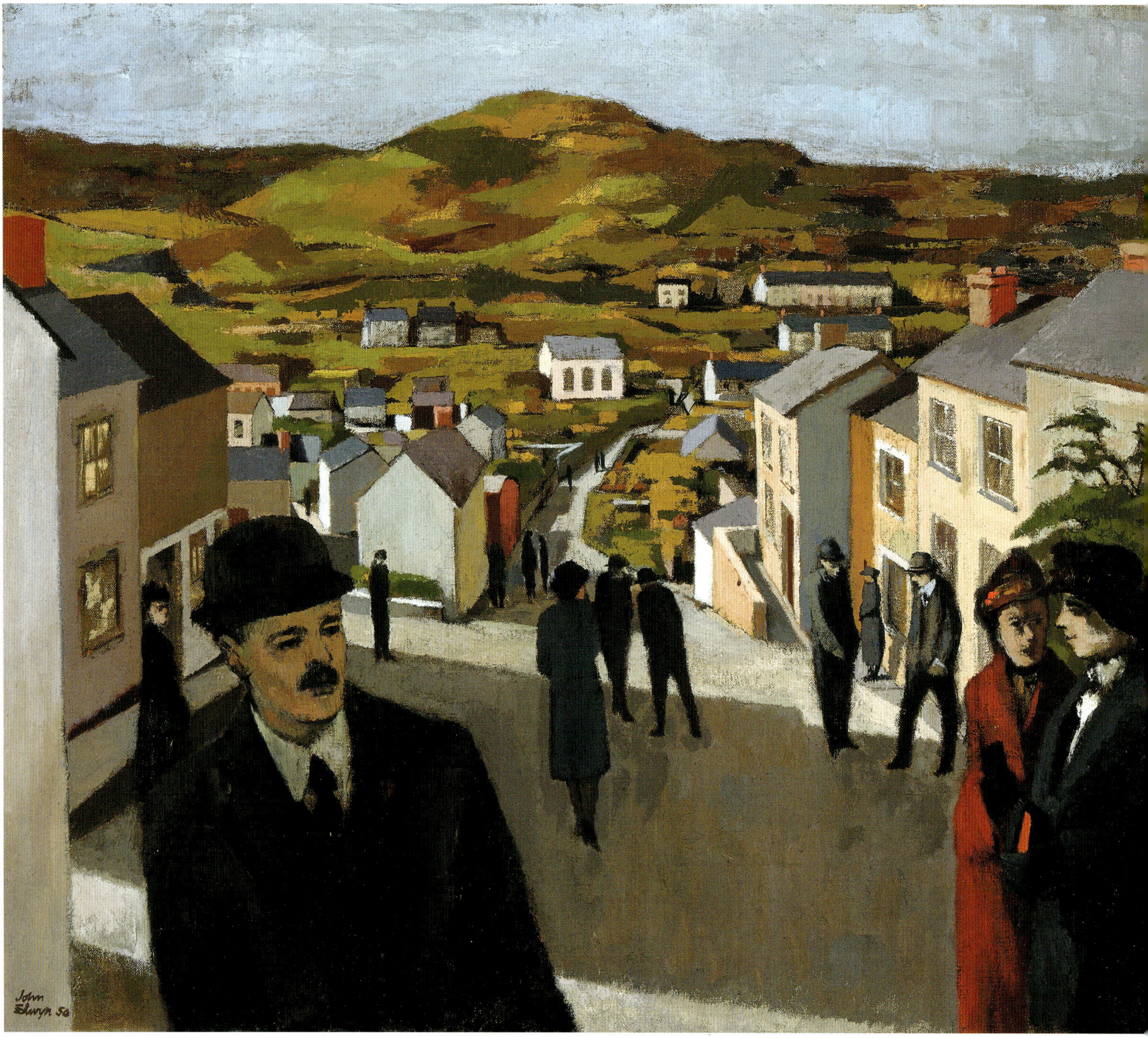

358. John Elwyn,
Bore Sul, 1950,
oil, 50.5x61

pictures, figures in landscapes, paint Wales' he would largely realise. Coombe Tennant found in him 'Something individual, not deviating, fresh, native and real', a response that predicted the affection for and identity with his work that would be felt by a broad public over the ensuing half century.[49] Remarkably, this affection developed in his absence, since he settled in Winchester, where for much of his career he taught in the School of Art.

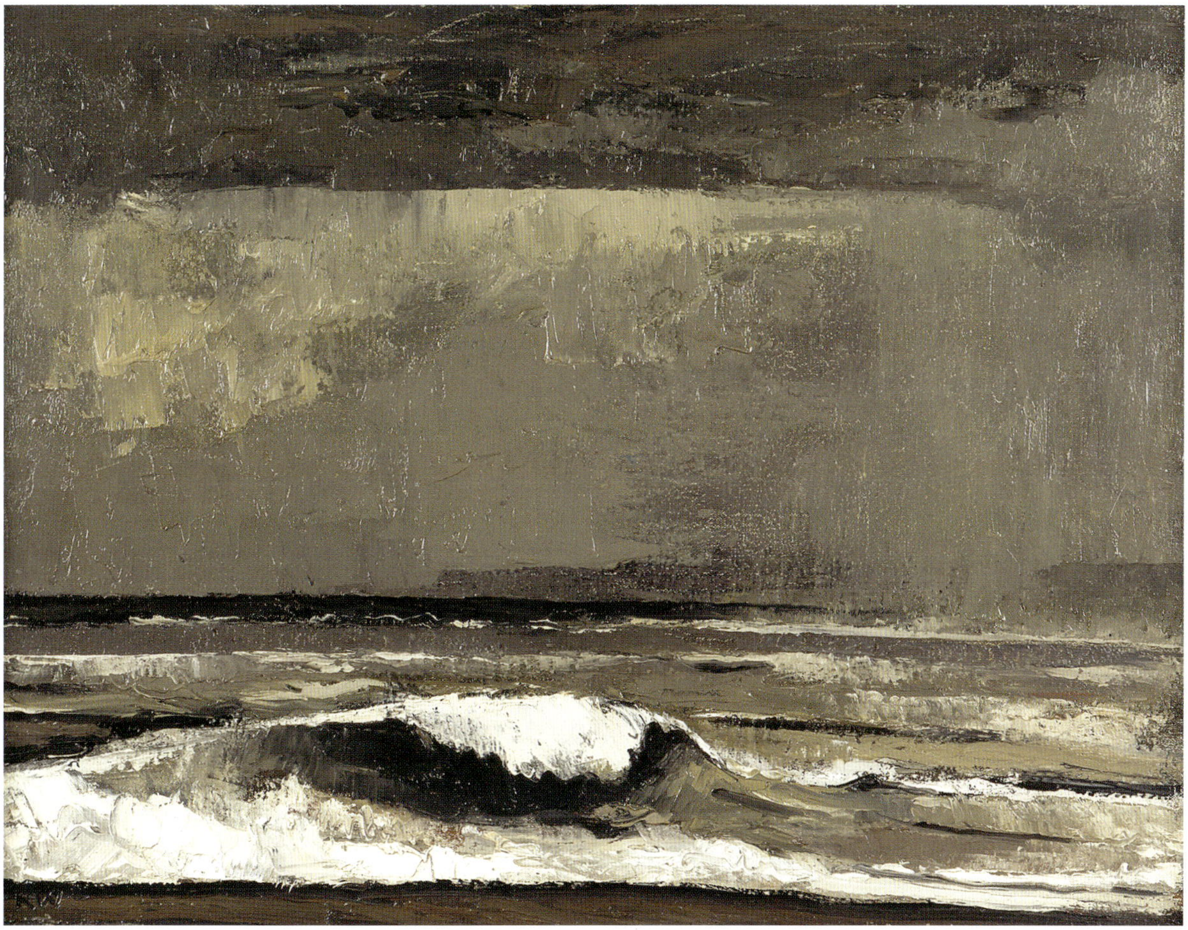

359. Kyffin Williams, *The Wave*, 1950, oil, 45.7x61

Though he returned to Wales to work from nature when not teaching, it was in the studio in England that John Elwyn created his refined images of landscape and community, rooted in childhood memory. It was a vision of continuity that appealed to a public increasingly conscious of the erosion of the values – whether real or imagined – that they represented.[50]

Though a very different personality, Kyffin Williams was able in the same way to touch in his painting a deeply rooted sense of identity that would eventually make him the most celebrated and well patronised painter of any period in Wales. Like John Elwyn, Williams was able to establish his position in the 1950s while teaching in England. Well connected socially through his Anglesey family, he was outgoing and forthright, in contrast to John Elwyn's quieter and more meditative manner. His sense of the landscape also differed markedly from that of his contemporary. Painting primarily upland and mountain locations, his imaging was frequently sombre and brooding, a mood reinforced by the drama of the palette knife technique that he developed early in his career. He was also a penetrating

49 The diary of Winifred Coombe Tennant, 29 June 1949, private archive.

50 Like John Elwyn, Williams also benefited from the patronage and encouragement of Coombe Tennant from the 1940s. For Williams see his own *Across the Straits, an autobiography* (new edn., Llandysul, 1993) and David Meredith and John Smith, *Obsessed: the Biography of Kyffin Williams* (Llandysul, 2012).

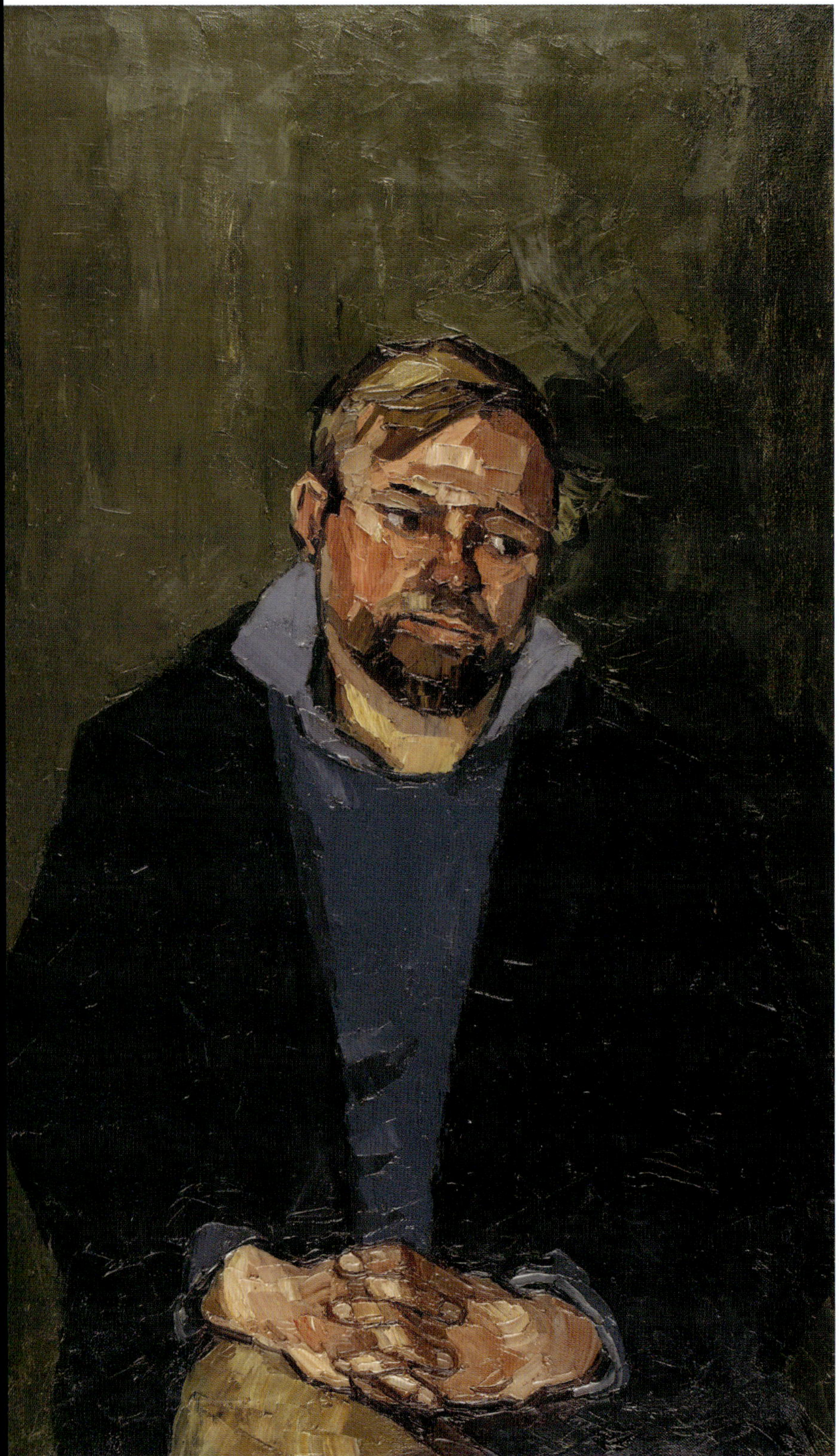

360. Kyffin Williams,
A Portrait of Jack Jones,
1969, oil, 90.5x55

portrait painter – though he maintained, with characteristic unpretentiousness, that he 'simply tried to get a likeness'.[51] However, the painter Jack Jones observed, after sitting to him, that 'he had captured not only my head but what was in my head and in my heart'.[52]

By the early 1950s, the unprecedented amount of painting being produced in Wales suggested that David Bell's aspiration to create the conditions for a Welsh school to emerge had been fulfilled. Also largely as a result of promotion by the Arts Council, the visibility of the work to the public had been enhanced. It remained for critics to identify a common characteristic with which it might be distinguished. The range of the work was wide, but John Petts sought to draw it together:

> The artist watches, records and
> selects: coaltips of the Rhondda,
> the piled fleeces of the upland clip,
> the pattern of Snowdon's screes, taut
> Bardsey fishermen, the chapel deacons
> grouped about the iron gate ...[53]

In 1953, Petts organised an Arts Council exhibition under the title 'Contemporary Welsh Painting and Sculpture'. In the catalogue, the selectors – David Bell, John Piper and Carel Weight – found a form of words which met the desire to identify a unifying ethos:

361. Ernest Zobole,
Llwynypia, c.1954,
oil, 96.5x156.2

> A feeling is conveyed in many of the pictures of love and compassion for humanity and a consciousness of the relation of men and women to nature, buildings and everyday life in Wales. This concern with environment seems to augur well for the future of a Welsh School of Painting.[54]

The notion of 'Welsh Environmentalism' was established, and even Saunders Lewis, philosophically no friend of industrial Wales, found cause to promote the idea of an underlying unity of vision among Welsh visual artists, when a reduced version of the exhibition toured to London in 1954:

> They tell us about Wales, about the disturbing dream-quality of a Cardiff dock, about the strange pressure of the sky mixing its colour with the colour of the streets, the amazing vision of Llwynypia, and about miners walking under the destiny-laden evening clouds. But one cannot translate from paint to language. One must stare meditatively and eagerly to receive what the picture says. Perhaps one can discover an akin-ness between M. Eldridge's Corris pen and the poetry of R.S. Thomas, but what is told the eye and what is told the ear are two different things ...[55]

51 Kyffin Williams, *Portraits* (Llandysul, 2007), p. 8.

52 For Williams's portrait of Jones, and the relationship between the two men, see Peter Lord, *Relationships with Pictures: an Oblique Autobiography* (Cardigan, 2013), pp. 177–188.

53 NLW Welsh Arts Council Archive, Exhibition Files, A/E/11.

54 John Petts, ed., Catalogue to the exhibition *Contemporary Welsh Painting and Sculpture* (Cardiff, 1953).

55 NLW, Welsh Arts Council Archive, Exhibition Files, A/E/11. The exhibition was entitled '30 Welsh Paintings of Today'. It also visited Scotland. For the apparent contradictions in the attitude of Saunders Lewis see, Jones, 'Exhibiting Welshness', p. 120. Lewis's introduction to the exhibition was printed only in Welsh, but the English version quoted is his own. His reference to the 'pen' of M.E. Eldridge was to the sheep-pen in her picture *Hill Sheep, Corris*.

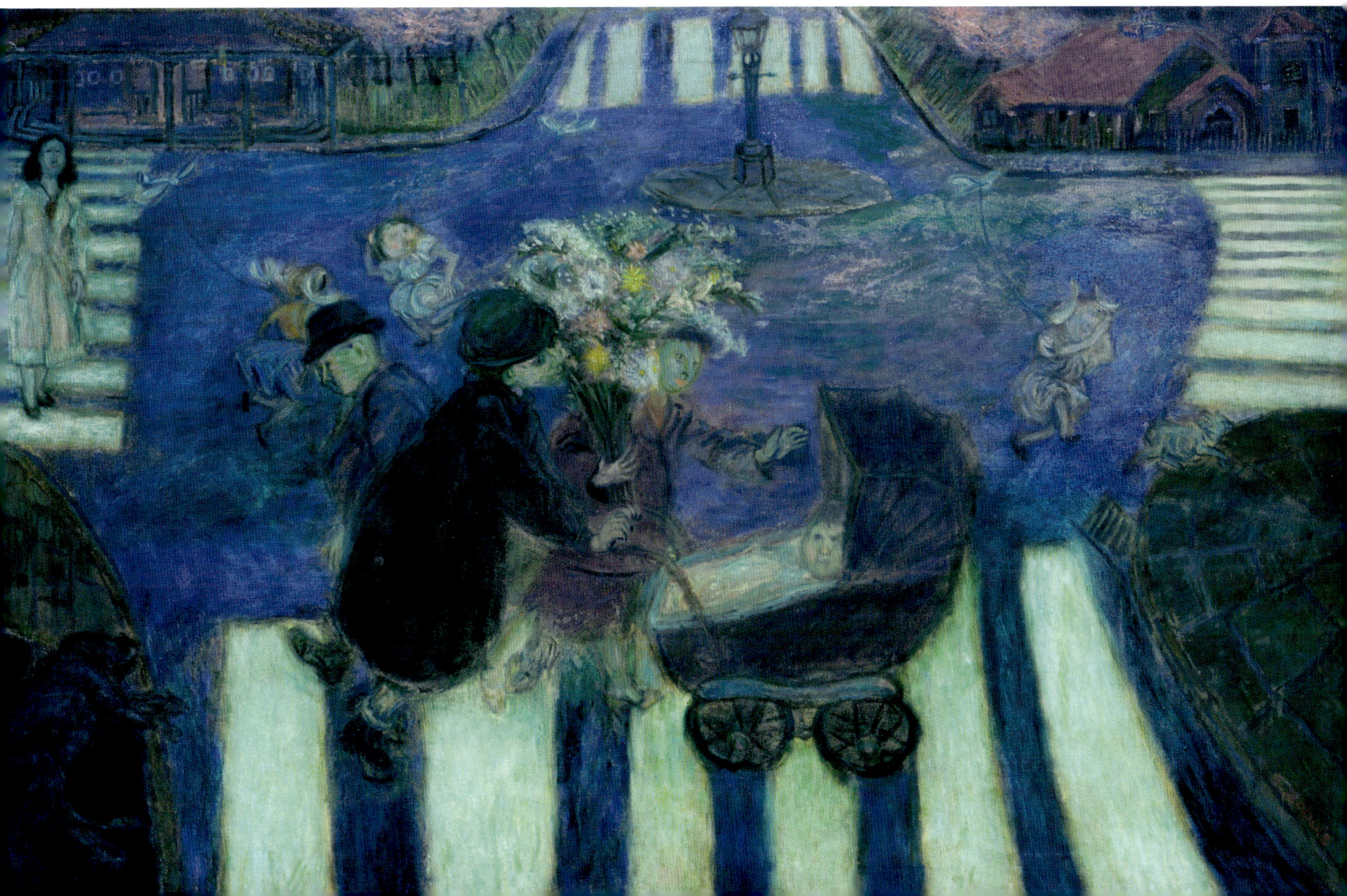

56 NLW Welsh Arts Council Archive, Exhibition Files, A/E/15. Levy's work in popularising the visual arts extended to a pioneering role in television. See Lord, *Relationships with Pictures*, pp. 170–172.

57 The work is now relocated to Glyndŵr University, Wrexham.

The success of the 1953 exhibition gave rise to a long series that became known simply as 'The Welsh Open'. Especially in the early years, the Open generated considerable excitement. Mervyn Levy, now established on his career path as a critic and interpreter of art, reviewed the 1955 show on the radio:

> Anyone who missed this sparkling exhibition at Cardiff should take the next suitable train or bus to Newport, or they can walk or run – but go they must, if it is at all possible, or if they have the merest interest in painting or sculpture. And if you haven't bothered a great deal about the visual arts before, well this is just the sort of exhibition that will kindle an undying love.[56]

opposite
363. Joan Baker,
Miss Cotton, 1949,
oil, 53.8x39.2

The humane ethos of much of the Welsh painting of the period stood in contrast to the global context of the developing Cold War. Although not widely acknowledged at the time, both tendencies informed one of the most remarkable large-scale works ever painted in Wales. M.E. Eldridge began a commission to decorate the nurses' refectory at an orthopaedic hospital near Gobowen in 1953.[57] In stylistic terms, *The Dance of Life*, which took three years to complete, revealed the painter's early association with English Neo-Romanticism and the work of Stanley Spencer. For her imagery, she drew on the landscapes and wildlife of Wales and Italy, familiar to her from before the war, to question the erosion of the relationship between human cultures and the natural world.

362. Mildred Elsie Eldridge,
The Dance of Life, panel 6,
1953–6, oil, h.160

Although she would maintain a relatively low public profile, the work of Eldridge also signified one of the most influential changes that affected Welsh painting in the post-war era. Along with Esther Grainger, Joan Baker, Nan Youngman, Brenda Chamberlain and Ray

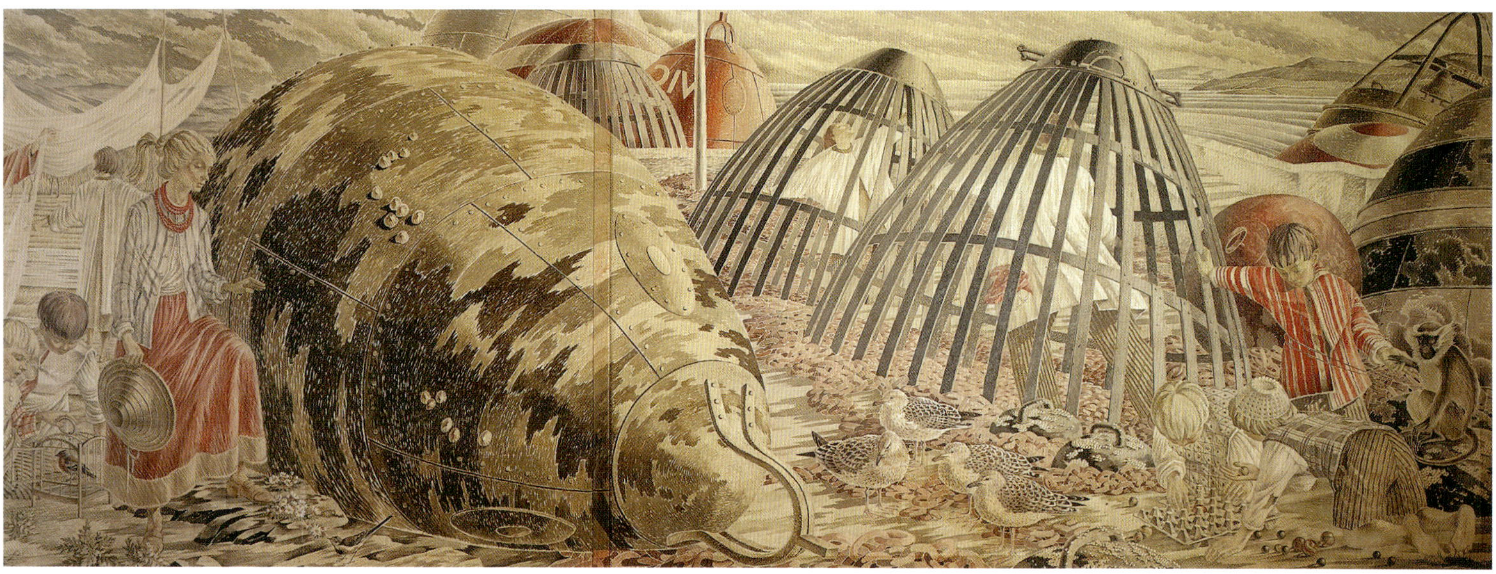

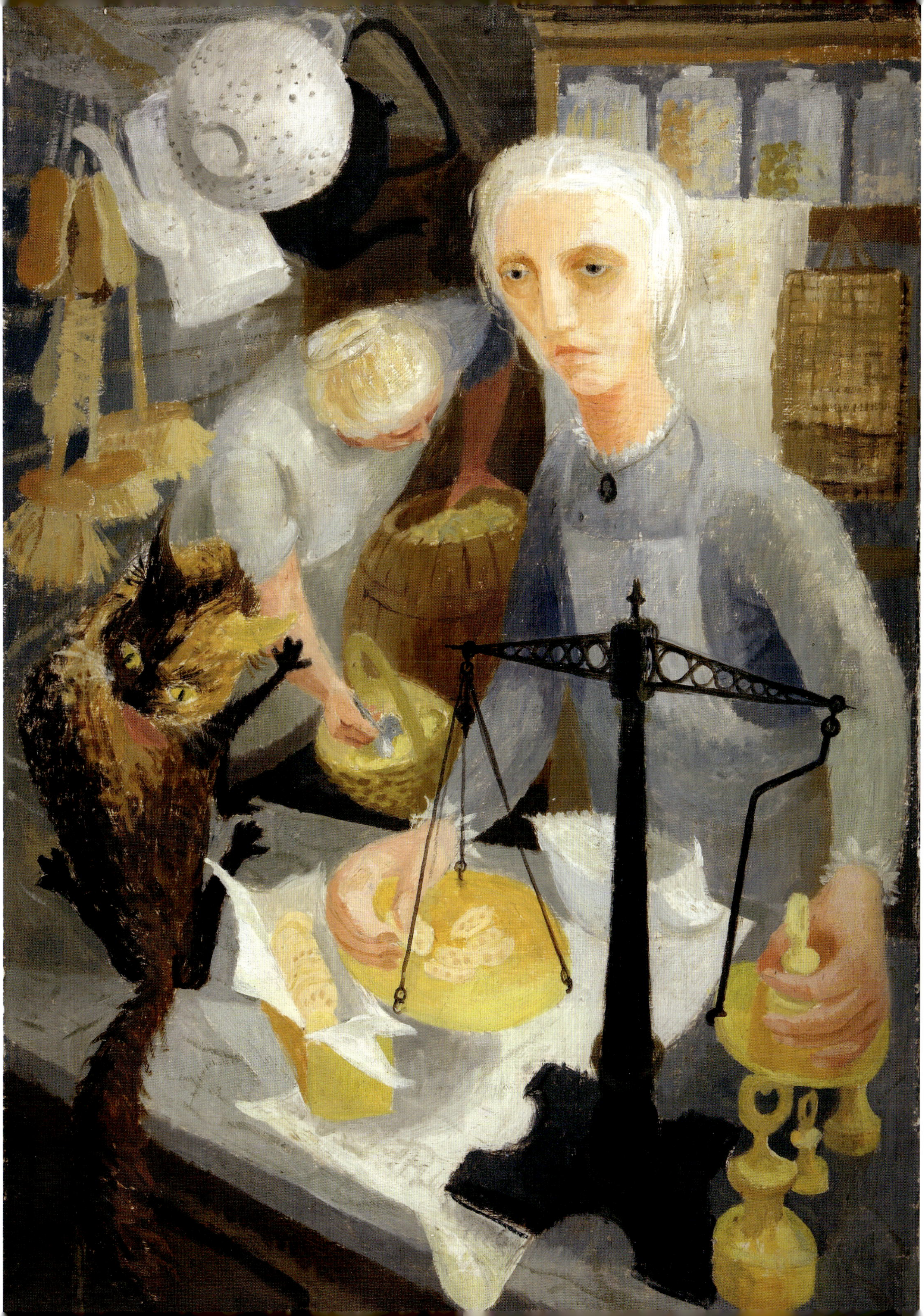

364. Claudia Williams, *Family on the Beach*, 1957, oil, 78.0x102

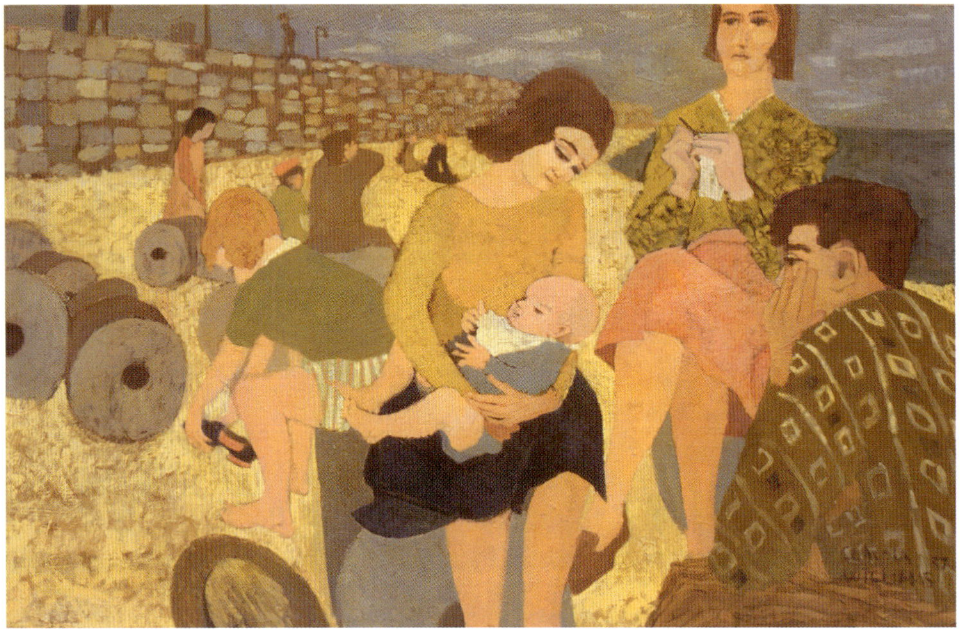

Howard-Jones, Eldridge formed part of an unprecedented influx of women into the art world. In 1952, Claudia Williams joined them in the public domain when she exhibited for the first of many times at the National Eisteddfod – though work made when she was still at school had earlier attracted press attention in London.[58] By 1957, when her picture

365. Vera Bassett, *Gossip*, late 1960s, watercolour, 34.2x45.7

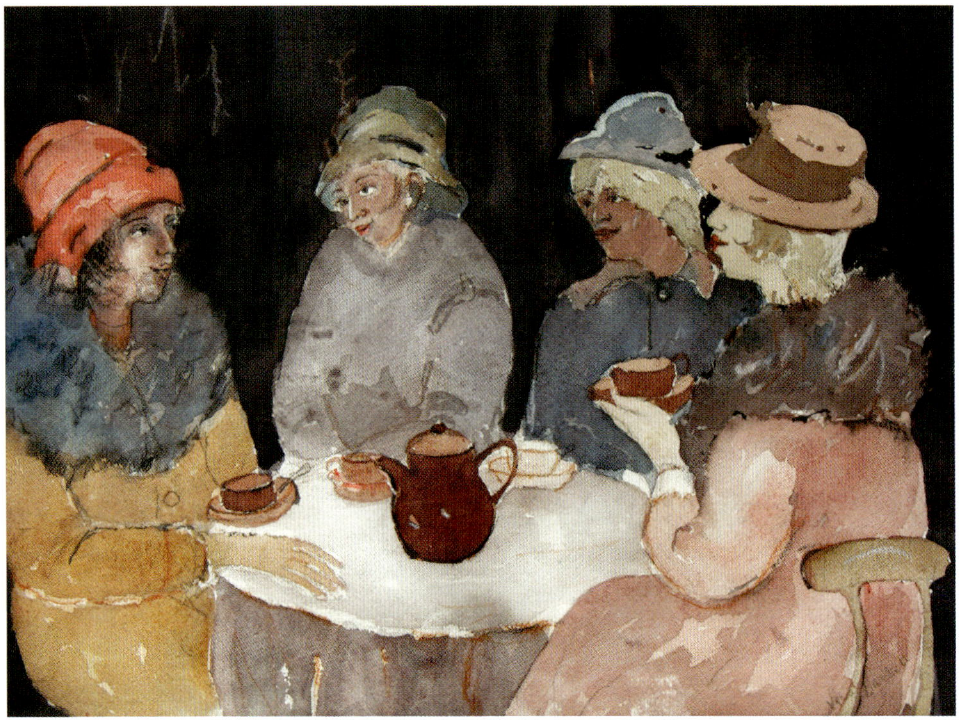

58 Harry Heuser and Robert Meyrick, *Claudia Williams. Intimate Acquaintance* (Bristol, 2013).

59 Mervyn Levy, 'Vera Bassett', *Dock Leaves*, 6, 16 (1955), p. 29. See also Michael Keen, exhibition catalogue *"A finely wrought line", The work of Vera Bassett 1912–1997* (Carmarthen, n.d.).

60 The exhibition was shared with the work of Frances Hodgkins and Ethel Walker.

61 Augustus John, *Finishing Touches* (London, 1964), p. 81. See also Holroyd, *Augustus John. The New Biography* (London, 1996), pp. 570–3.

62 For the painter in her own voice, see *Gwen John. Letters and Notebooks*, ed. Ceridwen Lloyd-Morgan, (London, 2004).

Family on the Beach was adjudged a close second to Chapman's Gold Medal winning *View in Merthyr Tydfil Valley*, her career was established. Williams's picture dealt with themes that she would pursue consistently throughout her long life – the social interaction of women, or of women and children, presented with a monumentality influenced by the work of Stanley Spencer, whom she had met as a teenager, and of Chamberlain, whom she met on Bardsey. Also emerging in this period, and taking women as her primary subject matter, Vera Bassett's idiosyncratic vision did not manifest the symbolist overtones of Williams, but relied instead on acute observation of the everyday world. Mervyn Levy particularly admired her work, and thought her able 'to express the very essence of the Welsh flair for interpreting aesthetic matters through the crystal flame of the lyrical, poetic eye'. He linked her to Innes, David Jones and, significantly, to Gwen John.[59] Largely forgotten in the metropolitan art world, John had died in 1939. Her brother organised a memorial exhibition at a private London gallery in 1946 which initiated a resurgence of interest, culminating in 1952 in a show at the Tate.[60] These exhibitions, and Augustus John's prescient remark that 'In 50 years time, I will be known as the brother of Gwen John', re-established her reputation and, in so doing, contributed to the beginnings of a slow process of change in the respect accorded to women artists in a male-dominated profession:

> Few on meeting this retiring person in black, with her tiny hands and feet, a soft, almost inaudible voice, and delicate Pembrokeshire accent, would have guessed that here was the greatest woman artist of her age, or, as I think, of any other.[61]

Despite the fact that as an adult she had little direct professional contact with Wales, her rising status added a prestigious name to the canon of Welsh artists, the importance of which would deepen markedly in the context of the resurgence of feminism in the 1970s.[62]

From her teenage years at home in Eifionydd, Claudia Williams figured in a complicated interaction of individuals, all of whom would play an important role in the evolution of the post-war art world. She met John Petts at the Caseg Press in Llanystumdwy, and as a consequence also Jonah Jones, who worked as assistant there. Jones was born and grew up in

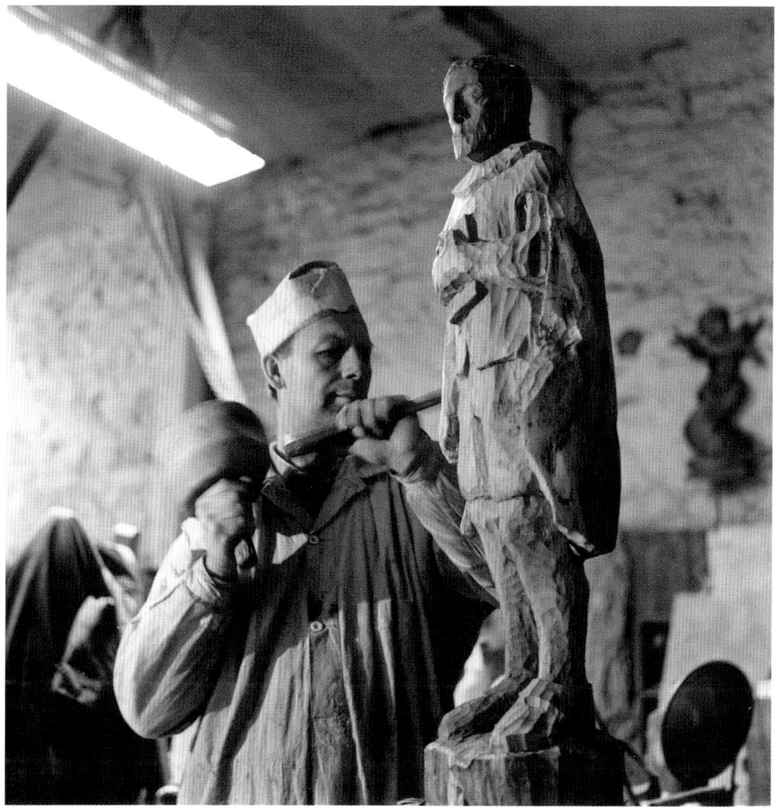

366. *Jonah Jones in his studio at Tremadog*, 1962

the north-east of England but, conscious of the fact that his grandfather hailed from the Caerphilly area, felt drawn to work in Wales. Meeting with Petts in the Forces proved the crucial event in propelling him into art as a career.[63] Jones temporarily left Wales to pursue a craft-oriented training in Eric Gill's workshops in England, but returned to settle in Caernarfonshire and in the 1960s would achieve a high profile both as an artist – primarily a sculptor – and as a commentator and interpreter of the Welsh art scene. But it was the last of the acquaintances made by Claudia Williams in Eifionydd that proved to be the most

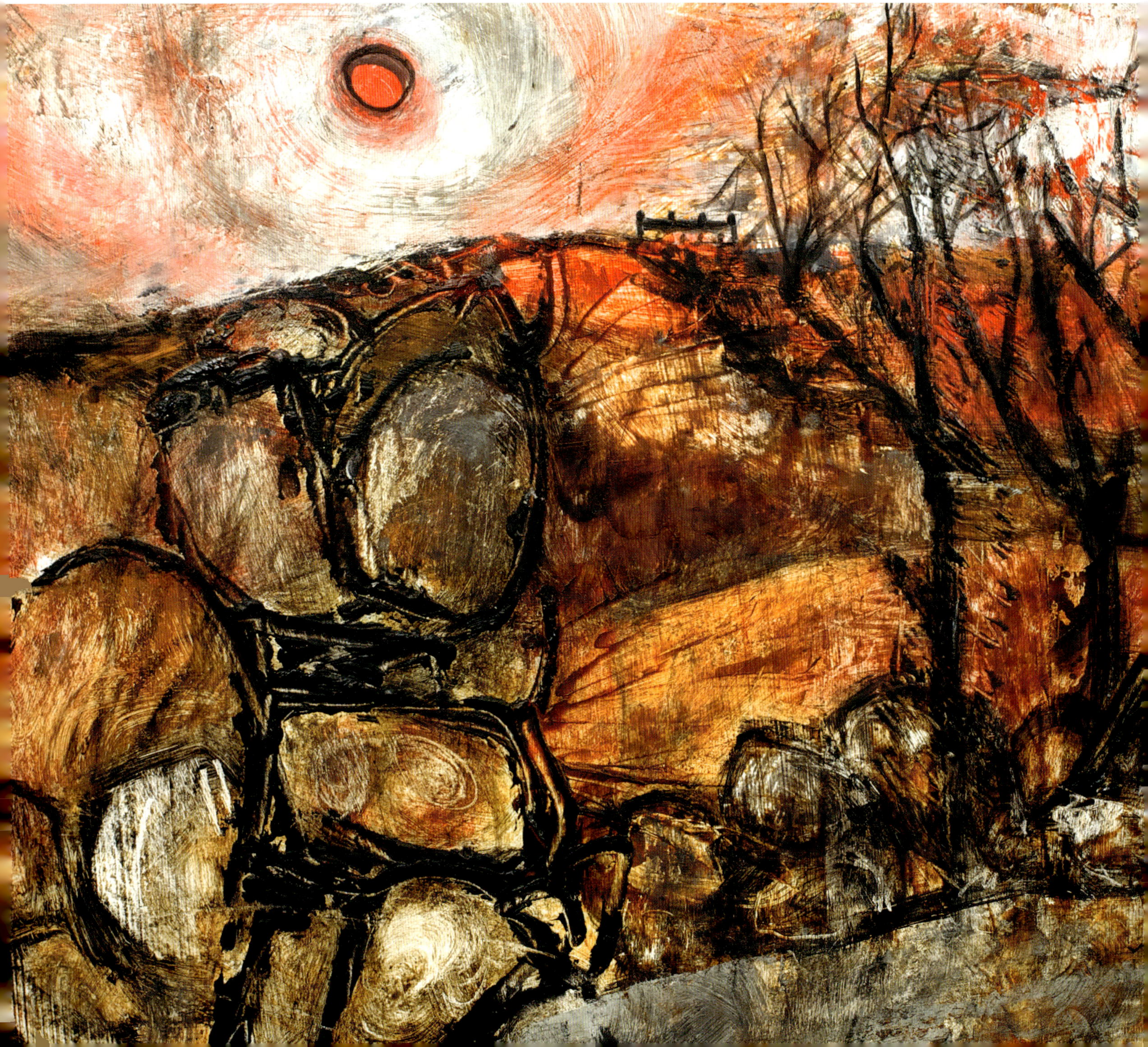

important to her. On holiday from Chelsea School of Art, she met a neighbour, Gwilym Prichard, newly released from National Service in the army and uncertain of his future direction. Williams's example stimulated Prichard to develop his interest in painting into a career.[64] In 1953 he went to Birmingham to train, where he was joined by Williams, and they subsequently married. It would develop into a remarkable partnership. Working in close proximity but always retaining distinct artistic personalities, Williams and Prichard would exhibit their work, often together, for over fifty years.

63 Jonah Jones in *Artists in Wales 2*, ed. Meic Stephens (Llandysul, 1973), pp. 104–6.

64 Harry Heuser and Robert Meyrick, *Gwilym Prichard. A Lifetime's Gazing* (Bristol, 2013).

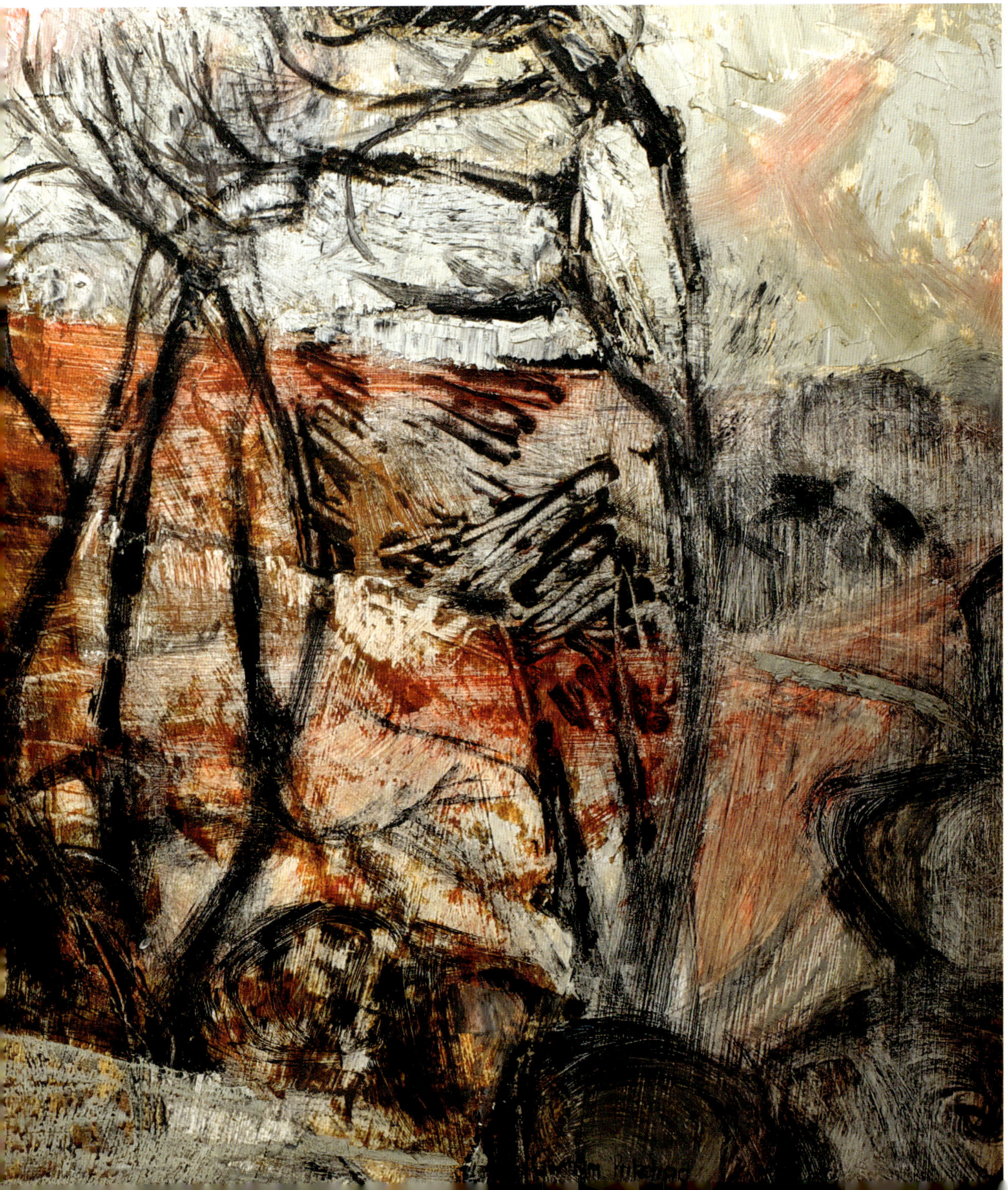

367. Gwilym Prichard, *Thorn Trees*, 1960, oil, 32x61

Modernism – two decades of the 56 Group

In 1957, in his book *The Artist in Wales* – the first attempt to write a narrative history of the subject – David Bell expressed the view that the 'awareness of environment characterizes the painting which is being done in South Wales today.'[65] For some, Welsh Environmentalism, widely exposed to the public in the Open and the annual eisteddfod exhibitions, remained a credible concept into the 1960s. As late as 1963, the Arts Council organised an exhibition that presented together the work of Zobole and Chamberlain, artists of 'very different background and experience', but who 'share, however, an ability to interpret through painting the places in which they work and their approach is lyrical and poetic.'[66] Nevertheless, despite the range and richness of this work, by 1956 suggestions were being made that Welsh Environmentalism, whether focussed on rural and upland landscape, human relationships, or the Valleys, had become a limiting convention, if not a cliché. Even Petts, who had played an important role both as artist and administrator in the evolution of the idea, began to sense a wind of change, blowing in particular from the direction of the United States. In 1956, in London, the Tate Gallery presented an exhibition of American abstract art that exercised a profound influence on aesthetic fashions in England. The transformatory effect was not unlike that experienced in the United States itself following the Armory Show of 1913, in which the Johns and Innes had participated, except that the influence, four decades later, travelled in the opposite trans-Atlantic direction. Within a short space of time, concepts of Englishness derived from the Neo-Romantic movement, and associated socially aware realist imagery, were relegated to the museum basement.

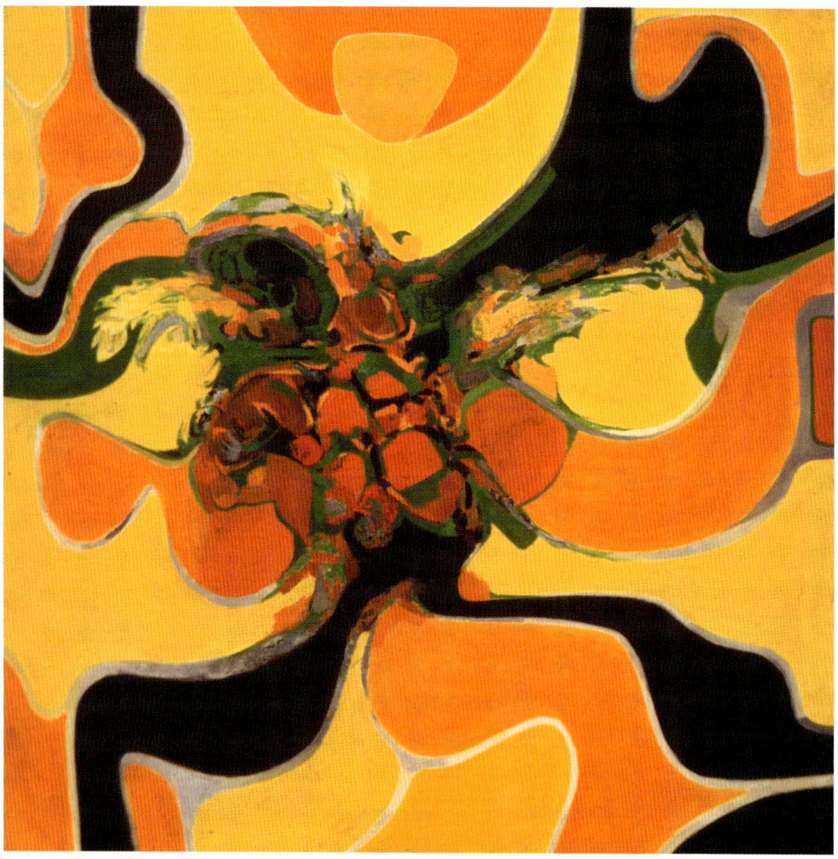

368. John Elwyn, *Enigmatic Blossom*, 1967, oil, 60x60

They were replaced by a tidal wave of non-figurative painting and sculpture – redefined as 'construction' – that emphasised the process of making art for itself, rather than the application of the process to the transformation of observed subject matter.

In Wales, some painters remained faithful to their earlier vision, though even in the work of John Elwyn and Ernest Zobole the formal influence of non-figurative painting was discernable in an emphasis on surface pattern that became evident in works produced in the 1960s. Others were entirely swept away. Koppel, working after 1964 in the art school world at Liverpool, abandoned the paint brush for the spray gun and devoted himself exclusively to making large, non-figurative colour-field works.[67]

In one of a series of informative artist interviews conducted by Goronwy Powell for the *Western Mail* in 1956, John Petts complained that Welsh artists 'persistently confine themselves to their own, often narrow, environments'. The virtue of cultural rootedness had became the vice of parochialism. Deep awareness of the particular would be, forthwith, shallow provincialism.

In Wales this philosophical shift created particularly stark divisions, coming as it did after a period of engagement by intellectuals with the exploration of the relationship between visual art (along with music and literature) and nationhood. Since the new art denied relationship to particular place, it tended to attract individuals politically unsympathetic to national aspirations, many of whom had no sense of personal identity with Wales and who retained a strong inclination to establish metropolitan reputations. Significantly, among the Powell interviewees in 1956 was the painter David Tinker, then in his early 30s. Powell sensed an 'air of rebellion' in Tinker, reacting 'against what he considers the prosaic, environment-ridden style of painting he sees done by Welsh artists.'[68] Tinker was a lecturer at Cardiff School of Art – one of many teachers from outside Wales who found work as a result of expanding provision of art education in the post-war period that continued through the 1950s and accelerated in the 1960s. Among his colleagues was Eric Malthouse, on whose suggestion moves were made to establish a small group of like-minded painters and sculptors who might exhibit together. The initial invitation to other artists included a vaguely worded manifesto but it was not adopted, since the thirteen involved represented a relatively broad aesthetic spectrum. They included Ernest Zobole, Will Roberts and Brenda Chamberlain, all previously associated by critics with Environmentalism. Chamberlain rejected the invitation, but Zobole and Roberts agreed, as did Arthur Giardelli, who would emerge as one of the two constant figures, alongside Tinker, sustaining the group over many years, as other members came and went.[69]

65 David Bell, *The Artist in Wales* (London, 1957), p. 172 For nearly thirty years, the book was considered by many to be authoritative in the field. However, its often patronising tone aroused some hostility from the beginning, for which see Mervyn Levy's review in *Wales*, 33 (October 1958), pp. 68–70. Bell had opened his text by repeating his belief that the Welsh, 'a small peasant people', had 'At no time since the Norman conquest at any rate ... had any visual artistic tradition.' Bell further observed that the term 'masterpiece' 'looks rather thin when dressed up in Welsh flannel.' The book's establishment pedigree was underlined by the fact that it was written at the instigation of Sir Ben Bowen Thomas, Permanent Secretary to the Welsh Department of the Ministry of Education. Before the war, Thomas had been the first warden of Coleg Harlech and a close associate of its founder, Thomas Jones.

66 Tom Cross, Foreword to the exhibition catalogue, *Two Painters. Brenda Chamberlain. Ernest Zobole* (Cardiff, 1963). Cross was then the Art Officer of the Welsh Committee of the Arts Council.

67 It is significant of the transitory nature of the fashion of the period that the publication associated with the retrospective exhibition of Koppel's work at Berlin in 2009–10 illustrates just one of these works made after the mid-1960s. Heinz and Renate Koppel acquired a house and studio in Ceredigion in 1969, and returned from Liverpool to live there permanently in 1974.

68 The *Western Mail* interviews were conducted in 1955 and 1956 by Goronwy Powell: Tinker, 27 January 1956; Petts, 2 March 1956.

69 The other founder members were Trevor Bates (Newport School of Art), Hubert Dalwood (Newport School of Art), Robert Hunter (Trinity College, Carmarthen), John Wright (Hereford School of Art until 1959, then Newport), Heinz Koppel (who left Wales for London in this year), George Fairley (Swansea School of Art). In 1964 Will Roberts became the first to leave, remarking dismissively, in retrospect, that 'The 56 Group was set up by art school teachers who wanted to sell their work.' Curtis, *Welsh Painters Talking*, p. 93.

Notwithstanding the range of original participants, the prime-movers of the 56 Group, as they called themselves, were motivated by antagonism to what they regarded as Welsh provincialism, and by their concomitant attraction to the metropolitan fashion for non-figurative, formalist art.[70] Tinker and the academic J. Roger Webster, an early supporter, were the most vocal:

> Wales has no tradition in the visual arts. This has often been discussed and analysed; but whatever may be said in explanation the situation remains and must be recognised by any contemporary artist working in the Principality.
>
> As a result, some Welsh artists have turned to the possibility of creating a tradition, and this is, perhaps, even more ludicrous than refusing to believe that such a tradition does not exist. How can a tradition be created overnight as some wish fulfilment? As far as Welsh art is concerned, it is apparently sufficient merely to paint pictures *of* Wales ...[71]

Crucially, as Director of the Welsh Committee of the Arts Council from 1961, Webster would persist in his emphasis both on the alleged poverty (or, indeed, absence) of visual art in Wales, and the associated idea that excellence was only to be found in the art of the metropolis. In 1965 he reflected that 'The appointment of specialist art teachers in schools and colleges throughout Wales in the past decade has meant that, for the first time, a number of professional artists have been able to live and work in the Principality.' This untruth, whether propagated through ignorance or politically motivated denial, became a received wisdom of those who considered themselves modernisers, repeated mantra-like into the 1980s. Webster enlarged on the serious handicap that working in Wales apparently represented to creativity. By this time, Tinker was head of the School of Art in Aberystwyth. Robert Hunter, one of the original members of 56 Group, worked at Trinity College, Carmarthen:

369. *56 Group exhibition at Tenby*, 1957, from left, the artist member George Fairley, Philip Jones, Assistant Director (Wales) of the Arts Council, with artist members Arthur Giardelli, Robert Hunter and John Wright in front of *Sorting Fish* by Eric Malthouse.

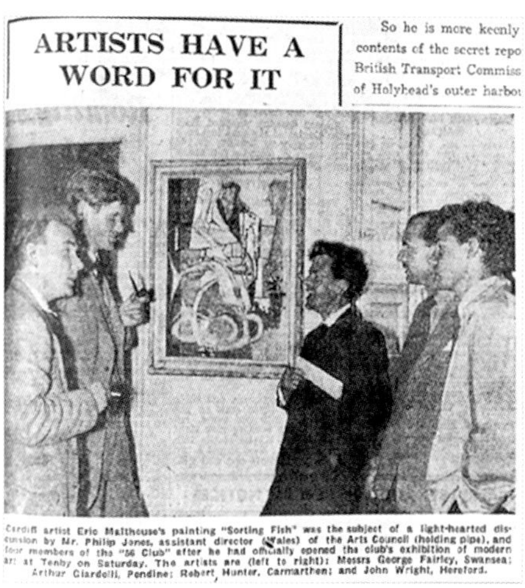
ARTISTS HAVE A WORD FOR IT

So he is more keenly
contents of the secret repo
British Transport Commiss
of Holyhead's outer harbo

Cardiff artist Eric Malthouse's painting "Sorting Fish" was the subject of a light-hearted discussion by Mr. Philip Jones, assistant director (Wales) of the Arts Council (holding pipe), and four members of the "56 Club" after he had officially opened the club's exhibition of modern art at Tenby on Saturday. The artists are (left to right): Messrs George Fairley, Swansea; Arthur Giardelli, Pendine; Robert, Hunter, Carmarthen; and John Wright, Hereford.

> ... these artists have many problems, the greatest of which is, perhaps, their isolation from metropolitan art centres ... Both Robert Hunter and David Tinker have triumphantly overcome this limitation. Although living in West Wales these painters have an intimate knowledge of contemporary art, and their work would look at home in any international exhibition.[72]

Characteristic of the rhetoric of the group was an assertion that the old guard of Welsh art had opposed them from the beginning. Tinker and Giardelli would long imply that they had been forced to go outside Wales for their first exhibition, which took place at Worcester in 1957. In fact, the group's initial approach to the Glynn Vivian Art Gallery had been welcomed by David Bell, and implementation was slowed only by the bureaucracy of a public institution. Furthermore, the Worcester exhibition was grant aided by the Welsh Committee of the Arts Council and it was opened by Rollo Charles, curator of art at the National Museum. The show transferred to the Museum the following month. The 56 Group was promoted by the national institutions from the beginning. By 1961 it was in receipt of an annual grant from the Calouste Gulbenkian Foundation, the Arts Council was represented at meetings, and Patricia Cross, married to the Arts Council's assistant director, was the group secretary. The Council was soon awarding them an annual grant. From the outset it was an 'official avant-garde', as Charles would later acknowledge.[73] In response, the painter Harry Holland remarked that 'To have an "official" avant-garde (if the words mean what I think they do) would be exactly like having an official revolution, which is no revolution at all.'[74]

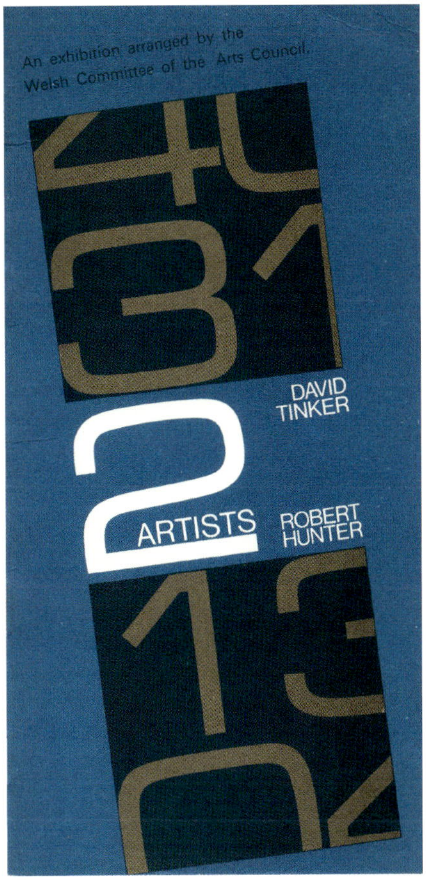

370. Kevin Eccleston, *Cover of the exhibition catalogue '2 Artists David Tinker Robert Hunter'*, 1965, 25x12.7

Arts Council support for the 56 Group through the 1960s did not result in the withdrawal of support from the exhibition of other artists, or from the creation of occasional historical exhibitions.[75] Furthermore, the Council assisted with grant aid a new private gallery which provided a commercial outlet in Cardiff for contemporary artists. The Howard Roberts Gallery opened in 1956, and showed work by a wide range of Welsh painters and sculptors.[76] Nevertheless, the high status accorded the 56 Group and its member artists by the establishment was regularly reinforced. In 1969, aligning itself with the highly divisive celebration of the investiture of the Prince of Wales at Caernarfon, the Arts Council embarked on a comprehensive review of art in Wales in the twentieth century, comprising three sections: 'The Early Years', 'Today', and 'Tomorrow ...?' The 'Early Years' were defined as 1900 until 1956, thereby iconising the latter year, a position emphasised by the division of the presentation of 'Today' into two exhibitions, one of them devoted exclusively to the 56 Group. The underlying politics of this decision, made by an arts establishment dominated by Labour Party sympathisers in a period of perceived threat to their long-standing hegemony in the south of Wales by the rise of Plaid Cymru, was

70 For the history of the group see David Moore, *A Taste of the Avant-garde. 56 Group Wales. 56 Years* (Brecon, 2012).

71 J.Roger Webster, 'National Tradition in the Visual Arts in Wales', *Welsh Anvil/Yr Einion*, viii (1958), pp. 108–18. Webster's reference to past discussion of Welsh tradition was surely directed at Bell's *The Artist in Wales*. From whatever side it came, all the rhetoric surrounding the issue obscured a fundamentally important conceptual distinction between the existence of 'tradition' and the existence of a body of works of art made in the past. Either wilfully or in ignorance, writers conflated the two, so that to remark on the absence of tradition was effectively to assert the absence of art. For a précis and analysis of this issue, see Peter Lord, *The Meaning of Pictures: Images of Personal, Social and Political Identity* (Cardiff, 2009), pp. 187–98.

72 J.Roger Webster in the catalogue to the Arts Council exhibition, *Two Artists: Robert Hunter, David Tinker* (Cardiff, 1966), no pagination.

73 Rollo Charles, in the exhibition catalogue *56/20:Grŵp 56 Cymru/56 Group Wales: Twentieth Anniversary Retrospective Exhibition, 1956–1976*, (1976), no pagination.

74 Harry Holland, 'Anniversary Exhibition of the 56 Group Wales', *Link* 4 (Summer, 1976), quoted in Moore, *A Taste of the Avant-Garde*, p. 45.

75 See Jones, 'Exhibiting Welshness', Appendix 2, 'Touring exhibitions organised by the Welsh Arts Council 1946–1981'.

76 Howard Roberts, 'The Howard Roberts Gallery', *Anglo-Welsh Review* 41 (1969), pp. 169–74.

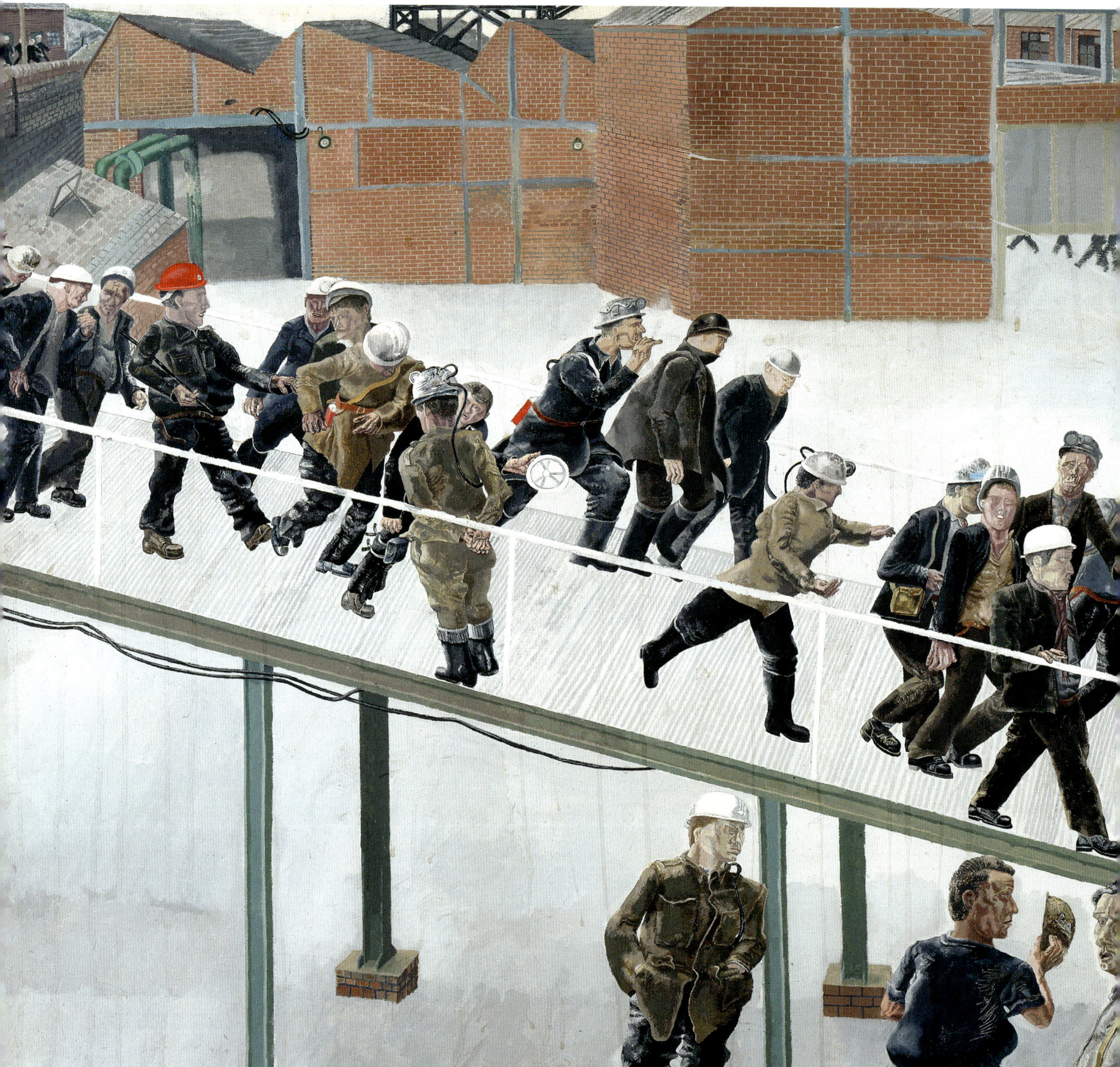

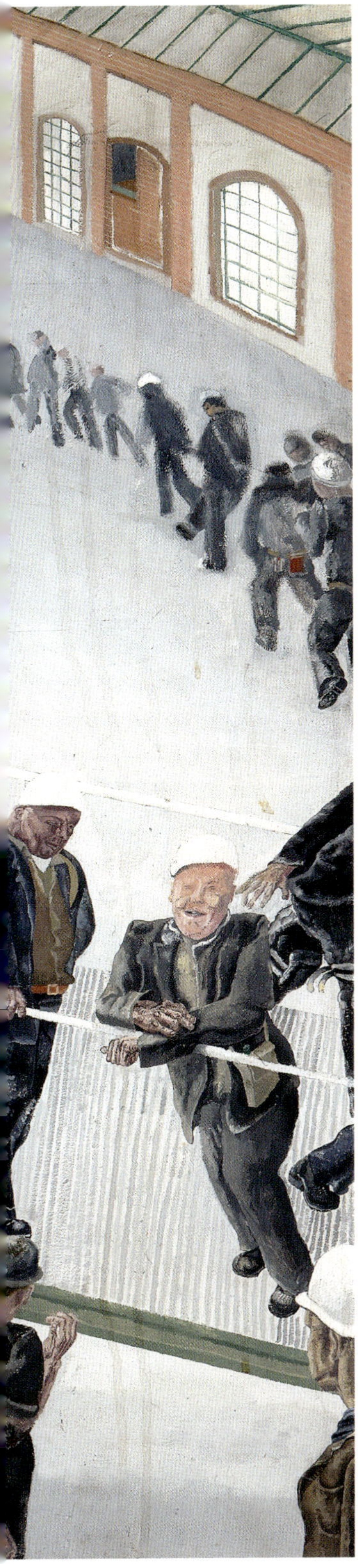

371. Jack Crabtree,
Going Down the Ramp,
1975, oil, 90.2x125.7

clearly expressed in the associated rhetoric. The exhibition catalogue noted the initiation of the Group as a 'protest against art which the founders regarded as narrowly and sentimentally nationalistic.'[77] The implication was that the formation of the 56 Group had represented the start of an enlightened era, now under renewed threat from regressive nationalists. All but three of the twenty artists shown were drawn from Newport or Cardiff colleges of art, and almost all produced non-figurative work. None was based in north Wales. Even in the complementary 'Today – Invited Artists' exhibition, of the twenty-two participants all but five were associated with the Cardiff or Newport colleges. Only one – Jonah Jones – was based in the north. Not a single woman was included in either exhibition.[78] This extraordinarily biased misrepresentation largely escaped critical comment, such was the authority of the Arts Council and the exclusive male, art-college network at the end of the decade. Five years after the 'Art in Wales' exhibitions, in 1974 the Arts Council opened 'Oriel', its own gallery in Cardiff. The 56 Group was again favoured, and staged the inaugural exhibition.[79]

Two years later, on the occasion of yet another Arts Council-sponsored exhibition of the 56 Group, celebrating its twentieth anniversary, the painter Bryn Richards observed that 'it must be considered more of an exhibition club for teachers who pass through the local Art Colleges than the spearhead of revolutionary art in Wales',[80] and indeed, many of those who participated in the group's exhibitions proved to be transitory figures. A few of them, notably Jack Crabtree, achieved a public profile beyond the art colleges during their stay, but it may well be significant that Crabtree, who joined the staff at Newport in 1966, was a figurative painter, whose images of the coal industry refreshed the long tradition.[81] His success pointed to a paradox within the agenda of 56 Group that had, in fact been grudgingly acknowledged by Webster at the outset. Professing

77 Edward Lucie-Smith, Preface to the exhibition catalogue *Today – 56 Group Wales*, (Cardiff, 1969).

78 The only discernable female involvement was the catalogue to 'The Early Years' exhibition, which was written by the art historian Shelagh Hourahane, working under Tinker at the Aberystwyth School of Art.

79 At a structural level, two changes occurred under the direction of J.Roger Webster that indicated a palliative response to the politics of the period. In 1967, the year after Plaid Cymru had taken from Labour the parliamentary seat of Carmarthen, the Welsh Committee of the Arts Council of Great Britain was reincorporated as The Welsh Arts Council, in practice a largely cosmetic change. The establishment in the north of the country of the first of three Regional Arts Associations would have more practical effect. See Jones, *Exhibiting Welshness*, pp. 135–7.

80 Bryn Richards, '56 Group Wales, Twentieth Anniversary Retrospective Exhibition, 1956 – 1976', *Anglo-Welsh Review*, vol. 26, no. 57 (Autumn 1976), pp. 274–6. Richards's observation echoed that made by Will Roberts, twelve years earlier, see above, n. 69.

81 See Tony Curtis, 'The Last Shift: The Welsh mining industry in art', in *Certain Welsh Artists*, ed.Iwan Bala (Bridgend, 1999), pp. 31–51.

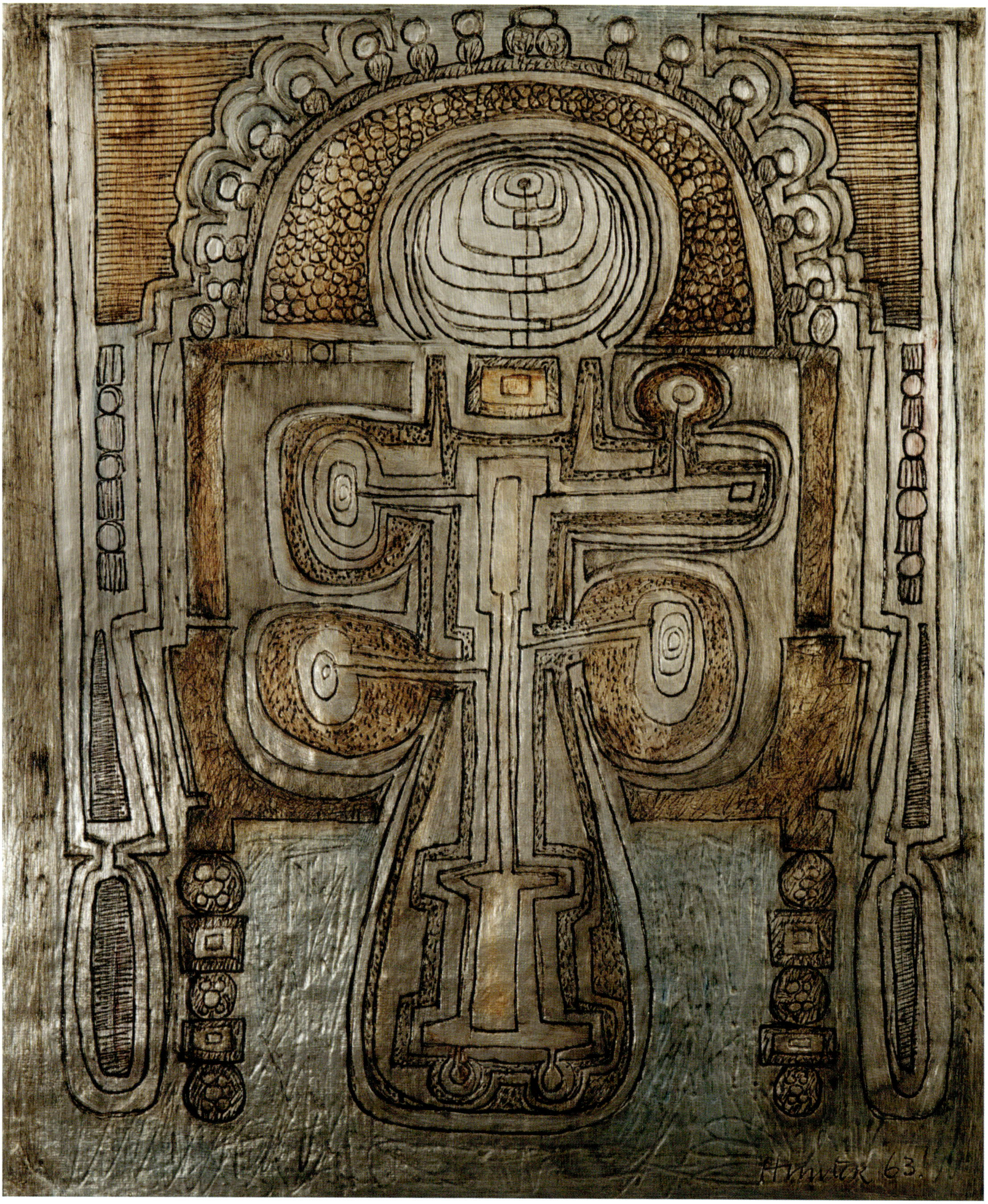

to be internationalists whose art transcended specificities of place, nevertheless they chose to come together on the basis of their particular location, even if acknowledged by some of them only in geographical, rather than socio-political, terms. Although not presented positively until 1967, when at Giardelli's suggestion the word 'Wales' was added to the group's official title, aspects of the particular context in which they lived became a factor in the work of artists such as Robert Hunter and Terry Setch, who settled and worked in Wales for a long period, and in that of those few who had been born or brought up in that country, notably Glyn Jones.

372. Robert Hunter, *Celtic Icon*, 1963, mixed media, 26.2x22

Robert Hunter's employment of patterns derived from pre-historic and Celtic Christian carving acknowledged the cultural particularity of the place in which he worked, though simultaneously acted as metaphors for his distance from it. He inverted the tradition of Celticists who had sought to adopt the symbol systems of the Welsh past as identifiers of a modern identity – and, indeed of contemporaries outside 56 Group, including Jonah Jones, who would employ the same references in works such as his memorial to the princes of Gwynedd at Aberffraw. Hunter 'put down marks which look as if they could be interpreted but confronted by them the intellect finds that it cannot go far enough, and it has to give way to an emotional acceptance.' His attitude to the living Welsh-language culture that surrounded him in Carmarthenshire echoed his response to these ancient symbols. His choice was not to learn the language, but to profess sympathy with it on the curious grounds that 'I like the sound it makes.'[82]

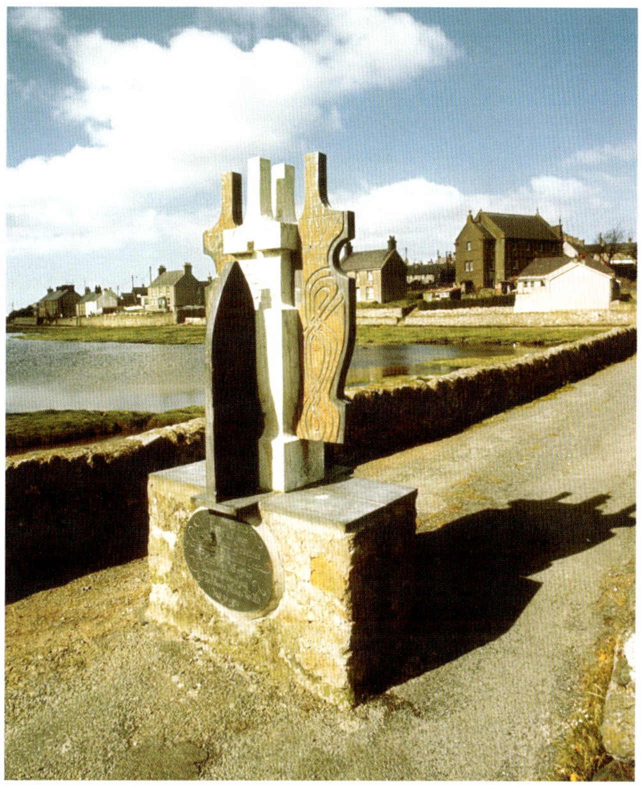

373. Jonah Jones, *Y Tywysogion*, Aberffraw, 1969, slate and Portland stone, h. 163

82 Stephens, ed., *Artists in Wales*, 2, p. 55, and previous quotation.

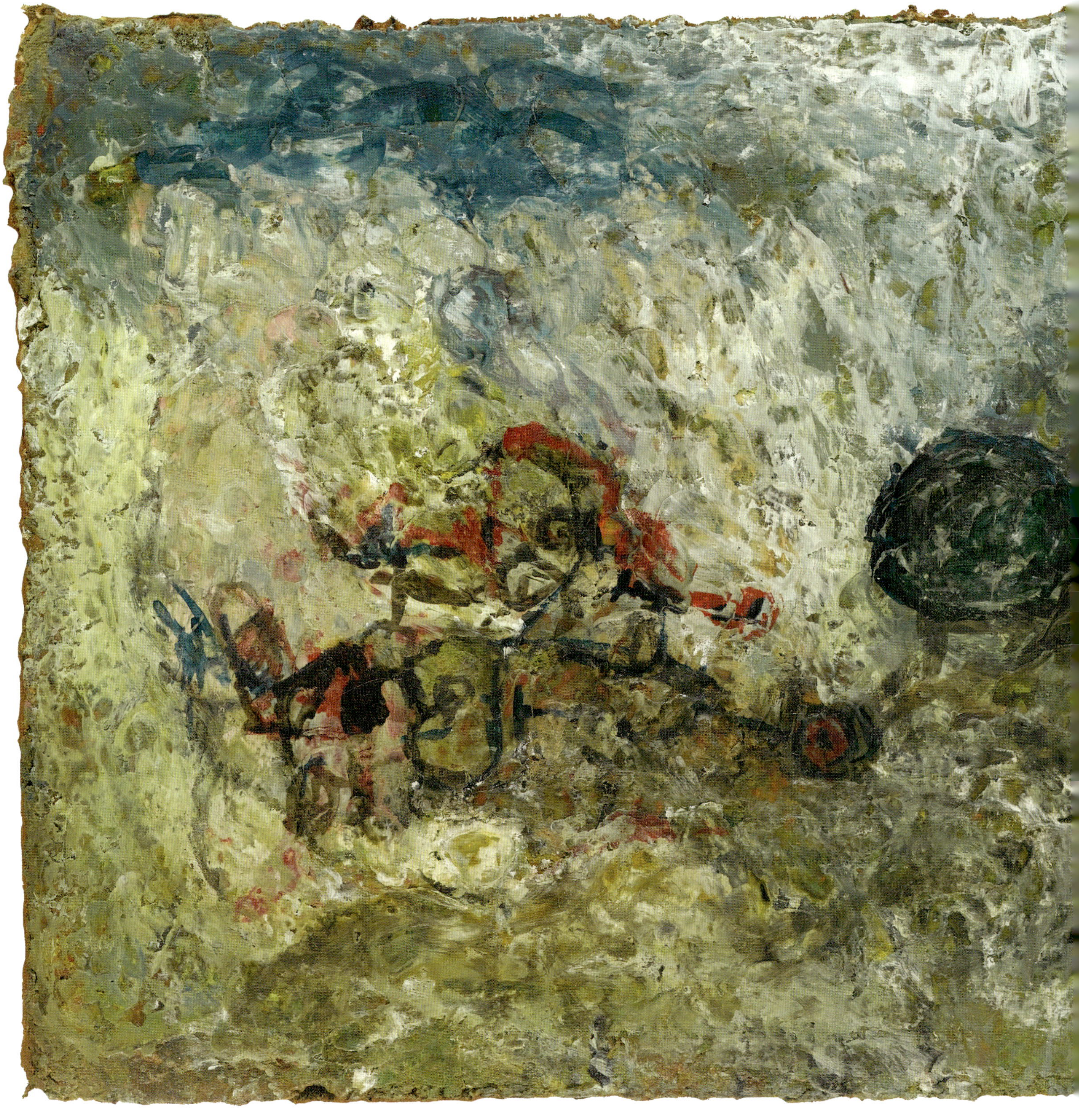

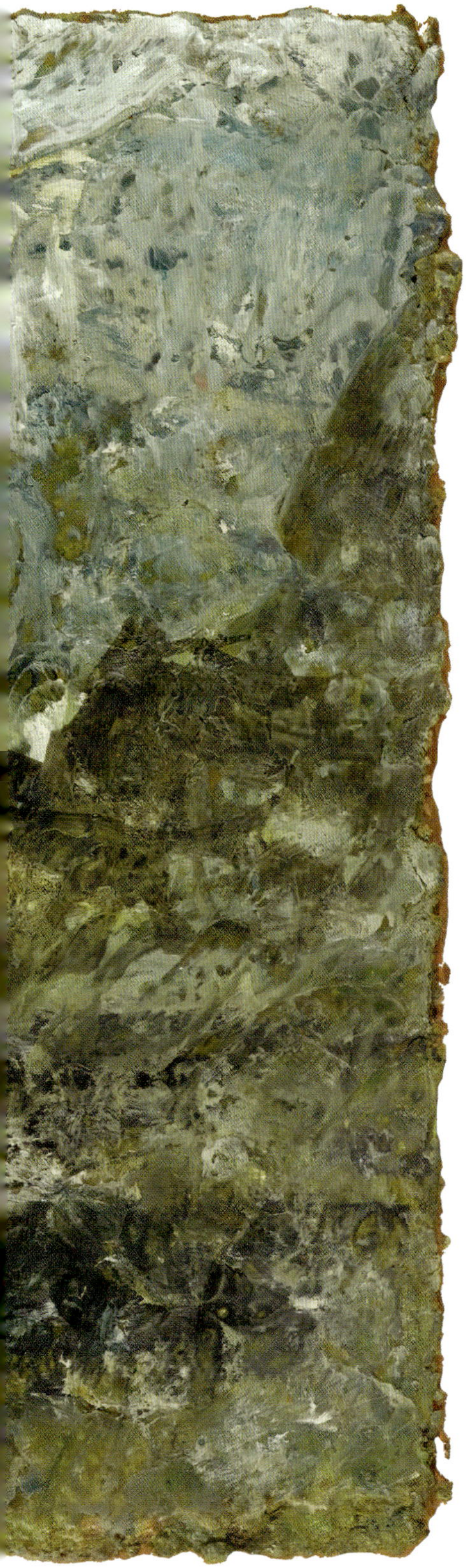

374. Terry Setch, *Car Wreck, Penarth Beach*, 1978, mixed media, 33.6x47.9

The effect of particular place on the work of Terry Setch was more deeply transformational – though it was a very different place to that experienced by Hunter. When appointed a lecturer at Cardiff in 1964, Setch was working in a design-conscious, hard-edged style. At the end of the decade he set up home at Penarth, where close contact with the sea-shore changed his attitude to work and correspondingly, to his manner of painting: 'When I first got here the shipping lane was still active. There was flotsam with jetsam – tyres, oil and tar slicks, rope, polystyrene crates. Incorporated into the painting these metamorphose and become a part of my art language.' Through observation of the intrusion of 'grotesque' elements into the natural landscape, Setch became politicised as an artist, presenting environmental issues related to those that had preoccupied M.E. Eldridge, twenty years earlier, in *The Dance of Life*.[83]

Of the 56 Group artists whose consciousness had been informed by growing up in Wales, John Selway, having trained initially at Newport, found himself at the Royal College of Art among a group of young painters (including David Hockney, R.B. Kitaj and Allen Jones) who would establish international reputations with the emergence of Pop Art. That period left its mark on work made by Selway after he returned to teach at Newport in the form of the intrusion of figurative elements into paintings that otherwise occupied an indistinct junction between landscape and abstraction.[84] Selway's close contemporary, Glyn Jones, trained at Cardiff in the early 1950s, where he met his immediate predecessors among the Rhondda Group. Jones continued his training and began his career in art education in England but from the outset, although adopting a non-figurative approach, his work made reference to his identification with the industrial landscape of the Rhondda. Returning to Wales as Head of Fine Art at Cardiff in 1972, he

83 Terry Setch interviewed by Sam Phillips, *RA Magazine* (Summer, 2014). 'It was the violent intrusion of something grotesque at a time when I was becoming politically conscious of waste and pollution.'

84 For Selway, see Osi Rhys Osmond, 'Illuminated from within. The Art of John Selway', *Planet* 147 (June-July 2001), pp. 17–23.

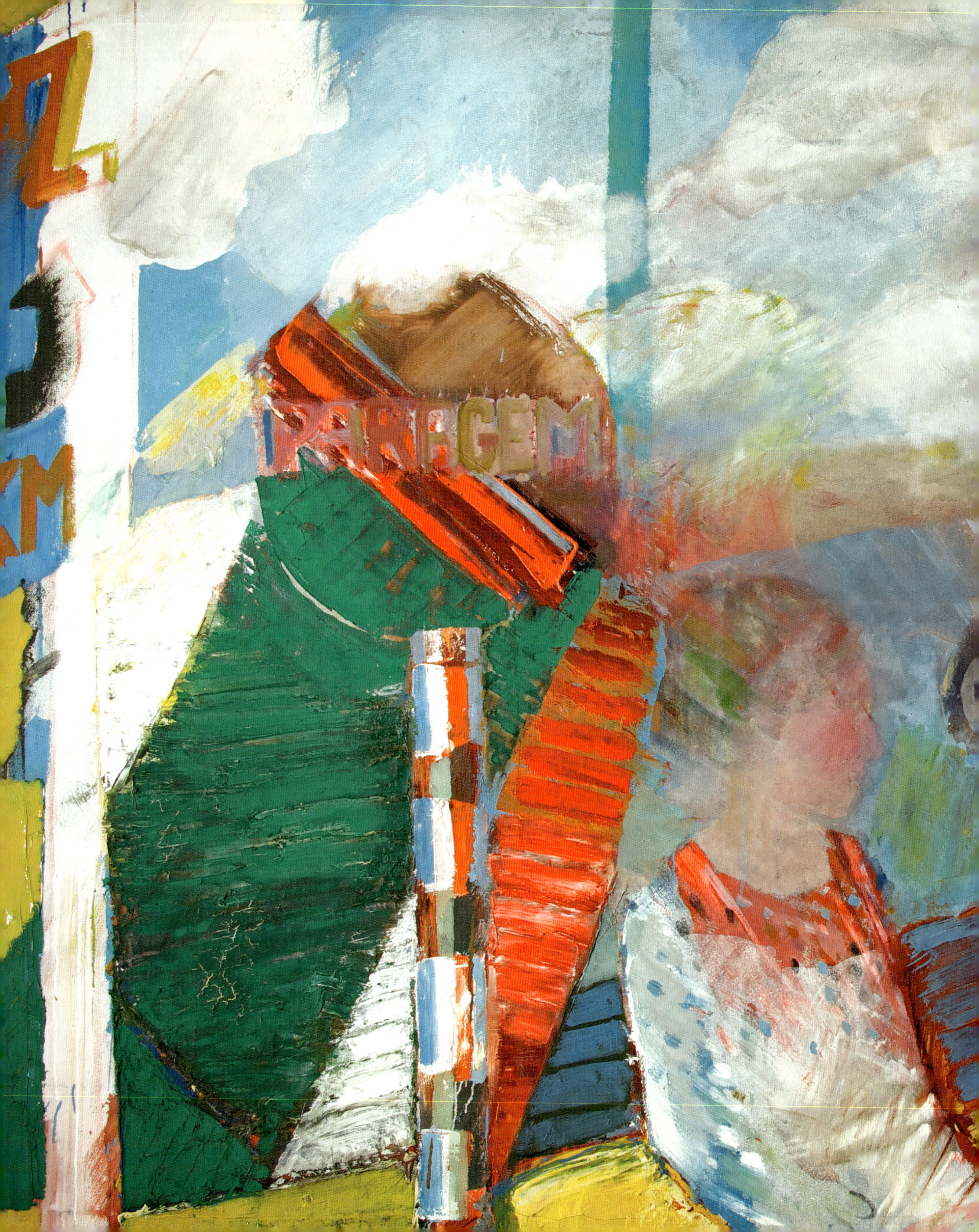

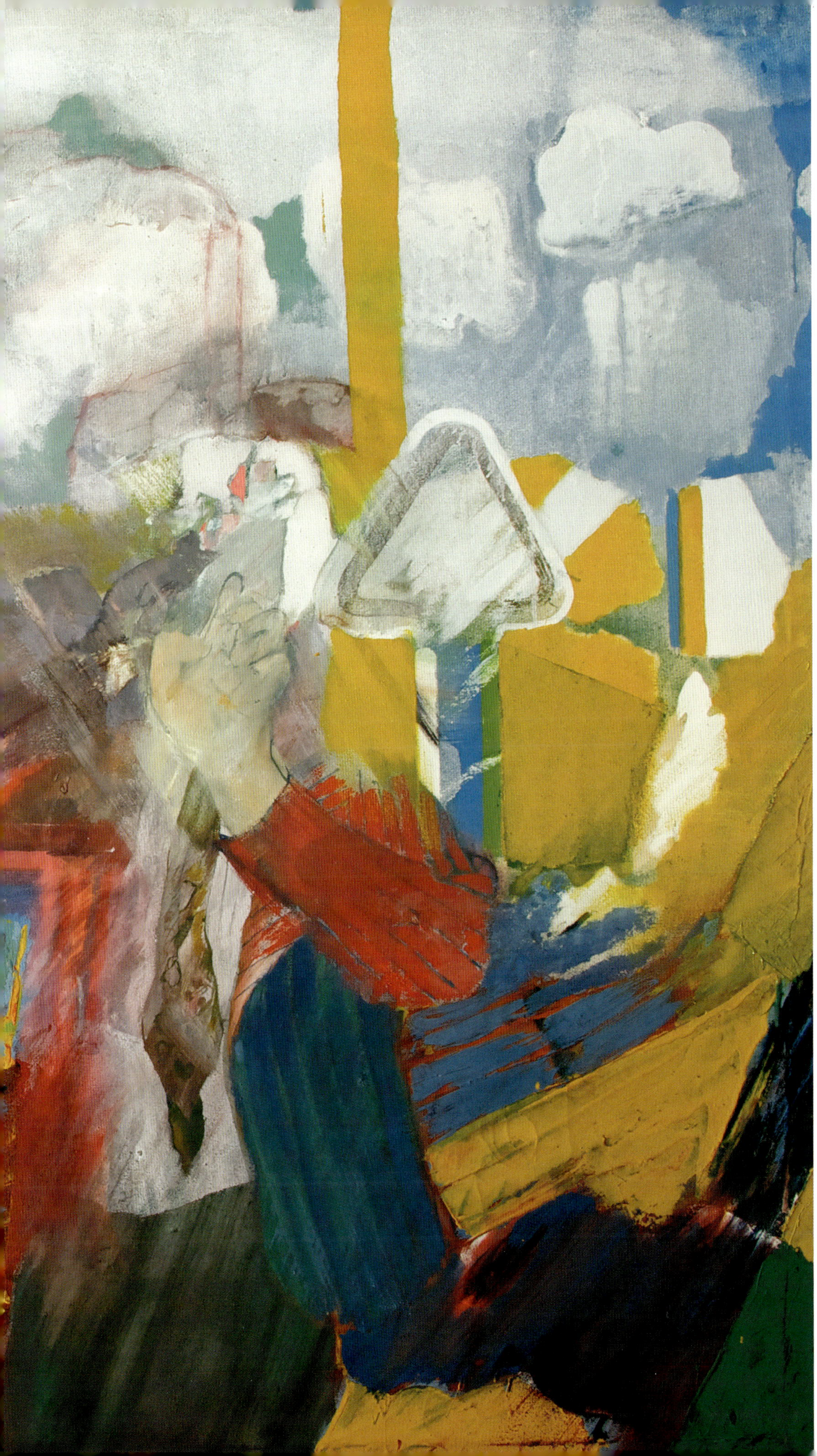

375. John Selway,
Innocents Abroad,
1968, oil, 135x194.6

became concerned with underlying and therefore universal issues of meaning, but again they were mediated through his particular Welsh cultural experience. Later, Jones would reflect on his understanding of how such issues could be made manifest in a non-figurative art, where resonance and equivalent stood in place of narrative:

> I sense that aspects of both Welsh and Celtic cultures share many of those values which offer an important alternative to the overt materialism of our secularised society. I particularly understand the spiritual dimension which in the distant Celtic past may have been 'magic' but became, centuries later, that glorious Celtic Christian Church and eventually the virile denominational mix, full of contradictions, which characterised the Wales of my childhood: the interwoven sounds and rhythms of choral music, the Welsh preacher as an instrument of the Holy Spirit chanting life-saving wisdom. Such things may surface in unexpected ways as one tries to fix an image which catches their reflection, each reflection being essentially formed and appreciated in our time and not that of the past.[85]

Nevertheless, non-figurative art proved problematic outside the art world.

85 Glyn Jones, 'Celtic Vision', *Link*, 53 (1986).

86 Quoted in Moore, *A Taste of the Avant-garde*, p. 6.

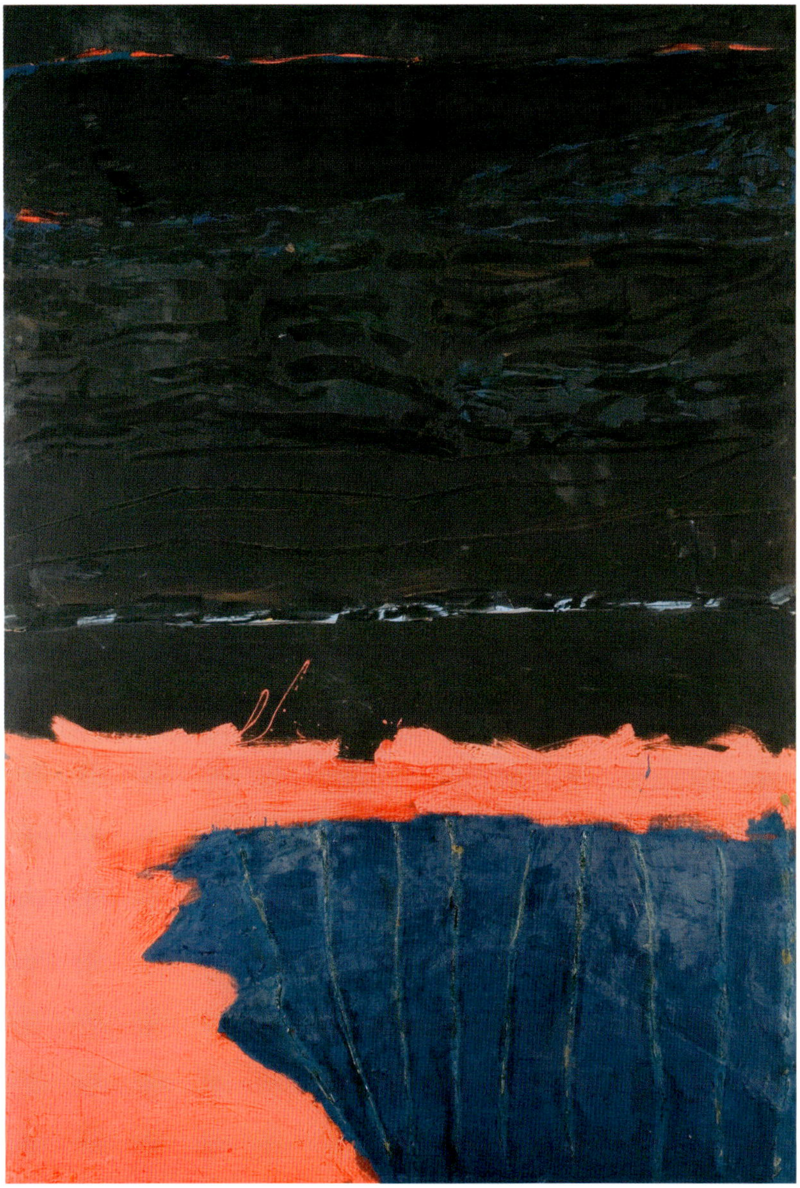

376. Glyn Jones, *Slag*, 1959, oil, 198.5x137

Paradoxically, the conspicuous absence of content in an art work may be an indicator of its underlying presence, even if that presence amounts to denial. David Tinker explained how 'The Hungarian Revolution [of 1956] made me want to convert the violent feelings which I felt into some visual art terms. The colour had to explode … From this point on I was a committed abstract artist.'[86] However, what may have begun as a visual metaphor, stimulated by an experience of political alienation, rapidly became an alienating art,

377. David Tinker, *Celestial Air*, 1961, acrylic, 114x 121.5

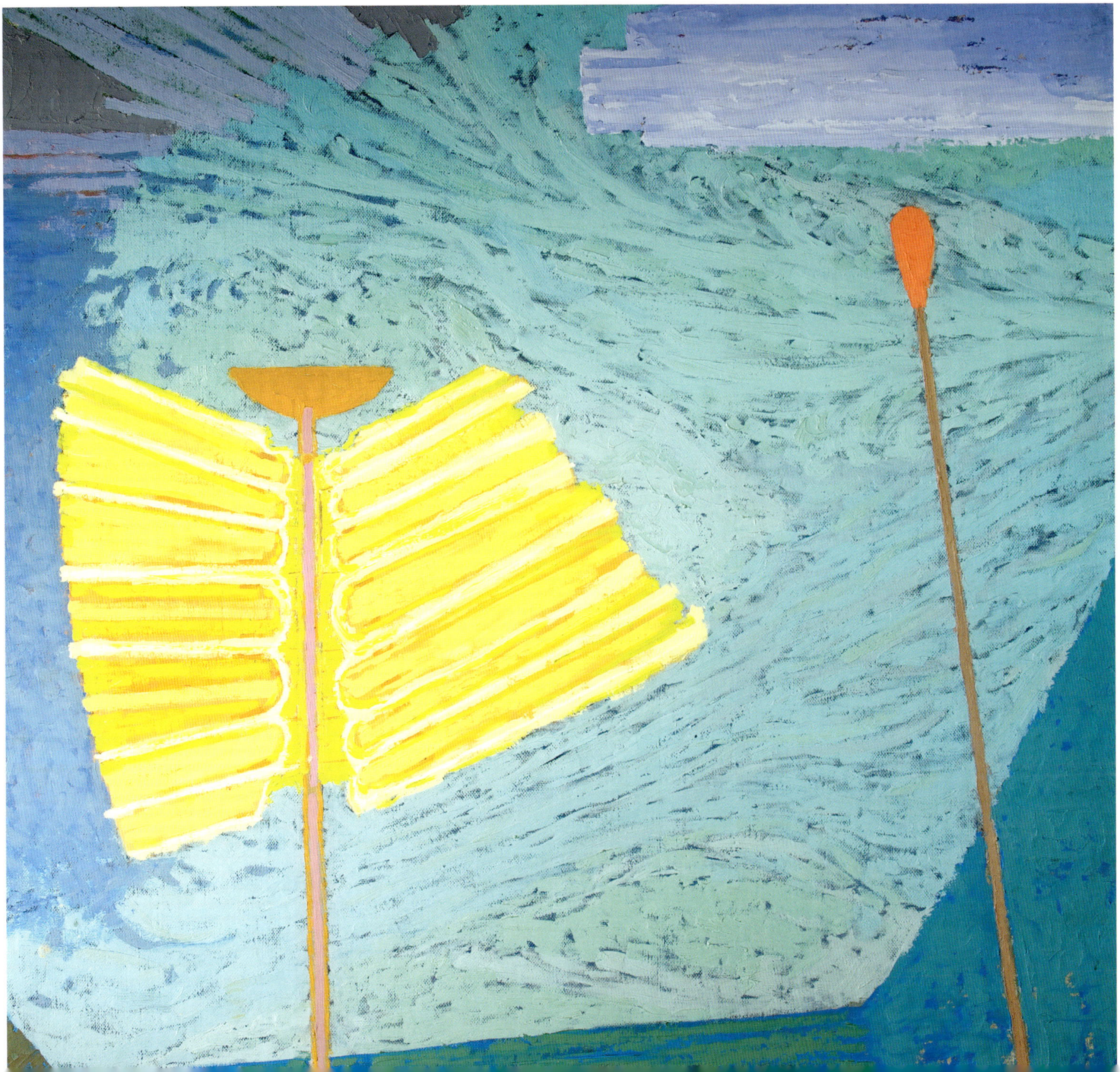

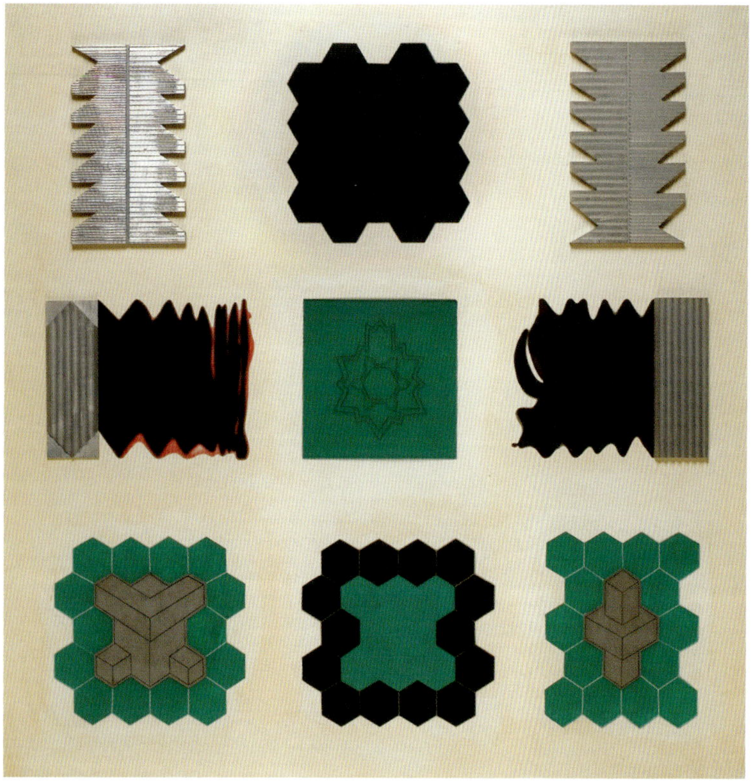

378. Tom Hudson, *Castell Britannica*, 1966, oil, 101x101

comprehensible only to the cognoscenti. In one of the innumerable 'artist statements' that characterised the exhibition catalogues of the 1960s, through which they attempted to explain non-figurative work to a sceptical audience, Tinker remarked of his 'exploring colour and tone relationships' that:

> The content is minimal in terms of exciting shape and form. This is done in order to make an 'unmemorable' image ...[87]

It was an artistic aspiration that many felt he and his colleagues fully achieved. In 1960, Lord Raglan, opening an historical exhibition of painting adjacent to the 56 Group's second appearance at the National Museum, made reference to 'atrocities ... over there', and some vandalism was reported.[88]

From 1964 until 1977 another 56 Group artist committed to abstraction, Tom Hudson, occupied the most powerful position in the art college hegemony as Director of Studies at Cardiff. There he introduced the notion of 'Basic Design' as the fundamental teaching method. The concept, based on principles established forty years earlier at the Bauhaus, replaced the teaching of drawing and craft skills with a pseudo-science of perception that stimulated the evolution of the succession of non-figurative fashions which characterised the period. Rejecting craft traditions and embracing impersonal and mechanistic ways of making reflected the direction of travel beyond the art college walls, where government response to the relentless economic and political decline of post-war Britain identified new technologies and industries based upon them as the means to regeneration. Government aspirations were evident in large infrastructure and development projects, such as the Severn Bridge and the Cwmbran new town on the one hand, and the wholesale sweeping away of the old urban environment on the other. The hard edges and clear colours of much of the non-figurative art of the period, and the quasi-industrial processes and new materials employed, especially by 'constructivist' sculptors such as Hudson, indicated the alignment of many artists with both positive and negative aspects of this agenda.[89]

Basic Design was often implemented by very young teachers, newly emerged from college themselves and with little experience of the world beyond. They presented a remarkable contrast with the previous generation, whose attitudes had been informed by the Second World War and National Service. The introspective cycle of college student to college teacher generated an art world most of the products of which seemed as far removed from realities outside these institutions as any art since that of the French court of Louis XVI. With the exception of the ironic engagement of Pop Art with consumerism, the modernist fashions of the 1960s and 70s, manifested in Welsh art colleges in ways indistinguishable from those in England, either declined to address issues beyond aesthetics, or declined to do so in a way that was apparent to a wide audience.[90]

While on the one hand continuing to promote such work, the Arts Council felt obliged to respond to the widening gulf between the general public and what was often perceived by them – rightly or wrongly – as the vacuity of 'modern art'. In 1967 the Council commissioned a series of abstract images for reproduction on the large advertisement hoardings that

87 Exhibition catalogue *Today – 56 Group Wales* (Cardiff, 1969), no pagination.

88 *Cardiff District News*, 3 March 1960. See also Jill Piercy, 'The Atrocities Over There', *Planet* 126 (December 1997–January 1998), pp. 88–94. On the other hand, among a few distinguished supporters from outside the establishment was Saunders Lewis, who bought a work by Tinker and in 1963 published a sympathetic, if fanciful, description of the artist's working methods. Saunders Lewis, 'David Tinker: an introduction', *Anglo-Welsh Review*, 31 (1963), pp. 21–5. Lewis had met Tinker as a theatre designer.

89 The pursuit of this agenda by some members of the 56 Group led to schism, and the resignation in 1970 of the founder, Eric Malthouse, as well as one of the original members, Ernest Zobole, and the more recently elected painter John Selway. As we have seen, Will Roberts, one of the only two Welsh-born members and not an art school teacher, had been the first to leave the group, in 1964.

90 This despite the fact that some of those involved for a time in Wales, such as Barrie Cook, were highly politicised individuals

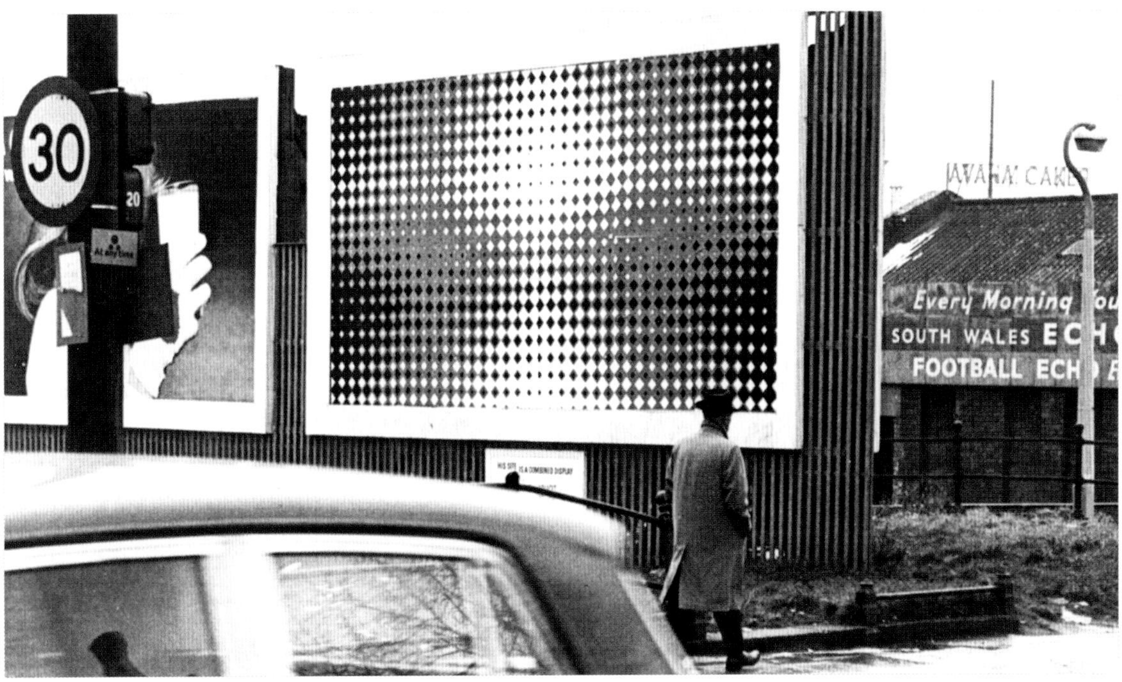

379. Julian Sheppard, *Poster Print by Jeffrey Steele at a Cardiff location*, 1967–8

punctuated the decaying urban environment of the period. Installation photographs taken by Julian Sheppard revealed a certain pathos in the indifference of passing individuals in this run-down world to the surrounding attempts to stimulate a taste for non-figurative art. Positioning themselves as radicals, in fact the commissioning body and the artists were applying the same top-down principles as the high-minded improvers of the nineteenth century, and more recently the creators of CEMA and the Arts Council. Ironically – and perhaps consciously – the documentary images of Sheppard, who taught photography at Cardiff, transcended the banality of the commissioned art works, which were their nominal subject.

The poster art experiment was initiated by the Swansea-born and trained painter Peter Jones, who had been appointed as Art Director of the Welsh Arts Council in 1965. With the same aim in view, but following a different philosophical tack, Jones simultaneously embarked upon a series of exhibitions that attempted to demonstrate the relevance of art to everyday life. Influenced by Marxist concepts, Jones broadened the subject matter of Arts Council exhibitions from high art to visual culture. Punctuating an intensified programme of exhibitions of contemporary Welsh art and imported shows featuring avant-garde artists such as the American Jim Dine,[91] Jones commissioned a series of thematic exhibitions that aimed to 'provide a basis for understanding pictures rather different from that contained in conventional art criticism.' Most of them were curated by Ken Baynes, head of the Design Education Unit at the Royal College of Art. For the initial exhibition in 1965, 'Background. The artist and his environment', Jones and Baynes visited four painters, including the Welsh-born Merlyn Evans, interviewing them and photographing their everyday lives: 'Anecdotal detail is not to be despised', asserted Baynes, 'it is the stuff of all good biography, and its fascination is that, by clarifying a person's character and surroundings, it throws light on whatever was the central theme of his life.'[92]

The co-operation between Jones and Baynes culminated in a series of exhibitions and associated books under the collective title 'Art and Society'. The series was proposed by Gordon Redfern, deeply involved with the wider social and economic regeneration agenda of the period as architect of Cwmbran. Redfern was unequivocal in his identification of the problem of 'modern art':

> Most art exhibitions as we know them, regardless of their quality and content, appeal by and large, to a very small part of the population. Such exhibitions are considered – often rightly in my view – by the majority to be esoteric, intellectual and incomprehensible. This may be an unpleasant truth for us to swallow but it is amply proven by fact and should, I feel, be of great concern to us.

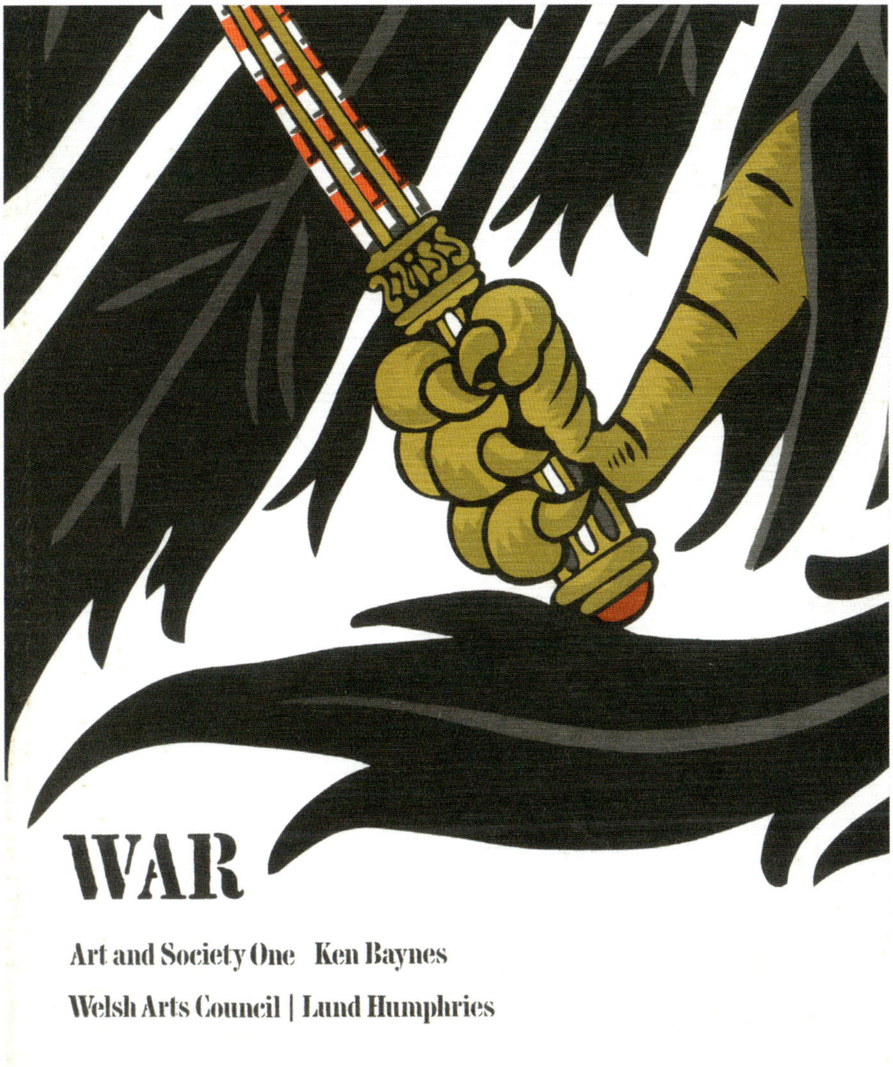

380. Ken Baynes and Steve Storr, *Cover of the catalogue to the exhibition 'War'*, 1970

Redfern felt that the Council 'should be spending some of the taxpayers' money, not only to amuse a minority or to push the particular fashion of the moment, but also to try to explain the relationship between art and life …'[93] The resultant exhibition series, and its associated publications, began in 1969 on the theme 'War':

> The origin of this series of books about the relationship between art and society is to be found in the dissatisfaction felt by the Welsh Arts Council for the traditional kind of art exhibition. Over a number of years, the Council has developed an approach to art and design which implies that they can no longer be contained within the meaning of labels like painting or sculpture or craftsmanship. Film, photography and television have found a natural place: so have magazines, advertising, toys, the work of amateurs, seaside souvenirs and

91 The touring Jim Dine exhibition was created by the Scottish Arts Council, and represented one of a number of co-operations with Wales in this period.

92 Ken Baynes in Ken Baynes and Peter Jones, *Background. The artist and his environment – Alan Davies Merlyn Evans Ivon Hitchens and Victor Pasmore* (Cardiff, 1965), pp. 2 and 3.

93 NLW WAC Archive, Exhibition Files, A/E/103, memorandum to the Arts Subcommittee. The text is quoted in Jones, 'Exhibiting Welshness', p. 191.

> a thousand other objects, humble and vulgar as well as grand and noble. A stage has been reached when the Council recognizes that the human phenomenon known as art has countless forms, and arises from equally varied impulses ...'[94]

'War' was immediately followed by 'Work' and 'Worship', though 'Sex' proved more troublesome. The book was published in 1972, but it did not emerge as an exhibition until four years later, politely transmogrified into 'Marriage'. The exhibitions proved their point by attracting audiences far in excess of those attending conventional shows. Among professional critics, the didactic tone of the texts, which expressed the authoritative status that the Arts Council had assumed by this time, irritated those who continued to see the role of the institution as the promotion of what they regarded as high art 'excellence'. Among them, J. Roger Webster and the writer Raymond Garlick, reacted along a spectrum that ranged from dubious to hostile.[95]

The exhibitions attracted considerable attention outside Wales and helped to establish for the Art Department of the Welsh Arts Council a reputation as a radical and creative body – a reputation which, ironically, overshadowed that of most contemporary Welsh artists. In 1969 the massive 'Play Orbit' exhibition, organised by Peter Jones, was shown initially at the National Eisteddfod at Flint but it transferred to the Institute of Contemporary Arts in London, where the associated book was published by Studio International. The ICA and *Studio International* magazine were focal points for the metropolitan avant-garde in the period.[96] The exhibition combined a history of toys with commissions to dozens of artists. They ranged from those with international art world status, such as Eduardo Paolozzi, to the young Welsh sculptor David Petersen.

Under the direction of Jones, the Art Department of the Arts Council also facilitated the elevation of photography to an art world status equal with that of painting and sculpture. Among those commissioned was David Hurn, at this time engaged in the development of a documentary photography school within Newport College of Art that would acquire an international reputation, as would the work of Philip Jones Griffiths, though it had yet to be fully recognised in his own country. From 1966, Griffiths' war photography in Vietnam exercised a deep influence on public opinion, especially in the United States.

In 1971, the exhibition 'Scoop, Scandal, Strife' and an associated book presented an 'analysis of the role of photography in newspapers'. In the remarkable catalogue, produced in large format on newsprint, Jones emphasised that the exhibition 'grows naturally out of the Welsh Arts Council's respect for photography':

94 Ken Baynes, *War. Art and Society One* (London, 1970), p. 3. Baynes reworked his introduction to the smaller exhibition catalogue of the previous year.

95 Responses are quoted in Jones, 'Exhibiting Welshness', pp. 194–7.

96 The exhibitions coincided with a related philosophical shift in the study of art history by academic historians, especially Marxists and feminists, later identified as 'The New Art History'. Characteristic of the new approach – though having taken over a decade to penetrate the English art historical establishment – was the radical interpretation of the work of Richard Wilson presented by David H. Solkin in the Tate exhibition 'Richard Wilson. The Landscape of Reaction' (1982).

97 Peter Jones, exhibition catalogue, *Scoop, Scandal, Strife* (Cardiff, 1971), no pagination.

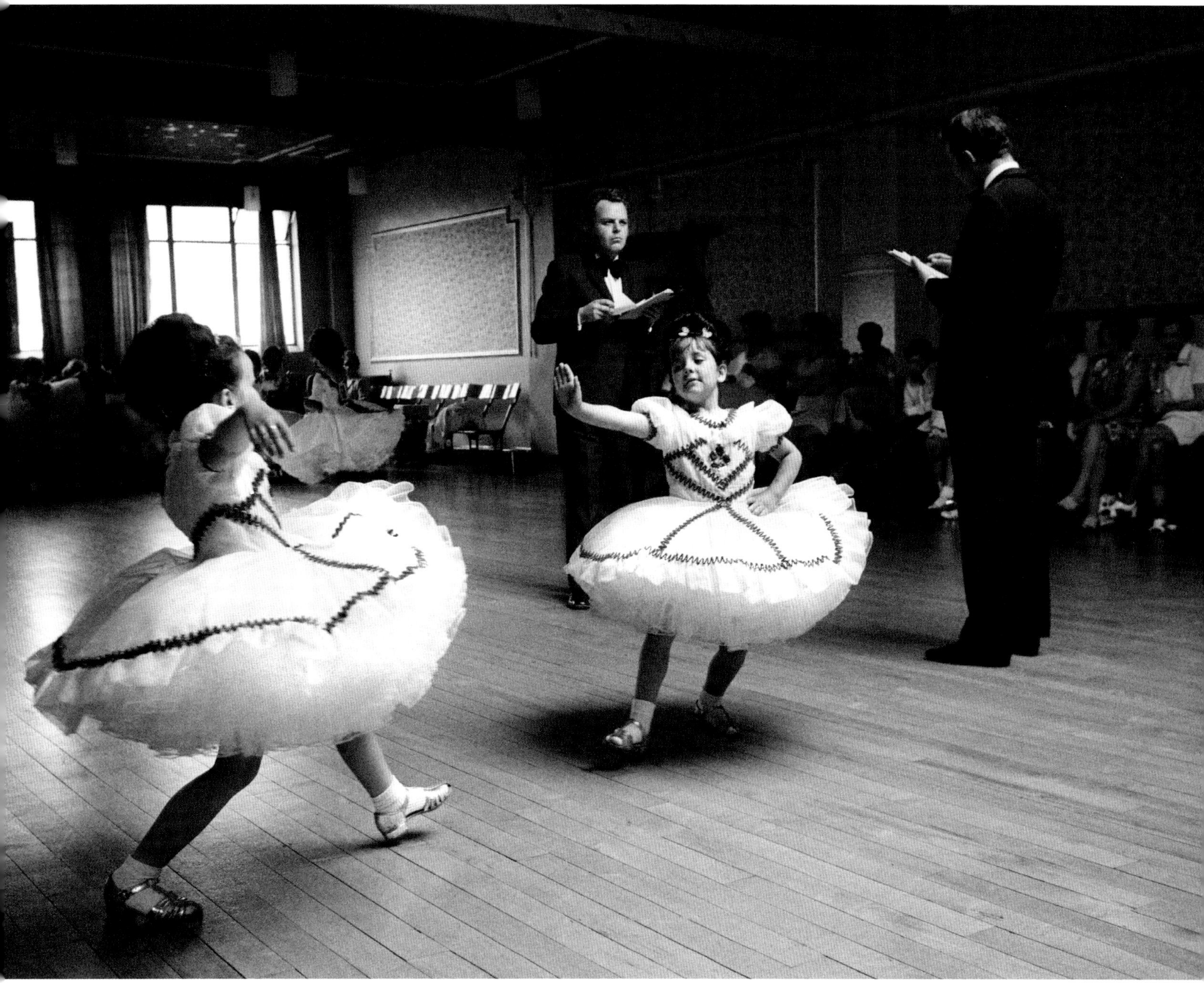

381. David Hurn, *Bargoed, Junior Ballroom Dancing*, 1973

The council was the first British art institution to organise an exhibition of work by a living photographer (Raymond Moore) and the first to commission a number of photographers to record the vanishing industrial scene in Wales (as part of the Recording Wales series of exhibitions).[97]

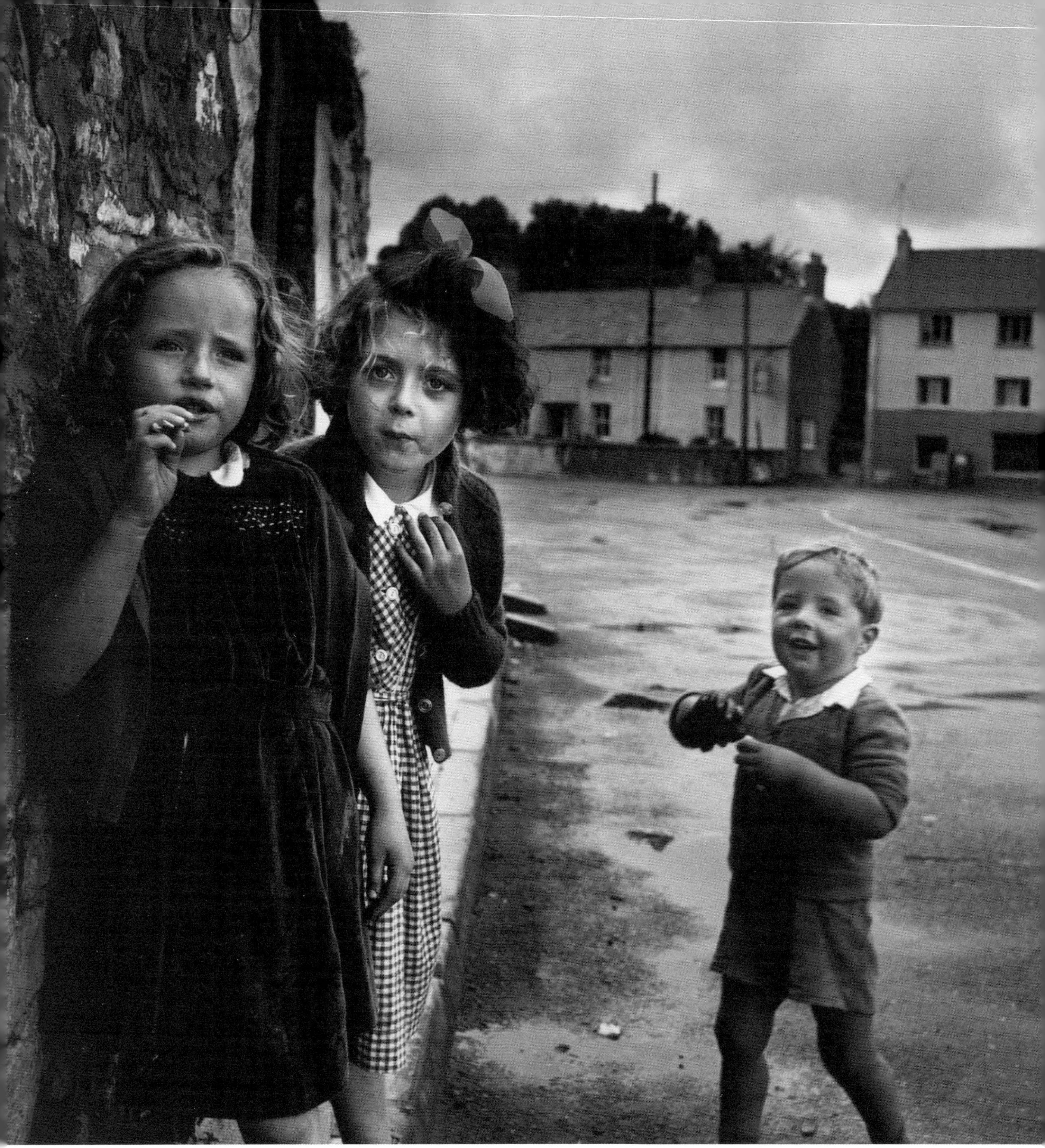

383. Peter Jones, *David Bailey, in the catalogue to the exhibition 'Snap'*, 1971

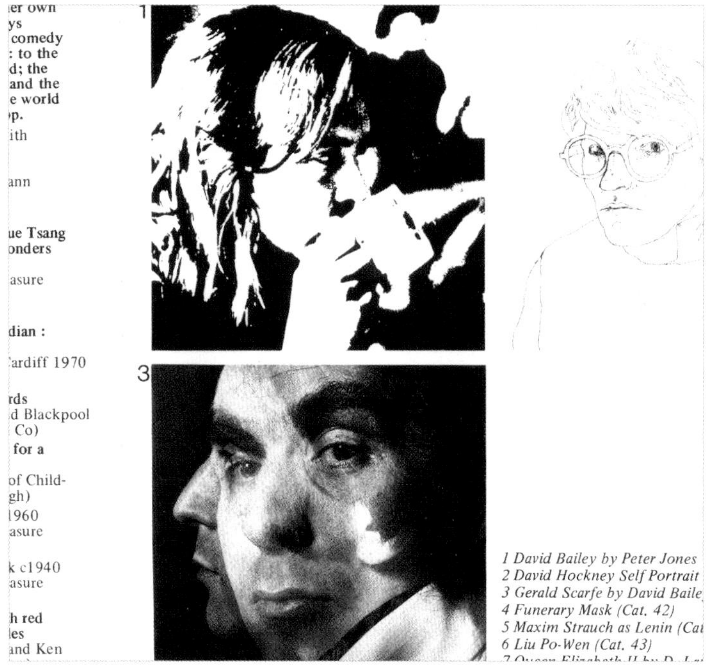

To produce 'Scoop, Scandal, Strife' Jones had once again worked with Ken Baynes. In the same year they also co-operated on 'Snap', which placed the Welsh Arts Council unequivocably at the centre of the London art world. The exhibition combined the inventive juxtaposition of historical portraiture with contemporary work by David Hockney and David Bailey, who himself was photographed at work by Jones for a slide sequence presented as part of the display. The catalogue introduction was written by Roy Strong, the Director of the National Portrait Gallery, another prominent figure in the trend-setting London circle then at the height of its international prestige in the arts.

However, there was a price to be paid for the establishment of a British reputation built around engagement with the London art world. The minimising of Welsh content in its exhibitions, combined with the dominance at home of the practice of internationalist non-figurative painters and constructivist sculptors, suggested a marginalisation of Wales itself in the Welsh art world, that was beginning to be a cause for concern.

opposite
382. Philip Jones Griffiths, *Children, Laugharne*, 1959 (kind permission Philip Jones Griffiths Foundation)

After internationalism

Opening an exhibition of paintings by Nicholas Evans in 1978, Lawrence Gowing observed that:

> We are suddenly privileged to see large quantities of pictures about something, after years of looking at pictures about nothing. We suddenly see pictures ... about ... sorrow, work, bereavement, courage, death and life ... Every trade union in the country should own one of these pictures because this kind of art gives the fullness of the realisation of the role of the working man.[98]

Although as a self-taught artist he was probably unaware of the fact, Nicholas Evans was enriching the remarkable body of imagery produced since the 1920s by painters belonging to the mining community.[99] Like Archie Griffiths, who was only five years his senior, he had

98 Quoted in Jones, 'Exhibiting Welshness', p. 224.

99 For the latter part of this period, see Tony Curtis, 'The Last Shift: The Welsh mining industry in art since 1970', in *Certain Welsh Artists*, pp. 31–51.

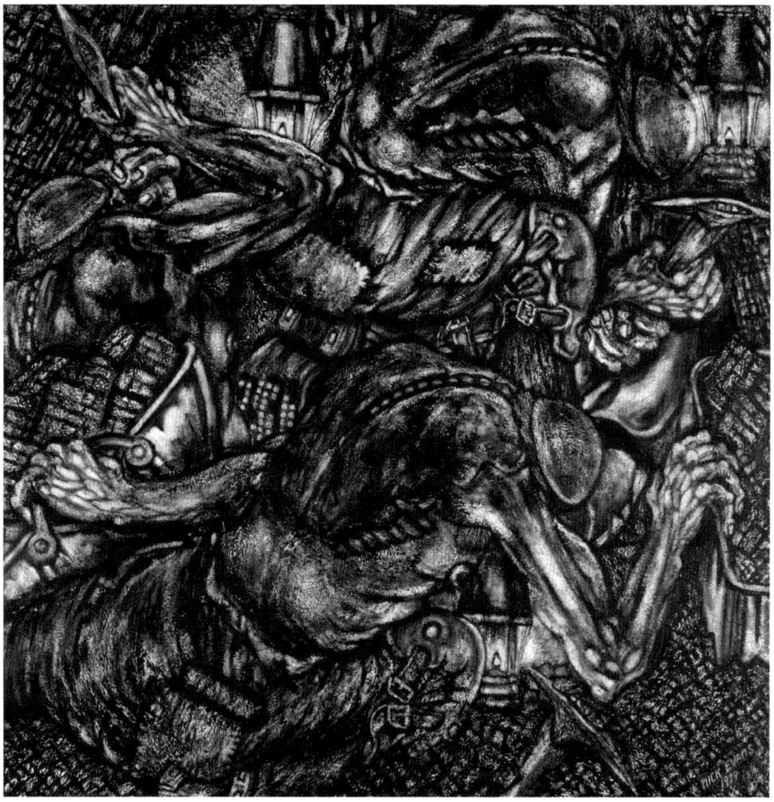

384. Nicholas Evans,
In the Coal Face,
1979, oil, 123x123

been born in Aberdare. He began his working life there as a collier, then became a railwayman but did not turn to painting until his retirement. His work first came to the attention of the public at Oriel in Cardiff in 1978, though Gowing's remarks were made on the occasion of his next exhibition, which was in the west end of London, and they were significant both for what they did and did not say. Clearly, the distinguished Slade Professor's breaking ranks with the metropolitan mainstream by celebrating narrative content in the work of Evans indicated that some among the cognoscenti were now ready to acknowledge the cultural limitations of non-figurative art. On the other hand, Gowing did not acknowledge one of the fundamental causes of public indifference to that art. Huw David Jones has observed that:

> Gowing failed to note how Nicholas Evans had approached the universal themes of labour through the particularities of his own Welsh Nonconformist background ... [T]he exhibition was presented through an interpretative framework that downplayed the work's national significance in ways which stifled the politics of Welsh nationalism.[100]

Unlike Roger Webster's dismissal of Welsh content in the work of Ceri Richards, made in 1958,[101] Gowing's British reading of the work of Nicholas Evans was given at a moment when such a standpoint could no longer be regarded as uncontentious. It came immediately prior to a referendum on devolution of political power to Wales, which represented the attempt of a Labour government in London to placate rising nationalist sentiment in the country, and the activism of campaigners for the Welsh language. Through the 1970s and 80s, this changed national context would find expression in the visual culture both in terms of philosophical debate and the production of art work, the content of which ranged from the passive acknowledgement of cultural particularity to the assertively political. As early as 1973 Jonah Jones had expressed publicly his unease with what he perceived to be the loss of specific cultural identity in art:

100 Jones, 'Exhibiting Welshness', p. 224.

101 'In making the journey from Gowerton to London he seems to have turned his back on Wales'. Paradoxically, Webster also offered the lame speculation that Richards's 'subtle and complex organisation' might be related to *cynghanedd* – a remark characteristic of a residual strain of 19th century cultural nationalism often detectable in Webster's otherwise bombastic internationalism. Webster, 'National Tradition in the Visual Arts in Wales', p. 111.

102 Jonah Jones, *Artists in Wales 2*, p. 103.

> The tide flows constantly, in and out, and internationalism, normally a curative for petty national rivalries and even wars, has flushed life out of too many communities at this late 20th century stage ... A return to sources is now required, to attention to the minutiae of landscape, people and living. Internationalism has the tendency to brush aside identity ...[102]

While continuing through its exhibition programme to promote its status as a radical player in the British context, the Welsh Arts Council began to demonstrate awareness of a change of mood in this period, especially in its co-operations with the National Eisteddfod. In 1974 it presented an exhibition under the title 'Iconograph of the Mabinogion', that brought together works by the immediate post-war generation (Morgan and Zobole), the 56 Group modernists (Hunter and Malthouse) and a new generation of artists with a stronger sense of Welsh identification, including Tony Goble and Ivor Davies. The career of Davies was

385. Tony Goble, *Confrontation*, c.1980, oil, 56.6x72.7

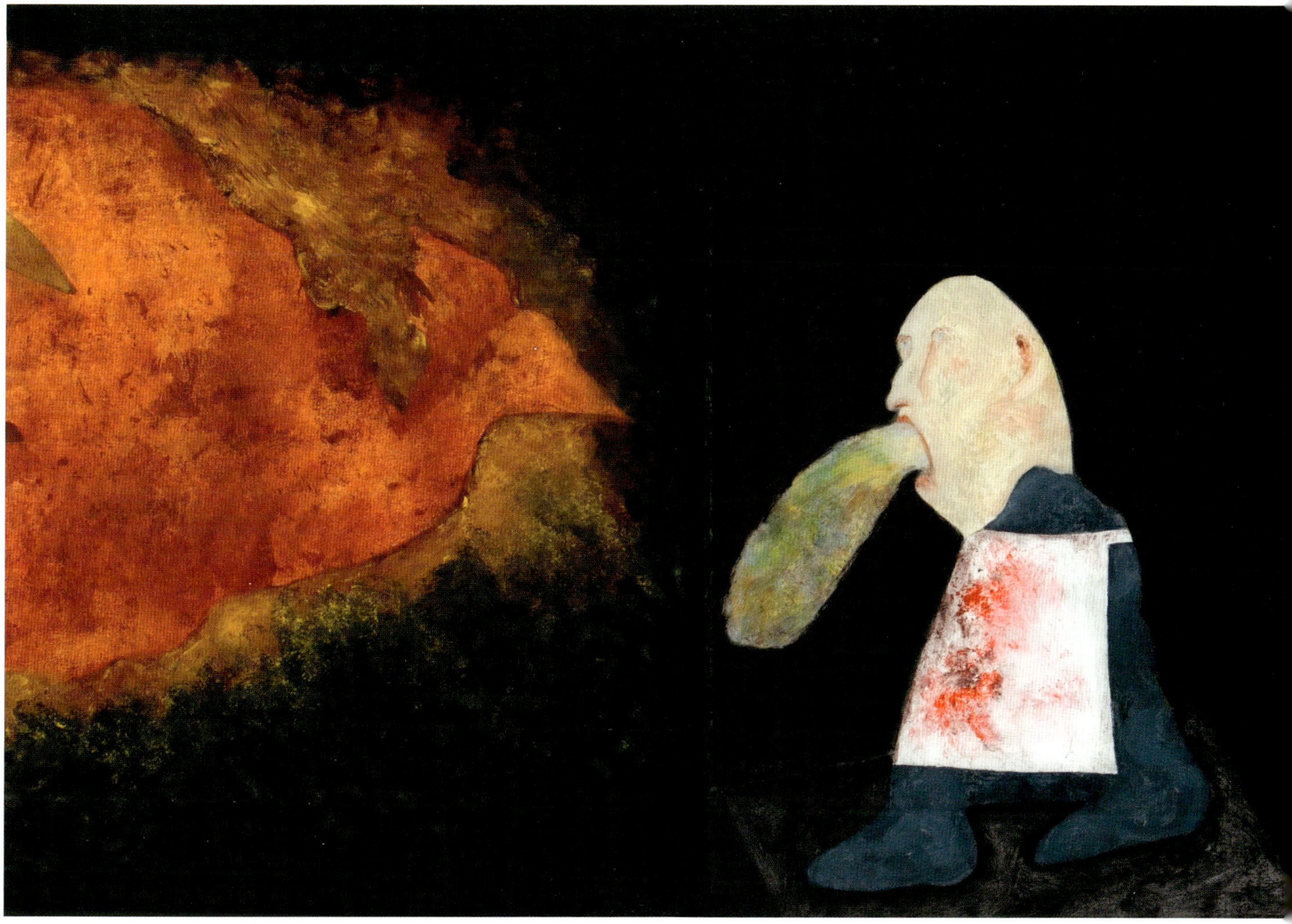

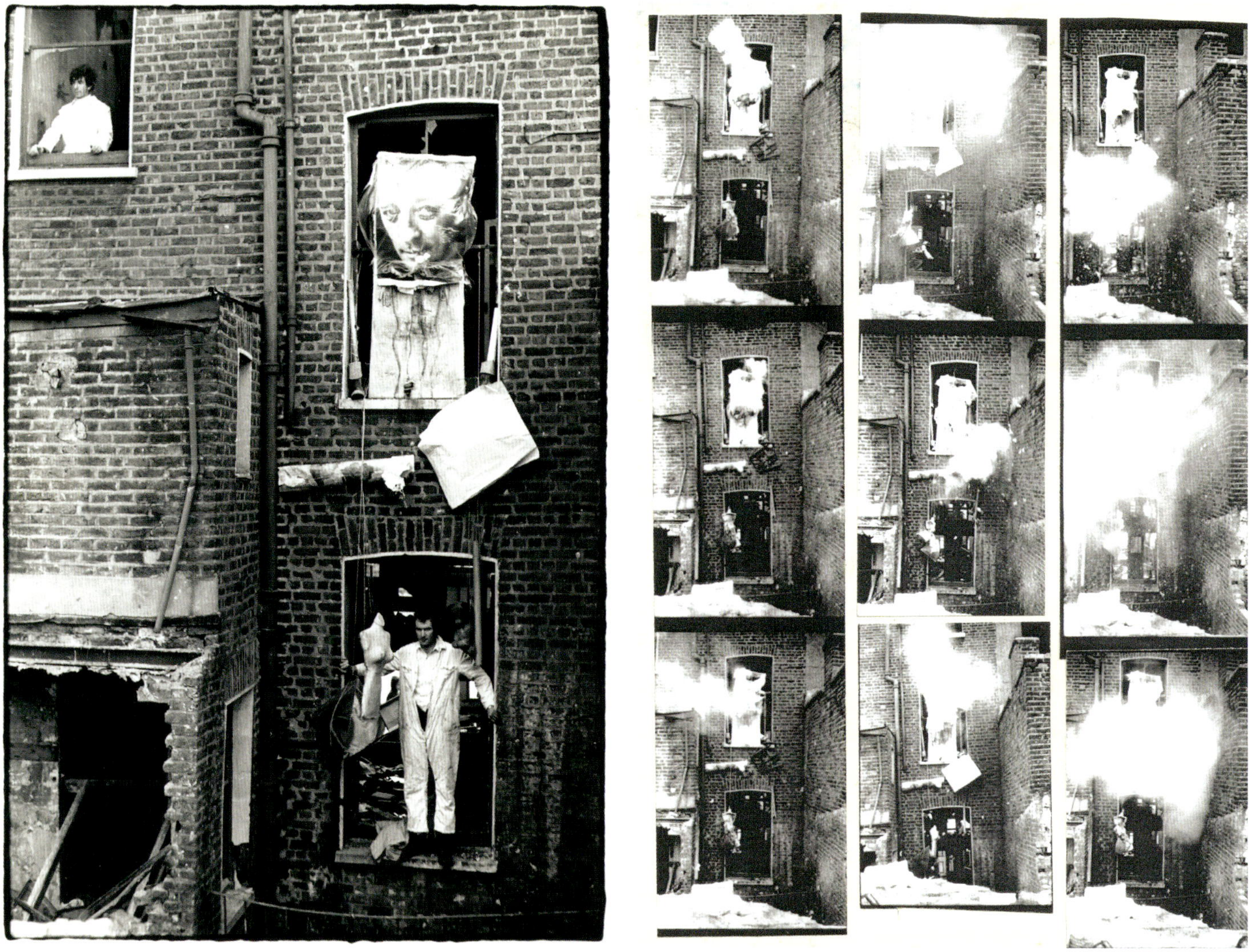

386. Ivor Davies, *Anatomic Explosions*, DIAS event, London, 1966

particularly significant in this respect. After training at Cardiff and Swansea, he began to exhibit his painting in Wales, but in 1963 moved to Edinburgh as a lecturer in art history. His particular interest was in the Russian avant-garde of the revolutionary period, and the development of his personal art work in the 1960s set him among the avant-garde of his own time. He was an organiser of the international Destruction in Art Seminars that took place in London in 1966, to which he contributed both at the theoretical level and by staging an event in which he used explosives to destroy a human image. Presenting art as an event or process rather than as a fixed phenomenon had its roots in the Futurist and Dadaist performances of half a century earlier, but reinvented as the 'happening' in the 1960s, became a commonplace of metropolitan art for a decade and more.

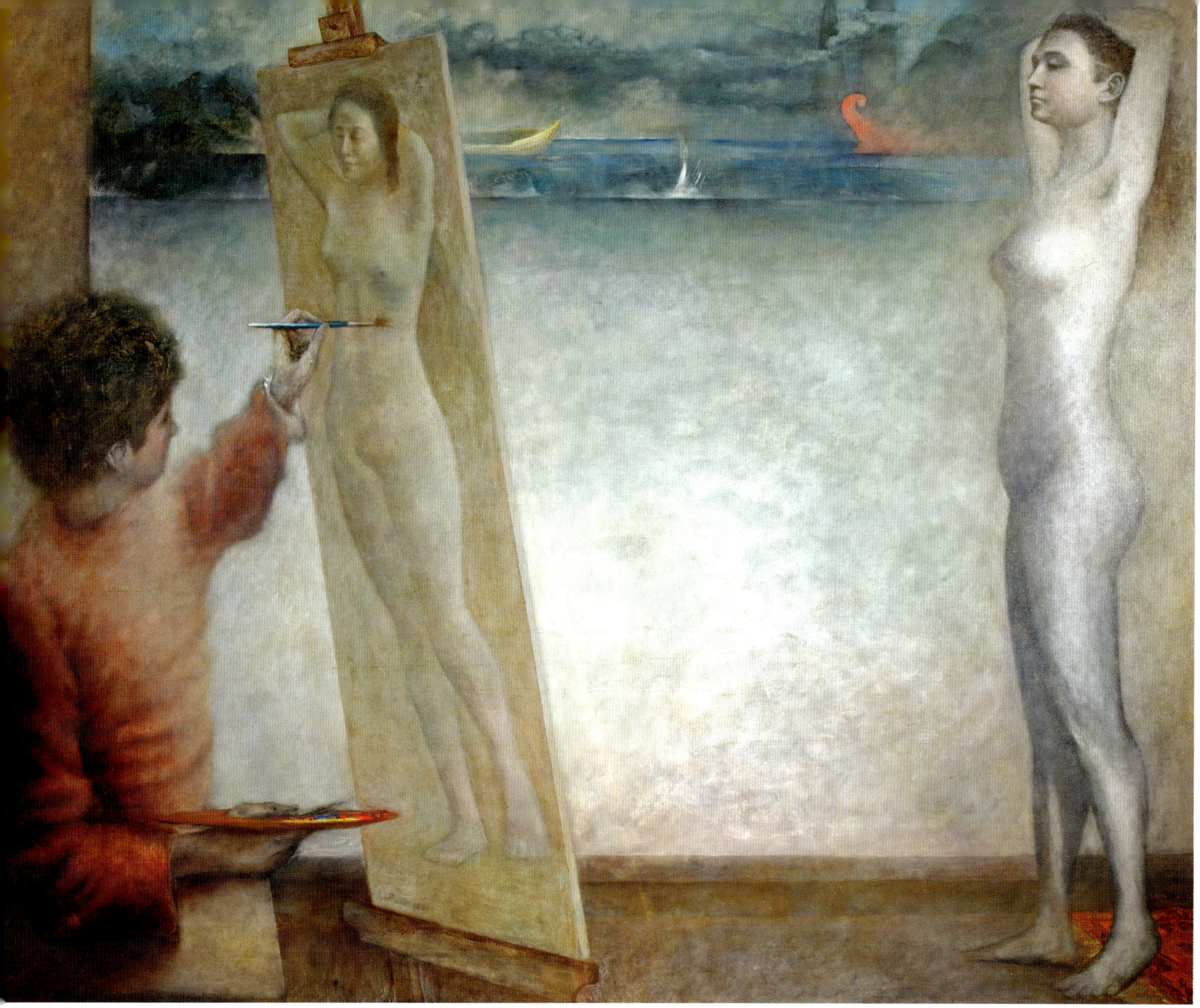

387. Ivor Davies,
Gwydion Conjouring the Illusion of Blodeuwedd,
*c.*1987, oil, 118x149

In 1977, the Arts Council sponsored the creation of a series of such events at the National Eisteddfod at Wrexham. Mindful of the current political climate, the brief advised the artists to create work relevant to the particular cultural context in which they were to perform, but the selection of participants, made by the London critic Caroline Tisdale, mitigated against sensitivity in this respect. Unable to perceive the relevance of performances that included the meticulous construction of a brick wall, subsequently demolished at a charge by its maker, clad in a crash helmet, audience reaction ranged from indifference to hostility, and there were accusations that the event was a waste of public money. However, the intervention of the artist Paul Davies, turned a fiasco into an occasion that, in retrospect, assumed considerable historical significance. Outside the

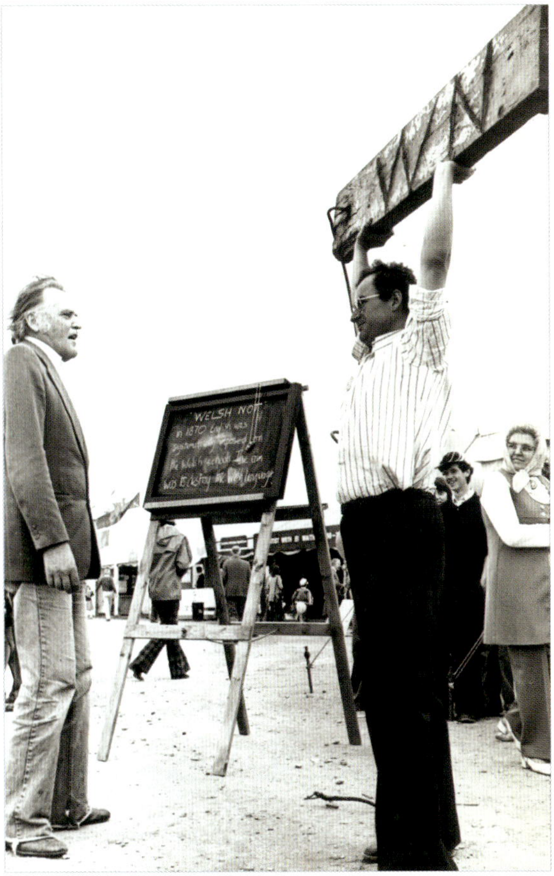

388. *Paul Davies confronted by Mario Merz*, National Eisteddfod, Wrexham, 1977

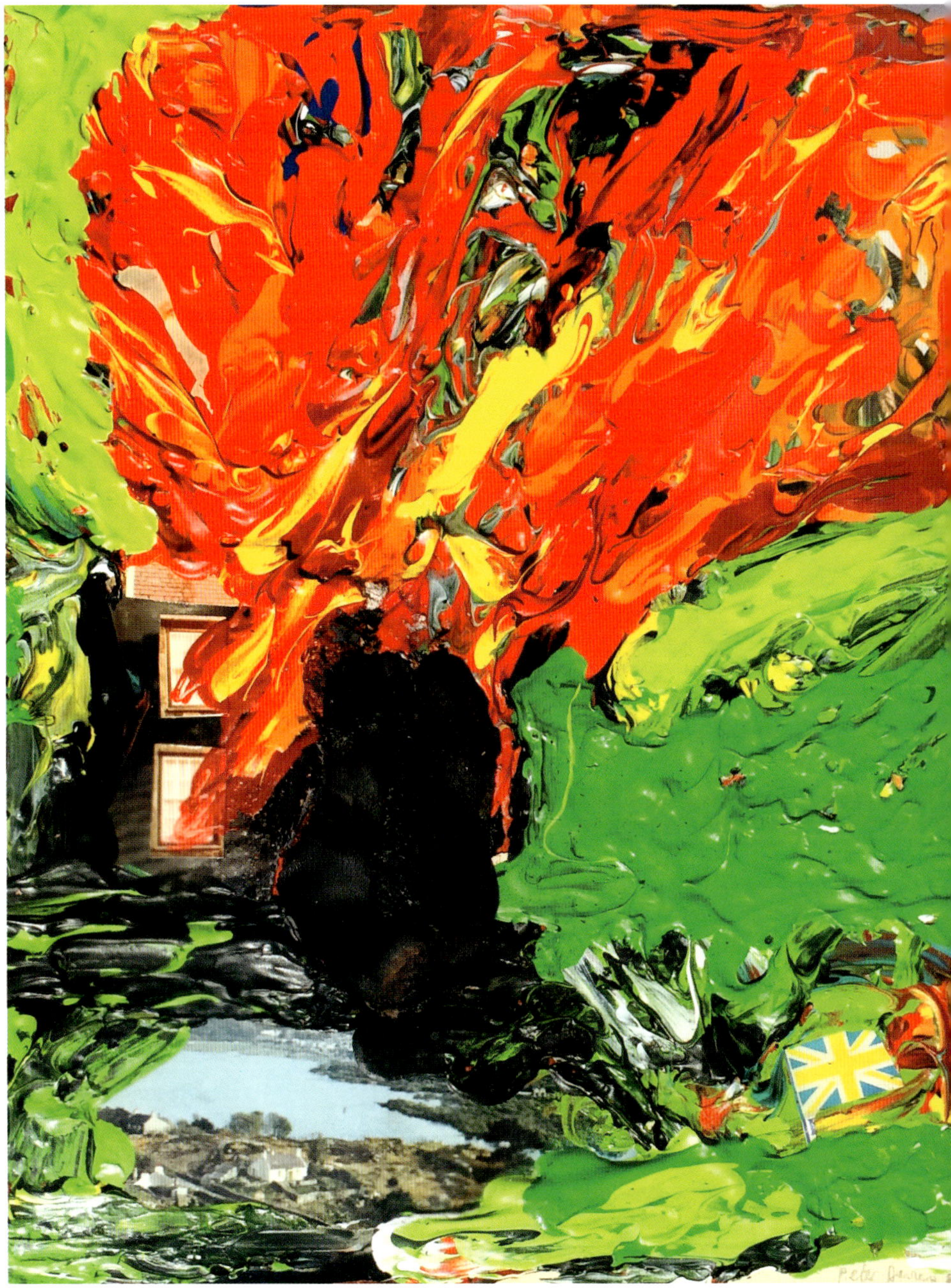

389. Peter Davies, *Tŷ Haf/Summer Cottage*, 1984, mixed media, 300x230

official performance area, Davies stood for long periods holding aloft a massive Welsh Not, drawing attention to the specific issue of the decline (and in his own case, loss) of the Welsh language, but also acting as a wider metaphor to challenge cultural imperialism, which the performances imported from London by the Arts Council seemed to exemplify:

> Paul Davies, arms raised high, carrying the roughly hewn 'Welsh Not' railway sleeper confronted by the Italian artist, Mario Merz … is the most potent image of contemporary Welsh art. It was an individual artist's public declaration of Welsh identity and content to the Welsh nation gathered at the Eisteddfod. A challenge of the dispossessed in their own land, the disempowered Welsh artist to the Welsh cultural establishment.[103]

As a student, Paul Davies had attended the Destruction in Art Seminars which Ivor Davies had helped to organise. The year after the Wrexham eisteddfod, Ivor Davies returned to Wales to live. He began to co-operate with Paul Davies and his brother, Peter, under the collective name Beca, in the creation of explicitly political imagery focussed on issues of Welsh identity.[104] In contrast to the art of the 19th and early 20th century national revival, which was characterised by aesthetic conservatism, Beca applied radical and, indeed, international aesthetic trends to the expression of these identity issues.

The public profile of the group was raised at its first exhibition at Bangor in 1983 when the gallery director removed *Tŷ Haf*, a work that referenced the burning of holiday cottages by the nationalist activists of Meibion Glyndŵr, then at its height. A year later, the extent to which the mainstream had been moved by the resurgence of political narrative art was revealed when Paul Davies was nominated by the landscape painter Peter Prendergast for admission to the 56 Group. Prendergast subsequently revealed his motivation:

> I thought he would be a conscience for us, a personality that would woo us out of complacency, someone to remind us of the indigenous culture of Wales, someone striving to make images that were Welsh …[105]

By this time, questions of Welsh identity in visual culture were beginning to be addressed also by the Arts Council's Art Department. In 1979, the advent of a London government that would no longer maintain the post-war social democratic consensus, contrary to the prevailing ethos within the Welsh establishment, undoubtedly contributed to a reorientation of policy. Political divorce directed attention towards the origins and contemporary meaning of Welsh, as distinct from British identities. Acknowledging that the questions arising applied in visual culture as in every other aspect of life, the Art Department promoted a series of conferences on theoretical issues. Among the speakers at the 1982 event, 'Artists and Politics'[106] (appropriately held at Gregynog), was the Plaid Cymru politician Dafydd Elis Thomas. Anticipating what would become a central concern in Welsh visual culture through the decade, both in terms of Welsh identities and feminism, Thomas remarked that:

103 Peter Davies, quoted in the catalogue to the retrospective exhibition of the work of Paul Davies, *A Mare in a Grey Sheet/Caseg mewn Cynfas Lwyd* (Wrexham, 1998), p. 3. See also Peter Lord, 'Homogeneity or Individuation? A Long View of the Critical Paradox of Contemporary Art in a Stateless Nation', in *Globalization and Contemporary Art*, ed. Jonathan Harris (Chichester, 2011), pp. 56–70.

104 The group name referred to Merched Beca (Daughters of Rebecca), the so-called 'Rebecca Rioters' of the 1830s and '40s, who attacked toll gates in south west Wales.

105 Peter Prendergast, 'Tribute to Paul Davies', Catalogue to the exhibition '56 Group Wales: Works on Paper' (1993), quoted in Moore, *A Taste of the Avant-garde*, p. 62.

106 Earlier conferences discussed 'Art and Patronage', 'Art and Morality' and 'The Judgement of Art'. Among the contributors was the influential English Marxist historian and critic, Peter Fuller.

107 Dafydd Elis Thomas, 'Imagination in Power' in *Artists and Politics* (Aberystwyth, 1982) pp. 2–3.

108 'It would seem that Welsh people notice mainly their friends, and that the surroundings melt into a kind of mist, as in the pictures of Beatrix Potter, which reflect the vision of a child.' Donald Moore, 'Art in a Small Nation: the Welsh Experience', in *Art in a Small Nation*, ed. Gwyn Davies (Aberystwyth, 1984), p. 87.

109 For a thorough analysis of these debates, see Jones, 'Exhibiting Welshness', pp. 226–76.

> Politics is about power. Art is about imagination ... My talk will be about the basic conflict and contradiction between the two words and concepts. But more specifically it is not just a historical or intellectual enquiry in a superficial sense; it is also about the possibility of establishing a new relationship between the two words, not just in language ... but as a historical event.[107]

Two years later, during the conference 'Art in a Small Nation', the art historian Donald Moore reiterated the archaic myth that Welsh people were peculiarly unvisual: 'Is the indifference to visual experience a matter of inheritance or simply of arrested development?' he enquired.[108] Meanwhile, in a contribution to the discussions made outside the conference building in Llangollen, Paul Davies created a huge relief map of Wales, on which he placed computer screens displaying unemployment and other statistics that demonstrated social deprivation in the country. The contrast of perceptions between the two commentators prefigured a debate that would shortly develop internally at the Arts Council, where it generated acrimonious confrontation between conservative and radical elements on fundamental matters of cultural policy.[109]

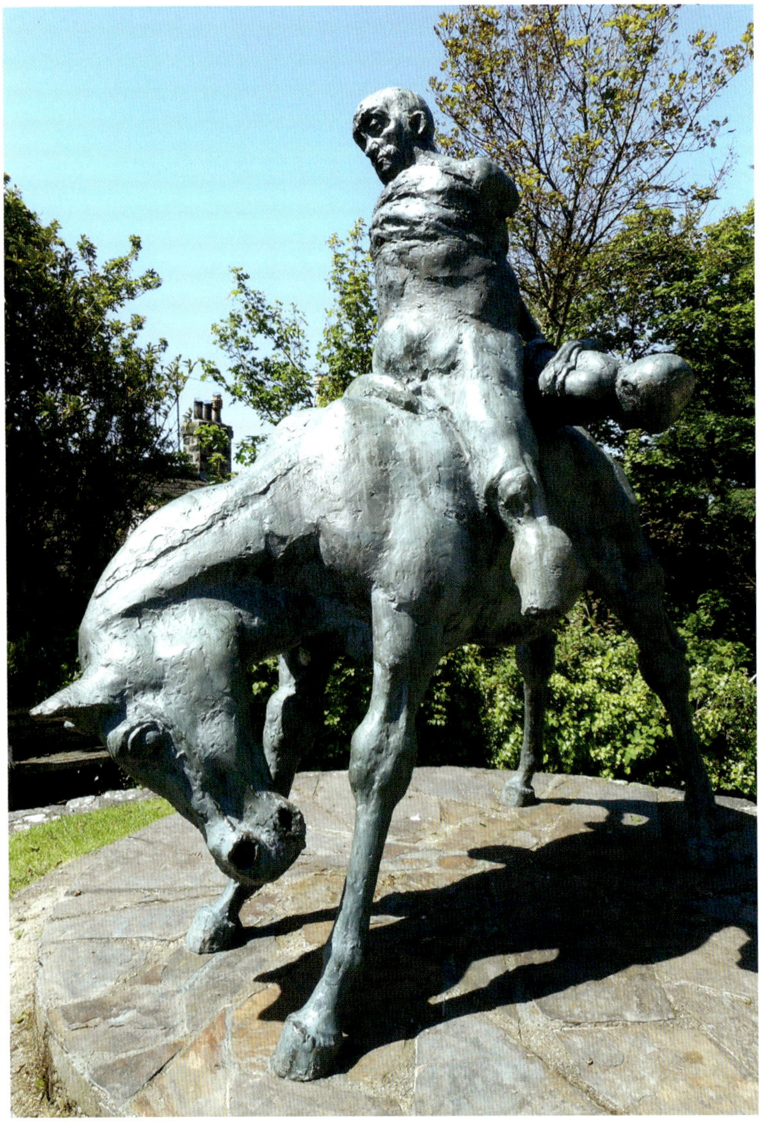

At a practical level, the gradual re-engagement of the Arts Council with issues of national identity was expressed in a series of commissions for public works. Nearing completion in 1982, as the 'Artists and Politics' conference was underway, was the first large scale equestrian statue commissioned in Wales since Goscombe John's *Viscount Tredegar* of 1906. The commissioned sculptor was Ivor Roberts-Jones, then at the height of his career, having completed bronze memorials to Augustus John in the early 1960s and to Winston Churchill in 1973. Based on a story in the Mabinogion, his image of Bendigeidfran carrying the body of Gwern,

390. Ivor Roberts-Jones, *Bendigeidfran*, 1983, bronze

killed during war between Wales and Ireland, was sited at Harlech, in the shadow of the castle walls.[110] In the context of the contemporary violence in the north of Ireland, it is interesting that critical comment on its potential interpretation as an observation on the wastefulness of war was minimal.[111] In two subsequent commissions facilitated by the Arts Council, to create memorials to Welsh leaders Llywelyn Fawr at Caernarfon and Hywel Dda at Whitland in Carmarthenshire, contemporary national resonance was more specific, since the subject matter was historical rather than mythological. The Hywel Dda Memorial, in particular, located in an area of intense political rivalry between the Labour Party and Plaid Cymru, became identified at the time with nationalist politics and proved contentious and divisive within the local community.[112]

Initially unaided by public patronage, the issues of Welsh identity central to the activities of Beca were taken forward by a widening group of participating artists, the most influential of whom was Iwan Bala.

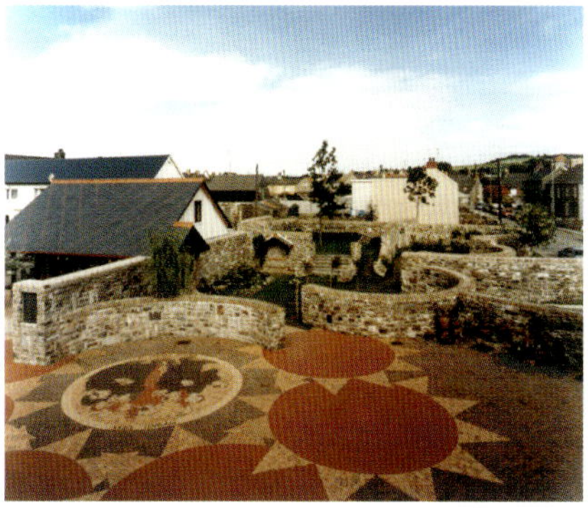

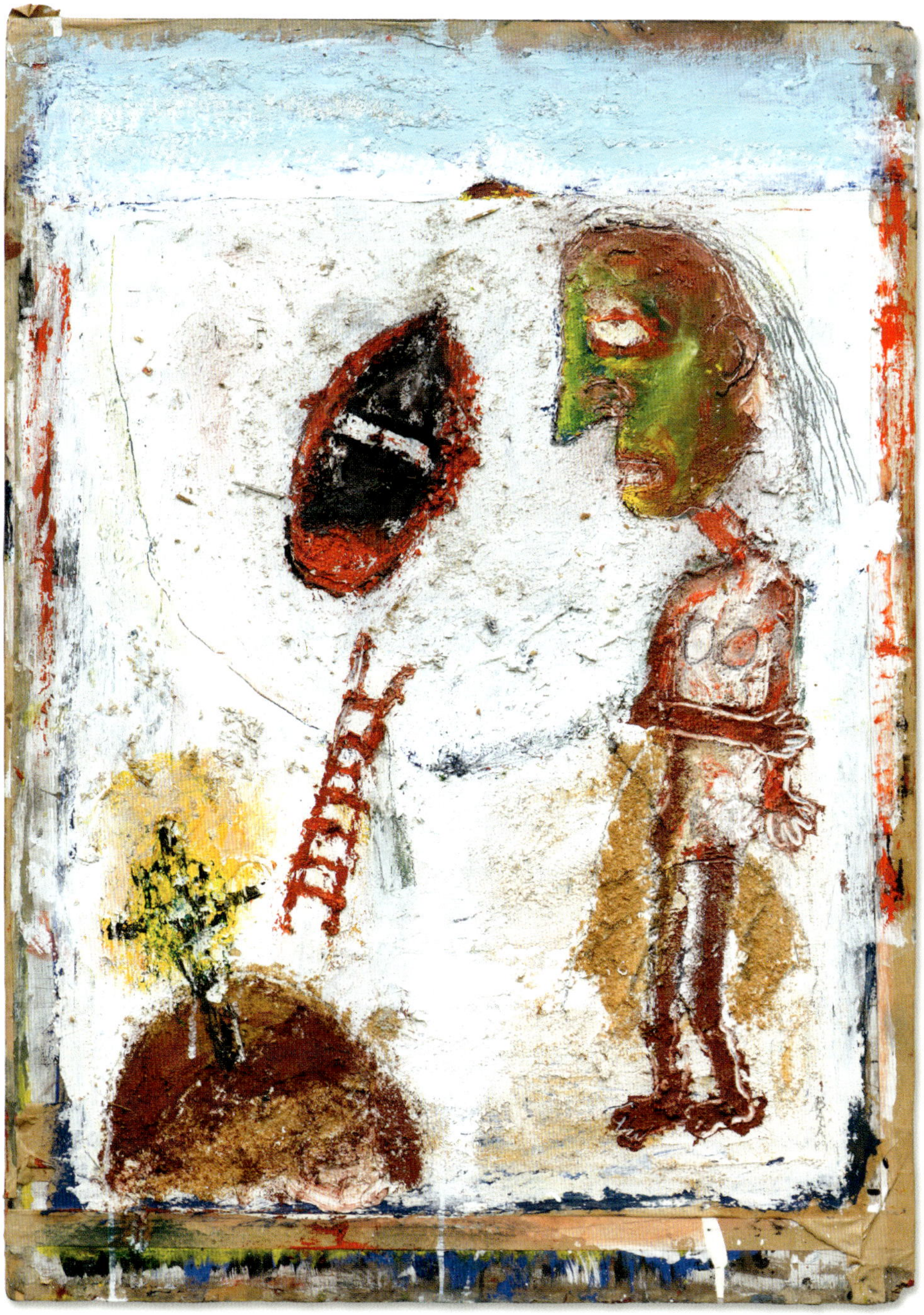

top
391. Peter Lord, *The Hywel Dda Memorial*, 1985, incorporating work by David Thomas, Maggie Humphrey, David Petersen and Glyn Rhys

392. Iwan Bala, *Galarnad i Arthur*, *c.*1990-1, mixed media, 76x56

110 Peter Cannon-Brooks, *Y Daith i Harlech/The Journey to Harlech* (Cardiff, 1983). Roberts-Jones was brought up in Oswestry, but identified strongly with his family origins in the Aberystwyth area. While working in London shortly after the Second World War, he became a close friend of Kyffin Williams.

111 Though see the comment made in 1982 by Dafydd Elis Thomas, 'Imagination in Power', p. 16. It is unclear whether it was made with the sculpture in mind.

112 See Peter Lord, 'A Narrative', in *Groundbreaking. The Artist in the Changing Landscape*, ed. Iwan Bala (Bridgend, 2005), pp. 100–11.

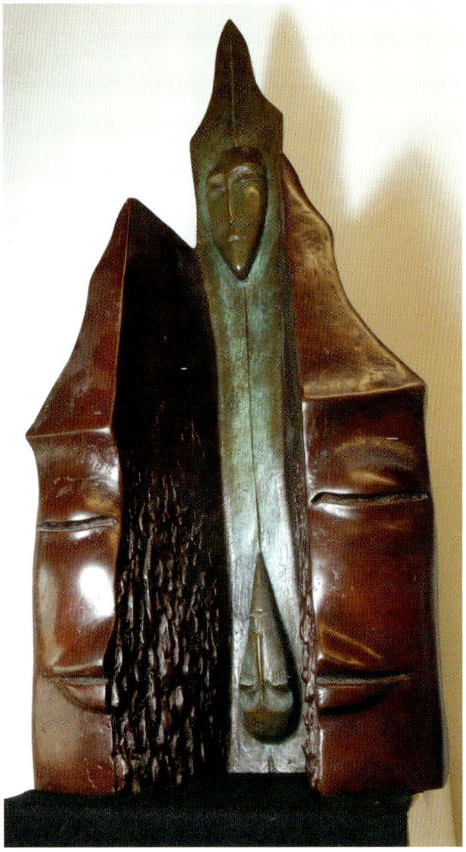

393. John Meirion Morris, *Oddi mewn i Chwi y Mae/It is Within*, *c.*1992, bronze

Emerging as a painter in the mid 1980s, Iwan Bala sought to comment on contemporary issues by the evocation of myth. By presenting landscape as the site of cultural memory, rather than as a vehicle for the conveyance of notions of beauty, he returned conceptually to the Classicism of seventeenth and eighteenth century high art. However, his use of primitive drawing and crude finish alerted the audience to the contemporary issues embedded in the work, by association with generations of European and American painters who had stressed their modernity by the rejection of polished academic technique. In the late 1980s, Iwan Bala had established links with Basque and Irish artists, and would be instrumental both in international co-operations and the development of post-colonial art theory in Wales. In 1990, he worked in Zimbabwe, enabling him to draw on an extended range of images that he used to associate his perception of Wales in a post-colonial world with other nations of comparable heritage.[113]

opposite

394. Clifford McLucas, *Artwork for the Bible Banners*, *c.*1986-7, watercolour, h.21

Over two decades before Iwan Bala, the sculptor John Meirion Morris had also experienced the manifestation of colonialism in visual culture by working in Africa. Although commissioned as a portrait sculptor on many occasions, the full development of Morris's work was constrained until relatively late in his career by his commitment to teaching, but began to flourish in the radical atmosphere of the 1980s.[114] Like Iwan Bala, he would reference Celtic mythology, and would not do so by the sterile repetition of defunct symbol systems, or the illustration of texts, that had characterised so much of the Celticism of the past. Like Ceri Richards, Morris attempted to draw from his understanding of the essence of prehistoric artefacts, insofar as they could be understood, to reach into the fundamental drivers of human consciousness. Earlier in his career, Morris had ventured occasionally into theatre design, continuing a tradition of interaction between visual art and literature that had, since the Second World War, engaged personalities as diverse as David Tinker and John Elwyn.[115] From the 1980s, the nature of such co-operations became more intense as distinctions between disciplines eroded. Iwan Bala co-operated with the playwright Ed Thomas, and the work of the visual artist and theorist Clifford McLucas – trained initially in architecture – became a central element in the work of the highly influential theatre company, Brith Gof.

113 See Iwan Bala, *Zimbabwe, Report of a Visit* (presented to the Welsh Arts Council, 1991). The visit was grant aided by the Arts Council.

114 Morris was closely involved, with others, in the creation of 'Gweled'. The organisation was established for those engaged in or simply interested by visual culture who were Welsh speakers, with the intention of counteracting the perception, heavily reinforced by the art school hegemony of the 1960s, that the visual arts were alien to Welsh tradition.

115 Remarkably, given their apparently different politics, Tinker had worked with Saunders Lewis, see above, n. 88. John Elwyn, along with many contemporaries, including Kyffin Williams, had co-operated on the illustration of Welsh texts.

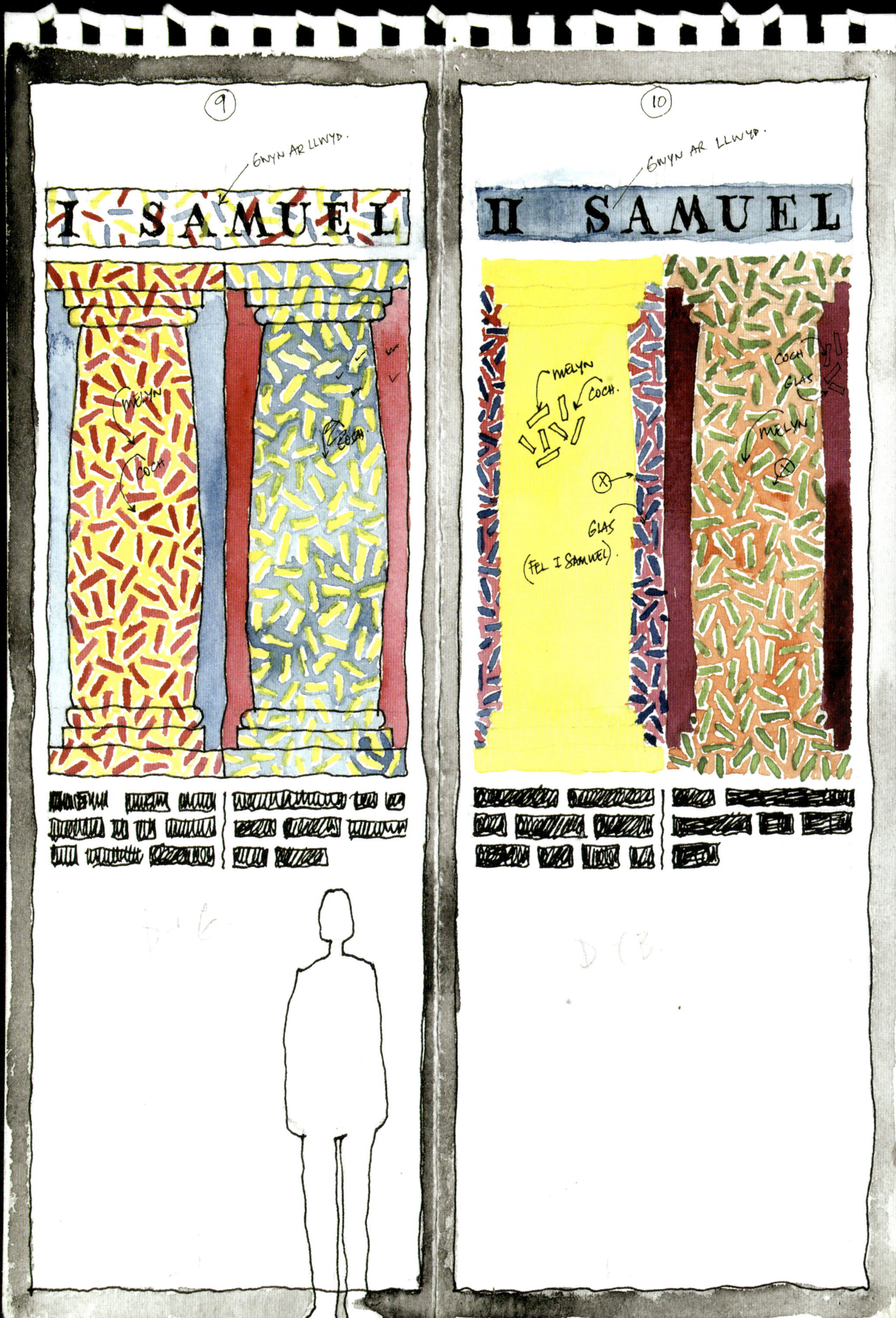
9
GWYN AR LLWYD.
I SAMUEL
MELYN
COCH
COCH.
10
GWYN AR LLWYD.
II SAMUEL
MELYN
COCH.
GLAS
(FEL I SAMUEL).
COCH
GLAS
MELYN

Since both revolved around the nature of power in social and political relationships, the thinking and practice of theorists and artists concerned with issues of nation and gender identities was interactive in the 1970s and 80s. After training and initially developing her career in England, the artist Eleri Mills returned to live in Wales in 1988, and was soon drawn to the same sources of imagery as Iwan Bala and John Meirion Morris:

> The land has always been there in my mind, beginning with a childhood helping on the farm. The passing on of the land from one generation to the next represents continuity and instils a deep sense of belonging. I grew up, therefore, in a place where history and tradition were relevant and my familiar landscape was connected by a network of mythic and cultural associations. The art of story telling celebrated life in all its forms, thus fuelling a culture founded on narrative as opposed to visual tradition, creating fabulous and complex imagery of the mind ...[116]

395. Eleri Mills, *Jwg*, 1985, paint, stitching and hand appliqué on cloth, 100x160

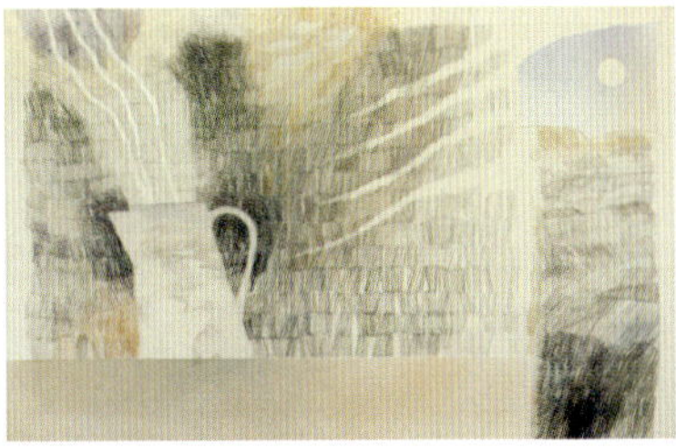

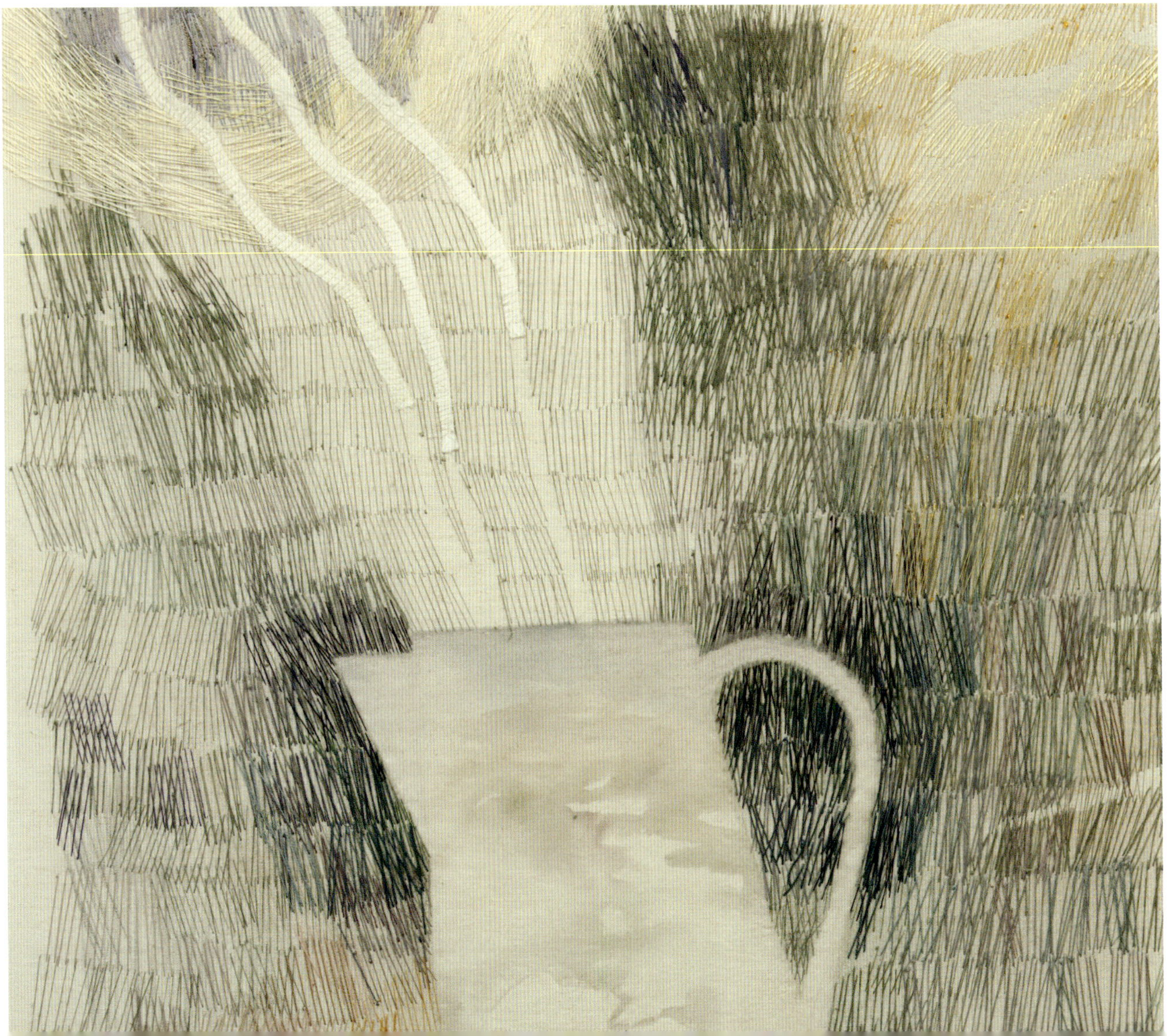

However, the means employed by Mills to translate her mythic imagery of the mind brought to the fore questions not only relating to geo-political identities, both local and national, but also to gender. In addition to painting and drawing, Mills employed fabrics and stitching to create pictures, which not only identified her as a craftsperson rather than as an artist, but in particular as a craftswoman, since the techniques and soft materials that she favoured had gendered associations. Both these identifications carried negative implications that were reflected in her art world status, along with that of many other women in the field. The extraordinary gender bias of the 56 Group had been broken only as recently as 1973, when the painter Mary Lloyd Jones – who, like Mills, sometimes used soft materials in her image making – was elected the first woman member. Further suggesting the impact that the rise of feminist consciousness would have through the next two decades, in 1974 Ray Howard-Jones became the first woman to be acknowledged with a one-person retrospective exhibition at Oriel in Cardiff.[117] However, it was ten years before change was sufficiently developed to be reviewed in the exhibition 'Women's Art in Wales' at the Mostyn Art Gallery – though the particularly apposite choice of venue appears to have escaped the attention of the organisers:[118]

116 Eleri Mills in the catalogue to the touring exhibition of her work initiated at the Ruthin Craft Centre, 1995, p. 45.

117 Nevertheless, the embracing of change at the official level was less than whole hearted. The 1977 'representative' touring exhibition, 'From Wales', reverted to male exclusivity.

118 See above, p. 215.

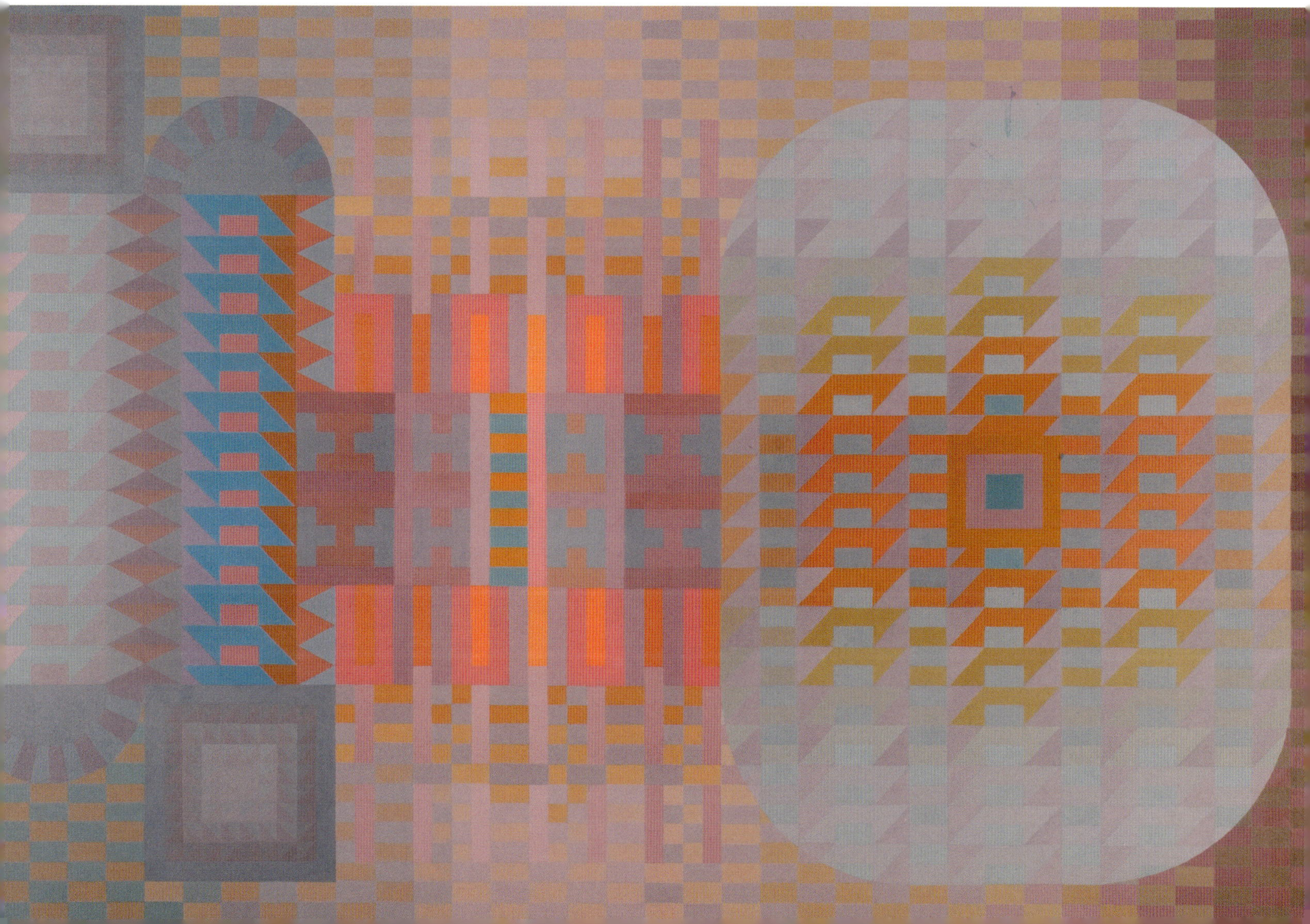

396. Mary Lloyd Jones, *Aubade*, *c.*1974, acrylic, 142x203

To the celebrated question, posed in 1971 by the American art historian Linda Nochlin, 'Why have there been no great women artists?'[119] the catalogue to the exhibition presented both main streams of feminist response – the exclusion of women from the development of a career path within the existing parameters of high art practice, and the more complex problem of the marginalisation in high art theory of those forms of expression which were particularly associated with women:

> Over the past ten years the growing debate concerning women's art practice has stimulated questions which have implications not only for women but for the whole of the contemporary art scene. The very definition of art is at issue – what does constitute an art work: the abstract painting, the patchwork quilt, the woodcarving, the knitted jumper? Why do we give higher value to certain traditions of art or to certain kinds of subject matter?[120]

397. Lois Williams,
An Unreconstructed Thing,
installation photograph
c.1994, mixed media

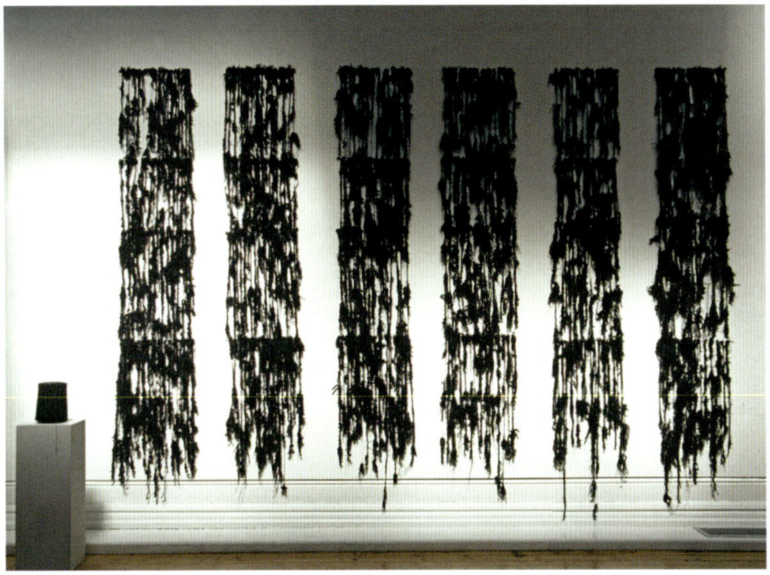

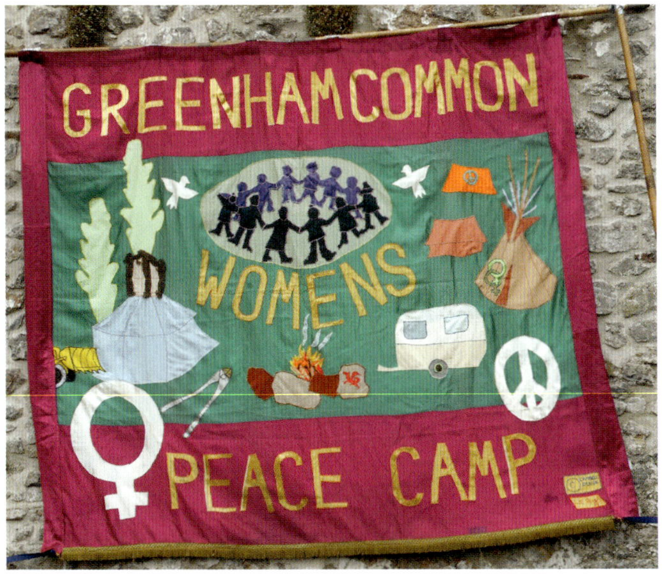

above right
398. Thalia Campbell,
Greenham Common Peace Camp Banner, 1983, satins, 200x240

The exhibition presented artists who worked both within and without the art establishment, in high art and marginalised forms. Working within the mainstream high art framework, but exploiting the breakdown that had occurred by the 1980s of boundaries between traditional forms of image making, Lois Williams reassembled and transformed collected objects and materials. Through them, inevitably she alluded to particular cultural context – though it was a context more often bounded by her farming background in a particular part of the country than by Wales as a whole. Beyond the confines of the art world, Thalia Campbell perhaps made the greatest impact among the public by the rejuvenation of a gendered form. Campbell was a founder member of the Greenham Common Women's Peace Camp, established by a march from Wales of women peace activists in 1981 to protest against the deployment of American nuclear weapons in England. Campbell reinvigorated the neglected political art of the banner, initially working directly on the subject of the Greenham Common protest, and subsequently widening her subject matter to include the broad range of political interests with which she was concerned.[121] Also drawn to Greenham Common by identification with the unique nature of the protest was the photographer Marian Delyth. Emerging in the 1970s, Marian Delyth worked initially in black and white in the documentary tradition, developing imagery that combined her engagement both with the gender issues that were the strong sub-text of the Greenham protest, and questions of Welsh identity, highlighted by the origins of the march. She would develop her career both as a documenter of political protest in Wales, and more personally in her explorations of Welsh identities in landscape and community.

119 Linda Nochlin, 'Why have there been no great women artists?', *ARTnews*, January 1971, pp. 22–39, 67–71.

120 Moira Vincentelli, exhibition catalogue *Women's Art in Wales/ Merched a Chelf yng Nghymru*, (Llandudno, 1985), p. 3.

121 See *100 Years of Women's Banners*, ed. Thalia Campbell (Borth, 1987).

399. Marian Delyth, *Greenham Common, Aldermaston*, 1983

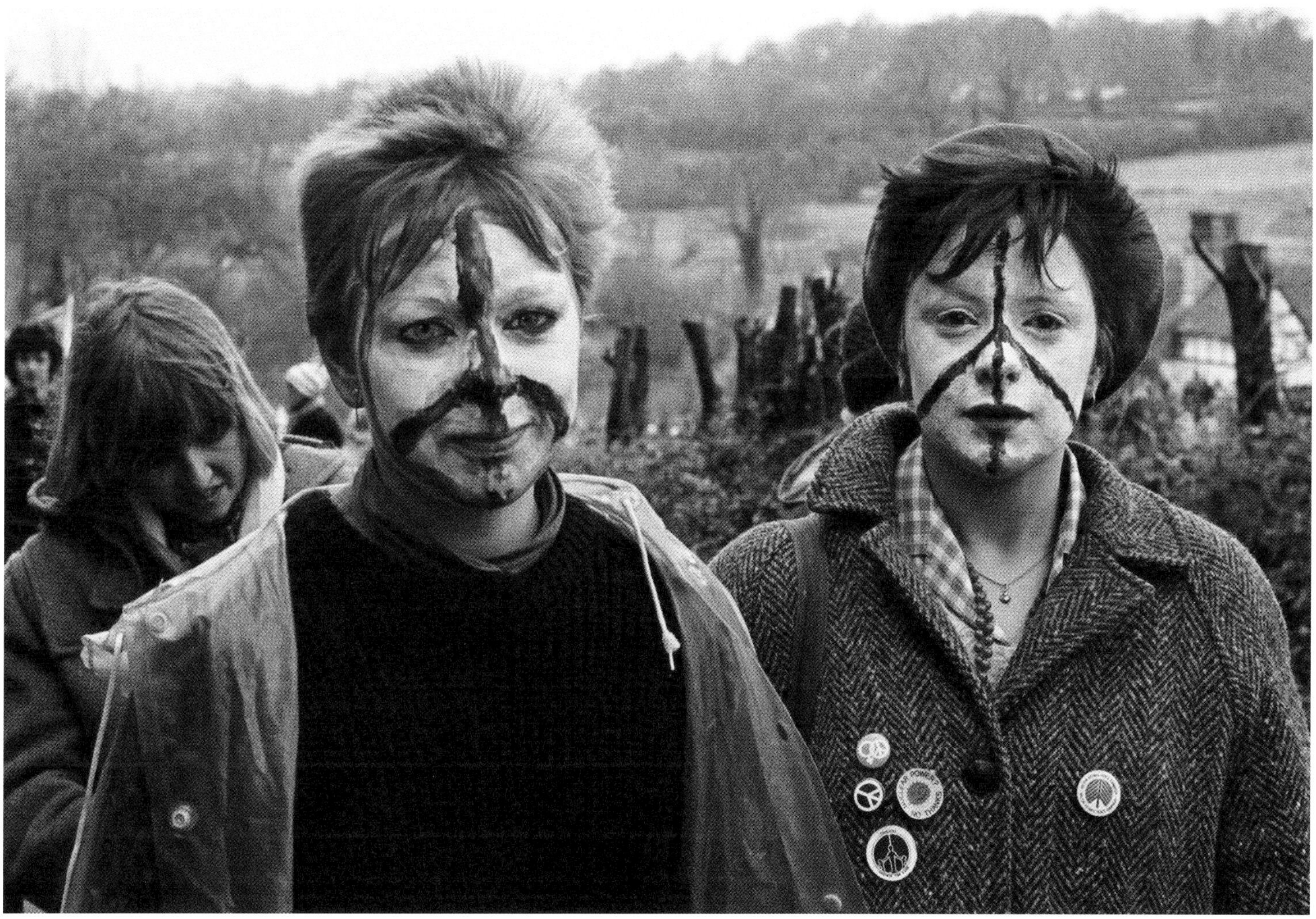

Maturity through diversity

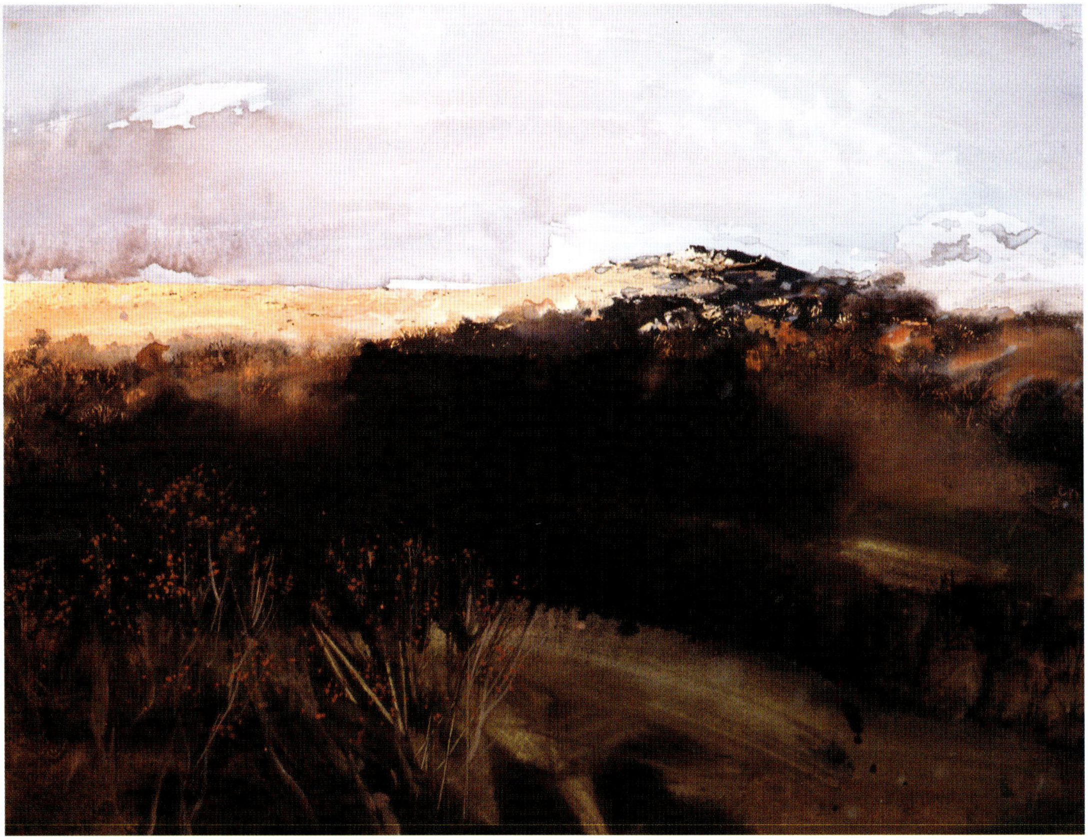

400. David Tress, *Carn Ingli, Late Sun*, 1990, mixed media, 56x76

below
401. David Nash, *Cradle and Bough*, installation photograph, *c*.1976, pine, h.198

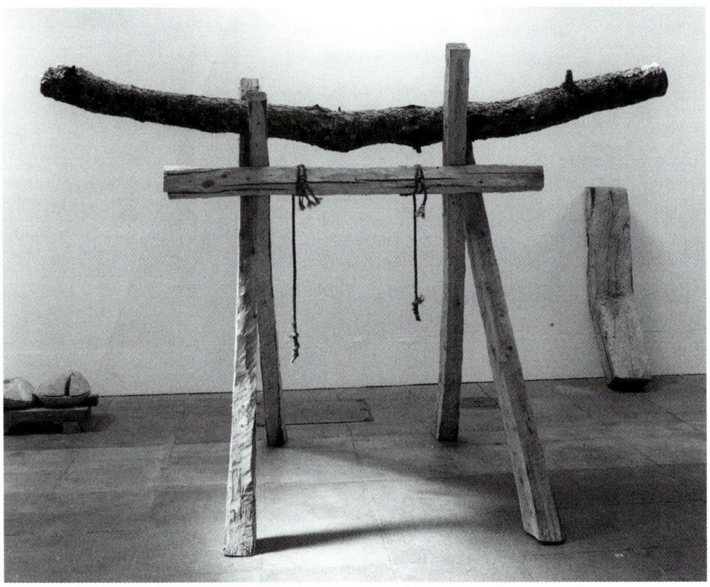

Although issues of nation and gender identity, more than any others, defined the 1970s and 1980s, their prominence contributed to a broader liberation of the visual culture from the strait-jacket of metropolitan and male dominance so apparent in the preceding two decades. Practice was remarkably diverse. For instance, the deeply rooted concern in Wales with landscape evolved both in the work of painters such as David Tress, who developed a distinctive vision within the painterly tradition, and in the radical approach of David Nash, directly moulding the material of the natural world, transforming both wood and live trees

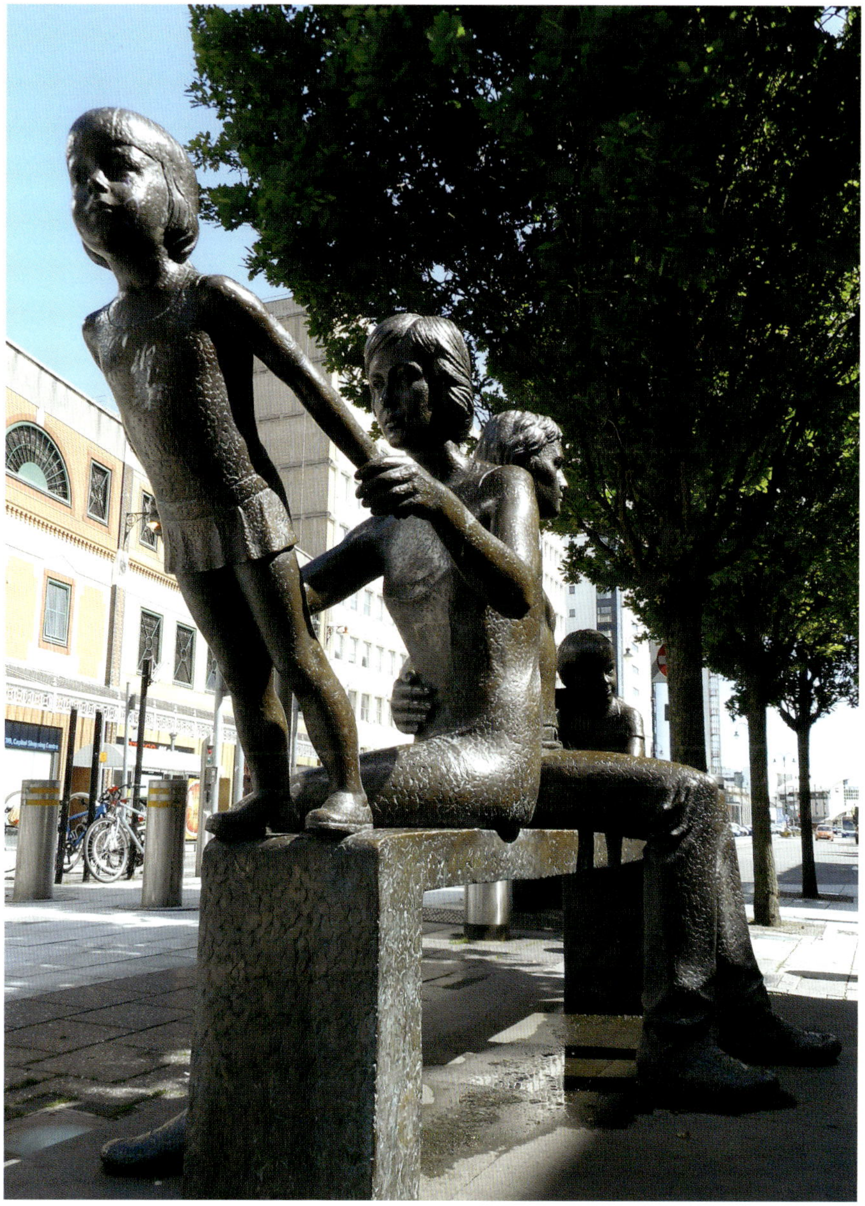

402. Robert Thomas, *Family Group*, Cardiff, 1985, bronze

in a tradition of engagement with environmental issues prefigured by M.E. Eldridge and Terry Setch. Two trends in particular sustained a more broadly based art practice than had been seen in any earlier period. Firstly, individuals such as Zobole, Ken Elias, Glyn Baines and John Uzzell Edwards, who had established their careers within Wales as young people, maintained their practice through a lifetime of image making and so provided an evolving background to the work of emerging younger artists.[122] The context they provided was reinforced by the return to Wales of a number of mature practitioners, who initially had developed careers outside the country. Prominent among those returning in the 1970s, and whose work would attain a high public profile, were the sculptor Robert Thomas and the painters Kyffin Williams and Ivor Davies. In the form of public sculpture, the work of Thomas, who had trained in Cardiff at the same time as the Rhondda Group painters, began to emerge at the end of the 1980s. The influence of Williams was felt earlier, both as a result of his public pronouncements on the state of visual art in Wales and beyond but also, largely unbeknown to the public, in the form of the encouragement and practical support that he gave to younger artists, such as Peter Prendergast. Secondly, art practice,

122 Like Zobole, John Uzzell Edwards had met Heinz Koppel at Dowlais in the 1940s.

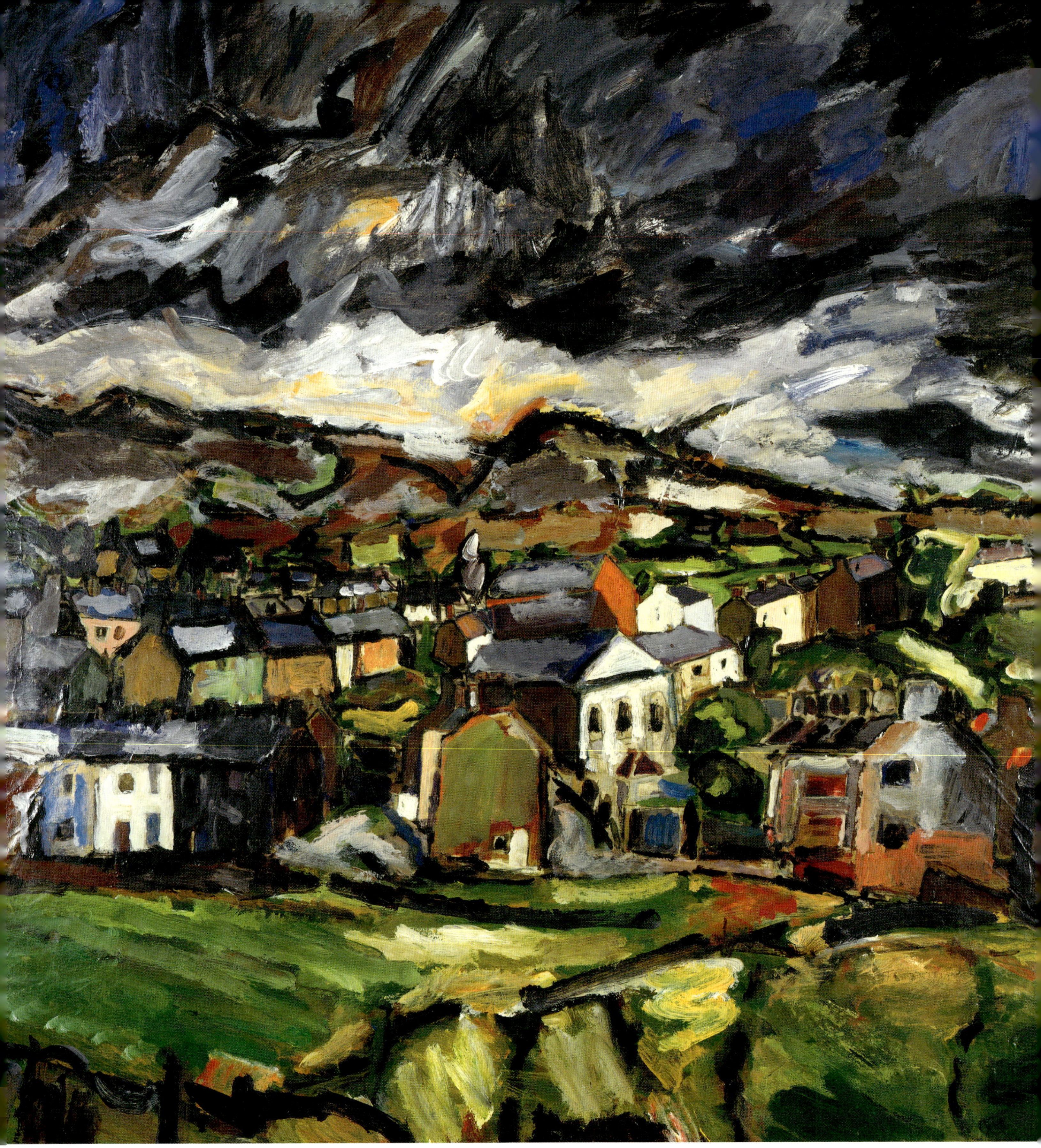

as exemplified by both Williams and Prendergast, became more evenly distributed throughout the country, both geographically and culturally. The work of artists based in the north, east and west, often in predominantly rural areas, was increasingly visible. It ceased to be perceived from a Newport–Cardiff art college axis as a secondary regionalism, and achieved equal status within a broadly-based Welsh practice. In a concomitant trend, the engagement of Welsh speaking practitioners increased markedly.[123]

Perhaps significantly, this broadening occurred alongside a precipitous decline in the influence of the Arts Council. Responding both to philosophical changes and to reduced funding that were the consequence of the election in 1979 of a Conservative government in London, which rejected the post-war social democratic consensus, the Arts Council withdrew from direct provision of exhibitions, from exhibition support and from the purchasing of works of art. Initially seeking to respond creatively to externally driven change, the Art Department redirected support towards the development of a small number of exhibition venues throughout Wales, and to the promotion of art through initiatives in marketing and project management. However, the ultimate consequence would be withdrawal of the Council in all the arts to a background role, following a policy of devolution of such direct funding as remained to new, quasi-independent bodies which also drew on other financial sources. This process began within the Visual Art Department.

In 1981, on the initiative of the art historian Shelagh Hourahane, the Welsh Sculpture Trust had been formed to promote the provision of sculpture in public spaces. Under the creative direction of Tamara Krikorian, the trust was prominent in a general revival of public sculpture, initially in open air exhibitions, but subsequently – taking advantage of increasing investment in urban regeneration – in the siting of large-scale individual works throughout the country.[124] Krikorian had been a pioneer of the use of video as a fine art format. She brought to bear her experience as an avant-garde practitioner, coupled with a particular sensitivity to Wales stemming from her Armenian cultural heritage, on the development of the Trust, which in 1991 evolved into a new organisation, Cywaith Cymru/Artworks Wales. The Arts Council's Art Committee devolved its long-standing engagement in the provision of public art to the new, independent organisation. In so doing not only did it complete its withdrawal from direct provision, but it signalled the end of the leading role that it had taken over nearly half a century in defining the intellectual context for the practice and presentation to the public of visual culture in Wales. As the Art Director, Peter Jones, acknowledged in 1991, the Welsh Arts Council was 'now on the sidelines ...'[125] The long post-war era, characterised by the direct involvement of the state in visual art provision for the benefit of all the people, was drawing to a close.

403. Peter Prendergast, *Carneddi on a Summer's Day*, 1978, oil, 110.5x106.4

123 See above, note 114.

124 The development of the organisation was reviewed in *Groundbreaking: the artist in the changing landscape*, ed. Iwan Bala (Cardiff, 2005). For the career of Tamara Krikorian, see the obituary by Michael Tooby, *The Guardian*, 6 August 2009.

125 Peter Jones, *The Welsh Arts Council's Commissions Service – Changes Afoot* (Cardiff, 1991).

Postscript – 1992

The engagement in visual culture of Wales's oldest national institution, the eisteddfod, was often undistinguished. However, occasionally it had provided a platform from which was signalled, with some force, a period of intense activity or of seminal change. There were the didactic exhibitions created by Cornwallis West at Ruthin and at Wrexham in the mid-Victorian era, for instance. The high ambitions of the National Revival at the end of the long nineteenth century were expressed in large exhibitions and by the challenge of the critical interventions of Hubert Herkomer. Against a background of unprecedented political tension, the professionalism and scale of Grant Murray's Swansea exhibition in 1926 represented a remarkable achievement. The Caerphilly exhibition of 1950 marked a point of fundamental change in the structure of the Welsh art world after the Second World War. Undoubtedly, the exhibition mounted for the National Eisteddfod held at Aberystwyth in 1992 should be included in this list of what its organiser, Jill Piercy, described as 'book marks' in the evolving story of the visual culture.

Though including also works by well established artists, the choices of the selectors of the art exhibition emphasised a new wave of practitioners who had emerged in the late 1980s, many of whom would form the core of practice in Wales into the twenty-first century.[126] Representative of their diversity were the winners of the Gold Medals for Craft and for Fine Art. Awareness of the importance of weaving in Welsh cultures had stimulated revivalist interventions by Lady Llanover in the nineteenth century, and by Winifred Coombe Tennant and Iorwerth Peate in the twentieth century. The father of the painter John Elwyn had been among the last to inherit the tradition. However, the weaver Cefyn Burgess was awarded the Gold Medal for Craft in 1992 not as a revivalist, but as an artist who, through a sense of Welsh identity rooted in his upbringing, was able to renew practice.

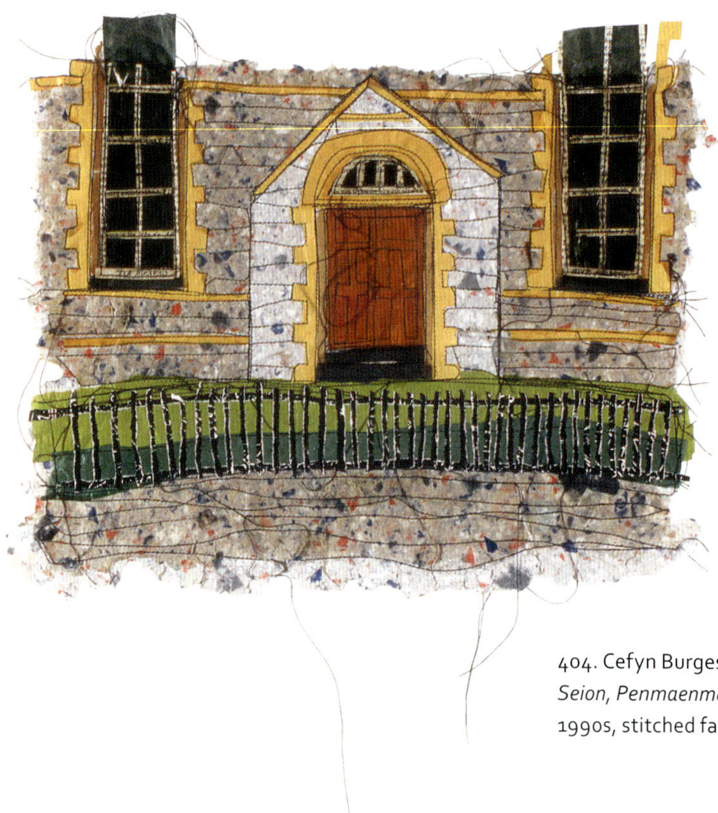

404. Cefyn Burgess, *Seion, Penmaenmawr*, early 1990s, stitched fabrics, 50x41

126 Four of the selectors were practitioners in their own right – Bill Davies, the architect, John Meirion Morris, the sculptor, Marian Delyth, the photographer, and Clifford McLucas, working across a broad spectrum of new media. The fifth selector was the art historian, Moira Vincentelli. The exhibition at the National Eisteddfod included a review of the history of art and craft in the eisteddfod movement, which signified a wider process of reassessment in the field that had begun in the 1980s.

The winner of the Gold Medal for Art, Shani Rhys James, emerged from a culturally more complex background. Her imagery was intensely personal, and rooted in the ambiguities of her cultural heritage, but was conveyed with a power, through the startling use of paint, that was soon to secure for her an international reputation. Beyond these two artists, much of the work shown at Aberystwyth in 1992, facilitated by the surrounding atmosphere of challenge and liberation, seemed characterised by an unusual sincerity of engagement. The exhibition revealed an unprecedented confidence in the expression of cultural identities that together, in their diversity, could define Wales as a maturing modern nation, in contrast to the search for the unique signifier of 'Welshness' that had constrained those concerned with the idea of national identity in the past. Crucially, in the practice of almost all those participating, there had emerged a unifying commitment to Wales as the home of a network of interacting creative cultures.

405. Shani Rhys James, *The Yellow Gloves*, 1987, oil, 127x189

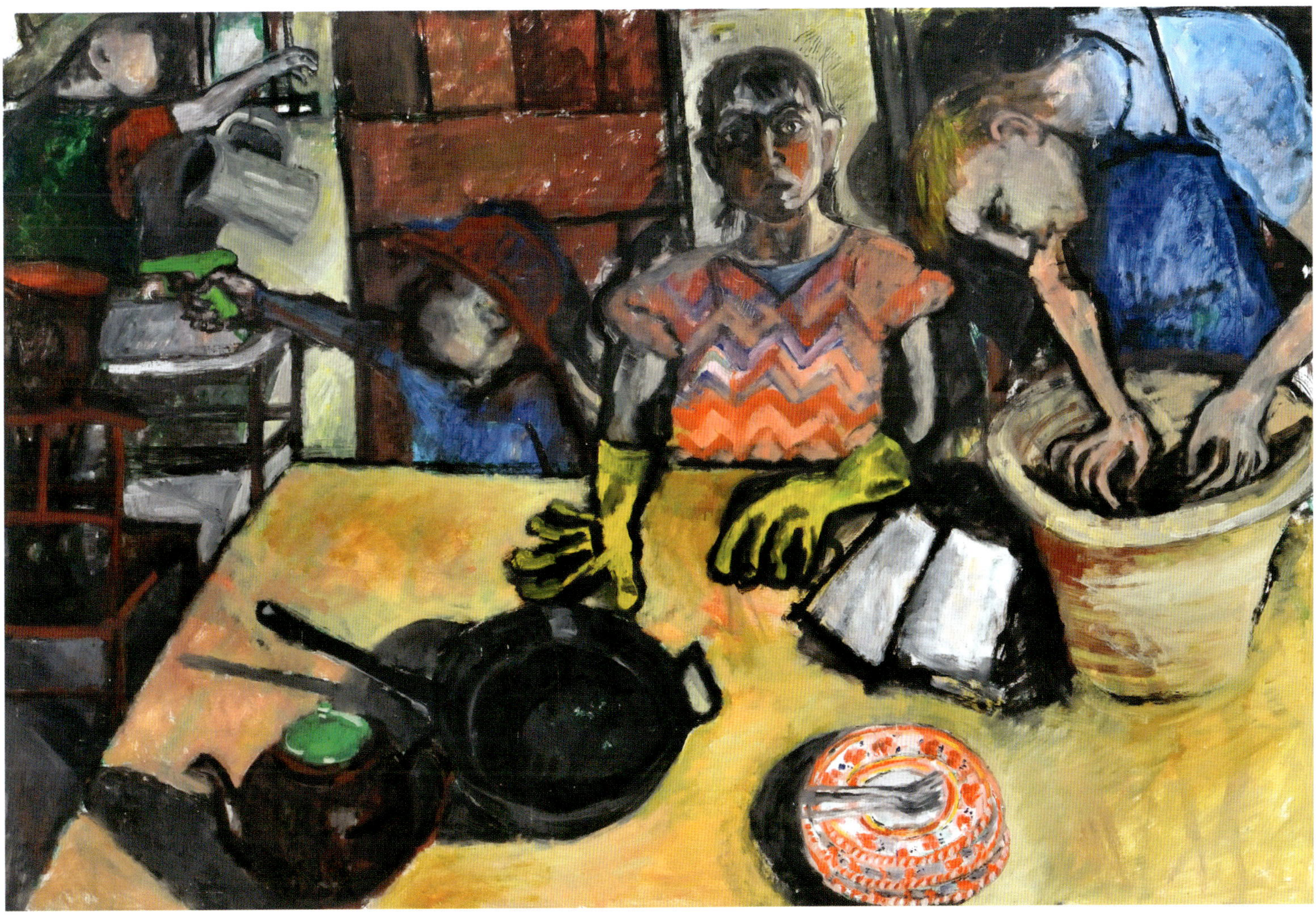

INDEX

General references are to pages, followed where appropriate by the ***number*** of each illustration in ***bold italics.***

ACKNOWLEDGEMENTS

Every attempt has been made to secure the permission of copyright holders to reproduce images. We gratefully acknowledge permissions granted by the following collections, copyright holders and photographers.

Aberdeen Art Gallery and Museums Collections, © Estate of Ray Howard Jones 328

Aberystwyth University 351 © The Estate of John David Roberts. By permission of the William Roberts Society, 367, 372

Aliki Currimjee, Fonmon Castle © 62

Archives de l'Université Catholique de Louvain 24

Arts Council Collection Southbank Centre, London 374 © Terry Setch

Bridgeman Images © 63

Brinsley Ford Collection 97

By permission of Amgueddfa Genedlaethol Cymru/National Museum of Wales 16, 20, 37, 38, 42, 44, 47, 54, 55, 60, 76, 82, 85, 86, 98, 103, 105, 109, 111, 113, 114, 117, 121, 124, 127, 128, 131, 132, 133, 146, 149, 151, 173, 174, 175, 176, 179, 180, 182, 190, 193, 197, 201, 218, 228, 229, 234, 246, 254, 259, 267, 269, 293, 295 with the permission of the Jones Estate, 301, 302 © The Estate of the late Cedric Lockwood Morris, 304 © The Estate of the late Cedric Lockwood Morris, 305, 313, 314 © The Estate of Ceri Richards. All rights reserved, DACS 2015, 317 © Estate of the Artist, 319, 321 © Mrs Clarissa Lewis, 325 © NMW, 335, 337, 341 © The Estate of Ceri Richards, 345 © Charles Burton, 346, 348 © The Estate of L.S.Lowry. All rights reserved, DACS 2015, 350, 353, 354 © Denys Short, 355, 356, 358 © Estate of the Artist, 361, 371 © Jack Crabtree, 376, 378, 382 © David Hurn, 384, 385, 386, 397, 401 © David Nash

By permission of Llyfrgell Genedlaethol Cymru/National Library of Wales 4, 9, 12, 32, 53, 52, 58, 80, 93, 95, 96, 106, 115, 116, 119, 130, 139, 141, 144, 145, 156, 158, 161, 164, 170, 183, 184, 185, 186, 188, 191, 208, 222, 223, 231, 235, 236, 243, 244, 248, 252, 255, 266, 277, 279, 284, 294, 296, 303, 316, 320, 331 © South Wales Evening Post, 344 © Estate of the Artist, 349, 360, 394

CADW Crown Copyright (2015) 31, 56, 57

Caernarfon Royal Town Council, Institute Building, Caernarfon 245

Canadian War Museum, Ottowa, Beaverbrook Collection of War Art CWM 201 10067-001, 265

Carmarthenshire Museums Service 3194, 196

Centre Historique des Archives Nationales, Paris 1

Charles and Patricia Aithie © ffotograff 3, 5, 6, 8, 11, 10, 13, 14, 15, 17, 21, 23, 33, 50

City and County of Swansea Glynn Vivian Art Gallery Collection 107, 166 Swansea Museum Collection, 230, 262, 280, 285, 311, 312, 315 © Estate of Ceri Richards. All rights reserved DACS 2015, 330 © Quentin Sandifer, 363 © Joan Baker, 403 © Estate of Peter Prendergast, All rights reserved DACS 2015

Crown Copyright, Royal Commission on the Ancient and Historical Monuments of Wales, 29, 34, 169

Fitzwilliam Museum, Cambridge © Bridgeman Images 258

Gwynedd Museum and Art Gallery, Bangor 159

His Grace the Duke of Beaufort 18 photograph Richard Bebb, 75

Holyhead Maritime Museum 163

Imperial War Museum © 332

Ivor Davies Collection 386

Kathy Davies © 35

Llandovery College © 199, 202

Manchester City Galleries 227 © Bridgeman Images, 334 © Estate of Ceri Richards All rights reserved DACS 2015

Martin Crampin photograph © 15, 30, 65

Martin Gregory Gallery, London, © 211

Marx Memorial Library and Workers' School, London © 309

Merthyr Tydfil Museums Service, Cyfarthfa Castle Museum and Art Gallery, 140, 150, 152, 153, 154, 177, 224, 327 © The Estate of the late Cedric Lockwood Morris

Monmouthshire Museums Service, Nelson Museum and Local History Centre 70

Museum Boijmans Van Beuningen, Rotterdam. Loan Museum Boijmans Van Beuningen Foundation. Photograph Studio Tromp, Rotterdam 263

Museum of Deinze and the Leie Region © 264

Museums Sheffield/Bridgeman images © 307

National Galleries Scotland 306

National Maritime Museum, Greenwich, London © 232

National Museum of Art, Architecture and Design, Oslo © 214

National Museums Liverpool 238

National Portrait Gallery, London © 67, 68, 89

National Screen and Sound Archive of Wales, 308 © NCVO

National Trust Photographic Library 19 Nicholas Riall, 22 Erik Pelham, 40, 45 Clare Bates, 46 Clare Bates, 59, 71, 73, 74, 77, 90, 92, 94, 99 John Hammond, 148 John Hammond, 318 John Hammond

Newport Museum and Art Gallery, 181 © Bridgeman Images, 268, 347, 375 © John Selway, 377

Nottingham City Museums and Galleries 216

Oriel Ynys Môn 299

Palace of Westminster Collection 198

Peniarth Collection 120, 189

Philadelphia Museum of Art: The Philip S. Collins Collection, gift of Mrs Philip S. Collins in memory of her husband, 1945, 27

Private Collections 30 photograph © Martin Crampin, 41, 84, 87, 88, 104, 142, 147, 155, 160, 162, 165, 167, 171, 172, 207, 209, 215, 217, 237, 240, 241, 260, 274, 278, 281, 283, 288, 289, 291, 292, 297, 298, 300, 310, 336, 338, 342, 359 © National Library of Wales, 364, 365, 368 © Estate of the Artist, 370, 380, 382, 381, 386, 388, 389, 392 © the Artist, 393, 395, 398, 399 © the Artist, 404 © the Artist, 405 © the Artist

Royal Academy of Arts, London 192

Royal Cambrian Academy 226

St Cadoc's PCC, photograph Kevin Thomas © 7

Sherborne Castle, by kind permission of Mr K.E.Wingfield Digby 39

Shrewsbury Drapers' Hall Preservation Trust, photograph Richard Bebb © 72

State Hermitage Museum, St Petersburg 123

Tate Gallery, London, 2015, 102, 122, 126, 137, 138, 143, 233, 242, 257, 256, 333

Tenby Museum 323

Thanks to Lord Mostyn and Mostyn Estates Ltd. © 36, 49, 187

The British Library Board All Rights Reserved © 2, 25, 28, 66, 157

The National Gallery, London, 2015 © 26, 125

The Stanley and Audrey Burton Gallery, University of Leeds, 261© Bridgeman Images

The Master and Fellows of Trinity College, Cambridge © 64

Tullie House Museum and Art Gallery, Carlisle 178

University Hospital of Wales Healthcare NHS Trust. Photograph: Matthew Keele Senior Photographer, Tempest Photography, Royal Military Academy, Sandhurst 270

University of Manchester, Whitworth Art Gallery 213

University of South Wales Art Collection Museum 387 © the Artist, photograph Public Catalogue Foundation 2011

Victoria and Albert Museum, London V&A Picture Library © 101, 129, 134, 135, 212, 221, 329

Worcester Art Museum, MA, Museum Purchase 1962.21. Image © Worcester Art Museum, 91

Worcester City Museum Collection 220

www.welshart.co.uk 83, 112 © Richard Davies-Cooke, 118, 120 with kind permission of the Peniarth Collection

Yale Center for British Art, Paul Mellon Collection 100, 108, 136

Picture captions: sizes are given in centimetres, height before width.